Cecil B. DeMille

Also by Simon Louvish

Man on the Flying Trapeze: The Life and Times of W. C. Fields
Monkey Business: The Lives and Legends of the Marx Brothers
Stan and Ollie: The Roots of Comedy: The Double Life of Laurel and Hardy
Keystone: The Life and Clowns of Mack Sennett
Mae West: It Ain't No Sin

FICTION

A Moment of Silence
The Therapy of Avram Blok
City of Blok
The Last Trump of Avram Blok
The Death of Moishe-Ganef
The Silencer
Your Monkey's Shmuck
Resurrections from the Dustbin of History
What's Up, God?
The Days of Miracles and Wonders
The Cosmic Follies

Cecil B. DeMille

A LIFE IN ART

Simon Louvish

Thomas Dunne Books
St. Martin's Press ☙ New York

THOMAS DUNNE BOOKS.
An imprint of St. Martin's Press.

www.thomasdunnebooks.com
www.stmartins.com

Library of Congress Cataloging-in-Publication Data

Louvish, Simon.
    Cecil B. Demille : a life in art / Simon Louvish.
        p. cm.
    Includes bibliographical references and index.
    ISBN-13: 978-0-312-37733-5
    ISBN-10: 0-312-37733-9
    1. DeMille, Cecil B. (Cecil Blount), 1881–1959. 2. Motion picture producers and directors—United States—Biography. I. Title.

PN1998.3.D455 L68 2007
791.43023'3092—dc22
[B]

                                                2007044599

First published in Great Britain by Faber and Faber

First U.S. Edition: March 2008

10 9 8 7 6 5 4 3 2 1

Contents

REEL FOUR

Let Us Go Down, and There Confound Their Language

REEL FIVE

So Shall It Be Written, So Shall It Be Done!

EPILOGUE

APPENDICES

Illustrations

PROLOGUE

The Champion Driver

Exodus, chapter 14, verses 14–25:

And the Lord said unto Moses: Wherefore criest thou unto me? Speak unto the children of Israel, that they go forward.

But lift thou up thy rod, and stretch out thine hand over the sea, and divide it, and the children of Israel shall go on to dry ground through the midst of the sea . . .

And the Egyptians shall know that I am the Lord, when I have gotten me honour upon Pharaoh, upon his chariots, and upon his horsemen . . .

And Moses stretched out his hand over the sea, and the Lord caused the sea to go back by a strong east wind all that night, and made the sea dry land, and the waters were divided.

And the children of Israel went into the midst of the sea upon the dry ground, and the waters were a wall unto them on their right hand, and on their left.

And the Egyptians pursued, and went in after them to the midst of the sea, even all Pharaoh's horses, his chariots, and his horsemen . . .

And it came to pass . . .

Charlton Heston, AD 1954:

Yesterday was the exodus, and I led them out. When we were discussing the scene the other day DeMille put it to me with apt awe, I think: 'When you lift your staff to signal the start of the Exodus, twenty thousand hearts will be beating in front of you.' . . . I don't think I can really convey to you what a genuinely moving experience it was to take part in this . . . I can only say that it was real. We are three thousand years from the time of Rameses II, and Egypt is the world's youngest republic, instead of its oldest empire, but DeMille succeeded in making again, on the sand at Beni Youseff, an instant in history . . . Moses the man makes a shadow in which the actor disappears . . . It felt magnificent, and as we walked I said again to myself the other words I'd spoken in the scene: 'Hear O Israel! Remember this day, when the strong hand of the Lord leads you out of bondage!'

And it came to pass . . . What is this moment, in which reality, myth, history, imagination, inspiration, dreams, delusions mix into the realm that we now call 'Hollywood', the American version of an art born of the marriage of modern science and the age-old gift of story-telling? The movies, as we know them, were born simultaneously in several countries: France, Britain and the United States primarily, but seized as a narrative form by pioneers in Italy, Germany, the Scandinavian countries and elsewhere by the first decade of the twentieth century. It was, however, that small town in California that made the cinema into the twentieth century's strongest cultural force, and, in that small town in California, Cecil B. DeMille was one of the men who made the movies what they are today.

So far, so familiar. The bare facts of DeMille's life story have often been told. He was born on 12 August 1881 to a family that was to be steeped in the theatre. His father, Henry Churchill De Mille, was at that time a jobbing actor but would soon be well known as a successful playwright and a co-writer with the mercurial David Belasco. His brother, William de Mille, born in 1878, would be a major American playwright, and Cecil would pursue his own play-writing career in collaboration with him. Their mother, Matilda Beatrice De Mille, would be a playwright, play broker, theatrical agent, founder of a school for girls and primary energizer and mentor for young Cecil after his father died when the boy was not yet twelve years old. *Cecil B. DeMille, Young Dramatist* was even to become the title of a children's book published in 1963 as part of a series entitled 'Childhood of Famous Americans'. The book informs us that when Cecil was born, in 1881, in Ashfield, Massachusetts, 'There were thirty-eight states in the Union. Chester A. Arthur was President' and 'the population of the country was about 50,155,000 . . . Thomas Edison', the book patriotically, if inaccurately, reminds us, 'invented the motion-picture camera, 1889.'

Many boys decide at an early age that their life is going to be legend, but few have persevered with such stubborn determination as Cecil Blount DeMille. At the family home in Echo Lake, New Jersey, 'an old pre-revolutionary house still held together on its original wooden pegs', Cecil dreamed, as 1963's *Young Dramatist* puts it, 'that he was the champion driver who rode a tireless, magnificent Arabian horse. He liked to pretend that people were in trouble and had sent for him. He would come galloping to the rescue, the sweat glistening on the sides of his trusty black steed.'

In 1919, already an established film-maker, the Champion Driver's steed had morphed into a big red aeroplane, in which DeMille had chosen to conduct, in the breathless words of *Photoplay* magazine's writer Elizabeth Peltret, 'the first interview which really took place in an aeroplane'. Ms Peltret described this historical moment:

We were moving slowly – that is, I thought we were moving slowly – over the oil fields on the outskirts of Los Angeles . . . I could not believe we were going at seventy miles an hour (though we were), and thought that something must have gone wrong. A glance at Mr. de Mille reassured me. He was smiling. He smiled every time I looked at him . . .

'I am,' he intoned, with an assumption of much gravity, 'a great believer in the philosophy which says that nothing in life is worth taking too seriously . . . but at the same time I take my work seriously – tragically so, sometimes.'

To conduct the interview, DeMille had shut off the motor, something which deeply disconcerted his passengers, whose faith in this new triumph of modern technology was shaky at best. DeMille's senior partner in the film business, Jesse Lasky, famously relayed his panic at this kind of manoeuvre when Cecil persuaded him, against his better judgement, to take to the air in the front seat arranged for student pilots. He would not have been reassured to know that, at this time, the pilot trainer at the back always took a heavy monkey wrench on board so that he could knock out the trainee and take control of the aircraft if the latter made any sudden and potentially fatal error. But the Champion Driver was in his element, sailing above the grubby fields. As Miss Peltret resumes:

Mr DeMille turned, several times, banking at only a slight angle, making as he said 'an easy figure eight,' and looking over the tilted edge of the wing I was treated to the unusual spectacle of being able to see equally well on both sides of a mountain at once . . . We were flying due west but the sun appeared to be below us. I most particularly wanted him to talk about God and that, too, he understood.

'My God is a God of nature, of bigness, rather than a personal God,' C. B. DeMille went on. (He was, by the way, brought up as a strict Presbyterian, notwithstanding his father's constant connection with the theater.) 'As a boy, I pictured Him as a sort of glorified man sitting on a throne in the clouds, pointing out individuals with a golden scepter saying, "Punish this man, and reward that one." Now I do not picture Him at all. I think, though, that he builds forever. I cannot believe that we are put here for fifty or sixty years and that after that there is nothing. If a man has a strong personality I do not see why it should not endure after death, but where and in what form it endures I am willing to wait to find out.'

Four years later, DeMille progressed forcefully towards a 'picturization', if not of the Almighty Himself, then of His agents upon earth with his first depiction of Moses in *The Ten Commandments* of 1923, the vital precursor of his last, Hestonian epic. Although this was not DeMille's first historical epic – that honour is due his 1917 version of the tale of Joan of Arc, *Joan the Woman* – it was the film that began to establish the legend of Cecil B. DeMille as master of the grandiose and of biblical sagas, a position that was cemented with his 1927 version of the life of Christ, *King of Kings*. This latter film, as if in premonition of our own day and age, sparked both adulation and rage across a wide spectrum, from fundamentalist Catholics to appalled Jews, who denounced the film as a vivid reminder of anti-Semitic Christianity. It also made vast amounts of money, over many years of revivals well into the 'talkie' age, and convinced DeMille and his backers that historical blockbusters were a sure-fire path to commercial heaven. The famous catchphrase 'Ready when you are, Mr DeMille', about the cameraman who failed to roll his camera when DeMille signalled the blowing up of a massive period set, marked an event that never quite happened the way it was told. But it denoted the director as indeed a King of Kings, master of the vast fantasies he surveyed from his own virtual hilltop throne.

And yet few other than film historians are aware that Cecil B. DeMille directed seventy motion pictures, all of them long-length 'feature' productions, that fifty-two of them were silent pictures, that only eight of these could properly be called 'epics', and only four of these – *The Ten Commandments* (1923), *King of Kings* (1927), *Samson and Delilah* (1949) and *The Ten Commandments* (1956 version) – were 'Biblical' films, with a fifth, *The Sign of the Cross* (1932), coming close to the New Testament era.

Of DeMille's silent pictures, the first twenty-four were all shot in the three-year period of his first avalanche of motion-picture making, from the end of 1913 through to 1916, when he was feeling his way, learning his craft, with few precursors in the art of the long-length movie. Thereafter he slowed down, a little, but still produced a further twenty-eight films before the end of the silent-movie era, the changeover years of 1928–9. To many critics, in fact, he was, by the time of the talkies, yesterday's man, a dinosaur whose best years had come a decade before, as the 1910s segued into the 1920s.

The curious, and somewhat stunning, fact of the life in art of Cecil B. DeMille is that most of his best, most intriguing, most masterfully crafted and indeed amazing movies remain invisible and unknown, even to film buffs who were brought up on the legendary sagas of this iconic movie-maker: the man who invented the stereotype of the swaggering director, with his desert puttees and rough-hewn casual get-up, the snapping generalissimo with his megaphone and his dedicated chair-boy, who always has the boss's chair ready for him to sit on wherever and whenever, without looking round. Many of these films are familiar only to a small group of movie historians, writers and archivists who have travelled across the world to view rare prints in film libraries dedicated to preserving films that have almost, but not quite, vanished into the great sinkhole of silent-movie oblivion. Some of these films, neglected for decades, are finally beginning to appear in new DVD versions that enable us to glimpse DeMille in his heyday: films like *Manslaughter*, *The Affairs of Anatol*, *Male and Female*, *Carmen*, *Joan the Woman* and *King of Kings* itself, now fully restored, some with the full glory of original tinting, toning and coloured intertitles brought back to shimmering life. Hopefully, as time goes on, more will follow. In due course, new audiences should be able to reel in disbelief at the bizarre, often delirious plot twists and visual pyrotechnics of movies like *Fool's Paradise*, *The Golden Bed* and *The Godless Girl*, or the early excesses of DeMille's almost hallucinatory saga of the Conquistadores and the Aztecs – 1917's *The Woman God Forgot*.

Long before DeMille was seen as Bible interpreter – or hack – he was lauded as the producer-director of Hollywood's most adult-themed entertainments: his series of husband-and-wife-divorce-and-remarry satires, most of them starring his youngest discovery, Gloria Swanson, whom he rescued from Mack Sennett's slapstick factory. These movies, with titles such as *Don't Change Your Husband* and *Why Change Your Wife?*, featured Miss Swanson and other ladies in exquisite gowns and headgear, living in exquisite homes with exquisite furniture and fittings, and usually with less than exquisite male partners, who might be swapped for sins such as neglecting their spouses, forgetting the wedding anniversary or overindulging on onions. Husbands would let go of their wives for incipient adultery, only to find their loss outweighed their gain. Long before he was holding forth about God's presence and plan for the universe, DeMille was telling Miss Peltret of *Photoplay*, in his aerial interview of 1919:

I am a great believer in goodness and virtue, but if a woman has made a false step, as it is called, I don't see anything to agonize over. She has had an experience, and if she only knows how to profit from her mis-step, she will become all the better.

Anyway, the best thing for her to do, in my opinion, is to forget it. Everyone else will forget it too. The 'ruined woman' is out of style; as out of style as the woman of the Victorian era who used to faint at every little alarm. The only reason why a fallen woman shouldn't get up again lies in her own foolishness, not the opinion of the world. Society will forget as soon as she will let it.

There is a stronger thing in life than love, and that is friendship. Friendship can exist with passion . . . My wife and I are friends, comrades in every sense of the word, true partners in life. And we do not in any way restrict each other's liberty. She has a sense of humor as keen as my own and for two people to be able to laugh at the same things is the best guarantee of happiness.

'There was a pause,' Miss Peltret wrote, 'once more the engine roared, and we rose. Then he shut off the motor and volplaned; an interesting and thrilling sensation. I was always thrilled when the motor was off and always relieved to hear it start again . . . Going back to the studio [in] the automobile seemed – tame? No, speedy in comparison . . .'

DeMille's public declarations about his marriage masked a complex relationship which ran in parallel with several other long-term partnerships in the director's life and determined his personal principles and practice in dealing with others. In many ways, DeMille's films comprised a battleground on which he played and replayed his ideas, emotions and peculiarities in matters of male and female sexuality and mores. The art is, in effect, more revealing of the man's inner life than the mounds of paper, the letters, notes, voluminous production files and records that he stockpiled and left for posterity to wade through. At a very early stage in his film career DeMille determined that he was to become a figure of at least national importance whose every move, gesture, thought and utterance should be left as a treasured artefact for the future. The major plus has been the preservation of the movies, which DeMille began to attend to in the mid-1920s. Even by then the negatives of six of his movies made between 1914 and 1917 had disappeared, and a seventh survives only in a truncated two-reel fragment, such was the cavalier attitude of the movie studio executives to their product: shoot, release, exploit and move on. But at least the other negatives exist, making prints and restorations possible.

In 1950, when DeMille, playing himself, featured in Billy Wilder's dystopian Hollywood satire *Sunset Boulevard*, the script gave Erich von Stroheim – as the chauffeur to ageing star Gloria Swanson, who reveals to the anti-hero, played by William Holden, that her driver was once her first husband and director – the line: 'In those days, there were three motion picture directors that mattered: D. W. Griffith, Cecil B. DeMille and Max von Mayerling' – the latter being von Stroheim's name in the movie. This was, when one substitutes von Stroheim's own name, unvarnished fact. Griffith's early masterpieces – flawed as his breakthrough *Birth of a Nation* (1915) was by racism, and crippled as 1916's *Intolerance* was by commercial failure – led to lesser and lesser works. Von Stroheim's films – after his first two – are justly celebrated, despite their survival as ruins of what should have been after they were curtailed, slashed and burned by the studios. In contrast, DeMille's silent films, from 1917 until the end of the silent era, are almost all precisely as the director wished them to be. For a full decade, he was the complete master and auteur of his films, though some were chosen by circumstance of war and the commercial desires of Jesse Lasky rather than artistic preference. And he continued to be the author of his films throughout the sound era too. For such an auteur, of such world-wide renown, the ignorance with regard to his best work must surely be considered peculiar, if not astounding.

And so this book is an attempt to tell the story of Cecil B. DeMille largely through his work: the Life *in* Art. It will form part of a process that appears to be unfolding as a rediscovery of DeMille's central place in the history of American cinema. This was begun by the fine, definitive filmography and production history of DeMille's movies by Robert Birchard, *Cecil B. DeMille's Hollywood*, published in 2004. As in all else, the study of DeMille engenders its own politics, and the heritage of DeMille as an American icon is shaping up as an important factor in the battle of ideas that is now raging in the body politic of America itself.

DeMille, once considered an artistic dinosaur, a purveyor of out-moded nineteenth-century standards, now appears, in the era of a new global American crusade, as a precursor to the 'neo-conservative' age of Ronald Reagan and George W. Bush. As the son of a socially pro-gressive, if morally conservative, playwright, DeMille imbibed both his Jewish mother's strong drive towards achievement and his father's Protestant ethos of sharp moral dichotomies, in an age in which modernity, the machine and the pursuit of money made America a battlefield of clashing values and temptations. Young Cecil embraced the birth of a powerful consumer society, the America of rising expec-tations and new sexual freedoms, until the old-time religion slowly began to waft down from his pervading childhood memories to infuse his films with strange, unanswered questions, and then emphatic, age-old answers. From a carefree dalliance with the burgeoning jazz age, replete with the syncopations of desire and pleasure – and delicious orgies – DeMille's films revealed a growing, nagging doubt about the salvations of secularity, until his eventual discovery of the potent power of presenting his modern dilemmas in their ancient settings.

Moses hefting the stone Tablets of the Law on Mount Sinai had more than a chance resemblance to the ambitious director who decided he now wished to reform a wayward world. America as a Biblical template for moral rearmament is an idea that DeMille did not invent, but he gave it its strongest portrayal in the twentieth cen-tury's most powerful and influential medium. In his political journey from soft left to hard right, becoming the scourge of left-wing unions and the communist menace, the imagery he presented upon the screen mirrors a cultural journey that America has forced the entire world to pay attention to, on pain of serious consequences. We must all pay heed now to these siren voices that came down, piggybacking upon the Founding Fathers' democracy, from America's pioneer origins.

Was Cecil B. DeMille savant or sinner, mentor or malcontent, artist or hack, a principled defender of American freedoms or a hypocriti-cal opportunist who embraced the Golden Calf of sheer commercial-ism? Was he, as his detractors insisted, a vulgarian who mixed sex and God in an unholy brew that made the box-office tills ring with Hosannahs, or was he indeed, as portrayed by his hagiographers, the master craftsman, a man loyal to wife, mistresses, long-serving crews and casts, and audiences, over his almost half-century of achievements? Garlanded with praise, the list of his awards fills pages of press releases, and he was the crowned king and progenitor of movie hype and merchandising, self-serving beyond a fault. Could he be all these, and more – the most complex personality of the American screen? Or does the collision of so many opposites reduce him to a chaotic mediocrity, like the Wizard of Oz, a thing of bells and whistles and puffs of coloured smoke but little substance in the end?

Here then is the pirate DeMille, the Champion Driver of his own imagination, the 'unauthorized' version of a pervasive puzzle that mirrors the larger puzzle, and contradictions, of America itself.

REEL ONE

The Play's the Thing

'Who Knows Where the Chain May Go?'

Soon after his seventieth birthday, as he planned his epic testament, his remake of *The Ten Commandments*, Cecil B. DeMille began another long delayed project: his autobiography. In keeping with a DeMille production, it was to be meticulously prepared and researched by his own long-term staff and his chosen book editor, Donald Hayne. Another writer, Art Arthur, hired as a publicist for *The Ten Commandments* in 1954, was later added to speed up the cumbersome process. By 1957, DeMille had amassed great folios of background material and voluminous research on the origins of the DeMille family. He had traced his father's patrimony back to one Gillis deMil, born in Flanders, today's Netherlands, in 1280. The lineage was followed down to Anthony DeMil, a Haarlem baker, who sailed to the New World in 1658. 'The first DeMil house in America', wrote the authors, in Cecil's voice, 'stood near the tip of Manhattan, in what is now Bowling Green.'

In contrast to his Dutch Reformed Church forebears, whom he continued to trace down the centuries, Cecil had little to say about the origins of his mother, Matilda Beatrice, except to mention that one of his great-great-grandfathers was a small merchant, Ralph Samuel, from Liverpool, England. It took another biographer, Anne Edwards, chronicler of the wider DeMille family saga, to pin down the immediate genealogy of Beatrice and the German Jewish origins of her ancestor, who had settled in England in 1779. Beatrice had been born in 1853, to Cecilia Wolff and Sylvester Samuel, a watchmaker. The family moved to Brooklyn, New York, in 1871, and it is probable (given the lists of ships' passengers through the previous years) that this was not Sylvester Samuel's first trip to America. The family was, in fact, part of the relatively wealthy and small Jewish merchant class which had prospered in England before the mass immigration of Jews from Germany, eastern Europe and Russia in the closing decades of the nineteenth century. Their arrival long preceded the desperate voyages of those 'poor, huddled masses' beckoned across the ocean by Miss Liberty's outstretched torch.

It is curious, and significant, that Cecil dropped the Jewish origins of his mother from his own tale, though this was consistent with his earlier insistence that it was from his mother, as much as from his Episcopalian father, that he derived his devout Christian beliefs. Her marriage to Henry Churchill De Mille, in 1876, took place against her parents' objections, though they were not, it appears, heavily orthodox, as they had enrolled their daughter with the Philokalia Musical and Literary Association of Brooklyn, a distinctly secular cultural group. Her acquaintance with Henry De Mille began, according to Anne Edwards, at the association's presentation of an Irish comedy on 4 November 1872, 'in which she played the flirtatious and frolicsome heroine, complete with Irish dialect', somewhat at odds with her 'exotic beauty . . . produced by the Sephardic Jewish background . . . olive skinned, almond eyed . . .' Henry, in contrast, is described as a 'fair skinned, effete looking, wire-thin Southerner with burnished red hair, myopic hazel eyes, and an aristocratic and aquiline nose'. Given Cecil Blount DeMille's robust physique and energetic temperament, one can conclude he took after his Sephardic, rather than his Netherlandish, background, notwithstanding his own reluctance to embrace it.

Henry was the son of William deMill and Margaret Blount Hoyt of North Carolina, where William was the mayor of the town of Washington and a successful, but apparently not slave-owning, merchant. Having joined the Confederate Army in May 1861, William served throughout the Civil War and was captured at Greenville, North Carolina, and imprisoned by the Union in February 1865. (This information was later presented on behalf of Cecil during the Second World War to obtain for him a 'Cross of Military Service' from the United Daughters of the Confederacy in 1942.) William's children were part of the many heirs of the South's defeat, but for Henry, the eldest at twelve years of age when the war ended, opportunity beckoned when he was sent to the Adelphi Academy – later named the Lockwood – in Brooklyn, New York. There, his theatrical and literary ambitions were nurtured, and his 'Valedictory Address' on leaving the Academy in June 1871 recalls his happy college days:

You all remember the story of Androcles and the lion – how the savage monarch of the forest (though confined three days without food) crouched

Henry C. De Mille

at the foot of his former benefactor, and licked the hand that had extracted from his foot the thorn. And shall not we, immortal beings, realize our own indebtedness to those who have labored with so much skill to extract from our hearts and minds the thorns of bad habits and ignorance?

We have been placed in a noble institution, guided by men and women of Christian character, of learning, and of talent . . . They have not contented themselves with casting out the evil spirit from our inner houses, and left them empty for its return. They have striven to furnish us with the means of resisting the manifold temptations of life, and to mark out for us the path of duty, which leads to the love and esteem of our fellow creatures and the approbation of our God . . . Every true pupil of this academy has stricken from his dictionary the words 'despair,' and 'I can't,' as expressions only fit for idlers and cowards, and substituting in their places those magic words, 'can,' and 'will,' he presses with vigor onward, his soul, as the poet expresses it, darting 'forward on the wings of just ambition to the grand result.'

Family lore has it that Henry's mother devoutly wished him to be a priest, but Beatrice, after she married him on 1 July 1876, strongly encouraged him towards a literary career. He had by that time graduated from New York's Columbia College and was teaching at his

5

alma mater, the Lockwood. Beatrice herself taught elocution at the same school. Their first son, William Churchill de Mille,[*] was born on 25 July 1878 at the home of his grandfather – and namesake – in North Carolina. The Federal Census of June 1880 finds them living at 408 23rd Street in Manhattan, a genteel residential area, listed as lodgers with a family named Lewis. Henry was teaching at Columbia Grammar School and had just sold a story in eighteen parts to a magazine called *Leslie's Weekly*. Soon after, the de Milles moved to Ashfield, Massachusetts, where Henry gave private lessons in Latin, Greek and mathematics, and where his second son was born and named Cecil Blount, after his maternal and paternal grandmothers, Cecilia Wolff and Margaret Blount.

Cecil writes that his father's diary on the auspicious day of his arrival noted succinctly: 'August 12th my little boy Cecil was born.' Cecil, or the ghostwriters of his autobiography, added: 'Eight words, after all, are a longer history than most of the world's population has had or will have . . . If any one who has ever lived had not lived, the whole history of the world might be different, for who knows where the chain may go?' That simple summer day had to be made, in retrospect, significant, though no comets had trailed through the sky. While imbued with the can-do ethos of his college days, Henry De Mille's ambitions were, as ever, quite modest. He had been bitten by the stage bug at an early age and saw his vocation in the writing of plays which would express the edifying tenets of his religious faith but which would also put forward new and progressive ideas. 'I do not for a moment wish to decry what is ethically right,' he wrote mildly in 1891 in the *New York Dramatic Mirror*, 'but I think that conventionalism often works much harm.' In 1888, when he became the Associate Director, with a Mr Franklin H. Sargent, of the American Academy of the Dramatic Arts, he told the *New York Times* writer who queried him about the 'primary work of the course':

The first thing to be accomplished is to teach them [the students] to read . . . They are not allowed to 'elocute,' but are required to act. Our idea is to teach them intelligently and well, and veil the fact that they have been taught

[*]The spelling of the family name has, as the reader can see, varied. Henry was 'De Mille', though most of the family retained the spelling 'de Mille'. Cecil began as 'de Mille', then used 'De Mille' and finally settled on the now official 'DeMille'. I will use the latter most often, but other spellings are used in the earlier chapters.

to read. They must be artfully artless in all their work . . . Serious work or comedy draws equally on the emotions, and the voice given, emotional power is the great instrument of the actor . . . The dramatic school is to be a powerful adjunct to the theatre of the United States of the future, and its capacity for good is only just beginning to be recognized . . .

By this time Henry De Mille had presented three of his own plays upon the stage, including *The Wife*, presented in 1887 and the first of those he was to co-write with playwright-producer-impresario David Belasco, soon to become the most dynamic force on the American stage. Before that, he had made his mark with his second produced work, *The Main Line, or Rawson's Y*, co-written with Charles Barnard and subtitled 'An Idyl of the Railroad'. (His first play had been *John Delmer's Daughters; or Duty*, a three-act comedy, briefly presented – for one week only – in 1883.) Presented by manager Daniel Frohman at the reopening of his Lyceum Theatre in New York, *The Main Line* was noted for its dramatic effects, in particular 'a scene representing a snow blockade in the Rocky Mountains, the realistic effect being greatly heightened by the passage across the stage of a full-sized locomotive and a "cyclone" rotary snow-plough'.

One can note how the theatre, several years before the first halting experiments by Thomas Edison and other pioneers to project moving pictures, was striving towards that condition of 'realism' which in the end only the cinema, and the De Milles of the future, could produce. The opening lines of Henry's railroad drama, however, could well have graced many a coming oater, as Little Prairie Flower, a 'very buxom, jovial-looking woman of middle age', enters on stage:

PRAIRIE F.: That 11:34 ain't in sight. Land O'Goshen! What on 'art am I going to do? Nothing here but them hackmetack doughnuts and pies that came C.O.D. week before last; guess now they're B.A.D. (*Calls*) Possy! Lands take the gal! If I was her mother, she'd toe the mark or my name ain't Little Prairie Flower. Possy! (*A crash heard in station.*)

This kind of frontier romance, combining heightened melodrama with 'realistic' characters and a moral dilemma resolved by true love, came in the historic period of the construction of the great transcontinental railways. The Northern Pacific Railroad was completed after twenty years' labour in 1883. A year earlier, Henry De Mille had been engaged by manager Daniel Frohman – who would play a great part in the career of the De Milles, father and sons, for many years – as a play reader at the new Madison Square Theatre. At the same time, David Belasco was hired as its stage manager.

This was a serendipitous meeting. Belasco was a suitable star in his production of his own mercurial life. Fact and fiction blended perfectly in his account of his early years. The son of Jewish parents who had, he claimed, been the first passengers to cross the Panama isthmus en route to a new life in gold rush California, he was produced in 1853 in San Francisco, a town full of opportunities for good folks and sinners alike. After his parents moved to British Columbia in 1858, Belasco claimed he had grown up among the native Songhee Indians of Victoria and had fallen under the influence of a Catholic priest, remaining two years in a monastery before decamping alone to the Rio de Janeiro Circus. Diligent biographers have cast doubt on this narrative, but all agree that young Belasco was back with his family in San Francisco in 1865 – where he was, despite the alleged Catholicism, properly bar mitzvahed.

Consumed by a powerful compulsion for the stage, young David produced his own plays and found a mentor in one Tom Maguire, redoubtable builder and manager of Californian theatres. Amid San Francisco's cyclical booms and busts, Belasco appeared for Maguire in such venues as the Egyptian Hall on Geary Street, which specialized in eerie stage illusions: 'Gas lamps were ingeniously concealed so as to give the impression of a phosphorescent light from ghostlike bodies . . .' Shadows were cast across a glass, which produced an illusion of ghosts shaking tables and chairs, while Belasco gave readings of 'The Maniac' and 'The Maiden's Prayer'. This apparent freakery was significant in sparking the young man's interest in the effects of imaginative stage lighting – which would, in the fullness of time and the twists and turns of collaboration, play a vital role in the younger De Mille's ideas of quite another medium. Without a pause, Belasco took every theatrical opportunity, performing the gamut of roles from Richard III to Dickens' Fagin, as well as producing plays and adaptations, including a controversial passion play which featured James O'Neill, father-to-be of playwright Eugene, as Jesus, removed from the cross not to the cave of burial but to the San Francisco jail. By 1882, San Francisco and Belasco had all but exhausted each other, and Gustave Frohman, brother of the aforementioned Daniel, beckoned him across the country, to New York.

It was Belasco who, as director, produced the spectacular effects that made the critics gasp at Henry De Mille's 'Idyl of the Railroad'. His collaboration with De Mille produced four successful plays between 1887 and 1890: *The Wife, Lord Chumley, The Charity Ball* and *Men and Women*. Despite this, he gave only a passing mention to his partner in his own account of his stage life, *The Theatre Through Its Stage Door*, published in 1919. The only partners in his ventures to whom Belasco offered any praise were actors. Since he produced plays with all three De Milles, Henry, William and Cecil, in turn over two decades, the omission is curious, until one hears the tale – to be recounted further on – of his great split with Cecil over the authorship of one of his flagship plays – *The Return of Peter Grimm*, produced in 1911. The De Milles were all but written out of Belasco's life, and he soldiered on well into the 1940s, becoming America's longest lasting theatrical mogul.

While Belasco excelled in the technical staging and production of the plays he co-wrote with Henry De Mille, it was De Mille who mainly attended to the text – dialogue, characters, plot, construction. Critics for the most part applauded the plays, though there was resistance, as an article in the 4 March 1893 issue of *The Illustrated American* entitled 'About a Certain School of Plays' reveals:

Mr. De Mille discovered the possibilities for entertainment in the utter commonplaceness and puerility of the humors, sentiments, and motives of the school of which Mr. De Mille was a chief exponent; but in comparison with the placidity and prudery of 'The Wife' and 'The Charity Ball,' the really mild effusions that Robertson, Pinero, Gilbert and Howard had in lighter moments sprinkled on the boards, proved strong drink . . .

An understanding of the distinctive and essential characteristics of Mr. De Mille's dramas is best attained by the circumstances and environment that must in all probability have exerted a forceful influence on his mind and method. At the beginning of his scenic experiences he was employed as a reader of plays in a little box of a theatre . . . under the control of some gentlemen more or less commercially concerned with virtue and piety . . . They set out to find in dramatic form the sentimental platitudes, the innocuous jocularities, the labored namby-pambyism, whose charm and attractiveness had brought prosperity to their religious periodicals.

These pious patrons of De Mille, the anonymous writer noted, had not only mentored a new type of play but also a new audience, whose previous diversions had been consigned to 'Sabbath-school picnics, strawberry festivals, sociables and possibly an organ recital'. To thrill this audience, the author stated, De Mille would sprinkle his anodyne dramas with a 'Damn!' or two, entrusted 'to some player whose personal purity and whose manner of performance would remove any hint of violence or vulgarity from the objurgation'. To further spice things up, 'an element of farce' was added, as the patrons of this type of drama 'insisted on getting a giggle for their money'. The writer continued to put the boot into De Mille, who by then was a posthumous target, by mocking his presentations of love:

From the calf love of the impuberal twain, to the senile amorousness of some pursy widower and anxious spinster, through all the gradations of childhood, youth, middle age, and ripe maturity, they showed us love in all its phases, forms and conditions save those of actuality. It squatted on hall stairs, in scenes that imitated the absurd decoration and construction of the prevailing mode; it coddled behind screens; it nestled and cooed in freaks of upholstery; it sniffled in the softened light of stained glass church windows; it moaned in the face of the calcium moon; but it never deceived anybody that it really was love. It was never passionate, or proud, or willful, or jealous, or exacting, or cruel, or vengeful. A homely, prosaic, polite and prudent emotion it was that De Mille and his disciples portrayed . . .

Henry De Mille's plays are indeed mild fare for our tastes, long preceding the modern American theatre of psychodrama and extreme emotions reflecting a deranged, corrupt and/or decaying society. *The Wife* is a tale of a woman 'parted from her lover through the machinations of an adventuress to whom he had rashly engaged himself in former years, and whose plot is helped on by the villain to further some political aims'. Of course, virtue triumphs in the end. *The Charity Ball* presented a clergyman as hero, who has 'the manly as well as the churchly virtues, and is neither a prig nor a canter'. The villain is 'only a human one, a victim of the ambitions and social tendencies of the day'. Love is good, money grubbing is bad. As the *Brooklyn Daily Eagle* summed up, in 1890: 'The whole play is an outcome and presentment of good impulses, moral and artistic, and the impression that it leaves is wholesome.' *Lord Chumley* is a piece of fluff set in a mythical England of Henry's American imagination, where people say 'By Jove!' and 'By Jingo!', and once again true love comes up trumps. *Men and Women* is a far more substantial work, if verbose and somewhat ponderous, set in the New York world of bankers and politicians. Subtitled 'A Drama of Our Times', the cast includes Israel Cohen, 'a rich Hebrew' and President of the Jefferson National Bank, a Governor of Arizona, an ex-member of Congress, a rich stockbroker, cashiers, etc. The combination of a liberal Jew, a conservative churchman, embezzlement and speculation made the play controversial, and despite being panned for failing to display any 'evidence of conspicuous originality' by the *New York Herald*, it was a hit with the public. Of all Henry's plays, it had the longest reach and was filmed twice – as a silent movie – once in 1914, under the direction of James Kirkwood, and once by Henry's son William, in 1925.

Henry's last completed play, *The Lost Paradise*, about 'the war of classes against masses', was produced on stage in August 1891 by Charles Frohman's company (Charles being Daniel's second brother). Its German roots seemed to free Henry to present more radical ideas about 'the cause of the . . . laboring man'. The 'finely-bred daughter of a rich factory owner', the *New York Times* summed up the original German play by Ludwig Fulda from which it was adapted, 'learns in time that her father's sturdy foreman is a worthier suitor than a Berlin military fop.'

By this time, Henry had split from Belasco, who had become intensely involved in his obsession with furthering the acting career of Mrs Leslie Carter, a twenty-seven-year-old millionaire's wife who had been sued for divorce on the grounds of her adultery with five male lovers, and in Belasco's own words, rose rapidly 'to the place of great distinction she afterward attained as a star under my guidance'. Henry turned to his teaching at the Theatre of Arts and to the writing of a new play, *The Promised Land*, which would deal with the struggles of American working people. But it was never finished. Late in January 1893, while attending a Charles Frohman production in New York, he fell ill and returned to the old 'pre-revolutionary' house he had bought in Pompton, New Jersey, with money inherited by Beatrice from her father. He was diagnosed with typhoid fever and died ten days later, on 10 February 1893.

The *Brooklyn Daily Eagle* noted that he had 'died in his prime . . . when he had given hope that he would yet be great'. Hopes for a dignified religious cremation were somewhat dashed, according to the press, when, 'while the author's body was being incinerated the body of Michael Krenzol, the New York cigar-maker who had committed suicide and left a request that a band of music should accompany his remains to the crematory and also provided that three kegs of beer should be drank, arrived'.

Even in death, and not for the last time, piety and the profane clashed to disorder the de Mille plans.

The Hereditary Germ

Two years after the death of his father, when he was not yet twelve years old, young Cecil Blount De Mille witnessed the death from spinal meningitis of his little sister, Agnes, who had been born in 1891. She was only four years old. In his autobiography, Cecil described the scene as his mother brought him into the parlour, where his sister's small body lay in its coffin: 'Mother made each of us boys put our hand over the dead child's heart and pledge that we would never treat any woman other than we would have wanted Agnes treated, if she had lived. Mother had a high sense of the dramatic.'

That was a trait she certainly passed on to her sons. Beatrice was determined to commemorate and continue her husband's artistic path. She began by attempting, with the aid of her eldest son, William, then barely fourteen, to complete his last play, *The Promised Land*, but it was not produced. To maintain the upkeep of her house, which she and Henry had named Pamlico after the North Carolina river and the boat Henry had remembered from his child-hood, she negotiated with David Belasco to represent, as artists' agent, the plays co-written by himself and De Mille. Beatrice became a play-broker and authors' agent, with an office in the Knickerbocker Building on Broadway. At the same time, she opened a school for girls, adjacent to Pamlico, which she named after the deceased Henry. Its prospectus offered 'Learning By Doing' and promised its pupils, and their parents, 'the combined advantages of country and city, without their disadvantages. Pompton is comparatively near New York, which makes it possible for the girls to attend good music and good lectures, under proper chaperonage, after which they return to the healthful surroundings and healthful sports of country life.'

With good ventilation, hygienic plumbing and the country air, the school offered a near-military regimen of 'prompt, unquestioning obedience, and . . . habits of neatness and precision . . . The aim of

Pamlico girls' school, 1890s

the De Mille school is to teach each "little woman" to understand and properly fulfill the three-fold relation she occupies: her duty to herself, her home and her country.'

Beatrice's boys too were to be subject to a training befitting their patrimony. At fifteen, Cecil was enrolled at Pennsylvania Military College. His mother, according to Anne Edwards, bicycled down with him to the grounds at Chester, Pennsylvania. Thriftily, she exchanged Cecil's enrolment fee for that of the college headmaster's daughter at her own school. The eldest son, William, was now at Columbia College, having earlier been sent for a stint abroad at a college in Freiburg, Germany. Beatrice wanted a more secure niche in life for her sons than her husband's somewhat shaky profession. Years later, interviewed by the *New York Sun* in 1905 about the 'Playwriting Epidemic in the DeMille Family', she revealed that 'When Mr De Mille died he said to me on his deathbed: Don't make the boys playwriters. Make them grocers, butchers . . . Why? Because the life of the playwright is one of uncertainties, indecisions, disappointments, heartbreaks, and he wanted his children to choose a career that had something strong and certain about it . . .'

Henry had wanted William to be an electrical engineer, but when he left college, she said, he wanted to write plays. Mrs De Mille, the *Sun* reported, 'contends that playwriting is a germ. She says also, that it is ineradicable, contagious and hereditary. She goes further, and says that, while in many cases it is merely sporadic, in others it is epidemic. She cites her own family as an example of this last assertion.'

Writing plays, however, was not merely a job but a vocation. As Beatrice said of her husband's work: 'He worked with untiring patience to write plays that should be sincere, refined and helpful. He firmly believed that the aim of the theatre is not alone to amuse, but to teach, encourage and inspire. Even in his college days it was his great belief that the Church and the stage could be brought together and be of mutual benefit.'

Two major influences acted on this principle, both crucial in the ideological development of both the sons, William and Cecil. The first, noted by Cecil in his autobiography, was the English writer, parson and 'Protestant controversialist' Charles Kingsley, to whose work Henry was introduced by a local reverend, Charles H. Hall, around 1878. 'For the next decade,' Cecil wrote, 'Kingsley helped form father's thinking on the deepest things in life. He gradually acquired Kingsley's works, read them, annotated them, made them his constant companions.'

Kingsley was born in 1819 and became both a clergyman and a champion of England's poor and working people. His first novel, *Yeast*, dealt with the plight of agricultural workers. Through the pseudonym of 'Parson Lot', he continued to convey his sympathies for Christian socialism. He wrote novels, plays, poetry and sermons in which his radical views were propagated. His best known work to a modern audience is *The Water Babies*, of 1863, a tale of child chimney sweeps in a harsh and polluted world. Kingsley's homilies and aphorisms were popular in the late Victorian world of rapid technological change and a Protestant work ethic that sought divine sanction, rather than secular reform, for good deeds: 'Have thy tools ready, God will find thee work – All we need to make us really happy is something to be enthusiastic about – There are two freedoms, the false, where a man is free to do what he likes, the true, where he is free to do what he ought.' But he was also critical of religious conservatives: 'We have used the Bible', he wrote, 'as if it were a Constable's handbook, an opium-dose for keeping beasts of burden patient while they are overloaded.' Part of his religious creed was fiercely anti-Catholic, and his ideas were also part of a philosophical trend in Victorian England promoting a 'muscular Christianity' that combined godliness and manliness by going back to the 'Teutonic' roots of English history.

Be that as it may, it was the socially progressive Kingsley who clearly fired up Henry De Mille and influenced his move, at the end of his writing life, towards plays that dealt with social evils. Immediate contact with the steelworking families that attended church at Pompton also influenced both Henry and Beatrice, and in her own social life Beatrice had come into contact with Annie Fox George, widow of the writer and social critic Henry George.

Henry George, born in Philadelphia in 1839, had been a sailor before becoming a printer and journalist in California. Self-taught, he published two books which would be an enormous influence on a generation of Americans: *Our Land and Land Policy*, in 1871, and *Progress and Poverty*, in 1879. The latter became a secular bible for millions and a major influence on the De Mille family, not least because, in 1903, William de Mille married George's daughter, Anna. Their union begat Margaret and Agnes de Mille, Cecil's nieces, the latter destined to become a major force in the history of American dance and a Georgist disciple to the end of her life.

George has come down to us in American social history as the propagator of the 'Single Tax' theory. 'He lived and worked', Agnes later wrote of him, 'in a rapidly developing society. George had the unique opportunity of studying the formation of a civilization – the change of an encampment into a thriving metropolis . . . And as he saw the beginning of wealth, he noted the first appearance of pauperism . . .'

What George argued was that progress engendered poverty if it did not allow the 'lowest class' to share in the abundance created. The root of this, he claimed, was renting and the ownership by the rich of land and property. Untrained as an economist, he found a single-minded solution to economic pressures – the single, sole tax to be levied on the site value of land. The income from this would, he argued, be sufficient for all the needs of the state. His main bogy was not the money-making entrepreneur but the parasitical landowner. Karl Marx wrote about him in 1881:

Theoretically the man is utterly backward! He understands nothing about the nature of surplus value and so wanders about in speculations which follow the English model but have now been superseded even among the

English . . . This is a frank expression of the hatred which the industrial capitalist dedicates to the landed proprietor, who seems to him a useless and
superfluous element in the grand total of bourgeois production.

Nevertheless, George was obviously prominent enough to come to
Marx's attention, if only to be scoffed at. He completed six tours of
Europe, where his lectures brought him more popularity than he
enjoyed at home, but his American audience grew apace. Several
more books followed on social problems, free trade and protection-
ism, philosophy and political economy. In the year of his death,
1897, he had run for mayor of New York as the 'incorruptible Henry
George', but he died before the election. His funeral, wrote Anne
Edwards, 'was a state occasion; "the catafalque was borne through
the streets to torchlight and followed by a crowd of fifty-thousand . . .
Poor people filed past the body for hours."'

At George's death, young Cecil De Mille was only sixteen and subject to quite different ideas of social harmony at the Military College.
Previous to this he had been schooled at another of his mother's good
educational establishments, a school at Pompton over Durling's grocery. There he was tutored by one Miss Acker and beaten up by a
local bully, Lester Smith, who at least spared him the blows of his
baseball bat. Or so he told the tale. His upbringing at what became a
girls' school is glossed over somewhat in his account. Clearly the educational cream was meant for brother William, with his European
stint and college years. The Champion Driver was being restrained by
the spartan rules of cadet life. His grades were not spectacular, but he
did boast a mark of one hundred in deportment. Friday night, Cecil
wrote, was bath night: the ordinary spigots by which the boys
washed were replaced by tubs 'ingeniously arranged under the floor
of our washroom . . . On Fridays the floor was lifted, and our tubs
awaited us. This was', Cecil adds, referring tongue-in-cheek to his
later penchant for spectacular bath scenes, 'my first, but not my last
association with sunken bathtubs.'

The cadet's uniform was quite an asset to the young man arriving
on leave at mother's girls' school, but Cecil is reticent about the
results. In his third year at the college, in 1898, the Spanish-American
war broke out, Cecil's first experience of a patriotic rush, though his
wish to enlist was thwarted by his tender age. Despite this, there is
scant evidence that Cecil enjoyed army life, for, just as the war wound

Cecil, aged five, with brother William, aged seven

up, in the summer of 1898, as he put it: 'with mother's encouragement, it was decided that I should leave Pennsylvania Military College and enrol that fall in the American Academy of Dramatic Arts'.

In all, it would seem that Cecil B. DeMille's childhood was at least in part idyllic, spent in the open air, amid woods and valleys, waiting for the pony which his dad's friend David Belasco – who impressed the boys as a great shaggy dog of a man – had promised, and listening to his father's Bible tales by candlelight. One can imagine the impact of the loss of his father on the young boy, but this too became part of his legend, somewhat toned down by the authors of *Cecil B. DeMille, Young Dramatist*:

Cecil found the house was a painful place to be during the days immediately after Father's death. He began taking long walks through the woods, but did not find much comfort there. One afternoon he met Bert Terhune who was also hiking. The older youth sat down beside the eleven-year-old Cecil on a log. Below them stretched the steep mountain road. 'See the bumps in that road, Cecil?' Bert asked. 'When I was your age I hated those bumps. They made coasting on a sled down the incline rough and unpleasant . . . Then one day I met a man who told me those bumps had been put in the road deliberately. They were there to serve as brakes to loaded wagons and to guide the rain water into gutters. I realized that sometimes bumps are put into roads for a good purpose. Bumps in our lives are put there for a good purpose too.'

Cecil was thoughtful. Losing Father was a terrible bump for all the DeMilles. But the road would go on for the rest of the family . . .

Bert Terhune, son of the local Dutch Reformed minister of Pompton Lakes, was a journalist and future novelist, a welcome mentor – and boxing teacher – for the fatherless boy. Further legends recounted about young Cecil included his one allegedly authentic feat as the Champion Driver, a horse ride across snowy ground to bring dynamite to break the ice endangering the Ramapo Dam above the Ludlum Steel Mill: '"If something isn't done soon the dam will break . . ."' "The DeMille boy here rides like the wind," said a young farmer, looking at Cecil . . . "I can ride fast and I can do it,"' says the determined lad, then only twelve years old. He rides off to the store to bring the dynamite: 'Nearer and nearer he came to Pompton. Would the dam hold? . . . All at once he could see the mill. Then he could see the men. A moment later they saw him and raised their hats and yelled. In a short time they had placed the dynamite and lighted the fuses. A great thundering noise shook the countryside as the dynamite went off. The ice jam was broken.'

Real life was less exciting, and more sombre. The death of his little sister deepened Cecil's dependence on both his mother and older brother. Apart from the outdoor pursuits of bicycling, boating, hiking, riding (with or without dynamite) and high-school football, young Cecil had, like any boy, a developed fantasy life. One of his first attempts to set this down in writing has been recorded by his adopted son, Richard de Mille, who in 1998 quoted childe Cecil's 'My Hunting Story', preserved by Beatrice down the years: 'When I was nine I had a verry small gun. I whent out to see what I could shout . . . It was snowing verry fast when I started for home . . .' A friendly dog comes to young Cecil's aid when he is attacked by a panther, but the boy's knife kills the dog by mistake. 'I thrwe him ofver my back and carid him home. And now he stands in the parler in the same possichon he was in when he saved my life.'

A very early rehearsal of the story-teller's future trade. But his main ambition at the turn of the twentieth century was still focused on the family profession – the theatre. Beatrice too followed in Henry's footsteps, writing, in collaboration with Harriet Ford, a play entitled *The Greatest Thing in the World*, which had a brief stage run in 1900. The two women had also, Beatrice informed the press in 1905, 'written a play that is in the hands of Beerbohm Tree, called "Rembrandt", in which we have used some of the dramatic events in the picturesque life of the great painter'. A third play, *A Dominant Chord*, was also mentioned, but neither of the latter two appear to have been produced.

Cecil began his stage apprenticeship, like his father before him, as an actor. His first recorded appearance was in a small part in a play called *Hearts Are Trumps* by Cecil Raleigh, produced by Charles Frohman at New York's Garden Theatre in February 1900. Appearances in *A Repentance*, *To Have and To Hold* and *Are You a Mason?* followed the next year, and in 1902, another small part, in *Hamlet*. Cecil wrote about these first modest steps: 'Kind-hearted publicists who have written about me have sometimes said that I became an actor in order to learn production. The facts are more elemental. I became an actor in order to eat.'

But *Hearts Are Trumps* was significant not only for its place in DeMille's career, for it was during its run that a young actress, Constance Adams, a New Jersey judge's daughter, joined the cast while it toured in Washington DC. At New Year's Eve at the end of the first year of the century, Cecil recounts, Constance and he were engaged. On 16 August 1902, at Judge Frederick Adams's home in East Orange, New Jersey, they were married, Cecil having just attained the proper age of twenty-one. Constance was eight years older. The *New York Times* reported that

Miss Rebecca Adams, a sister of the bride, was the maid of honor, and William C. De Mille, a brother of the bridegroom, was the best man. The house was decorated with flowers and palms. After a reception Mr. and Mrs. De Mille left on an extended wedding trip. They will reside in New York.

This dry item concealed the good judge's reluctance to give his daughter away to a jobbing actor, but Constance was determined enough to hold out. The wedding party, Anne Edwards informs us, was 'kept down to family members and very old friends. Except for Beatrice, the Samuel family was overlooked.' Cecil kept the Jewish branch of his genealogical tree firmly out of Gentile sight.

Brother William, for his part, waited another year before marrying Anna Angela George on 31 March 1903 at the George family home in Fort Hamilton. 'Although the weather was anything but agreeable,' noted the *New York Times*, 'the house was filled with guests from Brooklyn, Manhattan and out of town . . . John De Mille, an Uncle of the bridegroom, was the best man.' Constance and Cecil, we are told, were touring and not present. This was the first evidence of something of a gap, if not a rift, between the brothers: William, intellectual, handsome, sportive, attractive to a variety of women; Cecil, the more stolid, workmanlike second string of the family. Perhaps Beatrice too may have preferred that he become a grocer or engineer. But the hereditary bug had bitten, and both brothers were now embarked upon their intersecting careers.

'Intelligent Effort Along an Individual Line . . .'

The American theatre in the first decade of the twentieth century was, as ever, in search of the Great American Play. Show business glittered and pranced on the stages of Broadway, from the musicals of George M. Cohan to operettas and musical revues, as well as the continuing successes of David Belasco and the 'star maker', Charles Frohman. In 1905, the same year in which Cohan presented *Little Johnny Jones*, which featured the hit song 'Yankee Doodle Boy', the *New York Times* was discussing 'the Outlook for a Native Drama', as reflected in new plays by John W. Broadhurst, Clyde Fitch and William C. de Mille. Their plays, wrote the *Times*, represented 'intelligent effort directed with some success along an individual line . . . the general result has been such as to add to the hope, which recent events have created, for the future of playwriting in this country'. The future, one notes, but not yet the present, for the American stage was dominated by plays written not by Americans but by foreign playwrights, as it had been since the 1890s. At the end of the nineteenth century, the Norwegian Henrik Ibsen dominated the serious theatre, with works such as *Hedda Gabler* and *A Doll's House*. In a lighter tone, the Englishman Arthur Wing Pinero was popular with social plays like *The Second Mrs Tanqueray*, which dealt, controversially, with the marriage of a society gent to a woman with an immoral past. The play, performed in New York in 1893, was followed in 1895 by Oscar Wilde's *The Importance of Being Earnest*, while 1894 saw the first New York performance of a George Bernard Shaw play, *Arms and the Man*. A decade later, in 1905, Shaw's *Mrs Warren's Profession*, dealing boldly with prostitution, opened in New York for one night's performance only, after which the cast was carted off in a police van. J. M. Barrie's *Peter Pan* opened in November 1905, 'a pleasant antidote', wrote critics, 'to this Shavian unpleasantness'.

Among American playwrights, Clyde Fitch was amazingly prolific, earning at his peak over a quarter of a million dollars a year. In 1901, four of his plays were being staged simultaneously. He was, wrote the critic and theatrical historian Brooks Atkinson, 'a charming, modest man . . . everything about him remains attractive to this day – except, unfortunately, his plays', the most memorable of which was *Beau Brummell*, written with, or some said by, the star actor Richard Mansfield. William de Mille, however, was written entirely out of Atkinson's touchstone history, *Broadway*, in which the only de Mille mentioned is Agnes.

In 1907, William participated in a *New York Times* forum which discussed 'The Ideal Play'. This should, said William, be the play 'all of us who are writing plays hope to create some day. It should be an American play, of course. If an American playwright hasn't enough patriotism to wish his country to produce the crowning achievements of the drama, he should stop writing plays . . . The ideal play should be something more than a mere coterie of fashionably dressed people who exchange epigrammatic quips and stroll about showing off imported gowns and tailored suits.' William was exhibiting a common misconception of Oscar Wilde's work at this point. He added: 'I believe that the great play should get down underneath the veneer of society and convention and show human souls and human emotions in native strife. Strife, as Yeats has said, is the basis of all drama, hence it would overreach any semblance of melodrama or rant and hold audiences by its strength.'

The kind of strife that would, in due course, electrify the American stage and change it for ever was yet to come: it would arrive in 1915 with the young Eugene O'Neill, son of James O'Neill, David Belasco's old associate. But O'Neill's coruscating style, as it developed, would have been anathema to William de Mille. William's 'Ideal Play' would have to be 'treated in a wholesome manner, and the characters should be clean-cut and straightforward'. These principles informed the first play that provided William with success on the New York stage – *Strongheart*, produced at the Hudson Theatre in January 1905.

The play was set in an environment familiar to William: New York City's Columbia College, where the protagonist, an American Indian, fights prejudice to compete in the football team. In the subplot, a love affair between the Indian, Strongheart, and a student, Dorothy, is impeded by his duty to his tribe, who cannot accept her. Thus the play's initial anti-racist message becomes blunted by a matching Indian prejudice. Despite William's social pretensions, it becomes a typically American dilemma of an individual caught between love and obligation. This would become, in the fullness of time, a central mechanism of brother Cecil's motion-picture dramas.

The dialogue, realistic throughout most of the play, becomes highly stylized at the denouement:

BILLY: What's up between you and the boys?
STRONGHEART: The knife of prejudice has cut the ties of friendship.
BILLY: Is that straight?
STRONGHEART: Yes –
BILLY: Then I'm ashamed of my whole damn race, and I'll go and tell 'em so.

At the end, Strongheart is left alone on the stage, declaiming:

STRONGHEART (*raising his arms and face upwards*): Oh, great spirit of my fathers, I call to you for help, for I am in the midst of a great desert, alone.

William benefited from the talent and popularity of his lead actor, Robert Edeson, a major star of the day, who gained him good reviews, although the *New York Times* did snidely comment on the 'somewhat rather tiresome "race question" . . . There is nothing complex or subtle about the play,' wrote the *Times*, 'its appeal is simple, direct, such as to attract the "average theatregoer."'

While William was marking his first theatrical triumph, Cecil was labouring away at his own attempts to apply the family flair. From 1903 to 1904, Cecil was still eking out his living, with Constance, as a jobbing actor in stock theatre. On the New York stage he was sighted once more in *Hamlet*, as Osric, and in 1905 in a piece of froth, *The Prince Chap*, at Madison Square Garden, as the Earl of Huntington: 'Cecil B. DeMille was capital as the Earl and received a hearty round of applause, which was well deserved.' But between acts he too was scribbling away.

Cecil's first completed piece as a would-be playwright was *The Pretender – A Play in a Prologue and 4 Acts*, written about the same time that William was drafting his Indian college saga. The play was oddly set, not in any world familiar to the DeMilles but in Czarist Russia at the beginning of the seventeenth century. Its prologue takes place in 'Uglitch, Russia' in 1591, and the main events in 1602, in

Young Cecil in Henry De Mille's play

Russia and Poland. The tale was a rehash of a theme familiar to the Russians: of Boris Godunov and the false aspirant to the throne, Dimitri, a cossack captain who claims to be the son of Ivan the Terrible. Characters include Prince Vasili of the Supreme Council of Russia, the Dowager Czarina Marie and two Godunovs, Michael and Boris. Clearly Cecil was not in his element, with lines such as: 'Ah, Poland, my beautiful Poland, how quietly you sleep tonight,' or exchanges like:

MARIE: Are you the bearer of news from Moscow?
VASILI: Sad news, your Majesty.
MARIE: News from Moscow is always sad news, Prince.

As was the news from Robert Edeson, who was offered the play but preferred brother William's *Strongheart*. In fact, a 1907 article in *The Bookman* suggested it was Edeson who proposed to William de Mille that he should write him a part as an Indian:

De Mille worked for two years and a half on this play and wrote six distinct versions before one was finally evolved which met the requirements of actor, manager and playwright. It is a rather curious coincidence that even in his college days when de Mille appeared in college theatricals he took the part of an Indian. A little later he wrote a one-act play, 'Forest Flower,' in which the principal character was also an Indian. Then came 'Strongheart,' and finally in conjunction with his brother 'Son of the Winds,' a play in which all the characters are Indians. It would seem from this that de Mille was going hard after 'the American play.'

Son of the Winds, another unperformed play, was an even greater curiosity than *The Pretender*, set in a mythical Indian past in which the wind gods intervene to save a child who will become a great chief in the future. The prologue features Paguk (Death), Ka-Noka (the North Wind), Ka-Beyun (the East Wind), etc. The place is 'the Great White Plains', the time – 'before the white man came':

Scene: The Desert of the Southland at midnight. Great and weird formations of many colored rocks are on both sides . . . the Desert beyond: boundless, trackless, waterless, hopeless . . . The sage brush is grey and burnt . . . Great white patches of alkali are dotted here and there . . .
The mother calls: O Great White Spirit, stoop low and look upon the son of a chief, see the great wolf's head of his tribe burnt upon him like his father . . . It is the time when the spirits of the dead come back to earth. When the good Gods and the bad Gods meet in battle . . .

The mythological world appears to echo with old childhood fantasies shared by the brothers William and Cecil: the primeval landscape, the exotic-sounding names of the characters – Moanahunga (the Wanderer), Wa-Saw-Me-Saw (Roaring Thunder), Kee-o-Kuk (the Running Fox), Otaka (the Scalp Taker) – and the battleground of Good and Evil blend with the Champion Driver's boyhood imaginings into the play's ponderous soliloquies:

MOANAHUNGA: Take the trail that leads northward. Somewhere is a maiden who shall love you. Somewhere happiness awaits you. Many nations shall be your friend. Many seek to kill you. Unaided you must fight them. Using your wisdom, then your arrows . . .

'My warriors', the evil Otaka warns the primal hero, 'are waiting for the war cry, to kill the children and to burn the aged. Not one shall live to sing the death songs of your nation . . .'
It was the mundane necessities of life, however, rather than the

slings and arrows of imaginary enemies that were hampering Cecil's pathway to glory. Life on the road with his wife and the various companies of travelling players, he wrote, was tough, criss-crossing the nation in the old 'wooden railroad coaches . . . with the windows that were called poker windows because it took jacks or better to open them'. At one point, in West Virginia, the train crashed, the fire extinguisher falling and spilling chemicals on his head, and a travelling salesman 'began to chase the conductor down the aisle yelling that he didn't care about the wreck but wanted his mileage ticket back . . .' This event may have fuelled, twenty years later, the spectacular train-crash scene in one of his most bizarre silent sagas, *The Road to Yesterday*. But despite the rigours of the road, he wrote, 'it gave one a feeling of and for America – the America between the coasts', which the patrician East Coast boy would not have otherwise experienced.

The tours also helped him learn, he recalled later, the craft of the director, mainly by watching the great actor-director E. H. Sothern hone the performances of the cast, applying the kind of perfectionism that would become a DeMille trademark. From Belasco Cecil had learned the necessity of showmanship, the innate bravado of the theatrical magician who throws spectacle and drama at the audience until it has to pay attention.

As yet, there was no sign that either Cecil or William were paying much attention to the new unruly kid on the show business block – the motion picture, which was still very much in its infancy. Until 1905, movie showings in America were confined to fairs, small halls and the tail end of vaudeville programmes. The tailor-made 'nickelodeons' began to appear at the end of that year, and to proliferate to the end of the decade. Movies were short, mostly one or half-reelers, lasting between six and twelve minutes (or a little more, depending on the speed of projection). For the sons of Henry and Beatrice De Mille, the play was still the thing.

The peak of Beatrice's play-brokering business also came in 1905, with the *New York Sun*'s interviewer, in early March, finding her enthusing 'against an interesting background in her workshop at the Hudson Theatre Building, where the inspired and aspiring bring their masterpieces for her reading, criticism and approval. There is a model, which looks like a doll's house, of the college boys' room in "Strongheart," even to the stockings dangling from the chandelier, there are innumerable photographs of her talented family, a huge motto with Boucicault's famous words, "plays are not written but rewritten," and many other articles of vertu and virtuous endeavour . . .'

Continued the *Sun*:

The word enthuses is appropriate for Mrs De Mille has taken a 6 o'clock train from Middletown, N.Y., and at 11, when she talks to the interviewer, through breakfast, she has no signs of fatigue. In the course of the talk, busy people from all over the theatre rush in to say:

'Did he make good?'

Mrs De Mille explains that her youngest son, Cecil, has just opened at Middletown in 'Lord Chumley,' his first star part.

Her shining eyes and smiling lips are witness enough of his success, but she speaks of it with remarkable reserve, considering that she is a proud mother, seeing a favourite son act in a play written by the father . . . She laughs until she has tears in her black eyes, when she tells of the difficulties.

'Everything went all right but the orchestra; something had happened to it, and at the last moment the manager found a drummer . . . naively ignorant of what was expected of him . . .

'Fortunately for us the Middletownians do not demand Wagnerian orchestration between acts . . .

'Have we any fundamental principle, in our family, in our playwriting? . . . We have that left by the father of the family. I think I may repeat what so many of his friends wrote after his death, a sentiment repeated in the resolutions sent by the Lambs, the American Dramatists' Society, the Lyceum Stock Company and others – that he worked with untiring patience to write plays that should be sincere, refined and helpful. He firmly believed that the aim of the theatre is not alone to amuse, but to teach, encourage and inspire. Even in his college days it was his great belief that the Church and the stage could be brought together and be of mutual benefit.

'He certainly established an ideal for us to achieve, and though the boys have not followed his advice and become grocers I don't believe their incursions into the playwriting field will ever bring the name of De Mille into disrepute.'

In 1905, Mrs De Mille was still running both her agency and her much-nurtured girls' school at Pamlico, though the latter was soon to close in the wake of an infamous national scandal. This involved a young teenage showgirl she had taken on at Pamlico back in 1902, at the request of a wealthy architect in her social circle, Stanford White. The girl, Evelyn Nesbit, while being White's lover, was also pursued by the already famous young thespian John Barrymore, who continued wooing her in New Jersey. Nevertheless, Evelyn married another rich young man, Harry Thaw, in 1905. (William de Mille was on the sidelines of this story, having been engaged at Pamlico as Evelyn's 'fencing master'.) In June 1906, however, things came to a boil when, having discovered White was still Evelyn's lover, Thaw shot the architect in full public view at the Madison Square Garden Roof Theatre. As the case, its lurid background and Thaw's trial made headlines, alarmed parents pulled their girls out of Pamlico, and Beatrice was forced to file for bankruptcy in December 1907.

As it was now up to the De Mille sons to save the family's reputation, Beatrice had already taken on the representation of William and Cecil in their first full-blown collaboration, called *The Genius*. This was presented to the public at the Bijou Theatre in New York in October 1906. The De Milles had managed to capture one of vaudeville's best comedians, Nat C. Goodwin (who had made his reputation as 'The Happy Tramp'), to star in the show and produce it. Reviews were lukewarm at best:

[It is] the story of one Jack Spencer, who, unendowed with talents in the artistic line, sets out to buy them by the yard. He becomes the fad of the hour, and suffers all the attendant discomforts of lionism. He falls in love with a Trilbyesque model, named Nell Graham, but is engaged to Josephine Van Dusen, who loves him for his art's sake alone. He manages to convince the latter that to marry her would be to kill his inspiration, so she sacrifices her love upon the altar of art – with a capital A – and leaves the Genius with his model.

The farce, which is frankly such, with no attempt to dress itself up in the borrowed plumes of high comedy, is lively and wholesome. The satire is keen, and the play abounds with bright epigrammatical speeches and comical situations . . . If it is a little thin-waisted at times one does not go to a farce to stretch one's mental arm uncomfortably . . . (*New York Mirror*)

The *New York Times* was more scathing: 'All along there are laughs in spite of the staleness of William C. and Cecil de Mille's lines. But everybody who knows Mr. Goodwin on the stage will know how he makes that possible . . . The aim, of course, is to be a broad satire upon the misguided persons who dote upon Art and lionize Artists. It is but fair to add that some of the satire tells.'

Reputedly, *The Genius* was more the work of Cecil than William, and the published text certainly reveals more longueurs than shafts of genuine wit. Jack Spencer is a faker who presents himself as a genius, only to find that when he finally reveals himself as a sham, society is too vain to accept this. Jack raves:

JACK: Of all the concentrated, double-barrelled idiots I ever saw these peo-ple are the champions! Not one of them believes me, I wonder if, Good God! Maybe I am a genius. (*He sinks on central settee in despair*) . . . I have been branded a genius, and in spite of all I can do, I will remain a genius as long as I live!

His art being a fake, Jack can now divest himself of the society girl, Josephine:

JACK: If you marry me, the romance will go out like a candle . . . Oh, don't you see that a genius, because he's a genius, must marry a woman and not an artist? He must have someone to cook, and darn his socks . . . You can imag-ine the effect of a genius seeing his inspiration in curl-papers –
JOSEPHINE: Yes, you are right, I never thought of that before. Why, marriage is the worst thing that can happen to Art.
JACK: I give you my word, Josephine, that if you marry me, you will find my Art will soon die. If you wish to believe in my genius, you must not see me after Tuesday . . .

In reality, both Cecil and William had married society women, although one must assume that Constance DeMille, on the road, did her fair share of cooking, darning socks and sitting around in curlers. DeMille noted in his own account of his life that all he would say about his wife was that she was most aptly named. This did not cut both ways, however, as both brothers had a roving eye for the ladies, and Cecil soon found the age gap between himself and his wife reflected deeper libidinal issues. As described much later by his adopted son Richard de Mille, upon his marriage 'Cecil was barely twenty-one, an imperious, hot-blooded Edwardian ladies' man. Constance was already twenty-nine, a cool, restrained Victorian matron.'

Whether or not this reflected the realities at the time is a moot point. What we can surmise from a later letter, quoted by Richard, is their sexual incompatibility. Cecil preferred a strong, aggressive approach, to her obvious reluctance. As he wrote at the time of his departure late in 1913 to begin his movie career out west:

I love to feel your body next to mine and pressing close . . . Here then is my predicament . . . I must teach my wife those things the mistress usually pro-vides . . . But, shrieks the horrified god of morals, she is a good woman, she is so pure, she has no right even to know that such things exist, to feel such violent and evil passions . . .

Whatever her misgivings – about his unusual candour as much as his particular cravings, hair pulling being mentioned as one aspect – we know that Cecil and Constance conceived, and she bore a child, Cecilia, born on 5 November 1908, over six years after their marriage. 'I had to help the doctor deliver at home,' Cecil wrote, 'because we could not afford a hospital or a nurse.' Cecilia would be the first and last child born to Cecil and Constance, and their three future children would all be adopted.

Curbing his secret desires to have 'light, liberty and passion' in his love life or hiving his sadistic impulses off to suitable mistresses, unnamed in this early period, Cecil continued to deploy his boyhood fantasies in another playscript, first titled 'Sergeant Devil May Care' and later renamed *The Royal Mounted*. Meanwhile, he toured with the Standard Opera Company. We have no record of his singing prowess, apart from brief mention of his laryngeal exercises in shows such as *The Mikado* and *The Bohemian Girl*. As for William, he presented another college play, *Classmates*, written in collaboration with Margaret Turnbull, in 1907. Then, later in the same year, he found himself with another success, *The Warrens of Virginia*, which opened in December 1907. The play ran for 380 performances before closing in October 1908. Apart from being a hit, it also renewed an old collaboration – between the DeMilles and its producer, David Belasco.

4

Back from the Dead . . .

After his original collaboration with Henry DeMille, David Belasco had soldiered on with his own plays in New York. He had begun to specialize in plays set in the frontier west, such as *The Girl I Left Behind Me* of 1893, or in a Civil War setting, like *The Heart of Maryland*, produced in 1895. Free of De Mille's attempts at genteel social criticism, he deepened his own brand of theatrical effects, prompting critical grumbles about 'wild shrieking melodrama' and comments that 'Belasco is always the deviser, the contriver, the constructor of illusions and stage tricks.' While Belasco continued to shamelessly present himself as *sui generis*, script collaborators were sometimes acknowledged, sometimes not. He discovered a story by John Luther Long called 'Madam Butterfly' and adapted it into a play, which would later be made more famous by Puccini's opera, first performed in 1904. Fighting for his independence from theatrical managers like the monopolizing moguls Klaw and Erlanger, by 1905 he had his own theatre, the Belasco, where he presented another western saga, *The Girl of the Golden West*. *Rose of the Rancho* followed in 1906, lasting 480 performances.

These latter two plays were eventually to be movies directed by Cecil B. DeMille, but as yet neither the De Milles nor Belasco were paying attention to the medium that Belasco would describe, in his 1919 memoir *The Theatre Through Its Stage Door*, as 'the Drama's flickering bogy'.

The Warrens of Virginia was, like *The Heart of Maryland*, a Civil War tale. Although the writing was left to William de Mille, the new play bore a resemblance to the old one, both with plots involving a spy and love across the lines. In contrast with Belasco's melodrama, it displayed a deeper emphasis on character and social background, featuring the kind of old-school southern family that northern audiences loved to patronize. The fair southern daughter of the laid-back

General Warren is torn between her love for a northern officer and her duty to her cause. The northern officer is torn between his duties as a spy and his love for the southern woman he is betraying.

It is a classic DeMille dilemma which would later fuel many of Cecil's films – and indeed, *The Warrens of Virginia* would be another of his early movies. For the moment, Cecil had to content himself with a supporting role in the play, alongside a new child star called Gladys Smith, renamed for the purpose as Mary Pickford, who was at this time fourteen years old. The *New York Times* wrote: 'Mary Pickford and Master Richard Story played two children's parts very charmingly.' In a nod to Belasco and his collaborators' staging, the *Times* added that 'the scenery and effects were beautiful, and it is doubtful if anything lovelier has been disclosed than Ernest Gros' first act set in this play, showing a wooded copse with a little stream trickling down through trees and tangled underbrush'.

Cecil was to remember this staging, as well as the other lessons learned from Belasco's success in presenting hokum as quality. Belasco's innovations in lighting techniques derived from his desire to achieve a kind of heightened realism on the stage: 'It was my fortune', he was to write in his memoir, 'to come into the theatre during a time when lighting appliances and the use of illuminating effects were undergoing a great scientific revolution.' Years later, he was still striving to 'utilize to the fullest extent every new means by which the true effects of nature could be more closely reproduced in the theatre'.

Lighting, rather than the music of the 'melo'-drama, would represent the play's mood. Cecil would recall this when he began his own movie production, although he could not copy Belasco's more advanced experiments in the use of colours and hues. 'Romantic impulse', writes Belasco, 'springs from the half-lights, and thus the twilight, with its silvery blue, is the hour of lovers' trysts. Observe the effect of the yellow gleam of a lamp, shining from a window into the darkness, and note the feeling of half-fear that involuntarily steals over you. Yet courage comes in the clear white light of the noonday sun. Look at the sickly moon and detect at once a feeling of sadness . . .'

Many critics had long grumbled that Belasco's effects came at the expense of content, although it would fall to the eminent George Jean Nathan, in 1917, to put the boot squarely into Belasco's legend, writing of this 'clever man – the cleverest, and by all odds, in the native theatre . . . chuckling up his sleeve, for it is impossible to imagine him deceived by his own tin-pantaloonery, [as] he witnessed the canonization of his own simple humbug . . .'

Yet on the stage, as it would be in the cinema, the producer who scored multiple hits, even with a few failures in between, could do no wrong. It fell to William de Mille to try to square the circle of his own one-time enthusiasm to write the 'Ideal Play' and the exigencies of Mammon, as he told *The Bookman*, in 1907:

'The great American play? It will be written, but it will not be a single solitary upshot, it will be the best of a series of great American plays.'

De Mille believes that a play should have a message. Not that this message must necessarily be delivered in a heavy didactic way. Quite the contrary. The play must entertain first, and after that, if it teaches, all the better. But the message may be delivered through the medium of farce or of melodrama. A man should be catholic in his taste.

'I believe the man who writes the best stuff makes the most money. The converse is also true. That is, I mean the stuff must be good in its class, must be good farce, must be good melodrama, must be good for that public to which it is meant to appeal. But the test for all plays must be that they shall be close to the spirit of nature, that they shall possess artistic truth rather than naturalistic truth . . .'

The success of *The Warrens of Virginia* did, however, rub off on Cecil within a few months. In April, his own play, now called *The Royal Mounted*, was staged at the Garrick Theatre. It was presented, once again, as a collaboration with his brother. Opening on 6 April 1908, its robust, adventurous, northwest-frontier setting was perfect for the Champion Driver, its motto plain and manly: 'There are four stages to a murder in the Northwest. First, there's the murder; then there's the Mounted; then there's a hanging; and then there's peace.'

Belasco could not have put it more succinctly, but Cecil was ready now to set out his own stall. For propriety's sake, there is still an English aristocrat in the narrative, named for some reason O'Byrne (later O'Brian), who has been disinherited by his father Sir Gerald (of Castle O'Brian) and has therefore joined the Canadian Mounties. He is in love with Rosa, a wench as robust as he, having decamped from a Quebec convent to live in a cabin in the Great Elk. As O'Brian describes his amorous moment: 'I felt the same as I did when I was hunting my first bull moose.'

O'Brian is the Mounties' champion tracker, having gone out

'through three hundred miles of wilderness' to 'arrest and bring back an Indian murderer'. To correct the racial impression, his commander, Major Buckland, tells his men: 'Be careful . . . Bad white men are worse than Indians.' O'Brian's dialogue is Cecil's idea of Canadian wilderness brogue:

O'BRIAN: Oh, Major, you've never lived three weeks with an Indian who couldn't see a joke, and whose one fond hope was to get a chance to stick a knife into you – and turn it round once for luck. Twenty one nights in camp with a graven image, tempting the beggar to smile – with the choicest bits of Irish humor – and all I could get out of him was the most disgusted expression you ever saw, and a couple of grunts – for knowing the old son-of-a-gun would be hanged when we got home, I tried to make the trip as pleasant as possible, but nothing could please that Indian. I believe he killed his squaw because she made him laugh . . .

The murderer O'Brian is tracking this time, however, is Rosa's brother, a classic DeMillean moral dilemma, but in the end the slain man turns out to be a wanted assassin himself, and so it is revealed that no murder occurred after all.

The cast is replete with frontier names like Joe Hammer – Foreman of No. 13; Long Jack – the Uncertain, lumberman; Louis Trudeau – the Questioner; Mag Trudeau, Louis' sister, etc. The *New York Times* called the work 'A Story-Book Play', noting that 'the Canadian Northwest is a colorful country, the kind out of which the timber of real drama might be hewn. Somebody will do it some day. But he will know the life first hand . . . Twice during the evening the play gives a mild thrill of the unexpected; for the rest it is easily discounted out of familiar past experience. Such freshness as there is comes from the unusualness of the minor characters – taciturn Canucks, rough of manner and hesitant of speech, or speaking in queer phrases, as, 'My family, I hope he ain't be seeck,' which, considering that it refers to a wife and brood of twelve Canucks, means a pretty hard burden on one poor little personal pronoun.'

As well as writing the play, Cecil co-directed it, in tandem with the show's star, Cyril Scott. Another actor, Samuel Claggett, produced. But the play flopped, running for only thirty-two performances and closing the next month. Still, Cecil had his job in the cast of *The Warrens of Virginia,* and its fifteen-month run and subsequent tours kept food on his table throughout 1909. In his spare time, he penned another Indian play, *The Stampede*, written together with one of Beatrice's playwright clients, Lillian Buckingham. To put it on, Cecil sought a loan from David Belasco, but Belasco was not keen on the play. It was eventually produced by the Chicago Stock Company, but not to any resounding success.

Moving on from *Son of the Winds*, *The Stampede* tried to marry a tale of political skulduggery with the fate of an Indian tribe, the Chickasaws. John Morton, a 'Money Power', gets a young senator, Billy Bobbs, to sponsor the 'Witch Creek Bill', which will grant former Indian lands to white farmers. Unknown to the Indians, a money-making mine is situated on these lands. Dick Travers, a mining engineer, is in on the plot, but his lover Wanga, an 'educated half-breed', is caught in the familiar dilemma: her love for Dick versus her responsibility to inform her people of the scam, which will result in the Central Pacific Railroad running its tracks through the heart of Indian country. Dick tells her: 'You and I are worthy of each other. We are a splendidly matched pair. We both pretend friendship and we both betray those who trust us.'

Cecil could not shake off this kind of bombastic language:

MORTON: I can break a man as quickly as I can make him. There is no limit to the power of brains in combination with capital.

WANGA: You have all you need – money and power to satisfy an Emperor. In the name of Mercy – leave my poor people alone.

MORTON: Civilization demands that the Indians make way, they are of the past – the country belongs not even to the present, but to the illimitable future.

In the not so distant future, Cecil DeMille would return to the idea of rampant capital against the simple needs of folk again and again, reflecting a politics that we do not usually associate with his name. But at this point, Cecil may have thought Belasco could be brought on board by opportunities to stage a final spectacular scene, as the script sets out:

The roar of the stampeding cattle drowns every other sound – clouds of dust from the plain – thunder of hoofs, bellowing of cattle etc. Chapa and Joe stand on rock against skyline during the storm of sound – looking down at the plain – the sounds begin to recede . . .

Did Cecil consider, at this early stage, the possibilities of staging this kind of scene, not within the limited bounds of the theatre, but in another medium? After all, he does write that he had seen Edwin S. Porter's breakthrough *The Great Train Robbery* (made in 1903), albeit a picture with fairly static segments. As yet, in 1910, there is no sign of any such ambition. Belasco, in any case, was not tempted, but suggested paying Cecil to write a new play for him, which Belasco would produce if he wished to.

Cecil proceeded to this task. In his own account of the episode, he claimed that he went off to the woods of Maine to contemplate this assignment and saw the roots of his idea in the transformation of a grub into 'a beautiful dragonfly . . . It was the drama of eternal resurrection'. This gave him a religious epiphany: 'I had seen life come from death. If Our Father does this for a dragonfly, what must He not do for us?'

Such an autobiographical conceit might reflect more on the older and richer Cecil B. DeMille's requirement to give early events in his life cosmic significance than any accurate memory. At any rate, the play Cecil wrote for Belasco was the tale of a rich and ruthless businessman who had wronged his ward, a young girl, and who after death returned to right the wrongs he had done. What happened next soured the relationship between Cecil and Belasco for years to come. Belasco took the play, rewrote the characters, changed the ruthless businessman into a 'lovable old Dutchman of up-State New York – a grower of tulips and orchids – who returns to earth after his death in Act One to set right some things in his household which he left awry', and produced it on the stage as his own work under the title *The Return of Peter Grimm*, starring one of the leading actors of the day, David Warfield.

Belasco admitted to the press that Cecil DeMille had brought him the original idea of a man returning from the dead, but claimed his own memory of an appearance of his mother from beyond the grave, on the very night she died, had sparked his interest in the subject of ghosts. Buried in the small print of the lesser credits was the notation 'based on an idea by Cecil B. DeMille', which prevented effective legal action. But Cecil found it difficult to believe his father's friend and his own childhood idol had so blatantly plagiarized his work.

The Return of Peter Grimm opened in Chicago in January 1911 and was an instant success, despite at least one critic, Lewis Hillhouse in Cincinnati, pointing out its similarity to another source, 'a novel by Mrs Oliphant, called "Old Lady Mary; a Story of the Seen and

Unseen."' Cecil tried to fight his corner when the play opened in New York, accusing Belasco of taking credit for his work, but the press noted, wearily, that 'it is no new thing for Belasco to be charged with irregularities in the matter of claiming credit as author of plays . . .' The power of Belasco, as ever, prevailed.

By this time, Cecil had broadened his experience of the stage by taking on the direction and production of other people's plays. *The Wishing Ring*, a play by the prolific melodramatist Owen Davis, later to be a noted Hollywood scriptwriter, was directed by Cecil on Broadway in January 1910. Other plays produced but not written by Cecil would follow – *Speed*, *The Marriage Not* and *Cheer Up*, a play by one of Beatrice's star clients, Mary Roberts Reinhart, produced in 1912.

Beatrice, meanwhile, had weathered her bankruptcy over the Pamlico girls' school, opened a new office in the Astor Theatre Building and inaugurated a new business: the DeMille Play Company, star and money-spinner, William Churchill de Mille. By 1911, William was a prominent presence on New York's theatrical and social scene. He played tennis for the elite Skivi Club, and his views on life, art, the theatre and politics were eagerly sought by newspapers and magazines. A scribe from his old college, Columbia, enthused in their monthly journal, in April 1911, about the neatness and organization of William's study – a long-running DeMille trait, taken in the fullness of time to the furthest extreme by his brother – marvelling at the 'twenty-five hundred cards indexed, each bearing the name of an actor or actress he had seen with some pungent comment on their work . . . Other drawers were opened showing plays carefully filed for further elaboration and old ones laid away in different stages of revision . . . I wished that I still wore my hat that I might take it off in the presence of a dramatist who was a business man.'

William had continued to teach students at the American Academy of Dramatic Arts, where his father had taught a decade earlier, publishing, as early as 1906, a treatise on 'The Truth of the Unreal – Notes on Certain Principles Underlying Stagecraft'. This covered 'the nature of art – partly interpretive and partly creative', 'the principle of selection', 'the Problem – how can we make art our best medium of conveying truth', 'the principle of consistency', 'the paradox of acting – the emotion must be real and yet its expression must be artificial', 'stage movement', 'stage language – of which the principal fea-

Brothers in art: Cecil and William de Mille

tures are brevity and clearness' and 'complex emotions: The complex passions of real life are all simplified to a certain extent'. Further comments dealt with the various stage conventions of Japanese and Chinese theatre, Sanskrit drama, Elizabethan drama and the present day. 'However artificial may be our means of expression,' William wrote, 'we should always bear in mind that *that which is expressed* must be first, last and all the time – the Truth.'

Looking at the results, as far as the plays by William and Cecil are concerned, the gulf between Bill the intellectual and Cecil the Champion Driver and Story Teller looms ever wider. In Cecil's adventure plays, events tumble one after the other in a succession that seems to follow the writer's rampant imagination rather than the cool logic of brother William's teachings. What is The Truth, after all, that elusive grail of all art? While William worried away at this, Cecil got on with the job of learning his trade, though it seemed that he could never catch up with his elder brother, the family brains. Whatever the religious motivation that Cecil much later claimed for his idea of 'Peter Grimm', there is no evidence of any divine inspiration for the derring-do of *The Royal Mounted* or *The Stampede*. The politics of the latter appear to be a kind of raw native

Bolshevism, an angry cry at the rich dispossessing those whose nobility is composed of a different moral code, attuned to the 'natural' environment.

William, on the other hand, remained a devout 'Georgist', as his spouse wore the mantle of heir apparent to her father's philosophical legacy. From an early stage, he participated in the affairs of the Manhattan Single Tax Club, at whose dinner, in April 1907, he had presented a private play featuring an imaginary dialogue on matters of political morality between Thomas Jefferson, Andrew Carnegie and William Hearst. The rich men scoff at Jefferson's queries on the Single Tax: 'There are many people who think that Henry George makes cigars. But the cigars are punk.' Other speakers, less genteel than de Mille, made comments that were strictly anti-Semitic, one ex-Congressman ridiculing the mogul Jacob H. Schiff, an admirer of Rockefeller's business methods, as 'probably the richest Jew in the United States'. The dinner participants preferred the wisdom of an Indian, Chief Joseph, whose motto was 'treat all men alike'.

Away from the rarefied preferences of the Georgists, William de Mille aired his view that a great change was coming in American life, as he revealed to *The Bookman*: 'I think we are on the eve of a great social revolution . . . which may come with bloodshed, but which I believe will come gradually enough to be effected without violence through the ballot-box and for that reason be more radical and lasting. That revolution will mean the era of national mental activity, and the era of national mental activity in the history of every country has been the era of great literature and especially of great drama, because the drama more than any other form of literature reflects the mind of the people . . . Consequently I'm glad that my life has fallen in this period, for the chances are that my generation will do some of the biggest work in the history of the country.'

In 1910, William attempted to reflect his ideals of social equality in *The Land of the Free*, a play about an Italian immigrant who falls foul of grafters who try to prevent him bringing his wife and two children into the city from Ellis Island. 'Money talks,' says a corrupt city fixer, 'and I'm very fond o' hearin' its voice.' The Italian, Luigi, discovers bitterly that 'we get all the freedom we can pay for – an' no more'. The play opened in September in New Haven, Connecticut, but never made it to the stage in New York.

In October 1911, William scored another success, with *The*

Woman, and returned to the political fray, outlining to a *New York Times* reporter his developing views on art and life:

Every age has its own code of morality, and a wide gulf separates one from the other. There is as much difference between the morality of the age of Ibsen and Pinero, and that of Shakespeare and Euripides, and even in our own day the change has been so radical that the earlier dramas of Ibsen and Pinero might have been written eons of time apart from their later works . . .

Everywhere we are confronted with the necessity of readjusting our outworn and dying theories of what constitutes right and wrong. The dramatist and poet of the past had no cognizance of man's relation to society, with the result that his poetry and drama had to do merely with man's relation to the individual – to his wife, his sweetheart, his friend, his business partner, and in the case of the ancients, to his gods. Nowadays, thanks to our awakening social conscience, we are realizing as a people and as a race that man's relation to any individual, be he who he may, is of comparatively slight consequence . . . as compared with his relationship to his fellow-men . . .

The world would have long since come to a standstill, lapsed into barbarism, if its artists, its poets and dramatists had respected the popular traditions of the race and refrained from attacking decaying and outworn institutions. Take for instance the very immediate subject of chattel slavery. Today we look with horror upon this once ugly blot upon our civilization – but do you realize that 'Uncle Tom's Cabin' was only fifty years ago a blasphemous book to millions of excellent people, and that ministers of the Gospel of Jesus Christ preached from their pulpits the divine rights of the slave owner, just as a few of them still preach today of the divine right of the capitalist and inveigh against the new gospel being promulgated by the social reformer?

A fact that we always lose sight of is that the history of the drama is fundamentally the history of social reform and betterment . . . If it is the duty of the dramatist or the poet to record the feeling and thought and passion of the day in which he lives . . . and put it into concrete form to the end that it may become the common heritage of the race – and this has ever been the duty of the artist and the mission of art – if all this is true, we who are painting pictures, carving statues, writing poems or novels, and perhaps above all else we who are writing plays, have but one course laid before us – to record and interpret the age, our day, our hour.

In *The Woman*, William had finally grasped the nettle of contemporary American politics, focusing on a corrupt politician whose new bill 'will make railway over-capitalization legal, and once again provide a means to milk the public'. A rival politician seeks to stymie the bill, but he has a shady secret – an old alliance with a woman who was not his wife, two years before. The play's plot revolves round the attempts by the bill's supporters, gathered at a Washington hotel, to force a telephone girl at the hotel to divulge the number called by their rival, which they assume is that of his mistress, and thus unmask her. The irony, as the plot reveals, is that the mistress is in fact the wife of one of the plotters. The ordinary working girl on the telephone exchange, however, frustrates the politician's machinations.

The critics praised the deftness of the play's plotting, the naturalness of the writing and the performances. As this was a Belasco production, all praise went to the settings as well, Cecil's contretemps over 'Peter Grimm' not having affected William's own ties with his mentor. 'A splendid play by William C. de Mille dealing with graft in strong dramatic terms,' the *New York Times* summed up.

William was flying high, with Cecil still toiling away at ground level to make ends meet and feed his child. In the history of American playwriting, at the turn of the twentieth century's first decade, it seemed that the patrician heritage would tell and the elder son William would be remembered, while Cecil would be a footnote.

There was, however, a flutter in the wings. Someone else had walked onto this family stage, not from the elegant world of the legitimate theatre, but from its more raucous sibling, vaudeville. A man appears from the wings with a large cigar, a sharp suit and a determined air, eager to go places.

Enter, with a bow to the audience, Jesse L. Lasky.

Men Blowing Horns

Among the 'Jews who made Hollywood', Jesse Lasky was a most unusual sample. Unlike traders and merchants like Adolph Zukor or Shmuel Gelbfish, aka Goldfish, he had not arrived on the latest boat from Europe. His grandfather, so he claimed, told him childhood tales of his treks with the covered wagons along the Oregon Trail. 'My daydreams for years', wrote Lasky in his own account, *I Blow My Own Horn*, 'were peopled with redskins, punctuated with "ughs" and war whoops, and cluttered with flying scalps.' Further down the genetic trail, Lasky's father was 'part owner of the San José Baseball Club, a devotee of walking contests, and the best fly fisherman in the county'.

Born, like David Belasco, in San Francisco, in 1880, Lasky was barely a year older than Cecil DeMille but had lived a very different life. The childhood passion for fly fishing was followed by a craving for the brash sound of the cornet. Father had fallen on hard times, and the boy Jesse became determined that the cornet would be his tool of trade. He had a sister, Blanche, who was also hooked on music, but the boy was determined to strike out on his own. Low-paid jobs with Dr Crabtree's Indian Medicine Show or Witherall's Brass Band in San José were followed by an alliance with his second cousin, Jake Morris, dressing up 'like dandies in loud shirts, high choker collars, and puff ties' to impress the girls on Market Street. Lasky's romantic dreams, however, were dashed when it was found he had to wear eyeglasses.

Climbing up the pole, playing the Cloverdale Citrus Fair as 'Professor Lasky', his father's death set the boy off on a professional career, as the family earner, in small-time vaudeville. The Klondike Gold Rush tugged him north to Alaska in 1896 for an adventurous but unprofitable episode as a prospector. Lasky was to dine out for a long time on his tales of rough-hewn miners, gun-toting assassins and a night sharing his bed with a skeleton. Perhaps he merely read too much Mark Twain. From the pursuit of gold Lasky had to return to brass, with a job as a solo cornettist at the Orpheum Theatre in Honolulu. In Hawaii, his sister, Blanche, having learned the cornet in his absence, joined him to make the act a duet. After a series of small-time engagements, the duo progressed to major New York theatres and an accolade from vaudeville's legendary pioneer, Tony Pastor. As was the wont in vaudeville, chance linkings with other acts – in Lasky's case, with the magician Hermann the Great – led to managerial tasks, and soon the young man was producing a variety of different shows.

In the first years of the twentieth century, the golden years of vaudeville, Lasky became the complete showman. He swiftly became the king of brass-band acts, with shows like 'The Military Octette' or 'The Black Hussars', with 'tan lovelies' supporting the 'colored boys', who played solos, duets and ensembles in dashing military uniforms. That act toured Europe, though, Lasky noted sadly, he lost his tan lovelies in Berlin, Vienna and Paris, as they chose to 'remain in countries where there is no color barrier'. 'The Lasky Quintette', 'The Colonial Septette' and many more versions followed, produced with his partner, Ben Rolfe. Another early partner was exuberant theatre manager Henry B. Harris. For him, Lasky built 'the biggest phonograph in the world – with a box large enough to hold a twelve-piece brass band, including a trap drummer'. The 'Immensaphone' was duly consecrated, the precursor of another series of Lasky novelty acts, such as 'The Pianophiends', with several grand pianos on stage, and 'The Phiend Minstrels', the same in blackface.

Rushing around New York, whistling tunes, thinking out new ideas, Lasky soon acquired a wife, Bessie, née Ginzberg, who would remain with him through thick and thin. Dazzled by Europe, he convinced Harris to open a New York 'Folies Bergères', with a plethora of acts brought from Europe that included the Pender Troupe, eight acrobats on stilts, including a ten-year-old boy, Archie Leach, destined later to become Cary Grant. The centrepiece of the show was to be a play, *A La Broadway*, which would feature, among its stars, a young sassy showgirl named Mae West. This project, however, proved too expensive and was one of Lasky's few flops. Smitten, though, by the idea of grander revues and musicals, he procured an operetta called *California* and was, he recounted, in search of a proper playwright to write it as a stage sketch:

I went to see Mrs. H. C. DeMille, a play broker of high repute in the Hudson Theatre building, where I had recently had my own offices. Often we had exchanged casual greetings when we met in the halls, and I also acknowledged her son, William, a playwright who had to his credit a number of hits . . . But she also had a younger son, Cecil, who looked at me in a way that made me uncomfortable or ignored me in a way that made me more uncomfortable . . .

An aura of failure hung over Cecil after the lacklustre performance of *The Genius* and *The Royal Mounted* and the further discomfort with Belasco over *Peter Grimm*. 'I had no intention of entrusting my great idea to a lesser luminary than William,' writes Lasky, 'and certainly not to an actor who had made a couple of stabs at playwriting.' But Mrs De Mille, having glimpsed an opportunity for her lesser progeny, honed in on her target and insisted he should meet Cecil.

Cecil and I eyed each other suspiciously. Much against my better judgement I hemmed and hawed through the story thread of my operetta. But Cecil's eyes were taking on a glint of insight and I could sense his imagination was filling in the gaps, mentally picturizing how he would dramatize it. When I finished, he leaned forward and exclaimed, 'Say, I like that!'
The minute he said, 'I like that,' I liked him. And I've never stopped.

So goes Lasky's tale. In reality, William was far too busy, and prominent in 'legit' theatre, to undertake a sketch for vaudeville, though he did write a series of one-act plays, shorter satires, over the next few years. Cecil was a reasonable consolation prize. But there is no doubt that Jesse and Cecil clicked. Despite his eyeglasses, Jesse remained a keen outdoors man, and they both shared similar dreams of adventure. Jesse's background – his grandfather's Oregon Trail days and his own Alaskan interlude – was what Cecil might have wished for himself, much more in keeping with the Champion Driver than the staid upbringing at the Pamlico girls' school. 'We used to daydream', wrote Lasky, 'about exploring the South Seas someday,' and they took 'a month's vacation in the Maine woods, for which we bought outfits that would have been adequate for an expedition in the wilds of Tibet'.
Cecil remembered the friendship as beginning much earlier, and recalled Lasky seeing him through the debacle of *Peter Grimm* and he buoying Lasky up during the collapse of his Folies Bergères. Whatever the chronology, it was a serendipitous meeting. Of all

DeMille's mentors, Jesse Lasky was the most crucial to his career and his most long-lasting professional partner, carrying them both from one medium, the stage, into the whirlwind world of motion pictures. But this still lay some time in the future.

California was an ambitious production, though still only a one-act piece designed to be part of a full vaudeville show. It opened at the Colonial Theatre in New York City in January 1912, and was anointed by *The Billboard* as 'all-satisfying and delicately touches the fanciful imagination in an atmosphere that glorifies the west and brings home some of the trials and tribulations that were braved by the Indian aborigines and by the first Caucasian invaders'. Lasky had been talking up the production for a good while, telling the *Pittsburgh Gazette* in December 1911, in an interview headed 'BOUGHT MEXICAN BURRO TO MAKE SCENE REAL':

In producing 'California' . . . I have tried to give all the wealth of detail and care usually associated with the name of David Belasco. As an example . . . I may inform you that when we found a live burro was needed for the entrance of the principal comedian, we dispatched an agent to Southern California and secured a genuine Mexican burro, raised in the neighborhood of the locale of the story. Moreover, the dresses of the Indians, cowboys, Mexicans, surveyors and, indeed all the other characters that people the play of 'California,' were carefully made from correct plates and photographs of the period represented . . .

DeMille, who wrote the book of 'California,' is one of the ablest dramatists in America(n) today. His name and his fame is known to every patron of plays. It is perhaps most conspicuously associated with the production of 'Strongheart,' which, as you are aware, he wrote. He has been associated with David Belasco, as was his father before him, in many most successful productions . . . He has inherited the genius of his father before him, and at the same time kept pace with the period of progressiveness in which we are living . . . While providing a dramatic story he has also invested it with a rich flow of humor, combining the two qualities consistently . . .'

With a good showman's flourish, Lasky had blurred the difference between Cecil and William. The story Cecil had etched out appears as a template of many western tales that had passed before and were to come, with elements from his own play *The Stampede*: a lonely, isolated mission is 'threatened with demolition by a railroad company that claims the right to the ground on which it stands'. The engineer in charge, however, falls for a flirtatious girl, and both he and an Englishman are kidnapped and threatened with lynching. But the Englishman turns out to be the owner of the railroad, and the little mission is 'saved by the Englishman giving his word that the railroad will encircle it. Four good songs are offered,' continued *The Billboard*, 'Good By California, Save the Mission, The Tape and Chain and I Love You, My Own. Let me compliment the act by stating that it is really idyllic.'

For the first time, Cecil had a hit. Another sketch for Lasky followed immediately, also in January 1912, *The Antique Girl*: 'the story of a swindling antiquarian, who possesses, for sale, a wonderful singing vase, that is supposed to contain the spirit of a Persian Princess. When the vase is broken the "spirit" turns out to be the antiquarian's ward, Sally.' Music, as for *California*, was by Robert Hood Bowers, and this time Cecil had a co-writer, William LeBaron, who had written the doomed Folies Bergères show, *A La Broadway*. LeBaron, one of Lasky's regular writers, would also play a future part in the company that would rise from Lasky and DeMille's partnership, the kernel of the mighty Paramount studios.

Working for Lasky was quite a different matter from the slow, painstaking labour of writing for the serious stage. Everything was quick zip dash: by March, Lasky had a new, non-DeMille act to headline at Hammerstein's Victoria Theatre, something called 'Visions d'Art'. Meanwhile, another Broadway show, an operetta named *Baron Trenck*, was opening with a foreign star, Leipzig opera singer Fritz Sturmfel, who had been coached from a complete ignorance of the English language to warbling proficiency in no more than three months. When the show closed, Sturmfel departed to Germany, but the press announced he was booked to star in a vaudeville sketch later that year. This turned out to be *In the Barracks*, another Lasky–DeMille collaboration.

Meanwhile, Cecil returned to producing other people's plays, 'presenting', in May, *The Marriage – Not* by Joseph Noel. Total performances: eight, at Maxine Elliott's Theatre. *In the Barracks* was, however, much more fun, for the writer if not for the audience. The *New York Mirror* commented, on its September opening at Keith's Alhambra:

One pretty and charming song, 'Love is the Leaven,' sung by Fritz Sturmfel and Nellie Brewster, compensates for half an hour of rather indifferent entertainment. Mr Sturmfel's English is much clearer than when we last heard him in Baron Trenck, and his tenor voice can thus be enjoyed with far less irritation. Although Miss Brewster sings sweetly, her modesty makes her fancy it necessary to disguise her natural good looks by excessive make-up. Myles McCarthy, who furnishes comic relief by the simple but effective method of calling the Kaiser 'Emp' and defying the whole Austrian Army in American slang, is at times genuinely funny. The operetta, which depicts the quarters of Prince Karl in the barracks of the Royal Hussars, Vienna, is handsomely staged, and the military costumes are rich and pleasing.

The concoction featured characters with names like General Baron von Gardemark, Captain Prince Karl von Wollenstein (Sturmfel), and Lieutenants Max von Bruchholtz, Otto Stoltz and Ernest von Schlissel. Taking place on 'The Day of Presentation of the Iron Cross to Prince Karl for Bravery in Preventing the Assassination of the Emperor', it boasted such arias as 'The Call to Arms', 'Farewell to the Flag', 'The Emperor's Own Hussars' and 'You'll Have to Do the Turkey Trot'. Lyrics were by Grant Stewart, music once more by Robert Hood Bowers and book by Cecil DeMille. Cecil amused himself by naming the American love interest in the sketch 'Constance Adams', after his wife.

Sadly, this was Fritz Sturmfel's American swansong, as he drowned in a sailing accident at Lake Tegern, near Munich, on 6 August 1913. By then, Lasky had produced several more sketch shows, with titles like 'The Trained Nurses', 'The Gay Parisienne', 'Harnessing a Horse', 'The Three Beautiful Types' and 'The Water Cure', to name but a few.

But Cecil's career in vaudeville was short-lived. The friendship with Lasky could have enabled a succession of light farces, but clearly Cecil did not see these as his mission in life. He returned to another 'DeMille Play Company' production, Mary Roberts Reinhart's *Cheer Up*, which fared no better, in December 1912, than DeMille's previous 'presentations', lasting twenty-four performances. In 1913, he worked on a new collaboration with his brother William, a play called *After Five* – 'a farce comedy in three acts' which was produced at the end of the year. This was a strange concoction about an upper-class young idler who plans to have himself killed, as if by accident, so that the insurance will pay a debt he owes to the girl he loves, Nora, whose $150,000 he has vainly invested in 'Potash Preferred'. The play is indeed very silly and ran for an ill-fated thirteen performances at the Fulton Theatre.

William himself seemed to be treading water, having found a comfortable niche that allowed him to indulge in easy projects. He had obtained a summer home in upstate New York, at an artists' retreat called Merriewold, where he relaxed with his wife and two daughters – Agnes, born in 1905, and Margaret, born in 1908. There the family gave impromptu musicales, and William wrote short, pithy sketches in his rustic cottage. In 1912, he produced *In 1999*, 'A Problem Play of the Future', positing a world in which the women were dominant, a time when 'woman will have gained all the rights she has been so long denied, and mere man will have taken her place as the one who watches and waits'. Other one-act satires, *Poor Old Jim* and *Food, A Tragedy of the Future* (also titled *Fifty Years from Now*) – in which an egg is so scarce that a craving for one, smuggled from Europe, can threaten a marriage – followed.

In August 1912, in an echo of the controversy over *Peter Grimm*, Belasco as producer and William de Mille as writer were sued by a would-be playwright, one Abraham Goldknopf, who claimed de Mille's *The Woman* was plagiarized from his own work. In a dramatic response, Belasco (plagued all the while by such claims, justified or not) paid from his own pocket to produce Goldknopf's play for one night only, alongside *The Woman*, to demonstrate the chasm between the texts. The result was a theatrical coup, with the audience rolling in the aisles at the unfortunate Goldknopf's clumsy lines. 'Mr Belasco has staged the play', reported the *New York Times*, 'with absolute fidelity to the directions in the manuscript and with his familiar attention to details . . . It is impossible to convey any sense of the play's extravagance or the ludicrous effects of much that happens.'

Cecil DeMille must have breathed a sigh of relief that Belasco had not chosen this path with his own work. But his own patchy results on the stage clearly now made him more amenable to the medium that Belasco had dubbed 'the Drama's Flickering Bogy'. One day, Jesse Lasky relates, during one of their regular lunches at the Claridge, Cecil said to him: 'Jesse, I'm pulling out. Broadway's all right for you – you're doing well. But I can't live on the Royalties I'm getting, my debts are piling up, and I want to chuck the whole thing. Besides, there's a revolution going on in Mexico and I'm going down and get in on it – maybe write about it. That's what I need – a stimulating and colorful change of scene.'

It so happened, as Lasky tells the tale, that he had been badgered for some time by his new brother-in-law, businessman Samuel Goldfish, who had married his sister Blanche, to get into the growing motion-picture field. Just 'to keep Cecil from doing something foolish alone, I proposed we do something foolish together. I said, "If you want adventure, I've got an even better idea – let's make some movies!"'

And, Lasky writes:

His eyes gleamed, and before I was over the shock of hearing my own unconsidered suggestion, Cecil put out his hand, grabbed mine, and said, 'Let's!'

On that one resounding, impulsive word, Lasky proclaimed for posterity, motion-picture history was made.

REEL TWO

The Drama's Flickering Bogy

There's Some Movie Folks Working There

In January 1914, Jesse Lasky writes for the legend, he arrived by train at the Santa Fe depot in Los Angeles, hailed a cab and asked the driver to go to Hollywood. 'Get in, boss – we'll find it,' quoth the bemused cabbie. Eventually, they fetched up at a lone landmark, the Hollywood Hotel, where the driver suggested Lasky ask for more directions in the lobby.

I told the clerk my name and explained that I was President of the Lasky Feature Play Company . . .
  'I'm sorry,' said the clerk, 'I never heard of it.'
  'Perhaps I should have told you that the director-general of the company is Cecil B. DeMille,' I stated impressively.
  'Never heard of him,' the clerk said crisply.

Eventually the clerk directed the lost would-be mogul to go down the main road until Vine Street: 'It's a dirt road with a row of pepper trees right down the middle. Follow the old pepper trees for about two blocks till you see an old barn. There's some movie folks working there that might know where your company is.'

Sure enough, this was the barn upon which a sign was emblazoned – 'The Jesse L. Lasky Feature Play Company' – and where a reception committee awaited the boss.

Sparse as Hollywood village was at the time, Los Angeles and its movie business was never as primitive as portrayed by many, and Lasky and Cecil DeMille's entry into it was not so whimsical and spontaneous. *Motion Picture News*, one of the industry's trade papers, presenting the headline 'LASKY AND DE MILLE ENTER PICTURE FIELD' on 20 December 1913, wrote that rumours that the 'well-known theatrical producer was to enter the realm of the film' had been 'going the rounds in motion picture circles for the last eight months'. Another trade journal, *The Moving Picture World*, revealed

Founding the Lasky Feature Play Company: (left to right) Morris Gest, Adolph Zukor, Cecil DeMille, Jesse L. Lasky and Samuel Goldfish

on 3 January 1914 that the proposition to make motion pictures was made to Lasky 'some time ago', presumably by brother-in-law Goldfish, who, the same journal revealed in July 1914, had 'made a careful study of the industry for eighteen months'. Lasky did not agree at first, but 'his interest was aroused. He began going to picture houses . . . paying particular attention to features. "I realized at once," said Mr. Lasky, "what an opportunity there was for a producer of experience, particularly one accustomed to catering to types of vaudeville audiences and the great public . . . Cecil B. De Mille, who is associated with me, immediately took up the producing end of the business, and started quietly to secure control of well-known, successful plays."'

Already a businessman in the field of stage production, Cecil would have been well aware of the financial implications of entry into the pictures. By 1910, movies were already big business, with millions of dollars invested by a plethora of companies. In 1909, the Motion Picture Patents Company had been created, the instrument with which Thomas Edison and a cabal of other producers attempted to monopolize the industry by restricting the use of their patented movie equipment. The flight west to California was largely caused by independent producers decamping to avoid Edison's patent enforcers. But earlier pioneers had set up shop in Los Angeles as early as 1908. An old grocery store in the district known as Edendale was bought up by the New York financiers Kessel and Baumann and became, late in 1912, the Mack Sennett Studios. Carl Laemmle's company Universal was already a major player then, as was pioneer producer Thomas Ince, who set up his 'Inceville' at Santa Ynez Canyon, with an entire wild-west cast – cowboys, Indians and three hundred horses and buffaloes.

Since 1908, D. W. Griffith had been shooting short films for Biograph, a New York company founded in 1896. By 1914, when Griffith left Biograph, the films had already been getting longer. 'Features', defined at first as films longer than the standard one-reeler (which lasted between twelve and fourteen minutes, depending on camera-cranking speed), were an issue of hot debate in the trade press. When two-reel films became more common, the 'feature' was defined as any movie lasting three reels or more. Multi-reel pictures were known as early as 1909, when the Vitagraph company released *Les Misérables* in four reels. In the beginning, movie houses showed these films one reel at a time on different days, as serials, setting the basis for the great flowering of the silent serials, such as *The Perils of Pauline*, released in 1914. Theatre owners were often hostile to long films, as they preferred to clear the house and get a new paying audience for each quick set of one-reel films. But as long films were more expensive to make, more attention was paid by producers to quality, with the result that, as *The Billboard* wrote in November 1913, the 'multiple reel motion picture has come, figuratively speaking, as a general who has massed his forces, and because of public acclaim, has turned the tide of chaos towards success'.

An early pioneer of the feature was the now totally forgotten Pliny P. Craft, president of the Apex Film Company of New York, who produced his own multi-reel picture with Buffalo Bill's Wild West Show in 1910, then went to Europe and returned with the Italian five-reeler, *Dante's Inferno*. More period Italian epics followed, culminating in the ten-reel *Cabiria*, made in 1913 but shown in America in 1914 – and fuelling D. W. Griffith's determination to make his own longest film to date, *The Clansman*, aka *Birth of a Nation*, to be released in 1915.

In 1912, a Hungarian Jewish immigrant, Adolph Zukor – who had arrived in the United States at the age of sixteen and worked as an upholsterer and furrier before becoming, in 1903, an owner of street arcades showing the newfangled moving pictures – founded his own Famous Players Film Company and imported one of the new European epics, the French feature *Queen Elizabeth*, starring Sarah Bernhardt. The Famous Players Film Company was based, in Zukor's own words, on the idea that 'the moving picture man must try to do as artistic, as high class, and as notable things in his line of entertainment, as . . . Charles and Daniel Frohman were doing in the high-class Broadway theatres . . . What I wanted was a new idea which would be so startling in its departure from the old routine and so tremendous in its magnitude that the whole world would be as startled and surprised as a man would be who was suddenly confronted with a great transformation . . .'

His idea, beyond the usual showman's hyperbole, was 'to engage the highest salaried, the most highly respected, the most artistic actors in the world to pose in their greatest dramatic successes before the camera . . .' The slogan of 'Famous Players in Famous Plays' was to lead under Zukor's dynamic management to a project of releasing thirty feature films a year. Other companies followed suit, with entrepreneur Hobart Bosworth setting up Bosworth, Inc., in January 1913, signing an exclusive contract with author Jack London to produce feature films of his work.

When Jesse Lasky and Cecil DeMille entered films, it was logical and indeed imperative that they should focus on this new trend of producing long-length motion pictures. As Lasky himself contributed to the 11 July 1914 issue of the *Moving Picture World*, a 'Special Issue' on 'Trade Questions and Conditions by Leading Manufacturers and Producers' in the industry:

When contemplating entry into the field of Motography [*an old and now quaint term for the moving pictures*], I began a systematic study of the trade, from every angle. I decided that I would enter that branch which held the most glowing prospects for the future – the feature field.

Features, to my mind, offer a concrete, lasting future in that, within their short year of existence they have accomplished what the 'one-reel' subjects fail to attain, viz., the interest of the classes.

One must first view with the eye of a non-partisan, the sight in front of the theatre showing the feature and the house conducting strictly a one and two-reel programme.

Let us take, as an example, the beautiful Strand, the masterly Vitagraph Theatre, the Audubon or Hamilton Theatre and compare them with the New Comedy Theatre on Sixty-sixth street.

The programme at the Strand Theatre contained as a feature 'The Only Son.' Within one hour we counted fifteen automobiles and nine carriages draw up in front and at least thirty men dressed in evening clothes entering the Strand. At the New Comedy, where the small subjects are shown, the title of the pictures and condition of the lobby and interior speak for the audiences.

In other words, Lasky observed that the best profits would come from bringing the middle classes into the moving-picture theatres, leaving the old one- and two-reel cheapies for vulgarians like Mack Sennett, whose Edendale studio was churning out sufficient fodder for the working classes starring Mabel Normand, Ford Sterling, Fatty Arbuckle *et al.* and a young Englishman who had just been hired at the end of 1913, Charles Spencer Chaplin. Why take nickels from the poor immigrant masses when you could take a dime, a quarter or even more from the better off?

In all these strategic calculations, Cecil DeMille played a subsidiary part. Lasky was a friend and congenial partner, and Cecil had proved that, unlike the more patrician William, he could slum it in the world of variety sketches. Lasky sensed too that the man who often gave you an uncomfortable stare was full of an unconsummated passion and had a knack and a desire to embrace new challenges. Even in the coils of financial computations and market planning, the spirit of adventure still enveloped the movies.

DeMille's autobiography states, somewhat disingenuously:

I had seen a few motion pictures. The earliest I recall was a picture of a bull fight, lasting only a few minutes . . . The bull was about the size of a flea and hopped around the screen very much like one . . . Another picture, of a dur-bar in India, showed me that spectacle could be put on the screen more strikingly than it could ever be put on a stage. When I saw *The Great Train Robbery* . . . I discovered that you could tell a story in this medium, and . . . achieve both greater speed and greater detail than the stage allowed.

Since Edwin S. Porter's *The Great Train Robbery* was released in 1903, Cecil must have seen a great many more films than he wished to admit, though his training for the job in 1913 supposedly consisted of a day spent at the Edison Studio in the Bronx, watching crew and actors at work. The Jesse L. Lasky Feature Play Company was

founded with Lasky as president, Samuel Goldfish as general manager, Cecil B. DeMille as director general and Lasky's lawyer Arthur
Friend as its secretary. It had a formal capital of $20,000, though
only $15,000 was raised. Cecil claimed he tried to raise the remain-
ing $5,000 from William, who declined.

As its first property, the company obtained film rights to *The
Squaw Man*, a hardy theatrical perennial since its first production ran
for over two hundred performances in 1905–6. As a western, it could
be shot mostly outdoors without the expense of building a full-scale
studio from scratch. The playwright Edwin Milton Royle was at first
reluctant to join the rush to 'Famous Players'. He wrote to Lasky,
when finally deciding to accept his offer:

Ever since the first ingenious man conceived the idea of embalming actual
plays in moving pictures I have been honored with propositions for 'The
Squaw Man,' but I confess I could not take this movie madness seriously. Its
very popularity seemed to be against it. Whole communities, you know, used
to be afflicted with the smallpox. Every emotion in the raw, every situation
since the fall of man, was being grabbed with coarse, unskillful and sometimes thievish hands and smeared pell mell into pictures. It was all so crude
and formative . . . But I see signs that the kindergarten stage is passing or is
passed. You have helped me to a new view. The moving picture is fast developing into a new art form, a real art form, with a new distinct place, and a
future whose end no man can see . . . If you are to become an apostle of the
new art you must have more than an ambition to make money. I am putting
'The Squaw Man' into your hands with the understanding that you will do
fine and beautiful things in a fine and beautiful way . . .'

Royle seemed both shrewd and naive at the same time in contemplating the fate of his creation, given the raw beginners' enthusiasm
of the men to whom he entrusted the work. But Lasky took steps to
ensure his untried director general would be bolstered by professional help. An experienced director, Oscar Apfel, and cameraman,
Alfred Gandolfi, were hired to bolster Cecil's direction of the actors.
Apfel had shot films for the Pathé company, Edison and Reliance,
and Gandolfi had begun his career in Italy and continued with the
prestigious Pathé. As the film's star, a popular favourite, Dustin
Farnum, was willing and available. He was offered the same $5,000
block of stock that William had turned down as payment, but preferred to take a modest $250 per week in cash. As Cecil later noted,
a quarter stock in what was to become Paramount Pictures would

have made the actor a millionaire in due course. Not everyone in this enterprise had the same crucial combination of impulsiveness and vision, the pioneer's embrace of risk.

The play was set in Wyoming, but Arizona was the first choice for a location, perhaps because, Cecil later recalled fuzzily, the fares to get there were cheaper than going all the way to California, where everyone else was filming, and it was suitably western. But when the crew arrived in Flagstaff, so the story goes, they were met by a snowstorm and decided to continue further west. California became their second choice, and they leased a barn belonging to the Burns and Reiver Studio which that company had vacated. It had an outdoor stage and 'was known to be one of the best-equipped rental lots in Los Angeles'. It was hardly, therefore, a shack in the wilderness.

Proceeding within about seven days to production, Cecil and Oscar Apfel hired the necessary actors, including an authentic Indian actress, Red Wing, aka 'Ah-Hoo-Sooch-Wing-Gah', also known by the more user-friendly name of Lillian St Cyr, for the key role of Nat-U-Rich, the squaw of the title. The rest of the Indians in the picture were authentically white. Filming began on 29 December 1913, and the picture was shot in less than three weeks, ready for projection a bare week later.

Shooting *The Squaw Man* at the 'barn'. Cecil (right) in motion

The Squaw Man, the first of the majority of Cecil B. DeMille silent films previously available only to researchers, has recently surfaced in a new DVD. That we have a large deposit of these all-but-lost films is due to DeMille's early conviction of his own importance as a pioneer of the movies and the preservation of most of his negatives, starting in the mid-1920s. The researcher, however, must journey to archives in California, Rochester in upstate New York and Washington's bottomless Library of Congress to view most of the output – on film – of America's most famous motion-picture director. (A smattering of DeMille titles also reside in other archives, as far afield as Brussels and Moscow.)

In addition to the films themselves, DeMille kept voluminous paperwork (mostly from later projects), including a full set of his annotated film scripts, donated in later years to the University of Southern California. There one may fondle the actual scripts for *The Squaw Man* and DeMille's other early films, rare survivals of that pioneer era.

In legend *The Squaw Man* is the first American feature film, although, as we have seen, the 'feature' was already a familiar concept by 1913. Griffith's four-reel *Judith of Bethulia* was shot before *The Squaw Man*, but released later. *The Squaw Man* runs for six reels – about eighty minutes. The script, however, is a mere thirty-five pages, including 284 scenes, briefly and often summarily described:

1. Mess room – Henry prepares the fund – Jim and Henry made trustees – end of dinner.
2. Maudsley Towers – library – Diana – Lady Elizabeth – Lady Mabel – Henry and Jim on – Henry's affection for Diana – Jim's Explanation of Fund . . .
3. Kerhill box at race track – Henry and party. Henry lays bet in spite of Jim's warning. Lady E. overrules Jim – 'It is a gentleman's sport' – Bookmaker takes bet.
4. Start –
5. Box –
6. The Race –

In later years, silent-film scripts would often be divided into manuscripts that denoted the scenes and actions therein and a separate script listing the intertitles, which were almost always revised and set after the film was shot. But at the turn of 1914, none of the organizational machinery which would later characterize a 'Hollywood' studio was in place. D. W. Griffith, famously, proceeded to a shoot, even *Birth of a Nation*, without a proper script. The real joy in film-making was in making things up as you went along. When a 'Famous Play' had been bought, however, more rigour was expected and less leeway given by an audience which often knew the plot from its origin.

The plot of *The Squaw Man*, in fact, bears some resemblance to Cecil's own early forays into play-writing, particularly his championing of the Indians in such scripts as *The Stampede* and the 'Englishman' in *The Royal Mounted*. It may well be that these themes had some derivation from Edwin Royle's play *The Squaw Man*, which was first performed in 1905, the same year as *Strongheart*.

The tale, as it unfolds, is quite complicated, as the movie tries to follow the stage-born nature of its opening scenes, set in upper-class English society. As the film opens, Henry, Earl of Kerhill, and his cousin, James Wynnegate, are made trustees for the Orphans Fund of the 16th Lancers. Henry plunges heavily on the Derby – providing the race scene, with cheering crowd. He ends up owing $5,000. Title: 'Henry "borrows" from the fund, forging his own name.' This provides the basis for Henry to frame James, because Henry is jealous over the friendship of his cousin with his wife, Diana.

These first scenes are fairly static, given the restrictions of the Burns and Reiver studio stage, and the acting is fairly raw, histrionic in places. The embezzlement discovered, James is blamed for the forgery and is urged to go abroad to prevent disgrace. Diana tells him: 'Jim, I want you to go away, for my sake!' adding: 'If you are an honest man, you may kiss me goodbye.' He leaves without the kiss.

The next scenes are somewhat confusing, perhaps reflecting some lost footage: aboard a ship to America, an interloper breaks into Jim's cabin, and after a tussle, is tied up by Jim. This man is a detective on his trail. The ship sails. A child sets fire to a cabin. The fire spreads and Jim rescues the captain, but the interloper, whom we have last seen tied up, disappears from the tale – presumably drowned.

Title: 'Jim's party picked up by an American bound vessel.' Safe in New York, Jim intervenes when a girl tries to steal a man's wallet – 'James saves Big Bill from the light-fingered gentry.' The man he helped, a big-boned westerner, convinces him to 'Come out West – where folks keep their hands in their own pockets.'

Jim arrives in Maverick, where the white men appear to live amicably beside the local Indian tribes. A title introduces 'Tabywana, Chief of the Utes, and his Daughter, Nat-U-Rich.'

The strangely named Nat-U-Rich takes a shine to Jim. He buys a ranch and meets the cowboys working there. The Indians dance with the cowboys. But there is a flaw in this idyll: an Indian-hater, Cash Hawkins. Hawkins tries to cheat Tabywana in a cattle deal and ogles the lissom Nat-U-Rich. Jim protects the Indian girl.

The main scenes are set in a saloon through whose doors we see trains go by, almost a throwback to the basic set of *The Great Train Robbery* fully ten years before. We cut to a group of English travellers who fetch up in the town – no explanation is provided for this amazing coincidence. Among the travellers, Henry spots his cousin Jim. Cash Hawkins tries to provoke a fight with a call of 'To Hell with the English.' Jim stops him and offers Henry his friendship. But Henry says: 'I won't drink with a man who robbed the orphans of the King's soldiers.'

Meanwhile, Nat-U-Rich, in the train depot, is confronted by Cash. Jim comes in, drawing his gun, but Cash falls to another bullet, the Indian girl confessing to Jim: 'Me kill 'um.' He vows to keep her secret.

Later, riding in the snow, Jim is overcome by fumes at a geyser. Nat-U-Rich, who has been following him, overcomes her fear of the 'Evil Spirit' and rescues him, carrying him back on a horse-borne stretcher to the Indian camp, where the medicine man dances to revive him. Several months later, Jim makes a pledge to Nat-U-Rich. They hold hands. In the next scene they are living together; a child has appeared beside them.

Meanwhile, back in Europe, in the Alps, Henry climbs a mountain with Diana. He falls, and before his death, writes her a confession of his misdeed, stating that he was the one who robbed the orphans' fund. Diana's family vow: 'We are going to find Jim and bring him home.' Intercut between home and the west, where, in an election for sheriff, another local character, Bud Hardy, is told that to be elected he must find the killer of Cash Hawkins. Nat-U-Rich's pouch has been found at the scene and she is now suspected. Tabywana rides to warn Jim.

Jim, at this point, is broke and can't pay his cowboys. Tabywana and Jim smoke the pipe of peace, and the Indian warns Jim that Nat-

U-Rich is being hunted. As Jim despairs, a rider gallops up to tell him his name has been cleared at home: 'Your cousin's confession cleared your name – you are now Earl of Kerhill.'

Jim and Nat-U-Rich's child is now to be the future earl and is to be sent 'home' to England to be properly schooled. Nat-U-Rich protests, but Jim waves her away. She goes up the mountain to pray to her gods. Would-be sheriff Hardy comes to Jim's ranch, but Big Jim chases him off. The English party arrive in a cart to take the child. While Tabywana raises the Utes to fight, the cowhands say goodbye to the child. But the pursuers stop the departing cart, while the Utes ride to the rescue. In a field, Nat-U-Rich shoots herself. Tabywana carries her lifeless body to Jim: 'Poor little Mother . . .' THE END.

The film bears the scars of its adaptation from the stage play, as well as the discomfiting lurches of its hybrid narrative. The English society drama–western hybrid was a popular genre of the period, but in order to condense its convolutions, DeMille and Apfel had to make some leaps of faith and clumsy connections. At the time, however, this upset neither audiences nor critics. 'FIRST LASKY PRODUC-TION A HIT' headlined the *Motion Picture News*, proclaiming it 'scientifically superior to the original play . . . The thrilling scenes at the English Derby . . . the finely executed scenes of the burning schooner in mid-ocean . . . these, and others during the course of the six reels . . . represent the triumph of the pictures over the stage production.' The *Moving Picture World* lauded 'the touches of great beauty [that] contain a secret of success known only to screen presentation – they cause us to surrender ourselves more completely to the story that is being told and to love this new art for its own sake'.

Belasco's 'flickering bogy' was becoming sanctified in its own glory. It is certainly a challenge to today's viewer, with the experience of over ninety years of motion-picture production, from Griffith's *Intolerance* through John Ford's *The Searchers* to multimillion-dollar blockbusters like *The Lord of the Rings*, to see the ungainly lurches of *The Squaw Man* through the rose-tinted goggles of 1914. Even the *Moving Picture World* had to comment on the already old-fashioned theme of 'frenzied self-sacrifice on the part of a blameless man for the sake of a villain . . . "for the family honor" . . . all the more creditable to the producers that they have presented with exquisite charm what is no longer considered to be within the bounds of common sense'.

Curiously, given our knowledge of the racial prejudices of the age, there seemed to be no cavils about the overt theme of miscegenation between the white man and the Indian girl and the tragedy of her despair at her separation from their child. Sympathy for the Indians seems to have been much stronger in the first two decades of the twentieth century than was evident in a host of later westerns. Wrote *Moving Picture World*: 'Note the Indian maid "fighting it out alone in the foothills, only nature looking on," the distance tragically mellowed by a setting sun – how fascinated we become by this visible world of form and color –', suggesting, by the way, the original tinting already present in this early work – a process of colouring that would be standard, and pre-planned, in almost all DeMille's later silent movies.

The outdoor scenes were particularly praised, although the film was shot never very far from the Hollywood barn: some scenes in the San Fernando Valley, some at Universal's set and a few further afield. The Derby scenes were stock shots inserted in studio set-ups. Critics of the day seemed to assume that the film was essentially directed by Oscar Apfel rather than DeMille, but it is difficult to pin down the truth of this. There were other Lasky films attributed to Apfel in which DeMille was also involved, like *Brewster's Millions*, *Man on the Box*, *The Master Mind* and *The Only Son*, but once DeMille established his own canon he left those titles off his list. *The Squaw Man* had to be claimed as the hit that made the Lasky studio a going concern.

There are signs in the film of camera and lighting effects that would become DeMille staples: daydream images, as when a fashion-model photograph Jim sees in a newspaper mixes into Diana's face; moonlight and sunset on a mountain, as praised by the critics; and an early instance of side-lighting (the 'Belasco' light) through a tent flap on Jim's face as the Indian girl watches him.

All in all, Cecil DeMille had good reason to be pleased with his first go at moving pictures, given the glitches which famously attended its first screening. According to the legend, its cast and crew and their families, including Mrs Constance DeMille and Cecilia, the star, Dustin Farnum, and the head of the company, Jesse Lasky, were all seated comfortably when the film rolled in the projector – to utterly disastrous effect. From the first titles, the picture frame began to roll up the screen. As DeMille described it: 'The actors appeared, and as promptly climbed out of sight, sometimes leaving their feet at the top of the screen and their heads peeking up from the bottom.'

Whether the disastrous screening took place or not, clearly there were problems with the perforations of the film stock, which did not match the standards of the projector. Sam Goldfish, viewing an offending print in New York, took it to Siegmund Lubin's Bettsfield laboratory in Philadelphia, the most advanced plant in the country. There the Lubin technicians swiftly identified the problem: DeMille, it turned out, had bought a cheap machine – British-made, Cecil later recalled – to punch his negative sprocket holes that made sixty-five holes per foot instead of the standard sixty-four. The Lubin boffins simply glued a new strip of celluloid along the old perforations and reperforated the film. It was what we might call now a 'film school first term' type of error, though luckily today's students do not have to punch the perforations themselves. The film was saved and readied for shipping. All the stopped hearts could begin beating again.

'Raised in the Finest Traditions'

When William de Mille heard that his brother Cecil had decided to enter the motion-picture industry, he wrote him an anguished letter from his artists' perch at Merriewold. Accepting that Cecil had not flourished in the theatre, William still wrote: 'I did not suspect that you had reached the stage of utter desperation. After all you do come of a cultured family . . . I cannot understand how you are willing to identify yourself with a cheap form of amusement and which no one will ever allude to as an art . . . You, who were born and raised in the finest traditions of the theater . . . to throw away your future; end your career before it is well started and doom yourself to obscurity if not, indeed to oblivion, seems to me a step that calls for protest from those who really care what happens to you . . .'

The world that C. B. DeMille had embraced when he travelled west was indeed very different from the genteel milieu of the stage. He gave a rapturous account to an interviewer from the *New York Dramatic Mirror*, published on 14 January 1914, of his 'First Experiences Before the Camera':

When I first went out one glorious morning . . . to take the first 'stills', and actually began posing the artists, it felt to me just as it might feel to a prisoner leaving solitary confinement for the open air. Imagine, the horizon is your stage limit and the sky your gridiron. No height limit, no close fitting exits, no conserving of stage space, just the whole world open to you as a stage and a thousand people in a scene does not crowd your accommodations. It was a new feeling, a novel experience, and I was enamored with the way Mr. Apfel went about focusing his camera, getting his actors and actresses within range of the lens and the way in which our camera man followed the sun, tried to dodge a cloud, edged his camera into a more advantageous position, and then the artists.

I felt lost at first. I could not get the stage idea out of my head at first. I looked skywards for sets of lines, borders and drops. Then I entered right into the spirit of the thing. Within an hour I had my 'technique.' I learned all over again the art of directing. This time with a universe as a working basis . . .

Instead of a set mountain . . . I had a real honest-to-goodness mountain looming up in the background . . . I had a valley almost a mile deep . . . Cactus bushes burst into being before our very eyes . . . Our perspective was the upper chain of the Rockies, and our ceiling was God's own blue and amber sky. I felt inspired. I felt that I could do things which the confines of a theatre would not permit . . .

Our types, gleaned from the camps, mountain huts, and Indian reservations lent atmosphere to the scenes that could not be bought or manufactured in the theatre and nature did the rest . . .

The picture Cecil painted to the journal was an epiphany. Indeed, after years of effort and sweat trying to match the literary gift vouchsafed to Henry Churchill and William Churchill de Mille, Cecil suddenly found what the Champion Driver had been looking for all along: salvation in physical action; a medium for which the written word was just a blueprint, and an often clumsy one at that; a type of story-telling that required more emotional insight than the slow graft of typewriting or putting pen to paper at a desk. Even today, every film is to a certain degree an adventure for its creators, and much more so in the pioneer days, when Cecil shared his house on Los Angeles' Lexington Avenue with a tame prairie wolf obtained for *The Squaw Man*, a useful guardian against the idlers who hung about the studio barn at 6284 Selma, whom he suspected were plotting arson attacks on behalf of the Edison Trust. Sabotage took place at the laboratory, and anonymous letters arrived threatening death. Carrying a loaded gun everywhere and riding a horse to work over Hollywood's pitted roads was considerably more invigorating than attending a daily stage rehearsal for an indifferent, doomed play.

At one point during the filming of the burning schooner scene, the press revealed – or was fed the tale – that 'it was necessary for the purposes of the picture to ignite a hundred sulphur pots. Mr. De Mille arranged the pots and lighted them, and then discovered he had not planned for his own escape. The schooner was supposed to have been deserted and to show himself meant ruin to five hundred feet of film. There followed a terrific struggle between self-preservation and art, during which Mr. De Mille made a hasty mental calculation of the gross receipts and Jesse Lasky's anguish. Finally he covered his head with a piece of sail-cloth and awaited the cry of "Author!" The camera operator and several actors found him unconscious when they reached him and terminated his impersonation of Cassabianca.'

Brother William's ill-tempered letter, in fact, might have expressed a more selfish disappointment rather than the pious claim to speak for Cecil's best interests. In Merriewold, as we have seen, William had settled for the easy trophies of his middle-upper-class success: a comfortable family nest, established prestige. But there was no more talk of the pursuit of the Great American Play or proclamations on the social revolution that the 'New Drama' had to serve. His letter went on to chide Cecil about his decampment just as their latest joint play, *After Five*, was about to go on the boards, but when the play opened, the magazine *Vogue* provided a typically infuriating back-handed tribute of the kind critics love but creators dread:

The piece . . . displayed more novelty of invention and revealed a more accomplished craftsmanship than many other recent plays which have run successfully for many months. Success or failure with the public is by no means a reliable criterion of merit, and 'After Five,' which failed completely, should be remembered as a credit to its authors. They died in a noble cause.

Although William, playing from the bottom of the deck, accused Cecil of breaking his mother's heart, there is no evidence to suggest that Beatrice De Mille was terribly angry at her younger son's move. After all, it was she who had pushed him into the arms of the flamboyant Jesse Lasky in the first place. Recalling her husband's last cry, she might have consoled herself that a moving-picture director at least ranked slightly higher than a grocer or butcher, possibly on a par with an electrical engineer. At any rate, she followed her daughter-in-law Constance to Hollywood in the summer of 1914. By then, Cecil had directed another four films and was preparing a fifth. Beatrice could recognize a thriving business when she saw one, despite complaining about the climate that 'one might as well live in the Sahara'. In the event, William, whose East Coast options had run out like so much dry sand, was soon to join his brother in the physical and artistic desert that he had so forcefully derided. At this point, the power relationships within the DeMille family were irrevocably reversed: William, the senior, was to become the junior, and Cecil the superior and provider, until William too found his Hollywood niche.

The key element in this inversion of fortunes was the desire and ability to embrace change. Headlong industrialization, new construction, social developments all reached a peak in the America of the dynamic 1910s. Women's suffrage was a major issue, though it was not to be settled until 1919 in the passing of the 19th Amendment. The new assertiveness of women was expressed in national campaigns, images of the New Woman at work, smoking, drinking in bars, driving the new Model T 'Tin Lizzie' and even flying aeroplanes. Women's fashions became a major commercial force, and Cecil DeMille would make the 'battle of the sexes' a main theme of many of his peak-period silent pictures. The 'flickas' themselves were a crucial part of the marriage of technology and innovation. Magazines flourished to reflect a new culture of enlightened leisure: *Collier's*, *Life*, *Vogue*, *The Ladies Home Journal*, the *Saturday Evening Post*, whose first iconic Norman Rockwell covers would appear in 1916; ordinary punters would read in it short stories by the likes of Edith Wharton, Ring Lardner and Irving S. Cobb. There would be new intellectual voices – Sherwood Anderson, Walter Lippmann, Theodore Dreiser, even socialists like John Reed. Ironically, the theatre would at last be rejuvenated – after William de Mille had given up.

In short, William missed the boat, while Cecil leapt into his Viking warship and urged the galleys forth, sword flashing, towards the horizon of modernity. Freed of the shackles of old expectations, he could explore the new form of expression that 'picturization' provided. For it was not only the wide open spaces that could be embraced by the developing medium but also the atomic elements – though this was not yet common parlance – the hidden depths both of society and the individual's human emotions. Griffith had opened the way with his deployment of cinematic grammar, camera positions, close-ups, cutting and techniques of direction which drew wider implications from small gestures – the twist of a hand, the turning of a face, eye movements – that departed from the restrictive histrionics of the past. DeMille would learn from this, and from the sediment of 'Belasco lighting' carried from stage to screen, until he could find, in the language of movies, a way to express his innermost demons. Playing upon these discoveries, he explored the further, and eventually stranger, shores of narrative drama, until he found that he had travelled so far that critics and public failed to follow. But in 1914, this crisis lay a long way ahead.

After *The Squaw Man*, Cecil assisted Oscar Apfel in the next Lasky production, *Brewster's Millions*, based on a story by George Barr

McCutcheon. It was a social satire in which a young man has to divest himself of a million dollars so that he can become eligible to inherit $7 million from his eccentric grandfather. The difficulty a rich man has in losing money forms the core of the story. The hero, Monty Brewster, finally manages to impoverish himself, losing the greater sum to an absconding trustee but winning the real prize – true love. This tale became a Hollywood favourite and was remade four times: the first starring Fatty Arbuckle, in 1921, and the latest starring Richard Pryor, in 1985. (There was also a *Miss Brewster's Millions* in 1926!)

With two hits under his belt, Jesse Lasky proceeded to an alliance which cemented the fortunes of his Feature Play Company, forming a marketing combine with Adolph Zukor's Famous Players and Hobart Bosworth, the two other major forces producing feature films in America at that time. They were joined by Los Angeles business-man Frank Garbutt, two other film-company heads, Hiram Abrams of Master Productions and William Sherry of the Sherry Feature Film Company, and as a major lynchpin, the distributor W. W. Hodkin-son, president of a company called Paramount Pictures. The latter had originally been founded as Progressive Pictures, but Hodkinson discovered, early in 1914, that there was another company already registered under that name.

Hodkinson rates more than a passing mention in the history of motion pictures, as he was the creator of its most powerful financial weapon: the system which has come to be known as 'block booking'. Early producers struggled with the perennial problem of financing and then profiting from their pictures in distribution. Producers could either 'road show' their movies, taking them around the coun-try for individual screenings, or sell them state by state, a system known as 'states rights'. This latter was the way *The Squaw Man* was sold. Hodkinson, who had started as a distributor in the film business in Ogden, Utah, in 1907, suggested a system whereby distributors would provide advance finance to producers in return for exclusive rights to each movie, which would be distributed through a network of 'exchanges'. The distributor would also bear the cost of marketing and retain a high percentage – 35 per cent in Hodkinson's case – of the box-office take. The General Film Company Hodkinson worked for, which represented the Edison Trust (the Motion Picture Patents Company), turned down this idea, and Hodkinson went into busi-ness for himself.

In May 1914, Zukor and Lasky, with Bosworth and Garbutt, signed on to Hodkinson's system, signing five-year distribution contracts with his Paramount Pictures Corporation and aiming 'to supply the exhibitor with a program of such advanced standard as to elevate, dignify and perpetuate the exhibiting branch of the industry in all parts of the world'. Elevation and dignity were not long predominant, and this agreement was eventually challenged by accusations of double-dealing, strong-arm tactics and monopolizing that, in due course, embroiled Paramount in the industry's lengthiest trust-busting lawsuit. But this early step introduced the process that still defines Hollywood's distribution, and its hegemony in the movie market, to the present day.

Cecil DeMille was not in the executive hothouse of this grand deal, as he was shooting his second Lasky feature and the first credited solely to his own direction and script, *The Virginian*. Another western, based on a play by Owen Wister and Kirk La Shelle (originally a novel by Owen Wister), *The Virginian* is the earliest of DeMille's movies to be currently available on video, in a good quality, colour-tinted form – although the version that has survived, DeMille historian Robert Birchard has determined, is a 1918 re-release of the film with updated intertitles. Whatever the original titles, however, the film displays a quantum leap in structure and cinematography from the narrative lurches of *The Squaw Man*. This quality owes a great deal to a new cameraman, Alvin Wyckoff, who had worked previously with the Selig Polyscope Company. Wyckoff was to remain DeMille's cameraman for almost ten years, shooting all of the forty-three films he directed up to 1923. His contribution was vital to the visual development of his director, even if *The Virginian* was credited as 'Picturized by Cecil B. DeMille'. Film was never, even in the heyday of 'the director', completely the 'auteur' medium it was later declared to be by the theorists of the French New Wave.

We have no credit for the editor of *The Virginian* or any of the early Lasky quickies until three years later, but it certainly displays the seamless nature of a well-constructed film. Once again it starred Dustin Farnum, much more at home here as a rough-hewn cowboy than as the cod Englishman of *The Squaw Man*. The film opens with a beautiful shot of the classic rider on his horse, in grassland, with the hat, the gloves, the chaps and gunbelt. The opening title:

In the heart of the West, when cattle pastured in every valley, and solitary horsemen rode the ranges, there reigned supreme that romantic figure – the cow-puncher.

Westerns, of course, were as old as the cinema and one of the motion pictures' most familiar genres well before 1914. Early precursors were short 'actuality' items, like 1898's *Pack-Train on Chilkoot Pass*, and Edwin S. Porter's aforementioned *Great Train Robbery* of 1903. Griffith too shot his own quota of frontier tales. But *The Virginian* provides a template of the now classical western structure: the conflict between love (or friendship) and duty, the rough-edged life of the western town, the out-of-place girl from the east, the saloon confrontation, the duel at sundown and a wedding-day dilemma that directly presages Gary Cooper's in *High Noon*. (Cooper starred in the second of the four remakes – not counting the 1960s TV series – of *The Virginian*, an early talkie of 1929. Joel McCrea starred in 1946, and Bill Pullman in the most recent, in 2000.)

The Virginian – 'When you call me that, Trampas, you smile!'

The roughness of the town, and of the hero, is portrayed in quite harsh terms, with the unnamed Virginian delighting in such coarse pranks as mixing up babies at a dance for a lark, so that their parents drive off in their carts with the wrong children. He tells the girl, Molly, who exclaims, 'I hate such uncouthness!' – to which he replies, 'We're all uncouth out here, ma'am. But you'll learn to like the West an' you're goin' to love me.' Which, of course, she eventually does, but not until after she has vowed to leave when she learns that he has had to hang his best friend, who was seduced into cattle-rustling. 'My pal Steve was a thief, but I had to keep my word!' At the end, when the bad guy, Trampas, a surly moustachioed lout, comes to seek revenge on their wedding day, it's the classic 'I couldn't marry a man with blood on his hands – come away from here now!'

But then the final shoot-out has to take place. In an earlier scene, another classic dialogue trope is born when the Virginian joins Trampas at the gambling table. Trampas: 'It's your bet, you son of a –' The Virginian: 'When you call me that, Trampas, you smile!'

Early instances of DeMille's experiments with dramatic side-lighting are evident: campfires at night provide dramatic, high-contrast black and white, a departure from the blue tinting which was still used to denote 'day for night' night shots, though the strong flares in the campfires required for the effect made the bandits look rather foolish given their aim of trying to hide from the law. Light through a window highlights a romantic scene between the Virginian and Molly, and their final clinch is set again by a campfire, with the hero's horse looking over the lovers. The traumatic hanging of the hero's best friend is shown by the victim with his head in the noose, on his horse, followed by the chilling shadow on the ground of two hanged men. DeMille was learning the language of cinema in leaps and bounds.

Release of *The Virginian* was held back till September, when the film was widely praised by the reviewers. The *Motion Picture News* noted 'a deserving success . . . beautiful light effects and excellent photography throughout stamp the picture as technically perfect', while *Variety* wrote that 'in the main, the picture is spectacularly melodramatic, a picture of the West as it was and one that can fulfill its mission on its merits, not to mention the pulling power from the title'.

Lasky's policy of 'Famous Plays' was vindicated, as reviewers pointed out the familiarity of the stories that had been adapted from novels and plays. To increase publicity, 'novelizations' of the movies were published in *Photoplay* magazine, *The Squaw Man* appearing in May and *The Virginian* in November 1914, accompanied by stills from the films.

As *The Virginian* was released, the *Moving Picture World*, on 26 September, announced that 'William C. DeMille, one of the most successful playwrights of the decade and for the past ten years a leading dramatic author and teacher, left New York last Wednesday for Hollywood, California, where he will become the head of the scenario department for the Jesse L. Lasky Feature Play Company, working in conjunction with his brother, Cecil B. DeMille, Artistic Director Wilfred Buckland, and Oscar Apfel . . .'

Cecil's ascendancy over his brother was sealed, in film and in print.

'The Shaping of Lives'

William deMille recalled his arrival in the west in his own book, *Hollywood Saga*, published in 1939:

Suddenly I was in California. We had dropped down from the high altitudes of Arizona and were going through the Mojave Desert. Thrusting aside such book-learning as I possessed, I caught myself looking for caravans, and we paused at a little water-tank station named Bagdad. I pictured Haroun al Rashid and his ever-watchful vizier scouring the desert on pure white Arabian stallions . . . The sun was so beautifully bright that I risked my eyesight every time I tried to look out over the warm sands . . .

Cecil was not at the station to greet me, but his lovely wife was there . . . After a chaste family salute, she informed me that C.B. was out on the Lasky Ranch shooting 'The Rose of the Rancho,' and I was to put on old clothes and join him there without delay . . .'

Rose of the Rancho was the fourth of five more feature films Cecil B. DeMille directed after *The Virginian* in 1914. He was to follow them with thirteen more shot in 1915, racking up a total of twenty films made within two years of his arrival in California armed with only the most basic knowledge. By the time William reached him at the company location twenty miles north of Hollywood – 'several hundred acres of wilderness' – Cecil had morphed into the typical figure of the director that has since become a stereotype: William approached 'a solidly-built person, dressed in corduroy pants and puttees, a flannel shirt open at the neck, with dark sun-glasses, and a slouch hat pulled well down over his eyes . . . After looking at him closely I discovered that he was my brother . . .'

This costume was later rarefied by Erich von Stroheim by the addition of yellow gloves, thigh-length boots and a solar topee, but it was Cecil DeMille who established the iconic 'director''s look. As a correspondent for the *New Jersey Star* found him, in July 1915, at the original Lasky barn, well developed by then into a major studio: 'Flannel shirt, khaki trousers and puttees constitute the chief factors of a working garb that may seem unconventional, but that does look mighty comfortable, yes, and really businesslike, too . . . "It has been fascinating to watch this place grow under our hands like a garden," he said, "it was a garage and a stable eighteen months ago. No, I haven't been back East since the studio was opened. I haven't been downtown but four times except on business. You see, I write my own scenarios, and that keeps me going much of the night. I also cut my own pictures of course. I cannot understand a director not cutting his own pictures. To me that is inconceivable. Why, I do 20 per cent of my work in the cutting room. It means so much to be able to choose just where to place your climax and just where to cut it off – in other words, just where to ring down the curtain, where to change the scene . . .'"

Within these eighteen months, Cecil had stamped his mark on the medium, informing a reporter from the *New York Record* that '60,000,000 persons in the United States and Canada attend photoplays and motion pictures every week . . . How many others in different parts of the world also obtain entertainment and instruction from this medium is difficult to say. The photoplay appeals to almost as many persons as newspapers. The very nature of the appeal is swiftly developing a new world literature; namely, a narrative which reaches the mind and heart through the eye. The principles of sound and dramatic photoplay construction are different from those of any other universal form of reflective expression. The appeal is to the eye and we all know that sight is the most sensitive of all the senses, the quickest to grasp and understand. At the Lasky studios we are expending thousands of dollars every year in photodramatic experiment and in the maintenance of a photodramatic department composed of expert and well known writers who are specializing in this new and unlimited field. There is a responsibility in sending forth to millions of persons a product likely to have a deep influence on them. Our purpose is to make that influence one for good. The photoplay is filling its highest destiny when it aids in the shaping of lives . . .'

DeMille had ample opportunity to experiment, diversifying from his first two western sagas to a variety of different tales. The new partnership entered into by Lasky netted a new and much desired supply of story material from the DeMilles' old mentor, David Belasco. Cecil's prudence in not pressing his suit over *Peter Grimm* allowed him an amicable restart with theatre's unstoppable dynamo, and in June 1914, Belasco granted Goldfish and Lasky the rights to all his old plays and any future productions. Belasco had made his peace with 'the Drama's Flickering Bogy', writing to Lasky: 'For the past six months, in fact ever since dramatic successes became popular upon the screen, I have made a careful study of the situation. Personally I have seen numerous feature motion pictures and concluded after seeing the three productions already made by you that no other firm is as open to convictions as to the value of untried methods, no other firm as willing to innovate and no other firm allows their directors the freedom to create new methods of production to take the place of those which we have outgrown.'

Belasco admitted, in an interview with the *Moving Picture World*, on 13 June, that the Lasky company 'were indeed generous in the financial inducements offered', but insisted he had made his decision purely on artistic merit. He dismissed, interestingly enough, the idea of talking pictures, about which there was much kerfuffle in the trade press, which constantly promised this tantalizing development without any fruit appearing on the tree apart from short, uncommercial experiments. 'To me nothing can take the place of the speaking stage . . . I think this attempt to accompany pictures with imitations of sounds or of human voices is inartistic, unconvincing and unreal. The future of your art surely does not lie in that direction. Adding an echo to a shadow makes the entertainment artificial and mechanical. The pictures must speak for themselves . . .'

This was a view shared by Lasky, who had told the *Movie Pictorial* magazine in July 1914 that 'talking pictures' were unacceptable: 'No – absolutely no! . . . I think they spoil everything! Moving pictures are something new – silent drama. They depend on action – on the interpretation by silent methods.'

Cecil DeMille did not express a view on this issue, as he was too busy realizing the silent drama's unique action. After *The Virginian*, his next film was *The Call of the North*, another frontier tale, but set in Canada. This had been a play by George Broadhurst, based on a 1903 novel, *The Conjurer's House*, by Stewart Edward White. The settings were similar to the world of Cecil's own play *The Royal Mounted*, though the plot was quite different. (An adaptation of that play would have to wait a quarter of a century, until *North West Mounted Police* of 1940.)

The production history of each of Cecil's seventy films has been published in Robert Birchard's fine filmography *Cecil B. DeMille's Hollywood*, to which I refer the reader wishing for technical detail. To prevent the familiar frustration caused by specialists discussing obscure facts, I have included in this book's Filmography some synopses of those of DeMille's films that are so far available only in archives and that I have not chosen to look at in depth. Suffice to say, in summary, that *The Call of the North* deals with a tale of love and revenge in a fur-trading community dominated by a factor of the Hudson Bay Company, a man described as 'Lord of all temporal existence. Under his displeasure men were thrust unarmed into the wilderness. If starvation failed, his Indians did not. This was called the Journey of Death.' A man whose father was sent out on such a journey himself becomes a victim of the factor's malice. Various adventures with Indians, rogue trappers and the forbidding landscape ensue, before a last scene of atonement in which the factor realizes his vengeance against his original victim was based on a malicious rumour.

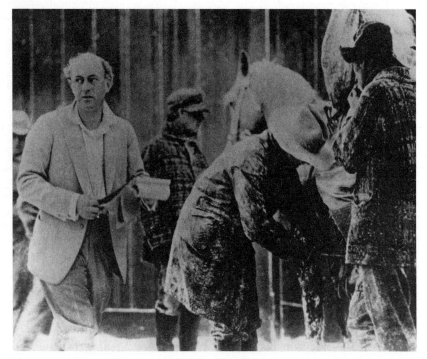

Call of the North – Cecil and the frozen north

The plot is complicated, but the scenery remains impressive, even though the entire film was shot in California and not in part at Moose Factory, Canada, as Lasky's publicity claimed. Log cabins, snowy landscapes and beautiful shots of canoes crossing lakes and rivers made the film another success. The star was stage favourite Robert Edeson, playing both the original victim and his son. Theodore Roberts, a burly and expressive actor, played the factor, the first of his numerous roles in DeMille films. Cecil's daughter Cecilia appeared as a small child.

As in *The Virginian*, DeMille presents frontier life as both romantic and harsh. Where in a John Ford film the frontier is a world of savagery awaiting the civilizing influence of the hero, DeMille's frontier is a more amoral place. Heroes are often not much better than the villains, being merely beneficiaries of chance. In later films, heroes or protagonists will often be weak, sullied or literally crippled, in an agonizing search for love. The landscape, rural or urban, is full of traps and pitfalls. Even jazz-age New York can be as hazardous a physical and moral backdrop for the DeMille hero or heroine as any lawless western town. Ultimate perdition lies in wait for the wrong, often momentary choice. There is a long way to go before DeMille begins to tackle religion as a direct subject, but, in hindsight, one can see even in the early films a religious dimension at the ethical crossroads of his characters. Henry DeMille's Christian socialism lurks somewhere in the underbrush like the vampire hunter with the wooden stake. But for some time it will remain in reserve.

Two more movies, *What's His Name* and *The Man from Home*, were shot during the summer of 1914. Both were modern tales, assignments to service the 'Famous Plays' bought by Lasky. *What's His Name* was a book by George Barr McCutcheon which had been serialized in the *New York Herald* in 1911, and it became the first of DeMille's film satires on modern mores and the 'battle of the sexes'. As such, it beckons us to linger a while.

Harvey, the 'Beau of Blakeville', is to marry Nellie the baker. But his uncle Peter kicks him out for such class infringement. They marry, bear a child, Phoebe, and are happy. But one day they see a sign for a musical comedy, *The Globe Trotters*, opening in town. A spiv goads Nellie with the intertitle: 'I'll give you twenty dollars a week to join the chorus.' Nellie is a success, and Harvey, now a soda-jerker, leaves with her for New York. In the big city the gender roles are reversed:

Harvey becomes the home-keeper and child-minder while Nellie earns the money, climbing the ladder of showbiz success.

The spiv recruiter tells Nellie: 'To be succesful there mustn't be any husbands around.' So Nellie establishes Harvey and Phoebe in Tarrytown, out of sight, and takes a new name, Nellie Duluth. Three years later, she has become a diva, the rage of New York. Meanwhile, Harvey battles with the consequences of his disempowerment – he can't even discharge the cook because he doesn't pay her wages. Enter a rich patron, Mr Leonard Z. Fairfax, who desires Nellie. When he dines with her, Harvey is introduced as 'What's-His-Name, Miss Duluth's husband.' As Nellie continues to meet with Fairfax, Harvey turns up one night, pulls a gun and chases the hangers-on off, so he can have dinner with his wife and child. Soon, Nellie is sending him a note to say she is off to Reno for a divorce. Fairfax visits Harvey, offering him 'twenty thousand dollars not to contest the divorce'. They fight, and Harvey is knocked down. He decides to gas himself, but survives. Husband and wife part, Phoebe staying with Harvey. They pack to return to Blakeville, Harvey taking down his sign 'GOD BLESS OUR HOME'. The newspapers trumpet: 'Nellie Duluth and Her Husband Separate: He is Charged with Cruelty, Desertion, Non-Support and Infidelity.'

In Reno, Fairfax visits Nellie and tries to kiss her by force. She resists. Meanwhile, back home, Phoebe lies ill. Harvey sends Nellie a telegram. Final scene: 'The Crisis is Past' – Nellie rushes to her daughter, and Harvey and Nellie reconcile over the child.

The theme of the story is unusually forthright for its period, and DeMille will return to it, with greater force and finesse – and repeatedly – some years down the line. The film starred stage actors Max Figman and his real-life wife, Lolita Robertson, with Cecilia DeMille, again, as the child. The actors are introduced with a device DeMille will revamp later: an artist looks at vignettes of his own creation which come alive for the credits. DeMille treats this story of the theatre with theatrical set-ups; much of the film is in the by now old-fashioned medium-long shots. Academic writer Sumiko Higashi, who has performed prodigious research on DeMille's silent output, has selected *What's His Name* as a prime example of the 'translation of domestic melodrama as an intertext from stage to screen . . . [representing] the ethical dilemma of middle-class families caught between the values of self-denial signifying moral character, on the one hand, and personality defined by commodities and performance, on the other'.

While it is doubtful that DeMille meant his tale quite this way, the jargon wraps round an important observation: that DeMille, for the first time, was dealing with aspects of modernity that were central to the moment – the rising aspirations of women to self-empowerment, the contradiction this entailed for prevailing male–female relationships in a barely post-Victorian era and the pursuit of material benefits at the beginning of what we today call the consumer society. The film also plays with the idea of reversal of fortune, which will become the dominant theme of DeMille's films in future years.

The Man from Home, shot a few weeks later, is a totally different comedy ragbag. Based on a Booth Tarkington novel, it satirizes the gulf between the 'honest American' and a bunch of effete English snobs, and is set mainly in a cod European setting populated by bizarre Russian revolutionaries and aristocrats. Daniel Voorhees Pike, the good American, loves his ward, Ethel Simpson, an heiress, who has been sent to Europe by her parents to get educated. Meanwhile, in darkest Russia, Ivanoff, a secret revolutionary, steals government funds for the revolution but is denounced by the dissolute Lord Hawcastle and sentenced to thirty years in Siberia. 'In Italy three years later,' says an intertitle, leaping over several coincidences, 'Lord Hawcastle decides to recoup his fortune by marrying his son to Ethel.' He instructs his creepy son Almeric to woo and wed the heiress, while they all swan about the elegant Hotel Tramontana. Meanwhile, in the Siberian mine, a maddened prisoner blows up the prison, and Ivanoff escapes by an abandoned shaft. Somehow, he arrives in Italy, in rags, chased by *carabinieri*.

So far so confusing, but there is more to come: in America, Daniel is to run for Congress, but, told that Ethel may be marrying into 'one of the great families in Europe', he rushes to her rescue. Meanwhile, in Russia, the Grand Duke Vassili (played with great verve by Theodore Roberts) sets off incognito for an Italian holiday. Some twiddle-twaddle ensues with Daniel meeting the Grand Duke and helping him to fix his stalled car. Ivanoff, still on the run, hides in the car, and Daniel protects him, presenting him as his chauffeur. In the hotel, Lord Hawcastle recognizes the fugitive, but Ivanoff has told Daniel how the treacherous lord betrayed him. Ivanoff is discovered, but the Russian duke pardons him, as a favour to his new American friend, the 'Man from Home'. Daniel tells him: 'You're all right, Doc.' And to Ellen: 'There goes your great European family.' The duke tells Ellen: 'You have noblemen in your own country, Miss Simpson.' Daniel to duke: 'If you're ever in Kokomo, be sure to look me up.' At the coast, Daniel and Ellen finally kiss. THE END.

The *Moving Picture World* called *The Man from Home* 'a shining star in the Paramount sky . . . a veritable triumph of screen dramatization. It emphasizes in a thoroughly convincing manner that, as a medium of dramatic expression, the film has no metes and bounds . . . Nothing in our art has now been demonstrated more clearly than the success of the American-made high-class feature with a typically American plot and atmosphere.' A somewhat odd statement given that almost all the film was set in a fantasy Italy and Siberia located in Lasky studios. 'The keynote of the play', wrote the ecstatic reviewer, the already influential W. Stephen Bush, 'is the inherent American love of truth and honesty, the American way of cutting the Gordian knot of European formalism and etiquette with the knife of wit and commonsense and the wholesome manliness of American men . . . For years I have been a careful observer of audiences, but never before did I see an audience so quickly drawn in sympathy to the screen . . .'

Though Cecil had never set foot in Europe at this time, unlike his German-schooled brother, he had a penchant for fantasy European settings, as his own very early unperformed play, *The Pretender*, revealed. Nevertheless, Americans revelled in the comeuppance of the effete English, and Cecil could display an early sympathy with the victims of Tsarist oppression which would flow, as we shall see further on, into a sympathy with Bolshevik rebels. That would have to wait a while though, as he had to return to the more familiar American west to process the first set of Belasco plays purchased by Lasky for 'picturization'.

Rose of the Rancho, *The Girl of the Golden West* and brother William's own *The Warrens of Virginia* followed in quick succession, released between November 1914 and February 1915. Each continued Cecil's experiments, with Alvin Wyckoff, in the expressive use of light and shadow. From *The Call of the North* too Cecil had been bolstered by the work of a new art director, Wilfred Buckland, who had known DeMille since both were students at the American Academy of Dramatic Arts and who had been a set designer for several Belasco plays. Sets began to be built that could serve the new lighting methods, filtering sunlight or night-time effects.

Rose of the Rancho is not among DeMille's best early efforts, despite its origin as one of Belasco smash stage hits. Juanita, the 'Rose', played by Bessie Barriscale, is the only daughter of the old house of Castro, in a Spanish California in which American 'Land Jumpers' are taking over the Spaniards' ranches as the state is claimed by the US. A white American, Kearney, who comes to investigate the land grabs, falls for the Rose, and then has to decide between his loyalty to his government and his love for the dusky Spanish maid. A night gunfight provides a fine early sample of sidelighting to enhance the drama. In the end, the lovers marry, but Juanita is ostracized and driven out by her own people – 'If you marry this gringo, you are no longer a daughter of the Castros.' End on marriage at a simple pueblo church, the couple alone at the fade out.

During the filming, brother William arrived and was immediately roped in by Cecil for movie service: '"Hello Bill," he said, grasping my hand. "How's Mother? Here. Put on one of these cowboy rigs and get on a horse – you're one of the attacking Gringos."'

Two cow-punchers, called 'Milt' and 'Tex', shepherded the new extra to a thicket, whence they broke loose at the signal, a gunshot from the distance, riding 'like bats out of hell' in a cloud of dust, the movie-shocked easterner praying not to fall under the thundering hooves, until they fetched up close to the camera, where 'I held my fire until I was right in the middle of the picture . . . Then I began emitting lusty yells and firing my gun.' Only after he had stopped did he realize the camera had stopped turning just before 'I had given what I considered an excellent performance.' As Cecil pointed out to him, 'in terms of the stage, play your scene while the curtain is still up'.

In another shoot-up, with real bullets flying and cutting through a barricaded door, William complained about the danger, only to be rebuffed by Cecil: 'Of course it's dangerous; who said it wasn't? But that's pictures. We don't fake anything in pictures; we've got to have the real thing.'

The real thing included a meticulous approach to detail, in the furnishing and dressing of the sets, props and costumes. If a certain antique Spanish side saddle could be useful to the production, DeMille would buy it, even if it was not catered for in the budget: 'If it can go on the screen and add to the story, it is worth its cost.' This credo was followed up in *The Girl of the Golden West*, where the saloon and miners' huts of the era are convincingly reproduced. The eponymous 'Girl' was Mabel van Buren, in a full-blown romance of the day when 'people from – God knows where – joined forces in the Golden West. They struggled, laughed and gambled – cursed, killed and loved, worked out their destinies, according to the virile code of their day. And one thing sure – they *lived*.'

Jake Rance, sheriff and gambler (the rambunctious Theodore Roberts again), wants to marry 'the Girl', who owns the Polka Saloon. The Girl falls for a bandit, Ramerrez, whom she helps when she finds him wounded at a stream, without knowing his true identity. Innocently, she entrusts the local miners' poke of gold to him. Ramerrez experiences an early DeMille dilemma: steal the gold or love the girl. More fine side-lighting is evident inside the Girl's cabin, in a night gunfight and in snow scenes. The west is once again portrayed harshly: the sheriff gambles a man's life in a card game; an Indian servant rushes gleefully to announce 'come see man hanging – lots of fun'. In the end, the gambling sheriff lets the bandit off the noose because the Girl has unmasked him as a card cheat, and we iris in to a mountain idyll, Ramerrez on his horse with the Girl beside him, as she prepares to leave with him – 'Goodbye, my California! Goodbye, my Sierras!' They ride off into the distance.

Cecil's last film in his Belasco trilogy, *The Warrens of Virginia*, was the first of his rare collaborations with brother William, here adapting his own Civil War play. Californian locations were once more used to great effect, but William struggled to find descriptive solutions to the full-blown stage dialogue. Many scenes are still stage-bound and static; perhaps Cecil felt more constrained in adapting his brother's material, less willing to 'picturize' it properly. The film is, however, famous for an apocryphal moment of movie history, when DeMille, Wyckoff and Buckland experimented further with side-lighting, leaving shadows on faces lit by lanterns, with portable small spotlights used to pinpoint light. When the film reached the New York theatres, the legend goes, exhibitors complained to Samuel Goldfish that 'if we showed only half an actor's face . . . [they] would want to pay only half the usual price for the picture . . .' DeMille's answer was to dub his new technique 'Rembrandt lighting'. For which, Goldfish wired back happily, they'd pay double.

A nice tale, were it not for the fact that side-lighting had been used in several previous DeMille productions, as well as by other directors. Even the sun-soaked foreign epic *Cabiria* and Scandinavian films of the time used the technique in certain scenes. Another American film of early 1915, *Alias Jimmy Valentine*, a seminal gangster picture directed by Maurice Tourneur, used dramatic side-lighting on faces. It was not that unfamiliar. But DeMille and his technicians were systematically learning to use it for dramatic and psychological effect.

The Warrens of Virginia was released formally on 15 February 1915. On 8 February, D. W. Griffith's Civil War epic *Birth of a Nation* had premiered in Los Angeles. In March, it opened in New York, sparking controversy, adulation, outrage, riots, calls for censorship and the biggest box office the movies had ever seen to date. DeMille, like every other film-maker of the time, realized that a new benchmark was being set. After all the battles over feature films, and the normal restriction to five reels, at most, for the standard length, Griffith's film ran a full twelve reels, over two and a half hours. As an independent production, it also consigned the Edison Trust to history and opened new opportunities, as well as perils, to film-makers.

If there was any doubt that movies could 'shape lives' and have an impact on society at large, Griffith's massive racial provocation dispelled any illusion. After *Birth of a Nation*, films could be as dangerous as dynamite and as effective in manipulating emotions as any religious or political agitation. Cecil DeMille had seen it coming. But he was still labouring, albeit with verve and enthusiasm, in Jesse Lasky's factory, bound to commercial necessity and still only testing his wings.

The Elemental Values, or The Many Faces of Cecil B. DeMille

The year 1915 was key for DeMille as a student of the craft of the movies. Having begun the year with the lacklustre *Warrens of Virginia*, he closed it with two productions shot back to back, *The Cheat* and *The Golden Chance*, both now judged as classics. This was the year in which American cinema came of age as an art form, and perhaps not coincidentally, the year in which America itself had to come to terms with its membership of a wider global fraternity of change and crisis, when the passenger ship *Lusitania* was sunk by a German submarine on 7 May, with the loss of over a thousand lives. The war had been raging in Europe since August 1914, but now it began to seem inevitable that America too would pay its toll.

In popular culture, however, the show went on. The vaudeville carnival continued to flourish, with W. C. Fields and the Marx Brothers sharing a stage at Keith's Theatre in Columbus, Ohio. Houdini had himself suspended forty-five feet from the office building of the *Minneapolis Evening Tribune* in a straitjacket and shook himself loose high above a crowd of gasping admirers. Mae West was being denounced as 'vulgar' in Detroit for shaking her breasts and singing suggestive songs to an audience that howled for more. Mutterings that something had to be done to curb the new licentiousness and moral laxity increased among the powerful reformers who were renewing their call for prohibition of alcohol. The movies too were under threat of censorship, as they had been almost since their very inception. Complaints from clergymen that the very atmosphere of their projection in darkened theatres led to the assault and seduction of children by perverts widened into agitation over the content of the films. 'CENSORSHIP NEWS FROM EVERYWHERE' headlined the *Motion Picture News* in March 1914, as it reported battles over attempts to pass state censorship laws in New York, Illinois, Ohio, New Jersey, Pennsylvania, Massachussets *et al*. 'Every reputable manufacturer has to be his own censor,' declared John F. Pribyl of the Selig Polyscope Company. The main concern of producers and distributors was to prevent a federal censorship bill, which would have put the industry into a straitjacket that even Houdini could not have escaped from. Although this was successfully fought off, state censorship continued to be a bugbear, as well as censorship in individual cities – Boston, Pittsburgh, Chicago or New York. Cecil DeMille's first brush with the censor was to occur in Pennsylvania over *Carmen*, starring the opera star Geraldine Farrar, in October 1915.

Across the country, however, DeMille's reputation grew rapidly. The *Moving Picture World* acknowledged him with a special feature as early as 27 March 1915, listing his successes to date and stating that 'such a series of extraordinary hits, all produced within a brief period of time, stamps Mr. De Mille as the foremost photo-dramatic producer in the world'. This, coming during the release of Griffith's *The Birth of a Nation*, was more than high praise and practically a coronation. Naturally, then as now, hype and publicity played their part in the trade magazines, and Jesse Lasky was a master at getting his films and his people noticed.

During the year, Cecil built up his team, the collaborators who would stay with him, some for decades, and add their considerable talents to the movies 'picturized' by the director. In addition to Alvin Wyckoff and art director Wilfred Buckland, personal secretary Gladys Rosson – part of a motion-picture family that included cameramen Hal and Arthur, who became Cecil's second-unit director on many pictures – came to work with him in 1914 and stayed for almost forty years. *Rose of the Rancho* had introduced another regular, soon to become a major lynchpin: a feisty, eccentric young actress with aspirations for a writing career named Jeanie Macpherson.

Jeanie Macpherson's life before and during her long tenure with DeMille has been the subject of much colouring, a fair patch of it by DeMille biographer Charles Higham, who describes her as being 'of mixed French, Scottish and Spanish descent [*sic!*] . . . her family was wiped out financially just as she was completing an expensive schooling at a lycee in Paris'. The record shows that, born in Boston, she was educated at the De Facq school in Paris and the Kenwood Institute in Chicago. She learned dancing with Theodore Kosloff, another name soon to become familiar in DeMille's repertory cast. She appeared on stage in a musical, *Havana*, and then got a part in

William de Mille's *Strongheart* in 1905. Higham describes her barging her way 'into D. W. Griffith's flourishing new Biograph Studio in New York. When he refused to see her, she sent him a letter which read, "I want a job. If you catch me on a Scotch day I will make money for you, and if you catch me on a French day I will act for you."' This enticed a call from Griffith to ask what day this was. 'She replied: "A French day." He said: "Put on a pretty dress and come over here."'

A pretty tale too, since the first Griffith film the record shows she appeared in was *The Fatal Hour*, an early short of 1908, made before Griffith was famous for anything other than his dynamic persistence at Biograph. She proceeded to become a Biograph regular, playing two roles, those of 'party planner' and 'nurse with buggy', in the first Mack Sennett special for Griffith, *The Curtain Pole*, in 1909. Between 1908 and 1909 she appeared in 137 short films. Moving to Universal, she was said to have written her first film script, for *Tarantula*, but researched credits note her first scenario as *The Sea Urchin*, a two-reeler directed by Edwin August and starring a very young Lon Chaney. There followed two writing credits for director Allan Dwan. Higham's description of her first meeting with DeMille is suitably vivid: 'She behaved rather as though DeMille was a butler whom she was considering for a job. She acted as though seeking work with him was the greatest possible way of flattering him and she was the greatest actress in the world.' When he ignored her, she flounced out, only to return two days later to demand an apology from him. DeMille stormed at her, she stormed at him, and eventually he said, 'Well, if you really want to act for me, I'll give you just one day's work.' Then he engaged her as a stenographer to take dictation of his scripts. Once again, a nice story, but doubtful given her acting experience. The fact that she appeared, albeit in a small role, in *Strongheart* suggests an early acquaintance with the DeMilles.

Once ensconced as the most valued of DeMille's crew, Jeanie Macpherson wrote most of DeMille's silent pictures from *The Captive* of 1915, and co-wrote his first two sound pictures. She also became his primary mistress, remaining close to him until her death in 1946.

Higham wrote that Macpherson 'had a masochistic streak, enjoying the agony of shooting. One of her favorite phrases was: "Only a thoroughbred can take a good whipping."' But claims that she slept

DeMille with Jeanie Macpherson in later years

her way to her jobs remain speculation. While she makes no great impact as an actress in *Rose of the Rancho*, *The Girl of the Golden West* or *Carmen* – in which she cavorts as a frisky Hispanic lassie – she clearly made an early impression both as a lover and as a writer who had ideas that fitted Cecil's own thoughts about the form and content of his work.

The first script that Macpherson stenographed, and possibly advised on, was *The Unafraid*, shot in January 1915. It was based on a novel set in Montenegro, exotically topical because of its vicinity to the assassination of Archduke Franz Ferdinand, which ignited the First World War in 1914. The story was a nonsense based around the rivalry between two brothers for political power, Count Stefan Balsic and his brother Michael, described as 'the Tool of the Dual Empire'. Delight Warren is an American heiress whom the scheming Michael spots on the Riviera and decides to marry for her money so he can finance his revolution. She decides recklessly to follow him to Montenegro, where, he has told her, 'the men are as rugged as the mountains – hating often – loving once'. But she is unafraid. In Montenegro, however, she is kidnapped by her suitor's brother, the count, who plans to force her to become his wife so that her money will be denied to Michael.

The ensuing shenanigans introduce the first hint of a sado-masochistic relationship into DeMille's oeuvre, a sign that he has worked out that a director can insert his own private fantasies into a story that he has not necessarily authored. While captive in Stefan's castle, fondling his immense dog, Delight appears ambivalent about her captivity. She is horrified at first, but when snatched back by Michael she discovers her suitor's brutal nature when he brings her to a torture cell to see the torment of a prisoner, forcing her with threats to sign a cheque. 'I will sell you his eyes, madame,' the intertitle chortles, while the prisoner and torture tongs are garishly side-lit. Bound and left in the castle as Michael rides out, she is rescued by Count Stefan, whom she embraces, telling him, when he offers to send her home: 'I am home, Monsieur.'

We might recall the letter sent by DeMille to his wife, Constance, when he departed westwards by train to begin his new life as a movie director, quoted in adopted son Richard de Mille's memoir: professing his particular sexual desires for his wife, he addresses 'the god of morals' whom he imagines denouncing him as a 'libertine'. 'My wife's my mistress and I'll teach her all a mistress knows . . . And I'll pull her hair to my heart's content, and you can go to the devil with your morality . . .'

Cecil's penchant for rather rough love-making does not seem to have been reciprocated by his wife, who expressed her own self-effacing tendencies by accepting her role as Constance by name and by nature. Cecil's long-term mistresses were the inevitable price she paid for allowing her husband outlets for his promiscuous desires while retaining the outward show of fidelity. In reality she became the perfect submissive to his drive for power and control. By the time of the arrival of Jeanie Macpherson, the DeMilles had adopted the first of three children who would be brothers and sister to Cecilia – John, a baby boy of unknown origin. Constance had begun work in a children's hospital in 1914, and according to family historian Anne Edwards, 'often brought home children from hospitals or orphanages for a weekend or a holiday'. The adoption of the DeMilles' next child, Katherine, would not occur, however, until 1920, and in 1922 Richard arrived, in circumstances which would not be revealed until he was thirty-three years of age.

And so, while his wife became Florence Nightingale, Cecil Blount DeMille could indulge his desires in reality and explore them in fiction, now that he had found a congenial partner who could insert these fantasies into his scripts. His next film, *The Captive*, was the first credited to Jeanie Macpherson as joint author of the scenario with her director. Another Balkan tale, set during the Turkish–Serbian war of 1912, it told the story of Hassan Bey, a Turkish officer, who is captured and leased as a working prisoner to a woman, Sonia, whose own brother has been killed by Turkish soldiers at the front. A working camaraderie, ripening into friendship as the woman is menaced by soldiers of both armies, forms the plot.

Macpherson's skills are instantly evident in this primal collaboration. This is the first original story directed by DeMille, and one can read into it various sly hints as to the relationship of the co-writers. Structurally, it is superior to the previous films. Stage actor House Peters plays Hassan most naturally, and Sonia is played by Blanche Sweet, already a motion-picture star. Her understanding of the nature of silent-screen acting is evident, and she plays the transition from loathing her captive to compassion and dependence with a subtle skill. Hassan's transition from sullen aristocrat to a man who learns to appreciate the hard life and fate of the woman left to farm her land alone, with only her kid brother to assist her, is well plotted in the narrative. At first prodded to work at pistol-point and locked in an attic behind bars, he finds the bars are fragile and easily removable. Yet he does not escape, realizing the virtues of the simple life and the attractions of his captor. When he is sent to wash clothes in the river and is laughed at by the local women, Sonia calls out: 'He's my captive! Don't you laugh at him!'

As against the rather ridiculous cadences of *The Unafraid*, *The Captive* flows in a much finer, harmonious style. As Turks and Serbs in turn attack the farm which has become an oasis of peace between enemies, a title announces 'THE DREGS OF WAR – THE LAWLESSNESS THAT FOLLOWS.' The burning farms seem an eerie precognition of a conflict that would rage in the same setting eighty years in the future. The instinctive pacifism of the DeMilles, and of America itself just before the *Lusitania*'s sinking, is powerfully expressed. The inversion of fortune continues as Hassan fights off a Turkish officer who is his own superior. When the war is over, on returning home this superior divests Hassan of all his lands and titles as an enemy collaborator. To ensure a happy end, Hassan, now penniless, chances across Sonia and her kid brother as refugees upon a

Lasky ranch crossroads. They move away together – he, she, boy and pet sheep on a lead.

During the shooting of the film, DeMille's demand for 'realism' claimed a victim in the form of an extra, Charles Chandler, shot in the scene of soldiers besieging the farm house. Whether the blanks that were supposed to be used had been replaced by mistake or whether DeMille had risked the scene with real ammunition remains open to argument. The widow of the dead man was kept on the payroll for many years, but this was an age when 'accidents did happen' on movie-studio lots, and DeMille escaped with only his conscience damaged.

DeMille's next three films are missing. *The Wild Goose Chase, The Arab* and *Chimmie Fadden* disappeared into the sump of indifference with which these conveyor-belt films were regarded once they had been exploited for their immediate profit. Film preservation was not even a tic in the eye of movie businessmen at that time. *The Wild Goose Chase* was an adaptation by William de Mille of one of his own plays, a piece of apparent fluff about a boy and a girl who are told they will inherit a large sum of money if they marry the daughter, or son, of a friend. They each run away and join a theatrical company, unaware that they are the respective objects of the money-grubbing exercise. Of course, love and money triumph together.

William had long surrendered to the idea that the drama 'must express the thoughts, or the point of view, the general psychology of its audience . . . Its deeper purpose is to formulate rather than form thought; to express to the people what they are thinking rather than tell them what to think.' In a commercial medium, could it be otherwise? A hit play may be seen by half a million people, but the motion picture had to reach an audience of millions. 'Therefore,' William later wrote, 'it must deal with values so elemental as to be a part of every man; it must have its roots deep in the soil of human nature, it must avoid subjects and motives which cannot be understood and accepted by the majority.'

Alas, we have no way of judging if in *The Wild Goose Chase*, as *Variety* wrote, 'the comedy by-play throughout easily makes the picture worth while seeing'. The next missing work, *The Arab*, received even warmer praise, *Variety* stating that it 'surpasses many of the previous Lasky releases and will set a mark for the others to aim at for some time'. The plot sounds like a precursor of the Rudolph

Valentino film *The Sheik*, if played for action rather than any sexual simmering. DeMille alone is credited with the scenario, which was based on a successful Broadway stage play. Stage star Edgar Selwyn played Jamil, the son of an Arab sheik who turns Christian and 'prevents a cleverly planned massacre of Christians by the Turks'. Desert scenes of camels ploughing through sandiest California were highly praised by the critics.

The third in the missing trilogy is *Chimmie Fadden*, a vehicle for comic actor Victor Moore, who had successfully played on the stage the role of a 'good natured rough-neck' living on New York's Bowery with his mother and trouble-making brother. Their verbal slang was reflected in the title. Although we cannot judge the transition from verbal to visual comedy in the film, the sequel, *Chimmie Fadden Out West*, made by DeMille later in the year, enables us to see how Cecil could direct for laughs, if he so wished. But he preferred drama.

While Cecil raced through these productions, Jesse Lasky continued to plough his profits back into his film-making factory. The 'ranch', purchased north of the old barn, consisted of 20,000 acres which included, in Lasky's words, 'some of the finest scenery in California. Mountains rise to a height of 6,000 feet. On the top we can get snow, while at the base there is an abundance of tropical foliage. Included in this property are three or four acres of remarkable desert and cactus.' In the original location of the barn, a new glass-covered studio measuring 100 by 80 feet had been built, 'so that we might take advantage of the rainy season', such as it was in Los Angeles. 'We also put in a plant of machinery for the making of all our properties as well as the more difficult carpentry work on scenery.' A special wardrobe department completed the new studio's independence. Not only the facilities but also the organization were streamlined, with a new scenario department put under the 'well known novelist' Margaret Turnbull. Jeanie Macpherson was as yet just a cog in this machine, of which DeMille was the director general.

In February 1915, the *New York Times* reported that Cecil B. DeMille was to accompany a cast of actors to Japan to 'make a movie version of Belasco's "The Darling of the Gods" . . . which it is planned to make one of the most elaborate yet produced'. Alas, this tantalizing prospect never materialized, as Cecil was far too busy in California. (Belasco had to fulfil his Japanese aspirations with a 1919 film version of his *Madam Butterfly*, *Harakiri*, made not in

Japan but in the German UFA studios by a new director, Fritz Lang.)

In May 1915, Lasky announced a new acquisition for his growing empire, signing a contract with the Metropolitan Opera star Geraldine Farrar. Miss Farrar was to spend eight weeks of every season making films at the Lasky studios. Some said she had been brought in as a competitor to Zukor's Famous Players' most profitable star, Mary Pickford. She, however, was twenty-three years old and Miss Farrar a good ten years older.

It might seem strange to engage an opera diva for the silent movies, but a star was a star. 'Jerry', as she was known by her admirers, had a legion of fans and a very modern-style coterie of female worshippers who were known as 'Jerry-flappers'. She was America's most prominent native-born opera singer – and the daughter of a star baseball player – who, in the words of W. Stephen Bush in the *Moving Picture World*, 'brought back from her conquests in Europe all that was worth learning . . . [and] gave to Europe more, however, than she took away. The ingenuousness of the true American girl, the modest freedom, the charm of innocence, the gay laughter of unspoiled girlhood . . . all these blessed things the young woman has brought back with her in undiminished and unimpaired form . . .'

As a rare movie lover among the snobby intelligentsia, Bush wrote, 'the resolution of this marvelously gifted young woman to employ her talents in the attaining of success in the films is the greatest step in advancing the dignity of the motion-picture, in freeing it from the bane of prejudice, in winning for it the good opinion of the public'. Jesse Lasky, who had begun his career in movies by counting the cars outside the feature-playing theatres and noting the sartorial superiority of their patrons to the slobbish riff-raff who attended one-reel comedies, had obviously figured the same way. He happily guaranteed her cash, chauffeur and a house in the sun for her mere two months per year of movie service.

Cecil girded his loins for the first of three productions he was to shoot with the great diva. But before that he released a small, modest film, shot in less than three weeks in the studio and marking a completely new and unexpected departure in both the subject matter and nature of his films.

From Tenement to Bull Ring: The Many Faces of Cecil B. DeMille, Part II

Kindling, a play set in the slums of New York's Hell's Kitchen, was written by Charles Kenyon and Arthur Hornblow and produced in 1911 at New York's Daly Theatre, to no great success – it ran for only thirty-nine performances. *The Billboard*, reviewing its opening in Chicago in 1912, wrote that 'Tears of Audience are Shed Copiously' and noted some effective scenes, but generally found the play a 'very uneven and disappointing work'. It was hardly, therefore, a 'Famous Play'. Its choice as subject matter can only be attributed to a nagging strand in Cecil's thought that recalled the social doctrines of his father's favourite, Charles Kingsley, and the anti-poverty agitation of Henry George. Some have called the film a 'socialist tract', but though there is anger at social conditions in the film, its dramatic thrust works towards the idea of self-improvement, while the overall emotion is of despair over any expectation of change.

Kindling is another of the many early DeMilles viewable, to date, only by scholars, but a closer look is well worth while. DeMille brought author Kenyon to Hollywood to help him adapt the script, which contains a mere 110 scenes. The written script introduces the main character and his milieu:

Subtitle: 'HONEST' HEINE SCHULTZ – A Stevedore.
Heine in flannel shirt. He carries dinner pail and has pipe in his mouth. Someone off scene says something Heine doesn't like. He turns quickly, taking pipe out of his mouth – pulls up his short sleeves. Showing bare arm, in threatening gesture, indicates, 'If you've anything to say to me, speak up!' Character off stage evidently explains satisfactorily and Heine smiles slow, pleasant smile and replaces pipe.

. . .

Scene 4. Fade in.
'Drop' of Lower New York – skyline with Brooklyn Bridge – sunset –

buildings are silhouetted against sky. Scene darkens to night – lights in windows come out one by one.

Scene 5. Ext. slum street at night – full view.
Typical summer night scene in New York slums. Light effect from all doors and windows. Light from street light on corner. Strong light directly over 'Private' entrance to saloon. One woman exchanges remarks from lighted doorway where she is standing to woman in lighted window above. Groups of men pass down street or lounge in doorways . . .

. . .

Scene 7. Int. cheap dive – back of saloon, night.
This is a dance hall of the lowest kind. Drinks are being served at tables to various types of crooks and toughs. In the center of the room, several couples are turkey-trotting. The Proprietor, a shrewd, stout, bad-faced man in shirt-sleeves with a large yellow diamond in his shirt and on his hand, mingles with the dancers laughing a great deal and disagreeably with his dirty-aproned bartender to see which and what couples are 'buying.' . . .

Heine and wife Maggie –
'When we ain't so poor we'll move to a place where it's safe to raise a family.'

In the finished film, the opening presents the title: '"Honest" Heine Schultz – A Stevedore – Thomas Meighan' and 'Maggie Schultz – Charlotte Walker.' Raymond Hatton, who was to be one of DeMille's regulars, having first appeared in a small Hispanic part in *The Girl of the Golden West*, is introduced as 'Steve – A Crook.' The street scene is introduced as 'Where the devil wins.' Rather than choosing a semi-documentary setting of a real slum, DeMille chose to shoot the entire film at the Lasky studio, which enabled him, with cameraman Alvin Wyckoff and art director Wilfred Buckland, to experiment to the full with what was becoming known as 'Lasky lighting'. The street lamp and windows of the saloon provide the 'contrasty' lighting that DeMille increasingly favoured to set the harsh mood of the piece. Another character, a detective, Rafferty, is introduced as being in cahoots with Steve to fleece the poor.

In contrast with the seedy saloon, a title, 'Where the devil loses,' introduces the Schultz home, where warmth and the wife's love for her husband mitigate the poor surroundings. A title, 'Victims of the City', precedes the poor queuing at a doctor's surgery. Maggie Schultz accompanies the doctor to a filthy room, where a woman and her ailing baby are shown beside a torn pillow on which a gin bottle lies, fitted with a teat. The doctor announces: 'The baby died from improper sanitation.'

Maggie's dilemma is that she is pregnant but is afraid to tell her husband, as he points out to her the terrible conditions in their neighbourhood. 'All the kids born here don't die!' she tells Heine, but he ripostes: 'The health officer says that half of them die – and the rest grow up to be crooks . . . When we ain't so poor, we'll move to a place where it's safe to raise a family.'

There follow scenes which critics, and censors, found hard to stomach, and most probably audiences too: a drunk man sleeping by a dustbin as a girl lifts his watch; another drunk feeding a child from his pail of beer as he exits the saloon; and two kids fighting over food from a dustbin. The script describes the scene as:

Dirty garbage pails and piles of refuse. Two children – a girl and boy eating from garbage can which is full of all sorts of decaying food and flies . . .
HEINE: I'd rather kill a child of ours the day it was born than send it up against a game like that . . .

Maggie confides in her mother, having bought a cheap cradle from a pawnshop: 'I don't dare tell Heine: he says babies born down here burn up like kindling.' Her mother tells her of a government plan to set up folks in a farm out west. DeMille follows this with a double exposure: from the slum to an idyllic farm scene, with children playing in the open fields.

'The Toll of the Tenements': as the story unfolds, the woman whose baby died can't pay her rent, which is due to a rich woman living outside the city. Her good-hearted niece, Alice, persuades her to take a trip down to the tenements to see how her tenants really live. Meanwhile, Heine has come home, unemployed because of a strike. When the rich landlady appears to view them in their squalor, she offers Maggie Schultz five dollars a day to come and sew a garment – for her dog. Steve the crook, overhearing this, offers Maggie one hundred dollars, the exact sum needed to get a home out west, if she will help him get into the landlady's house to rob it.

'In the House of Wealth': Maggie sews a bonnet and lace for the dog, and steals a brooch for herself. A French maid gives her instructions for the dog's toilette: 'Bebe's bath must not be more than 70 degrees.' Maggie rages silently: 'She'd do this for her mutt – and let my baby starve.' She agrees to help the crooks, breaking a tap in the bathroom so that a plumber is called. Steve calls as a plumber and proceeds to rifle the house. When the real plumber arrives, the theft is discovered and Maggie suspected. She goes and pawns the brooch, while Steve hides his stolen stash under her bed. When the detective Rafferty finds her pawnshop money, she claims the landlady's niece, Alice, loaned her the cash. Alice, realizing her desperate situation, connives in the lie. Heine, entering into the scene, realizing the truth and the pregnancy, confesses to the robbery. Maggie cries out, as the cuffs go on Heine: 'He's goin' to prison in my place to save his baby from bein' born in jail!' She cries out to the landlady: 'I lied – I fought – I stole – to keep my baby from bein' born in this hell-hole of yours!' Rafferty puts cuffs on Maggie, but the aunt says: 'I won't prosecute!' Niece Alice gives Heine the money: 'Here's $100 – take her out west.'

Mix – to Heine and Maggie in an open field, then back to their room as they fondle baby clothes . . .

Variety's reviewer hated the picture heartily: 'The story . . . is extremely morbid and in the film version is doubly so . . .' The scene of the kids fighting over the garbage should be eliminated, the reviewer wrote: 'it is revolting . . . this scene is so strong as to cause one to become ill in viewing it'. Which, one assumes, was the director's purpose. While praising the '"night scene", evidently done with the aid of flares', the reviewer found nothing to praise in any of the performances, apart from that of Thomas Meighan – soon to be another DeMille favourite – who 'walked away with the acting honors'.

DeMille's fan at the *Moving Picture World*, W. Stephen Bush, could not have differed more profoundly about *Kindling*, writing on 3 July 1915:

A Genuine Film Masterpiece Featuring Charlotte Walker and an Ornament to Any Program

I do not hesitate to say that this is one of the best samples of the Lasky school of motion picture art. When at its best this new school beggars comparison. It is pleasing, it is powerful, it scores in every scene and there are no weak links . . . The director has handled [the actors] to the greatest possible advantage, creating many stirring moments, moving our pity and arousing just anger . . . I must dwell on the director's ability to show atmosphere. To portray atmosphere and surroundings in one or two brief touches is art of the highest order . . . The scene entitled 'Where the Devil Wins,' depicting a typical section of the tenement district of a big city, is as graphic as anything that ever came from the hands of Hogarth or Rembrandt . . .

Just as the periscope draws a complete ship with its surrounding seascape within its small compass, giving a view in miniature, the screen is capable of doing this very thing in portraying all the phases of life. This film play gives a very fine example of it. All through the picture we find the very reverse of padding; this director epitomizes, abbreviates and condenses. Space forbids a further amplification of the extraordinary merits of this film.

The *Motion Picture News*, in contrast, gave the film grudging praise for its technical prowess and realism, but agreed with *Variety* in grumbling that 'nothing is actually pleasant in it'. The argument about 'realism', which rages on to this day in the discussion of movies, was already rife in these days of dawn and experiment. In an intriguing article in the same issue of the *Moving Picture World* that so praised *Kindling*, another critic, Louis Reeves Harrison, wrote, under the heading of 'Fallacies of Realism', in the somewhat overblown style typical of that period:

Worse than ignorance is a false idea that takes possession of healthy human minds and perverts what might otherwise be good judgment. Such is the mistaken association of realism in drama and literature with unvarnished truth . . . The true artist appropriates the facts of life as so much rough material from which he constructs an existence more marvelous than that we daily look upon . . . He depends largely upon his imagination. To critically ignore that is to attempt to solve the problem of creative art by denying its source . . .

The story may be cunningly realistic or openly romantic – to impose critical limitations on it in either respect narrows the field and dulls variety of presentation. An author deeply interested in social problems may present scenes and characters as he thinks he sees them from a purely personal point of view or from that of an artist engaged in revealing what is unknown to them . . .

Many of the absurd notions, false conceptions and pernicious practices that we deplore in human existence have been created by realists and naturalists who argued wrongly from fundamental truth. Peculiar quality of the unfettered poet and of the fiction-maker who does not waste his time in acquiring a heavy burden of useful information is a gift of exaggeration that is often inspiring and even prophetic. The romancer writes fiction because he loves it, the realist as if he had a painful duty to perform. The man who loves his work is sincere. He is drawing from the exhaustless font of his sympathies and not attempting to deceive us by presenting dull facts under the illusion of fiction, yet he accurately pictured the submarine fifty years ago and set the whole world thinking with the purely romantic characters of Dr. Jekyll and Mr. Hyde . . .

Trying to pin down Cecil DeMille at this stage in his film-making would be like trying to skewer a light beam. Resolved to produce at least one feature per month, he was moving too fast, leaping from one genre to another. To all these genres, there was already a background and a context. Kevin Brownlow, in his crucial book *Behind the Mask of Innocence*, alerts us to the wide variety of 'Films of Social Conscience in the Silent Era', most post-dating, but many preceding, 1915: films about social conditions, crime, prostitution, juvenile delinquency, the troubles of immigrants, prison conditions, drug abuse. (Many of these films disappeared in the 'kindling' of prints which consumed the majority of movies made in the silent era, their celluloid melted down for the cosmetic and other industries, the rest having to await the historian restorers of our own age.) Films were not only made by the burgeoning studios but by independent forces such as trade unions, highlighting labour problems. Foreign matters were not neglected either. The tyranny of Russian czarism, for example, was a subject for film-makers: William de Mille's fourth film, 1916's *The Sowers*, dealt with rebels against Russian tyranny one year before the Russian Revolution itself. Both brothers had grown up with a sympathy for the enemies of despotism in Russia, and this was to emerge in strange forms in Cecil's future oeuvre. Another of William's 1916 films, *The Blacklist*, dealt with a miners' strike in which strikers are shot down ruthlessly by the mine guards. The heroine, played by Blanche Sweet, was the daughter of a Russian anarchist, and the *New York Dramatic Mirror* called the picture 'a socialistic drama'. The film caused William to be put on an FBI list of early Hollywood radicals.

Following *Kindling*, however, Cecil could neither rest on his laurels nor brood over critical abuse, as he had to attend immediately to the triumphant arrival of New York's queen of opera, Geraldine Farrar. She had been enticed to Hollywood by theatrical manager Morris Gest, who had wooed her with the chance to have her smash-hit performance of *Carmen* adapted for the motion-picture audience. The masses were already captivated by her voice on records, but this way, *sans* singing, her face could become as familiar.

On her arrival in San Francisco, *Photoplay* magazine recorded, she was 'met at the train by Mayor Rose of Los Angeles and 500 school children, who strewed a pathway of flowers from the singer's private car to her motor. Traveling in Miss Farrar's entourage are her parents . . . her personal manager . . . two maids, a secretary, a man-servant, a chef, a hairdresser and a chauffeur.'

The roughnecks of the Lasky studio in Los Angeles awaited her appearance with some trepidation. Although they had worked with 'famous players', those were still only jobbing actors, bearing fan mail perhaps, but also the stains of sweat and greasepaint. Unremembered as she is today, Geraldine Farrar was the first celebrity Cecil B. DeMille had to deal with. Would she put on airs, be recalcitrant, Wagnerian, obstructive, and worst of all, totally ignorant of the inferior medium? In the event, everyone at the studio was surprised by Farrar's lack of pomp, her willingness to co-operate and learn how to function as a silent actress. As *Photoplay* declared in its September issue:

Cecil de Mille . . . declares Miss Farrar one of the most satisfactory persons to direct in pictures.

'I love it,' said Miss Farrar. 'It is glorious and free.' William, her pet goat, looked at her and sighed. She hadn't had her arms around him since morning . . . So William wandered away, leaving Miss Farrar exclaiming her delight at moving picture acting . . . 'In grand opera, every gesture, every movement has to be in perfect accord with the score . . . But here. Ah, here it is different. At first I asked Mr. de Mille if there were any time limit to playing certain scenes. He said: "You act them just as long as you please." So now I emote for fifty, seventy-five or a hundred feet if the spirit moves me.'

Miss Farrar had not yet realized the ruthlessness of the cutting room. She had been hired primarily to film her version of *Carmen*, but DeMille thought it might be better for her to test her skills in the new medium with another picture, so that she would not risk being seen as an awkward learner in her star role. He had another property, also a Spanish love story: *Maria Rosa*, an 1890 play by Angel Guimera which had been adapted for the New York stage in 1914. Shoot this movie first, Cecil suggested to Lasky, and then hold its release until after that of *Carmen*. Success of the second movie would ensure an audience for the first.

And it came to pass . . . *Maria Rosa* was shot over twelve days in June 1915, and *Carmen* in less than three weeks later in June and into the middle of July.

Maria Rosa exists so far only in archive, while *Carmen* can be found in a fine DVD version, the earliest of DeMille's films to have been fully restored with tinting and score. The first film is a piece of fluff about a Catalan peasant girl who is loved by two glowering hulks: Andres, a vineyard labourer, played by Wallace Reid, and Ramon, played by Pedro de Cordoba. Another suitor, the fish-peddler Pedro, is killed by Ramon with Andres's knife. Andres is condemned to prison for the murder, only to return after being released for saving a small girl from death at a quarry, at the very moment when a feast is laid out for the marriage of Maria and Ramon. Andres reveals himself to Maria, Maria gets Ramon to confess in a drunken stupor, and the end features the obligatory stabbing, of Ramon by Maria.

DeMille experimented further with 'Rembrandt lighting': shadows on walls, candlelit scenes, dramatic side-light at the end as Andres leads Maria off through the door. But its critical impact came with the film that was shot shortly afterwards.

Geraldine Farrar recalled some of the technical challenges of her first film in her autobiography, *Such Sweet Compulsion*, published in 1938:

As work progressed, Mr. DeMille evolved many effects to heighten the expression of our drama. It was the day of the close-up innovation, but there was a certain peril in this exaggerated facial display for my features. In the 'shot' thus enlarged, my grey eyes, under the glaring Kliegs, faded out so completely that I had the sightless orbs of a Greek statue. When I saw the first studio 'rushes' I nearly fainted from the shock! But Mr. DeMille repeated these 'close-ups' the following day, with an assistant holding a large square of black velvet just behind the camera on which the pupils of my eyes were focused intently, the retina expanded and darkened in its usual normal expression. Many a scene we repeated for the sake of Kliegs that cast villainous shadows and left some of us quite toothless in what was supposed to be a seductive smile!

Farrar noted that DeMille's long theatrical experience gave him 'an uncanny reading into his actors' psychology. Thus, with me, he outlined briefly the scenes, their intended length, the climax – and with the minimum expenditure of precious energy in preliminaries, set his cameras at all angles to catch the first enthusiasm of a scene, which spontaneous impulse was always my best interpretation . . .' This suggests that DeMille was using multiple cameras in certain scenes to avoid retakes and provide a wider coverage. Farrar also wrote of another reason for her enthusiasm for the silent pictures: 'After the responsibility of a long singing season and anxiety over a troublesome and delicate larynx, this was a carefree heaven indeed for me.'

Both *Maria Rosa* and *Carmen* were written by William de Mille, but the *Carmen* project was complicated by the copyright owners of the libretto demanding an obstructively high fee. William had to discard his first draft and write the story as if it were formally based on the original novel by Prosper Mérimée. Writing about the film twenty-four years later, William commented:

Just twenty years later I had occasion to look at our picture of 'Carmen.' It was hard to believe that what I saw upon the screen was actually the same work upon which so much effort had been expended . . . Our beloved 'Carmen,' which had been hailed as an achievement in 1915, was as much like a modern motion picture as . . . the earliest 'horseless carriage' is like the streamlined, high-powered automobile of today . . . Looked at with 1935 eyes, our picture was badly photographed, the lighting was childish, the acting was awful, the writing atrocious and – may Allah be merciful – the direction was terrible. The only interesting thing about our work was the fact that we had taken the same pride in it as Henry Ford took in his Model T, or the Wright brothers in their first plane . . .

If William de Mille had looked at the picture today it might have appeared somewhat different. In 1935, the silent film was an embarrassing anachronism, dead and buried by the glorious talkies that were dancing noisily on the non-talkies' grave. Today, after so much restoration, we are more ready to appreciate the silent cinema as an art form in its own right, not just as a precursor of sound movies but as a universal medium that could appeal across borders and language barriers with a mere intertitle change. As audiences that take the trouble to see these restorations – in good 35mm prints or video derivations of them – can appreciate, they have a visual beauty that is quite distinct from the often functional images of the early talkie film. The picture was all, and 'telling a story in pictures' was the alpha and omega of the craft.

Seen in this way, *Carmen* can be regarded, despite its relatively low budget and the short schedule of its production, as the first proper 'Cecil B. DeMille' saga, with the melodrama leading to the obligatory spectacle of the denouement at the bull ring in Seville. Carmen, the gypsy free spirit who gives her love to whomever she chooses, vows

Carmen – Geraldine Farrar choking Jeanie Macpherson

to seduce the honest officer Don José, played by Wallace Reid, so that her smuggler clan can get its goods into town. Meanwhile, she is wooed by the bullfighter Escamillo, played by smouldering Pedro de Cordoba. Along the way, she has a wild fight at the town cigarette factory with Frasquita, a feisty *chiquita* played by Jeanie Macpherson – an opportunity to glimpse Cecil's long-term writer-cum-lover in a couple of fairly lengthy scenes. Goading Don José to fight for her and kill a fellow officer, Carmen then spurns him for the bullfighter, only to be followed by a jealous José to the finale, where the inevitable knife thrust ends her vivacious and reckless life.

With its restored tints, we can appreciate the quality of the early monochrome prints, the orange, red and blue providing added mood and atmosphere to the scenes. Here, 'Lasky lighting' finally comes of age, with dramatic effects in the Spanish tavern and at night, when Carmen learns her fate from the tarot cards dealt by an old crone in the shadows. At a later stage, DeMille would claim intellectual roots for the movie designs he and art director Wilfred Buckland developed in the work of German stage master Max Reinhardt. But he could have claimed more native roots in the direct influence of David

Belasco. The experiments of German film-makers, in the mood light-ing that begat 'expressionism', lay some time in the future, and American audiences did not view the breakthrough *Cabinet of Doctor Caligari* until 1920. Early Scandinavian films using similar techniques just might have been viewed by DeMille.

Lea Jacobs, in an article in the magazine *Film History* in 1993, analysed in some detail the techniques originally used by Belasco on the stage and compared them with film lighting. In brief, Belasco was using, by 1902, a switchboard that varied the intensity and colour of theatrical lights, and he had used dramatic lighting variations even earlier. The 'Rembrandt' effects used by DeMille and Wyckoff were created by 'minimizing diffuse light and creating isolated pools of directional light', with small 'baby' spotlights and other variations in the great carbon arcs of the day. Belasco's influence was more in inspiration than actual methods, which could not be transposed directly from stage to film set.

The difference between the way the American and the German (and Scandinavian) film-makers used these techniques was cultural. The Germans were developing a concept, the mood or *stimmung*, which would stand as a metaphor for the inner life, the contrasts of the movie characters' mind or soul or of society and its discontents, a psychological, sometimes magical and even occult effect. The Americans, despite Louis Reeves Harrison's caveats about fictional narrative, were still looking to a heightened 'realism'. DeMille him-self was still banging on about this in a *New York Times* piece that appeared under his name in September 1915, in which he discussed the difference between the stage and the screen under the heading of 'THE REEL AND THE UNREAL':

The producer for the legitimate stage is ever trying to construct a fabric which may be built up and torn down in its entirety . . . as often as his drama is acted . . . The legitimate producer's work is toward illusion. His practica-bilities are limited to the boundaries of the theatre. On the other hand, the photoplay director is working limitless realism. His stage of operation is boundless. His proscenium arch is the horizon; his scenery is nature's own fields, mountains, forests and streams . . . If the demands of his photoplay command him to blow up a train or destroy a mountain, he does either or both and does not have to worry about putting either the train back on the track for the next performance or restoring the mountain in time for the moonlight scene . . .

In this Cecil DeMille was being, and not for the last time, disingenuous about both his methods and his artistic aims. His statement serves the myth of the director who allegedly destroyed a massive and complex set in a great explosion, only to find that it had not been caught by the cameraman, who uttered the apocryphal words after the act: 'Ready when you are, Mr DeMille.'

In reality, DeMille aspired to be as magical in his results as the Germans would ever prove to be, within the realm of American practical concepts. Drama, after all, was not real life but a condensed, emotionally intense representation of it, and the more intense and emotional the better. Perhaps, in his public interviews, he did not wish to frighten the natives about the true course of his ongoing experiments. After all, business was business, and the immediate worth of *Carmen*, beyond the enthusiastic reviews – which praised its artistry, its panache and its vision – was the fact that it cost, according to the record (compiled by researcher David Pierce), $23,429.97 to make and grossed $147,599.81.

The Future of an Illusion

Following *Carmen*, Cecil took advantage of Geraldine Farrar's eight-week contract to shoot a third film with her, *Temptation*. This is yet another of DeMille's missing films. According to the record, it was a modern-day story, with Farrar as an opera singer engaged to a failed composer but tempted by a powerful impresario to accept both a role and his advances, only to find that she has given up her true love in vain when the impresario is shot by another mistress. Pedro de Cordoba played the struggling composer and Theodore Roberts the rich tempter. *Variety* was not impressed, stating that 'in spite of the excellent acting . . . the fine photography and even the Farrar name, the story is hardly worth more than being utilized for a two-reeler on a jitney program'.

Late in August 1915, Farrar headed back east, seen off at the Santa Fe station by a horde of well-wishers who filled her private car with flowers. Gushed *Motion Picture News*: 'The natives won't forget her for years, and the neighbors probably never will forget Miss Farrar's farewell party which started last Saturday night and which ended last Sunday night at midnight.' For the guests, cast, crew and critics, she sang several arias from *Carmen* and *Madam Butterfly* in full costume. The picture went on general release in November – after some early censor twitches about the bawdiness of the gypsy girls' fighting – to general ecstasy, despite the simultaneous opening of a second version of *Carmen*, made by the Fox studios, starring Theda Bara and directed by another up-and-coming talent, Raoul Walsh. This tantalizing rival film, alas, has not survived to our day.

The Lasky studios, meanwhile, continued their expansion, despite a fire which gutted their colleagues' Famous Players studio in New York and in the teeth of a rival movie merger, the creation of the Triangle Film Corporation encompassing D. W. Griffith, Thomas Ince and Mack Sennett. Paramount, under W. W. Hodkinson, was well positioned to crush this new would-be monopoly, girding itself to fight dirty and wield the full power of its block-booking methods. 'Ten million persons in the United States can and must see Paramount pictures every week,' Hodkinson ominously declared.

If these strictures were to be followed, the film-makers would have to work overtime, as indeed they did. Partly to answer his fellow directors' complaints that they were overworked, DeMille later claimed, he took on a unique project, directing two films at the same time. By late October 1915, he had produced his sequel to the Victor Moore franchise, *Chimmie Fadden Out West*, an amiable western caper which wielded a 250 per cent profit. (Even *Temptation* grossed five times its $22,000 cost, capitalizing on its popular star.) By this time, two Lasky purchases had been stacked up, and Lasky wanted them shot before the end of the year. As the other directors at the studio were working flat out, DeMille took both on, back to back. But although they were assignments, both *The Cheat* and *The Golden Chance* provided opportunities for Cecil to combine the social strand opened up with *Kindling* with the melodrama of his films with Farrar.

According to the production records, shooting began on *The Cheat* on 20 October and on *The Golden Chance* on 26 October. For two weeks at least the productions overlapped, so DeMille directed the one by day and the other by night, in the studio. This is an astonishing feat, given that both films were the most accomplished made by DeMille to that date. (The script of *The Golden Chance* in the University of Southern California archive reveals that the production was 'restarted November 5' and continued until 26 November, i.e. at least part of it was shot after the overlap!)

Both *The Cheat* and *The Golden Chance* now exist in restored DVD versions. *The Cheat* that we can view today is, in fact, a 1918 reissue, released with altered intertitles to change the original character of the Japanese businessman, Tori, into a Burmese named Laka Arakau. The racially charged portrayal of Tori, played by Sessue Hayakawa, outraged Japanese viewers, and when the US entered the First World War, with Japan as her ally, Japanese opinion had to be soothed. Burmese nationals were not thick on the ground in America at that time and presumably could be offended with impunity.

Hayakawa already had the distinction of being the American screen's only non-white star. Trained on the Japanese stage, after an abortive attempt at a naval career at home (and an equally abortive

The Cheat – Sessue Hayakawa and Fannie Ward

attempt at hara-kiri), he came to the US at the age of nineteen and was spotted on the Los Angeles stage by producer Thomas Ince. By his twelfth film, 1914's *The Typhoon*, he was receiving voluminous fan mail, mainly from swooning women. Hector Turnbull, who had written the script of *Temptation*, wrote the scenario that Lasky had purchased.

The ambivalence with which America viewed the Japanese is apparent in DeMille's film, in which all the stops are pulled out to dramatize a highly lurid story: Edith Hardy – played by veteran stage 'flapper' Fannie Ward – is the flighty wife of a businessman, squandering his money on clothes to keep her social position. As treasurer of the Red Cross fund, she is entrusted with $10,000, which is to be sent to the Belgians, gallant victims of the war in Europe. Her husband also disapproves of her friendship with Tori, a rich Japanese who is courted by the social set. In the first shot of the film, we are introduced in spotlit close-up to Tori's habit of branding his oriental figurines with his personal brand, heated in a small brazier. Edith, wishing to help her husband get rich quick, hazards the funds on a reckless investment. Of course, it is all lost and she faces ruin. Tori, who clearly lusts after her, offers to pay her debt for a price – her body. When all seems lost, her husband lucks out on his own investments. But as she tries to buy back her pledge at Tori's house, the Japanese refuses to release her from her promise and attempts a rape among his oriental trinkets and an impassive bust of Buddha. As she resists, in his rage he brands her on the shoulder, marking her as his property. In the tussle, she finds a revolver and shoots him, wounding him in the shoulder. She runs out, and her husband, who has followed her, rushes in and is arrested in the house, gun in hand. At his trial, Tori names him as his assailant, but as Hardy is found guilty, Edith leaps forward, and baring her brand, tells all to the jury of gaping white men. The men in the courtroom surge forward towards Tori, who hides behind the judge. The charge against Hardy is dismissed and he leaves the courtroom with his wife, to general applause.

The film electrified audiences, who were not accustomed to this degree of emotion in a tale dealing with rampant sexual desire rather than erupting volcanoes, battle scenes or men on horses charging over the countryside. Hayakawa took the opportunity to develop a mastery of silent acting that broke new ground. Racial hostility to the Japanese in America was quite widespread, but instead of trying to soothe it, he faced it head on with a smouldering display of desire for sexual power. Restraining both his bodily gestures and facial expressions, he managed to convey in a glance or a twitch of the eyebrows his contempt for the wife's moral weakness. Writing in 1924 in *Motion Picture Magazine*, Hayakawa told writer Harry Carr that 'I was always taught that it was disgraceful to show emotion. Consequently . . . I tried to show nothing in my face. But in my heart I thought, "God, how I hate you." And of course it got over to the audience with far greater force than any facial expression could.'

Watching the film today, it is still a masterclass in silent-film acting on Hayakawa's part, an object lesson on how a great actor can – almost – overcome an ugly racial stereotype. The rage on the faces of the men in the courtroom when the wronged woman, who is nevertheless The Cheat, tears her dress off her bare shoulders to expose her scar is not only righteous but a startling expression of sadistic titillation, the same frisson that rippled through the audiences who may well have experienced, in the violent branding scene, the closest to a pornographic moment as could be imagined then in a 'legitimate' film. Given Cecil DeMille's own deeper desires, it must have given him great joy to shoot it.

Critics gushed. W. Stephen Bush predictably declared that 'features like this one put the whole industry under obligations to the Lasky company'. Even *Variety* succumbed, in part, noting that 'here certainly is one of the best yellow heavies that the screen has ever had . . .', though it somewhat cryptically took the writer, Hector Turnbull, a former New York newspaper reporter, to task for having 'lost his perspective . . . otherwise he would never have suffered a director to stage a court room scene as theatric as the one which closes this picture'.

'There are some fascinating lighting effects,' *Variety* had to admit, and indeed there are major developments in the dramatic portrayal of faces caught in a pool of light amid deep shadow. When Edith confesses her financial blunder to Tori during the Red Cross party held at his house, we can see the shadow of her husband conversing with a friend upon the latticed paper wall. Confronted with the challenge of a short shooting schedule and limited sets, Cecil came up with solutions which would be echoed over thirty years later in the movies we now define as 'film noir'.

The same solutions are evident in *The Golden Chance*, DeMille's ingenuity not deserting him in the exhausting night shoots. As with *The Cheat*, the story opens in high society, but then veers off to become the first of DeMille's many films contrasting rich and poor and the sparks that fly when one attempts to pass for the other. 'Mr. and Mrs. Hilary of the Smart Set' are introduced playing chess. They are desperate for half a million dollars to 'swing the Baldwin contract', but their close friend, millionaire Roger Manning, played by Wallace Reid, doesn't want to invest in their project, as he is 'going out west'. Mrs Hilary plots to keep him close by inviting him for a special dinner to meet 'the prettiest girl in the world'.

Meanwhile, on the other side of the tracks, in a tenement room and with a drunken husband passed out on the bed, lives Mary Denby. A newspaper headline from *The Pompton Bulletin* of five years before tells us who she is: 'Mary McCall, Daughter of Judge McCall', who has eloped with Stephen Denby – 'a Young Man of Questionable Reputation'. With the rent unpaid, Mary takes a job as a seamstress with the Hilarys. As she prepares for her important guest, Mrs Hilary is told that the pretty girl she had invited is ill and cannot come. Looking for an immediate substitute she notices Mary's genteel manner and promises her good clothes and extra pay to play the part of the alluring guest. Of course, millionaire Manning is smitten, and the Hilarys persuade Mary to continue her subterfuge and join them with Manning for a long weekend. Mary tells her husband she has a '3 day job in a laundry in Newark' and departs, leaving him to fend for himself.

Enter DeMille's favourite rat, Raymond Hatton, as a crook who tells Mary's husband: 'The cook at 27 Harrington Drive says a swell dame is stoppin' there with sparklers as big as your head.' The scene is set for a disastrous meeting between husband and wife in the night. The crooks break in, and husband Steve, shining his torch in the 'swell dame''s bedchamber, handles the fine lingerie of the sleeping woman, unaware she is his wife. His curiosity leads him to play his light on her face, and she turns, in a moment of recognition . . . As Steve rushes off, he is discovered down the stairs by Manning, who grabs his pistol, the intertitles taking up the story:

Steve: 'I just came to see my wife.'

Mary: 'I never saw that man before – he is a thief! Search him!'

Mrs Hilary, taking Mary aside: 'All that time you were working the "inside" so that he could rob us!'

Mary to Mrs Hilary: 'You must let him go – do you want your friend to know how you have fooled him?'

In the confusion, Steve escapes, to tell his pal Raymond in the bar: 'That swell dame with the sparklers was my wife!' The crooks decide to blackmail Manning, persuading Mary to send him a letter asking him to come to her house, to which she manages to append the words: 'Don't come.'

Manning arrives in any case to meet Mary. The blackmailing husband barges in, demanding $10,000. But Manning has told a boy outside the building to call the cops if he is not out of the house in five minutes. Manning gets in a fight with the crooks, the police rush in, and Steve is shot by the cops as he climbs down the fire escape. End on a close shot of Manning and Mary, as they realize Steve is dead: she looks out of frame and he looks down, downcast, to the fade out.

The Golden Chance is the first of DeMille's classic, fully achieved riffs on the theme of the reversal of fortune, though both he and writer Jeanie Macpherson will get more sophisticated, if hardly less contrived, in their handling of construction and plotting. But what is more significant in this film than in its predecessors is the extent to which its characters are seen as chess pieces in the game of prestige and money. Everyone is angling for a better deal, and pretending to be what you're not is both enticing and a trap for the unwary. By a fluke of chance, Mary gets to be what she was 'born and bred' to be, but is cast by her benefactress as an impostor. The women, nevertheless, are schemers, whereas the men are vacillating, weak or criminals. Sumiko Higashi writes, in her analysis of DeMille's silent films in terms of their reflection of American culture, that both *The Cheat* and *The Golden Chance* show that 'the moral dilemma represented by women as consumers is displaced onto lower class and racial components in the body politic'. A fancy way perhaps of saying that in these films women who try to step beyond their preset social – and racial – bounds face punishment for their presumption. In *The Cheat*, the woman is rescued by her husband's love when she finally confesses her transgression, while in *The Golden Chance* the ending is more ambivalent: we do not know if love wins through, although fate has freed Mary of her inadequate spouse and provided a possible return to her birthright. DeMille is beginning to make moral judgements on the conduct of his human puppets, though they all, male and female, end up with their essential fragility exposed. They have become truly psychologically naked in the camera lens's pitiless glare.

The goal that evaded William de Mille, of the ideal play that would 'get underneath the veneer of society and convention and show human souls and human emotions in native strife', was being achieved, albeit in rough clay, by his brother Cecil in a medium that thrust back words and expressed itself through light and shadow. Setting *The Golden Chance* mostly at night, reviewer Peter Milne wrote in *Motion Picture News*, ensured that 'the countenances of the players are clearly defined by rays of light that strike them full in the face, leaving the backgrounds totally dark . . . aiding the suspense of the story beyond measure'. It is certainly a film in which, under the surface of 'realism', there is a strong sense of nightmare, of fantasies of displacement and a fear of chaos that afflict the central characters.

It was Jeanie Macpherson's first full-blown original scenario for DeMille, and it reveals that she understood his aspirations and desires as a motion-picture director clearly and was able to articulate them in a script much better than he could on his own. Their pairing as a partnership of the dominant and the submissive crossed the divide between the personal and the artistic and would stand the test of time in both aspects.

Cecil DeMille approached 1916 immeasurably strengthened in his new medium. Where Griffith was still seen as the revolutionary pirate king of the movies, DeMille was recognized as the driving force behind the motion pictures' first corporate empire. Lasky and Goldfish, who had entered the field with him, would continue to build on their success, but they were aware that the creative ingenuity of their company rested with their third partner.

On 2 January 1916, the *New York Times* announced that the motion-picture industry now ranked 'fifth in importance among the industries of this country', after agriculture, transportation, oil and steel. At least $500 million, the *Times* revealed, was estimated to be invested in movies. Ten million people, 'one out of every ten men, women and children in this country[,] visits a photoplay theatre weekly'. The monopoly that the Edison Trust had wielded six years before was thoroughly broken. The future of this business was up for grabs. 'The motion picture industry', wrote the *Times*, 'has also developed a new type of artist . . . the director. Five years ago the motion-picture director who received a salary of $50 weekly considered himself fortunate. Today there are directors whose annual income is equal to that of the President of the United States.'

On a Noble Eminence, or Moving Towards the Light

In the third year of his labours, Cecil B. DeMille rested – but not for very long. Having shot thirteen pictures in 1914 and seven in 1915, he directed only four in 1916. Three were regular pot-boilers, but for the fourth, Cecil girded himself for his most extravagant production to date.

In truth, Cecil was not resting at all, apart from his regular breaks for hearth and home. His home life was a secure compartment where, as his niece Agnes was to describe: 'Aunt Constance gave him his dinner every night herself, prepared it and served it no matter what hour he came in, and sat and talked to him until he grew rested enough to sleep.'

By 1916, Cecil was a wealthy man, and he began to look for the creature comforts wealthy men might expect. First he moved from what he called his 'little cottage on Cahuenga' to a great house with ample grounds south of Griffith Park, across Los Feliz Boulevard. The area was then known as Laughlin Park. The original prospectus had described the property as 'a residential paradise on a noble eminence, a replica of Italy's finest landscape gardening linked to the city by a perfect auto road'. Two classical-style houses had been built side by side, and Charles Chaplin would soon move into the other. In 1926, when Chaplin moved elsewhere, DeMille bought his house and expanded his refuge into a semi-palatial nirvana. Here mementos and items from his movies, little *objets d'art*, old movie cameras and endless plaques and awards were housed, with a classical symmetry that would exemplify his mania for order – he was one of those people who organized his books on their shelves according to their height. Later on, the seclusion of the property was somewhat dented by the building of other adjacent houses, into which moved other Hollywoodites like Deanna Durbin, W. C. Fields and Anthony Quinn, after he married Cecil's adopted daughter

Katherine. Eventually the linking road would be named DeMille Drive.

To augment this refuge, which also became his office, umbilically linked to the buzz and bustle of the studios, Cecil found another, much more secluded property in the Santa Monica mountains, in the 'Little Tujunga Canyon'. His lawyer, Neil McCarthy, urged him to avoid it, telling him: 'It's the wildest, most terrible place you ever saw in your life.' Access was only by the narrow entrance to the canyon. DeMille bought it at once. There, over the years, he set up his ranch, which he named 'Paradise', purchasing land adjacent to it and setting up a true sanctuary where he could hide, brood and contemplate nature – the hills, deer, foxes and the universe at large. Like a much smaller Hearst Castle, with fewer trimmings, 'Paradise' became a place to which DeMille invited his close friends, producers, actors and anyone he wished to impress – and dominate, as they would in later years be obliged to dress up in costumes provided by their host (or captor): 'silk Russian blouses and cummerbunds, in a variety of colours'. Cecil strode around the property in a cloak, bearing a gun which, he insisted, was to guard against rattlesnakes. 'I do not deny that I enjoy "dressing up,"' he wrote later, bemoaning the loss of sartorial diversity that occurred when, in the nineteenth century, everyone, with the exception of 'soldiers and sailors and the clergy, judges, and professors on occasion . . . began to dress all alike and as drably as possible'. The director's costume became an expression of his own desire to stand out.

The ranch would also house DeMille's private library, including a mint collection of European erotica which was witnessed many years later by actor Charles Bickford, who described the books as 'beautifully bound and illuminated' and including 'a privately printed three-volume edition of shockingly illustrated works of François Rabelais'. Other activities at the ranch were in keeping with the literary ambience but would come to reflect, in due course, the more licentious decade of the 1920s.

The ranch was also a refuge from wife Constance and mother Beatrice, who had settled in Hollywood, where both her sons now laboured. Though Cecil's will held sway over his immediate family, wrote Agnes, 'before his mother, Bebe, his spirit sometimes quailed. She talked to him about all his work. She would sit opposite him at dinner decked in the extraordinary collection of laces and beads and flowers with which she covered her beautiful grey curls and talked to him sometimes very sternly. He always listened . . . more to her than to the critics.'

Cecil managed a kind of hold over his mother thanks to the fact that she now lived on his earnings. As Agnes described the family at Christmas, Cecil presided 'like a Pasha at the head of table carving the roast pig. All the females lined the sides murmuring and attentive, with Father [William], the older brother, somewhat sardonic, tucked away among them.'

By now, Cecil was well on his way to establishing what became widely known as his 'harem'. Jeanie Macpherson was number-one mistress, with Gladys Rosson, the permanent secretary, consigned as number two. Number three, Anne Bauchens, had arrived as William's secretary and would become, from 1918, Cecil's regular and trusted film editor, a major authority on cutting motion pictures. Then there were actresses far from immune to the charismatic power of the Master. The narrow pass of Tujunga, the sagebrush and rattlesnakes were perfect guardians of Cecil's secrets.

Beyond the sanctuary, there was no let-up in the financial and technical advances of the film industry. In March 1916, *Motion Picture News* reported on the newly opened laboratory of the Lasky company, which would, when complete, 'represent an outlay of $125,000' and have 'the distinction of being the most modern and efficient building of its kind . . . It was designed by Cecil B. DeMille, director general of the Lasky Company, and Alvin Wyckoff, director of photography.' Solid concrete, three and a half storeys high and with its own viewing theatre, great care had been given to protecting the dark rooms and the developing film, so that 'from the negative developing room to the shipping room, the film never doubles on its course, but moves systematically forward'. All employees donned white coats with 'white rubber soled shoes and white gloves'. Filtering, heating and refrigerating plants cooled and replaced air in the building, and the perforating and printing machines were 'especially made for the Lasky Company', so the shame and humiliation of that first screening of *The Squaw Man* would never be repeated again.

In corporate politics, Karl Marx's predictions of the monopolizing trends of modern capitalism were being played out in moviedom's back rooms. Jesse Lasky, on one side, and Adolph Zukor, on the other, already linked to the distribution juggernaut of Paramount, were coming to the same conclusion: that they would be more powerful together than apart. Rumours of a merger went around for several months until, in June 1916, it was announced: Lasky's Feature Play Company and Zukor's Famous Players would combine as Famous Players-Lasky, with Zukor as president, Lasky vice-president, Goldfish as chairman of the board of directors and Cecil B. DeMille as the only working film-maker on the company board.

This shake-up was, however, just part of an even larger battle, in which W. W. Hodkinson, Paramount's founder, was replaced at a stockholders' meeting by Hiram Abrams, who then opened the door for Zukor and Lasky to take a 'controlling interest' in Paramount Pictures Corporation, i.e. to take over their distributor. Hodkinson departed to form his own company and, in the shuffle, Samuel Goldfish was pushed aside, departing to form his own company with Edgar Selwyn – the Goldwyn Pictures Corporation. Soon Samuel was to change his own name to Goldwyn, although his detractors said he should have combined the names differently, so as to rename himself 'Sel-Fish'. The combined stock of Famous Players-Lasky and Paramount stood at $22,500,000, making them the most powerful force in the business.

The Napoleon of this empire was Adolph Zukor, the diminutive merchant who had come out of Hungary with nothing but pep and ambition, a personal template of the Great American Success Story. He had come a long way since his first 'Crystal Hall', a moving-picture theatre above his 'Automatic Vaudeville'. Cecil later claimed that his first encounter with him was at the fire that consumed Famous Players' New York studio at 26th Street in September 1915. As he and Lasky watched, one man among the milling crowd stood still, saying only, when Lasky and DeMille approached him to commiserate about his studio: 'Thank you. We'll build a better one.' In fact, most of his negatives were stored elsewhere, and a plot in uptown Manhattan had already been purchased for the new Zukor studio.

Nevertheless, the merger marked yet another turn of the wheel that was cranking up the power of Hollywood. Paramount moved, under Zukor, to overtake and undermine the other movie companies, in particular the upstart Triangle. Block booking was used mercilessly, with theatre owners persuaded to take Paramount product under threat of a rival theatre being built beside them, stocked with

Paramount films supplied more cheaply. Triangle itself would pretty soon buckle, and the conglomerate formed originally by Harry Aitken with Griffith, Sennett and Ince would itself be subsumed into the Paramount empire in 1917.

More than ever, Cecil B. DeMille was in the right place at the right time. But there were, of course, other great beasts in the jungle. Carl Laemmle, at Universal, William Fox, producer of the rival *Carmen*, and independents like Griffith and Ince were forging ahead, although the Metro-Goldwyn-Mayer lion was only a distant growl in the future. While DeMille was learning his craft in leaps and bounds, Griffith had, as we have seen, released *Birth of a Nation* and was known to be shooting the greatest epic yet attempted, soon to be released as *Intolerance*. In May 1916, Thomas Ince presented his own epic, *Civilization*, a 'sermon based on the uselessness of war' set in an imaginary Germanic kingdom. Scenes of the horrors of war were linked to a tale of redemption, in which the hero, Count Ferdinand, is revived by the Saviour, who takes him on a Dantesque journey through hell to preach peace and the end of all warfare. The film fed into the strong opposition in America to involvement in the war in Europe and allegedly helped the re-election of Woodrow Wilson, who campaigned on a ticket of neutrality while his opponent, Charles Evans Hughes, campaigned for 'mobilization and preparedness'.

The ten reels of Ince's saga were eclipsed by the twelve reels of Griffith's *Intolerance*, which repeated the theme of the evils of war, religious bigotry and injustice on an even grander scale. With its four interwoven stories of ancient Babylon, Christ's Palestine, France of the Saint Bartholomew's Day Massacre and the modern poverty story it had all evolved from, 'The Mother and the Law', Griffith's film stunned the critics, who hailed it as the 'Apex of Motion Picture Art'. The 'intolerance' that Griffith was targeting might also be seen as deriving first and foremost from his own pique at the attack by liberal opinion on *Birth of a Nation*, but, being Griffith, he drew it on the widest canvas. Whatever the misgivings at the time about his experimental structure, the battle scenes, the dynamic cross-cutting and the massive sets of the Babylonian episode, never since surpassed, made this the proverbial 'hard act to follow' – by Griffith himself or anyone else.

The first film that Cecil DeMille directed in 1916 was *The Trail of the Lonesome Pine*, an adaptation of a 1913 play by Eugene Walter, itself based on a novel by one John Fox Jr. It was a hillbilly tale of the moonshining Tolliver family and the love affair between the family patriarch's niece, played by Charlotte Walker, and a government 'Revenue' agent, played by Thomas Meighan. Theodore Roberts played the scenery-chewing 'Devil' Judd Tolliver. According to legend, the playwright and novelist watched the film and one commiserated to the other that 'at least they kept the lonesome pine'. 'No,' said the other, 'it was a redwood.' But critics and audiences enjoyed the hokum. Sample dialogue: He: 'You can't shoot me, because you love me!' She: 'I reckon I do love yo' – but I'll shoot your head off – if yo' cross that door!'

The Heart of Nora Flynn, another original story by Hector Turnbull and adapted by Jeanie Macpherson, starred stage star Marie Doro, who, DeMille wrote, 'had the largest and most beautiful eyes I have ever seen', and Elliott Dexter, who would become another staple of DeMille films for some years. It was, like *The Cheat*, a tale of a cheating woman, but on a much less lurid scale. The easy adulteries of the rich are set against the honest love of Nora Flynn – nurse to the adulterous Mrs Brantley Stone's two children – and Nolan, the chauffeur. Nora is set up as the fall girl for the cheating nobs, until her employer's dishonesty is exposed. Robert Birchard has pointed out that the film reveals 'DeMille's growing sense of staging scenes for the camera . . .' Unlike Griffith's favoured close-ups, 'DeMille preferred to explore character by showing actors' interactions and also by relying on illustrative props . . . In part, this was simply practical technique. The closer one worked, the more one could save on building sets.' It would continue to be characteristic of DeMille that he deployed what would become the more conventional form of presenting actors on the screen, although his films would eventually diverge from what was to be Hollywood convention in directions which may have surprised even himself . . .

The third 1916 film, *The Dream Girl*, is another work that has vanished, described thus in *Motion Picture News*:

Mae Murray, as Meg of the slums, is the center of attention. It requires a considerable stretch of imagination to believe that a girl, reared in the most sordid surrounding could be so deeply influenced by a volume of 'King

Arthur' . . . Again, we have a crook posing as an English Lord . . . 'English' Hal finds it easy to get himself into the good graces of the rich Merton family, and very soon we find Meg there also. Tom Merton falls in love with her. Meg gives Hal's identity away, and Hal, in turn, explodes Meg's assertion that she is the daughter of a minister . . .

In the end, love across the class barriers wins through, but we have no way of judging the quality of this apparent fluff. The film was released in July and was preceded by the delayed release of *Maria Rosa*, Geraldine Farrar's precursor to *Carmen*. Farrar had returned to Los Angeles in June for her second stint of making movies for the Lasky company. She arrived with her new husband, actor Lou Tellegen, whom she had met the year before on the Lasky lot, and moved into the usual 'handsome residence'. The press reported that she would make several pictures for DeMille, photoplays of five, seven and ten reels respectively, though the titles and themes were not divulged.

In fact, DeMille had decided to make just one more picture in 1916, and to stake his claim as a rival to both Griffith and Thomas Ince in the field of the spectacular film.

The subject was unveiled to the trade press in September, when Farrar departed back east, having completed a film of twelve reels: 'The title for the picture has not been selected, there being several under consideration. Miss Farrar appears in the role of Joan of Arc, supported by Wallace Reid, Hobart Bosworth, Theodore Roberts, Tully Marshall, James Neil . . . and more than fifty others known upon the stage and screen. In all more than four thousand people took part in the production which required more than thirty large sets for interiors and exteriors, and will need five more before other scenes are completed. DeMille will spend about a month making the scenes, and it will be fully a month before the film is cut, tinted, colored sections made and ready for release.'

Various shenanigans ensued concerning schedules, titles and Farrar's initial desire to have her husband play the lead, against the absolute determination of both Lasky and DeMille to prevent this. But Farrar took her defeat on this matter with good grace. The film eventually opened early in January 1917, the last of 1916's triumvirate of major epics. Finally named *Joan the Woman*, the title exemplified DeMille's intention, unlike Ince, to tell, as he put it, 'an absorbing personal story against a background of great historical events'.

Unlike Ince or Griffith, DeMille wished to pull the emphasis away from the grand theme to the drama of individuals. Jeanie Macpherson, on the other hand, writing the script, had her own particular set of ideas which never let go of a strong thematic thread. In a real sense, from now on there would be a tug of war, unknown and invisible to the audience, between the director and his writer/lover which would enrich the coming works and imbue them with their own peculiar, sometimes eccentric, sometimes downright bizarre effect.

Macpherson's persistent theme, which would colour so many of DeMille's silent productions, was an occult sense of historical determinism and notions of reincarnation that led her to either include various historical flashbacks in an otherwise modern narrative, or in the case of *Joan the Woman*, to construct the whole film as an extended flashback from the modern day. The opening intertitle of the picture perhaps expresses more about Jeanie Macpherson than the historical Joan:

> Founded on the Life of Joan of Arc,
> The Girl Patriot,
> Who Fought with Men,
> Was Loved by Men
> And Killed by Men,
> Yet Withal Retained
> The Heart of a Woman.

There follows a flurry of titles positioning us in France in 1429, 'on the verge of becoming an English Province', with Paris in English hands and the 'shabby court' of her weak king, Charles VII, while in the village of Domrémy lives a 'simple peasant girl, the daughter of Jacques D'Arc'. An image of Farrar at a loom in a hut introduces the 'sturdy country maiden' who 'gave her all for France – and her reward was Martyrdom' – cue Farrar in dramatic pose, hands outstretched, mixing to her crucified against the light of the fleur-de-lys. But 'Joan of Arc is not dead. She can never die – and in the war-torn land she loved so well, her spirit fights today –' Fade in title: '1916, AN ENGLISH TRENCH SOMEWHERE IN FRANCE.'

At this point, DeMille faced an awkward political problem, as he was telling a tale of English villainy against the oppressed French at a time when France and the British were united in battle against the

common enemy, Germany. This is dealt with by the first of Jeanie Macpherson's peculiar reincarnation sequences: an English soldier, played by Wallace Reid, is chatting with his comrade in their dugout when he senses some object in the earthen wall and pulls out an old, jagged sword and muses: 'I wonder what queer old chap carried this sword to battle in the old days . . .'

Meanwhile, his superior officers are calling for a volunteer for what amounts to a suicide mission, someone to 'attempt the destruction of Enemy Trench Number 2 with this bomb'. The volunteer was given till midnight to decide, because 'the man who goes will not come back'. As Reid lights his pipe in his dugout – Lasky lighting by now routine – Joan, attired in armour, appears to him in a double exposure, declaring: 'The time has come for you to expiate thy sin against me.'

'INTO THE PAST' – we enter the main story, almost four minutes into the film. The pastoral scenes of the village which follow have been beautifully rendered by Wilfred Buckland's sets and Alvin Wyckoff's photography. DeMille's two collaborators gave of their best in this film, from the countryside scenes of Joan driving her flocks of sheep, to the low-lit skulduggery of the chambers of power, to the sweep and mayhem of the battle scenes, which have the scope of an Uccello.

The major problem of the film for today's audience, its strange bookending modern segments apart, remains the casting, which was at the time an obvious advantage, given Farrar's stardom. She was, however, thirty-four years old when the film was shot, and the standard histories of Jeanne D'Arc of Domrémy portrayed her as merely seventeen when the events that made her famous occurred. She was said first to have heard the voice of God speaking directly to her at the age of twelve and was executed at the age of nineteen at Rouen. The whole point of the tale of Joan of Arc was that she was a teenager, practically a child, leading an army against the occupiers of her country.

DeMille, of course, was not the only one to cast against age in this story: Carl Theodor Dreyer's landmark 1928 film, *The Passion of Joan of Arc*, shot mainly in coruscating close-ups, cast Italian actress Maria Falconetti, who was thirty-five years old. Geraldine Farrar, however, does appear on screen looking more like Joan of Arc's mother than Joan, despite her undoubted verve and charisma.

The voices from God are presented obliquely in DeMille's version, emanating from a messenger in noble robes or in the image of a flaming sword, or later in the film, a winged 'black horseman', signifying her own doom. The exigencies of Protestant America might allow many portrayals of Christ, the human saviour, but not of the divinity Himself. But DeMille's Joan is more patriot than saint. As DeMille defined her, she was 'a woman of flesh and blood, whose heroism was as much in her victory over herself as in her victory over the English. That is what real saints are like, I think.'

Agnes de Mille described the shoot in her book *Dance to the Piper*:

Farrar was given a suit of silver armor to spare her the weight of the men's irons. She spent days in the saddle and whole days in a fosse up to her waist in muddy water, a cowboy guard around her dressed in bobbed wigs and fourteenth century hats, fending off broken spears, falling beams and masses of struggling extras. The Sunday the battle of Les Tourelles was shot out at the studio ranch, every director on the Lasky lot was commandeered as a lieutenant to Cecil; George Melford, Frank Reicher, Donald Crisp, James Young, Pop [William de Mille], all stood in full costume on the line. Each director was responsible for the authentic appearance, acting and physical safety of a company of soldiers . . . Farrar's understudy, an equestrienne of stamina, rode at the head of four hundred men on a white horse carrying a white silk banner. We sat around in open cars with picnic baskets. It was something like an English hunt breakfast . . .

Watching the film one can see that, unlike Griffith's penchant for dynamic camera movements – the spectacular camera sweeps over his Babylon sets, the car-mounted camera racing ahead of galloping horsemen, the pounding parallel shots of rushing cars and trains – DeMille favoured a static camera capturing dynamic action in the frame, in a montage building into a dramatic crescendo. He was the first director to pay proper attention to the individuals within a crowd. Rather than just a milling mass, as Agnes noted, he was eager to create a scene where the extras acted as they would individually in the real circumstances of the action. The result is an unusually convincing portrayal of the chaos and mayhem of battle. Kenneth McGaffey of *Photoplay* magazine observed the shoot, describing it thus:

To prevent any fakiness in the hand to hand fight, Mr. DeMille offered a bonus to the English if they succeeded in capturing Joan, and to the French if they prevented it . . . The objective point was the breach in the fortress wall. Every inch of the distance was contested. Cameras whirred and hummed, directors shouted, and many a head was sadly battered . . . Surrounded by her soldiers, Joan finally reached the moat, and there she stood in the water up to her waist for nearly three hours. Mr. DeMille asked her if she didn't want to come out of the water and rest – but 'Our Jerry' replied – 'If the boys can stand it, I think I can.'

Farrar's popularity among the 'troops' was such that extras volunteered, according to McGaffey, to follow DeMille's wish for them to fall rather than jump off the battlements into the moat, a much more dangerous procedure, so that none of 'Our Jerry''s scenes should be cut out: 'Next day the scene was re-taken and the wall rained struggling men. They fell in twos and threes into the moat. Several were slightly injured by having other steel-clad companions clash down upon them, but the doctor was always there and . . . nothing serious befell them. In fact, both armies seemed to glory in their wounds, for the next day they had the pleasure of being asked by "Our Jerry" if they were all right.'

The plot of the film has Joan's peasant patriotism opposed by the English and their French puppets: a slimy royal adviser, 'The Spider', 'L'Oiseleur – the Mad Monk', who denounces her as a witch, and 'the Traitorous Bishop Cauchon', who 'Seeks his King's Destruction to Further his own Ambition' – a full-blooded villainous turn by Theodore Roberts. DeMille cast Raymond Hatton, previously assigned to petty crooks and spivs, as the spineless King Charles. A less convincing plot line charts the central relationship between Joan and the English knight, Eric Trent, who is to morph into the modern wartime soldier. After she protects him and nurses him back to health following the sword wound he suffered during the looting of her village, they meet again at the siege of the towers, when he is captured and realizes the peasant maid who leads the French armies is the girl who saved him before. He is the man, however, who is ordered in the name of his king to capture the betrayed Joan – the original sin that is to be expiated centuries later. Wallace Reid looks suitably woebegone in his scenes, perhaps seeing, in the mist of prophecy, and beyond his halcyon years as a matinee idol, his own sad ending as a drug addict in a Los Angeles sanatorium some years down the line . . .

'DAWN BRINGS ON THE DAY – BIG WITH FATE.' Wyckoff and DeMille's awareness of classical painting is evident in scenes in which the captured Joan is mocked by soldiers – one is reminded of Hieronymus Bosch's famous image of the mocking of Christ. At her trial and torment, again shot with static compositions, hooded figures portend her doom. As she is shackled over a boiling cauldron of fire to terrify her into signing her confession, the medieval imagery, looking forward to as yet unfilmed sequences by Fritz Lang, almost slips into the future parodies of gothic horror movies. And is the goggle-eyed, grinning face of the Mad Monk in the lower-left corner of the frame that of Cecil's own sadistic alter ego? All stops were pulled out for the climactic sequence of Joan's burning at the stake, commencing with a powerful montage that opens with a long shot of the empty town square:

Long Shot: *Town square, a cart piled with twigs and brush enters towards the stepped scaffold with bare stake at its center. A dog barks at the cart.*
Close Shot: *In chamber – Eric Trent's despairing look.*
Close Shot: *Cart driver tosses sticks on scaffold.*
Close Shot: *Joan in her cell, taken out by guards.*
Long Shot: *Crowd surges round the scaffold – camera iris in to stake.*

Long Shot: *Aftermath of King's banquet orgy at court, a soldier bursts in to tell him:* 'They are burning Joan the maid.'

Close Shot: *King, indifferent, glazed eyed, waves soldier away; then slowly realizes import of news, staggers among the sleeping banqueters, picks up the Jester's staff and mask.*

Close-Up: *King with Jester's staff.*

Long Shot: *He falls, face in hands.*

Medium Shot: *Joan bundled onto cart . . .*

As the crowd circles the stake, hysteria mounts, the cart approaches, the Mad Monk, belatedly, begs forgiveness and the executioners light the brushwood. For these scenes, DeMille deployed a new colouring technique, the 'Handschiegl' process – literally hand-coloured portions of the frame – to redden the fire. The flames rise up, with angels awaiting Joan on either side, as she makes her last call: 'My Voices were of God – they have not deceived me!' And then the raging fires mix to a candle in the modern trench, and we are back to 1916 and the closing of the circle, with the 'reincarnated' Eric Trent sacrificing his life upon the barbed wire of the enemy trenches. As he dies, the figure of Joan stands over the field of corpses . . .

Agnes de Mille wrote of the execution scene:

During the burning, Uncle Cecil stood at the stake for hours trying out smoke. He never asked an actor to do what he would not do himself. Farrar stood until she was obliterated by smoke and flame although everyone said it would do her voice no good at all. But when they burned the dummy and its hair caught and flaked off in a single shower of fiery cinders, she turned sick and had to go to her dressing room . . .

Farrar gave her own account of the moment in her autobiography, *Such Sweet Compulsion*:

For my climax at the stake, my clothing, skin and hair were treated with a fluid to make scorching impossible. I had cotton, treated with ammonia, placed in my nostrils and mouth . . . For the final immolation, in the long shots a figure of wood was used, cleverly arranged with shrouded, drooping shoulders and the face well forward, covered with disarranged locks. For the 'close-ups,' I was placed in the middle of tanks filled with oil; their ignition and the spectacular flames together with clouds of rolling smoke, gave a perfect illusion in the 'cut-backs.' It was a supremely lovely film – and I never played any screen part that inspired my love and enthusiasm as did this beautiful story.

Joan the Woman was the first film in which DeMille tested his skills as a cinematic general leading his cast and crew into battle, and he saw, in the evening and the morning of each shooting day, that it was good. The theme of Divine Intervention in human conflicts and the ultimate dramas of war and conquest was a grail first glimpsed on the transformed battlefields of the Lasky ranch in the summer of 1916. The missing ingredient, the emotional tension of sexual desire, was not yet present, except perhaps obliquely, in this tale of virgin Joan's sublimation of desire to her duty. A seed had, nevertheless, been planted, although its buds were not to sprout above ground, in true biblical fashion, until seven years passed . . .

The film was rapturously received and made the name of Jeanie Macpherson, who had been elevated in the opening credits to pride of place under the main title, which read: *Joan the Woman, by Jeanie Macpherson* – although the *Moving Picture World* noted that it was 'above all a director's picture. Mr DeMille has splendidly staged his subject . . . His pageantry is superb . . . There can be no question that "Joan the Woman" will live long in a field that has witnessed many triumphs and of which this surely is one.' Even *Variety* finally succumbed to the general cries of 'Huzzah!' and 'Bravo!', stating that 'hardened motion picture and dramatic critics, who imagined they were proof against any possible surprise from the other side of the footlights, came out of the 44th Street theatre last Saturday afternoon in a state of bewilderment . . .'

This new epic flourish seemed to have come without any great fanfare of preparation or any great pre-publicity of the kind that had preceded both Griffith's *Intolerance* and Ince's *Civilization*. In unusually gushing tones, *Variety* reported it was 'impossible to describe in detail what producer De Mille accomplished with such a wealth of material. Suffice to say that no one else could have done more and few, if any, can have done as much.'

But life, commerce and global events can lie in ambush even for the most fortunate. For whatever reason, the studio cut down the twelve reels of *Joan* to a more manageable length, and the film flagged as it proceeded along in its initial 'road show' phase, showing in many cities around the country before settling down in Los Angeles and New York. It had been DeMille's most costly film at just over $300,000, ten times the budget of his most expensive previous film (*The Warrens of Virginia*, at $28,000). Although *Joan* did eventually gross $600,000, its high distribution costs practically swallowed the profit, and Jesse Lasky preferred a return to the norm of lower budgets and higher relative returns.

DeMille had to postpone plans of further epics for a while. To complicate matters, the story's anti-English slant suddenly became highly undesirable, when, on 6 April 1917, Woodrow Wilson, despite winning re-election on the neutrality ticket, finally took the United States into the war in Europe, alongside both Britain and France.

America's Sweethearts

After the formal declaration of war upon Germany, America mobilized. Men were drafted, women prepared to take their place in the factories, and those who couldn't tighten rivets were urged to 'Knit Sox for the Boys'. Civilians who were in the public eye spoke at rallies to sell 'Liberty Bonds'. Douglas Fairbanks and Charlie Chaplin warmed up the crowds on Wall Street under the statue of George Washington. Everyone wrapped themselves in the flag, which another George, Cohan, would soon serenade in song. On 21 April 1917, *Motion Picture News* was already advertising 'a Timely, Up-to-the-minute, Authentic Photoplay in 5 Parts – How Uncle Sam Prepares', quoting Washington: 'If we desire peace, it must be known that we are at all times ready for war.' Modern American Eric Trents were lining up to deliver that new bomb across enemy lines to destroy the enemy trenches.

Movie-studio workers were formed into a company of the Coast Artillery Reserve, with the Lasky studio forming a Home Guard unit, of which Cecil DeMille, naturally, was the captain, with brother William as 'top sergeant'. Jesse Lasky recalled that 'our director-general drilled his "army" with real Springfield rifles, up and down Vine Street with as much relish as though he were showing General Pershing how to do a scene. The drilling was accompanied by a brass band composed of prop men, carpenters, grips, and actors from our lot.'

Tiring of this pretty soon, Cecil applied for an army commission but met the same indifference as when he had volunteered for the Spanish-American war in 1898. Then he had been too young; now, at thirty-six, too old. However, he was told, there was one skill the army needed that was so rare that 'we'll commission you if you're aged ninety'. This was the ability to fly an aircraft.

'I had another motive,' Cecil wrote in his autobiography, 'in addition to the patriotic one, for wanting to learn to fly. That was fear. All

Cecil B. DeMille, aviator

my life I had had an unreasoning dread of heights . . . That was something to be conquered.'

Jesse Lasky, whom we have noted as one of DeMille's early passengers, described the experience:

There were two places in the flimsy little biplane. I sat in the forward one, gripping the side of the cockpit as though I were trying to hold the thin fabric together. To my amazement we took off without ground-looping, and I was just getting fairly well-adjusted to the idea of still being alive when Cecil shouted something to me. I looked back and he kept shouting, but you couldn't hear a thing over the roar of the motor, and the goggles gave him a terrified expression. I thought we might be in trouble. I shouted that I couldn't hear him. Suddenly the motor cut out and so did my heart. All I knew about flying was that when the motor conks out you're a dead pigeon. I began reading big black headlines all over the sky. But Cecil had just shut off the motor for a moment to warn me that he was going to demonstrate some fancy turns. He needn't have bothered. My stomach was already demonstrating fancy turns without benefit of the pilot.

I couldn't bring myself to go up in a plane again for years.

Another early and more enthusiastic passenger was Julia Faye, a young actress who joined the DeMille menagerie for his next epic outing with Geraldine Farrar, *The Woman God Forgot*. She was certainly not forgotten by Cecil, who added her to his long-term cast and, pretty soon, to the roster of long-term mistresses.

Despite these aerial adventures, there was no let-up in the pace of production at the Lasky studios and the Cecil B. DeMille movie factory. By the time war had been declared, Cecil had directed a new western, *A Romance of the Redwoods*, and within a week, on 13 April, he began shooting another film, *The Little American*. Both movies starred Mary Pickford, whom DeMille had first met on the stage in his brother's *The Warrens of Virginia*, when he was playing her older brother. By 1915, she had become America's highest-paid actress, graduating from the role of 'Little Mary', which had been her monicker since her early years with Griffith. A shrewd businesswoman in her early twenties, she then managed to extract $10,000 a week from Adolph Zukor's Famous Players company and was well on her way to becoming 'America's Sweetheart', her only rival being Mabel Normand, Mack Sennett's ever-peppy comedienne. Zukor also had to allow her her own dedicated studio on the East Coast and her own company, the Mary Pickford Film Corporation.

The distribution and block-booking wars continued apace, with Mary Pickford's new distributor, Artcraft, undercutting Paramount's terms. In May 1917, Zukor absorbed Artcraft, as he would soon swallow Mack Sennett, Thomas Ince, William S. Hart and even Griffith. Chaplin, as ever, remained outside the big tent.

As a small part of this empire building, Cecil DeMille got to direct his two Pickford movies. The first, *A Romance of the Redwoods*, was a remake of *The Girl of the Golden West*, with a better constructed story co-written by Jeanie Macpherson. Mary was the girl come from out east after her mother dies to live with her uncle, who, unbeknown to her, has been killed by Indians and his identity stolen by an outlaw, 'Black' Brown, played by Elliott Dexter. A full roster of lively western characters is added to the well-stirred stew. The rough cabin where Mary discovers that her 'uncle' is the outlaw and the robust miners'-town saloon are vividly drawn, with 'Lasky lighting' in full flow in the flickering firelight and fine interplays of light and shadow. The burgeoning theme of a DeMillean moral dilemma is played out in the girl's realization that the outlaw is her only defence in a lawless place, until she wins the hearts of its rough-hewn citizens. The outlaw, falling in love with her, vows to 'go straight', but a last robbery in which he is found out leads to one of Pickford's most curious moments, in which she pretends a doll's clothes are intended for a child she is pregnant with by the bandit. Abashed and unwilling to leave her in disgrace, the townspeople spare the man and the presiding 'Justice of the Peace' marries them on the spot, with the rope still round 'Black' Brown's neck. When the townsfolk discover the doll, her local benefactor tells them ruefully: 'Boys, I reckon when twenty men have been fooled by one small woman – they'd better take their medicine.' And the unlikely lovers are allowed to make their way through the redwoods towards a new life.

The movie was an unusually light confection for DeMille, with an abiding charm that provides yet another surprise for those who think Cecil B. can easily be pinned down. Unlike in *Joan*, there is a greater use of close-ups in the claustrophobic atmosphere of the small cabin in which Pickford and the outlaw find a new lease of life. The critics noted DeMille's growing versatility across a range of genres, and *Variety* praised the film for enabling Mary Pickford not just to 'pout for effect' but to act, and 'in such a manner as to land her points with surprising effectiveness. This Artcraft release is one that will be a money maker of the first line.' And so it proved to be, bringing the smile back to Lasky's face.

With this turn of fortune realized, Cecil could proceed to shoot the war drama he had originally favoured as his first Pickford project, which had been held back because of its perceived anti-German bias in a still neutral America. The film must have clearly been scheduled before the US entered the war, as it began shooting just a week after. It could not have been more timely, although the film tempered the newly popular Hun-bashing by making the German-American protagonist a tragic hero rather than a villain.

The Little American – Mary as society girl Angela Moore – is introduced with a close-up of her saluting in front of the Stars and Stripes. Mary is courted by two suitors: the French Count Jules de Destin (Raymond Hatton) and the German Karl von Austreim, played by Jack Holt. On a fourth of July celebration, in 1914, von Austreim is recalled to Germany to join the army preparing for war. A short while later, the French count is recalled as well, breathlessly telling Angela: 'I'm sailing at once! France and Germany are at war! Mademoiselle – 10,000 Germans have been killed.' At which Angela asks: 'Do you know if Karl was with them?'

In France, the count is wounded and marked for the amputation of his arm. Angela decides to sail for France on the *Veritania*, but en route the ship is sunk by a German submarine. Rescued by a fishing boat, she arrives in France at her aunt's chateau to find the aunt has died and she has inherited a staff of maids who are terrified as the French retreat from the area and the Germans march in. When the French bring their wounded men into the chateau and Angela meets her armless count, she decides to stay and agrees to help the French hide a telephone so she can inform them about German gun positions.

The German soldiers break in, brutally shooting the butler, and rush to find and assault the women. Karl, who is with his corps, chases Angela around a darkened room before realizing who she is. Shamed, he nevertheless cannot prevent the rape of the maids, which is sanctioned by his superior officers. As an American citizen, Angela is humiliated but spared. She witnesses a massacre of civilians by firing squad and decides to help the French by calling them secretly on the hidden telephone. The French shell the German guns, and Karl is sent to find whoever is giving away their positions. Angela is caught and sentenced to death by summary court martial. Karl finally breaks down and denounces the German army's atrocities. He is sentenced to be shot as a traitor beside her, but at the last moment the French open fire and the firing squad is blown up. The Germans retreat and

The Little American – Mary Pickford surrounded by the beastly Huns

Angela and Karl stagger wounded through the bombed town. Found by the count and his men, Karl is spared and becomes a prisoner, but in the end wins his freedom thanks to Angela's pleading. They kiss through the barbed wire of the prisoner-of-war camp at the end.

Distinctively, DeMille and Jeanie Macpherson had decided to highlight the dilemma of the German soldier, the son of a German father and an American mother. The Little American is a naive neutral who first tries to stand her ground at the chateau by brandishing the US flag and declaring: 'Gentlemen, you are breaking into the home of an American citizen – I must ask you to leave!' But at the end she tells the court martial: 'I was neutral, till I saw your soldiers destroying women and shooting old men. Then I stopped being "neutral" and became a human being.' The moment when Karl pursues her with a rapist's lust before discovering she is the woman he loves will be reused by DeMille in his 1926 Red Army film, *The Volga Boatman*.

In the sinking of the ship, DeMille pulled off one of his finest scenes of cataclysm and terror, recreating the real-life sinking of the *Lusitania* only two years before. The passenger liner is fired on at night, in the midst of a ball, tipping the dancers in all their finery into an oily sump. Alvin Wyckoff used the searchlight of the German U-boat to sweep across the hull of the doomed ship and the sea, picking out in flashing pools of light the bodies falling, the passengers drowning and the desperate struggle to get aboard the lifeboats.

Unlike *Joan the Woman*, with its glorification of combat in a just cause, American pacifism and reluctance to go to war are vividly expressed in scenes of purposeless carnage, the shelling of the town, mass executions, the assault on the women, the spectacle of fleeing civilians and, not least, the degradation of the German-American, forced to become a beast under orders. In the end, his rebellion is against becoming a cog in the warrior-caste system, the 'Prussian efficiency' which wipes out any concept of mercy. As he and the Little American stumble through 'the Valley of the Shadow of Death', as an intertitle puts it, the bombed town is dominated by a burning church, whose outsized Christ remains standing even when church and cross are blown away. The heroine lurches towards the figure, hands outstretched, and is found the next morning by the French army and her count, lying under the Saviour's nailed feet. It is the first overt sign of divine intervention in a contemporary movie by DeMille. But very far from the last . . .

Despite the call of the flag, declarations of patriotism and stirring editorials in the film magazines for the motion picture to be 'called into the service of the country and humanity', business as usual continued to be the dominant theme in the movie industry. No let-up in the surge towards monopolization is detected in the rapacious march of Paramount to domination and countermeasures by other companies like First National and Metro, which increased its capital by 600 per cent. In fact, the war, and the immediate choking of European commerce, had greatly benefited the American film industry, as New York overtook London as the 'Film Capital of the World'. Movies previously shipped worldwide through England were now routed via New York and San Francisco. 'Prominent foreign film men' told *Motion Picture News* in June 1917 that 'now is the time for American film men to jump in and corner the markets of the world'. American movie-making was booming, Mary Pickford had bolstered DeMille and Lasky considerably, and Lasky urged Cecil to get on with the third tranche of Geraldine Farrar summer productions, still contracted to go ahead. But, Lasky warned DeMille, no more gargantuan productions. Two Farrars for the price of one would do just fine for the year.

DeMille, however, having expressed himself on the war, had prepared another extravaganza, a lush epic set in post-Columbian Mexico, with Geraldine Farrar as an Aztec princess. Jeanie Macpherson had written the original script, fuelled by who knows what rush of fantasy fulfilment crafted between her and her director lover. The preamble to the script was suitably bizarre:

Ages ago – a certain people of White Skin – possibly Carthaginians – sailed over the seas and conquered the ancient coast tribes of Mexico.

Blonde and blue-eyed was their Leader – who came to be worshipped by the dark skinned Mexicans – as the Fair God.

His followers refused to accompany him when he returned to his own land; and centuries later their children's children became known as the 'Aztecs' – who looked ever after for the Promised Coming of the Fair God . . .

Something in Cecil's youthful idealization of the American Indians, and his old play, *Son of the Winds*, may have played their part in this exotic conception. Vast sets had been planned by Wilfred Buckland, along with the most luscious costumes, finally allowing DeMille to properly undress Farrar and the Aztec maidens who were to be sacrificed to the gods. Lasky, however, insisted on curtailing his troops: DeMille would make two Geraldine Farrar movies, each not exceeding six reels, which together should not cost above the reasonable average for the present fiscal year.

The result is one of the most tantalizing of DeMille's hidden treasures, another archival marvel awaiting rediscovery. *The Woman God Forgot* unfolds as part epic, part hallucination, dream-like in the intensity of its settings and theatricality of its acting.

In the kingdom of Montezuma, king of the Aztecs (most bizarrely played by Raymond Hatton), the great gong is struck when 'the hour of sacrifice is at hand!' While the white conquerors, Cortés, the Spanish adventurer, and his favourite captain, Alvarado (Wallace Reid), land on the beach, Montezuma's daughter Tecza (Farrar) shields her handmaiden, who has been chosen for the lethal ceremony. Here finally is the DeMille scene we have all been waiting for: the exotic princess on her bed with flower-clad girls and lute-plucking servants, amid exotic parakeets preening in the 'Court of the Birds'.

The film introduced another DeMille regular-to-be, Theodore Kosloff, Russian ballet dancer extraordinaire. He had been a member of the original Diaghilev Ballet Russe, training at the Moscow Imperial School and then dancing in Paris with Nijinsky. Summoned to America, he toured the vaudeville circuits with his wife, Maria Baldina, and a dancer called Winnifred Hudnut, who was renamed Natacha Rambova. Agnes de Mille described her first sighting of him as he appeared as one of Uncle Cecil's Aztecs:

When I first saw Kosloff he was naked in feathers, leaning on a feathered spear. He had painted himself horned eyebrows in the Russian Ballet style, and his gestures were real classic pantomime, involving clenched fists and the whites of the eyeballs . . . Here was passion and here was sincerity in amounts. Every expression was performed with a force that could have carried him across the room and over the wall . . .

Everyone else seemed to take their acting cues from him: Montezuma, apprised that 'from across the sea come fair skinned strangers – who burn our temples and destroy our Gods!', vows to sacrifice one maiden a day till the invaders leave. When Tecza/Farrar hides the first maiden, Montezuma vows that twenty maids will be sacrificed for the one. Meanwhile, Kosloff, as 'The Tiger', offers gifts to the

Spaniards to leave, but Cortés refuses: 'All thy land must kneel before the cross!'

Unusually, in the burgeoning DeMille theology, religion is presented in this film as a destructive force on both sides: the Aztecs' religion is barbaric, ignorant and powerless, and the Christians' cross is an instrument of conquest and slaughter. Most probably Jeanie Macpherson got the better of Cecil in this one. The 'moral dilemma' here is Tecza's growing love for the foreigner Alvarado, whom she shelters when captured, and Alvarado's love for the heathen he has come to vanquish. As an intertitle grandly proclaims: DURING EVERY CRISIS IN HISTORY – SOME WOMAN'S HAND HAS ALWAYS TWISTED THE OUTLINE OF THE WORLD'S MAP!

Tecza's love for her enemy leads her to open the city bridge for the Spaniards to destroy her people and save Alvarado from being sacrificed. Cortés has mendaciously given her his word that he will leave when Alvarado is rescued, but all is over for the Aztec way of life. Montezuma curses his daughter: 'No land wherein thy dwelleth shall ever prosper . . . All the Gods, yes, even the Christian God – shall evermore forget thee!'

At the end, by a waterfall and beside a small hut, Alvarado and Tecza, like the redwood lovers of Cecil's Pickford western or Angela Moore and her German soldier, find peace in their mutual love, the one thing that is 'stronger than hate!'

Art director Buckland built for the movie what appears as a great wall, with steps worthy of Eisenstein for the final sweep of the Spaniards towards their bloody victory, although the sets were restricted by a reduced budget and had to be shot only from certain angles.

Geraldine Farrar later enthused about the great novelty of 'the feathered attire of the men and women . . . the soft rugs . . . riotous in exquisite colors [*which, of course, we cannot see*], blocked and handwoven in lustrous patterns, copied painstakingly from authentic designs of this picturesque people . . . The whole studio was enclosed in fine wire netting, with lush tropical greens screening the protective walls. In another sequence, my boudoir was hung with ropes of huge fresh magnolias, renewed twice daily. This floral magnificence was in itself an incentive to passionate action . . .'

And yet, after all this opulence, DeMille simply moved on to his second contracted Farrar film, *The Devil Stone*. This is a three-quarters lost film, as only its last two reels exist. These show the denouement of a murder story, in which a detective traps Geraldine Farrar into a confession, pleading self-defence. Farrar wrote that the film included 'an interesting flash-back to a former incarnation of the heroine, as a Norse Queen of cruelty and vigour. The equipment was the prescribed Valkyrie pattern, and I must say, seated in my high chair with two vicious wolf hounds at my feet, I had somewhat the vicarious thrill of playing Brunnhilde, even if it was a voiceless one with no battle-cry!' Alas, all this is lost to posterity.

The screenplay was supposedly based on an original story by Cecil's mother, Beatrice, and one Leighton Osmun. There seems to be some continuity with the theme of the previous film, as the script opens with the credo: 'Throughout all ages – man's stumbling block has been SUPERSTITION!' The 'Devil Stone' has come from a Viking helmet, and its pilferer is cursed: 'Since thou hast robbed this stone to serve the devil – this shall it do, henceforward, unto thee: Not by day or by night shall thou know ought of happiness or rest condemned to wander homeless on the earth – till thou dost bring this stone unto our God!'

The Devil Stone cost just over half as much as *The Woman God Forgot* ($67,000 and $115,000 respectively) but grossed almost the same ($290,000 as against $340,000), further convincing Lasky that Cecil's sagas were an indulgent luxury. Geraldine Farrar returned to her autumn opera season, and these were her last films for DeMille. She was unhappy over Lasky's refusal to let her husband, Lou Tellegen, direct movies, and soon signed a deal with Goldwyn Pictures.

But she would never find another Cecil B. DeMille.

The Thunder and the Whispers

Of the eight DeMille movies released in 1916 and 1917, all but one were vehicles for female stars. Almost all told the tale of strong, assertive women, if not all in the full Brunnhilde mode. And of Cecil's previous twenty films, about half had revolved around the dilemma of the role of women in a man's world.

The only conventionally obedient woman in DeMille's life remained his wife. While Cecil indulged his fantasies, Constance DeMille busied herself with a constant flurry of charity work for hospitals and orphanages, as well as looking after her daughter and adopted sons.

Agnes de Mille described her aunt on one busy afternoon rushing from a children's hospital committee to help the desperate family of a drowned child: 'she went to the victim's home, cleaned the house, prepared supper for the brothers and sisters, comforted the mother, returned, bathed and dressed, put in a brisk half hour hunting flies and ants for her small son's neglected alligator, presided at the dinner table of her own children, sat with them while they studied, and at midnight was found trailing alone around the cellar in a red velvet negligee in search of the special Liebfraumilch which Cecil liked with his late supper'.

Cecil quoted this passage approvingly in his own autobiography, thanking his niece for reminding him of what he clearly took for granted. Like a medieval potentate, the master had his women well pigeonholed, and this would remain his pattern throughout.

And yet DeMille's abiding feature was his unending fount of energy, which flowed into his work. The reader may well experience synopsis fatigue because of the sheer volume of films DeMille was directing on his unstoppable conveyor belt. One longs at times for some trivial gossip to lighten up the Herculean labours of this Vulcan hammering at his celluloid block. As noted, another member of the long-term harem, Miss Julia Faye, joined during the Aztec epic, playing a 'lady in waiting' to Princess Farrar. Forty years later, she was still appearing for Cecil, in *The Ten Commandments*. Perhaps not so trivial a relationship after all, if but one of many . . .

The Lasky–Zukor engine, meanwhile, continued pumping away. 'Something Going On Every Moment of the Day and No Lost Motion', headlined *Motion Picture News* on 29 September 1917. Business was as big as ever. A million dollars was set aside for advertising – in newspapers, magazines, electric lights. 'Our decision to spend this sum', said Zukor, 'is only another indication of our implicit faith in the wonderful future of motion pictures and our stars.' More new stages were being built for Lasky feature films. The creative team was more and more a mere part of the whizzing wheels and cogs. In November, Jeanie Macpherson stepped out of the background to give her first interview for *Motion Picture News*. Described as Cecil B. DeMille's 'left hand brain', Macpherson told the magazine:

'Sixteen hours is frequently a day's work . . . Hard work? Yes; but I like it. You can't be youthfully imaginative when you're fifty, and the pictures demand the energetic expression of youth. Do you agree with me?'

The reporter agreed with her emphatically, adding that he wanted to hear something more about that remarkable DeMille system of feeling out the public's likes and dislikes.

'We keep a constant record of opinions from exhibitors in all parts of the country. They send us a report at frequent intervals, telling us not how they liked certain productions, but how their patrons liked them. Sometimes the exhibitor himself adds a postscript to his report, saying he doesn't agree with the patrons. We often go farther than that and admit that we do not agree with either patron or exhibitor. These waves of public expression – just as accurate as if we had photographed the national mind – often wreck what we call our artistic opinions. That's why Lasky pictures never "run amuck." They stay on the track. They have the uncanny knack of giving the audience what it wants when it wants it. Often we sacrifice what we consider to be wonderful artistic possibilities for the public's terrible taste. Maybe that's why our concern is making money, and their exhibitors are making money, when some of the more "artistic" producers tumble into the mud occasionally.'

This embryonic 'market research' fell far short of the complex procedures employed in the present day, and expressed more of an aspiration than a working method. By now, Cecil B. DeMille was powerful enough to make his own decisions about the movies he would like to make. And despite the tug and pull of commerce, there was still Art, with a capital 'A', which he was determined to explore. He had already spoken out, alongside art director Wilfred Buckland, about the necessity for motion pictures to advance from the straight-forward picturization of reality, citing Max Reinhardt's idea of 'suggestive settings . . . The audience is made to feel the background rather than see it . . . We are beginning to pose our people in the settings as a painter would pose them . . . with consideration for the perfect balance of the painting . . .' Taking the movies beyond the simple technique of the early 'Rembrandt lighting', Buckland explained:

The present obvious method of photographing nature is lacking in the higher class of artistic expression and is not the ultimate end of motion picture possibilities . . . Art expresses the sentiment an object inspires and is not the reproduction of the object itself. For example, Corot, when a student, painted a tree as faithfully as he could reproduce it. Corot, when a master, painted the same tree so it expressed the mood and sentiment of nature, but his tree was no longer photographic, so in art 'photographic' is a term of reproach . . . [But] photographs taken by Whistler and Wm M. Chase prove that it is possible to paint with the camera as these men painted on the canvas, as backgrounds, figures, grouping and action are treated according to the laws which govern a painter's composition and chiaroscuro . . .

The method which we are gradually introducing substitutes imaginative for realistic scenery, and depends for its effects on art lighting . . . One does not need plains and mountains and the sun from which nothing escapes, for in any suggestive art more depends on what is left out than what is put in.

This was a far cry from the marvellous freedom DeMille had extolled in his earliest movies of being able to use real mountains, deserts and streams instead of theatre backdrops, and he and Buckland had already employed this new approach in *The Little American* with the powerful economy of lighting used to portray the stricken passenger ship. But he was about to take this further in his next production and demonstrate an economy of style that would both fit in with a restricted budget and achieve a greater freedom to experiment with different, less 'realistic' narratives. He was going to try a new kind of film-making which would plumb deeper into both human emotions and social mores – to look within the human soul rather than at the external and the apparent world.

This film would be *The Whispering Chorus*.

*

Since the publication of Robert Louis Stevenson's horror tale *Dr. Jekyll and Mr. Hyde* in 1887, there had been an abiding interest in tales of the multiple faces of man, the good and the bad that affect the human soul. Several movie versions of Stevenson's tale had been made, the first dating from 1908. But the story influenced a genre already populated by ghosts and other spectral voices that stretched back to before the nineteenth century. DeMille and Jeanie Macpherson chose as a source for their new film a story by a prolific but now little known writer of adventure stories, Perley Poore Sheehan, whose fantastic tales, often laced with an exotic mysticism, had titles such as *The Abyss of Wonders*, *The Copper Princess* and *Captain Trouble*. The latter tale, still in print, features an American adventurer who 'fights to become the successor to the great Kubla Khan'. *The Copper Princess* featured a resurrected Incan princess, a band of Russian revolutionaries and the Tsar's secret police.

Sheehan was also a budding screen writer, and was eventually to rack up twenty credits as story originator or co-writer, notably of one of the silent cinema's lost treasures, 1927's *The Way of All Flesh*. The movie starred Emil Jannings as a solid middle-class man who is seduced and robbed on a train, kills a criminal and leaves his family behind as he descends into degradation – a tale quite similar to *The Whispering Chorus*.

The theme of the reversal of fortune, as we have seen, was already obsessing both Macpherson and DeMille. Their new screenplay began with a close focus upon the man who will be at the core of the drama:

FADE IN. INT. AGAINST BLACK VELVET, NIGHT.
Suggestion of Tremble's desk. He is working at open ledger, and wears an eye-shade. He looks up a little from his work and removing the eye-shade he runs his hands wearily over his eyes, then he glances at small clock on desk, it is ten o'clock. He turns with disgust to his ledger and shuts it with a bang, then he leans wearily on his desk, his head in his hand – his face tired and bitter . . .
The 1st Face (disembodied) faces in over his right shoulder and says:
'What do you slave your nights away for, just to make a rich man richer?'
The 2nd Face (this is a sulky, discontented face), fades over his left shoulder and says:
'After all, good work is always appreciated in the end.'
This is a kind, calm face, it fades.

*The 3rd Face fades in over the top of his head and looks down pointing a
ghostly hand at him and says:*
'Don't be a fool! Did you ever hear yet of your esteemed President giving
anybody anything as a reward?'

In the finished film, an explanatory intertitle is inserted before the
disembodied faces appear, commenting on 'these echoes which none
but yourself could hear! The secret, private life of every man and
woman is lived away in a Hall of Echoes – to the music of this
Whispering Chorus . . .'

The hectoring faces fade in and out of the blackness surrounding
John Tremble, '2nd Assistant Cashier of the Clumley Contracting
Company', sitting isolated at his desk. At home, his mother and wife
await his return from work in their genteel poverty, ready to accept
their fate, while he rages over unpaid bills and the shabbiness of his
coat and shirt. Meanwhile, his nemesis, George Coggeswell, 'a far
seeing young legislator', is introduced, his own desk dominated by a
figure of justice with her tipping scales. At Christmas Eve, Tremble
goes out to buy his wife the 'cheap dress' she craves, but is diverted
by a work colleague to a gambling den, where he loses the little
money he has. Returning, he tells his wife the dress was already sold,
the first lie that precedes the great deception that is about to over-
whelm him.

Seduced by his voices – 'Don't be a fool, no one will ever know!' –
Tremble alters a $25,000 entry in his books to $15,000 by a simple
erasure and pockets the difference. But in the corridor a workmate
shows him a newspaper headline which announces that the company
is about to be investigated by Coggeswell for graft, and Tremble's
embezzlement is sure to be discovered. Urged by the bullying voice to
'clear out – if you don't want to go to jail!', he leaves a note to his
wife that he is going away on business, climbs aboard a boat and is
gone.

The fraud uncovered by Coggeswell, Tremble is sought. But ven-
turing from his shabby hideaway cabin to fish in the lake, Tremble's
hook catches the hand of a dead body in the water. Once again, the
voices have advice: 'If that dead man were you, all your worries
would be over!'

Tremble drags the corpse into the cabin, and despite his horror at
his own deed, smashes its face in with an iron, then fakes a note that

implicates an imaginary enemy, 'Edgar Smith', who supposedly wished him to defraud the company, prompting his refusal and escape. Shaving his beard and moustache and now unrecognizable, Tremble leaves the cabin, a man now perpetually on the run.

DeMille cast his regular actor-of-all-trades, Raymond Hatton, as the anti-hero John Tremble. Having eked out his apprenticeship as secondary crook, spiv, brother to Chimmie Fadden and the like, and then graduated to become King of France and Emperor of the Aztecs, Hatton finally found the role he could excel in: a squirming weasel of a man, exuding fear from every pore. The nightmare Tremble descends into is a perfect visualization of his inner state. As the body that is assumed to be his own is discovered and then identified by his distraught wife, Tremble transforms into a seedy dock worker and is then lamed in an accident by a cascade of falling barrels. Meanwhile, Coggeswell climbs the ladder of social success and is elected governor of his state, while he woos the 'widowed' Jane Tremble to become his wife. Homesick in his hovel, Tremble writes a letter to his mother back home, pretending to be a 'friend of John Tremble' who needs her help. The letter enables the police to trace him, but he manages to escape from an undercover agent and boards a ship headed for Shanghai.

The Whispering Chorus – Raymond Hatton and shadow

The film relentlessly cuts between Tremble's decline and his wife's rise at the side of her new lover-husband, the rich dinner party set against the embraces of an opium-addicted woman and the background of the chaotic Chinese New Year (Sheehan had to insert his orientalist fantasies somewhere). Two years later, a title tells us, Tremble has returned back to near his home, a pathetic street-seller of toys, while the new governor dines with his 'charming lady', who is now pregnant with their child. Tremble's voices urge him to visit his mother, the only person who will understand his plight. When she first sees him, she assumes he is a beggar, but then recognizes him and faints. As he tries to call a doctor, he is caught by a cop, and then finds his mother has died from the shock before she can save him by revealing his true identity. He is left with the promise she asked him to make with her last breath: to 'save Jane even if it killed you'.

The trap now closes around Tremble, who is identified as 'Edgar Smith' and put on trial. Brought before the defendant, his wife declares that 'I never saw him before in my life.' Found guilty, he finally bursts out: 'I never thought it could be done – but they've done it! They've convicted a man of the murder of himself!'

Hysterical, he tries to tell the truth to the jury, but Coggeswell tells Jane that the man must be insane.

Title: 'God moves in a mysterious way!' – divine intervention beginning overtly to invade DeMille's intertitles. Jane visits Tremble in jail and recognizes him, to her horror. Back in her governor's mansion, her future child appears spectrally to her. In his jail cell, Tremble is tormented by faces gibbering at him from the stone wall, reminding him of his promise to 'save Jane even if it killed you'.

Jane tries to ask for a pardon for 'Edgar Smith', but is faced by the next twist of the dilemma: if 'Smith' is Tremble, then Tremble killed 'Smith' – there is still a corpse to account for. She visits Tremble again, in his death-row cell, asking him to assure her he is not guilty of 'the other man's murder'. He remembers his pledge and tells her: 'When I pay the price – there will be no miscarriage of justice.'

Another divine title intervenes, declaring: 'And knew that somewhere in the world – God's dreadful dawn was red!' In the cell, like the accountant he is, Tremble crosses the last day off his wall calendar. The death sequence is one of DeMille's finest scenes, a masterclass in economy of style:

– Tremble, holding the single rose Jane has left with him, walks through the iron door towards the electric chair.

– In his home, Governor Coggeswell sits hunched in chair.

– In death chamber – executioner holds the switching lever.

– Close-up – Tremble's hand, clutching rose, tied to arm of chair. His fingers fondle the rose.

– Close-up – switching lever pushed.

– In her room, Jane falls stricken to table.

– In his seat, Coggeswell tautens.

– Close-up – lever pulled back.

– Close-up, foot of electric chair, as shredded petals fall to the floor.

In their home, Coggeswell and Jane view their town through an open window. As their new life begins, the ghost of John Tremble, hands outstretched, walks through them. He has left them a false confession to save his wife, writing as 'Edgar Smith' that he had indeed killed John Tremble. Coggeswell pledges, on this third anniversary of his bigamous marriage to Jane, that they can now repeat their wedding, 'in the presence of Almighty God'.

DeMille, Wyckoff and Buckland's deployment of their new theory of 'art lighting', paying as much attention to 'what is left out' as to 'what is put in', emphasized the metaphorical rather than naturalistic sense of the film, and Jeanie Macpherson excelled in rendering the lurid, pulp-fiction source into a moral, sensationalist fable, appropriate to the days of modern press hysteria and the corroding force of the emerging consumer culture. Clothes make the man – appearance is a motivator, as the shabby Tremble, literally trembling at his post, physically caresses, unseen, the sleek fur cuff of his employer, whose hand rests on his desk. The creeping religious message – one slip and man is damned – can only be mitigated by the ultimate sacrifice, which is, in true nineteenth-century mode, LOVE. The strange combination of old-fashioned moralistic values and the ultramodernism of the 'new' psychology permeates the film, presenting it to us as a full-blown precursor of the German expressionist *stimmung* or the later film noir.

It seems to have been long believed that DeMille experimented with this style and then dropped it due to the box-office failure of *The Whispering Chorus*. The record shows, however, that the film did well at the box office, taking in $242,000 for an outlay of $72,000. The two Mary Pickford films had cost much more, due to Pickford's staggering salary for the time – about $80,000 per film. The film was well received, *Variety* commenting that 'as a feature production, *The Whispering Chorus* stands with the best', though other critics found the death scene 'gruesome' or 'morbid'.

DeMille and Macpherson were to develop further the narrative ideas explored in the movie, in particular the reversal of fortune theme, although the 'less is more' visual style was never again used quite as boldly throughout. Jeanie Macpherson had explained her philosophy of screen-writing in some detail for the same issue of the *Moving Picture World*, in July 1917, that had showcased DeMille and Buckland's lighting ideas:

We have found out it isn't necessary for a photodrama to have only one dramatic scene, but each scene must be a drama in itself. The whole picture must be made up of a series of small dramas. This makes the completed drama a mosaic of little ones. Scenes that have no dramatic value in them, or say nothing, must be eliminated. So the scenario writer must bear in mind at all times not what he can put into a picture, but what he can leave out. If each scene has a why and a wherefore and an excuse for being, then you get a perfect continuity . . .

I find that in a great many pictures the writers deviate from their main theme – that they have two or three themes wandering through the story, which necessarily makes it complicated and hard to follow. If the writer will take a simple single theme, then work up the detail, decorate it with embroidery and lace, every little bit different from the last, but have each bit of trimming pertain directly to the main theme, he will have a much better story. Instead of that, writers branch off with a counter-plot or sub-plot which is upsetting and makes the story hard to follow.

Note that Macpherson, though a female writer, seems constrained to announce herself in male terms! Her argument, of course, was largely a reproach to Griffith, with his multiple *Intolerance* tales, and she would certainly have stood with the executives of MGM who would butcher Erich von Stroheim's grandiose, many-stranded *Greed* some years later. But her principles do serve to explain, at least in part, why Cecil DeMille veered away from formal experiments to what is now counted as a conventional narrative, though both he and his screen-writer would often favour a type of sensationalist, lurid and ultra-dramatic contemporary story similar to *The Whispering Chorus*. The experimentation would be internalized in the content of the piece. When asked by newspaper writer Monroe Lathrop in

March 1918: 'What is the keynote of *The Whispering Chorus*?' De Mille answered:

Simplicity, directness and repression. I have swung to the other extreme from my former methods. I am a convert to the conviction that the motion picture is capable of finer and more telling subtleties than the stage. There is greater dramatic power in an individual's intensive thought clearly and graphically conveyed than in the pictured clash of the most tremendous material forces . . .

If DeMille had stuck to this credo, he would have had a very different name in history from the one he has today – the master of spectacle and historical sagas. DeMille was uttering these words at the time of a very apparent clash of tremendous material forces – the all consuming European war. DeMille would pay his dues to this later in the year, when he would shoot a fairly negligible pro-war propaganda movie, *Till I Come Back to You*, full of good Belgians, evil Germans and heroic American soldiers who save a bunch of local orphans from the Huns. But this was an aberration, and his only other war movie of this period, *For Better, For Worse*, shot in 1919 after the war had ended, would plug into his already accomplished series of wife–husband adultery and upper-middle-class sophistication movies. For all his avowed patriotism and zeal for America, as a film-maker Cecil DeMille was a lousy flag-waver, and his openly patriotic films are without doubt his worst.

As ever, the fascination of DeMille lies in his paradoxes, the many contradictions of his mercurial enthusiasms. This was the last director you would expect to find philosophically contemplating his navel and scratching his head in indecision over the nature of his next project. Scripts were piling up on his desk and the next was in the schedule as *The Whispering Chorus* was being shot. The boss of the studio, Jesse Lasky, was not very excited about artistic aspirations and claims for a new kind of cinema. Ever the vaudeville entrepreneur, he wanted the widest variety of shows that would entertain the public, especially in wartime, when great anxieties and fears for loved ones overseas troubled the American audience.

The principle outlined by Lasky immediately after *Joan the Woman* still stood: 'What the public demands today is modern stuff with plenty of clothes, rich sets, and action. Nothing prior to the Civil War should be filmed.' Lasky continued to bombard DeMille with notes urging him to get more 'commercial'. He had a novel about an adulterous husband, by one David Graham Phillips, that he wanted DeMille to 'picturize'. DeMille was not terribly keen on it but one film made to please Lasky would certainly do him no harm. So he agreed to direct *Old Wives for New*. And therein lay yet another crucial and unexpected turning point in DeMille's long movie march.

REEL THREE

The DeMille Commandments
or
Civilization and Its Discontents

Take an Idea and Add Money

From *Theatre* magazine, February 1919:

Seymour bathing suits will be de rigueur this season . . . if you are impatient for verification you might run down to the beach any time next summer – but no, perhaps 'twould be better to go see de Mille's new Artcraft production, 'Don't Change Your Husband,' to adorn which these high visibility bathing costumes were designed . . .

Not that Cecil B. went after *weltmacht oder niedergang* in the realm of Fashion with malice prepense and aforethought. It came about as naturally as falling in love. You see for ever so long de Mille has been so intricately involved with them [motion pictures] that it would be hard to say whether de Mille made motion pictures, or whether motion pictures made de Mille . . .

De Mille's formula is: Take an Idea and add money until the treasurer begs for mercy . . . de Mille has demonstrated that ideas do not necessarily injure a photoplay; while as for the financial aspect, his motto is 'Cast thy bread upon the waters; and after many days it shall return to thee with butter on it.'

This thing of lavishing money on a production with a scoop shovel involves more than is apparent at first glance. It means the employment in the costume department of the ablest designers the country affords. It means retaining an art director who stands at the head of his profession and who is supplied with a staff as large as that of a field marshal. It means the retention of a young army of specialists, experts and master workmen in every line of activity touched upon by up-to-date photoplays, which include more forms of human endeavour plus everything else the scenario writer can think of.

More women see de Mille's pictures than read fashion magazines . . . Now do you suppose for one moment that a woman could be true to her sex if she did not want every stunning dress and pretty hat she saw upon the screen, especially if she could not afford them? And when she sees five whole reels just crammed and jammed with beautiful creations, what is there to do but go home and order hubby to go without lunch and cigar money until he saves up enough to buy at least some of the finery that de Mille doped out?

Gloria Swanson, modelling modernity

Yes indeed! And then there are the tips on interior decoration and home furnishing wherewith the Art Director and his staff of professional aesthetes adorn each scene. It is within bounds to say that the taste of the masses has been developed more by Cecil B. de Mille through the educational influence – Good Lord! The beans are spilled. Nobody will read any further than that word 'Educational . . .'

The end of the Great War unleashed a grand parade of thanksgiving and celebration that the forces of 'democracy' had prevailed over 'the Beast of Berlin', as the German Kaiser had been named by one of the many war-propaganda movies that had sprouted during 1918. 'Police Take Notice,' said one ad in April. 'Any Rioter Who Resents Seeing "The Kaiser – the Beast of Berlin," Is an Enemy of America.' Simultaneously, as trivia has it, an early version of Edgar Rice Burroughs' *Tarzan of the Apes* was taking up to $749.40 'In One Day! It would get blood out of a turnip!' gushed the publicists. American hyperbole, like America itself, was accelerating at an unprecedented rate that expressed the underlying energy of a nation most emphatically on the move. The 'culture of momentum' that had been manifest since 1910's Model T 'Tin Lizzie' encompassed both the real growth in production, from automobiles, steel and construction to fashion, and new developments in creativity, in literature, plays, movies and the greater use of marketing and advertising. Since Europe had bled on the battlefield for three years before America entered the war, America was well positioned to profit from the paralysis of the old empires. It was, as the cultural historians have reminded us, the beginning of a new 'consumers" society, and the motion-picture industry was ready and eager to play its part, in peace as it had in war.

'Peace for the Exhibitor,' announced Fox Films in December 1918, meant that 'profits are what interest you. One picture that you know will be a box office power is safer than all the untested productions combined . . . It is your assurance . . . that your money, time, energy and advertising will not be wasted. And this is the sort of pictures William Fox offers you.'

Everyone else in business was eager to prove they were on top of this principle. 'Giving the public what it wants' was no new commercial adage, but the public had to be made to want the products of the consumer boom, whether they knew what it was they wanted or not. The marketers and advertisers had to figure out how to make people desire not only useful products but those that might be merely decorative or that common sense might suggest they could do without. Americans' belief in themselves, strengthened by winning the war, could be turned to a belief in secular miracles: mind over matter, the idealization of technology and social mobility. Sigmund Freud, when visiting America, had noted that personal diagnoses were difficult, since Americans were prone to two kinds of mania: a healthy urge to break with old forms and engage the new, and a pathological condition that worshipped energy for its own sake.

To accomplish more in the new consumers' paradise was to buy more, and all who wished to sell had to maximize their market. This meant, in the social reality of post-war America, that no one could afford to ignore that half of the consuming public which had up till now played a lesser part in commercial decision making – America's women. And as women were still considered mainly as homemakers, this meant a greater emphasis on things like furnishings, fittings, decorations and costume.

In this production of desire itself the movies were, of course, paramount. When Jesse Lasky rained messages upon Cecil DeMille to get going on films that featured 'plenty of clothes' and 'rich sets' in contemporary situations, he was perceiving the changes already taking place at the centre of American culture and fashion, New York; changes that were not yet as obvious in a place that had been until very recently little more than a hick town at the other side of the continent. DeMille himself was no model of the new sartorial man – despite his own vainglory – as a gossipy item from the very East Coast *New Jersey Telegraph* reported on 29 September 1918, under the heading of 'What They Do on the Coast':

Cecil B. De Mille nearly starved to death one night recently. For nearly two hours he wandered around the streets of Los Angeles hunting for a neck scarf. It happened this way:

Mr De Mille spent all of one Sunday afternoon at the aviation field tinkering with an aeroplane; he was so warm that he took off his tie and unbuttoned his collar. Still warm and uncomfortable, he drove back to town. Arriving in Los Angeles he decided to go to the fashionable Alexandria for dinner and much to his consternation found that he had no tie and naturally could not appear in such an aristocratic eating place without being properly garbed.

He immediately dispatched his chauffeur on a hunt for a tie and also started a search himself. No haberdashery stores were open, so finally in desperation he went into a drug store and tried to buy some of the trimmings off a candy box. The frightened feminine drug clerk looked upon him with great suspicion and informed him that they had no candy boxes with ribbon on them that could be sold. Mr De Mille then asked her if she had anything else that would do for a necktie. The clerk was then more suspicious than ever and held a whispered consultation with the other employees in regard to summoning the police. Seeking safety in flight Mr De Mille then went out into the thoroughfare and tried to stop somebody and buy his necktie . . . A great crowd gathered. Several of the curious offered to sell their ties, but those who would sell wore ties that Mr De Mille would not, and those wearing ties desirable, would not sell.

Finally, after exhausting all the possibilities on the highways, and followed by a crowd, Mr De Mille went to the Alexandria and nabbed a bellboy, offering to buy his tie . . . . [The bellboy needed it] but told him that the tie could be rented, and so, for the sum of $1, Mr De Mille was able to rent the tie for two hours and, decorating his throat, departed to a much belated dinner.

By this time, DeMille had completed and released the first of his 'trilogy' of domestic dramas featuring errant husbands and wives, *Old Wives for New*. It would be followed in October by *Don't*

Change Your Husband and, as a belated addition, *Why Change Your Wife?*, made a year later in the autumn of 1919. In between, as was his wont, Cecil squeezed in five more films: another missing title, *We Can't Have Everything*, the ridiculous Hun-baiter *Till I Come Back to You*, a remake of *The Squaw Man*, a war-cum-domestic drama, *For Better, For Worse*, and his biggest hit to date, *Male and Female*. Four of these eight films starred DeMille's new discovery, ex-Mack Sennett comedienne Gloria Swanson.

Old Wives for New was an adaptation of a novel by David Graham Phillips, a crusading reporter and novelist who had been much concerned with political corruption and social issues. He had become famous in 1906 with a series of articles in *Cosmopolitan* magazine entitled 'The Treason of the Senate', revealing how senators were paid by corporations. In 1911, he was murdered by a man who believed his novel *The Fashionable Adventures of Joshua Craig* was a libel on his family. *Old Wives for New* had been published in 1908 and dealt with the social and economic position of women, charting the gulf between young, idealistic love and the troubles of marriage in middle age:

In rural Indiana, young Charles Murdock once wooed young, elegant Sophy. Twenty years later, however, as the official press release for the movie put it: 'Murdock is still a young man comparatively, but his wife has become vulgarly fat, lazy and quite content to drift idly down to an untimely desuetude.' The couple have a son and daughter, teenagers in our own parlance, 'both high spirited and quite fond of their parents. Murdock has become wealthy and has just closed out his business with his partner, Berkeley, a man of the world with the temperament of a rake.'

DeMille cast Elliott Dexter as the husband and Sylvia Ashton as the wife, with Theodore Roberts as the dissolute Berkeley. The love interest, the woman Charles Murdock falls for, dressmaker Juliet Raeburn, is played by Florence Vidor. The film still opens with a somewhat less than feminist title credo:

It is my belief, Sophy, that we Wives are apt to take our Husbands too much for granted . . . We've an inclination to settle down to neglectful dowdiness – just because we've 'landed our Fish'! It is not enough for wives to be merely virtuous any more, scorning all frills. We must remember to trim our 'Votes for Women' with a little lace and ribbon – if we would keep our man a 'Lover', as well as a 'Husband.'

The landed 'Fish', Murdock, gazes wistfully through his executive window towards a young couple chatting by the oil derricks, thinking, 'They don't own the house they live in – and they haven't any automobile, but they're happier than I am, because they have love!'

Morning in the Murdock household presents a bathroom in which the wife's comb is thick with her hairs, Murdock cleaning the grimy sink while Sophy is slumped in bed. She goes sighing into the bathroom, shuts the window which he likes kept open, complains of a headache and goes back to bed. At the breakfast table, the son and daughter read matching newspapers, while hubbie is left contemplating his lonesomeness. The scene resembles the typical W. C. Fields household of small-town American domestic misery that Fields was later to depict on stage and screen, but without the laughs. Murdock looks at a photograph of his wife aged eighteen, prompting a flashback to the day they met: he fishing, she demure by a stream, her bare feet in the water, her dress caught in his hook. He reels her in and kisses her. DeMille follows with a clever cut directly back to the 'old' wife at the door, as if looking in upon the past idyll of her husband with some winsome rival, as she asks him angrily: 'Charles Murdock – what on earth are you "mooning" about?'

The film was ground-breaking in its depiction of divorce as a valid solution to a failed marriage, as Murdock tells his wife: 'It's a degradation for two people to go on living together who no longer care for each other.' She, however, is conventionally appalled: 'Are you proposing to divorce me – the mother of your children?' This idea of a non-moral approach to divorce was shocking at the time, and Adolph Zukor even considered holding the film back, fearing a hostile reception by audiences.

Giving his wife three weeks to make up her mind, Murdock goes off hunting with his son and meets a younger woman, Juliet, a fashionable city dressmaker. They both shoot at the same bear, but Juliet's guilt at killing the animal is soothed by Murdock telling her it was his bullet that had done the deed.

Intertitle: 'Murdock the Cynic, the Disappointed, comes at last to know what a woman – the Right Woman – can mean to a lonely man.'

The film continues with a series of melodramatic incidents and coincidences: Murdock saves Juliet from going over the rapids, but she rushes off when he confesses his married status. Sophy Murdock discovers that her husband has been with Juliet and vows that she will refuse to divorce him. She rips apart the photograph of her younger, happy self. DeMille depicts her in bed, weeping and stuffing herself with chocolates as she reads the Bible: 'Therefore shall a man leave his father and his mother, and shall cleave unto his wife: and they shall be one flesh.'

Meanwhile, Berkeley, Murdock's dissolute and adulterous partner, invites Murdock to forget his worries in a bawdy cafe – speakeasies were still in the future, with Prohibition not kicking in till a year and a half later. As a ripe intertitle announces: 'Better be merry with the Fruitful Grape – than sadden after none, or *bitter* fruit . . .'

The cafe scene provides a template of Cecil B. DeMille's portrayal of what would later be called the 'jazz age'. From the start, a delight in the ambience and the promise of easy pleasures in the twirling smoke of cigarettes and spotlit performers in scanty attire, and on the other hand, a sense of moral laxity and loosening of social bonds. The shadows of exploitation, deception, lies and an inevitable retribution are combined. Dancing, balloons, Viola the Vamp smirking under her huge transparent hat, Murdock drinking 'to the Death of Memory!' Meanwhile, at home, his wife also takes up her own flirtation, with Murdock's creepy private secretary, Blagden.

While Berkeley peels off hundred-dollar bills at his table, the Vamp flirts with Murdock. But nemesis beckons with a payback delivered by Berkeley's old flame, Jessie, when the old rake flirts with a new girl. Following Berkeley home, Jessie shoots him. Murdock is called and conspires with the girl to take his partner to die in a hotel, thus avoiding ruining his firm's reputation. The girl confesses to Murdock: 'I killed him – he was a beast! No man ever knows what another man is with a woman!'

DeMille has returned to the world of *The Cheat*, but the setting, with all its convoluted plot points, is devoid of its racially provocative fantasy and turned to recognizable social dilemmas. When Murdock's dalliance with Juliet is revealed by Sophy to the newspapers, they attribute the rake's death to a scandalous love triangle. Murdock goes overseas with the Vamp, Viola, to throw the press off Juliet's trail.

The wronged wife, meanwhile, is persuaded to undergo a new beauty treatment by Blagden, who tells her: 'There's a certain French beauty doctor, who can restore your natural charm.'

'The Rejuvenation of Sophy' follows, as the previously frumpish wife is rolled about on the floor by a team of nurses, placed in a steam bath up to her neck and her corsets hauled in painfully tight. The Old Wife is now herself New, not for her old husband, but for the new – his former secretary, Blagden. And now the plot can be wrapped up, as Murdock is reunited with his new love, Juliet, in Venice, having paid off the 'cats-paw', Viola, with a rapturously accepted fat cheque. As the Old Wife remarries, the New is clasped on a balcony in the Venetian night, overlooking the rippling waters of the canals . . .

Adolph Zukor's anxiety over releasing the film proved unfounded. Audiences flocked to the theatres by word of mouth, forcing extra screenings. Critics continued to praise DeMille: 'All the characters are drawn so faithfully that there is never the slightest temptation to question the probability of the action,' said *Motion Picture News*. 'An admirable product,' *Variety* stated, adding that 'what may be considered immoral is counter-balanced by the pointing out of a moral and thus the picture should encounter no serious censorship.' After all, both husband and wife had abandoned a failing partnership to conclude new ones with more congenial partners, surely the essence of American progress.

DeMille reports in his autobiography that, as an experiment, he had his secretary Gladys Rosson copy the script and send it to her sister in New York in order to submit it as her own original screenplay. Of course, it was rejected as 'quite unsuitable for pictures'.

Old Wives for New was the movie which DeMille presented, in his own account and with tongue firmly in cheek, as his 'original sin' – the point at which he was accused of 'bidding a last good-bye to integrity and art' and cleaving to the commercial imperative. This was, of course, nonsense, as the extended chronicle of his work to the middle of 1918 shows quite clearly. Commerce and art had gone together in his calculations from the very first shot of *The Squaw Man*. His profession, wrote DeMille, was 'making motion pictures for popular entertainment'. He could do no different, having discovered in his theatrical career the cost of failing to satisfy the audience's taste.

Old Wives for New set a benchmark for films of contemporary situations with stories that dealt with the tangles of modern marriage, the new assertive woman and her oft bewildered husband, with fixtures and fittings that practically advertised the latest fashions and designs, as *Theatre* magazine aptly noted.

The style that can be seen in Cecil's 'domestic satire' movies was part of a mode of design that would later be given a specific name: art deco – though the definition of the concept would derive from a 1925 exhibition in Paris called the 'Exposition Internationale des Arts Decoratifs Industriel et Modernes'. Preceding movements in this field have been categorized as 'art nouveau' and 'art moderne'. Modernity was its calling card, in furniture design, crafts and glassworks, poster art, sculpture, painting, and most of all, in architecture, hugely affecting the skyscrapers that shot up to create the skyline of Manhattan. It was affected by new ideas in art – French Cubism, Italian 'Futurism', even Russian 'Constructivism' – as well as geometrical designs based on faddish 'oriental' styles, particularly following the Egyptian craze sparked by Howard Carter's discovery of Tutankhamun's tomb in 1922.

If Hollywood might be thought to be a little remote from the sparkling centres of culture, we have nonetheless already seen that both DeMille and art director Wilfred Buckland were well aware of European trends. Watching the DeMille movies of this period one can see the close attention paid to every aspect of set design, decorations, props, furniture and costumes, which not only mirror the new fashions but often anticipate them. The case is clinched in 1920 when DeMille appoints as art director of one of his most noted social dramas, *The Affairs of Anatol* – based on an Arthur Schnitzler play – Paul Iribe, French designer and one of the founders of the new 'art deco' movement.

Alas, we can pass no judgement on Cecil's next production, *We Can't Have Everything*, as no print appears to have survived. This is particularly galling, as it included scenes of a movie studio in action shot on the Lasky premises, incorporating shots of a fire that consumed part of the sets – an accident that was turned to good effect, according to the critics, who wrote of these shots that 'no one can claim that they are short on realism'. The movie was a comedy take on the husband–wife merry-go-round, with Elliott Dexter and Kathlyn Williams as the main lovers who dip in and out of divorce and marriage to other people. Lauding the film, *Motion Picture News* wrote that 'the society which revolves about the divorce court, the road house and the wife whose intellect is blonde, can be looked at on the screen with the same awe that it is looked at stepping out of a taxicab and floating into Sherry's'.

Cecil proceeded briskly to *Till I Come Back to You*, the vaunted return in the title being that of King Albert of the Belgians, whose promise to a small Belgian orphan boy can be kept due to a heroic American soldier. The evil German officer, Karl von Krutz, all strutting moustache and brutality, was a minor addition to the flood of anti-Hun pictures that included *Crashing Through to Berlin*, *Who's Afraid of the Hun?*, *The Woman the Germans Shot* and *The Kaiser's Finish* – 'a Stirring Photoplay Prophecy of The Day When the Yanks March into Berlin. It's Big! It's Timely!' Alas for the movie-makers who wished to cash in on the last push to end the war, a body blow was delivered to the industry and daily life in America (and throughout the globe) by the influenza pandemic that struck in October 1918, cutting a swathe through the younger part of the population and emptying theatres and movie houses as people shunned crowded spaces. After killing millions, the pandemic had spent itself by February 1919, though theatres dared to open the previous November, after the European Armistice of 11 November cheered up a depressed population. In the midst of this, however, Cecil DeMille was still not idle, releasing his remake of *The Squaw Man*, which, against all odds, was a box-office success. This too, however, is missing, apart from its final reel.

The stage was set for the next instalment of DeMille's social comedy dramas, which Jesse Lasky was eager to produce and present on the screen as quickly as possible. Despite his prolific output, Cecil was getting a little weary of the grind, as a brusque cable to Jesse Lasky of 4 February 1919 suggests:

Think it very serious mistake to try make me finish this picture for March release . . . If you want me to make good pictures I absolutely cannot be rushed in my work. If our policy is to really make good pictures and fewer of them let's start now. I cannot possibly make more than five pictures a year and have them of the kind we all want . . .

The DeMille mill would begin to slow down from 1919, with only four films produced, and then just three in 1920. But 1919 would begin with a new face, which would provide the next two years' pictures with the grace and attraction to take the Lasky–DeMille oeuvre to its next level. Cecil at last cast a star who could highlight the gowns, the decor and the stories with a new flair and sophistication, presenting the perfect image for the new age.

He had found Gloria Swanson.

Don't Change Your Star

Glimpsing Gloria's Gorgeousness
Small talk with Miss Swanson about her new picture,
And mostly about her lovely clothes.
By Media Mistley (*Picture Play* magazine, March 1919)

I had come to see Gloria Swanson's clothes, and not Gloria, and I made no bones about telling her so. Gloria's a love, and I like to remind her of it every once in a while, just to see that white neck and arms of her go all pinky. Not that she doesn't like it; she does. Remember, Gloria Swanson is just a girl – like you or me – which is the best compliment that I can pay to any woman who has been through the picture mill the way she has. But I like to tease her.

'Glory,' said I, opening her dressing room door and flopping into an absurdly comfy wicker nest which she calls her 'day bed,' 'Glory dear, I want you to give me a line o' talk on your clothes. So bring on your newfangles and your slithy, swanky evening clothes, and let's have the lecture illustrated. You're adorable today in that thing. What is it, anyway?' . . .

'Why, it's this fish-net stuff, my dear. Funny, isn't it?' she remarked, looking down at the skin-tight cuffs of coarse silk net that reached from her elbows to the knuckles. She had some more of it bound softly round her head. But that wasn't what made her eyes seem that color. They've always made me think of mermaids – they're so big and cold and clear. But then, Glory's mostly Scandinavian, though she has a dash of French, Italian, and Polish, too, in her ancestry, I believe . . . She moves with a lithe gracefulness that would have raised an ancient sculptor to ecstasies and that drives modern poets to verse, so I'm told.

And then the clothes began to come in – armfuls of street gowns and walking suits and evening things and mostly soft frilly negligees. At last I understood why Gloria is called the best dressed girl on the Lasky lot, which is a big compliment for a newcomer to the force, for that's what she is.

'Gloria!' I fairly squealed in delight. 'But why the thousand and one negligees? Why, you have enough there to spend the rest of your life in bed – gracefully.'

'I got them for my last picture, "Don't Change Your Husband." You remember De Mille's "Old Wives For New," don't you? Well, "Don't Change Your Husband" is an answer to the questions raised in the other picture. You know how in the first story the wife was terribly careless about her appearance, and so she lost her husband's love? Well, in this new story, the wife is exactly the opposite. Leila is just a little girl wife, used to having her own way and all the pretty clothes she wants. And she always has plenty of money to spend on clothes – until she leaves her husband, at least . . .'

Gloria May Josephine Svensson had been born on the move, the daughter of an army transport man who moved around US bases from Florida to Puerto Rico, although she spent her school years in Chicago. A talented child actress and singer, her mother wanted her to succeed in the theatre, but Gloria took her first job with the Essanay movie studios when she was seventeen. Her early fascination for clothes and costumes was somewhat dented by a spell at Mack Sennett's Keystone studios, where she found the slapstick, pie-in-the-face vulgarity and the 'giggly girls' of the Bathing Beauties a poor substitute for a career. In her inexperience, she also collected a husband, Wallace Beery, a Sennett heavy whom she had first met in Chicago but was teamed with in the Keystone comedies. Unfortunately, Beery was a brute both on and off screen, manhandling her as he chained her to a railroad track in Keystone's *Teddy at the Throttle*, and according to her own account, raping her on her wedding night.

Gloria was soon promoted sideways, within the Keystone-Triangle kingdom, to dramas and features. Her first encounter with DeMille occurred during this period, when DeMille's casting director, Oscar Goodstadt, tried to poach her from Triangle early in 1918. Gloria described the event in her 1980 autobiography, *Swanson on Swanson*:

Mr Goodstadt started to tell me how to get to the studio, but I said I knew where it was. Everybody knew where it was. It took up a whole block at Sunset and Vine. It was where Mary Pickford worked. And Douglas Fairbanks. And Almighty God himself, Cecil B. De Mille.

Any notions I may have had of style or elegance evaporated the moment I was ushered into Mr. De Mille's paneled office. It was vast and sombre, with tall stained glass windows and deep polar-bear rugs. Light from the window shone on ancient firearms and other weapons on the walls, and the elevated desk and chair resembled nothing so much as a throne. I felt like a peanut poised on teetering high heels.

When he stood up behind the desk, he seemed to tower. Not yet forty, he seemed ageless, magisterial. He wore his baldness like an expensive hat, as if it were out of the question for him to have hair like other men. A sprig of laurel maybe, but not ordinary hair. He was wearing gleaming boots and riding breeches that fit him like a glove. He came over and took my hand, led me to a large sofa and sat down beside me . . .

At that point DeMille could not offer her a contract as she still 'belonged' to Triangle, an obstacle that was soon removed as Triangle slid towards bankruptcy. When the summons from DeMille came again, Swanson had already appeared in eight features and was just over twenty-one.

At the Lasky studio, she was delivered to the hairdressers, a team of ten to fifteen girls under the aegis of 'Hattie, a tiny black woman . . . standing at an old-fashioned ironing board ironing a long switch of dark-brown hair'. She was Gloria's guide on the modus operandi of the DeMille set. DeMille, everyone knew, was a perfectionist: 'Everything had to be just so or he sent it back. He never started work until ten in the morning and he never overworked his artists. He had a violinist playing on the set to create a mood and make the actors feel good . . .' The jewels to be worn with her costumes on the set were brought in by three Pinkerton detectives: 'Mr. DeMille always had his actresses pick out the jewellery they wore in his films so they would act as if they owned it.'

DeMille 'entered like Caesar, with a whole retinue of people', which included Jeanie Macpherson and Sam Wood, the assistant director. 'He peeled off his field jacket and a Filipino boy behind him caught it as it left his hand. When he was ready to sit down, the Filipino boy deftly shoved a director's chair under him.' The 'chair carrier' would be part of the DeMille legend for ever. Sticking to the great man like a limpet, the chair boy was always poised to place the seat as the director sank back without bothering to see if it was there. It always was.

In her first scene, Swanson wrote, she had to pack a trunk. He didn't tell her why or even, she claimed, tell her the name of the film. Many actors recalled that DeMille would not supply them with what we today call 'motivation'. As Swanson relates him shouting at a young actor who dared to ask him how to play a scene: 'This is not an acting school. I hired you because I trust you to be professional. *Professional!* . . . When you do something wrong, *that* is when I will talk to you!' Many years later, when DeMille's reputation was practically mythological, actors were to continue to quail before this iron-clad dictum. Yet for those who accepted his faith in the craft of those he cast in his movies, DeMille was a loyal and generous employer.

As she became conscious of the complex relationship between the director and his writer, secretary and now permanent editor Anne Bauchens, Gloria may well have wondered whether she too was slated to join the harem. DeMille's adoption of the phrase 'young fellow' in his dealings with Gloria left her at least with some leeway. In any case, she was not divorced from Wallace Beery until 1919 and had another lover, the millionaire socialist Craney Gartz, and in due course a new husband, film distributor Herbert Somborn. Gartz introduced her to Friedrich Nietzsche, Karl Marx, D. H. Lawrence, George Bernard Shaw, Henrik Ibsen, James Joyce and Sigmund Freud, while Somborn introduced her to life at a level which did not make her utterly depressed to go home to a working actress's apartment after a day with the latest fashions and gewgaws. 'Working for De Mille', she wrote, 'was like playing house in the world's most expensive department store.'

Gloria Swanson was most fortunate in her first starring role for 'Almighty God'. *Don't Change Your Husband* was the first Cecil B. DeMille film marked by a newly heightened, aggressive press publicity campaign, a prototype of much that was to follow. From February 1919, ads spread over several pages of the trade magazines announced, putting first things first:

Gorgeous Gowns, Beautiful Women and A Startling Story of Married Life. Cecil B. De Mille has done it again. He had put married life in a show window, with all its heart aches, misunderstandings – with all its joy and genuine beauty.

A production of superb radiance.

A story of lost love, of happiness regained.

A tale that reaches the hearts and souls of every home, that bares the false and scorns the sham.

For every husband who sometimes bores his wife.

For every wife who sometimes is an enigma to her husband.

A full page featured 'An Appreciation' of the film by John C. Flinn, Director of Publicity and Advertising for Famous Players Lasky, who hailed it as 'another great step to supremacy'. A 'Special Service

Section' harangued theatre bookers with advice on how to profit from 'the wonderful allegorical episodes of which De Mille is capable'. For example: 'Gloria Swanson . . . swinging over a huge pool with a background of flowers and dozens of girls in attendance . . . This picture should be advertised well in advance of the first presentation. It should be the same sort of advertising that you would expect from a big society event.' Urging a 'teaser campaign', the piece suggested, 'you have a chance here with a single word to attract a lot of attention. Simply mail to your patrons a card bearing the word, "Don't." Better still if you can follow this up a few days later with an added word, "Don't Change" . . . and then coming along with the full title of the picture . . .'

Whole Exploitation of This One Should Be 'Special'!
Get this line . . . taken from the titles in the picture:
She cast off a husband because he ate onions, because he went to sleep with a cigar in his mouth, because he forgot the wedding anniversary. And she married the man whose niceties so contrasted. But she learned . . .
Keep the adjectives out, but aside from that you can go to the limit . . . It doesn't matter about the people to whom you have to appeal. Everyone married or thinking about getting married or against getting married.
'Don't Change Your Husband' – use that in the biggest type you have in the shop. And don't forget Cecil B. De Mille.

There was little chance of that. After this level of hype one might consider the film itself to be a let-down. But it was, in fact, a significant advance over its predecessor. Once again, a restored DVD version enables us to enjoy the film anew: Elliott Dexter, a specialist in DeMille's strong, silent men, excels as the onion-eating husband who loses his wife because he doesn't care about his appearance, forgets their wedding anniversary and is too tied up in his work. Gloria's friend, the well-dressed heel, Schuyler, woos her with: 'Leila, Jim regards you too much like an old shoe.' As her snooty set prepare for their masked ball, Schuyler entices her with concepts that she sees in her mind's eye: Pleasure, Wealth and Love, with Gloria in lush sets, African servants bringing her trunks of jewels, and then in an Arcadian garden, where she is seduced by flutes and luscious grapes – mix to Schuyler's attempted kiss on the sofa. At the ball, hubby is attired by his rival in jester's cap and absurd curved shoes – 'for the Apparel oft proclaims the Man'.

Jeanie Macpherson's dialogue intertitles mix the poignant with the absurd as Schuyler tells his rich hostess: 'Why should you blame me for trying to get what another man is too fond of *onions* – to try and keep.' The onion motif keeps recurring in all its plebeian horror. Gloria decides she can't stand this 'corn beef and cabbage existence any longer'.

Swanson wrote of her impressions of the way DeMille handled the scenes of intimate and private emotions, pointing out a key scene with Elliott Dexter:

The most moving scene in the whole picture for me was the one in which he realizes I've left him. He looks into the camera stunned, miserable, alone and full of regret. I watched the rushes of the scene over and over, until it finally dawned on me what motion pictures could mean to the audience if they were wonderfully acted and directed. Here was what every woman who had ever left a husband wanted to see – how he looked when he first understood that she was gone. Motion pictures allowed her to be a fly on the wall at the most secret moment of her husband's life. No wonder people sat enthralled in darkened theaters all over the world in the presence of these big close-ups . . .

Gloria may well have been thinking of the effect she wished for Wallace Beery. Clearly the audience responded strongly to these finely observed small moments. The irony of Leila's divorce from her first husband and marriage to Schuyler is that her new husband proves to be just as clumsy as the other: smoking in bed, leaving his butts on the carpet, smelling of booze and complaining about her tastes, 'Can't you find anything to wear in the mornings, Leila, besides that queer oriental junk?' Schuyler even reads the newspaper at breakfast – and dunks! A wastrel, his failed business ventures eat up the capital of Leila's hard-won jewels. Soon, New Hubby is flirting with a new girl, 'Toodles', the ever flirty Julia Faye.

Meanwhile, Old Hubby has spruced up his act: shaved, fit and newly accoutred, he's successful in his trade. While Schuyler dines with Toodles, Gloria runs into her ex – 'Fate Sometimes Lurks in Christmas Shopping' – and the unseen narrator's intertitle comments: 'Of the external forces which combine to make us what we are – DRESS is the most potent. It covers our ideas no less than our bodies – until we finally become the thing we look to be.'

No finer explication of the consumerist motto could be made. Semiotic historian Sumiko Higashi comments about DeMille's marital satires that 'as the middle class became more immersed in consumption as a way of life, the lower class, especially women, found that the democratization of luxury was accessible for the price of a movie ticket'. The movies had come a long way in less than ten years, from a point at which they were still mainly marketed as an entertainment for those Jesse Lasky had observed as the shabbier end of society and the immigrant masses who flocked to low-class comedies.

At any rate, the dictum that 'clothes make the man' is followed to the utmost in *Don't Change Your Husband*, as Leila ditches Schuyler and hooks up again with Hubby Number One, while Schuyler woos a new girl with his standard 'pleasure, wealth and love' spiel. End Title: 'And now we know what every woman comes to know, that Husbands, at best, are pesky brutes, and at worst – are unfit for publication.'

Leapfrogging over the next two films DeMille directed, the final panel of the triptych was made in the autumn of 1919, with Thomas Meighan replacing Elliott Dexter as the husband and the roles of the previous film inverted: in *Why Change Your Wife?*, it is the husband who is dissatisfied with marital life, preferring a little dallying at the cabaret to staying in with boring Gloria, who has allowed herself to get quite dowdy and 'whose virtues are her only vice'. Tiresomely intellectual, she replaces his record of 'The Hindustan Foxtrot' with 'The Dying Poet' and worships the foppish foreign violinist played by Theodore Kosloff. When hubby meets a new girl, Sally, played by Bebe Daniels – 'legally a widow and optically a pippin' – new romance blossoms and the old fades. After the divorce, however, Gloria is converted to the joys of a new makeover, morphs into a ravishing beauty and flirts with Kosloff at a spa hotel. By coincidence, her ex and Sally turn up at the same resort and the DeMillean '*la ronde*' can occur. Gloria falls back in love with her husband, and Sally ends up with the violinist, but not before a most un-American cat fight between the two ladies over the stricken husband, who has, most mundanely, slipped on a banana peel thrown by an urchin on the street and lies concussed in Gloria's bed. Sally's attempt to throw acid on Gloria fails when the acid turns out to be eyewash, and she flounces out with the final word: 'The only good thing about marriage, anyway, is the alimony.'

The film combined elements from *Don't Change Your Husband* and *Old Wives for New* in a frothy concoction that the critics noted was becoming somewhat derivative. But as *Variety* noted, DeMille had 'worked in some good sex stuff camouflaged carefully for the benefit of the censor. His moral may be chocolate coated with women undressing, but it will get by just the same.' In fact, the script for this retread derived from a story by brother William, stirred and well shaken by Olga Printzlau and Sada Cowan, rather than Jeanie Macpherson, and the project had begun as a William de Mille film in the first place. William had well established himself by now as a director of social dramas, with fifteen features under his belt since 1916. The early radical dramas like *The Sowers* and *The Blacklist* had been left behind, and he too had succumbed to the fashion for fashion and bourgeois travails.

In his final intertitle for *Why Change Your Wife?* Cecil ended his trilogy with an admonition that mirrored his own private credo regarding his life with Constance:

And now you know what every husband knows – that a man would rather have his wife for a sweetheart than any other woman. But Ladies – if you want to be your husband's sweetheart, you simply must learn when to forget you're his wife . . .

By now, DeMille had become quite the pontificator on the ins and outs of marriage, and not only in his films. After his comments on fallen women while in his aeroplane with *Photoplay*'s Elizabeth Peltret, he would be interviewed, towards the end of 1920, by Hollywood's most prominent gossip writer of the era, the redoubtable Adela Rogers St Johns, who was supposed to know where every skeleton in the film colony lay. 'What Does Marriage Mean? As Told by Cecil B. de Mille', also in *Photoplay*, caused a furore as Adela revealed, in her typically hyperbolic style, DeMille's views on marital infidelity:

He [DeMille] stimulates a keen, mental enthusiasm. He seems vitally, almost painfully alive – a driving, compelling yet pleasing force . . . It is, I think an unusual welding of the ability to think with the ability to feel. Most men who have a capacity to do one to the limit, neglect the other . . . The welding of the two in de Mille accounts for the combined magnetism and compelling force of the man . . .

I am quite, quite sure that because of the things he said to me that night I shall be a better wife.

He opened doors to me, as a woman, that had been discreetly veiled if not tightly shut to me . . .

[Said DeMille]: 'If a woman has the mental strength to stand the gaff, her husband will always come back to her . . . If she just has the moral poise to weather his yieldings to the beast within. Every husband would go back to his wife if she stood pat . . .

'A man does something he ought not to do. I make no excuses . . . I do not condone. It seems the nature of the beast, that's all . . . He strays, falls from his allegiance to his wife. In reality to him it's a matter of small importance, so far as his feeling for his wife is concerned . . . It isn't a thing he's at all pleased about . . . He goes home, crawls home, curls up at his wife's feet and says, "Lady, please step on me . . ." He probably buys her a diamond, or a lot of roses, or a new car. It isn't to buy her off. It's a sincere attempt to show her his love hasn't been changed.'

Proclaiming himself as almost a prophet determined 'to batter down' the door of the taboo on the discussion of sex – 'the object only of hushed voices, lifted fingers, drooped eyes' – DeMille told St Johns: 'I am not creating an imaginary thing. It is. Fidelity to the marriage covenant – the most sacred of all obligations – is not to be gained by encouraging women to rail against their husbands . . . it is to be gained only by showing wives how men may be, if not lifted entirely above sex, at least taught to hold it within the bounds of moral law and decency . . .'

Mrs St Johns was obviously an adept at tempting her interviewees into indiscretions, or making them up, as DeMille ventured into his own private arena:

Women get into a habit of picking. It's a habit . . . Such a habit in a wife should be handled instantly.

I married a girl from an old New England family . . . My wife had been brought up to believe that if there was a scratch underneath the piano the whole house had to be sent out and repolished.

After our wedding, we traveled to a little place that we had arranged. It was charming full of delightful old furniture . . . Now I must be comfortable. All my life I have had a habit of tipping back in chairs. I always sit in a straight chair and tilt back, rocking myself gently with my foot. I do it when I am directing. I always do. Always have.

I did then. I settled down blissfully, put my foot on the rung of a beautifully, highly polished old mahogany desk and tipped back. My wife – I don't think she had taken off her hat – said, 'Don't do that, you'll scratch the desk.'

I got up. I stood on the desk. I climbed on top of it and jumped. I stood on all the chairs. I turned them sideways and stood on the sides. It resulted, of course, in a wild outburst of tears, which I soothed with joy and willingness. But in eighteen years of happy married life, the word 'Don't' has never been said to me again . . .

I have been married eighteen years. In eighteen years I have never passed a Saturday night at home. In eighteen years I have never said where I was on a Saturday night, nor what I was doing, nor with whom I was.

And in eighteen years, I have never been asked . . . Consider for a moment the immense amount of strength, of character, of moral stamina it takes for a woman to refrain from asking that fatal 'Where have you been' every Saturday night for eighteen years. Think of the respect it creates in the mind of the man. Think of the ability to control her own emotions it gives a wife.

If I had ever been asked that question, I should simply have stayed away for four or five days next time.'

DeMille's presentation of his home life as an extended training session for the obedient and unquestioning spouse brought in thousands of letters, according to St Johns, prompting a 'Second Episode of "What Does Marriage Mean?"' in the May 1921 issue of *Photoplay*. 'It's amazing,' DeMille was quoted as responding, 'astounding that a few words about marriage, stripped of ancient traditions and outworn creeds, should start so many echoes.' Women, of course, were outraged, and DeMille had to comment that Mrs DeMille had asked him to state that 'you should let everyone know that of course you accord me the same privileges of personal liberty that you ask for yourself'. Of course, no one needed to ask where Mrs DeMille was on Saturday nights, as everyone knew she was dutifully at home, tending her daughter and her adopted flock. The magazine properly published a picture of Mrs DeMille in the garden of her home – 'a small, graceful woman, giving forth a deep serenity, very sure of herself, yet gracious, pleasant, keenly humorous. A woman of reserves, of depths, of accomplishments.' She herself, of course, was not interviewed.

'Women always forgive the men they love,' asserted Cecil. 'To my mind the really good woman . . . is the broad, wise, pure, understanding woman, who with every right weapon she can grasp tries to kill the beast in man . . . helping him to overcome the Adam inheritance of lust and dust that eventually lead to ruin . . . With Browning, I could say:

'Youth ended, I shall try
My gain and loss thereby;

Leave the fire ashes, what survives is gold.'

This would be the last time Cecil DeMille would open the Pandora's box of his marriage in public to reveal the jumping Jack-in-the-box held down by its lid. In the future, as before, he would continue to explore those hidden tensions between men and women in his films. There, as he achieved the mastery of his art alongside an unparalleled authority to control his own productions under Lasky's aegis, and with the box-office tills happily ringing, he could manipulate his human puppets in the doll's houses of his imagination, in shadow and light, to the full.

The Monarch of All He Surveyed

Apart from the husband–wife trilogy, Gloria Swanson only made four more films with DeMille. Her films for Cecil had made her a star, continually appearing in movie magazines and grilled about her taste in everything, from gowns and hats to the art of acting. She became, in today's parlance, a trendsetter, as *Photoplay* declared in August 1919: 'The vast majority of our younger set are not keenly intrigued by the shut-down of theatres in Germany, the campaign against lynching, or the build-your-own-home-in-Bay-City movement. On the other hand, Gloria Swanson's newest head adornment means a lot to them.'

Within a year, she had her new husband, Herbert Somborn, and then a child by him and a new, much improved contract by Jesse L. Lasky. She eventually moved on to directors like Marshall Neilan and Allan Dwan, and in the twilight of the silents, to her ill-fated artistic tryst with Erich von Stroheim in 1929's *Queen Kelly*, the film she would be watching as Billy Wilder's reclusive madwoman in *Sunset Boulevard*. In all, she would collect four husbands.

By that summer of 1919 she had appeared in two more DeMille films, the first of which was *For Better, For Worse*. This was a wartime drama starring Elliott Dexter as a surgeon who declines to enlist for the war in order to stay and tend his hospital full of sick children. The film is a strange concoction of high melodrama, social comment on the vexed issue of draft dodging and an almost ghoulish obsession with physical disfigurement that will recur as a fetish in several future DeMille films.

The surgeon, Dr Ned Meade, and his friend, Dick Burton, both love priggish Sylvia Norcross, played by Swanson. As war and the flag waving break out, Dick enlists, but Ned is persuaded by 'the Cry of the Children' to stay behind, despite Sylvia's insistence that 'I couldn't love a man who stayed home – when brave men are going

out to die.' Another girl, Betty, loves Dick, but he wants to marry Sylvia before he goes to war – cue a bizarre series of flashbacks to Gyda blessing the spear of Harald the Dane as his Viking ship sails, Richard the Lionheart and the Lady of Navarre, and the 'untrained lads of Lexington – to whom a woman said – I love you' – a shot of Gloria in the Revolutionary war, handing her husband his flintlock gun and powder horn . . .

Sylvia and Dick plight their troth with the flag in a sombre wedding – 'for better for worse, for richer for poorer, in sickness and in health – till death us do part'. While Dick is at the front in Europe, Sylvia works to help needy families. But when a little girl is hit by a car and might 'never walk again', she finds all the good doctors have enlisted, except Ned Meade, who has been denounced in the press as 'yellow'. When he takes on the girl's case, Sylvia tells him: 'I'm beginning to understand how brave you really are!'

Meanwhile, in France, Dick is crushed, under fire, by a falling church spire – Christ literally smashing his face. He lies, maimed and disfigured, in hospital and instructs his friend to tell Sylvia he is dead.

Back at home, Sylvia has watched Ned nurse the little girl back to health.

Against all odds, army surgeons restore Dick's face to a heavily scarred but tolerable state. He returns, in the midst of Sylvia and Ned's 'surprise' engagement party. Having met Betty, the girl who loved him from the first, he goes up to an empty room to wait, lurking behind the door in shadow. Sylvia enters, turns and faints as she sees him. In a funereal scene, Dick is introduced, instead of the engagement, as the surprise of the party and is feted under the slogan: 'His arms were her Defense – her arms his Recompense.'

The ending is ambiguous, overwhelmingly sombre, as Betty convinces Dick she truly loves him, while Sylvia confesses to him she really loves Ned, who is waiting with the cured child, hoping for a fairy-tale end to his own yearning. It comes with Sylvia's final statement: 'It isn't a question of bravery, it isn't a question of war – it's a question of love,' as they tentatively kiss.

DeMille, who never went to war, clearly wished to present the dilemma posed by the clash of patriotism and a different sense of duty – to one's own calling. It was an unusually critical approach to a cause still strongly defined as the 'War for Democracy' and the 'War to end Wars'. In the failed engagement sequence, the ubiquitous Stars and Stripes seem to suggest a shroud more than a flag.

The studio publicity highlighted critical acclaim, but *Variety* sounded a very sour note, suspecting that 'it looks as if the Cecil B. DeMille–Artcraft feature, "For Better, For Worse," written by Edgar Selwyn and Jeanie Macpherson, was produced before the war was concluded and was afterward altered to meet present conditions'. This was not in fact the case, as the picture was shot from the end of January to late March 1919. But, said *Variety*, 'it is a most unsatisfactory tale and the conclusion cannot be anything but distasteful, whichever way it breaks'. Nevertheless, it was 'admirably produced by DeMille, and hence interesting . . .'

DeMille was aware that this project might not be to everybody's taste, and even before the film's shoot had his eye on another, quite different vehicle for Gloria, much more in keeping with the flighty wife of *Don't Change Your Husband*. Jesse Lasky had acquired the film rights to *The Admirable Crichton*, the 1902 play by the author of *Peter Pan*, J. M. Barrie. This, both Lasky and DeMille determined, was to be their big production of the first post-war year.

'Big' was the operative word in 1919 as the entertainment boom escalated: 'Millions Invested in New Film Theatres,' trumpeted *Motion Picture News* on 9 August, 'Country Seething With Big Building Boom and New Playhouses That Will Rival Best in the World Spring Up Like Mushrooms.' The demand for motion pictures was at its peak. This called for more 'plants and organizations . . . a large selling machine . . . manufacturer–dealer co-operation'. Luckily for DeMille, he was positioned perfectly in just such a corporate enterprise. *Male and Female*, declared Adolph Zukor, ahead of the film's release, 'is DeMille's best – one of the finest productions of all time'.

Barrie's play had been renamed, so legend has it, because a telegram operator had once mistaken the 'Admirable' for 'Admiral'. And so the movie became 'Male and Female (Created He Them)', the biblical allusion added and then dropped. In reality, the script by DeMille and Jeanie Macpherson required the altered emphasis.

The Admirable Crichton was a play about class, a tale of a group of upper-class Englishmen and women who embark, with their kitchen maid and butler, on an ocean cruise which ends in shipwreck on a desert island. On the island, the practical skills of the butler, Crichton, reverses the power relationships, as he becomes king over his useless superiors, until their rescue re-establishes the 'normal' facts of social life.

The main reversal, in the play as in the film, concerns the relationship between Crichton and the spoiled Lady Mary, in whose role DeMille cast Gloria Swanson. To play opposite her, Cecil cast Thomas Meighan, described by *Photoplay* as 'homely as manly beauty goes' but endowed with the quality to 'get it over'. In 1915, he had been the stolid Heine Schultz in DeMille's *Kindling*, but by 1919 he had played opposite Mary Pickford and Norma Talmadge, and had accumulated a female fan base sufficient for him to progress from 'leading man' to star. 'Not So Darn Homely As That' headlined his special plug in the magazine. DeMille added upcoming Lila Lee as Tweeny, the kitchen maid, Raymond Hatton as a lazy upper-class twit and Theodore Roberts as the head of the household, the cigar-chomping Earl of Loam.

The desert-isle part of the film was shot on Santa Cruz Island, one hundred miles from Los Angeles, where the surf pounded on a rocky coast. Production supervisor Howard Higgins brought several hundred sago trees from Florida, as well as two hundred cactus palms, two hundred orange and lemon trees, banana trees, avocados and fifty crates of tropical rushes, according to *Picture Play* magazine. Writer Edna Foley described the scene, in October 1919, under the heading 'On a Typical, Tropical Isle':

Santa Cruz Island . . . hundreds of years ago, was a Spanish prison island. An offender against the law was sent there with enough sheep, goats and pigs to keep him alive. For a long time now it's been a desolate place inhabited only by a few wild goats and hogs . . . When it had been transformed De Mille's company for 'Male and Female' joyously set sail, making the expedition a regular picnic trip. Gloria Swanson, Lila Lee, Margaret Reardon, Thomas Meighan and the rest of them prepared to be shipwrecked with pleasure. John Barrymore went along just by way of adding a bit of excitement to his restful summer . . . Altogether there were forty people, and if their month as castaways wasn't an enjoyable one we've heard no reports to that effect . . .

'De Mille was the monarch of all he surveyed,' read the caption on one of the essay's photographs. It was pretty clear who Cecil identified with in this vintage wish fulfilment. The film seemed the perfect choice for DeMille to explore his favourite theme, the reversal of fortune. But a comparison between the text of the play and DeMille's screen version provides some revealing clues about his take on the age-old war of the classes, of character versus society.

Barrie's playscript contains detailed descriptions of the upper-class characters, introduced to the audience at 'Loam House in Mayfair', but when he comes to Crichton, the playwright writes, tongue firmly in cheek:

It would not be good taste to describe Crichton, who is only a servant; if to the scandal of all good houses he is to stand out as a figure in the play, he must do it on his own, as they say in the pantry and the boudoir.

One of the central quirks of Barrie's play is that the master of the house, Lord Loam, is a lapsed aristocrat who believes in equality and tries to lecture his butler:

LORD LOAM: Can't you see, Crichton, that our divisions into classes are artificial, that if we were to return to nature, which is the aspiration of my life, all would be equal?
CRICHTON: If I may make so bold as to contradict your lordship . . . The divisions into classes, my lord, are not artificial. They are the natural outcome of a civilised society. (*To Lady Mary*) There must always be a master

and servants in all civilised communities, my lady, for it is natural, and whatever is natural is right.

LORD LOAM (*wincing*): It is very unnatural for me to stand here and allow
you to talk such nonsense.

While James Barrie's inversions are those of the European ironist,
Cecil DeMille's are those of an American moralist. Crichton in the
film is no believer in the social order; he is rather an American-style
democrat, a frustrated egalitarian who daydreams about the very
reversal of fortune that fate will soon bring about. Viewers of the film
might puzzle over the central part played by a book of poems by
William Ernest Henley, British Victorian poet and friend of Robert
Louis Stevenson. We find Crichton in the Loam library mooning with
the maid Tweeny over the poem:

> Or ever the knightly years were gone
> With the old world to the grave,
> I was a King in Babylon
> And you were a Christian Slave.

This idea of reincarnation, which will spark the film's central flashback sequence, appears as if it had been inserted by DeMille and
Macpherson in keeping with their continual obsession with this
theme. But in fact the poem is present in Barrie's play and fuels
Crichton's transformation on the island into the same dominating
personality that Lord Loam believes cannot exist in the proper state
of nature:

CRICHTON (*to Lady Mary*): A king! . . . I have occasionally thought of late
that, in some past existence, I may have been a king. It has all come to me so
naturally . . . as-if-I-remembered. 'Or ever the knightly years were gone . . .'
[etc.] It may have been . . . I am lord over all. They are but hewers of wood
and drawers of water for me. These shores are mine. Why should I hesitate;
I have no longer any doubt . . .

In the play, it is the servant who believes more firmly in the rule of
established power than the master, a precursor of present-day novelist Kazuo Ishiguro's classic English butler in *The Remains of the Day*.
DeMille has no sympathy or empathy with this. His Earl of Loam is
a clownish brute, weaselly biding his time in subservience but ready
to take over again when the tables are turned back.

DeMille – and Hollywood – is, of course, more interested in the interplay between Crichton and Lady Mary – Tom Meighan and Gloria Swanson – as, for example, in the London mansion scenes, when she complains to Crichton about her spoiled toast and is outraged by his double-edged reply: 'Are you sure it's only the toast that is spoiled?' Once the cruisers' yacht is wrecked on the desert isle, Crichton takes over as the man of all trades, giving the aristocrats a near-Bolshevik creed: 'Those who are not willing to serve – are apt to find themselves both cold and hungry!' The aristos cower in the open air while Crichton sips his self-made soup in his self-made shelter, till Gloria begins to doubt her own class: 'Is it possible, Ernest, that a Graduate of Oxford knows less than a Butler, how to keep a shivering woman warm?'

Crichton forces the spivs to fetch and carry, despite their attempted rebellion against him. Meighan's taming of Gloria in the movie is more taming of the shrew than true love, with the maidens, upper or lower class, vying with each other over who will serve the new lord and master his dinner, while old master Loam snaffles the dessert. One crucial scene has Crichton shooting a leopard to save Lady Mary, then returning to camp with the slain beast draped over his shoulder. DeMille had the animal drenched in chloroform for the scene, only to find his actor panicking when it began purring in his ear. But the most crystallized moment of DeMillean madness came in the 'flashback' scene prompted by Crichton's fantasizing about his Henley poem as a literal memory of times gone by. This was DeMille's most exotic set since the Aztec palace in *The Woman God Forgot*, as Gloria Swanson recalls:

Mr De Mille had saved the most dangerous scenes . . . the 'vision' in Babylon – until the very last. Except for a dozen black slaves in leopard skins . . . the only other characters in the scene were Tommy Meighan, Bebe Daniels, and half a dozen lions. Tommy as the King of Babylon has me brought before his throne. He tells me to renounce my religion and become his bride or face a den of lions . . . I choose the lions, of course, and Mr. De Mille said I should confront them in the manner of a very dignified Christian saint.

The set, dressing, costumes and bizarre headgear are all the epitome of an orientalist's dream. Steps led down through arches to the den, entered through a golden gate. Out of shot, trainers with whips and guns stood by to control the lions. Gloria's costume was so heavy 'two maids had to help me carry it when I was not on the set. The

Male and Female – Gloria and her latest admirer

gown was made entirely of pearls and white beads . . . and the towering headdress was made of white peacock feathers.' The crowning
sequence was the one in which Gloria, the martyr, lay supine beneath
the chief lion. Swanson claimed DeMille was ready to omit it, after
two earlier shots almost ended in disaster when the lions made a
move towards Gloria and she had to be whisked away bodily by the
trainer before ending up as lunch. But Gloria insisted: '"Oh please,
Mr. De Mille . . . you've said right from the start that you wanted the
scene of *The Lion's Bride*." . . . "All right, young fellow," he said,
almost bursting with anticipation, "Let's go," and with that he took
me by the hand and down the steps to the lions' arena.'

As she lay down, one of the trainers whispered something to
DeMille, who came down and asked her a question no woman would
wish to be asked in these circumstances: 'Are you menstruating?'
Luckily she was not. Gloria continues:

I could hear the lion breathing near me. They put a piece of canvas on my
back to keep the lion's manicured claws from making the slightest scratch.
Then they brought the lion up to me and put his paw on the canvas. Ever so
slowly they pulled the canvas aside until I could feel his paw on my skin.

Every hair on my head was standing on end. I could hear the camera grinding and then the crack of the trainer's whip. Every cell in my body quivered when the animal roared. His hot breath seemed to go up and down my spine.

To cap it all, Gloria's father, the army officer, was on the set, 'his eyes almost popping out of his head'. One wonders what his thoughts of DeMille were at that moment. And all this for $350 a week!

DeMille's reaction at the end of the scene was, according to Swanson, to sit her on his knee and offer her the choice of 'a velvet tray covered with brooches, rings, necklaces, and a whole array of beautiful jewelry'. She chose 'a delicate little gold-mesh purse with a square sapphire in the center'.

Cecil was certainly getting a pretty good deal. Today, when almost any effect or combination of images can be created on screen with computer wizardry, it is hard to know what a contemporary audience might make of this splendiferous long shot, beauty under the beast, with the long train of her gown stretching back up over the steps of the den. It is certainly one of the great images of the silent screen, of any film since the first whirring of the cameras of Edison and Lumière. And, of course, it is completely superfluous to the needs of the plot!

Zukor's forecast for the film was borne out by the box office. *Male and Female* became the first DeMille movie to gross over $1 million. At a cost of over $180,000, it was Cecil's second-most expensive movie, after *Joan the Woman*, but it was Paramount's most successful release to date.

Gloria Swanson was now one of Hollywood's biggest stars, at the age of twenty-two, and it was only a matter of time before she would realize, her eyes opened by Herbert Somborn, that she was being paid peanuts under her current Lasky contract. 'Everyone is cashing in on you, darling,' Somborn told her. 'It's about time you did too.'

At the end of the Crichton tale, Lady Mary returns to her previous fiancé, Lord Brockelhurst, and Crichton goes off with kitchen maid Tweeny to a new life farming in the American west, although in Barrie's play he replies to Lady Mary's claim that 'you are the best man among us' with: 'on an island, perhaps; but in England, no'. 'Then there's something wrong with England,' says Lady Mary, but Crichton rebukes her: 'My lady, not even from you can I listen to a word against England.' The servant, as ever, remains the best guarantor of the persistence of power.

Swanson would remain, for a while, in DeMille's repertory company, partnering Thomas Meighan in the next movie in line, the aforementioned *Why Change Your Wife?* This too gobbled $1 million at the box office.

If ever DeMille had thought he was being constrained, he was not now. He was indeed the monarch of all he surveyed. But still something was nagging at him. The perfect job. The perfect life. The perfect wife. The perfect, discreet mistresses. Yet something was not right in this best of all possible worlds. Despite the boom in business, there was still turmoil in the nation and abroad. Europe was recovering from cataclysm. Revolution had transformed Russia, quite in what way no one was sure. In America, the great Red Scare of the last months of 1919 had made foreigners, immigrants and trade unions suspect. Blacks were being attacked, Jews stigmatized. The reformists had triumphed with the Prohibition of alcohol, but 'Normalcy' had not banished poverty, nor found enough jobs for returning soldiers.

Cecil, unlike brother William, had never been a social crusader, but the liberal bent of his family left marks, dents and dimples on his thinking. Some whispering chorus, a paternal ghost perhaps, appeared to be murmuring in his ear that a force other than box office might intervene in this world.

Thought Trained Upon a Deeper Motive

From the *New York Dramatic Mirror*, 12 June 1920:

THE HEART AND SOUL OF MOTION PICTURES
By Cecil B. DeMille

Motion pictures are like people in many respects . . . There are good people and bad, clever people and stupid, interesting people and dull. It is the same with motion pictures. But when all is said and done we return to the sincere person whose understanding of the word charity is literal, whose love of his fellow man is something more than a mere profession.

The motion picture which is brilliant, sumptuous, lovely in investiture of thought, and has as its core something that touches the fibres of our being; which partakes of the essence of humanity and warms us with its fund of sympathy – is an ideal worth striving for . . . [The producer] must realize that the world is peopled by millions of human beings, each with a set of human opinions and thoughts; that these comprise his audiences and that to them he must tell a story that is understandable to the least as well as the greatest . . .

Out of the war has been born a great wave of mysticism that is sweeping across the world. It finds expression in everything from table rapping to the outcropping of new religious movements . . . All of this may be superficial in a degree, but beneath it some tremendous truth is struggling for expression . . .

What is the heart and soul of motion pictures?

What is it but the truth about man and woman? The utmost of realism, the highest of ideals, the sincerest of life.

Problems must vanish in the light of truth. By depicting these problems and elucidating their solution, we can do a service for humanity, even as we entertain . . .

I recognize certain faults, for example in my earlier productions which I have been able to eliminate in later ones. I have grown closer and closer to the heart of the people, I think . . . Motion pictures are something more than mere amusement. They have a distinct value as an educational institution, and as a moulder of public opinion are far superior to the newspaper. The producer cannot merely say: 'I will make an amusing picture.' Behind it there must be thought trained upon a deeper motive . . .

'I shall make better pictures next year', wrote DeMille, 'than this, just as I believe I made better pictures last year than the year before.' Self-improvement was ever the way to set an example, in private as well as in public life. The home life of the DeMille family was now settled into the structure that Cecil had decreed and then stamped his authority upon, just as he stamped on the desk and chairs at his honeymoon. In 1920, the DeMilles adopted another child, nine-year-old Katherine Lester, an orphan whose father had died in the war in France and her mother of tuberculosis soon after. The English family from which her father came had disapproved of his marriage and would not take charge of the child. Constance DeMille gathered her up from the orphanage, and she joined twelve-year-old Cecilia and seven-year-old adoptee John. The fourth child, Richard, was to appear in 1922. The paterfamilias now had a suitably large brood, augmented by brother William's own fifteen-year-old Agnes and twelve-year-old Margaret, to grace his Christmas dinner table. Cecil DeMille had many good reasons to be thankful for his lot in life, and proceeded to apply his thoughts and principles to the widest possible audience.

Post-war America, as DeMille had noted in his article, was struggling to come to terms with the creative and destructive elements of science and technology and the age-old search for a spiritual 'truth'. The secular jazz age and its hedonistic embrace seemed, from the start, to afflict Cecil with a deep feeling of ambivalence. On the one hand, he was building his fortune from the depiction of its excesses. It was enabling him to examine the emotional dramas of his time, just as brother William had attempted in his era on the stage. Success might be seen to be its own reward. But the search for a spiritual dimension was no new fad for the DeMilles. It echoed down the years from Henry De Mille, the father lost in childhood, a siren call of old Protestant cautions.

Strange auguries of divine intervention, as we have seen, had found their way into Cecil's films, from the enduring Christ of *The Little American*, through the sombre intertitles of *The Whispering Chorus*, to the opening credo of *Male and Female*, presenting, after portentous opening shots of sky, sea and canyon, the lines of Genesis 1:27:

'So God created Man in His own image; in the image of God created He him; Male and Female created He them.'

Although in his first five years as a film-maker DeMille had not attempted any biblical narratives, he was beginning to look for a project that would fit the quest for spiritual meaning. Lasky had offered him a script based on Maurice V. Samuel's 1917 play *The Wanderer*, a Bible spectacle based on the parable of the prodigal son. David Belasco was apparently keen on this idea. Religious pictures had been made since the first years of the cinema. The Italians had produced the epic *Quo Vadis* in 1912, and the US had seen many efforts, from *From the Manger to the Cross* to Griffith's *Judith of Bethulia*. By 1915, there had been four versions of *Samson*, and 1914 had seen a first feature version of *The Sign of the Cross*, the tale of Nero and the Christians – which DeMille was to remake in 1932.

The Wanderer was eventually made in 1925, not by DeMille but by Raoul Walsh. As ever, various proposed projects came and went, and DeMille had no shortage of options. He chose to make *Something to Think About*, an original script co-written with Jeanie Macpherson. It was to be DeMille's first overtly religious film, but it was still set in contemporary America.

This is the first title of a small group within DeMille's oeuvre that might be dubbed 'Cecil's Arcana', films that represent DeMille operating with his greatest freedom from studio convention but also with his most extreme eccentricity.

The plot line is frankly bizarre: in the small town of Clearwater lives David Markley, a 'young' philosopher (played by Elliott Dexter) who is avowedly secular and collects artifacts of non-Christian cultures, like Japanese figurines. He has a housekeeper, played by Claire McDowell, whose stern edicts on God rain down on him like bolts from the Protestant Avenger: 'Someday you'll wish you knew Him better.' But Markley does not believe. Perhaps for this reason he is a cripple, moving around on crutches.

Elsewhere in town lives Luke Anderson, the blacksmith, the 'Iron Man' – Theodore Roberts – and his teenage daughter – Gloria Swanson. David Markley teaches her geography and pays to send her to be properly schooled. On her return, he contemplates the 'Pygmalion' he has created and falls in love, but is bound by his crutches. Her father suggests she owes David the debt of marriage, but there is a rival in town, a young virile man, Jim Dirk – played by Monte Blue.

Gloria becomes engaged to David. But at the county fair, where the 'Iron Man' displays his prowess in the Strong Man contest, a fairground lout makes eyes at Gloria and jeers at her companion. Dirk cries out: 'Can't you see he's a cripple?' and beats up the lout. A clown, played by Theodore Kosloff, states the edict of Fate to David: 'The strongest man always wins!'

As Jim decides to leave town to seek his fortune elsewhere, the inevitable happens: Gloria elopes with him, leaving David alone in 'the room of dead hopes'. The clown mocks him in the mirror, and the housekeeper tries to console him, to no avail: 'Not the strong man wins – but the right man . . . God has given you the right to happiness.' The 'Iron Man', Luke, utters a curse on his daughter: 'I never want to see her face again.' He promptly gets his wish and goes blind.

In the big city, Jim Dirk toils to build the subway, while Gloria counts her pennies, poor and pregnant. In a spectacular accident scene which DeMille will revisit again and again, the river bursts into the underground works and Dirk is drowned. Gloria learns of this from a newspaper headline: 'CAVE IN ON NEWTON TUNNEL'. The body is not recovered.

Gloria falls. Toiling in a laundry but too fatigued by her condition, she loses her job. She considers suicide in the river and sinks down on a bench in the park. A beggar steals her purse, but advises her to go back to her folks if she has any. The purse is empty.

Back in Clearwater, the 'Iron Man' now packs boxes for the poorhouse. Gloria finds him and reveals herself, but he rejects her. 'I guess I can go the rest of the way alone,' she muses. DeMille takes her into a dilapidated, bat-ridden barn, where a rope swings, appearing as the shadow of a noose on the ground.

Miraculously, David Markley finds her before the deed. She tells him: 'Jim's dead. I've seen my father. There's nothing left.' He sees the baby cap she's holding and realizes her situation. He offers to marry her for 'the protection of my name . . . I'm not asking for love – for mine is dead.'

In the years that follow, the loveless marriage drags on. There is a small boy in a sailor's suit. David and wife eat at either end of a long table. And the housekeeper's Voice of God intervenes: 'When are you going to give up worshipping PRIDE and BITTERNESS – and give

LOVE a chance.' But David still rejects the 'Sunday School talk'.

While Luke fishes in the river, the small boy approaches him, asking for a bite of his apple before realizing the old man is blind. In the household, the housekeeper works on Gloria: 'Dear little girl, you have tried every human means to bring your husband back to you, and failed! Let's drop the human mind, for a while, and work with the Divine!' Close-up on the Holy Bible. 'God's Law does not fail! – Love is Stronger than Hate!' Cut to child, telling Luke his own grandfather is blind too. Luke recognizes this is his own grandchild and hugs him. They catch the fish. The housekeeper and Gloria pray for David to hear 'the Call of God – the Unbeliever shall Believe – for Truth destroys the false Gods!' David drops his crutches and walks towards Gloria – the intertitle proclaiming: 'Many waters cannot quench love, neither can the floods drown it.' The old man and the child, with fishing rod, enter the gate of the house. The housekeeper holds the crutches: 'I thank thee my Father – thou hast heard me!'

Spotlight on her face – and THE END.

Although Paramount trumpeted the film as 'A Picture that Will Be The Talk of America', critics were puzzled by the sudden switch in the inclinations of the erstwhile master of the satirical domestic drama. DeMille 'has taken upon himself the burden of giving expression to the spiritual drama,' said *Motion Picture News*, 'thus stopping the critics who took him to task for reveling in sex.' While 'the production itself is flawless . . . the subtitles are often preachy and too much drama is told through them.'

Variety complained that 'the "faith cure" episode is exceedingly implausible and difficult to swallow and at other times the motives and emotions of the characters are obscure and unreasonable.' And the *New York Times* noted that 'all this may be impressive to some . . . but its effect upon others is unmistakeably indicated in the overheard exclamation of a woman, neither frivolous nor cynical by nature, who said impulsively, at the story's most ecstatic moment, when David was about to drop his crutches and reveal the miracle of his new-found love and strength, "Look what stunning patch pockets Elliott Dexter has on his coat."'

'Praise and blame for the authorship of the story', wrote the *Times*, 'must go to Jeanie Macpherson.' Which must be so, as DeMille had apparently given her a free hand in the project. It was indeed the first production under a new five-year contract that DeMille had negotiated with Famous Players-Lasky. He had also formed his own new company, Cecil B. DeMille Productions, with his lawyer, his wife and Constance's stepmother Ella King Adams, who also happened to be his script reader.

The family concern provided an extra layer of protection in case of trouble – a wise precaution, as things turned out. The industry, as ever, was consumed with its endless financial shenanigans: would Adolph Zukor continue to control the studio? Who would earn what for whom? and so forth (the Famous Players-Lasky Corporation posted a profit of $3 million at the end of December 1919). Artistically, *Something to Think About* was the first DeMille film on which cameraman Karl Struss, who was to become one of Holly-wood's most proficient and prolific directors of photography, was brought in to work with Alvin Wyckoff. The spare, very contrasty black-and-white images in Wilfred Buckland's spare and uncluttered sets contributed mightily to the sombre look of the film.

There was no getting away, however, from the profusion of symbols that cascaded from the screen: the cripple's crutches, the 'Iron Man' who becomes a blinded giant, the oriental idols, the oracle jester, the underground cavern in which Dirk is drowned, the soulless city, mirrors, water dashing on rocks, the blind man's fishing rod and apple. DeMille seems to have intended the God-obsessed house-keeper to be a fount of inspiration, but why then did Jeanie Macpherson write her as a fanatic? The tensions between writer and director on religious themes would recur when they were to tackle the monumental subjects of *The Ten Commandments* and *King of Kings*.

Like the woman noted by the *New York Times* who preferred to focus on Elliott Dexter's snazzy patches rather than the moral uplift, it was clear that many people saw the film as mere claptrap. Nevertheless, given DeMille's track record, and with another Lasky–Zukor ad campaign hammering the message home, it still grossed over $900,000 for a cost of $169,000.

The man who couldn't stand still moved on again, producing on a lavish budget – double that of his previous film – a remake of his own 1915 film *The Golden Chance*, with the title *Forbidden Fruit*. Better sets, more lavish costumes and more pointed comparisons between the rich and poor characters did not, however, make it a better film. The tale of the fallen society woman who gets a chance to impersonate a woman of the class she once belonged to, only to be enmeshed in a criminal act by her ne'er-do-well husband, remained the same. DeMille inserted a 'Cinderella' sequence, with a masked costume ball and opulent fountains, to point up the symbolism of the story and used inserts of this scene in the corner of some intertitles, a neat and economic trick. When her husband Steve thinks of his scheme to blackmail the rich couple who have traduced his wife, dollar signs appear in his eyes. Unlike the ambivalent and poignant glance between the lovers which ends the 1915 version, the 1921 remake offers an epilogue on a country-house porch in which Prince Charming finds his lady of the slipper, only to find her foot is too big.

The fine clothes that were only in the domain of the very rich have now become attainable as lifestyle accessories, no longer fabulous but mere brand names: gowns by Poiret, perfumes by Coty, jewelry from Tiffany's. 'Think how Cinderella would envy you,' says the snobbish hostess, Mrs Mallory.

American movies had, in general, made a quantum leap in the two boom years since the end of the war. February 1921 saw the release of Rex Ingram's *Four Horsemen of the Apocalypse* – with its new young star Rudolph Valentino an instant sensation – which was lauded as one of the 'few immortal pictures that have been produced'. There were new benchmarks to be surpassed.

At the end of January 1921, DeMille completed his fortieth picture since *The Squaw Man*, at about half the cost of *Forbidden Fruit*. It was to be the last of his classic social-satire dramas, and his last movie starring Gloria Swanson. It was also his first film without his regular art director, Wilfred Buckland, who had left him to join director Allan Dwan's new independent company rather than toil on in the Lasky mills. To replace him, Cecil recruited the previously mentioned Paul Iribe, the French designer of all things ultra-modern. Iribe had designed some of Swanson's costumes in *Male and Female*, and he helped to deliver the best-looking film of DeMille's silent period. Its imagery was also enhanced by Alvin Wyckoff's new fellow cameraman, Karl Struss.

The film began its life with the working title 'Five Kisses', but it was released, with one kiss shorn off on the way, as *The Affairs of Anatol*. Luckily, it is available today in an excellent DVD version, with its original colour tints and ornate titles restored in all their gaudy pinks, purples, reds and blues. This enables us to see DeMille at the height of his powers as a master of cinema, presenting:

The Affairs of Anatol
by Jeanie Macpherson
Suggested by Arthur Schnitzler's Play of the Same Name

The opening credit, with the addition of an 'appreciation' to co-writers Beulah Marie Dix and Elmer Harris for their 'literary assistance', contains its own caveat concerning the script's source. *Anatol* had been a cycle of ten short plays, the earliest dating from 1892. Later Schnitzler plays, observing the merry-go-round of turn-of-the-century Vienna's moneyed elite, were influenced by the new theories of local savant Sigmund Freud, whose *Interpretation of Dreams* was published in 1899. By the 1920s, Freud's name had long been familiar in American circles too.

The plays' anti-hero, Anatol, comments at one point in Schnitzler's text that 'I've sometimes fancied I have a sort of evil eye turned inwards, to wither my own happiness.' Schnitzler introduces him, in the first one-act play, *Ask No Questions and You'll Hear No Stories*, as:

Anatol, an idle young bachelor, lives in a charming flat in Vienna. That he has taste, besides means to indulge it, may be seen by his rooms, the furniture he buys, the pictures he hangs on the walls. And if such things indicate character, one would judge, first by the material comfort of the place and then by the impatience for new ideas which his sense of what is beautiful to live with seems to show, that though a hedonist, he is sceptical of even that easy faith . . .

DeMille and Macpherson's adaptation mutated Anatol – played in the film by Wallace Reid – from the amoral charmer who flits from woman to woman to a less censorable 'romantic young man who has a passion for saving ladies from real, or imaginary difficulties'. To armour-plate him further from the reformers who, flushed with the success of Prohibition, were about to pass a censorship bill in New York state, the screen-writers gave him a wife, Vivien, played by Gloria Swanson. Her role during most of the picture is to be ornately petulant and smoulder. And so the story begins:

At the Green Fan, a lush nightclub, Anatol and his new wife are out with his best friend Max (a staple of the Schnitzler plays) – a restrained role for DeMille regular Elliott Dexter. At a nearby table,

The Affairs of Anatol – Wallace Reid and Gloria Swanson

Anatol spots an old school sweetheart, now good-time girl, Emilie (played by Wanda Hawley), who seems to be elegantly suffering under the yoke of glowering, brutish Theodore Roberts as Bronson, her 'theatrical backer' and sugar daddy. A title tells us he is yet another 'Man of Iron', also known in the night haunts as the 'Man of Dough'. Anatol vows to save Emilie with Vivien's help, but Vivien refuses to be part of this process. Emilie is eager to be saved by Anatol but loath to give up the lovely jewels gifted her by Bronson. And thus a typical merry-go-round unfolds.

Schnitzler's Vienna morphed into DeMille's New York, a studio-bound fantasy, from the art-nouveau fittings of the Green Fan to the oriental lamps, curtains, statuettes, goblets, ornate tables and dressers carefully placed in every scene. The only exterior shots in the city represent the Brooklyn Bridge, from which Emilie is made to cast her boxes of jewellery into the river, though she has stashed the gems and only throws away the empty boxes.

More exteriors, shot near the Lasky studio, occur in the second seduction sub-plot, in which Anatol falls for a flighty farmer's wife, who has purloined her husband's church funds to buy dresses, is found out and attempts to drown herself in the river. Fortunately she splashes down just as Anatol and Vivien, out to escape the 'rotten life' of the city in the 'pure' countryside, pass by in a boat. Anatol rescues her, but she plays him for a sucker, stealing his wallet and a kiss while Vivien is calling a doctor. She arrives just in time to catch the kiss, and Anatol is misunderstood again.

Back in the city, Anatol, angered by his wife's 'unreasonable' suspicions, goes out to the most sordid place he can find: the boudoir of exotic dancer Satan Synne, 'the most wicked woman in New York' – a star vamp turn by Bebe Daniels. Here the set design becomes positively outlandish, with Miss Synne's black bed, pet leopard lurking beneath it, dominated by Hades-like painted clouds and a bat-winged mirror. The maid is dressed in oriental mode with matching chains. As if realizing they have gone too far, DeMille and Jeanie Macpherson have given Satan Synne an ironic 'honest' secret: she is ready to sell body and soul to pay for an operation to save the life of her badly wounded off-screen husband, a war casualty now forgotten by his country. Anatol, of course, unfurls his cheque book. 'The Devil's not a man, but a WOMAN!' the un-wicked Synne tells him. 'That's what every woman knows, but doesn't tell.'

As if this were not enough, we have already had a cameo by Theodore Kosloff hamming it up as Nazzer Singh, a Hindu hypnotist who makes Vivien take off her shoes and stockings in a trance. Wyckoff and Struss have shone two baby spots in his eyes, a trick F. W. Murnau was to use to great effect for Emil Jannings' Mephistopheles in his 1925 *Faust*.

Even in this sleazy milieu, the divine retains some oversight, the stern words of DeMille interposing in the intertitles: 'No sooner is a temple built to God – but the Devil builds a chapel hard by.' Fun, in *The Affairs of Anatol*, is invariably presented as decadence. Emilie's apartment buzzes with her friends, assertive and chic women who smoke and drink in private – 'It's Anatol! Quick, hide the cocktails!' And her big party with Bronson and his rakish mates is interrupted by Anatol, who proceeds to wreck the joint, smashing the table, chairs, mirrors and furniture, throwing a sofa through the window and even managing to demolish the piano. As poor Emilie sobs in the ruins, Bronson's hand, dangling a string of pearls, comes into frame, brushing her face. 'For centuries,' the intertitle intones portentously, 'the Moth has been lured by the Flame, and no amount of moralising can keep it from the Flame.'

To sugar the pill, the American Anatol has the option of returning to his real sweetheart, wife Vivien, who, towards the end, decides that two can play at the game of kicking over the traces and goes out on the town with Anatol's best friend Max. As a *deus ex machina*, hypnotist Kosloff enters at the finale, conveniently placed to put Vivien under so that her husband can question her to see if she really loves him. But should he ask, thereby proving his own fundamental mistrust of her, or should he take her true love on faith? Buy the DVD and find out.

In the end, one feels that DeMille would agree with Shakespeare that the answer lies 'not in our stars, but in our selves', although there is not much sight, in this delicious concoction, of DeMille's pledge to the *New York Dramatic Mirror* to train the film-maker's thought 'upon a deeper motive . . .'

DeMille's male lead in *Anatol*, Wallace Reid, returning after a long absence from the DeMille repertory crew, had come a long way from the moment he had been spotted as a muscle-bound blacksmith in Griffith's *Birth of a Nation*. He had matured and had learned to project a kind of manly melancholia which made his legion of female fans swoon. But there was a poisonous snake in his garden. The official tale has it that Reid had been badly hurt in a train accident during the filming of *The Valley of the Giants* in 1919, and had become addicted to the morphine he was prescribed in hospital. Alcoholic depression added to his woes, and even his rugged physique began to crumble. Other gossips claimed he was a primary source of the 'joy-powder' happily adopted by the movie colony's nouveau-riche carousers.

Rumbles against the Hollywood high life – in more senses than one – were to culminate in the moralists' backlash that occurred over the Fatty Arbuckle scandal: on 10 September 1921, just before *The Affairs of Anatol* was due to open, the famous and popular comedian was arrested on suspicion of raping an actress, Virginia Rappe, during a rowdy film-makers' party at a San Francisco hotel. The girl died soon after. Arbuckle was tried three times before being acquitted, but the damage to Hollywood had already been done. Ex-postmaster general Will Hays was brought in as the industry's own censor to purge the movies of their sins. Another scandal, the mysterious killing of director William Desmond Taylor, which involved rumours of drug-taking, multiple love affairs, occult connections and homosexual relations, followed in February 1922, prompting ever louder calls for a clampdown.

In March of the same year, Wallace Reid's wife, the actress Dorothy Davenport, committed him to a sanatorium, and his drug addiction was revealed to the world. He had managed to appear in nine more films after *The Affairs of Anatol*, but he died in the asylum on 18 January 1923, just short of his thirty-second birthday.

Fool's Paradigms?

Not everybody loved *The Affairs of Anatol. Variety* moaned in its usual manner that, despite the galaxy of stars, it was 'not a good picture. Perhaps too many cooks tend to spoil the broth, or it may have been the scenario . . . The impression of the auditor as it unfolds is that situations are forced. It lacks spontaneity, suspense and comprehensive appeal.'

But despite the atmosphere of anti-Hollywood moralizing, the film was another million-dollar hit for DeMille. Paramount published ecstatic notices from exhibitors around the country. From the Rialto Theatre, New Haven: '"Anatol" opened yesterday to biggest crowds in history of Rialto, breaking all box office records . . .' From Kansas City, Missouri: 'They fought like mad to get in.' From Youngstown, Ohio: 'Thousands turned away. Congratulations to all responsible for this wonderful attraction.'

Nevertheless, censorship and the moralists' backlash would have its effect on future films. Henceforth, the wormwood drip of absinthe into Anatol's cup or the funny cigarillos of Satan Synne, branded with her own 'SS' mark, would be much more difficult to get away with. Earlier in the year, in the spring of 1921, Jesse Lasky had come out strongly against the curtailment of movie themes by any force other than the audience itself, the 'power of public opinion'. He criticized those 'loose thinkers [who] have criticized certain pictures because they could not take their children to them. This is really arrant nonsense. Let us have done with the thought that the photoplay is primarily for children . . . We makers of screen drama aim to serve the majority and not any specialized group. The motion picture, with the help of the public, is just beginning to fulfill the mission that the intelligent families of the nation are demanding of it.' But by the autumn of 1921, this argument was losing ground. The moral guardians had a further feeding frenzy that summer upon Erich von

Stroheim's *Foolish Wives*, released about the same time as DeMille's *Anatol* and an even sleazier tale of adulterous vice. Stroheim's 1919 movie *Blind Husbands* had introduced American audiences to characters who made Cecil's wayward spouses look like wedding-cake decorations. But the funeral bell was tolling for this particular theme.

More worrying for Lasky was the traditional downturn in the business cycle, which forced Paramount to cut its production costs by 25 per cent in July 1921. Throughout the year the company had been pressurizing its directors, DeMille included, to hold budgets down, at the very moment that DeMille was negotiating a new five-year contract with the studio. Agitated cables had passed back and forth between director and mogul over the cost of his next film, which was shot, as usual, before the previous one was to open. To cut its overall costs, the Lasky company was closing its New York studios and concentrating on the West Coast. DeMille was flirting with First National and United Artists, but in the event he stuck with Lasky and Zukor, and they stuck, for the moment, with him. He was, after all, a consistent money-maker. The next film, *Fool's Paradise*, though failing to breach the million-dollar mark in gross profits, was still a tidy earner.

Less well-known than DeMille's social-satire cycle, *Fool's Paradise* nevertheless is another entry in 'Cecil's Arcana', and arguably the strangest movie he ever made. To date, it is one more of the many Cecil B. DeMille films seen only by a handful of archivists, who tend to reel away from the viewing table with minds awhirl at a plot line which only DeMille could prevent from spiralling into utter chaos.

As in *The Whispering Chorus*, DeMille chose material from a popular but second-echelon writer, in this case Leonard Merrick, another fairly obscure name today. Merrick was a prolific author of lush tales that were described by one of his prefacers, A. Neil Lyons, as 'sermons' demonstrating that 'people who go out deliberately to look for happiness, to kick for it, and fight for it, or who try to buy it with money, will miss happiness; this being a state of heart . . . more often to be found by a careless and self-forgetful vagrant than by the deliberate and self-conscious seeker'.

The name of the original tale was 'The Laurels and the Lady'. The screenplay was not by Jeanie Macpherson but is credited to Beulah Marie Dix and Sada Cowan (co-writer of *Why Change Your Wife?*). Alvin Wyckoff and Karl Struss performed their usual magic with the camera.

Fool's Paradise unfolds as a savage dream, set in a world marked from the outset with DeMille's brand of the reversal of fortune. The first informative title of the movie tells us that:

The Arabian Nights offers no magic compared to a new oil town on the Mexican Border. As if some modern Aladdin had rubbed his silver lamp – what was yesterday gray Dust and Cactus flows now with Golden streams. Frenzied hope and black despair unheedingly brush elbows –

The story focuses on Arthur Phelps, a failed poet and ex-First World War soldier 'whose assets are all losses' in a place where 'Love and Life – and Derricks, are "For Sale" – cheap!' He lives in poverty with his dog, while all around him are the once low who have struck it rich: 'In a topsy turvy world where you see your Boot-Black in an automobile de-luxe and your Garbage Man in diamonds, it is poor consolation to live in a shack made of Packing-cases, Tin Cans – and Dreams.'

Arthur dreams of famous French dancer Rosa Duchene, whose picture and figurine decorate his meagre abode. He remembers her as an angel of mercy, come to the hospital at the front where he was recovering from shrapnel wounds to his eyes. She left him her handkerchief, which he still treasures. As he gazes at her figurine, it comes to life, dancing on his table.

Meanwhile, at a cantina on the other side of the border in Mexico, Poll Patchouli – 'Flower of the cactus, Untamed as the Desert Wind' – is fending off all-comers, including her protector-boyfriend, the knife-wielding Mexicano Rodriguez. In the dance hall, Poll saves a young innocent girl from being pawed by the customers and then flees Rodriguez's wrath, across the border. She fetches up at Arthur's shack and falls for him, but he is fixated on Rosa, who, he sees from a poster, is due to dance in the town. Poll goes off in a huff, and when Arthur next visits her cantina, she gives him, as a practical joke, an exploding cigar.

Arthur pockets the cigar as he goes to the stage door to greet his dream beloved, Rosa. As she steps from her coach, she recognizes him as the soldier she once gave her handkerchief to, but then hurries within. The day is blustery and cold. At the stage door, musing of his dream come true, Arthur lights the cigar, which explodes, right in his damaged eyes. A hairy, claw-like hand closes upon his face. He staggers into the theatre, watching Rosa's dance of *The Snow Queen* through a grey, rippling blur. A whirl of activity on stage relates the magical tale of the lover bewitched by the queen, who cries out: 'Nevair shall you return to ze mortal Love you have throw aside! For your heart ees ICE – and belongs to me!'

In the midst of a bizarre swirl of sledge-carrying bears, fake snowflakes, a bevy of ice-skaters and a magic carpet on the stage, in the audience Arthur goes blind, shouting out, as the performance ends: 'Why don't they turn on the lights?' Poll rushes to him as he staggers in the empty theatre, but recognizing her voice, he cries at her: 'Don't ever touch me again – or I'll kill you!'

The scene is now set for the central twist of the tale: Arthur seeks work, but no one will employ a blind man, and he is mocked at the cantina. Poll, entering his shack, pretends to be Rosa, and he tells her his blindness was caused by the woman who gave him an exploding cigar. Caught by her own subterfuge, and knowing he will reject her if he discovers the truth, Poll stays with him as Rosa, listening as he reads her his rejected poems. She declares: 'I love you – and I stay wiz you always!' He cries out: 'You mean you'd marry a blind, penniless failure like me?'

Intertitle: 'And so begins the strangest masquerade that a woman ever dared! When Arthur, believing that he is marrying the woman he loves – weds the woman he hates – and the sunlight denied his eyes dwells at last in his heart!'

The subterfuge deepens when Arthur's poems come back rejected by the publishers yet again, but Poll, reading their letter, pretends that he has been accepted, presenting him her cookbook, *Cooking for Two*, as his newly published poems.

Time passes, and then the plot twists again, as we see Poll reading a newspaper headline: 'BLIND MEN MADE TO SEE – Dr J. B. Sanders, the Famous War Surgeon, has come to El Paso – the Saviour of the Blind'.

A demonic title pops into Poll's mind: 'If he stays blind – he's yours! If he's cured – he's hers!'

Her better self prevails, and he becomes set on the miracle cure. DeMille the story-teller hurries the narrative along, lest we have time to dwell on its crazy lurches. The operation is performed: 'As the young Doctor of Hope City removes the bandages – he sees!' Arthur realizes the truth, that 'Rosa' is Poll Patchouli, the very cause of his tragedy, and his 'poetry' book is just the cookbook. He realizes his 'Fool's Paradise' –

Just then, a group of men rush in suddenly to tell Arthur that 'Blake's Wildcat Well, next to your land, has come in with 50,000 barrels – your land is worth a million!'

Reversal of fortune strikes again, and Phelps, sighted but embittered, is now a millionaire. He leaves Poll and goes forth to find 'the woman I love'. She is left alone, viewing herself in the mirror, bitterly reflecting: 'You've worked for him, and cooked for him, and slaved for him – and the OTHER WOMAN gets him!' She sets fire to Arthur's photograph and his shack, lighting a cigar with his burning poems.

Just when you think this story can't get any weirder, we segue into a completely different setting: while Arthur Phelps has been in his Fool's Paradise, Rosa Duchene has been touring the exotic Far East, 'studying the ancient temple dances of Siam'. Cue pagodas, elephants, Thai dancers. Rosa is now the beloved of the local ruler, Prince Talaat-Ni, whose wife is smouldering with eastern jealousy. 'Half way round the world', Arthur, now rich, has tracked down Rosa. He enters the temple and faces her. Once again she remembers the soldier, as he approaches her exclaiming: 'If you give me an hour – I have the strangest story to tell you, that a man ever told a woman.'

While, in El Paso, Poll lights Rodriguez's cigar with a $5,000 cheque she has received for the annulment of her marriage to Phelps, in Siam, Arthur recites his poems to a bored Rosa, who prefers playing with a monkey. In his mind's eye, though, he sees the image of home-loving Poll . . .

Rosa still cleaves to her princely Thai lover, who invites her to the ceremony of 'the Living Sacrifices to the Sacred Reptiles'. She agrees to come, with Arthur as her American escort. Arthur kisses her, while her monkey screams.

Siam at night: the prince's barge floats downriver to the temple and the pit of crocodiles. A living sheep is thrown down to the reptiles. Arthur, outraged, rescues the sheep. Riot and confusion in the profaned temple. Rosa allows her glove to fall in the crocodile pit. Playing with the rivals for her hand, she declares she'll love the one who's man enough to get her glove. The prince climbs down into the pit.

Arthur: 'Is that your idea of *Love* – sending a man to his death – just to satisfy a whim?' The prince falls; Arthur jumps in to save him, beating off the crocs. The princess helps him get the prince back up

Blind love and sacrifice in *Fool's Paradise*: Conrad Nagel,
Dorothy Dalton and Theodore Kosloff

and cradles her hubby. Rosa to Arthur: 'You were wonderful – my soldier boy!' Arthur: 'The prince is entitled to your embraces – he got your glove!' He is disillusioned: 'You've never loved anything except yourself – but you've shown me the Heaven I've lost – and I'm going back to find it!'

Rosa, rejected by both prince and pauper, starts thinking about 'The Dance of the Prince's Glove', while the crocs slink frustrated in their pit.

And now DeMille's long-awaited intertitle motto:

'Not in the plaudits of the Throng – Nor in the Crowded Street – but in Ourselves – Are Triumph and Defeat!'

Back in Mexico, Poll dances in her saloon, Rodriguez wooing her with a wedding dress, but suddenly Arthur's dog is at her feet, and then Arthur, rushing in to tell her what a fool he was – 'It's you I love!' But she spurns him, embracing Rodriguez. The Mexican throws his knife at Arthur, but it strikes Poll, who has moved to protect him. She breathes out to Rodriguez: 'I love him!' Arthur carries her inert body out of the saloon.

Title: 'But the ONE who sees everything – always gives his Blind Children one more chance – to come up into the light'. Poll is nursed back to life in a rest home, as Arthur greets her with his dog.

'Will you marry me now, with eyes open?'

Apparently she will.

THE END.

It is difficult enough to convey in words any film, least of all a tale as fundamentally extravagant as this. Without Jeanie Macpherson's flashbacks to mythologically 'significant' moments, the story unfolds in seamless order, Anne Bauchen's cutting taking the scenes effort-lessly from moment to moment, until one loses sight of the fact that none of it makes 'normal' sense in the real world most of us inhabit. Whereas Satan Synne, faux exotic as she may be, could be easily imag-ined in New York's 1920s night-spot phantasms, the convoluted tale of Poll Patchouli and Arthur Phelps is consistent only in its inconsis-tency with what DeMille himself would usually describe as 'realism'. But the story-teller/film-maker's craft is evident in every sequence, making the most unlikely events convincing, in that ultimate suspen-sion of disbelief craved by any author. And yet *Fool's Paradise* is not a genre tale of fantasy, horror or gothic melodrama but a story set, in its own manner, in the contemporary world. Unreal, but real – the essence, surely, of the twentieth-century motion picture.

DeMille knew, as many makers of films from their 1890s begin-nings understood, long before intellectuals deployed the Freudian impact on narrative, that all films are dream-like, though some more so than others. One does not require complex theories to grasp this, merely the experience of sitting in a darkened theatre. But I have no doubt that, by choosing certain source material, Cecil was experi-menting with the effect of making an audience believe the utterly unbelievable.

From this point on, in fact, Cecil's films, though shot in a conven-tional manner, as far as composition and the by now standard light-ing for mood were concerned, were to slip further and further away from the Hollywood convention of realism. One might call these ele-ments of his work surreal, were they not combined, more and more, with a moralizing tone which conveyed Cecil's growing unease with what he saw as a promiscuous and dangerous age. The stage was being set for the foray to come into the overt embrace of religious themes, which was to be Cecil B. DeMille's most enduring legacy. From here on, the fantastic, the outlandish and often the bizarre would be major tools in his arsenal, his box of cinematic tricks that would continue to dazzle and confuse those who thought they could pin DeMille down.

In terms of casting, *Fool's Paradise* was another turning point. Gloria Swanson had departed to other pastures, and gone were Wallace Reid, Elliott Dexter, Raymond Hatton and even Theodore Roberts, all long-term regulars. Arthur Phelps was played by Conrad Nagel, one of Hollywood's longest-lasting actors. He had moved from stage to screen in 1918 and would clock over one hundred and ten film appearances, as well as live television performances, before his death in 1970. (He was a co-founder and later president of the Academy of Motion Picture Arts and Sciences, but was blacklisted by several studios in the 1930s because of his founding of the Screen Actors' Guild.) Nagel gave Arthur a desperate integrity which carried him through the thorny assignment of making his absurd folly work. Dorothy Dalton, already a silent film star, portrayed the mercurial Poll Patchouli. She too would live long, surviving till 1972, but retired from the screen in 1924 after marrying theatre mogul Arthur Hammerstein.

Rosa Duchene, femme most fatale, was played by Mildred Harris, fresh from a divorce from Charlie Chaplin, whom she had married, aged only sixteen, in 1918. She had been a child star in the movies, making her debut in 1912, and would appear thirty years later in two of Cecil's wartime talkies, *Reap the Wild Wind* and *The Story of Dr Wassell*. DeMille had the proverbial elephant's memory and a fondness for his actors that never dimmed. Julia Faye, his long-term mistress, had her part as the luscious Thai Princess Samaran. Theodore Kosloff bagged the role of the jealous knife-wielding Mexican.

Despite its strange narrative, the critics gave *Fool's Paradise* an easy ride, with even *Variety* praising the lavish production. Special presentations at local premieres boosted promotion. For the opening at New York's Criterion cinema theatre-owner-cum-musical-director Hugo Riesenfeld arranged an 'unusual surrounding entertainment', featuring a 'prologue' that included a live ballet with a Colombine and 'Baby Doll'. In Seattle, when the film opened in April 1922, a special lobby display featured a Mexican cantina, with Spanish dancers and a mock-up of the 'alligator den, with cut-outs of the alligators, open-mouthed, in the foreground'. The ushers in the theatre wore Mexican costumes, and the prologue was a live replica of the movie's 'Dance of the Ice Palace'.

The promotional campaign also featured a full-page ad acclaiming 'CECIL B. DeMILLE'S HORN OF PLENTY FOR EXHIBITORS', with

money spilling out of a horn emblazoned with all of DeMille's titles, from *Old Wives for New* through to *Fool's Paradise*, a cornucopia of box-office delights. The ad was prefiguring Cecil's next production, *Saturday Night*, which followed hot on the heels of its predecessor. There was no sign, as yet, of the horn of plenty emptying. It seemed to retain an endless, miraculous capacity to renew its cargo of box-office gold . . .

Towards the Tablets of the Law

DeMille completed three films in 1922: *Saturday Night, Manslaughter* and *Adam's Rib*. In all three, Jeanie Macpherson kept God at bay, though in *Manslaughter* that was just by a whisker. All three were structured round the by now familiar theme of the reversal of fortune.

Saturday Night focused on two groups of characters, rich and poor, whose fortunes are symmetrically reversed. Laundry girl Shamrock O'Day and her neighbour Tom McGuire become entangled in the lives of blue-stocking Iris van Suydam (played by Leatrice Joy), who is 'one of the Lilies in Life's Hot House – who "Toils not, neither does she Spin"'. Her rich fiancé, Richard Prentiss (Conrad Nagel again), is 'tired of the silken women' of the upper classes. Their paths cross when Shamrock delivers laundry and falls down the stairs; Richard falls for her, and later Iris falls for Tom, who has become her chauffeur. Shamrock finds herself married to the snob set, bored and ostracized. Iris finds herself in Tom's noisy apartment by the railway line, mopping the floor, trying to learn to cook and vainly drawing a bath for Tom, who complains: 'Why a bath? It's only Tuesday!'

Shamrock gets Tom to be her chauffeur, and they end up at Coney Island, where they're trapped by a mechanical fault in the ferris wheel. Richard, searching for her, goes to Tom's home, where he finds Iris, who utters the immortal intertitle: 'Dick, you can't bind the woman you love with Pearls and Limousines, when she wants Chewing Gum! Nor can I hold Tom with Poetry – when he's hungry for Pie!'

So now Iris loves Tom, Dick loves Shamrock, Shamrock loves Tom, and it's time for the *deus ex machina* – the house catching fire. Tom rescues Shamrock, and Dick goes back into the blazing house to rescue Iris. Conclusion by Iris: 'I thought you both had forgotten me! But in the end, Dick, it's always – kind to kind!'

The film is DeMille in lighter mode, with many amusing scenes of social dislocation. But the previous ambivalence towards social trans-gression, wife switching and the temptations of hedonism has veered towards a clear-cut decision: the attempt to cut across the classes, however laudably democratic the aim, will not end well. Love, after all, cannot conquer class, even in movies. Despite the playful tone, the outcome of the story is pretty dour, and conformist to an unusual degree.

The technical and artistic qualities, however, were as strong as ever. Paul Iribe was now DeMille's regular art director and delivered lush settings for the upper-class mansion. Some old faces were back: Theodore Roberts as a stern uncle and Julia Faye as Iris's snobbish sister. Ex-child star Edith Roberts played Shamrock with great verve, but it was her only film for DeMille. Leatrice Joy, another veteran silent star, was at the time married to star actor John Gilbert, and her daughter claimed in a later biography that this marriage broke up due to Gilbert's accusation that she was having an affair with her director – a tale more likely than not.

Cecil B. DeMille was now forty-one years old and paterfamilias to an ever-growing brood. The DeMille family was about to gain a new member as a result of the birth, on 12 February 1922, of Richard, a baby who, it was announced to the press by family lawyer Neil McCarthy several months later, had been found on Cecil's doorstep and adopted in addition to John and Katherine. This scenario would hold for the next thirty-three years, until William de Mille's death in 1955. It was only then, after the funeral, with Richard himself already a father, that Cecil revealed to him the dramatic truth, as Richard relates in his 1992 book *My Secret Mother, Lorna Moon*:

'Before you were born,' Father said, 'your Uncle William and I agreed that whichever of us died first, the other would tell you about your parents. Your father was your Uncle William. Your mother was a writer. This is a book she wrote.' He handed me a slim black volume. The title was *Doorways in Drumorty*. Inside was an inscription: 'To my friend William de Mille, very tenderly, Lorna Moon.' It wasn't a name I recognised or remembered hear-ing before.

Cecil certainly preserved his flair for melodrama to the end! Lorna Moon had been a Scottish woman, married to an Englishman who was then killed in the Great War, leaving her with a daughter whom she in turn left behind with friends when she emigrated to New York. There she established herself as a writer, going to Hollywood as a scriptwriter in 1919. Brother William, ever the ladies' man, swept her up. In fact, she was his subsidiary mistress, as he was already engaged in a long-term relationship with another writer, Clara Beranger, who was to become his second wife in 1928. The birth of a child, a brother to Agnes and Margaret, to a mistress was clearly impossible to acknowledge. Lorna Moon, who was suffering from tuberculosis, felt she could not keep the child, and so he was 'found' on Cecil's doorstep at the age of nine months. This would have occurred during the filming of *Adam's Rib*.

Cecil's cornucopia continued with *Manslaughter*, shot between May and June 1922. The scenario by Jeanie Macpherson was this time an adaptation of a book by Alice Duer Miller. Cecil was not well during the shoot, as he had caught rheumatic fever while on a vacation to Europe, accompanied by Paul Iribe and his Japanese valet, Yamabe, taken immediately after completing *Saturday Night*. Robert Birchard suggests this weakened state may have accounted for the poorer quality of *Manslaughter*. But I do not think the film is poor. It simply represents an important shift in the direction and concerns of DeMille. What might be more significant is Cecil's claim that during their European tour he and Paul Iribe had gone to the Vatican in Rome for a prearranged audience with the Pope, Benedict XV. Dressed in their best attire, they presented themselves at 'the bronze doors of the Vatican', only to be turned away by the Swiss Guards. The Pope had died that very day, 22 January 1922.

This strange happenstance contrasted with another near encounter on that trip, with a 'very beautiful young lady' DeMille met in Paris, at Maxim's. She invited him to her home, expecting him to accept with equanimity her double life as family woman, with husband and children, and high-class prostitute after hours. 'If I put that scene in a motion picture,' DeMille wrote in his autobiography, 'it would hardly be believed.'

DeMille does not tell us why he was seeking an audience with the Pope in the first place. He was, after all, a Protestant born and bred. The Fatty Arbuckle scandal, the previous September, had embroiled Hollywood in much moral breast-beating, but Cecil's trip meant he was absent when the killing of William Desmond Taylor, on 1

February, struck a second blow to Hollywood's image. (This enabled him to be left out of the enormous list of potential suspects, a real boon in the ensuing Hollywood panic!) But this was ten days after the projected papal meeting.

Was the desire for spiritual guidance sparked by Cecil's knowledge of the child about to be born of his brother William's transgressions? Or by the accumulation of his own? There was certainly no sign of DeMille changing his way of life, his Saturday nights resolutely spent Not At Home. But we might be allowed to sense the glimmer of some deep-seated moral malaise.

This feeling, indeed, was poured into *Manslaughter* as into a sacral vessel. The story's author, Alice Duer Miller, was an essayist, poet, novelist and later habitué of the famous – and liberal – 'Algonquin Round Table'. Her tale of a rich girl who plunges into the lower depths of prison and poverty when she gets a speed cop killed in an accident had at its centre an ethos of social responsibility. Cecil DeMille and Jeanie Macpherson turned it into an unabashed moral sermon:

Lydia Thorne, who 'has everything in the world she wants, except a mother and father', is 'speed-mad and geared too high'. She races a motorcycle cop in her car at 55 miles an hour and tries to bribe him to let her off with a bracelet that she leaves in his hand. Her high life is explored in a carnivalesque New Year's party, in which she drinks and flirts with a rich politician while the man who truly loves her, district attorney Daniel O'Bannon, tut-tuts and suffers on the sidelines. DeMille cast Leatrice Joy as Lydia and returned to an old hand, Thomas Meighan, for the upright O'Bannon. It is true that the directorial hand seems off the tiller here, for Meighan performs with an unusual stiffness, like a clothes horse for uplifting ideas. On the other hand, there are no holds barred for the carousing, complete with a ladies' pogo-stick race and an elaborate flashback to an orgy in Roman times, introduced by O'Bannon's lament:

We're no different today than Rome at its worst! This dance, with its booze and licence, is little better than a feast of Bacchus!

Paul Iribe went to town on the Roman hall, with Lydia barely costumed on a throne while the boys 'n' gals frolic below, slurping the Bacchian grapes. Gladiators armed with swords and tridents enter, their combat cutting to a modern women's boxing match.

Meanwhile, back in the present, Lydia's maid, Evans, is in torment, as she needs money to send her sick boy to California. Distraught, she steals her mistress's diamond ring, only to be caught by O'Bannon, who is called in by Lydia to investigate. At the trial, O'Bannon hopes Lydia will turn up to plead for mercy for her maid, but she has been trashed by the previous night's jazzy carousing and sleeps through the verdict: three and a half to seven years in the state jail.

Divine justice, however, is about to catch up with Lydia. The traffic cop's wife finds Lydia's bracelet and shames him into giving it back. He chases Lydia's car again on his motorbike, but she accelerates and tries to shake him off with a skidding turn which instead sends him crashing into her car, fatally injuring him on a rock.

Arrested, she assumes her social position will get her off with a fine, but the upright O'Bannon determines to prosecute her and send her to jail: 'I'm going to put you behind bars, Lydia! You're heading straight to hell! And I'm going to save you – because I love you!'

And so O'Bannon convicts the girl he loves, regaling the jury with yet another Roman-orgy flashback: 'The over-civilized, mad young set of wasters – to which this defendant belongs – must be STOPPED! Or they will destroy the Nation – as Rome was destroyed, when Drunkenness and Pleasure drugged the Conscience of its Young!' Cue the entrance of the Vandals, destroyers of Rome, with Meighan doubling as their chief, complete with winged helmet and whip, as he threatens to chastise Lydia while his club-wielding proles wallop the effete youths and drag off the girls: 'Loot, plunder and Kill! No man deserves his Treasure who defends it not!' Such treasure, one assumes, being not the fiduciary kind but the honour of its class and its women.

This is the first instance of DeMille going wholly over the top in his denunciation of the jazz age, offering a lethal comeuppance with lip-smacking sadistic overtones. Lydia's descent into the hell of the prison is, in contrast, portrayed with harsh realism, as her finery is removed, her ears and mouth probed, her hair cropped and her degradation witnessed by mocking prisoners. Worst of all, she is subjected to the contempt of her own maid, who has become a trustee. Lydia's agony, however, and her delirium, which prompts her to see herself shooting the district attorney in a hallucinatory replay of her trial, triggers off a redemptive pity in the former maid, Evans. She resolves to save Lydia, who is herself lifted by this example and survives to become a model prisoner. Meanwhile, in a parallel reversal of fortune, O'Bannon succumbs to an overwhelming guilt about the horror he has wrought upon his beloved. He resigns his post and sinks into a world of booze and pawnshops, disappearing into the lower depths.

When Lydia and Evans are paroled, Lydia declares to her fellow prisoners: 'I had to come to prison, to learn the meaning of Freedom! To be locked in a cell, to know that I had a soul!'

Dedicating herself to helping others, she doles out 'Free Coffee and Doughnuts' to the breadline. It's New Year's Eve again, this time in dismal snow and poverty. O'Bannon, having given his last pennies to a street kid, joins the line and then sees Lydia. She tries to take him back, to save him, but he declares he has to fight the booze alone.

There follows what can only be described as a free advertisement for the virtues of Prohibition. Tempted, O'Bannon withstands the evil brew, and a lazy intertitle informs us that after three years he has risen 'like a phoenix from the fires of fate' and is running for governor against Lydia's old flame, the rich politician. Lydia is now engaged to him, but at the climax, discovering that as a 'jailbird' Lydia could not inhabit the governor's mansion, he renounces the governorship that the polls tell him is in the bag in order to marry her.

The early 1920s were obviously ripe for this kind of preaching. The accelerating pace of change was bewildering for the general public, while at the same time political life was apparently stabilized under the new president, Warren Gamaliel Harding, the epitome of 'normalcy'. (The 'Teapot Dome Scandal' which would mar his legacy would not break out until 1924, after his unexpected death.) Prohibition promised a new era of social sobriety and conservative morals but unleashed the very evils reform was designed to combat, the licentious speakeasy culture that district attorney O'Bannon thundered against. The criminal empire of bootlegging that soon emerged was, however, not yet a movie staple, and the 'bootlegger' who tries to entice the fallen O'Bannon is a very weedy Raymond Hatton.

There was, indeed, a religious backlash building, felt fiercely in Los Angeles, where the powerful Pentecostalist Aimee Semple McPherson was planning to make her headquarters in what was to be, in 1923, her Angelus Temple. She had been preaching in the city since 1918, and her travelling crusades drew tens of thousands. In 1922, she proclaimed a vision of her 'Foursquare' gospel – spiritual and physical healing through Jesus Christ as Saviour, Healer, Baptizer in the Holy Spirit and King to Come. Curing the blind and the crippled and the 'laying on of hands' were major parts of her mass performances.

Cecil DeMille kept his distance from all this. Following on the heels of *Manslaughter*, another film was begun in the autumn of 1921, another grand production, with the largest set the Lasky corporation had reputedly ever built. In February and March 1923, DeMille presided over the release of *Adam's Rib*.

Like *Fool's Paradise*, it qualifies as one of 'Cecil's Arcana', but with an even more confusing story. This time the young jazz-age 'flapper' would be not a selfish villain but a happy-go-lucky young girl. Tillie Ramsay is the daughter of 'a very modern Father and Mother'. Dad is Michael Ramsay, a Chicago business mogul. Mother is neglected and finds solace with an exotic foreigner, Jaromir (who else but Theodore Kosloff), who is the exiled King of Morania. Tillie is in love with Nathan Humboldt Reade, distinguished anthropologist, 'vertebrate palaeontologist – and confirmed Bachelor'. Elliott Dexter played this precursor of Cary Grant's shy egghead in Howard Hawks's future talkie, *Bringing Up Baby*. He's busy with Tyranno-saurus rex, but Tillie thinks his 'little pets' are cute. He is secretly smitten but indignant: 'You're an inexcusable, impertinent product of the movies – woman suffrage – and the war. And you don't belong in a museum, except for purposes of research.'

When Tillie confronts him at night in his museum, their argument about whether men have always trusted but been fooled by women, or whether men have always unfairly blamed women, segues into an Arcadian scene in the redwoods, 'Then as Now', as prehistoric man and woman play out their primal game. This massive studio set of primeval jungle was created by old hand Wilfred Buckland, brought back to imagine a scene beyond the scope of Paul Iribe's modernity.

The Arcadian scenes, for once, were absurd rather than glorious. Kosloff capers grotesquely in a leopard skin with a flute, while the Thinker, the cave-age professor, constructs the first bow and arrow: 'Throughout all time strong men have fought for fair women!' The rest of the film descends into a messy quadrangle between the busi-nessman, the wife, the ex-king and Tillie, who is suspected of being the rakish foreigner's lover. In order to convince her true love, the professor, that she is innocent, she has to follow him thousands of miles to an archaeological dig in Honduras, climaxing in a reprise of the finale of *Anatol*, when the professor tears up the written proof she brings him without reading it, to show that he does indeed trust her.

Reviews were mixed, with DeMille stalwarts at *Motion Picture News* proclaiming it 'DeMille at his bizarre best', while *Variety* called it 'a silly, piffling screen play . . . but a picture that is obviously des-tined to make a lot of money'. In reality, it did not make as much as it required to cover its $400,000-plus budget, grossing barely twice that sum. There were clear signs that DeMille was cobbling together stuff from several previous productions, without treading any new ground.

Perhaps sensing this dearth of inspiration, DeMille handed his publicists an unusual assignment: to announce a contest for members of the public to suggest the subject for his next picture. The *Los Angeles Times*' Hallet Abend set to work, promising a $1,000 prize for the winner. What began as a publicity stunt mushroomed into a mountain of correspondence from all over the country and even from overseas, letters 'from men and women of every station, creed, and trade'. Proposals of every kind, from the sublime to the ridiculous, inevitably poured in, but, DeMille noted, an unexpectedly large number focused on religious themes. Of these, eight different people all suggested the biblical Ten Commandments.

Quite how much of this search was genuine and how much was hype to cover a decision already made is hard to judge. DeMille did pay eight winners $1,000 apiece. The chronology reveals that the subject was presented by DeMille to Jesse Lasky and Adolph Zukor long before he finished filming *Adam's Rib*. On 11 November, Lasky was reporting to Cecil 'considerable enthusiasm in mind of Zukor' over the Ten Commandments idea. By December, the project was already budgeted by DeMille's office at well over $1 million. This the executives of Paramount back east in New York were not so keen on. After all, Cecil B. DeMille was known and celebrated as a maker of contemporary domestic dramas, not of overblown period pieces, let alone a biblical film. The last two period sagas DeMille had directed, *Joan the Woman* in 1916 and *The Woman God Forgot* in 1917, were emphatically not included in the studio's box-office hall of fame.

DeMille himself, however, most certainly was: a 'jury' of one hundred of his peers invited by *Motion Picture News* voted him among the twelve 'greatest people of the motion picture industry' in December of 1922. 'Creator of Artistic Productions Embodying High Box-Office Value' was the rubric granted him by the magazine. 'He has been criticized at various times for [his] vision scenes, at times seemingly introduced without adequate reason,' wrote the editors, 'but it must be remembered that the public has been extremely slow to accept the costume picture, and that such visions, inserted in modern dramas have been the one way of gradually "selling" the fans on the desirability of the historical drama.'

Everything seemed to be converging on the publicity campaign for DeMille's next picture, the one that would keep him in that hall of fame and brand him in the public eye for ever.

'A Powerful Preachment'

'It's just like we're living in dem times when we got the Torah, and
now we're getting it all over again by Mr. DeMille.'
Jewish lady employed as an extra on *The Ten Commandments*

On 30 December, the penultimate day of 1922, the *New York Times*
reported that Cecil B. DeMille's yacht *Cecilia* had been destroyed by
fire when her engine backfired during a three-day speedboat race off
the Los Angeles harbour. The captain of DeMille's yacht was 'blown
into the water and narrowly escaped drowning. De Mille was
unhurt.'

On 23 February 1923, the *Times* filed another report, headed
'LIQUOR ON DE MILLE YACHT': 'A quantity of high priced liquor and
rare wines was said by customs officials to have been found on the
Seaward, a yacht owned by Cecil B. De Mille . . . just returned from
a voyage into Mexican waters . . . They found the liquors and wines
in a secret compartment below decks. No arrests have been made,
but Putnam [Deputy Collector of Customs] said that hereafter all
yachts returning from Mexican ports would be searched.'

It would come as no surprise that in those parched days DeMille
and company might have sorely needed some libation before embarking on their massive enterprise. From the beginning the whole affair
was envisioned in the grandest terms. Eight months of preparation
were mentioned, which meant that the inception of the project must
have come ahead of the October 'Nationwide Idea Contest' that had
supposedly come up with the theme. Many hundreds of drawings,
designs and plans had to be prepared for the massive sets that were to
be built further north along the Californian coast, at Guadalupe. This
location, south of Pismo, provided desert-like dunes in an environment more congenial to human survival than Death Valley, in which
Erich von Stroheim was about to shoot his rigorous finale of *Greed*.

Cecil the sailor man

The sensational discovery of the tomb of Tutankhamun by the archaeologist Howard Carter was later said by many to have inspired DeMille's designs. But as this occurred on 22 November 1922, it was in fact a serendipitous coincidence, which hugely increased public interest in the Pharaonic theme.

Before the sets and the designs, Jeanie Macpherson had to agonize with DeMille over the structure of the scenario. How could such a subject be dramatized? Unlike with Joan of Arc, the original biblical story could not be altered or transformed beyond the familiar myth that both Jews and Christians were taught from the crib. In what detail should it be told? Should it be episodic, focusing on the highlights? When should it begin or end? Or should it instead be metaphorical and played out in a modern, contemporary setting?

In the end, Cecil and his screenwriter settled on a mixture of the episodic and the metaphorical. The biblical tale of Moses the Lawgiver would form a prologue, albeit an extended one, to a modern feature-length story which would reflect the unshakeable 'truth' of the Ten Commandments in an American city. The city chosen was San Francisco, itself a powerful metaphor of rebirth after the earthquake and fire of 1906.

Hundreds of costumiers, fashion designers, artists and illustrators laboured at the Lasky studios until, at the end of May 1923, an army of film crews, actors and extras headed up the coast from Los Angeles. The statistics were staggering: DeMille employed over 2,500 people and shipped more than 3,000 animals – horses, sheep, goats, camels, oxen, chickens, ducks, guinea fowl and dogs – for the two-week shoot of the Exodus segments. The location covered twenty-four square miles. Three hundred and fifty carpenters, plasterers and other builders set up Camp DeMille and the great set of the city of Rameses. There were, according to *Motion Picture News*, 'hydraulic engineers, telephone linesmen, electricians, stenographers, doctors, artists, architects, dressmakers, musicians and cooks. The camp comprised 550 sleeping tents, two huge mess tents, each with a capacity of 1,000 diners; a big recreation tent for dancing and other amusements, four tents forming a camp hospital . . . twelve tents for wardrobe and property use and a separate unit of twenty tents for the guards of the animal corrals.' Four miles of sidewalk had to be laid, and water pumped to provide 36,000 gallons of water daily, with thirty shower baths for the men and twenty-four for the women. Costumes and props consumed sixteen miles of cloth, three tons of leather made into Egyptian chariot harnesses for two hundred and fifty chariots, two tons of talcum powder to whiten actors' faces, five hundred gallons of glycerine to grease their bodies and two hundred pounds of safety pins, despite one anecdote about a Mrs Rosen and a Mrs Kaplan, in which Mrs Kaplan says: 'Take dat off'n you, Mrs Rosen, or the director will be mad mit you. Mr DeMille say in olden times dere wasn't no safety pins.'

Among the extras, DeMille had recruited what the promotion called '250 Old World Israelites', new immigrants and elder members of California's Orthodox Jewish community. These were served by a camp synagogue, overseen not by Moses but by a bona fide Aaron, Rabbi Aaron Markovitz, who was assisted by an interpreter for the Yiddish speakers. These 'Old World' extras had to be placated after protesting about the standard allocation of ham sandwiches for the location lunch.

The extras got $10 a day per adult and $7.50 per child, which would have landed DeMille with a bill for actors' salaries – including his featured actors – of well over $30,000 a day. Local journalists witnessed the arrival of the Jewish specials: 'Old men, infirm of step, feeble with long hair and patriarchal beards. With their belongings tied up in newspapers or in battered old suitcases, they huddled together.' Strict standards of conduct were enforced at Camp DeMille by guards and deputy sheriffs. Men's and women's tents were divided by a 'Lasky Boulevard'. Eventually, the new arrivals got a kosher kitchen and settled down to learning their roles, which would be no great problem, as, according to one extra: 'We know this script, our fathers studied it long before there were movies.'

As Camp DeMille grew in the desert, anxieties were beginning to grow at Camp Zukor, back at Paramount's main office. At a time of contraction, the company was uneasy, despite Lasky's stated enthusiasm for the project, about the money pouring into the sands. The studio had already invested heavily in another 'blockbuster', James Cruze's *The Covered Wagon*, which critics lauded as a 'monumental achievement' when it opened in New York in March. Hot on its heels, Paramount boasted in July that DeMille's saga 'represented the biggest single location feat in the history of motion picture production'. And yet, while the cash flowed, the modern section of the movie had not even begun shooting yet. This too would involve a large interior set of a church being constructed in San Francisco. The budget was sure to top a million dollars, and in the end it consumed $1.4 million.

Apart from the sets, DeMille was planning sequences shot in the new Technicolor process. The Technicolor company was eager to demonstrate to the major studios that its process represented the future of movies rather than another in a series of gimmicks that had not caught on. The colour camera used a 'subtractive' two-colour system which did not reproduce the entire colour spectrum. (The later three-strip Technicolor that ultimately triumphed would deliver better results, with three simultaneous films.) Several scenes, mainly the mass exodus of the Children of Israel and their pursuit by Pharaoh's army, were shot in this two-colour Technicolor, and other sequences, like the parting of the Red Sea and the pillar of fire holding back Pharaoh, were tinted and toned or used the 'Handschiegl' (colour stencilling) process.

Technical director Roy Pomeroy constructed a studio model with gelatin mounds that could be flooded in a special tank and then combined with the mass scenes shot on location to show either the waters receding – in reverse motion – to allow the Children of Israel to pass or cascading in to drown Pharaoh's army. In the film, it is startling to see how economical these sequences are. The essence of special-effects scenes (until our CGI-rich time) was to keep individual shots as short as possible, before the audience could spot the tricks. In the event, the effects appeared stunning, and remain largely convincing even today. 'FEAR YE NOT, STAND STILL, AND SEE THE SALVATION OF THE LORD!' cries out Moses. And, by Holly-wood's grace, so we do.

The Ten Commandments marked the end of DeMille's traditional partnership with cameraman Alvin Wyckoff. Some have said they clashed over the quality of Wyckoff's 'contrasty' photography, but that sounds unlikely, as in the old days this was DeMille's trademark 'Rembrandt lighting' of which he was so proud. Nevertheless, a new generation of cinematographers had flourished in Hollywood, and DeMille chose Bert Glennon, who had just shot a desert movie, *Burning Sands* (1922), for director George Melford. Glennon was to be another of Hollywood's ace photographers, shooting his first film in 1916 and his last in 1963. The camera still remained largely static in *The Ten Commandments*, building the epic mostly by the accumulation of its great compositions, but broke into a succession of dynamic travelling shots following Pharaoh's vengeful chariots over the plains.

Paul Iribe designed some spectacular sets, combining classic Egyptology with a spare hall of columns in Pharaoh's palace that echoed with his art-deco ideas. Rather than featuring the ornate hieroglyphic inscriptions and well-known pictorial art of ancient Egypt, Pharaoh's hall is like the great den of a glowering beast of prey. DeMille cast a French actor, Charles de Roche, as Pharaoh Rameses II. He was, according to the movie's promotional brochure, in 'private life' the Count Charles de Rochefort, related to the Bonapartes (on his mother's side). His movie record shows that he began as a comic actor in 1910 in Max Linder movies and had appeared in the 1923 remake of DeMille's *The Cheat*, directed by George Fitzmaurice. He was therefore a Lasky contract player, and his hulky physique and great beaked profile was ideal for Moses' adversary.

DeMille cast his most veteran stalwart, Theodore Roberts, as Moses. This was strange, as Roberts was sixty-two years old at the time and had spent many of his twenty-three films for DeMille play-

ing irascible uncles, corrupt capitalists or villainous rakes. The closest he had come to the Hebrew Prophet of the Exodus was as the blinded 'Iron Man' of *Something to Think About*. The casting was probably affected by DeMille's fondness for one of the foundation stones of his design for the picture, Gustave Doré's Bible illustrations. These, the most sombre of all Bible drawings, companion pieces to Doré's set of illustrations for Dante's *Inferno*, Cecil remembered from his father's home. Looking at them, one might be struck by the thought that they correspond more closely to the original contrasty 'Lasky' lighting than the Rembrandts more often cited. The lowering light in the hall of pillars when the firstborn are slain, or Moses striking the rock, silhouetted against the sky, or the shaft of lightning as Moses smashes the Tablets of the Law could be classic cinematographer's dreams. And indeed Doré's Moses, a muscular but elderly figure, with his chiselled face and beard flowing like lava from a human volcano, is a closer fit for Theodore Roberts' craggy visage than, for instance, Michelangelo's sculpture.

Unlike the 1956 remake, *The Ten Commandments*' 1923 'prologue' proceeds as a series of fabulous, episodic set pieces: the Children of Israel in bondage, dragging stones to build the city of Rameses. Moses the Deliverer urging Pharaoh to 'Let my People Go!' The Plague of the Firstborn (the tale is picked up when the previous Nine Plagues have already struck Egypt). The death of Pharaoh's own son. The casting out of the Israelites. As they pour out of the city, its massive temple and double row of sphinxes are clearly modelled on the well-known Temple of Luxor. Jewish writer Rita Kissin, who had joined the shoot as an extra as well as a witness, recalled that, at the parting of the sea, Theodore Roberts 'stood on a rock on the Pacific shoreline, surrounded by the children of Israel. As sunset approached, clouds blocked out the light, threatening to ruin the shot.' Just then the clouds parted and sufficient sun broke through to enable the shot: 'a gasp went through the crowd. The faces of men and women reflected the light, tears trembled on wrinkled cheeks, sobs came from husky throats. For many, the world had moved back 3,000 years . . .'

Once Pharaoh's chariots are drowned, the picture cuts directly to its next tableau, upon Mount Sinai. Moses has already been ensconced there, waiting for the great explosions in which the words of the Commandments thrust out of the screen towards the audience.

Meanwhile, at the foot of the mountain, the impatient Israelites have built their Golden Calf. Once again the tangled masses of Doré's illustrations are recreated in the studio. Recalling *Joan the Woman*, DeMille paid close attention to the individual actions in the crowd. Modern computer tricks can simulate any number of figures in a throng, but nothing matches the reality of different people, their faces, gestures and thrusting limbs. The girl who becomes a leper crawls to the feet of the patriarch, who comes down the mountain to face the disastrous heresy of his people. Jeanie Macpherson wrote in the original script:

The scene should look like a group in Dante's inferno . . . Finally, in a great gush of wind, the remainder of the tent is blown down – and everything is uprooted and blown from one place to the other. So that Moses and Joshua, and Aaron and Miriam, with their huddled group – are standing out under the storming sky, with the overturned calf flaming up, fanned by the terrific wind. Miriam is weeping and covering her head, and Aaron can only hold out his hands, begging Moses' forgiveness. At the end of this scene we have *FOUR* elements (A) wind / (B) lightning / (C) rain / (D) fire.

NOTE: If this could be in *special color* it would be very wonderful!

But only the ultimate mercy of faith can cure the guilty, and as Moses casts down the tablets and the Golden Calf is struck by lightning and turned to dust, the picture mixes into the opening scene of the modern story. As described in Paramount's brochure:

Departed is the picturesque splendor of the days when history was written in stone . . . A primly dressed mother sits at a table in a modern room. She is reading from the Bible to her two sons . . . One son, Dan, is bored and cynical. The other son, John, is tolerant and more than half-impressed; at any rate, he is deferential to his mother.

The modern story, a contemporary fable to match the well-worn historical tale, remains the Achilles heel of *The Ten Commandments* and one of the weakest of DeMille's moral narratives. Dan and John McTavish, played by Rod La Rocque and Richard Dix, are a plaster villain and saint, the one a brash atheist who says the Ten Commandments are 'bunk . . . that sort of stuff was buried with Queen Victoria!', and John, who in the words of Jeanie Macpherson's synopsis 'is the garden variety of human being, which believes in the Ten Commandments as unchanging immutable laws of the universe. He is not a sissy or a goody-goody. He is a regular fellow, an ideal type of man of high and steadfast principles, who believes the Commandments are as practicable in 1923 as they were in the time of Moses.'

There is also Mary, 'a girl who doesn't bother about the Ten Commandments at all. She is a good kid, but she has spent so much time working that she hasn't learned the Ten Commandments . . .' All these are judged against the mother, Mrs Martha McTavish, who in Macpherson's original script 'keeps the Commandments the wrong way. She is narrow. She is bigoted. She is bound with ritual. She is representative of orthodoxy. Yet withal she is a fine, clean, strong woman, just like dozens we all know.'

Therein, of course, lies the problem of the modern story, as the characters are 'representative' of this and that attitude, emblematic rather than real, contradictory human beings. DeMille's conception of Mrs McTavish deepened the problem, as he presented her, despite her rigidity, as the moral core of the tale, much like the housekeeper in *Something to Think About*. She is, rather than bigoted, righteous. And to make sure we don't miss it, DeMille lumbers her with a massive, half-ton Bible to carry about from room to room.

Everything in the modern story heightens the unreality, despite the realism of some of the settings. DeMille used a real church in con-

struction, St. Peter's and Paul's in San Francisco, to shoot sequences on its high girders, with a majestic view of the 'phoenix-like' city. The 'meeting ground of East and West', the city provided DeMille with a bizarre sub-plot, in which a Eurasian woman, Sally, played by Nita Naldi, has escaped from an eastern leper colony to the Golden Gate, where she infects Dan McTavish with the biblical plague as he dallies with her while his girl, Mary, pines. McTavish reaps the wages of sin when the church he is building with rotten concrete to save money for his own profit collapses on top of his mother and kills her. Discovering how Sally has infected him, he shoots her dead. DeMille's portrayal of the killing, with Sally shot behind a shower curtain, anticipates Hitchcock, the curtain hooks snapping one by one as she falls. Dan McTavish has now broken all Ten Commandments and qualifies for perdition, perishing at sea when the boat he has escaped on is dashed against the rocks. Poor Mary, who has become leprous through her contact with him, is cured miraculously when she kneels by the good John McTavish as he declares his love for her. John has related to her a vision of Jesus curing the leper peasant girl, and Mary looks at her own hands against the rising sun:

'Look, John! In the light, it's gone!'
And John answers: 'Yes, Mary – in the LIGHT – it's gone.'

The Ten Commandments opened just in time for Christmas 1923 and was an immediate sensation. As *Motion Picture News* reported:

For hours preceding the start of the performance crowds of people eager to obtain seats had jammed the lobby of the [George M. Cohan] theatre and overflowed out into the street . . . It was shortly after 8:30 when the huge tablets which formed the scenic background for the presentation slowly opened outward and the introductory title was revealed on the screen. From that moment until the end, three hours later, there was not one second's abatement of interest, while the applause and cheering at times were deafening. Waves of handclapping swept over the theatre in crescendo with the pursuit of the Children of Israel by the Egyptian charioteers, the opening and closing of the sea, the pronouncement of the Commandments and with the climax of the modern story, and at the conclusion the calls from all parts of the house for the producer were inevitable.

After five minutes of insistent applause Mr. DeMille walked upon the stage and it was several minutes more before he could speak. 'We will feel indeed grateful,' he said, 'if our great effort shall lead to a reawakening of interest in the world's greatest book. It is difficult to tell whose work this picture really is. Mr. Zukor and Mr. Lasky with their enthusiastic interest – the inspired pen of Miss Macpherson – the cast, cameraman, camel drivers, draughtsmen, assistant directors, wardrobe assistants – all worked with the light of a great purpose. Each believed that he was doing his bit towards the consummation which, after all, all of us are striving for – the Brotherhood of Man.'

Indeed, most of those who counted for 'Man' in Hollywood were present in the audience: Messrs Zukor, Lasky, Will Hays and William Randolph Hearst, as well as the cast and crew, Mrs DeMille and family, and William de Mille, with his mistress Clara Beranger. Messrs Zukor and Lasky spake not, as they might have recounted the dramatic shenanigans occurring behind the scenes from July, when mounting location costs began to convince them that they should either shut down the production or allow DeMille to take over the financing of the picture himself. The final straw, DeMille claimed, was 'the bill for Pharaoh's two black horses', which would have cost $200 in Hollywood, but 'I had paid ten times that for a pair.' Paramount's financial secretary, one Elek J. Ludvigh, a good company lawyer, told Zukor that 'this wild and irresponsible director . . . was ruining the company'. DeMille's own lawyer, Neil McCarthy, got a pledge of a quarter of a million dollars apiece from producers Joseph Schenck and Jules Brulatour, but the most important pledge came from an influential friend, banker A. P. Giannini, who was willing to loan half a million. DeMille was involved in the banking business himself, having become vice-president of the Federal Trust and Savings Bank of Hollywood in 1922 and of the Commercial National Bank of Los Angeles in 1923, heading its advisory board on movie loans. This was small beer compared to Giannini, a son of Italian immigrants who had founded the Bank of Italy in San Francisco in 1904, opening more banks all over California, and who would, by 1930, consolidate his holdings to form the Bank of America.

Despite the financial back-up, Zukor was still ready to pull out of *The Ten Commandments*, until another Paramount founder-executive, Frank Garbutt, suggested to him 'don't sell what you haven't seen'. Production continued under the aegis of Famous Players-Lasky. And the rest, as they say, is history. The picture grossed over $4.5 million, the greatest profit, in the silent era, for a Cecil B. DeMille movie.

DeMille was entitled to declare, as he had, that though 'Our Modern World defined God as a "religious complex" and laughed at the Ten Commandments as OLD FASHIONED', they packed a 'mighty punch'. As the preamble to the film stated:

The Ten Commandments are not rules to obey as a personal favour to God . . . They are not laws – they are the LAW.

'A great picture – great in theme and story, great in technical excellence, great in acting and great in box-office worth,' wrote *Motion Picture News,* 'a powerful preachment combined with all the thrills, heart-interest and melodramatic effects that the screen, at its best, knows.' Exploitation angles, wrote the critic, were almost unlimited, as 'every institution in every community can be enlisted because here is a film that will be a positive benefit to civilization'.

The *New York Times* did complain that the modern story was 'uninspired' and 'extremely tedious', though the prologue was certainly a 'wonderful spectacle', but curmudgeonly *Variety* succumbed, predicting that audiences would 'mob the box offices . . . No picture-goer will be able to resist seeing it . . . It's a great picture for the Jews. It shows the Bible made them the Chosen People, and also . . . it will be as well-liked by the Catholics for its Catholicity.' This po-faced encomium was penned by 'Sime', the journal's founder-editor Sime Silverman, a hard-boiled showbiz mentor who had seen it all. Despite the 'hoke', Sime wrote, 'it may have been the magnificence of the big scenes that dwarfed all else, acting and people, with Mr. DeMille having swallowed up his picture and people . . . exactly as he made the Red Sea swallow up the greater host.'

The Guadalupe dunes indeed swallowed up the gargantuan set of *The Ten Commandments*, with all its artworks, props and chariot harnesses, animal corrals and safety pins. According to legend, it was effects man Roy Pomeroy who suggested that, rather than bear the cost of shipping everything back to Los Angeles, better to bury the whole lot in the sand. DeMille oversaw the demolition, the decapitation of the sphinxes, the breaking down of the temple, the statues of Pharaoh ploughed under as if he were but the latest dynast burying the old in order to preserve the primacy of his own personal vision. As family historian Anne Edwards recounts:

It took almost a whole day to complete the task. By nightfall, C.B. . . . and his company were gone and the city of Pharaoh was covered with sand. No one in Guadalupe took much notice of this incident. Most of the residents [population 1,130 in 1923] assumed the city had disappeared the way it had arrived, by trucks that would transport it in pieces back to Hollywood via State Highway 1.

It would be fully sixty years later, in 1983, when a local rancher led three zealous film archaeologists, Peter Brosnan, Bruce Cardozo and Richard Eberhardt, to the site, showing them the curious items that had been exposed by the shifting sands: shards of statues, a pharaoh's foot, parts of a sphinx's head, fake Egyptian vessels. And so excavations began. The Lost City of DeMille is now a tourist destination and a cause for film buffs. Alas, DeMille built in plaster rather than stone, and the artefacts of his amazing celluloid dream tend to turn to dust when exposed. 'Ground-penetrating radar', we are told, 'has located about 23 large pieces' that are believed to be 'intact enough to reassemble'. Over twenty years, many smaller pieces of costumes and props have nevertheless been extracted, among them, suitably poignant and redolent of another lost age, 'a bottle of Quality and Purity cough medicine, which was popular in Prohibition for its high alcohol content'.

And the Band Played On

From the press book for *Triumph* (1924):

Putting It Over Right

The name of Cecil B. De Mille, well known previously, has recently received barrels of wonderful publicity on account of 'The Ten Commandments.' It is safe to say that there isn't an adult in the United States above the grade of moron who hasn't heard of De Mille and doesn't know he is a director of fine motion pictures. The regular movie fans have always been crazy about De Mille. If there were people among the non-theatre crowd who didn't know all about De Mille before, 'The Ten Commandments' has made them acquainted . . . In other words, the De Mille of 'Triumph,' his first picture since 'Commandments,' is the best and most favorably known, the most widely advertised and the easiest-to-put-across De Mille you have ever sold . . .

The Ten Commandments was released as a 'roadshow' movie, a special presentation showcasing in major cities before settling for its 'normal' run. The screenings lasted throughout 1924, and into 1925 in some cities – New York clocked sixty-two weeks. By this time, DeMille had shot three more movies in 1924 alone: *Triumph, Feet of Clay* and *The Golden Bed*. All were projects that DeMille had contracted to film for Famous Players-Lasky, on moderate budgets and in contemporary settings.

In all, DeMille shot five films between his first biblical epic and his second, the New Testament *King of Kings*, produced in 1927. It was a strange period for DeMille, because he remained as busy as ever, never pausing between one project and the next, but his return to contemporary subjects, complex and ambitious as they were, seemed to critics to be less than satisfying when judged against his greatest achievement so far.

Nevertheless, DeMille was at the height of his powers, prestige and financial standing in 1924. This was a banner year for Hollywood, unchallenged in its own hegemony over all other American arts. In literature, Sherwood Anderson, Lewis Mumford and Edna Ferber published new books, while the new voice of Ernest Hemingway was still tuning up in Paris. In drama, Maxwell Anderson and Laurence Stallings' *What Price Glory?* was judged the great American First World War play. On the popular stage George S. Kaufman, the Marx Brothers and W. C. Fields sparkled alongside the regular George M. Cohan shows. In music, jazz was reaching its widest audiences, in a year in which Louis Armstrong accompanied Ma Rainey and Bessie Smith, Duke Ellington played on Broadway, and Gershwin's rhapsodies and Paul Whiteman's band demonstrated that white folks also got rhythm, more or less.

But the movies were America, technology and art in perfect syncopation – apart from the pirate and spoiler Erich von Stroheim, whose razzberry to American triumphalism, the cut-down and mutilated *Greed*, finally opened in November to thunderous disapproval. Even the normally generous *Motion Picture News* denounced it as 'the most morbid, sordid, uncompromising movie ever shown . . . Serves no entertainment . . . Will probably disappoint patrons through being consistently grim and morbid.'

DeMille's first film of 1924 was the product of yet another 'Nationwide Idea Contest', its subject chosen by the public. It was, so the publicist claimed, a runner-up in the original contest which had been won by the Ten Commandments idea. Apart from a Bible tale, the 'outstanding cry' of the public had been, said the press men: '"Give us more stories of business, of industry." Said the husbands: "We want to see men on the screen like those we know." Said the wives: "We want to see the movies but it's hard to get our hubbies to stir out in the evenings. They say they just don't like love stories. Give them something of their own stuff, and our job will be easy!"'

And so *Triumph* was made. Its theme was yet another version of the classic reversal of fortune. Rod La Rocque and Victor Varconi played two rivals, King Garnet and William Silver, both sons of the founder-owner of the Garnet Can Company, the latter by an illicit affair. The old man left a will that disinherited King if he failed to be usefully involved with the company and handed the ownership of the factory to Silver, an arrogant social climber and proclaimed socialist whose motto was: 'No able bodied he-man would live off another's labor!'

The ironic tale tells how King, the rich wastrel, is humbled and has to rise again through the shop floor, while Silver becomes an unfeeling boss who also takes over King's sweetheart, Ann, helping her make the breakthrough in her singing career. Ann gets her name in lights in Paris, while Silver toasts their mutual rise in the world: 'I drink to TRIUMPH! To the world's applause – and to the golden bauble of success!'

A fire in their hotel, however, overcomes Ann, and the smoke ruins her voice. Silver too is ruined when his investment in Cambodian oil fields turns out to be a fake. Fortune is reversed back again: King Garnet on top, Silver agitating the men against him. In a final act of magnanimity, King rehires Silver as his manager, but also gets the girl, who loved him all along.

Despite the trumpeting of the movie's virtues by the publicists – 'scenes filmed amid the thundering cogs of the factory, a fight between the rival lovers in a limousine going 90 miles an hour, spectacular café and modiste-shop scenes, a daring fire scene, a charming vision episode involving "Romeo and Juliet" . . .' – the film did not gel with either critics or audience, though DeMille's name kept it modestly profitable. As the critics noted, the old formula that had sustained DeMille at the outset of the jazz age was now considered passé as the full blast of the 'roaring Twenties' set in. Cars now had to be faster and better, the high-class settings richer, the contrasts between success and failure sharper and more rapid, reflecting an age of increased social mobility that papered over any economic gulf.

The *New York Times* in particular lambasted *Triumph*: 'Originality and subtlety are not favored in Cecil B. DeMille's new pictorial effort . . . Mr. DeMille has bowed to what is termed a showman's idea of a picture, and the result is that one has to sit through a mile and a half of hokum.' The paper added, in a further feature review on 27 April, that 'to us this is the worst picture that DeMille has ever made, and one of the worst we have seen'. Although other reviewers were kinder, DeMille was certainly not used to this kind of reaction. He had no time to mope, however, because within two weeks of the latter notice he was back on set, shooting his second film of the year, *Feet of Clay*.

This, once again, is a film that is missing, though there is great confusion as to how and when it got lost. When, around this period, DeMille began gathering his negatives, there were already gaps in the archive. *Feet of Clay*, on the other hand, remained available but vanished in the following decades somewhere in the confusion of shifting corporate titles and properties. Charles Higham's short 1973 biography of DeMille suggests the author had viewed it, but Robert Birchard insists the print was lost many years before. It is by far the most irritating loss in the DeMille oeuvre, since all indications are that it was one of his most distinctive films, a companion piece to *Fool's Paradise*, but even more bizarre, if that were conceivable.

Based on a popular novel by Margaretta Tuttle, serialized in the *Ladies' Home Journal*, the movie dealt once again with rich young people dealt a series of dramatic blows by fate. The original story was about a soldier who returns lame from the war, having lost the toes of one of his feet. This, Charles Higham suggests, fed into DeMille's kinky foot fetishism. Cecil was also inspired to add some topical mystical and occult elements, mainly derived from a play by Sutton Vane, *Outward Bound*. That told of a ship carrying a motley group of passengers who are in fact dead, between this world and the next. It would be filmed once in 1930 with Leslie Howard and then again in 1944 as *Between Two Worlds*, with John Garfield, Eleanor Parker and Sydney Greenstreet. DeMille wanted to purchase the property but Lasky couldn't secure the rights, so the resulting concoction used similar material from a play by Beulah Marie Dix entitled *Across the Border*. Dix co-wrote the film script with Bertram Milhauser.

The tale of *Feet of Clay* went something like this: at an 'acquaplane' race off Catalina Island, with shapely maidens attached to surfboards, one of the boats is blown up and the driver, Kerry Harlan (Rod La Rocque), is thrown into the water and attacked by a shark. His foot mangled, he is unable to work, and Amy (Vera Reynolds), his young bride, goes to work as 'a mannikin in a style emporium'. As *Motion Picture News* continues: 'While the wife is away, Bertha Lansell [Julia Faye], wife of the surgeon who is treating Kerry [Dr Fergus Lansell, played by Robert Edeson], tries to win Kerry for her own. In attempting to evade her husband, she falls from a ledge and dies of her injuries. Tony, Kerry's rival, attempts to get Amy to marry him following this scandal, but Amy remains true and returns to Kerry, finds him supposedly dead from gas fumes. She attempts to take her own life. Both are saved.'

'One of the real novelties of the season,' wrapped up the *News'* critic, Frank Elliot. Indeed, many critics, like the *New York Times'*

Mordaunt Hall, employed a great deal of head-scratching trying to come to terms with the film. Reporting on audience reactions, Hall wrote that 'one man told us that he wondered whether the revolving bandstand in this picture made the musicians dizzy. He added that it seemed strange to him that the weird shark in Pacific waters not only showed the dreaded "triangular" fin, but also a good deal of its tail. He opined that rubber sharks usually acted that way.' A great deal was apparently made of the injured foot, with the young sufferer tortured by a plethora of dance offers. Hall poured scorn on a scene of the surgeon, suspecting his wife has visited Harlan, looking out of the window but failing to spot her standing on a narrow ledge, clinging to telephone wires: 'Then one sees a shot showing the distance below, about six stories. The absurd hero cannot muster up sufficient courage to look out of the window, and finally, one by one, the nails holding the telephone wires give way and the deceitful Mrs. Lansell falls to her death.'

As the 'deceitful Mrs. Lansell' was portrayed by Julia Faye, Cecil's long-term lover, the scene would have had an ironic frisson to those in on the private joke. 'Mr. DeMille obtains his suspense', wrote Mordaunt Hall, 'by elementary methods, much on the order of a serial like the "Perils of Pauline." The necessary and often impressive details are sacrificed for the spectacular effects, which detract from the thread of the story.'

The most spectacular of these, indeed the most painful loss of any scene in the canon, is a great 'Bridge Between the Worlds', where the lovers, Amy and Harlan, having committed suicide, find themselves in a fantastic limbo, as described in the script, scene number 479:

(*Amy, thinking Kerry dead, inhales gas, falls:*)
INT. BEDROOM. FLAT.
Window. Light beyond window increases, and window starts to lose shape. Kerry comes into picture, moving towards window hesitatingly, with his back to camera. He stands silhouetted against the light beyond the window, as the window slowly assumes the form of a Bridge, running off to a tremendous length, with nebulous shapes of people, moving in groups of two or three, who become every second more and more distinct. These people come from behind Kerry, and pass along toward infinity, all in one direction. By the time their density is equal to that of Kerry, the window is entirely dissolved. We have Kerry standing, dazed, bewildered, in the midst of the slowly moving groups of people, of all nationalities, ranks and ages.

As Kerry and Amy stand among the dead, they see a peasant woman knitting, a crumpled soldier and a murderer with the rope round his neck, who, when he asks an old woman to untie it for him, is told: 'That is a knot that cannot be untied!' A policeman is carrying a black baby he has died trying to save. The script notes: 'We want a negro child, so that people will understand this is a stray baby he has died trying to save, not his own.' They are all heading towards the Book-Keeper – 'the focal point of the people moving along the Bridge'. A Chinese man says to Kerry and Amy: 'Be not afraid. He but speaks what you have ordained. He will send you to a destiny you have yourself shaped in your mortal life.' The murderer, consumed by his own crime, tries to tear the page of his judgement from the book, in vain, for the page is like a tablet, and he rushes off 'running to edge of Bridge and hurls himself over into the gulf below'.

As the Book-Keeper seeks to separate the couple, sending Amy on but Harlan back, they are left behind as 'lost souls – lost forever!' They look back along the Bridge, 'into infinite distance – the way the Dead come, endlessly. There is no further shore on which this Bridge is seen to rest.' They walk back through the Dead, as, in 'reality', both Harlan and Amy stir on the bed. An alarm clock rings and she

Feet of Clay – on the bridge of the Dead

throws it through the window, shattering the glass and letting the lethal gas escape – an ending clearly taken from the unused source, *Outward Bound*. Love has brought them back to life . . .

How much of this was shot and in the final film we cannot tell, but there certainly was a 'tremendous climax' that showed 'the two leading characters fighting their way back through the promenade of death to life'.

Publicity for the movie vigorously highlighted the playboy–playgirl aspects of the film, with images of the 'acquaplanes', swimwear-clad girls and shark: a 'real picture! . . . Typically DeMille . . . luxury, gorgeousness . . . a picture with a smash climax, the like of which you've never seen before – a scene you'll talk about just as everyone did of the opening of the Red Sea in "The Ten Commandments"!'

With impeccable bad taste, the press book suggested 'semi-humorous tie-ups with all shoe and hosiery stores . . . The night before the show opens, make footprints on all the sidewalks leading to the theatre. Stencil could be cut out so that the title, "Feet of Clay," would appear on each footprint.'

The author, Margaretta Tuttle, according to Charles Higham, pestered DeMille during the shoot, sending him letters written 'on purple notepaper', typed with a 'mauve ribbon' and gushing with encouragement and advice: 'You who know love, know its Feet of Clay, set upon good Earth . . . Love begins with clay; molding it as a child molds clay, and the clay is not enough. It must have living tissues to mold . . .' Tuttle visited the set, but responding to reporters, told them: 'It is only the feet that interest him.'

Nevertheless, 'DeMille had turned Catalina into an authentic millionaire's paradise for the film. The beach, originally stony, was converted into a lovely crescent of white sand, imported from Hawaii at great expense. Each day, the cast was served by white-coated servants, off tables loaded with solid gold, Spode and Wedgwood plate. They ate rainbow trout in aspic, truffles, pâté de foie gras and pyramids of crystallized fruit.' DeMille's own yacht was moored off the beach, and white-flannel-trousered dinners were common. At the end of filming, the director left for two weeks' cruise on his yacht while Anne Bauchens cut the film.

Censorship and lawsuits plagued the post-production and release. The Pennsylvania State Censor Board wanted to change the word 'Passion' in one title to 'Love', and the author of *Outward Bound*,

Sutton Vane, sued for plagiarism. DeMille was also being sued by a woman in Atlanta, Mattie Thornton, who claimed that Jeanie Macpherson's script of *The Ten Commandments* was lifted from her own text, which she had offered Lasky back in 1918 as an unsolicited script. Mrs Thornton did not win her case, and Vane's more serious challenge was settled out of court.

But this was grist to the mill of pictures, the everyday hazards and struggles to keep the truffles and pâté de foie gras coming through. Reorganization continued apace in the industry. In May, the great merger of Metro-Goldwyn and Louis B. Mayer was announced, 'intended to eliminate waste in production, to make bigger and better pictures at less cost, to furnish better service to exhibitors, and to accomplish a tremendous saving in distribution'. The dream of W. W. Hodkinson's primeval Paramount was now being cast in the steel of Mayer's determined corporate enterprise. DeMille, Jesse Lasky and Adolph Zukor had fearsome rivals all around.

Censorship, in this period, was being redefined by the 'leadership' of ex-postmaster general Will H. Hays. In April, an attempt at the repeal of censorship in New York state failed in the state's assembly. But Hays presented himself as the friend of the industry, declaring that 'political censorship is un-American'. The best censorship, he proclaimed, was applied by good citizens patronizing good, wholesome pictures and steering clear of 'the stupid picture, the picture of bad taste and the picture possibly suggesting unwholesomeness'. These would vanish before the good taste and sense of the public. But there was iron in this soulful approach too, as Hays told an interviewer for the *People's Home Journal*: 'We can do this work together. Right now, especially, is this public co-operation and sympathy necessary, for right now our association is engaged in a most earnest effort to prevent the more or less prevalent type of book and play from becoming the prevalent type of picture.'

No Upton Sinclair adaptations then, and no hairy apes from Eugene O'Neill. 'We who make pictures are the public's servants,' said Hays. 'We are not only willing but most eager to provide for the public the most perfect pictures that our artistic geniuses and our wizards of the camera can make. But we must know just what *you* want. And there is one way in which your answer can be registered unmistakeably.'

Cecil DeMille was quite happy, as we have seen, to present his own work as a response to the overriding public will. But in his heart of hearts he knew that this was not his primal motivation in film-making. Every director becomes addicted to playing with 'the greatest train-set' a child could have, as Orson Welles once defined it. For the Champion Driver, the factory bustle of the motion-picture set – with its make-believe realities and dreams made true – was a total culmination; if he could deploy this pulsating machine, this demigod-like dynamo to make a film that popularized the Bible, or the Divinity, he could climb the summit of Mount Sinai and remain there, throwing ever more exhilarating thunderbolts. What could be more fulfilling? But Cecil knew that Adolph Zukor, the money-making gnome of the movies, less beholden than the human face of Hollywood moguldom, Jesse Lasky, to old friendships and the comradeship of dreams, would continue to obstruct his climb up his personal Olympus, where he could disport himself as he wished. This mutual knowledge lay at the root of the continual jousting between DeMille, in Parnassus, California, and the Paramount executives, in the Vulcan forges of New York.

In the end, the Vulcans wished to bend him to their will. A significant move, in the summer of 1924, was their signing of D. W. Griffith, the bowed but still not completely beaten master mason of Holly-wood, to a three-picture contract. DeMille knew Griffith was in decline and would accept the vassalage. The cracks were widening in the house that Zukor, Lasky and DeMille had built with such mutual enthusiasm in the pioneer years. When box office is all, something has to give in the shotgun marriage between art and commerce that had so defined the motion-picture industry.

Back at the factory floor, there was a third movie already in the works, although for this one DeMille and his company moved east, shipping through the Panama Canal rather than going overland in order to shoot his next Paramount production at the Famous Players' studio at Astoria, Long Island. This move, Cecil assured the press, 'is not to be interpreted as meaning that I am leaving Hollywood. My entire life is centered here and will continue to be. I am simply going to make one picture in the East.'

That picture was to be *The Golden Bed*.

The Candy Ball, and Other Indulgences

Once upon a time, there were two families: the House of Peake, 'muffled in tradition', a fine, colonnaded house, with ancestors in picture frames 'leaning on the shoulders of the past'; and the House of Holtz, 'muffled in the smoke of factories, ancestors unknown – POVERTY AND WORK, grasping the hand of the Future . . .' Shot of a lopsided wooden sign – 'Mrs Holtz, Peppermints and Washing' – and a row of shacks below a great belching chimney.

Thus begins Cecil B. DeMille's *The Golden Bed*, his forty-eighth film, 'a dramatic exposé of the morals and marriages of today', as it was hyped in its press book when it approached completion in the winter of 1924. Classified by many critics as one of DeMille's 'oddities', it remains another archival film invisible to all but the coterie of movie historians and the small audiences that have attended its few revivals.

The source was once again a popular novel, by Wallace Irwin, first serialized in *Pictorial Review*, which as a result was 'selling like hot cakes in every city and town in the land'. Jeanie Macpherson wrestled it into the most powerful of Cecil's reversal of fortune fables.

The past, as has often been pointed out, is a foreign country, and the silent cinema is a very foreign landscape for those whose horizon stops with the earliest talkies. Hollywood's fabulism ran riot in a realm where gesture and image could be both symbol and ersatz reality at one and the same time, and in Hollywood, DeMille's world had long become a separate island, adrift from the main. 'Filmed with DeMille's Super-Gorgeousness' was the publicists' consistent mantra.

The introduction continues with two separate beds: the Golden Bed of the House of Peake, a 'gift of Louis XV', in which, dominated by a great gold swan, lies the 'petted, golden-haired hope of decaying grandeur', our tragic heroine, Flora Lee Peake. In the 'Other House – the bed of Admah Holtz is Iron'. As a boy, the young Admah sells his

with
Rod La Rocque,
Estelle Taylor and
Victor Varconi

THE story of two sisters – one
a tigress tearing out men's
hearts for the fascination of the
game. the other all sympathy and
tenderness – and their lovers – one
a self-made millionaire, the other
a fortune-hunting nobleman.
Against the backgrounds of an
American city, of Paris and Monte
Carlo, De Mille shows you these
four people living their lives of
passion, conflict, and final happiness. Produced with characteristic
De Mille lavishness of gorgeous
gowns and women from Wallace
Irwin's Pictorial Review serial and
best-selling novel.

Cecil B. De Mille's
production
The Golden Bed

Screen play by Jeanie Macpherson
From the novel by Wallace Irwin
Presented by Adolph Zukor and Jesse L. Lasky
A Paramount Picture

mother's candy, flirting through the great gate of the rich man's house
with little goldilocked Flora, while her sister, the plain but loving
Margaret, has to take second place. Admah gives out free sweets to
Flora, but not to her . . .

Ten years pass. At Flora's wedding, the fortunes of the House of
Peake have changed. The patriarch, Colonel Peake – played by
Griffith's iconic southern hero Henry Walthall – has to mortgage the
house, pawning its gold plates and furniture 'for a last brave show'.
Flora (played by Lillian Rich) is about to marry the Marquis de San
Pilar (Theodore Kosloff, of course), 'the Goose that is to Lay the
Golden Eggs'. Meanwhile, the candy boy Admah has grown to a
candy man (Rod La Rocque) who now owns his own business,
Candy Holtz Ice Cream, made only with the 'purest ingredients'.
Flora, glimpsing him as he tends to the catering, tosses him a rose.
But it is the plainer sister Margaret (Vera Reynolds, hardly plain at
all) who turns up at Admah's candy store looking for a job, convinc-
ing him that she can add 'some class' to his plebeian enterprise.

Three more years pass in a cut, and in the Swiss Alps marquis

Kosloff returns early from his day's climb to find his wife Flora in the hands of a new lover – with foreground fireplace flames framing the lovers in a satanic embrace – the suave and even richer Duc de Savarac.

Charles Higham tells the tale of DeMille's location journey to shoot the Alpine section in Washington State, braving snow, ice and the dangers of avalanche to realize the most unrealistic sequence of the marquis cutting the rope to drop both himself and his rival into a crevasse, ignoring the duke's plea: 'For God's sake don't cut the rope – no woman is worth a man's life!' As the legend has it, DeMille and his crew ran into blizzard conditions when shooting on Mount Rainier: 'Lillian Rich, Jeanie, and Claire West [costume designer] had to be carried by the male members of the team in the final stages, and DeMille had to run for his life, leaving a tent and twenty thousand dollars' worth of equipment behind. His journey back across treacherous ice made good telling when he got home at the end of the month.' (The whole scene, oddly enough, has a strong studio-bound feel to it, as if realism no longer seems feasible for DeMille.)

And so Flora too experiences the turn of fortune: as Admah flirts with his employee Margaret, Flora, blonde and destitute, turns up at the candy shop, with only her pet monkey, Louella, left from the marquis' riches, denied her when he had cut her out of his will. Admah goes off with Flora, while the monkey trashes Margaret's carefully mounted shop-window candy display.

'So Admah listens to the Song of the Lorelei – the enchanted Song of Destruction.' As Flora, now his wife, combs her long tresses at the mirror, DeMille indulges in the film's only 'symbolic' scene – Admah climbing on rocks towards his siren. But his fortune too has changed, and now he spends his hard-earned money keeping Flora in the manner which she insists on preserving – one bill he is faced with paying reads: 'Duplicating Mrs Holtz' gowns for monkey – $550.00.'

Admah falls into debt but still cannot resist his wife's desire to outshine the society snobs' Hunt Club Ball by planning her own affair. Of course, she is also flirting with a new beau, 'Bunny' O'Neill (Warner Baxter). Admah has one day to repay a $40,000 banker's loan, so he embezzles the money from his own firm, while mounting for Flora a 'Candy Ball' – a sombre intertitle virtually shaking its head in sorrow: 'A Man's Honor Spent for the Triumph of a Woman's Spite.'

The Candy Ball is one of DeMille's most outstanding sequences, a tour de force of exquisite vulgarity, planned and executed in meticulous detail: the entire set, fittings and props are made of candy, including a central pavilion with a chocolate dais and liquorice columns. The candy band plays on candy instruments, and one male guest eats the candy flowers off a girl's shoulder, while, centre stage, the Candy Slavemaster enters, his skin oiled, clad in candy bracelets and chains and with a row of lollipops stuck in his head, calling out: 'How many lollypops am I offered for these beautiful slaves in Candy Chains?'

The scene follows the original script closely, preserved with all its colour-tinting instructions:

Reel 6, Roll 5 Heavy Orange:
Heart shaped box and steps. At steps – MS – slave master and slaves in background – crowd in foreground, bidding . . .
At pavilion, SCU – Flora and Bunny in background . . .
Bunny: 'Flora, you're wearing CANDY chains too – only – you're afraid to break them!' . . .
Scene 64 – Garden and other part – MS – on crowd of men taking marshmallows off of girl.
Garden – SCU – girl dressed in marshmallows – men eating off of her.
At steps, SCU – Admah and Amos [the banker] – marshmallow girl enters to them – Admah takes one – girl exits – Amos says: 'I didn't come to play! I came to tell you that unless you pay your note tomorrow, I'll take over your factory – WITHOUT your services!'

As Flora and Bunny kiss in the pavilion, a shower of wrapped condiments descend from the ceiling on tiny parachutes. Admah catches the lovers *in flagrante*, but Flora flounces off, refusing his demand that she sacrifice her jewellery to stave off his impending bankruptcy. He is left in ruins, and in despair pushes down the columns of liquorice, like a modern, fake, empty-handed Samson knocking down the Philistine temple. He stands in the ruins as a monkey drums on a toy drum, and then unwraps a last stick of gum, shrugs and goes off with the police, who have discovered his embezzlement and have come to take him away.

Title: 'So the State takes its five year toll from Admah Holtz. And only one little flame shines through the despair of his first three years.' In jail, he receives letters from Margaret, who now keeps his candy store going: 'After all, Admah, what do prison walls shut out? They can't shut out my faith and my affection.'

Once again, the years pass, and Flora has been deserted by Bunny and has shrunk to a ragged, wandering waif, fetching up outside the old House of Peake, now a boarding house. Outside it, an organ grinder's monkey capers. She walks in, up the stairs – DeMille, twisting the knife, mixes to a flashback of her wedding day. Her shadow looms on the stairway as she climbs up towards the room with the golden bed –

And there Admah finds her, as, released from jail, he wends his way back to the house where Flora's sister Margaret awaits him with 'Life, Warmth and Expectation'. On the way, he passes by the Peake house, and on impulse, steps within and asks the landlady to see the old golden bed. There Flora lies, shattered, deranged, perhaps a victim of drugs. Recognizing him, she begins to apply make-up, murmuring: 'You're the Candy Man – I haven't forgotten – you were a guest at my wedding . . .'

Downstairs, one of the boarders is playing the piano. Flora looks up as she hears it: 'Maybe that's the jazz band – in hell!'

Cut to morning, and Admah approaches the candy store. Margaret is within, still waiting, and as he enters he tells her: 'I've just come from Flora,' and then: 'She's dead!' Outside the windows, workmen are building a new store –

Margaret: 'It's Tomorrow, Admah, and we're going to be like those men – BUILDERS – with Yesterday behind us!'

THE END.

Once again, it's so difficult to convey in words the utter weirdness and intense emotional claustrophobia of *The Golden Bed*. By now, DeMille's relationship with the jazz age closely resembles that of Moses with the worshippers of the Golden Calf. The pleasure principle receives its most atavistic and child-like aspect with the Candy Ball, the lollipop slavemaster and his chocolate chains. They may be easily and deliciously consumed, but they are as strong as steel nonetheless. A man succumbs to the wiles of the 'fallen woman' at his peril, even if he is as decent and hard-working as Admah Holtz, the primal 'Adam' of this grim modern fairy tale, in his enticing gingerbread house. All along the good 'Eve' awaits him, but he is grist to Lilith's will – the original spouse, who, according to legend, would not bend to Adam's will and flew off to copulate with demons. Despite the publicists' blather about the DeMille 'Super-Gorgeousness' and the apparent bending of his own will to Lasky's desire for modestly budgeted modern stories, the director had delivered yet another sermon, his own gospel in modern dress.

It was, as it happens, the last film produced by DeMille for Famous Players-Lasky. The last straw, according to Robert Birchard, was an ultimatum from the head of sales at Paramount, Sidney R. Kent, who cabled DeMille from New York on 18 December: 'It is not your [cash] advance that we object to so much as the added expense caused by your separate unit from which we feel you get no return commensurate with the expense it costs us . . . Mr. Zukor feels that this must be taken off our backs.' This was not the kind of Christmas present DeMille was expecting or thought he deserved from the company he had helped found at the end of 1913.

On 10 January 1925, DeMille's contract with Famous Players-Lasky was terminated. The *New York Times* announced, on the 11th, that 'Mr. DeMille, his wife, and a party of eight others, including Jeanie Macpherson, scenario writer; Mrs. E. Claire O'Neill, Mitchell Leisen, Peverell Marley [now DeMille's new lighting cameraman], Julia Faye and Mrs. Louis Covell, had booked passage to sail yesterday on the steamship George Washington . . . As a result of the sudden termination of Mr. DeMille's contract, the bookings were cancelled at the eleventh hour. Mr. DeMille said that he had decided not to leave now because of the conferences which his new plans for the future necessitated . . .'

DeMille had booked to sail in order to prepare the shooting of a new Lasky film, *The Sorrows of Satan*, based on the novel by Marie Corelli – which would eventually be filmed in 1926 by D. W. Griffith. The tale, with its personification of a grieving Satan searching for someone he cannot corrupt, might have seemed tailor made for DeMille, but Madame Corelli disapproved of Cecil, perhaps because he wasn't religious enough for her peculiarly fiery opinions. In the event the film was a very troubled production for Griffith, recut and released to a hostile reception.

By mid-January, 'DE MILLE LEAVES PARAMOUNT' was big news, and the trade press reported that he would now join United Artists. He was also known to be negotiating the purchase of Thomas Ince's studios at Culver City, after Ince had died in November 1924: at home in bed, according to the press; on William Randolph Hearst's yacht by a misjudged bullet, according to conspiracy theorists.

Cecil was bullish with the press: 'I will produce pictures of the same calibre as my past work,' he told all and sundry. 'The new situation permits me to carry out plans for enlarged activities which I have long had in mind. I am now laying out a schedule of stories and stars to appear in them which will offer the most ambitious program I have ever attempted . . . I feel that the program I have in mind can best be carried out independently.'

The Golden Bed opened at the end of January, to mixed reviews. *Variety* thought it was far too long, at ninety minutes, while Mordaunt Hall of the *New York Times* weighed in with a heavy dose of scorn, judging that, although 'technically, Cecil B. DeMille's fantastic production, "The Golden Bed," is interesting . . . as a story it is hopeless . . . Mr. DeMille has a weakness for factory details. In this picture one has a chance to see how certain candies are made, and Admah is pictured as an incurable gum chewer . . . Admah's mind is devoted to his wife and his candy business . . . The dainty Flora has a weakness for a pet monkey . . . [which is] at the ball, and one is continually disgusted by its repugnant presence. One wonders how the men could lean up against the sticky pillars with such nonchalance, and the constant feeding on candy petals must have been somewhat satiating . . . And yet,' the prominent critic had to admit, in contradiction, 'this picture as an entertainment is much more effective than either "Feet of Clay" or "Triumph."'

In February, DeMille announced an affiliation with a group called the Producers Distributing Company to form a new concern, the Cinema Corporation of America, with capital of $10 million. Pledging to bring over the stock company he had built up at Lasky, both crew and cast, DeMille also planned a vast schedule of projects that he would produce but not direct. As part of their severance agreement, Lasky amicably ceded to DeMille camera and lighting equipment, as well as the library of prints of his own movies that had built up over the years. Robert Birchard, as ever, has recorded the minutiae, quoting Lasky letters: 'We are willing to let you have . . . Hattie the hairdresser, though we are sorry to lose her . . . We will turn over the Magnavox [public address system] outfit to you with the understanding that you will agree to lend it to us whenever we need it . . .' All these mechanical and human resources were soon ensconced at Thomas Ince's former studios, and DeMille moved into his new premises at Culver City, regretfully abandoning the Hollywood and Vine site of the original barn.

A key figure in the financing of the new company was Jeremiah Milbank, an investment banker and philanthropist whose later charities would endow studies on infantile paralysis and diphtheria and who was also a devout Christian. DeMille claimed that the main attraction for Milbank was an early discussion of an idea that was to match and even surpass *The Ten Commandments*, now due to go on general release after its 'roadshow' period, in May 1925. His greatest wish, DeMille claimed he told Milbank, was to 'make a film on the life of Christ. I wanted simply to take the four Gospels and tell the story of Jesus of Nazareth . . . a figure no less human than divine.' Milbank swiftly signed on the dotted line, but the Jesus film had to be put back for other, more commercial concerns. DeMille production documents suggest, however, that the idea for the Jesus project came later, and Milbank was primarily attracted to DeMille's reputation as one of Hollywood's most consistent high earners. In 1925, DeMille also became president of the Culver City Commercial and Savings Bank, a holding bank for his friend A. P. Giannini, shoring up his financial credentials and adding to the two bank vice-presidencies he already held.

In July, the trade journals advertised the first three of the new company's productions: *The Coming of Amos*, 'a graphic picturization of the world-famous William J. Locke's most popular novel'; *Hell's Highroad*, 'a smashing drama of the New York "gold coast"'; and *The Road to Yesterday*, 'a production to which the word stupendous can be fittingly applied'. The first two were directed by Paul Sloane and Rupert Julian respectively. Only the third was directed by DeMille.

'Big in theme, spectacular in action, rich in scenic investiture,' *The Road to Yesterday* was Cecil and Jeanie's most direct experiment with the concept of reincarnation. It was not a new story, having been presented on the stage by Beulah Marie Dix and Evelyn Greenleaf Sutherland in 1906 and running for 216 performances, well into 1907.

The tale appealed to DeMille's kinks because he could feature another maimed anti-hero, in this case a newlywed husband, Kenneth Paulton, and his wife, Malena, who cannot bear the touch of his crippled arm. On a camping holiday at the Grand Canyon, they meet a flighty flapper, Beth, and a rugged, manly scoutmaster, Jack

Moreland, who turns out to be a reverend. They meet again on a train bound for San Francisco, which crashes en route, catapulting all four of them back into the past, to seventeenth-century England, where lords and commoners cavort and clash. Once again, as in *Joan the Woman* and the 'flashback' scene of *Male and Female*, the present-day wound turns out to be the result of an act of un-redeemed evil: in this case, the rapacious lust of Lord Strangevon, the past persona of Paulton, whose wish to marry the rich heiress who is the modern-day Beth leads him to torture her true love, the future Moreland, and deny his gypsy wife, the modern Malena. As Moreland in his death throes knifes the lord, the gypsy girl is burned at the stake and mouths her curse: 'Through lives and lives – thou shalt pay and pay!' At which point the characters, having realized their ancient fates, are catapulted back to the train, where Paulton miraculously regains the use of his arm and redeems his past sin by rescuing his fellow passengers.

To serve this strongly stirred stew, DeMille cast several newcomers to his stock company. As the withered hero, he chose the stage and film actor Joseph Schildkraut, the son of German Jewish stage star Rudolph Schildkraut. Joseph had begun his career as a child actor, appearing on Max Reinhardt's stage and in several German films from 1915, before coming to the US with his father in 1920. For the wife, DeMille engaged a French actress, Jetta Goudal, who turned out to be too much of a prima donna and sued – successfully – after he refused her further employment. The flapper was steady youth-culture girl Vera Reynolds, and the reverend was played by William Boyd, a young man who had been a regular bit-part player in DeMille's films since he had first appeared, uncredited, in *Old Wives for New*. His big break would occur in Cecil's next movie, *The Volga Boatman*, but his fame would be assured in 1935 when he would first play that hardy western perennial – Hopalong Cassidy, a role he reprised in fifty-three films.

The Road to Yesterday featured a number of extraordinary shots of expressionist-like shadows, 'emanations' of the past that threaten the tormented newlyweds, and several set-piece sequences, the most memorable being the head-on train collision. Described as 'one of the most vividly sensational train wrecks ever filmed', it is another trade-mark DeMille cataclysm, albeit on a less cosmic scale than the part-ing of the Red Sea. The art directors, Paul Iribe, Mitchell Leisen and

The Road to Yesterday – train wreck with Joseph Schildkraut and Jetta Goudal

their team, had a 'duplicate' built of the K-4 passenger engine, 'with twelve driving wheels seven feet in diameter and a length overall of eighty feet . . . A special rack was built as retakes were impossible.' The mechanical beast was flung off its rails and the dishevelled actors then picturesquely wedged in a slew of tangled and burning wreckage, undergoing a modern trial by fire. 'Mr. DeMille', the publicists explained, 'stationed a battery of cameramen strategically so that when the spectacular tragedy occurred, it was filmed from every angle.'

The art directors were equally flamboyant in reconstructing Olde England on the Culver City lot, 'quaint, beautiful and historically correct in every detail', according to the publicists. Pity about the acting in these sequences, which delves deep into the overdone and the ridiculous. Like any mortal, Cecil B. DeMille excelled either in what he knew or in those imagined realms that best expressed his inner muse or demons. Period England, which attracted so much Hollywood hokum, was not his forte. Ten years on, he would be able, nevertheless, to portray its colonizing hordes with visceral force in *The Crusades*, but that, of course, involved his core concerns – fanaticism, faith and religion – organically integrated in the story. *The Road to Yesterday* resonates with bathetic religious bombast, with the now familiar awakening of the crippled atheist to the 'Kingdom and the Power and the Glory' in the final scene, which is set, of course, in a church, under the sign of the cross.

The *New York Times*'s Mordaunt Hall, despite his lack of enthusiasm for DeMille's pictures, took time out to lunch with him in his 'private studio suite' in Los Angeles during the shooting of the film, and wrote up his impressions of the encounter for the 19 July issue:

I came away filled with admiration for DeMille's discipline, which is emulated by his subordinates. He is a man of millions, who works just as hard as if he were starting out on his first picture . . . He was directing a scene just before 1 o'clock, the hour set for luncheon. With one leg slung over a high stool behind the camera, he was studying the poses of the players . . . A word of praise from Mr DeMille brightens up the face of the person to whom he refers. He has obedience such as perhaps no other director obtains. His assistants, his property men, skip about with alacrity, never wanting to be a second behind in giving Mr DeMille that which he wishes . . . They always see that a chair is ready for him, no matter where he moves. Mr DeMille sits down knowing that the chair will be ready to receive him, and in the years that he has been directing not once has the property man forgotten to place that chair . . .

Mr DeMille is as careful concerning his luncheon in the studio quarters as if he were in the Ambassador Hotel. The servant waits on him in the most punctilious manner, making next to no noise and observing Mr. DeMille's countenance as he eats . . . This servant knows that Mr DeMille dislikes calling a servant or even asking for what he wants. He thinks that it ought to be there. When Mr DeMille was sipping his iced tea he made a wry grimace, which instantly brought sugar to his side . . .

Hall described the lunch room as 'fashioned after the cabin of a sailing vessel', a design inherited from yachting fan Thomas Ince. 'It pleases Mr. DeMille. He has, however, his own special office, which is an elaborate spacious place with the skins of several animals decorating the floor.'

The devotion of the stooges was noted again and again: 'If he walks three paces forward, they walk three paces forward. If he retreats, they go back too. While I was watching a scene that afternoon, Mr DeMille called for Miss Macpherson, and four heads turned anxiously looking to see if Miss Macpherson were present, while only one of them called out her name.'

When the film was released, however, Hall, properly distanced from the hypnotic gaze of the basilisk, damned it with faint praise, noting that 'DeMille adheres tenaciously to his queer flamboyant style . . . The story lacks necessary clarity,' though he joined the acclaim for 'the finest conception of a train wreck ever projected on a screen, and it is regrettable that the other episodes do not measure up to this exciting sequence'.

Despite massive publicity, the film did not prosper. Its grosses barely exceeded its costs, the first financial failure ever for a DeMille film. Clearly the audience did not share the DeMille–Macpherson penchant for the elaborate flashback, reincarnation themes or crippled heroes. Had the Jesus project been uppermost in his mind, one might have thought that DeMille would have turned immediately to this ideal way of restoring his fortunes. Instead, he embarked on what was perhaps the most unlikely project of all those that he had ever embarked on, since his quickie Balkan War films of 1915.

Before *The Road to Yesterday* opened at the end of November 1925, he was already on set, shooting a movie that glorified a Russian communist revolutionary entitled *The Volga Boatman*.

Red Cecil, from the Volga to the River Jordan

Cecil DeMille's romance with Russia was an old story. We might recall his first attempt as a playwright, the Tsarist-era play *The Pretender*, with its prologue set in 'Uglitch, Russia' and its tale of the false tsar, Dimitri. 'News from Moscow is always sad, Prince' was a line that reflected both American and western European conceptions of that domain of autocracy and repression. As a member of the cultural elite, Cecil would have had an essential acquaintance with Russian literature, at least with Turgenev and Tolstoy. Every red-blooded democratic soul in America knew that tsarism was appalling and barbaric, and sympathy for the Russian revolution, in particular with its February 1917 outbreak, was widespread. Bolshevism, however, as exported in the form of class-based revolutionary politics and trade-union agitation, was not so favoured. The *Beast of Berlin* picture cycle of late 1918 was swiftly followed by such movie productions as *Bolshevism on Trial* (April 1919), with Liberty holding back the ragged hordes under the heading 'Columbia's Sword Unsheathed to keep Bolshevism from the Land of the Free!' As the era of resurgent business advanced, organized labour's attempts to get a slice of the growing cake was countered by paranoid accusations of Red subversion as the spearhead of a takeover by Lenin and Trotsky, although the Communist Party in America in 1919 numbered at most 60,000 followers.

The Big Red Scare died down after a few months, but hostility towards the Bolsheviks did not. In 1923, William Fox released *Red Russia Revealed*, a 'documentary' featuring the 'First Pictures out of Russia in Two Years'. Posters showed a flame-tongued wolf with outstretched claws snarling over a throng of helpless refugees, as onion-domed churches burned in the background.

However, both William and Cecil continued to be sympathetic towards the Revolution and were unconvinced by the claims of the restorationist 'Whites' who had fought a devastating civil war in Russia to stifle it. We might describe William's views today as those of a typical upper-class socialist, whose principles lay at an odd slant to his own comfortable way of life. Some of his early films, like *The Sowers* and *The Blacklist*, clearly showed his sympathy for working-class struggles. The ideas of Henry George served him as a perfect vehicle for resolving the contradictions between the soundness of capitalism in principle and its impact in practice upon working people. Cecil's own views were, as we have seen, refracted through his penchant for hyperbole and melodrama and Jeanie Macpherson's semi-occult ideas. The reversal of fortune theme presented a format in which they could express their social sympathies while also suggesting a 'hidden hand' that ultimately decided human fortunes. Macpherson saw it as a mystic principle of predestination and fate. DeMille had by now decided it was God.

The opening intertitle of *The Volga Boatman* expresses this sleight of hand quite clearly, as an apologia for Cecil's unexpected political slant: 'Ours is not a story of a Crusade, a Struggle or Victory,' declares the title disingenuously, 'it pleads no cause, it takes no sides. It is a story of people – a Prince, a Lady and a Volga Boatman . . . plunged into a maelstrom of flame and terror. To explain Revolution is not a task of ours – Man cannot explain it.'

Which suggests the curious proposition of the Russian Revolution as an act of God, a unique DeMillean claim. In fact, DeMille's interest in revolutionary Russia had survived all the Red-baiting scares and propaganda. In September 1921, he had sent a letter to Adolph Zukor at the Paramount New York office, suggesting that he could pursue some commercial possibilities for the company on his coming 'rush trip' to Europe. DeMille wrote that 'Theodore Kosloff has approached me on the subject of the vast possibility of the Russian market. Mr Washington B. Vanderlip, who has just returned from Russia, where he obtained from Lenin the Kamchatka concessions, is very sure that the time is ripe to sell pictures to Russia. He has assurances from the Russian Ministry of the Interior that every aid possible will be given the exhibition of pictures throughout the country . . .' DeMille suggested to Zukor that, at a very 'light expense', he could dispatch Kosloff to Moscow and 'have him go thoroughly into the possibilities of selling our product in Russia'. Cecil ended his letter with a personal note: 'I am sorry not to have been east during the recent political activity but I am sure that you know, without my repeating it, where my loyalty is. With kind personal regards, Cecil B. DeMille.'

The 'political activity' DeMille was referring to had nothing to do with revolution in Russia or America but was the great trust-busting suit that Paramount was now immersed in over its block-booking policies. Zukor replied to the letter suggesting that Cecil postpone his trip to be on hand for the promotion of his 'horn of plenty' of titles, including *Manslaughter*, *The Affairs of Anatol*, *Fool's Paradise* and *Saturday Night*. He thanked DeMille for his loyalty and added: 'As to Kosloff, I have the matter up with Mr E. Shauer who is at the head of our foreign department. He tells me we are in constant touch through our own European representatives with the Russian situation and he feels that there is not a thing that Kosloff could do for us. I want to thank you nevertheless for bringing this to my attention . . .' In short, DeMille was blown off.

Kosloff's involvement is interesting as Russian émigrés were in general wildly opposed to Bolshevism. He had, however, arrived in America before the Revolution and was not part of the post-revolutionary 'White Russian' exiles, who would form their own artistic community, mainly in Paris.

DeMille admits in his autobiography that if he were making *The Volga Boatman* now, i.e. the 1950s, he would be hauled up before the Un-American Activities Committee. 'In 1925,' he writes, 'most of us were more naive politically.' As we have seen, it is only the reader of his book who might be so naive as to accept this. DeMille claimed the idea for the film was sparked by, of all things, an advertisement for Mazda lamps portraying a bunch of people with bowed heads, except for one who was looking towards the light. 'It reminded me of mankind's long struggle for freedom, led by the few who dared to raise their heads out of the shadow of oppression.' In fact, the image of the Volga boatmen in the film is posed exactly as the figures in a famous and much reproduced Russian painting by Ilya Repin, *Barge Haulers on the Volga*, dating from 1873. The Russian nationalist critic Vladimir Stasov, a contemporary of Repin, saw the painting as 'a commentary on the latent force of social protest in the Russian people', a central theme of the original book by Konrad Bercovici.

For Cecil to have chosen the Bercovici book in the first place was significant, as Bercovici was a communist of Romanian Jewish origin who had made his name as a journalist and an expert on the various immigrant communities in the US, notably the Poles. His book on the gypsies was a major source on the Romany communities in Europe. He would later write on biblical subjects such as Moses and the Exodus, and become involved in what is known as 'Revisionist' Zionism, supporting the efforts of a group of influential Hollywood-ites, including Ben Hecht, to finance Jewish refugee immigration to Palestine and support for the anti-British 'Irgun' militia (or 'terror-ists', as they would be termed today). In the late 1930s, he grew dis-illusioned with Stalin's purges, and was also noted for his 1940 feud with Charlie Chaplin, a close friend for many years, whom he sued for stealing his original idea for *The Great Dictator* (a suit eventually settled out of court).

The posing of the Volga boatmen might, of course, have come from the art directors, Max Parker, Mitchell Leisen and Anton Grot, but it is such a central image for the movie that one might reasonably suspect the director's crucial hand. Bercovici's novel was a human story rather than a propagandist piece, portraying the dilemma of people on either side of the revolutionary divide. It was a perfect example, in fact, of Cecil's reversal of fortune theme – an entire coun-try and society turned upside down – though once again Jeanie Macpherson sat this one out and the script was written by Lenore Coffee, later known as a specialist in 'women's pictures'. She was to clock up eighty credits between 1919 and 1960, and had the added honour of being a descendant of General John Coffee, chief of staff to Andrew Jackson at the Battle of New Orleans in 1814. Perhaps the military background qualified her for this particular task.

DeMille considered shooting the picture in Russia, but his new partners in the Cecil B. DeMille Pictures Corporation rejected this idea. As it was, the chosen location on the Sacramento River was expensive enough, and the executive producers insisted that the bud-get be kept well below the $400,000 that DeMille wanted (it would eventually cost almost $480,000). DeMille engaged a new camera-man, Arthur Miller, already a veteran of twelve years' experience and known today as one of Hollywood's greats. Production documents, however, reveal a great deal of screaming and yelling by DeMille about the levels of light, given that he had agreed with Miller on the use of the new panchromatic film stock, which rendered colours bet-ter in black and white and removed the necessity for heavy make-up on the actors' faces and hands. Behind the scenes, and without news-paper interviewers present, DeMille was often more temperamental than his public image suggested. No one wanted to be on the receiving end of a major rant from him, and he could be as unpleasant in his wrath as he was supportive to those who obeyed him. After several arguments with DeMille, Arthur Miller departed from the set, and shooting was continued by Peverell Marley.

The cast for *The Volga Boatman* was led by William Boyd in his first starring role, Elinor Fair as the Russian princess Vera and Victor Varconi as her White Russian officer fiancé, the love triangle in the film. Veteran stage actor Robert Edeson, who had turned down Cecil's original play *The Pretender* to play Strongheart for brother William twenty years before, co-starred as Vera's stern father, Prince Nikita. Julia Faye and Theodore Kosloff provided semi-comic relief as a Tartar hussy and a dumb blacksmith who later become Red Army fighters. Boyd, as Feodor, gives a handsome dignity to the Boatman, who bears – and often bares – the scar of the rope with which he pulls cargoes up the river and dreams of the dawn of free-dom under the red flag.

Despite the opening credit's disclaimer, the sympathies of the film are not in any doubt. At a castle on the banks of the Volga, the 'per-fumed' aristocrats of old Russia enjoy their last moments of luxury while, below them, the simple folk struggle to survive and the boat-men, the 'human mules of Russia', drag their load against the drift of the river, singing their repetitive 'Song of Work and Hope'. When Prince Dimitri confronts Feodor the Boatman and demands he wipe the dirt off his shoe, the ensuing blow he strikes across the Boatman's face for his insolence is answered with: 'Our blood flows now – later other blood will flow.'

The prince's plea to Vera, who has responded emotionally to the boatmen's song, is: 'Can you find the soul of Russia in these animals?'

Revolution comes, a boat of Red commandos rushing dramatically up the river with the red flag. Semi-Eisensteinian scenes of rapt faces listening to Feodor's call to arms follow, though DeMille would not have been able to see Eisenstein's recent *Battleship Potemkin* before he shot his picture – first screenings of *Potemkin* abroad took place in 1926.

The Reds, with Feodor now leading them, break into the prince's castle at dinner time and force old Nikita and Vera to serve them

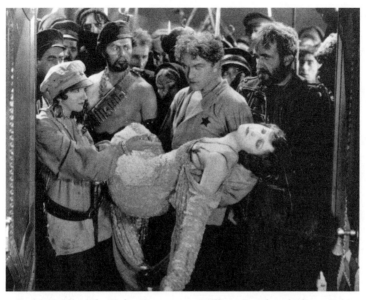

Red DeMille: *The Volga Boatman* – William Boyd and Elinor Fair

food off their gold plates. In a scuffle, a young Red is killed, and Feodor is assigned to shoot Vera in reprisal. Impressed by her courage, however, he saves her, and they escape to an inn as a married couple. The Whites, led by Dimitri, take the inn. Dimitri is in a fury because he has been told Vera has been captured by the Reds. When he hears a Red officer and his 'wife' are at the inn he orders his men to 'do to their women what they have done to ours!' There follows a reprise of the scene in *The Little American* between Mary Pickford and her American-German lover, as the White officers lasciviously mock Vera, whose garments are torn off off-screen, till Dimitri enters and realizes he has ordered the humiliation of his own fiancée.

Feodor, in turn, is condemned to execution, but Vera bars the firing squad's way till, in the next twist, the Reds attack. Feodor is forced to prove his loyalty to the Revolution by condemning the Whites, including Vera, whom he loves. The Whites are sentenced, men and women, to be roped to the Volga boats in order to drag the jeering Red soldiers up the river. Defiantly, Feodor joins the haulers, and all three, Feodor, Dimitri and Vera, get to sing the Volga boatmen song. In the end, at a tribunal, Vera agrees to join the Revolution so that 'the blood of old Russia' will help to build 'the new Russia', while Dimitri chooses exile, the Red judges having, in most unlikely fashion, been impressed by Feodor's speech about love.

Press releases dated 10 May 1926 reveal that there was an alternative ending to the picture, less friendly to the Red tribunal: 'Feodor demands the privilege of disposing of Vera and Dimitri, and, in view of his service to the cause, his demand is granted. He escorts the pair to the border of Russia and commands them to cross it and never return. But when he leaves her side, Vera breaks away from Dimitri, and hurries after Feodor. The dumbfounded boatman takes her in his hand and, together, they wade through a raging snow storm towards the Volga river, while Dimitri resigns himself to his fate and leaves his country behind.' This scene must have cost a pretty penny to shoot, but most probably DeMille thought that a final victory for love, rather than a reluctant retreat from Feodor's ruthless Bolshevik principles, would resonate better with the American audience. As indeed it did.

It is easy to see *The Volga Boatman* as ridiculous, and indeed Mordaunt Hall in the *New York Times* – against a mostly positive critical response – poured scorn over the 'weird Hollywood dream of the Russian Revolution, which was presented last night with due pomp before a critical audience in the Times Square Theatre. In this feature panting men and women pause during dramatic interludes and seem to accomplish the impossible. There are contrasts that are often grotesque or absurd, but some scenes are emphatically stirring . . . The production as a whole, however, causes one to reflect that it is unfortunate that Mr. DeMille has nobody to say him nay.'

This was true in a sense, though DeMille was surrounded by executives who were naying him on a constant basis. While directing his film, Cecil was also continuing to produce the first tranche of his new company's titles with other directors, comprising ten films for 1925 and 1926. The second year's season, 1926–7, would comprise sixteen films, and the third year, to 1928, a staggering twenty-five titles! DeMille was stretching himself to the limit, and his greatest task was just about to commence . . .

Nevertheless, if one sets aside the conventional expectation of a 'realistic' narrative, *The Volga Boatman* once again demonstrates DeMille's talent for constructing an incredible story so as to make it dramatically convincing. The film can at least be properly judged by present-day viewers, as it exists in a fine video presentation, with original colour tones restored. Photography, settings, furnishings, props are once again exemplary, and the acting – despite the often ludicrous plot turns – is relatively restrained, an improvement on the gothic grotesquerie of *The Road to Yesterday*. All three protagonists extract some genuine emotion from their emblematic status as representations of three clashing ideals: proletarian solidarity, upper-class consciousness and patriotic Russianness. It is indeed a Hollywood dream, but also yet another of Cecil DeMille's peculiar visions, full of odd kinky moments, sado-masochistic lashings and the casting of his lover Julia Faye as a shameless and vengeful wench.

One can see that the DeMille craft is as strong as ever, but the philosophical underpinnings are beginning to break up. King of his own castle, DeMille can indeed, as Mordaunt Hall noted, do what he wants, but the question now looming is: what is it exactly that Cecil B. DeMille wants to do? The obstacle was not the absence of external control, since the financiers and lawyers of the Cinema Corporation of America could hardly have made any useful creative contribution. If Cecil had thought new partners would give him more leeway than Zukor and Lasky, he was sorely mistaken. The ace in the hole was Jeremiah Milbank, and the promise that DeMille made to make another biblical film. But if the executives were anxious about the budgets for more modest projects, how could they be brought to back yet another period epic?

To cover his back, Cecil reverted to the old gimmick: a competition launched with the *Los Angeles Times* in February for, yet again, an idea for his next movie. Prizes amounting to $2,100 were offered. Letters, containing basic ideas and of no more than two hundred words, were to be addressed to the DeMille Contest Editor and were to arrive by midnight 27 February. The letters poured in while DeMille hied off to New York to joust with his financiers and executives. The results were forensically analysed in *Motion Picture News* on 3 April: 38,517 proposals were submitted, as against the 29,100 ideas of 1922. People wrote in from 'every State in the Union and sixteen foreign countries. These suggestions came from college professors, doctors, lawyers, priests, ministers, rabbis, bank presidents and executives in practically every great commercial industry; as well as from authors and artists of world-wide reputation; artisans, clerks, miners, and laborers in every field of human endeavor.'

And the winner is . . .

On 13 March, *Motion Picture News* had reported that although biblical themes had once again led the field in the early stages, there had been a 'sharp decline in the number of Biblical suggestions' towards the end of the contest. Nevertheless, on 3 April, it was found that 14 per cent of the ideas were biblical, 12 per cent other historical and 11 per cent were post-war stories, while there were ninety-five suggestions relating to industrial topics, the rest involving 'Prohibition, married life, crime and young love', in that order.

One hundred and fifty-seven proposals favoured the same subject – The Deluge – and so on 17 April the press announced that this was indeed to be DeMille's next film. The first prize, $1,000, was awarded to Miss Catherine Comstock of Long Beach, California, 'because of the manner in which she described and presented The Deluge as a motion picture theme'. Thirteen other 'meritorious' prizes were awarded. Said DeMille:

The Deluge will come as a suggestion from the public. 'The Ten Commandments' was a tremendous pleasure in its development, and I foresee equal pleasure in the growth of 'The Deluge' into final form.

In fact, 'The Deluge' was thoroughly prepped, including a spectacular poster depicting the ark and the flood. However, in May, soon after *The Volga Boatman* opened, the press announced that work on 'The Deluge' had stopped 'owing to the fact that Warner Brothers had previously filed plans with the Hays office to make a production titled "Noah's Ark."' (That was eventually directed by Michael Curtiz in 1928 as a partial talkie; its flood scene cost the lives of three extras, but one of the uncredited swimmers, a young John Wayne, survived.)

Finally, by serendipity, DeMille was able to proceed to the project he claimed his main financial backer always wanted him to make. By another stroke of fortune, *The Volga Boatman*, helped by a massive publicity campaign, was striking gold at the box office. Double-page ads lauded DeMille with glowing superlatives:

The Master-Craftsman of Motion Picture Production and Star Maker of a brilliant galaxy of box office favorites, transcends with each succeeding production the triumphs that have placed him in an exalted niche of his own.

The creative genius that produced 'The Ten Commandments' and 'The Volga Boatman'; the prophetic vision that was responsible for the development of such great stars as Gloria Swanson, Thomas Meighan . . . [*etc., etc.*]

the forceful executive ability that had organized and welded together into a perfect production unit the amazing group of super-craftsmen responsible for P.D.C. product; these are the potent and fundamental faculties that Cecil B. De Mille has brought to the monumental task of motion picture production on a colossal scale.

To cap it all, Cecil had now brought brother William, with his creditable record of a string of modest hits and finely judged dramas as a director, to his new outfit. 'His name never has been identified with a failure' was the new studio puff. The two DeMilles for the price of one were unstoppable. But William continued ploughing his own quiet furrow, while Cecil approached Jeanie Macpherson with 'the most important assignment of her life'. This time there would be no counter-balancing modern story, no brothers or mother McTavish to blur the essential message. This time it would be true to itself, pristine and fundamental, the genuine article, The Greatest Story Ever Told.

Coasting to Golgotha

Foreword from the *King of Kings* brochure:

> AT NO TIME in the World's history has Humanity so
> hungered for the Truth. Science has declared there is a
> God. And a groping, eager World cries,
> How may we find Him?

Cecil B. DeMille's movie *The King of Kings* sparked a controversy as agonized and passionate as that prompted seventy-seven years later by Mel Gibson's 2004 film, *The Passion of the Christ*. The battleground was essentially the same and involved accusations from major Jewish organizations and their leaders that the tale as told on the screen reignited the primal Christian libel against the Jews as the assassins of the Saviour. Was this 'The Most Dangerous Anti-Semitic Photoplay in Filmdom', as some raging critics maintained? Or was it, as DeMille insisted, his honest and sincere attempt 'to give the peoples of the modern world the same opportunity to see the wondrous life-drama of Jesus as was given to the citizens of Judea nineteen hundred years ago'?

Knowing his Bible, his audience and his industry very well, DeMille prepared himself in advance for this onslaught, bringing to the set Catholic and Protestant ministers, as well as a number of rabbis. The first day of shooting began, according to DeMille, with a prayer service combining participants of the Catholic, Protestant, Jewish, Buddhist and Muslim faiths.

The most enthusiastic of the clergymen witnessing the production was, however, Father Daniel A. Lord, one of the most prolific Catholic scribes of the century, who could boast the authorship, among his three hundred pamphlets and essays, of the Production Code of the Motion Picture Producers and Distributors Association. He set down his memories of the shooting in his 1959 autobiography, *Played By Ear*.

Father Lord arrived, he related, after news of the extravagance of the production had been lampooned by *Vanity Fair*'s cartoonist, who made the set look like 'Ziegfeld at his most sumptuous, Frank Buck at his most ferocious, Rome at its most luxurious, and a faint trickle of Scriptures struggling through a jungle of scenery and costume'. The location was Catalina Island, standing in for Galilee and the Nazarene carpenter's home. As Lord described the scene:

H. B. Warner, playing the part of the Lord, was kept in a sort of tented cloister addressed not at all until he was out of costume. An unfortunate lady, cast as Mary, was under a morals contract that she violated by divorcing and marrying again before the picture was well released . . . The waving of armies of extras past thousands of feet of celluloid, the systematic confusion of the old silent pictures, burst upon my head. And DeMille welcomed me, like the emperor he is . . .

The Protestant minister had come and gone, and would return. The rabbi seemed to have disappeared once the Old Testament had dissolved into the New . . .

I became aware of the slavery that attached to the office of an author in Hollywood. Jeanie Macpherson was the scenarist, swiftly killing herself with an intensity of work and a passion for precise detail that kept her on a sixteen-hour-a-day schedule during the long months of production . . .

Of DeMille, Lord wrote:

He was a strange and fascinating blend of absolute monarch and charming gentleman, of excellent host and exacting taskmaster, of ruthless drive on the set and a complete letdown the moment that the day's shooting had come to an end; a Renaissance prince who had the instincts of a Barnum and a magnified Belasco; frankly in love with hokum (which he liked to discuss and reduce to terms of understandable basic emotion) . . . an excellent listener and a voice that spoke with the most compelling possible command; an Episcopalian whose mother (deeply beloved) was, I think, a Jewish convert to Christianity; a man with the Midas touch (who loved to know) . . . his backers were worried at his extravagance, while all the time he never lost sight of a penny or really wasted a single foot of film.

This was the first time that Cecil's 'half-Jewish' identity became a factor, both for his supporters and his detractors, although he made no particular effort to play on it. His introduction to the reading of the script, in August 1926, to cast and crew acknowledged the need to be ultra-sensitive to religious divisions, 'to treat all classes fairly and particularly the Jew, because the Jew is put in the most unfortunate place of any race in the Bible, because it was not really a matter of the Jews having persecuted Jesus, it was Rome, Rome with her politics and graft'.

Cecil was dissimulating, as he well knew the central problem that bedevils inter-faith issues and 'fundamentalisms' to our day: that each of the three monotheistic religions are blasphemous to each other. Jews and Muslims do not accept the divinity of Jesus, and Christians consider Jews and Muslims heretics for that reason. The spiritual message of the Christ – and Judaism and Islam – can be drawn on for principles of tolerance, but the iconic drama, which DeMille was about to film, had to include the scene of the Hebrew crowd baying for Barabbas and the crucifixion of Jesus, with the dreadful cry: 'His blood be on us, and on our children' (Matthew 27:25). DeMille omitted this line, the primal fuel for Christian persecution of Jews down the ages. But he cast two prominent Jewish actors, the father and son Rudolph and Joseph Schildkraut, in key controversial roles – Joseph as Judas and Rudolph as the High Priest Caiaphas. The latter projected undeniable authority, but he was a well-known actor on the Yiddish stage. And he certainly 'looked Jewish', to risk the stereotypical charge.

In fact, one earlier announcement of DeMille's new film, as reported by the *New York Times* on 13 June 1926, was that the subject of the picture was to be Judas, 'the most despised character in Biblical history . . . The question of priority of right,' the *Times* wrote, 'seems to be the predominant issue.' The title of this film was 'Thirty Pieces of Silver', and it was to be just one of three productions based on the same theme that year, the second being a Famous Players-Lasky project called 'Pieces of Silver', 'from a magazine story published two years ago, as a feature for Emil Jannings, and the third a version of a drama "The Kiss" by screenwriter J. Stewart Woodhouse'. Woodhouse's theory that Judas was maligned and 'acted from justifiable motives in the betrayal of Christ' (an ancient Gnostic contention) would probably not have been well received, and it was never filmed. Nor did Emil Jannings play the part.

Father Lord, ever the wry observer, noted that in the opening scenes of *The King of Kings* scenario DeMille and Macpherson had written 'a love story that would satisfy the morons' desire for red meat' (the morons being, in Lord's words, 'Minnie and Jake (those mythical and all-powerful Gods of the box-office)'). As Lord put it:

A moment of prayer before the Christian epiphany, as seen by *Vanity Fair* in 1926

'Out of some ancient and little-known German legend of the Middle Ages had been resurrected the love story of Mary Magdalene and Judas. Judas, a handsome young fellow with ambitions that the Gospels hint at, had fallen in love with Mary Magdalene, a courtesan in the very best Broadway, penthouse or villa-on-the-Riviera style . . . There was even an indicated desert scene with Mary at the door of the tent of Christ and Judas raging in jealousy. I confess that my heart sank at the possibilities of this plot.'

Lord asked to see this section and reported 'DeMille at his most DeMille-ish. A Roman banquet with roistering drinkers, dancing girls, zebras harnessed to a chariot, and a Mary Magdalene, played by the beautiful but soon to disappear Jacqueline Logan, who combined the charms of generations of females of the fatal stripe.' Cecil explained to the good father that modern audiences needed to be led into the picture: 'They could not be introduced to burlap and desert sands, but must have a sense of luxury and beauty, the kind of life they would themselves like to lead.' A simple carpenter in an old robe clearly could not do the trick, at least not from the start. The showman who wanted to make every woman want to wear what Gloria Swanson was wearing in his last movie couldn't quite fade away. In the event, the opening Magdalene scene became a pretext for another experiment in two-colour Technicolor, the other colour bookend of the film being the sequence of the rising from the tomb. The

Magdalene's rush with her zebras to reclaim Judas from Jesus leads to her cleansing of the Seven Deadly Sins, who all depart, leaving her a contrite disciple.

What converted Father Lord to the project, despite his misgivings, was the particular aura of DeMille's choice for the role of Jesus, H. B. Warner. He was, at fifty-two, way over the age for the part and had been in movies since 1914. DeMille wanted a physically imposing, authoritative Jesus, a man among men, rather than what he called 'the effeminate, sanctimonious, machine-made Christs of second-rate so-called art, which used to be thought good enough for Sunday schools'. This Christ would be expected to scourge the moneylenders from the temple but also exhibit the more tender characteristics of compassion and humour, as well as a virile intelligence. Father Lord noticed how Warner could 'walk through make-believe scenery and yet dominate the hushed audience of actors, technicians, and make-up people, who watched him and hardly breathed'. Christ, as Lord observed, 'began to take over', to the extent that DeMille began utterly to merge him with the role, leaning over to the priest and saying: 'He's great, isn't He?' 'Warner?' asked the priest. '"Jesus," he replied. "He is great."'

By November, the trade magazines were reporting that *The King of Kings* was 'Half Complete' (while eleven other Producers Distributing Corporation films, merely produced but not directed by DeMille, were in progress!). 'Some of the largest sets ever erected for a motion picture' had been constructed, including an 'unusually large set representing the Temple of Herod'. It contained two hundred and ninety-five great pillars, had been built by two hundred and fifty carpenters working in shifts and in some shots contained three thousand extras. 'The materials used included four hundred thousand feet of lumber, sixty thousand lath, forty-five thousand square feet of tar paper, thirty tons of plaster, seventy-thousand square feet of cement for the floor,' and so forth. And yet, DeMille told *Motion Picture News*, 'this set will be dwarfed by that representing the Judgment Hall of Pontius Pilate, which is now in course of construction under the supervision of Art Director Paul Iribe'. Not being built in the dunes, all this would have to be dismantled at the end of the shoot at great cost, though the sets were left standing for 'several months' in case of retakes.

The production wrapped on 17 January 1927, and DeMille was

said to have scheduled eight weeks for the editing. So short a period for so complex a project might seem unbelievable in our day, but it was the custom of editors to begin cutting the film as soon as shooting began, and Anne Bauchens was obviously not expected to get any sleep for two months. The basic principle was not to allow money to lie idle. The final cost of the picture topped $1.2 million.

The King of Kings premiered at the Gaiety Theatre, New York, on 19 April. Musical arranger Hugo Riesenfeld presided over a thirty-six-piece orchestra and a choir of forty singers who accompanied the score. This time the critics universally raved, even *Variety*'s sourpuss 'Sime', who called it 'tremendous in its lesson, in the daring of its picturization . . . and tremendous in its biggest scene, the Crucifixion of Christ'. Mordaunt Hall reported in the *Times* that 'so reverential is the spirit of Cecil B. DeMille's pictorial transcription of the life of Jesus of Nazareth, the Man, that during its initial screening . . . hardly a whispered word was uttered among the audience. This production is . . . the most impressive of all motion pictures.' *Motion Picture News* described it as 'the greatest sermon of all time . . . The appeal of this picture is not of the dramatic. Rather it is of the church and cathedral,' though one of the three critics the journal sent to the picture, L. C. Moen, thought it nevertheless failed 'as entertainment'.

'Sime' did note that the film 'looks predestined to provoke many and strong arguments, according to the faith . . .', and so indeed it did. Even before it opened, the movie had opened up a rift between Catholics and Protestants at the Motion Picture Producers and Distributors Association, headed by Will Hays. The Hays Office noted a sermon, preached on 10 April by the pastor of St Paul's Presbyterian Church in Los Angeles, about 'Filmdom's Most Notable Religious Picture'. The pastor was much less forgiving than Father Daniel Lord of DeMille's use of the Magdalene to enter the tale of the Christ, which, first of all, presented 'a photographic reproduction of the Son of God'.

'Can the Church Endorse Such a Picture?' asked the pastor. 'Has Cecil B. DeMille sold Christ, as did Judas of old, in commercializing the most Divine Tragedy in the History of the Race?' Cecil's sins were legion, as he had reportedly confessed that he had to have 'a sex lure in order to sell this picture . . . WHAT IS THE TROUBLE WITH CECIL DeMILLE? His father was a lay reader in the Episcopal Church – held services when the Rector was not present – took offertory once in a while. DeMille needed to raise three million dollars, by his own testimony, to make money on the life of Christ . . . I WILL STAND against that sort of thing morning noon and night – the idea of photographing of a human being to represent, to me, my Saviour, and that human being to go outside, smoking a cigarette!'

This screed was based on a report by another Protestant minister, Reverend William E. Barton, in the *Dearborn Independent*, the weekly published by Henry Ford and noted as America's most scurrilously anti-Semitic propaganda sheet. Following his son, Bruce Barton, to the set, the reverend met and liked Jeanie Macpherson, 'a competent and attractive young woman' who emphasized her good Scots descent to him. But he did not like the Magdalene tale. DeMille must have rued the day he had allowed clergy on the set, when Barton advised him to 'cut out the Raising of Lazarus . . . it is recorded by only one of the evangelists . . . the Feeding of the Five Thousand is your best chance in this film to show a crowd'. However, he had accepted DeMille's assurance that 'this film should be a religious lesson to America and the world'. Barton concluded: 'I brought away an impression of a deeper religious spirit in this film than I had expected to discover.' One Hays Office internal memo to the censor, Colonel Jason Joy, citing the Barton piece, noted that 'You will appreciate the value of this article to the motion picture industry because of the previous critical articles which the *Dearborn Independent* printed . . . I think it would be a splendid thing to send to all the religious editors.'

Protestant wrath was eventually assuaged, but Jewish anger mounted against the film through its major run from April to the end of 1927. In October, the President of B'nai B'rith, Alfred Cohen, the liberal Rabbi Stephen Wise and the 'dean of American Rabbis', David Philipson, viewed the film and declared war. The film, claimed the influential leaders, 'revived the ancient slander that the Jews had killed Jesus', an accusation that had caused great persecution, dispossession and countless Jewish deaths over centuries. Nobody understood why Rudolph Schildkraut had undertaken such a scenery-chewing role as Caiaphas, who, counter to any Gospel source, is actually the first to cry 'Crucify him!' in Pontius Pilate's ear. To balance this, DeMille has Caiaphas, after the crucifixion, addressing God after the temple has been rent (and a candelabrum bursts into flame): 'Lord God Jehovah, visit not thy wrath on thy people Israel – I alone am guilty.' But by then the damage had been done.

The Jewish leaders first tried to call for the banning of the film, but this was not in any case feasible, and they fell back on a plea to prevent its distribution abroad, particularly in European countries rife with anti-Semitism, such as Hungary, Romania, Poland, Austria or Germany, the home of the annual passion play that so often sparked anti-Jewish violence. Rabbi Wise protested that Schildkraut's Caiaphas was 'more of a five and ten cent Shylock' and excoriated the intertitle that introduced the temple: 'To the faithful of Israel, the dwelling place of Jehovah, but to the High Priest, a corrupt and profitable marketplace.' Other Jewish critics attacked the Jewish executives of Hollywood and Sid Grauman, who had opened the film in his new Chinese Theatre in Los Angeles, for shamelessly supporting the calumniation of their own people.

What DeMille had done, more clearly than any film-maker before him, had been to blur the distinction between the commercial, artistic and advocating power of the medium. From the beginning of film, producers and directors, camera professionals and art directors had known that they were acting, at least in some way, on the cultural bases of society, on the way people thought, on the decisions they made about how they lived their lives, on what they bought, on how they dressed, on how they spent their leisure hours, and more than anything else, on how they daydreamed in the movie theatres. Religious propaganda, at least in the western world, was always a part of motion pictures, though the smart money tended to shun it. What delights the adherents of one faith can clearly outrage those of another. The worst charge that could be brought against a film-maker who earned his bread and butter by entertaining the public was that he was a bigot. The greatest good for the greatest number was ever the mantra of Hollywood.

Among the Jewish leaders, DeMille had sought in particular the support of Rabbi Edgar Magnin, a member of B'nai B'rith's Anti-Defamation League, which had been formed in 1913 precisely to combat the stereotyping of Jews in plays and the new motion pictures. Magnin, unlike Wise, declared that the best response by Jews would be to accept the picture, let it have its run and move on. 'If the picture succeeds,' he said, 'it will be because the Jews have attacked it. Nothing makes a play go like attacking it.'

This certainly seemed borne out by the box office. The film took off, and continued flying well into 1928 and in numerous revivals afterwards. Many special showings were held, among them a screening at Grauman's Chinese Theatre, on 16 August, at ten in the morning, to close to a thousand nuns (excluding the Carmelites and Cloister Dominicans) who had been given special privilege to see the movie. As Grauman's publicist described the event:

The entire sisterhood of Southern California were represented there. All were dressed according to their Order. Some with the black robes, others in white with black robes over, then again those in navy blue, still others in grey and the refugee Sisters of Mexico with a touch of red on their habits . . . This in itself was a solemn but picturesque sight.

A number of Sisters who attended were eighty, eighty-five and ninety years of age, who had always lived secluded lives, having lived through the evolution of the auto, radio, etc., and had never seen a motion picture.

DeMille, despite the unique success of the film, was badly stung by the accusations of anti-Semitism and countered, for a long time, with many tales of the good that was done by the picture. He kept a book of almost six hundred pages consisting entirely of typed transcripts of the many letters he had received from people of all walks of life, the famous and the obscure. From a Maybell G. Heaton, on 24 October: 'The King of Kings has awakened in my soul the beautiful faith I seemed to have lost . . .' From Mrs Elizabeth Terrell: 'Beloved Mr DeMille, Just a few words to say I saw your glorious, beautiful, uplifting, entrancing "The King of Kings" last Monday. I am going again soon . . . Yours in the service of God and humanity . . .' From Pastor Ralph Welles Keeler: 'Congratulating you on your vision and thanking you for making the vision concrete . . .' From Harmon Eldridge (aged fourteen): 'The most perfect picture I have ever seen.' From James M. Darst: 'In the mass of present day trash . . . your production stands as a landmark . . .' From Mack Sennett, who said he would urge his mother in Canada to rush to see the picture: 'My sincere enthusiasm for your great picture . . .' From Miss L. E. Grant: 'It does seem as though Christ had worked thro you to give this beautiful message to the world . . .'

Some people wrote long letters with their own poems. One lady wrote that 'the attached letter was dictated to me by a blind man . . .' Letters came from converted Jews, from the First Church of Christ

Scientists, from the Boy Scouts of America and from Spanish distributor Julio Cesar, who wrote: 'Had private exhibition KING OF KINGS in Palace Pedralbes to King and Queen of Spain now in Barcelona for a season. Full triumph. King says film is marvellous and the best he has seen . . .' And Monte Katterjohn, Hollywood screenwriter, wrote to him:

Your picture caused me to recall the wonderful moments when, as a little boy, I sat on my grandfather's knee and, while showing me beautiful, colored plates of the life of Christ, he related incidents in the same simple, direct and much the same unassailable manner as presented by your picture . . .

Whatever one's take on the controversy which, after all, only transferred to popular culture the same dilemmas and issues that had pre-existed in the New Testament's relationship with the Old, there is no denying the pictorial beauty of the film. Fortunately, *The King of Kings* has been blessed by an exemplary DVD restoration, including the original 155-minute version and a shorter version (112 minutes) with musical soundtrack released in 1928. The bookending Technicolor sequences have been gloriously recovered, despite some notable fogging on the Rising section, which some might think is mystical in origin but is probably merely the usual damage to a negative exposed eighty years ago. Two-colour Technicolor has a particularly unrealistic look as the full range of the spectrum is not represented, but the red and mauve costumes of the rich revellers egging on the Magdalene with her pet leopard and zebras are a proper feast for the eyes. The austere black and white of the bulk of the picture has been marvellously rendered by Peverell Marley, with Fred Westerberg and J. A. Badaracco manning the two extra cameras clearly seen churning away in surviving behind-the-scenes shots. These fragments of publicity shots and off-cuts reveal just some of the milling chaos that exists on the set of any large-scale movie, with its Judaean beggars chatting over their crutches, sheep and children racing the wrong way, and the general confusion – one marvels that anything coherent can be put together at the end of the day. Only innocents like Father Lord could conceive that DeMille never 'wasted a single foot of film', since the amount of film exposed and discarded was prodigious. DeMille presides over the melee from a specially constructed high chair, wielding a megaphone, the trademark leggings and all-weather pants in place. The silent-film set – unlike the

later talkie set, with its trademark yell of 'Silence!' – was a cacophony of barked orders and often the clattering and banging of other sets being built as cameras rolled.

The finished film proceeds, in the manner of *The Ten Commandments* but shorn of its indigestible 'modern story', as a series of tableaux, with dramatic tension generated by the classically composed relationships between characters in the shots. Although there is often a swirl of action within the shot, camera movements are kept to a minimum. DeMille's trademark direction of crowds is apparent everywhere: the small blind boy who wanders through a throng; the people surging towards the central figure; the masses at the temple compound celebrating the rout of the moneylenders; the temptation of Christ by the devil, who shows him the massed ranks of armies that could spring to his bidding; the 'Crucify him!' mob; and the crowds swirling at the foot of Golgotha as the penultimate act of the drama unfolds.

Jeanie Macpherson's scenario proceeds through all the familiar stations of the Gospel narrative: the healing of the blind, the raising of Lazarus, the tale of rendering the coin unto Caesar, the plotting of the Pharisees and Caiaphas, the chasing of the moneylenders from the temple, the Last Supper, the capture at Gethsemane, the scourging and the crown of thorns, and in most orthodox mode, Pontius Pilate's '*Ecce homo!*' DeMille set Pilate on a throne encased in a gigantic eagle, the power of Rome looming as a colossus. But as Rudolph Schildkraut as Caiaphas creeps forward at Pilate's elbow, with the wicked leer of his malevolence, DeMille falls into a moment of sheer anti-Semitism, the most misjudged shot of the film.

Judas, as played by Rudolph's son Joseph, is presented as a handsome and proud rebel who wants Jesus to proclaim himself an earthly king, with Judas as his princely deputy. He betrays him when he realizes this will not happen, hanging himself in terrible remorse at his deed.

At the crucifixion, DeMille indulged in his most apocalyptic sequence, as dark clouds gather, lightning rakes the sky and great fissures open up in the earth, the most 'Gustave Doré'-like moment in his entire oeuvre. But before the special-effects men were let loose, he celebrated his culminating scene in a manner recorded years later by his adopted daughter Katherine, who recollected to author Anne Edwards the moment when, in the shadow of the three crosses, the day's shoot ended at about 9 o'clock in the evening of Christmas Eve and the extras began to scatter:

All of a sudden, his voice boomed across the set. 'Ladies and gentlemen, if you'd stop for just a moment . . . I would like you all to take five minutes . . . for you to just think about what you have seen tonight – and to remember that what we've seen tonight is the filming of something that really happened . . . I'd like you to take a few minutes of quiet. I've asked the orchestra to play some music.' He had an organ on the set and first only it could be heard. Then the orchestra joined in. I think it was Bach's Christmas oratorio . . . There were many who wept. Some got on their knees facing the cross . . . In a few minutes he said, 'Thank you, ladies and gentlemen. Let's go home to our families – have a wonderful Christmas . . .'

DeMille could never resist the grand gesture, on or off screen. He may have scorned the Sunday-school art of a mundanely comforting Saviour, but his film is shot through with compositions that echo the devotional poses of traditional and Renaissance art. At the centre of it all, H. B. Warner expresses a quiet and determined authority that was not equalled in screen portrayals of Jesus until Pier Paolo Pasolini's startling neo-Marxian revolutionary in 1964's *The Gospel According to St Matthew*. It is no wonder that Christian audiences in

1927 sat entranced by the image as DeMille's lighting cameramen enveloped the actor with a luminous sheen of light, culminating in the final figure of Christ floating over an iconically modern city with the words 'Lo, I am with you always' shimmering upon the screen.

It is significant that when modern critics, particularly the opinion-forming movie fanatics of the French New Wave, began to anoint certain Hollywood directors as 'auteurs', they chose John Ford, Howard Hawks, Raoul Walsh and other journeymen of the studio factories, but not DeMille, who controlled his own films to a much greater degree than any of the regular canon. DeMille was passé, naive, unsophisticated, a degradation of the true sacrality of Hollywood, which was to express the American dynamic as a set of symbols of human progress. Henry Fonda walking out towards the bare wooden frames of a church constructed in the prairie of *My Darling Clementine* expressed the classic Fordian idea of civilization overcoming the wilderness. And this civilization, even as a church, was avowedly secular, a communal and practical ideal.

DeMille's declaration in *The King of Kings* that 'Science has declared there is a God' would be strictly nonsense to the secular sensibility, whether of the French left of the 1960s or any secular liberal – or even conservative – of our own age. But it resonated strongly in the slew of evangelistic movements which had spread across the US for decades before the film was made, from Mary Baker Eddy's Christian Science movement to Aimee Semple McPherson, Billy Sunday or a host of others. And it resonates too in the growing influence, in our own day, of American Christian fundamentalism and the creed of 'Intelligent Design'. Cecil Blount DeMille, disciple of Henry George as well as of Henry De Mille's Episcopalian faith, may well have cavilled at present-day arguments that accept the evidence of dinosaurs as long as they are dated no more than five thousand years ago to fit in with biblical chronology. He was not a 'literalist' who believed in the absolute truth of every word in the Bible. As a storyteller, he could recognize a rattling good fable when he read it. But he was becoming more and more convinced, as success and acclaim from one side of the religious – and political – argument was set against decreasing praise from the socially 'progressive' modernists of film and cultural comment, that destiny intended him to proclaim certain messages. The chair on which he sat as a director was getting higher and higher. Could there be any way ahead but down?

Twelve years after *The King of Kings*, Jeanie Macpherson and brother William de Mille prepared a script for Cecil on the subject of Mary, the mother of Jesus, which was tentatively titled *Queen of Queens*. Father Daniel Lord described his own reactions as he read the scenario: 'It was completely dreadful. The story focussed around the love affair of Judas, this time with Salome, the daughter of Herodias. The climactic scene occurred during the dance of the seven veils, with Mary in the garden outside the house of Herod, and the camera swinging back from the dancing Salome to the suffering Mother in the shadows as she tries to save John the Baptist.'

Lord convinced the DeMilles that this fowl would not fly, as the Catholics would 'raise the roof' at anything short of total reverence, while non-Catholics would consider the film as pure pro-Catholic propaganda.

The Queen of Queens was never made.

In Godless Hollywood – the Last Silent Hurrah

From the *Brooklyn Eagle*, 9 September 1928:

INSIDE A CINEMA CZAR'S SANCTUM
By Mayme Ober Peak

The approach to the De Mille sanctum is interesting because the sharp contrast it presents to the rest of the studio is an index to the nonconformist creating it. The big white building, located in Culver City, is of Colonial architecture, and was formerly owned by the late Thomas G. Ince. Set back on a wide expanse of green lawn, with white pillared front, dormer windows and long low wings, it is a replica of Mount Vernon. Over the broad front door is a typical colonial fanlight, on it a brass knocker which one hardly lifts before a colored butler in blue swallertail swings it open with the air of the old-school darkey.

You step into a Colonial hall where a grandfather's clock ticks softly and antique chairs are drawn up before an open fire blazing on gleaming brass andirons. On the wall are old portraits with mellowed gold frames. But for the telephone operator, seen through a small arched window, the last place on earth you'd imagine yourself would be in a motion picture studio!

The operator quizzically questions you, telephones the inner regions in a low tone and if you pass muster presses a magic button that opens a paneled door.

Neither the flapper nor the austere business type of secretary would suit the De Mille setting. You appreciate this the moment Miss Rosson takes you into the exotic study of her chief, who is purposely missing. Otherwise the reporter would have been unable to concentrate on anything but his dominant presence.

It is an enormous square room with beams and panels of stained wood. Trophies of hunting and fishing are all over the room. The head of a fine caribou, shot by De Mille in New Brunswick, is mounted over the mantel. On the hardwood floor, and thrown over the chairs and soft, deep divans, upholstered in wine red velvet, are the skins of a leopard, lion, wolf and bear.

The walls are brilliantly splashed with color – here is hung some priceless relic sent by his collectors abroad, there a souvenir of one of his productions. The coat of mail worn by Wallace Reid in 'Joan the Woman,' together with the famous armor that covered Geraldine Farrar . . . Close by hang the banners from the 'King of Kings,' also the crown of thorns which reposes on a red velvet cushion . . .

To the writer his heavily carved desk was especially interesting. Both in size and design it reminds me of the desk made from the wood of an old Resolute that graces the President's private study in the White House. It is broad and spacious with top covered with a soft Persian rug instead of blotter. DeMille's methodic neatness and thoroughness are indicated by the neat piles of carefully assorted mail, reference books with markers, his open engagement calendar. The sentiment of the man is seen in the gold framed miniature of his mother, Beatrice DeMille. Several of her photographs are on tables – the only likeness of a woman in the DeMille study.

A glass-topped platform with velvet sides is mounted in the open space under the DeMille desk. By pressing a button the producer turns a Klieg light in this platform, so located that it throws an illuminating glow on the face of the speaker opposite him . . .

The white bearskin rug . . . occupies a psychological position directly in front of DeMille's desk. It is impossible to cross the room without passing over it and equally difficult to avoid stumbling over the enormous mounted head . . . DeMille had that rug placed there to test the poise of his callers. 'I have punctured many a balloon with that rug,' I was informed he said . . .

Cecil DeMille would make one last silent film before the deluge of talkies closed noisily over his head. Many silent-film practitioners drowned, but many more were able to swim to safety. Synchronized sound had been an old ideal of the movies, and throughout 1926 and 1927 various experiments brought its fulfilment closer. October 1927's premiere of Al Jolson singing 'Mammy' in *The Jazz Singer* was just the culmination of a process, but many studios were slow and reluctant to retool.

So studios continued making silent pictures well into 1928. Cecil DeMille had produced twenty-five of them in 1927 alone – no wonder he had no time to meet Mayme Ober Peak in his office. In April of that year, in the very week of the premiere of *The King of Kings*, DeMille's Producers Distributing Corporation had announced a merger with another distributor, the Pathé Exchange, having already been joined by a group of financiers from the Keith-Albee-Orpheum group, whose principal proprietors had been in business since the early days of vaudeville. One of these ancient monsters, J. J. Murdoch, the original Mr Tight-Wad, had already become a major thorn in DeMille's flesh. DeMille and Jeremiah Milbank were only two players in a crowded locker room.

In October, when Al Jolson's warble was just about to be unleashed, a four-page ad in the trade press trumpeted DeMille's greatest achievement, in which he would undertake 'a production task unparalleled and unprecedented in the history of the business. Plans were laid for the production of twenty-six program pictures embracing stories of an unusual and sensational type . . . ten big DeMille Studio Specials, based on famous stories and plays offering the maximum in showmanship and exploitation possibilities . . .' Even disasters, in this grand folly, could be heralded as opportunities: 'In the midst of early production, fire swept the DeMille studios, completely destroying one big stage, property building, paint shop and equipment valued at more than $200,000. The following day every scene that had been scheduled was taken as if disaster had not touched the studio. And within a week a new great stage, the largest in the world, measuring 300 feet in length and more than 200 feet in width began to take form over the still-hot ashes of the ruins.'

Resurrection was now the norm in DeMille's world. But despite the baying of the press agents, these productions were not reaping the promised harvest: *The Fighting Eagle, The Country Doctor, His Dog, The Rush Hour, The Wreck of the Hesperus, The Wise Wife, The Forbidden Woman, Let 'Er Go, Gallagher, Rip Van Winkle, A Blonde for a Night, Chicago*, etc., were barely breaking even, if not showing an actual deficit. (*Chicago* was a version of the popular stage musical, touted at first as a DeMille-directed project but credited, on its release, to Frank Urson.) On the other hand, close by, on the other major lot at Culver City, rival MGM was cutting the mustard, with *Old Heidelberg, Quality Street*, King Vidor's *The Crowd* and Victor Seastrom's mature masterpiece, *The Wind*, with Lillian Gish.

The truth was that even the Champion Driver Cecil had bitten off more than he could chew. The new partners, like Murdoch and Pathé Exchange boss Joseph P. Kennedy, were none too pleased, and by March 1928, the press was reporting that DeMille was negotiating his separation from the company. Once again, speculation mounted that he would join United Artists.

By this time, DeMille was completing the shoot of his final film for the company, his last silent, *The Godless Girl*. Once again he confounded the critics by embarking on a project that seemed an unlikely, even perverse choice, and disconnected from his previous work: a film about 'boys and girls' reformatories'. In a cable to Charles Beahan, his East Coast story editor, quoted by Birchard, he wrote: '[I] understand the inmates of these institutions use sign language, that they are not allowed to speak to each other except at certain times, that there is no beauty whatsoever inside the walls, that they are taught to spy on each other . . . Secure as much data as possible.'

These preparations were set in motion as early as June 1927, a mere two months after *The King of Kings* opened and in the midst of his complicated mergers. DeMille did not seem to be happy unless he was juggling at least a dozen balls in the air at any one time.

It is difficult to tell what drew DeMille to this subject. His own adopted boys, John and Richard, were somewhat unruly, John in his teens and Richard an apparent terror in primary school, though his expulsion at the age of seven would occur two years after *The Godless Girl* was conceived. Constance's charity work for orphanages and hospitals would have resonated with stories of young people

DeMille at home with family (*c.*1936): (left to right) Cecil, Constance, John, Katherine and Cecilia

who had fallen off the edge of society. His disillusion with the jazz-age 'flapper' was evident in the run-up films to *The King of Kings*. Issues of religion were still, naturally, haunting him in the aftermath of his grand testament.

In addition, the subject of religion and youth was in the news, with anxious revelations about atheist societies agitating in high schools. The echoes of the 1925 'Monkey Trial' of John Thomas Scopes for teaching Darwin's Theory of Evolution at the Central High School in Dayton, Tennessee, were still reverberating round the country. Cultural commentator Frederick Lewis Allen, writing twenty years later, described the sudden realization by the general public that such secular ideas existed as an awareness 'that our behavior depends largely upon chromosomes and ductless glands; that the Hottentot obeys impulses similar to those which activate the pastor of the First Baptist Church . . . that sex is the most important thing in life, that inhibitions are not to be tolerated, that sin is an out-of-date term, that most untoward behavior is the result of complexes acquired at an early age, and that men and women are mere bundles of behavior patterns, anyhow'.

All this was at odds, of course, with what DeMille himself had just been preaching with great force from his film-set Golgotha. But, again, DeMille confounds us with his contradictions, because he was, after all, also a man of science, a master of technology – the movie camera, projectors, film laboratories, the alchemies of modern life. Out of this cross-current of ideas and reflections, Cecil and Jeanie Macpherson concocted an original script dealing with an ideological rift between young people that leads to a cruel accident and lands the protagonists of the story in a state reformatory. Into the tale they incorporated the factual findings of their researchers, as set out in a special report of May 1928 in *Motion Picture Magazine*:

DeMILLE INDICTS THE REFORM SCHOOLS
A Crusade in Celluloid
By Dorothy Donnell

When Cecil B. DeMille decided to make a picture exposing the horrors of some of the reform schools, he knew he was starting something. But he did not dream just how much he was starting. To be sure of his facts he hired a special investigator – an ex-detective whom we will call Mr. S. . . . The reports which Mr. S. made to the studio, the sworn affidavits which he collected from paroled inmates of these reform schools, fill two immense books at the DeMille studio. Perhaps they are the most expensive books ever written, for up to date the investigations have cost nearly two hundred thousand dollars . . . As representative of MOTION PICTURE MAGAZINE, I have seen these books and read in them things so revolting that they will probably never be printed . . .

Some of the things that the magazine did print included:

A girl of fourteen . . . hanging by her thumbs from a cell bar in a central Southern institution for wayward girls. Her tiptoes touch the floor. She has been in this position for three hours because she spoke to another girl in the silence . . . A ten-year-old boy locked in a windowless, solitary confinement cell like a wild beast, without a bed, with only bread and water to eat. The cell is sound proof so that the guards will not be annoyed by his cries . . . He tried to run away from the reform school. In another school there are desperate twin criminals three years old, who helped themselves to candy when the grocer's back was turned and confined as thieves by the law of the land until they shall be twenty-one years old! These things are not happening in Russia or China, but in our own United States . . .

The eventual script of the film opened with a disclaimer stating that: 'WHILE MANY OF THE INCIDENTS IN THIS DRAMA ARE BASED UPON ACTUAL HAPPENINGS, NO CHARACTER IS THE PORTRAIT OF ANY LIVING PERSON, AND NO PUBLIC INSTITUTION IS PATTERNED AFTER ANY SPECIAL SCHOOL OR REFORMATORY IN ANY PARTICULAR COUNTRY OR STATE.'

Production of *The Godless Girl* proceeded amid a great deal of press interest, with the *New York Times*, on 19 February 1928, reporting that more than twenty state governors had written to DeMille 'commending the idea' of a film on juvenile reform schools. Word had also got around that DeMille intended to attack atheism, prompting 'a telegraphic objection from Charles Smith, the President of the American Association of Atheists', to which DeMille had replied:

The subject of my next picture will be high schools and the inadvisability of propaganda of any sort being circulated through the schools. It is not an attack upon any creed or sect to force belief in its own doctrines. Your telegraphic suggestion that I eliminate the thought of God from my future pictures I must discard, inasmuch as up to the present time this is a free country and I feel that I have as much right to use my medium of expression to give the world my thought as you have the right to use your medium of expression to give the world your thought.

Of course, when DeMille published his exchange of messages with Mr Smith, many letters of commendation descended upon him from assorted clergy. The *Times* continued:

While up to the present time the angle of the picture concerned with atheism has received more publicity . . . the reform school material will constitute the greater and more important passages of the production. On the DeMille lot at Hollywood there has been constructed a five story building representing a reform school which will be burned down to provide the climax for the action of the picture . . .

There is a peculiarity about the cast in this picture. Virtually all the characters are just boys and girls. There are older persons, of course – Noah Beery as a reformatory guard, Kate Price as a matron, Marie Prevost as a 'trusty' . . . Robert Edeson, Fred Walton and others.

Members of the California Women's Prison Commission were involved on the set, and the DeMille publicists saw to it that their approval for the reforming message of the picture was suitably presented to counter the opposition expected from proponents of the illiberal status quo. The *New York Times*, 11 March: 'After working for several hours on the sets, Secretary Buwalda is quoted as saying: "We feel that 'The Godless Girl' will do more to make the ordinary taxpayer of the State willing to adopt a progressive and humane policy toward its delinquent women than any other single factor."'

By the time the film went on general release in February 1929, the silent picture was to all intents and purposes dead in America, and DeMille had had to shoot a final reel using the new sound process, with some embarrassingly clumsy spoken dialogue. If it were not for the fact that the reel featured the same actors, one might have thought it belonged to a totally different picture. But the preceding eleven reels are an intriguing addition to what I have called 'Cecil's Arcana'. Sensationalist, unusually brutal in places and with moments of high melodrama tinged with religious hysteria, the picture stands with the oddities of DeMille's oeuvre and is among his strangest and arguably most 'DeMillean' films.

Reversal of fortune once again provides the central dramatic theme: at a privileged American high school, students are at loggerheads over a brash and aggressive atheist campaign, introduced by the movie's opening title:

It is not generally known that there are Atheist Societies throughout this country attacking through the youth of the Nation the beliefs that are Sacred for most of the people. And no fanatics are so bitter as youthful fanatics.

Pamphlets and posters urging 'JOIN THE GODLESS SOCIETY TO KILL THE BIBLE' fill the screen. A harassed headmaster calls out: 'This blasphemy is spreading throughout the school like a plague! It must be stopped!'

The story focuses on two antagonists: Judy, 'Disciple of Atheism', and 'Bob, Son of Gospel', presented as 'Intolerance versus Intolerance' – it was still a Jeanie Macpherson script after all, and she may well have been trying to get her own back after the over-righteous Mother McTavish. In a shabby hall, 'where little rebels blow spitballs at the Rock of Ages', the student atheists gather. Their battle cry: 'This is a scientific age – do we need God?' The atheists have brought along a monkey, perhaps a refugee from the Scopes trial, and call out: 'Come and get a pamphlet from Koko – he's your cousin!'

Young Bozo Johnson is about to be initiated into atheism, but when he pulls back, saying, 'Does that cut out my Christmas holidays?' he gets pelted by the atheists. Meanwhile, Gospel Bob and his friends break into the meeting and a fight ensues. A janitor calls the police, but the melee spreads to a rickety stairwell, which collapses. Judy's younger sister slips – a dramatic shot of her falling from a great height towards the camera. As she lies dying, cradled by Judy, she whispers: 'Judy, tell me you're wrong – tell me there's something more!' But it is the Irish cop who comforts her: 'Don't be scared – He's waiting there to take you in his arms!'

The film then moves on dramatically: shadows talking on telephones follow a headline: 'SCHOOLGIRL KILLED IN RIOT – THREE HELD FOR MANSLAUGHTER'. Judy has accused Bob of pushing the girl. Both she, Bob and Bozo Johnson are sent to the reformatory, introduced by the title: 'Bricks . . . Barbed Wire . . . Iron . . . and Rebellious Youth.'

DeMille's scenes of the reformatory are indeed some of the harshest scenes ever filmed by an American director in the silent period. The regimented brutality in both the boys' and girls' sections of the prison is portrayed with grim precision: the shearing of the hair, the shapeless uniforms with stripes on the boys' pants – 'so they can pot you if you try to get away!' – the strict rules of silence, the regime of gongs for the inmates to wake, wash, eat and sleep, and the violent

The Godless Girl – the prison escape

punishments, beatings and dousing with hoses meted out by the head guard (Noah Beery), who is described as possessing 'the muscles of an ox – the brains of a sheep – the mercy of a Hyena . . .' So bleak are the images that DeMille had to insert a special intertitle: 'The conditions in this story actually exist in certain reformatories – the great majority, however, are humane and progressive – thanks to those who are striving to help our Delinquent Youth to become good men and women . . .'

Judy is befriended by Mame, a Bible reader, and her anti-religious convictions begin to soften when Mame covers for her in a conflict with the matron. Later, while carrying their respective sections' garbage to the dump, Bob and Judy meet on either side of an electrified fence. But when they entwine their fingers through the wires, the sadistic guard turns on the juice, leaving Judy literally with the stigmata of a cross burned on her palm.

Bob and Judy break out and experience a brief idyll in the fields, with Judy bathing in a stream – a long shot suggesting nudity. But they are caught, and Judy is handcuffed in her cell in the condition documented by DeMille's researchers. A black cat overturns a lantern that sets the jail on fire, but the head guard orders the gates locked. The girls raise the flag of revolt and seize the keys, leaving Judy in her burning cell. Bob climbs over the fence, fighting the guard for his keys, as Judy prays. The guard runs from the scene, but is electrocuted by falling wires. Bob frees Judy, and they rescue the burning guard, who gives witness, on the point of death, to their heroism in saving him from the fire.

The rescue of the guard and the release from prison of Judy, Bob and Bozo constitute the final, spoken reel, as Bozo asks Bob: 'If you had to save somebody – why did you have to save this guy?' Judy: 'He's human and he's suffering.'

Cringeworthy dialogue continues, as the guard dies in Judy's arms: 'Tell the warden I recommend their release.' And a repentant Judy: 'Forgive us our sins, as we forgive those who have sinned against us.' As Judy and Bob exit the prison gate, DeMille cannot resist the coda:

Judy: 'It's like coming out of the dark . . .'
Bob: 'Only the Godless are in the dark.'

The Godless Girl was apparently, on its foreign release, an unexpected hit in the Soviet Union. But this was allegedly because the pious dialogue and the repentant final reel were removed, so that the film was seen only as a graphic denunciation of the brutality of the capitalist penal system.

As with so many of DeMille's silent movies, the bare description belies the atmosphere of heightened tension, severe anxiety and melodramatic stylization. The final burning of the jail, with its massive wall in whose windows the rioting inmates are silhouetted against rising flames, has echoes of the Gothic settings of a Murnau or Fritz Lang. Hokum and religion have combined with youthful lust and frustration in a cocktail of hysteria that was emphasized in some of the movie's posters: a boy and handcuffed girl kissing in darkness, or figures writhing in a slew of hate-filled faces –

Vivid! Colorful! Realistic! The emotions, the hate and the love of youth – radiant and rebellious – thrown against the most absorbing background in the annals of the screen – a never-to-be-forgotten picture that will be written about in every newspaper and talked about in every home!

Blather and hype could not mask the revolution in the picture industry, and *The Godless Girl* flopped badly, grossing under half a million dollars against its cost of over $700,000. Throughout 1928, only wishful thinking stood in the way of the talkies. In July of that year came the headline: 'King Vidor Decries Dialogue Films'. The prestigious director, who had made the classic hit *The Big Parade* in 1925, told *Motion Picture News* that he saw sound as '"only a fad that will run its course within a year . . . Motion Pictures were just getting somewhere," said Vidor, "when the upheaval came along. They had reached a point that neared perfection and they were developing artistically along lines that argued well for the future . . . Sound pictures, those with dialogue that runs continuously, will do away entirely with the art of motion pictures . . ."' Joseph M. Schenck, president of United Artists, concurred: 'Talking pictures will never displace the silent drama.' Even in December, Adolph Zukor stated: 'So-called sound pictures will not displace silent films . . . We would be surrendering all that we have achieved. I think our future lies in the silent film, with sound and dialogue as adjuncts.'

Jesse Lasky, on the other hand, the man who skulked about motion-picture theatres to see what the patrons really wanted to watch, had already 'predicted that in five years there would be no more silent pictures'. He was clearly reading his own trade papers assiduously: in August, *Motion Picture News* reported that two hundred sound pictures were 'Definitely Planned for 1928–1929'. The writing was no longer just on the wall but leaping out from the billboards of every theatre: audiences wanted talkies.

Meanwhile, DeMille had thrown in the towel in his marathon bout with the financiers of the Producers Distributing Corporation, Keith-Albee-Orpheum, Joseph P. Kennedy and all. The *New York Times*, 3 August 1928:

CECIL B. DEMILLE QUITS AS PRODUCER
Signs Contract to Join Metro-Goldwyn-Mayer Films as a Director. Selling His Own Studio.

Fifteen breathless years had passed since the first contract had been signed by DeMille, Jesse Lasky and Sam Goldfish to found their own company to make feature-length pictures. Between them they had produced hundreds, if not over a thousand films. Cecil DeMille had directed fifty-two pictures and produced several dozen more. He had spent millions and made millions. His previous film, *The King of Kings*, still wowing the masses, was just set to begin its 'regular' run – in its music-synchronized version – in October 1928, after eighteen months of 'roadshow' screenings around the country, a record sur-passing even *The Ten Commandments*. As newspaper woman Mayme Ober Peak had discovered, he was an icon even in his absence, the souvenirs of his triumphs, so boldy mounted in his office, epitomizing the man: Joan of Arc's armour, the skins of majes-tic animals, the prop department's crown of thorns.

As he quit the role of master producer, the *Times* reported that 'Mr. DeMille declared that the future of the motion picture was brighter than ever before and that the educational value of motion pictures was just beginning to be realized.'

Not for the first time, DeMille was predicting the birth of another brave new world.

Let Us Go Down, and There Confound Their Language

'Couldn't They Stop that Horrible Sound?'

Just before New Year's Eve 1928, a thirty-seven-year-old actor named Charles Bickford arrived in Los Angeles from New York City. He had enjoyed an outstanding success on Broadway back in 1925 in a Maxwell Anderson play called *Outside Looking In*, co-produced by Eugene O'Neill. Bickford played the starring role of Oklahoma Red, 'swaggering and burly, glib of tongue, mocking and reckless all at once', as the *New York Times*'s critic noted. Another red-headed smart guy cast in the play was a veteran vaudeville hoofer, James Cagney.

Both continued treading the boards, looking, for the moment, no further than the footlights for fame and glamour. But when, three years later, Bickford starred again in another Anderson play, *Gods of Lightning*, based on the Sacco and Vanzetti case, the new talking pictures firmly beckoned. At last, being 'glib of tongue' was a recommendation rather than an irrelevance.

And so MGM imported Charles Bickford to Hollywood, with the promise of a movie that he assumed would be 'blessed by the Midas touch of DeMille'. The famed director had seen him on Broadway and wanted him for the part of Hagen Derk in his first full-blown talkie.

Welcoming him to Los Angeles, Bickford recalled in his autobiography *Bulls, Balls, Bicycles and Actors*, published in 1965, the great director invited him to a pre-Christmas open house on the famous MGM lot. Warning of the unreliability of Bickford's memories, DeMille historian Robert Birchard notes that Bickford left New York on 26 December and so could not have been on the West Coast that Christmas. The bulk of Bickford's tale of his Hollywood arrival, however, involves DeMille's subsequent New Year party, which Bickford would have been well in time to attend, and so the intimate detail of its sequences still stands, with the usual caveat about oral histories and their often fuzzy chronology. Bickford wrote of the moment he met Cecil:

The party at the DeMille bungalow was merry, but decorous. Of the twenty or more celebrants present, I spotted but one drunk. The others, sun-tanned and dressed in sports clothes, were standing in groups as they vivaciously discussed the important question of the day, namely, Who is doing what to whom?

A sturdily built, sun-bronzed man came toward me with his hand extended in greeting and although I had never met DeMille, nor seen a picture of him, I knew that this must be he. The pongee sports shirt, well-tailored riding breeches, leather puttees and Napoleonic stride seemed to proclaim the fact that here was the director to end all directors. 'My God,' I thought, 'It's an American Benito Mussolini.'

Restraining a compulsion to give him the fascist salute, I grasped his hand. The man had a grip like a bear trap . . . Although he was smiling, I detected the glint of antagonism in his eyes. It was difficult for me to believe that a man of his position would resort to such an infantile method of intimidation but as the pressure continued I realized that he was serving notice to me that he was king of the mountain.

Bickford stood his ground but failed the next Hollywood test, which was to accept an obligatory 'producer's girlfriend' for the ride home. This refusal, he wrote, earned him the lady's abuse as a 'faggot', a charge which required him to prove his masculinity at the subsequent New Year's party at the 'American Mussolini''s mountain retreat of 'Paradise'. Bickford recounts that he realized word had got around when DeMille's telephone invitation included a query about his '"preference in women . . . Don't get me wrong, Charles. I strive to please. I want you to have a good time. Which is it to be – blonde, brunette or redhead?"'

'"Make it one of each," I said, modestly. "All I ask is that they be dainty, feminine, shapely, beautiful, intelligent and passionate."'

A selection of three appropriate beauties was apparently on hand, with the man himself in his car, when DeMille arrived to pick Bickford up from his hotel on the day. They drove up into the mountains, turning into DeMille's private road and 'suddenly engulfed in a subtle perfume, emanating from acres of lime, lemon and orange trees . . . The road ended at the center of this enchanted forest, disclosing an attractive sprawling ranch house, a pool, handball and tennis courts. Radiating from the major house were several shady lanes, or lovers walks, each leading to a picturesque little guest bungalow.'

Cecil's 'Paradise' was certainly a sybaritic retreat, in which the great central living room boasted red leather-clad sofas and armchairs, a giant fireplace and, 'most impressive in those prohibition days – a practical bar which boasted a breath-taking stock of pre-war liquors'. DeMille proudly showed his guest his collection of erotica, though Bickford was somewhat disappointed by his own uncomfortable reaction, born of 'my streak of inherent Yankee Puritanism' – of which the urbane and cultured DeMille was noticeably free. It was at this point that Bickford was presented with the 'privately printed three-volume edition of shockingly illustrated works of François Rabelais'.

As was the form in DeMille's private universe, the guests were all assigned clothes by their host, with male guests required to wear red Russian blouses. It was always 'white, yellow or black' for DeMille himself. The girls were allowed more varied plumage. The dinner, after this build-up, was somewhat mundane, Bickford recalls: 'the pièce de résistance was corned beef and cabbage', and 'after dinner two teams were organized to play charades'. Bickford's hopes for an orgy began to recede at this point, but after the obligatory 'Happy New Year' toasts, he was summoned to DeMille's own bungalow, where the hidden delights of the party were then revealed in a large 'play-room' under a spotlight:

A girl, beautiful, blonde and petite, was dancing. She was nude but for a diaphanous veil which she cleverly manipulated as she writhed, python-like, to the beat of Ravel's Bolero.

Three men: DeMille, the Broadway leading man, and one of the juvenile actors . . . watched avidly as they sprawled on the carpet just outside the circle of light.

Three girls, the cream of the crop, catered to the gastronomical desires of the men from a table laden with a Lucullan display of food and drink.

A 'sort of strip-tease dice game' then ensued, which developed into 'quite a shindig' with 'some cute capers cut'. Bickford draws a discreet veil over the rest and cuts to the next scene of his Hollywood triumph, the purchase of a used automobile.

DeMille's secret life, in this account, seems more in tune with the opening Magdalene scenes of his Gospel epic than the later crescendos of pious uplift, though one might point out that by the standards of Hollywood's more outré revellers, smackheads and coke fiends it would appear tame by comparison. Nevertheless, out of sight of his wife, and even of his long-term harem, Cecil could indulge as his jazz-age voluptuaries, rakes, Pharaohs, Aztec princes and Knights of Olde had in their movie *droits de seigneur*.

Having explored California and the lower dives of Mexico just across the border, Bickford was ready for his first day's work on DeMille's first talkie. This commenced, Bickford relates, with a mammoth reading by the producer-director of the entire script, which Bickford describes as 'a mess of corn' with terrible dialogue. Daring to question its quality, the actor found himself at the sharp end of DeMille's disapproval. Three professional script-writers had laboured on the project, which was, they insisted to Bickford, 'tailored to your measure'. In which case, Bickford said, 'you must have used a lousy yardstick'. DeMille still insisted, however, that 'I know what I'm saying when I call this an excellent script.'

Despite the misgivings, Cecil kept both his actor and writers in line, and in the third week of January 1929, the movie in question, *Dynamite*, went into production. It was completed nearly three months later, a lengthy – and costly – period for a contemporary drama. A large chunk of the time was spent shooting a silent version for movie theatres that had still not been adapted for sound.

When the film was released in December, DeMille's nemesis at the *New York Times*, Mordaunt Hall, gave him the usual credit for being 'a master of technical detail and a director who is able to elicit from his players thoroughly competent performances' but lambasted him for 'artificiality vying with realism and comedy hanging on the heels of grim melodrama. Even in the work of the performers, there are moments when they are human beings and then, at times, they become nothing more than Mr. DeMille's puppets. The dialogue is a potpourri of brightness and banality and it was no wonder that the audience in the Capitol yesterday afternoon found humor in scenes that were intended to be serious. Most of the film holds one's attention, but toward the end the incidents become a trifle too bizarre for one's peace of mind.'

The fact we face, when dealing with Cecil B. DeMille's sound films, is perhaps the central paradox of a director whose name is recognized for a handful of pictures made in the latter part of his career, rather than the fifty-two films he made before – apart from his two silent Bible epics. That is that the best, most scintillating, brilliantly crafted and socially significant films made by DeMille are all clustered among those fifty-two silents, and the rest, the twenty-eight sound pictures, contain most of his dross and his lesser work, and are often his clumsiest projects – even if successful – reflecting a director in decline.

Very few of DeMille's silent films – of those extant – are negligible, and even the most uneven contain moments of brilliance and scenes of finely crafted technical prowess. In contrast, very few – in my estimation six, including the culminating remake of *The Ten Commandments* – of DeMille's sound films are of particular merit as movies, though several more are historically significant in terms of Hollywood lore.

The point, of course, is arguable, as all opinions of movies necessarily are, as the familiar cries of contempt and abuse sparked by any list of the 'best' films in cinema history continually demonstrate. Is there a general, agreed yardstick? Everyone has favourite films that are not necessarily the 'best': influential movies from childhood or films that are enjoyed for their lurid transgression of rules of narrative, good taste or the very qualities that define the well-made picture. Nevertheless, most movie-watchers would recognize qualities of intent, planning, execution, craft, technique, performance and a director's talent and ability to draw all the disparate elements of film-making together – to master the machine and create what we can recognize as art.

Some purists might stop here, deciding that if one wants to celebrate Cecil B. DeMille, 'Great Film-maker', one might as well quit the story at its zenith, at the point at which our hero bestrides his own world, having made his major contribution to motion pictures and represented, for his brief moment, the cutting edge of social transformation in America's golden movie age.

As talkies came in, many movie professionals found themselves flummoxed by the new technology: actors' squeaky voices were revealed, while directors were incarcerated in the glass soundbox and made slaves to the flaws of early microphones – the kind of tales made movie legend by Stanley Donen and Gene Kelly's *Singin' in the Rain* of 1952.

The reality was more drawn out and complex. Throughout 1928, producers struggled with the poor quality of spoken sound. Comments like those of Mordaunt Hall in the *New York Times* about one Warner Bros. film, *On Trial*, were common: 'There is quite a lot of lisping as the players utter their lines . . . periods when the speech is slightly muffled . . . to avoid explosive phases of the Vitaphone.' MGM, which was late changing over, broke through in 1929 with *The Broadway Melody*, a smash hit that helped inaugurate the 'all-talking, all-singing, all-dancing' motto of the Hollywood musical.

DeMille's *Dynamite* was one of MGM's earliest sound films, and the lack of experience in the medium certainly tells. The three writers mentioned by Charles Bickford would have been Jeanie Macpherson, Gladys Unger and John Howard Lawson, the latter a renowned playwright whose Marxist credentials were clearly no impediment for DeMille at this stage of his life (he was later to become one of the imprisoned Hollywood Ten). Despite the expertise, these three turned in an almost indigestible screenplay of 218 pages. Its opening sequence, credited on 22 November 1928 to Lawson, read like this:

Scene 1:
Courthouse: Derk's Condemnation:
JUDGE: I sentence you, Hagen Derk, to be hanged by the neck until dead – for the murder of George Clark – and may God have mercy on your soul!
MARY ANN: Oh don't let them take you away from me – please don't let them . . . (*the even knock of the Judge's gavel*)
DERK: Sorry, Judge – my kid sister – we're kind a' worried – her an' me, about what's to become of her.
JUDGE: (*as his gavel strikes again*) The Court orders this child to be removed – in the care of proper persons.
DERK: There ain't nobody, Judge, she's got nobody in the world but me to look after her . . .
MARY ANN: Don't take him away – he didn't do it . . .
DERK: Take it easy, Baby, we don't holler when we're hurt. I'll fix things up fine – don't you worry, just you leave it to me . . . smile at trouble, Baby – an' I'll be smilin' too!
THE GUARD: Get a move on, Hagen Derk, you got a long trip to make.

The script begins at least to address the possibilities of sound, using the judge's gavel as a counterpoint to the dialogue, but the old DeMillean corn, albeit with a new twist on the reversal of fortune, prevails: Hagen Derk, a rough and rugged coal miner, is sentenced to death for a crime we later learn he has not committed, leaving his kid sister destitute. Meanwhile, among the rich and spoiled, young heiress Cynthia must marry within a month of her grandfather's death or forfeit his fortune. She is in love with a married man, whose wife, her friend, is willing to allow an uncontested divorce in return for a cut of Cynthia's inheritance. Her dilemma seems solved when she sees a newspaper item with Hagen Derk's offer to sell his brain and body to science for $10,000 to look after his sister. Cynthia hies to the jail and offers Derk a proposition: she will marry him in the shadow of the gallows, and thus be swiftly widowed and free, having fulfilled the terms of Grandpa's will. Derk agrees, and the prison chaplain marries them in the death cell, as the carpenters hammer at the scaffold and a Mexican prisoner strums his guitar.

Unfortunately, her scheme comes unstuck when, in a bar, the real murderer, goaded by his friend as the clock's hands tick by to an innocent man's demise, breaks down and confesses. Derk is set free, the uncouth coal miner now married to a society heiress. He turns up at her party and spooks her rich friends. Meanwhile, Cynthia discovers that by the terms of the will she must live with her husband for at

Dynamite – Charles Bickford and Kay Johnson make an unlikely match

least a week. She begs Derk to take her in as his wife in his shack in the company town.

The tale then gets almost too convoluted, as Cynthia's rich lover, Roger, goes down the mine to tell Derk to his face that he is going to reclaim Cynthia, and both men and Cynthia are caught in a mine collapse. The only way out is for one of the men to hammer in a stick of dynamite and blow a hole that will allow the other two to flee. They draw lots. Roger loses and hammers the dynamite in. Derk is saved, and Cynthia confesses she loves him, as he carries her through a cleft in the rock. Labour and capital united, as it were, in love.

Dynamite would have been a proper addition to 'Cecil's Arcana' were it not for the inherent clumsiness of the staging and the total demise of DeMille's deft dance, in the silents, between 'realism' and fantasy. Only in the earlier part of the film does DeMille attempt to break out of the sound camera 'glass box' by filming a 'hoop race' of swimwear-clad girls, the camera tracking in parallel.

Nevertheless, the film remains archival in value, one of the curiosities of the nascent talkies. The highlight is probably the 'wedding' scene in the prison cell, with the prison chaplain intoning the vows: 'the Holy state of Matrimony, which is not to be entered into unadvisedly or lightly, but reverently, discreetly . . . soberly . . .' Cynthia crying against the hammers: 'Couldn't they stop that horrible sound?' Derk: 'I'd like it stopped a lot more'n you would.' And the chaplain, continuing: 'Wilt thou have this woman to thy wedded wife, to love and keep her as long as ye both do live?' Derk, with a smile: 'Just about that long . . .'

The rough-edged nature of early sound pictures apart, DeMille had never before portrayed modern marriage quite as sourly – a ceremony of commerce totally unspoiled by sentiment. Did the cynicism perhaps come from Jeanie Macpherson, fifteen years a wife in waiting in her *seigneur*'s busy harem? Or did it derive, at least in part, from John Howard Lawson, who would join the Communist Party four years later and clearly revelled in the comparison between the immoral cruelty of the upper classes and the rugged integrity of the working-class hero? Charles Bickford gamely managed to provide this character with the integrity of his stage performances. He would then move on to play opposite Greta Garbo in his next but one contract film for MGM, *Anna Christie*, which, he later claimed, earned him an invitation to San Simeon, William Randolph Hearst's palatial retreat in the mountains, an extravagance that eclipsed DeMille's.

There was always, in Hollywood, someone higher up the food chain. Cecil B. DeMille, regardless of his past record, would have to fight tooth and nail for his supper, as he prepared his second talkie – *Madam Satan*.

Lucifer's Consort, or Where Do We Go from Here?

DeMille may have made only one film during the crossover year to sound pictures, but he was not idle on other fronts. As ever, he was never happy unless several irons were glowing in the fire. Family life had settled down, with no new adoptions and Constance presiding over the great mansion on DeMille Drive. Early in 1928, Cecil had been elected president of the Association of Motion Picture Producers, the most powerful industry lobby group and the buffer between Will Hays and Hollywood's film-makers. He was seeing off two plagiarism law suits over the copyright of *The King of Kings*, one brought by a seventy-year-old woman, Mrs Joan Armstrong Alquist, and another by one Valeska Suratt, 'former stage and screen star', who owned the rights to a book about Mary Magdalene by one Mirda Ahmed Schrab. Each plaintiff claimed a million dollars. Neither collected. In July, DeMille was also embroiled in a stock-issue scandal involving several film and theatre people who had invested in the Julian Petroleum Company, whose dealings appeared not to be wholly above board. Charges of usury were brought over a loan of $45,000 at 'an illegal rate of interest'. The charges were later dismissed. In December, yet another hopeful, William T. Trautmann, sued for plagiarism over *The King of Kings*. Some people just couldn't get over this story being in the public domain.

In the same month, DeMille eulogized Theodore Roberts, who had died at the age of sixty-seven, having left the mark of his vigorous personality on so many DeMille films, although, like Moses, he had never quite reached the promised land of movie immortality. Having completed the shooting of *Dynamite*, DeMille then became embroiled, as president of the producers' 'union', in fighting another union, the actors' Equity, whose New York office, led by Frank Gillmore, sought better conditions of employment in movies. Equity's efforts to foment a strike in Hollywood failed, to DeMille's satisfaction, who declared that 'as producers we regard ourselves merely as the medium through which the public decides which of the actors and actresses shall be presented for their entertainment. The motion picture industry has brought contentment and prosperity to thousands employed therein. The conditions of employment are fundamentally sound . . . We believe that many of Mr. Gillmore's supporters were recruited in part from the ranks of those who unfortunately were out of employment and in part from those who have never been able to obtain employment.'

This typical piece of bosses' nastiness did not quite inaugurate a new DeMille, as his old liberal concerns for society's underdogs had already metamorphosed into a set of moral rather than economic criteria. In principle, Cecil was still attracted to ideas of social justice and the inequities of formerly dominant classes, but in practice he was adopting the familiar attitude that, as America was constitutionally classless, these standards did not apply to matters more closely at hand. Having fought so long for his financial independence as a producer, he had become adept at ascribing his personal interests to the general principle of 'giving the public what it wants'. Others might call this hypocrisy, but that was, after all, despite constant denial, the abiding sin of his own class.

Then came 24 October 1929, the day on which 'Wall Street Lays an Egg' and the Great Stock Market Crash sent its shock waves through America. Like many investors, Cecil scrambled to instruct his secretary, Gladys Rosson, to sell his stocks, but he was too late. He lost $1 million, but he had another $2 million in 'more stable and fluid investments', notably in some Californian oil wells, and in February 1930, he was able to host his twenty-one-year-old daughter Cecilia's wedding to Francis Edgar Calvin, the son of a retired railroad executive, at the family home and endow the newlyweds with a home of their own 'just down the hill'.

Of the other DeMilles, William was also adapting to sound, having directed *The Doctor's Secret*, based on J. M. Barrie's play, and *The Idle Rich*, based on a play by Edith Ellis, in 1929 (William had also moved to MGM). This latter title is considered one of MGM's superior early sound pictures, with a good variety of camera angles mitigating its stage origin and single set. Conrad Nagle, the lead actor, weathered the transition to sound better than most. Despite this, William was only to direct three more movies – *This Mad World*, *Passion Flower* and *Two Kinds of Women*, the last in 1932 – before bowing out of movie-making. The new rising star of the family was Agnes, who performed in her first ballet in New York in December 1928. She then appeared in *The Black Crook*, a revival of the very first, nineteenth-century American musical, gaining her first credit as a choreographer, which was to be her forte. By 1930, the *Los Angeles Times* would embrace her with the headline 'DeMille Girl Makes Good'.

William simply came to the end of his reversal of fortune with his younger brother. Agnes wrote, much later, in her personal obituary of her uncle that while the contest with his elder brother strengthened Cecil, 'I think in some ways it broke William. They loved each other, but as years passed they saw less and less of one another, and before my father's death [*William passed away in 1955*] they met only a couple of times annually. They had been very close as boys and later as collaborators in plays and ventures. There was only one way for them to talk to each other – just plain. But Cecil had grown out of the habit, and father disturbed him.'

William was to make a new career for himself as an academic, a teacher of film to young people. Agnes wrote that she had never heard of Cecil 'helping young talent. He hired talent, if useful and convenient. He never endowed it. He considered slow development a form of weakness, and could not forgive psychic disabilities. It follows that he thought Freud idiotic. The young, the gifted, the ambitious were not to be nursed. If you had guts you could get what you wanted. He had.'

This was not totally fair, as the record shows that Cecil gave several young actors great chances. But like many a man who had pulled himself up by his own bootstraps, or convinced himself that he had, Cecil had little tolerance for anyone who lacked the same gumption or ability. He still considered himself, in the early sound era, a Jeffersonian Democrat, and voted, in 1932, for Franklin D. Roosevelt. But this appendage of a liberal upbringing was soon to wilt and drop away. William had spent his life in theatre and cinema pursuing the chimera of a progressive narrative that nurtured a humane and humanistic outlook, and where had it got him?

Back to 1929, and the aftermath of the Wall Street Crash: in November, the National Museums of France made a special presentation to DeMille at the MGM studios of a bust of Voltaire, in the presence of Louis B. Mayer. Three weeks later, Cecil made a speech at a meeting of the Western Motion Picture Advertisers, on behalf of his Association of Motion Picture Producers, defending the concept of 'Hokum':

I used to be insulted when people called me 'The King of Hokum,' now I consider the term the highest of compliments . . . Hokum is the most important phrase in the language of the drama.

We should give thanks that the motion-picture business is built on hokum; that it clung to it when the stage veered off into other paths . . . Seventeen years ago the critics called my first picture, 'The Squaw Man,' 'a piece of hokum,' . . . To avoid the allegation I made a picture based on the Old Testament, a picture called 'The Ten Commandments.' But they called that 'hokum.' Then I went to 'The King of Kings,' a story of the life of Jesus of Nazareth. And that was decried as 'hokum.'

So it began to dawn on me that those who misuse the term denominate as 'hokum' all the tender virtues of life. A scene of parents mourning over a sick child, that's 'hokum.' Scenes of self-sacrifice, they are 'hokum.' Mother love is 'hokum.'

At the end of his speech, DeMille assured his audience that as long as it were up to him, 'the screen will not part with hokum'.

On this, he most emphatically kept his word. As the 1930s began, Cecil was ready to embark on his second film with Metro-Goldwyn-Mayer, a project that would mark a decisive break with the jazz age and all its licentious excursions. Mayer was pressing him to make a musical. Jeanie Macpherson, working again with Gladys Unger and John Howard Lawson, and also with veteran vaudeville star Elsie Janis, had produced another arcane and bizarre script which rang the bells of all Cecil's obsessions with money, adultery, sexual titillation and American urban decadence.

DeMille surged ahead and in two months, from March to May 1930, *Madam Satan* was filmed. This would be arguably DeMille's weirdest film, although his continuing inexperience of sound shooting places it well below *Fool's Paradise* or *The Golden Bed* in terms of quality, pace and performance. DeMille cast English-born Reginald Denny, specialist in stiff-upper-lip roles, as his male protagonist, Bob Brooks, and Kay Johnson – who had cut her sound teeth on the character of Cynthia in *Dynamite* – as his betrayed and vengeful wife, Angela. Another Englishman, Roland Young, whose creepily 'umble Uriah Heep would immortalize him in 1935's *David Copperfield*, was cast as Bob's friend and fellow carouser, oil man Jimmy Wade. Cecil cast his nineteen-year-old adopted daughter Katherine as an extra, sensing that she, of all his brood, was meant for a movie career.

The film falls into two distinct parts. For almost an hour, we are treated to a slow-moving, almost interminable unfolding of the plot line: Bob and Jimmy come back from a night out on the tiles and try to convince Angela that 'Trixie', whose card she has found, is not Bob's bit on the side but Jimmy (the confirmed bachelor)'s wife. Some less than frenetic action between Jimmy, Trixie – played by Lillian Roth – and Angela, hiding behind bedroom doors and, at one point, with Trixie concealed under the sheets of Jimmy's bed, leads to the wife's despair at her husband's conduct and her exit in order to remake her life and regain both her lost husband and her dignity. On the way, we are treated to some tongue-in-cheek dialogue that surely reflects Jeanie Macpherson's familiarity with DeMille's own marital kinks, as Bob pleads with his wife: 'Don't you understand? Love can't be kept in cold storage. It's a battery that has to be charged, every day. I've tried to be your lover as well as your husband. But you don't know what love means!'

'You don't know what marriage means!' she ripostes, to which he counters: 'It's a schoolroom, and you're the teacher. Well, I've graduated.' And he walks out.

The musical element is ladled in as Angela's maid convinces her in song that she has to fight to get her husband back. Confronting the flighty Trixie, who tells her barefacedly: 'I jazz all the dullness out of him. All I have is a body, made out of flesh and blood, and I'm not ashamed of it,' Angela declares: 'I'll get my husband back from you. I'll give him perfume and jazz until his head reels. He wants some hot stuff – I'll give him a volcano! He'll have to call the whole fire department to put me out!'

The second part of the film is entirely taken up by Jimmy Wade's 'Masquerade' ball, which is held on board a Zeppelin moored at a tower overlooking the New York skyline. (In an untypical self-referential touch, the Zeppelin is named *C.B.P-55*, i.e. DeMille's fifty-fifth picture – by his own count!) Hordes of costumed revellers 'walk the catwalk' to the dirigible, warbling: 'We're going nowhere, we're going somewhere, we're going everywhere . . .' while Theodore Kosloff, as 'Electricity', cavorts in an Aztec-like mask festooned with lightning bolts. Compères in aviators' uniforms call out the arrivals: 'Mr. and Mrs. High Hat . . . Miss Conning Tower . . . Mr. and Mrs. Hottentot . . . Mr. and Mrs. Henry the Eighth . . . Miss Movie Fan . . .' and so forth.

The ballroom scene is a variation on *The Golden Bed*'s Candy Ball, with the ladies in exotic plumage revealing more than the censor might desire. In fact, the censor, Jason S. Joy, had sent DeMille an eleven-page letter in January listing the manifold transgressions of *Madam Satan*'s script and requesting a large number of cuts. Among lines that might fall foul of censorship, the inappropriately named Joy listed:

Page 3: 10: (Bob) 'I'm not sorry for any cat that's a bachelor!'
Page 5: 28: (Bob) 'Because they're orphans! Poor li'l orphans want a popper!'
Page 24: 134: (Angela) 'Thanks! I've no desire to mingle with ladies who are being auctioned!'
Page 47: 289: (Jimmy) 'It's the kind of bed that turns on you in the night!'
Page 73: 460: (Trixie) 'I didn't take him – I found him straying!'

Kay Johnson is *Madam Satan*

Page 78: 484: (Angela) 'All right! You're on, a fight to the finish! And we each use the same weapons! Passion and deceit! (*lifting drink*) And may the wickedest woman win!'

As ever, it is difficult now to fathom some of the censor's sensitivities, though page 14 – 'Angela picks up Bob's coat from the floor and takes out a tiny toy balloon, which has been blown up and busted' – definitely tweaked Jason Joy cruelly. The Zeppelin ball, somewhat trimmed, is dominated by the dramatic appearance of 'Madam Satan', a demonic, cat-like masked figure, whom husband Bob of course fails to recognize as his own once dull wife. Spurning feathered Trixie, he bids $3,000 for Madam Satan in the auction for the 'Queen of the Ball'. The revelries, however, are cut short as thunder and lightning cut the dirigible loose from its moorings and send it plunging towards fiery doom. As Satan/Angela unmasks herself, the aviator-caterers hand out parachutes to the guests so they may leap out to safety.

Like the sinking of the *Veritania* in *The Little American*, the fall of the Zeppelin provides DeMille with a classic catastrophe, this time reflecting not the horrors of war but the inevitable wreck of a demented society. As Bob Brooks, invoking the spirit of the *Titanic*, conducts the band in a last rendition of 'Where Do We Go from Here?', the upper-class girls and boys shoot out into the stormy night, flimsy dresses fluttering, legs kicking, screaming under their parachutes. One is tempted to link this hallucinatory imagery with the tropes of surrealism – or its precursor, the madcap artistic antics of Dada – as the art-deco designs of the floating ballroom with its fizzing machines and 'futuristic' props are crushed in an inferno of broken metal and the blimp's giant deflating shroud. It is without a doubt DeMille's most bizarre scene, and one of the strangest in twentieth-century cinema.

But unlike the Dadaists and the surrealists, who had declared their own revolution against social convention and hierarchies, social etiquette, class repression and religion, DeMille's grand apotheosis is a profoundly conservative statement. Here is Cecil Blount DeMille's final farewell to the jazz age, which he had embraced with the gowning of Gloria Swanson and then lampooned and castigated in *Male and Female* and *Manslaughter*. Bloated by its hypocrisy, drunkenness and sexual lust, its defiance of all moral standards and the Law of Moses – and of Christ – it finally implodes and explodes, raining its jaded, cowed and terrified fallen youth out of the black sky over Sin City New York.

In movies, of course, even the damned survive, and a '*Daily Bulletin*' headline suitably yammers: 'GAY PARTY IN PERIL WHEN BOLT HITS ZEP: ALL SAFE'. All the celebrants had their parachutes except Bob, who gave his to Angela, who gave it to Trixie, while Bob fell into the city reservoir. He is back with his wife, bickering but content – he knows that exciting Madam Satan now lurks behind the cosy and dull exterior.

DeMille, however, was not succoured by *Madam Satan*, which lost money. The aftermath of the shooting was marked by physical setbacks. He broke his ankle while sailing his yacht the *Seaward* round Catalina Island in stormy weather. Then, in November, he went under the knife in the Cedars of Lebanon Hospital to have his appendix removed. He had been working on the scenario for his next film, yet another remake of *The Squaw Man*. Shot and released in 1931, it too failed at the box office. Of his three films for MGM, DeMille had just about broken even with the first, and struck out with numbers two and three.

Was DeMille already a dinosaur, a great but defunct creature of the industry he had helped create? Garlanded with honours, he was celebrated by a cartoon in *Photoplay* tracing his life from a boyhood ambition 'to be a policeman', through his first job as a 'carriage washer', to his 'outstanding productions – Ten Commandments – Feet of Clay – Volga Boatman – Dynamite and his best – The King of Kings'. He was, the cartoonist reminded the readers, 'Pres. Motion Pictures Prod. Ass'n; Vice-Pres. Bank of Italy . . . 32nd degree Mason – Shriner', member of the Lambs Club, New York, the Athletic Club of Los Angeles, the Tuna, Beach and Vermejo Clubs. Verily a man of substance.

But was he doomed, like his near contemporary, D. W. Griffith, to a swift decline, in practice as well as principles, a rendezvous with disappointment, melancholy and the bottle, the loss of assets, friends, admirers and prestige? Would he too fall from the sky with *C.B.P.-55*? The omens were not good. MGM did not renew the first three-picture contract, and for the first time, Cecil had to close the production office of his own company. Staff were scattered, and even Anne Bauchens was forced to look for work at other studios. DeMille looked abroad for other opportunities, movies to be made perhaps in Europe, in England, Italy or even further afield.

No one, not even MGM or Paramount, flailing in the first year of what people were beginning to label 'the Depression', was exempt from the economic fall-out of the Wall Street Crash and so many business failures. Could Cecil replight his troth with Jesse Lasky and the little Napoleon of the cinema – Adolph Zukor?

But an even more puzzling question could be asked by those following the fortunes of Hollywood's luminaries in the summer and autumn of 1931 as they scanned the trade magazines and newspapers over their breakfasts: what was Cecil B. DeMille, renowned movie capitalist, doing cruising down the Volga River in communist Russia, heading southeast from Moscow towards Stalingrad?

Shall We Gather by the River?

In future years, DeMille would cast his Soviet trip primarily as a fact finding tour about the possibilities of movie production. 'I was struck', he wrote in his autobiography, 'by the contrast between all the doors closed to me in Hollywood . . . and the recognition given to directors in Russia.' Nevertheless, he added, Soviet film officials made it clear to him that individual freedom was subordinate to the collective decision of all the studio workers. This was a blatant deception, as it was not the way films got made in Russia in 1931, or even in their heyday in the mid-1920s, when, as quoted by film historian Jey Leyda: 'All films when finished are submitted to about twenty people to ensure that they are sound from a Communist viewpoint.'

'All was friendliness,' however. The 1957 DeMille still had to admit that his trip a quarter of a century before was a voyage of discovery into the reality of ordinary life in Russia, as he and Mrs DeMille, with Theodore Kosloff and their inevitable official guide, Mme Levina, took the boat down the river he had recreated in Sacramento for *The Volga Boatman*. They then boarded the ever-crowded train from Stalingrad to Vladikavkaz, in the heart of Russia, continuing on over the mountains to Tiflis (Tbilisi) in Georgia.

Few western travellers and even fewer Americans made this kind of journey during this period. Harpo Marx's breakthrough trip to Russia, arranged by Alexander Woollcott, would not take place till two years later, in the winter of 1933, as part of the diplomatic thaw with the Soviet Union set in motion by President Roosevelt. DeMille was travelling in the Hoover years, when Stalin's Soviet Union was still portrayed as a ravening wolf out to swallow poor Europe whole. But there is little doubt that DeMille, like Harpo Marx after him, swallowed large dollops of Soviet propaganda while he was on the road.

In 1931, Stalin was not yet a dictator but the powerful chairman of a board of many squabbling voices yet to be silenced, and it was true that there were still considerable reserves of social idealism, particularly among the young urban elites. Back in January 1930, however, the Communist Party had passed a resolution to enforce the complete collectivization of the Soviet Union's rural areas by 1932. In 1931, the country was in the grip of unrest and shortages induced by these measures, as peasants resisted the seizure of their smallholdings and killed their livestock rather than letting it fall into state hands. In 1932, actual famine resulted in many regions. But DeMille was steered clear of most problem areas by his government minders.

'Nothing you have heard about it is true,' he told newsmen on his return to America, adding, 'there is more drama in one block on a street in Moscow than I have ever seen in an entire city anywhere else,' though he recalled, in 1957, the lack of freedom and the terrible poverty of the majority: 'It was a land of bewildering contrasts, from the bright and airy prisons shown to foreign visitors, to the hotels so primitive and filthy that at least once Mrs. deMille slept fully dressed on a sofa rather than brave the uninviting bed.' During his trip, DeMille kept a diary which described the daily sights along his itinerary in a succession of cinematic notes as if for a movie that would never be made: 'Funerals, one old horse pulling a wagon with four white posts on the corners. The coffin tied to the body with rope . . .' Down the Volga: 'The woman pulling the inside of the fish and eating it. The tea made out of apples. The drunken boy . . . the bales of goat skins cut in small pieces . . .'

One in ten faces that he saw, he noted, was marked with smallpox. And yet he still enthused years later over the 'thrilling muster of nearly half a million Russian youth pouring . . . into the Red Square to be reviewed by Stalin'. Summing it up, he noted that, despite the poverty and hardships, 'two experiments started at the same time. Prohibition has failed and socialism succeeded.' At a women's prison he noted the humane conditions, but observed too that one of the prisoners was serving two years for hiding wheat from the authorities.

Red Square enthusiasm, clean jail, the works – DeMille was properly done over by his hosts. Nor did Russian-speaking Theodore Kosloff seem to disabuse him at the time. DeMille wrote that Kosloff only agreed to enter Russia under the protection of his American friends and was searching for his sister, who had been left behind and whom he found 'on the street in Moscow, selling cigarettes'. Had he tried to undermine the flimflam fed his companions, her life, if not his, would not have been worth a nickel.

The 1957 DeMille admitted he had been naive, but the 1931 version voiced very few doubts. 'Russia', he told the Los Angeles press in December, 'is the most interesting place in the world. They even begged me to direct a picture. The theatres are packed to the doors, and they are ahead of us in using pictures as one of their principal educational mediums in the schools . . .' He had seen the 'first Russian-produced talking picture, "Passing Through Life,"' and noted that 'it contained propaganda, as all Russian films do'. The distribution of the films, however, had to 'await the introduction of electric power', which was absent outside the urban centres.

The main question he was asked by people of all walks of life in Soviet Russia was: 'Why do the Americans hate us?' As he told the press: 'The majority of Russians do not think highly of activities of American Communists,' thus enlisting his Russian interlocutors, strangely, to the ranks of his anti-union cause.

The DeMilles journeyed 1100 miles by boat down the Volga River. DeMille said he was impressed by the similarity of the Volga and Sacramento Rivers. 'The boatmen who tow the boats still sing at their work, and I was pleased to see that the section of the film, "The Volga Boatman," which was taken on the Sacramento River, was a faithful reproduction,' he said.

Europe, according to the American traveler, appears to be far worse off from a business standpoint than the United States, but 'has learned to grin and bear it better than we have.'

DeMille's growing inability to divide movie from common reality was, of course, a typical Hollywood syndrome. In his pro-Soviet leanings, he echoed the views of many who, in the white heat of the Depression – when capitalism itself seemed to be imploding – had doubts about their government's demonizing of the Russian 'experiment' and were ready, indeed eager to be convinced that there was merit on the other side – as long as those ideas, which might be right for peasant Russia, were not transferred to the very different reality of the US. Jobbing actors like Harpo and Groucho Marx, or James Cagney, or writers like John Howard Lawson could be home-grown socialists, but an employer like Cecil B. DeMille could not be expected to take kindly to such shenanigans in his own backyard.

So unusual was DeMille's inland journey that he was debriefed on the way back by the American ambassador in Istanbul, Joseph G. Grew. The ambassador was later to become a staunch anti-communist, sidelined during the alliance with Stalin in the Second World War and a prominent sponsor of such later projects as the 'Crusade for Freedom', which spawned 'Radio Free Europe' in the 1950s and is now known to have been funded by the CIA. Individuals would be urged to make the following pledge:

I believe in the sacredness and dignity of the individual,
I believe that all men derive the right to freedom equally from God,
I pledge to resist aggression and tyranny wherever they appear on earth,
I am proud to enlist in the Crusade for Freedom.

In 1931, however, it was not quite clear what sort of crusade Cecil DeMille might sign up for. His journey east continued, after Turkey, to Greece, Egypt and Palestine, where for the first time he trod the real sites where his 'King of Kings' had walked. In Cairo, he met Charles Watson, head of the American University, a pivotal institution (still prominent in Egypt today), who introduced him to the tolerant imams of the ancient Islamic university of Al-Azhar. DeMille became a member of the American University Sponsors and donated a print of *The King of Kings*. Toleration was in short supply, however, in Palestine, which was undergoing yet another turn of the screw in the Jewish-Arab unrest, policed uneasily by British colonial troops.

Cecil returned, after his detour in search of new meaning abroad, to an America still in economic turmoil. His own affairs were in a pretty pickle, as he had to appeal against an income-tax demand for over $1.6 million and dispute the government's calculations of his profits, grosses, expenses *et al*. At the end of December, he attended the eighteenth-birthday celebration of Paramount Studios, held in the old barn on Selma and Vine where the first *Squaw Man* had been shot. Melancholy thoughts of the fate of the talkie version could not have been far from his mind, but it was an opportunity to remind Jesse Lasky of his own movie production debut in 1913.

Cecil DeMille was in dire need of a resurrection, as was all of Hollywood, which was enduring a heavy battering from the Depression, whose consequences had been mitigated for a while thanks partly to the novelty of the talkies. On 20 October, *Variety* banner-headlined the sombre message 'END OF SILENT FILMS', as the studios halted all distribution of intertitled pictures. The last casualties were 4,000 deaf mutes in Chicago, whose La Salle Theatre had been catering for them to the end.

With studios on a mission to slash costs, many careers were on the line, at the top as well as the bottom of the totem pole, as *Variety* noted slyly in January 1932:

HOLLYWOOD'S SOCIAL UPHEAVAL

The Hollywood blue book is in confusion with none knowing just how the other fellow should rate socially. Shifting of jobs at the studios, with some out and others demoted, has left its mark on parties, teas and other social events . . . With everything changing so rapidly in setup of the lots, an exec's wife can't figure how to treat the wife of another exec who is out, on the verge, or just plain down and out . . . Example is one studio big boy who moved right next door to his superior on the lot . . . The head man was let out recently, and the other man given his job. Now the wives don't know how to act toward each other. Which should adopt the superior attitude?

Much more pain, however, was being felt at the lower end of the scale, by actors, writers and directors who now had to scrabble for jobs with a shrinking number of employers. As *Variety* reported on 19 January, 'the world's center of motion picture making has only six major companies now producing films. All other outfits have either been merged out of existence or shut down.' But United Artists, Columbia and Pathé had only been temporarily paused, with Paramount, Universal, Radio (RKO), Warners, Metro and Fox all still standing, some on pretty wobbly feet. Extras were being laid off en masse as producers were favouring 'former employees who previously filled other jobs than acting'. Economics apart, there was a new medium sopping up attention: broadcast radio, which penetrated practically every home and which didn't entail standing in line.

And so DeMille scrambled with the others. At the end of February 1932, he left Hollywood for New York to hobnob with Paramount heads there. Zukor, despite his misgivings and vivid memories of Cecil's extravagance, was willing to chance at least one movie deal, as long as DeMille kept the costs down. At the same time, hedging his bets, DeMille was dropping hints of a return to the stage for 'legit production', as he was said to be 'carrying two scripts' for the purpose. In the event, he remained, of course, in movies.

The nature of talkie scripts was a vital issue at a time when new writers who excelled in dialogue were driving a pick-up truck through the conventions of the old silent-era Hays Code. The producers of early talkies even had enough chutzpah to argue that, as spoken speech was not specifically mentioned in the Code, the recorded soundtracks of the talkies were not themselves subject to censorship. No judge, however, would uphold this, and Father Daniel Lord and others were zealously engaged in rewriting and tightening the Code, a process that would bear its bitter fruit in 1934. Meanwhile, maverick stage and newspaper writers had hit town, men like Gene Fowler, who rode about the streets of Hollywood on a bicycle, scoffed at the pretensions of 'execs' and boasted that the only decoration in his office was a simple head of cabbage.

The 'dialog model' for Los Angeles's movie people, *Variety* reported on 8 March, was Ernest Hemingway, despite the fact that he had only sold one novel to the pictures: *A Farewell to Arms*. Other writers popular as models were Alexandre Dumas, Zane Grey and Edna Ferber. None of these had been or would be suitable exemplars for DeMille's gang, especially not for Jeanie Macpherson. Cultural tastes were, as ever, changing, but DeMille stayed rooted against the new grain. This was an obvious problem.

DeMille's solution, after his flirtation with Soviet exoticism and social sermons, was to return to the tried and true source, the Rock of Ages, the themes and stories that had made him the most money. Elsewhere in Hollywood, Frank Capra was producing *The Miracle Woman* with Barbara Stanwyck, a searing satire on evangelist Aimee Semple McPherson; Gene Fowler was writing the morally ambiguous *State's Attorney* for John Barrymore; Mae West was being introduced in her pilot film with George Raft, *Night After Night*, and Paramount executives were scheming to film her transgressive play *Diamond Lil*; Marlene Dietrich was about to be *Blonde Venus* for Josef von Sternberg; and Radio Pictures were about to unveil the 'Eighth Wonder of the World – *King Kong* – The Strangest Story Ever Conceived By Man!'

Once upon a time, DeMille might have been expected to be at the forefront of these kinds of outrageous challenges to the expectations and conventions of his time, a leader of trends rather than a follower, far less a film-maker who turned his back on the high wire of experimentation in favour of the safety net. But in the summer of 1932,

Cecil B. DeMille was on the Paramount lot again, shooting *The Sign of the Cross*.

This was a different Paramount from the mighty juggernaut that had seen Zukor, Lasky and DeMille rolling over all their movie rivals. The New York banks were urging all the studios to install new fiscally ruthless managers, and the old boys were on the chopping block. Some, like Zukor, hung on in power. Lasky, however, had to take an 'indefinite vacation' in May from the studio he had co-founded, though in June he was back 'in supervision of a special phase of production that is being worked out for him'. Fellow executive B. P. Schulberg had been tossed overboard – though he soon returned as an independent producer – and the new kings of the lot were Emanuel Cohen and Sam Katz, managerial executives to the bone. On 23 August, *Variety* revealed the terms which the new moguls enforced on DeMille, whose 'contract with Paramount on "Sign of the Cross" provides for a maximum cost of $600,000 but with the proviso that DeMille personally pay all costs above that amount. Result is that DeMille is slicing the salaries of the cast with many taking only 25% of their announced salaries for the honor of being discovered by DeMille.'

Soon after, Lasky too was confirmed as an independent producer for Paramount, with overall control over DeMille's productions. Somehow, the old guard had negotiated a new lease of life, no longer kings of the jungle but respectable carnivores nonetheless.

To work with DeMille clearly still had cachet, as demonstrated by the famous anecdote from the filming of *The Ten Commandments*, when Theodore Roberts and James Neill, exasperated with having to wait for the director to sort out some problem, announced their presence to DeMille's secretary Gladys Rosson with: 'Moses and Aaron have come to see God!' Of all the giants of the silent screen – Griffith, von Stroheim, Thomas Ince, even Keystone's Mack Sennett – he was the last man left standing, apart from wily old Ernst Lubitsch, still active and directing at Paramount. Other veteran silent directors were still working, such as King Vidor, Henry King, Clarence Brown or John Ford, but none were already enthroned in legend.

Nevertheless, he was a cut-price colossus. To construct Nero's Rome and the great Colosseum where gladiators slashed each other to death and the pious Christians were cast to the lions on a restricted

The Sign of the Cross – Charles Laughton, Claudette Colbert and Fredric March

budget for *The Sign of the Cross* was a particular challenge, albeit one DeMille had faced before, with the Aztec temple of *The Woman God Forgot*. Although some sets could be built in miniature, others had to be built to scale for the actors, with camera angles suggesting much larger crowds than were actually there. But the Colosseum was impressive by any standard, an amazing feat by art director Mitchell Leisen.

In keeping with his own dictums about 'hokum', DeMille launched his comeback with the verve and gusto of a Roman lion who had not eaten a Christian for ages. The press book of the film set the tone boldly:

THE LOVES, THE BLOOD-LUST AND THE GLORY OF ROME
IN DeMILLE'S NEWEST BOX-OFFICE SUPER-SPECTACLE!
THE SIGN OF THE CROSS *is the circus of the screen!*

It has THE LURE OF THE FLESH – the bacchanalian revels that made . . . and still make . . . the world gasp. Beautiful slave girls . . . courtesans . . . harlots . . . their only purpose to outdo each other in the orgiastic rites loved by a lustful Caesar. A flesh-mad emperor . . . Nero . . . loving . . . living . . . laughing a crimson streak across the world . . . painting the ancient city red

. . . with the warm blood of his victims . . . just for a sadistic thrill. Naked women . . . their helpless beauty pitted against the ferocity of frenzied animals . . . while Nero licks his lustful lips . . .

Of course, religious uplift had to be provided: 'THE FAITH OF CHRISTIANS AGAINST THE SEX-MAD PAGAN LUST . . . the cradle of Christianity . . . the suffering of the martyred followers of Jesus Christ . . . the passive battle of the Christians against the cruelty . . . of Caesar and his Roman horde . . . a page flaming with soul-stirring action . . . with heroism and treachery . . . death and everlasting life . . .' And as the poster for the Colosseum games offers: '30 BARBARIAN WOMEN FROM THE NORTH TO FIGHT PYGMIES FROM AFRICA . . . 100 CHRISTIANS TAKEN IN TREASON TO BE EXECUTED . . .'

To play Nero – 'the body of a woman, the heart of a hyena, the soul of a snake!' – DeMille cast Charles Laughton, whose stage career had been augmented by bit parts in three British silent films and leading roles in a couple of early Brit talkies, and who was signed up for a trio of Hollywood movies, the most notable being James Whale's *The Old Dark House*. DeMille claimed to have picked him out on the London stage when attending the stage play *Payment Deferred* during his visit in the summer of 1931, but he might equally have found him at the Broadway run of the same show, which opened on 30 September that year. Cecil recognized the unique talent of the stout actor, who was far removed from the Hollywood idea of either a hero or a heavy but inhabited both roles with a particular relish. It was an inspired choice, as Laughton slurps and slimes his way through the role, establishing the film as an early camp classic by hamming his lyre-plucking doggerel as he enjoys the burning of Rome.

DeMille's second casting triumph was Claudette Colbert, who had starred (in place of Clara Bow) in the sound remake of DeMille's own *Manslaughter* (directed by George Abbott in 1930) and had acted in five films in 1932 alone. Born Lily Claudette Chauchoin in 1903 in Paris, she had grown up in the US and begun her acting career on Broadway in 1923, adopting her new stage name then. DeMille, seeing her potential in the 'fluffy, lightheaded roles' she had been playing for Paramount, claimed he had stopped her on the lot one day and asked her: 'Claudette, how would you like to play the wickedest woman in the world?'

No actress could pass that up. And so she became Nero's wife, Poppaea: 'the red-headed woman of 65 A.D. – Goddess of silken flesh . . . men loved her . . . only to die!' For the male love interest, DeMille engaged Fredric March, who had also starred in the talkie *Manslaughter*, in the Thomas Meighan role, and would soon be awarded an Oscar for 1931's *Dr. Jekyll and Mr. Hyde*. He was given the more difficult part of a besotted Roman prefect who hates his job, falls in love with the Christian girl, Mercia (played by Elissa Landi, an Italian actress in Hollywood from 1931), and fights off Poppaea's lusty advances.

The Sign of the Cross generated a fair number of mythological anecdotes which have been oft repeated, whether they were true or not. DeMille's best 'bathtub scene', the grand pool of asses' milk in which Poppaea slithers, softening her skin – and is that the single-frame flash of a nipple? – was supplied with genuine milk, which curdled under the lights after several takes, giving off the most pungent smell. A later DeMille biographer, Phil Koury, who joined DeMille's team as an assistant in the 1940s, described the adventures of a young animal trainer called Melvin Koontz, hired to handle the large number of lions obtained for the climactic scene: Koontz, dressed as a Christian and 'kneeling in final prayer' in order to be mock-mauled by one of the male lions, was nonplussed when 'something else caught the lion's attention – a lightly clad girl, tied to a post and judiciously garlanded with flowers. Amid dead silence, the animal sniffed at the shackled beauty and might have loitered in the vicinity indefinitely had not Koontz leapt to his feet and chased the amorous beast into a cage with a pick handle.' Goaded by the trainers, the animals began doing what animals do when flustered, so that 'a wrathful DeMille, stalking Koontz on the dampened sands, thundered: "This is an outrage! Those goddamn lions of yours are urinating on my Christian martyrs!"'

The most iconic tale has DeMille taking the reins from the cautious animal trainers and chasing the lions single-handedly up the dungeon stairs with a chair in one hand and an axe handle in the other when they were loath to perform. 'The startled beasts', writes Koury, 'looked at DeMille as if to say, "Where are the trainers? Why don't they protect us from this man?"'

The whole movie narrative was a piece of balderdash whipped up by scriptwriters Waldemar Young and Sidney Buchman, based on a play by an Englishman, Wilson Barrett, written in 1894 and already filmed once in 1914. The play was apparently penned after an Easter meeting at a St Louis hotel between Barrett and Robert G. Ingersoll, the famous nineteenth-century free-thinker, enemy of religion and priests and scourge of all believers in the literal truth of the Bible. Galvanized by the challenge, Barrett vowed that 'I will write a play . . . that will appeal to the same classes that Colonel Ingersoll's lectures reach. He ridicules the Christian religion across the footlights; I will show across the same footlights the beauty and strength and purity of that fate.' This was, we might note, a year after the death of Henry C. De Mille, the gentle dramatist of moral plays.

The story is easily summarized: mad, bad Emperor Nero is persuaded to blame the Christians for the fire that has ravaged Rome. The Christians in Rome are living secret lives, under constant threat of death. A beautiful Christian girl, Mercia, tries to intercede when her guardian, Titus, and a pilgrim from the Holy Land who has witnessed Jesus's preaching are seized by Romans. A passing prefect, Marcus, falls for her and becomes her protector. But when Mercia's younger brother is caught and tortured, giving away the venue of the Christians' secret meeting, they are all killed or captured. Marcus, who has been spurning the advances of the emperor's wife, Poppaea, pleads for the life of the Christian girl, but when she discovers her people are condemned to die at the arena, she opts to join them. Marcus is so moved by her refusal to renounce her faith despite the certainty of death that he joins her in her final march up the steps towards the lions' claws and fangs.

The Sign of the Cross retains to this day all the hallmarks of the classic good bad film. No opportunity has been ignored by DeMille to enhance the 'hokum' of the story. From Laughton's raving emperor, through Colbert's slinky excesses, the near nudity which challenges the censors' most sensitive organs and the lip-smacking relish of the brutality in the arena scenes, it all brings DeMille's old sadistic kinks bubbling openly to the surface. 'Bread and circuses', the old Roman cry, echoed in theatres as audiences weary of the Depression flocked in to enjoy at least part of the promise. As the gladiators clash, blood squirts from faces and eyes, a head is lopped off and Hollywood's finest midget extras in blackface are spitted on Amazon spears or take their revenge by sinking their tridents into the midriffs of the 'barbarian' girls. Elephants crush a man's head and drag corpses off by their feet. Slaves pull a cart piled with gladiator corpses as the drooling, perspiring nobles put their bets on the Thracian with the net or bicker about getting stuck with tickets for the worst seats. Nero nibbles at a flower as he deploys his thumbs down to send yet another sword plunging into the belly of another muscle-bound loser. Whips lash the backs of bare-shouldered women and hissing crocodiles slink up from their pit towards a terrified tethered maiden.

It is all a far cry from the piety, compassion and exemplary compositions of *The King of Kings*. Cinematographer Karl Struss delivered some eye-catching crane shots that swoop and sweep along the crowd in the arena, and there are some sombrely dark scenes in the dungeons, though none to match the quality of silent days. Oddly enough, the only scene the censor objected to seriously was the 'lesbian dance' in prefect Marcus's palace, in which a pagan dancer, Ancaria (played by Joyzelle Joyner), prances around Mercia chanting her odes to drown out the singing of the condemned Christians outside. It was an 'alluring' dance, as DeMille described it, but the Catholics on Will Hays' board found it too alluring for comfort.

According to DeMille's own account, Will Hays called him on the phone to ask him what he intended to do about the scene. DeMille answered: 'Not a damn thing.' The record shows, however, that on 16 November 1932, Hays enforcer Colonel Jason S. Joy wrote to Paramount that 'ordinarily we would have been concerned about those portions of the dance sequence in which the Roman dancer executes the "kootch" movement. But since the director obviously used dancing to show the conflict between paganism and Christianity, we are agreed that there is justification to its use under the Code . . .'

Others, beyond the Hays Office, were less lenient. One good reverend who had been sent the script by Paramount's advertising department, obviously hoping for a testimonial, blasted back:

The picture 'The Sign of the Cross' as shown in the script sent to me is repellent and nauseating to every thinking Christian. It endeavors to get a lot of lewd scenes and sex appeal exhibitions on the screen and then dresses the whole with a cheap and unhistorical hodge-podge of hymns and incidents from sacred Christian martyrdom. Only an ignoramus concerning Christian history, feelings and facts would compose such a script.

It is a cheap and disgusting attempt to present lewd performances under a sacred name and shielded by an ignorant notion of religion . . . The whole picture is suggestive, unclean and unworthy of a great company like the Paramount Publix Corporation. It will cheapen and dishonor the sacred emblem, the cross, and bring opposition from every loyal 'believer' in Christ.

I confess I feel chagrined to think that you had such a cheap notion of me as to think I would in any way commend it.

Yours in disgust,

CHRISTIAN F. REISNER

But the critics, nevertheless, raved. 'Spectacle of a type they haven't seen in a long time,' wrote *Variety*. '. . . It's going to make the church element dizzy trying to figure out which way to turn . . . Religion triumphant over paganism. And the soul is stronger than the flesh. Religion gets the breaks, even though its followers all get killed in the picture. It's altogether a moral victory . . .' Of the slaughter scenes, the magazine noted: 'Most of it will be nearly nauseating to those with sensitive stomachs, but all of it is holding. It makes the heart pound faster for almost a solid hour . . . If any picture around just now has a chance to go out and get big money it is "Sign of the Cross."'

Mordaunt Hall in the *New York Times* wrote that, although 'there is an abundance of imagination throughout . . . One feels, however, that the players must have been relieved when the production was finished, for all work hard and thoroughly, even to those who merely figure for an instant or so in a death scene in the arena or the more fortunate who are spatting about their seats.' The critic astutely noted the energy DeMille put into directing his extras, as well as his principal actors, making a crowd not just a conglomeration of figures but a living, spitting, dynamic force of individuals straining to emerge from the mass.

In the end, hokum won the day and the spoils: for a total of just over $690,000 spent, a gross return of over $2,700,000. A net profit, with all spending on promotion, advertising and distribution covered, of over $600,000 – real gold at the height of the Depression. The film, with all its pomp and circumstance, mass crowd scenes, orgies, animal sequences and baths of milk, had taken just over eight weeks to shoot.

Even before he had begun, DeMille was regaling the press with the similarities between ancient Rome and modern America, with particular emphasis on his own current tax woes: 'Multitudes in Rome were then oppressed by distressing laws, overtaxed and ruled by a chosen few. Unless America returns to the pure ideals of our legendary forebears, it will pass into oblivion as Rome did.'

The confusion of movies and reality was now almost complete. Discarding the mythology of socialism Russian style, DeMille was back-pedalling to another source that would feed into his own long-term legacy: an unashamed flag-waving patriotism that would, in its unfashionable religious linkage, be dismissed by many but would return, in the ironic workings of history, long after he too was gone . . .

This Day? This Age?

Despite his success with *The Sign of the Cross*, DeMille was not yet ready to dump all his aspirations to film more contemporary stories. Before his comeback epic opened, he had already agreed to make a low-budget movie that would re-establish him as a regular Paramount hand. After seeing the returns of *The Sign of the Cross*, Zukor offered a three-picture deal. The first film, *This Day and Age*, was shot in less than five weeks in the early summer of 1933, and the second, *Four Frightened People*, was begun in September.

Despite the massive publicity deployed for both movies, they remain DeMille's least-known sound pictures, much argued over by the archival community. Is *Four Frightened People* DeMille's weakest film or is it, in the words of the kind-hearted Robert Birchard, a 'highly amusing social satire'? *This Day and Age*, certainly, has few partisans these days and at the time was rejected in Holland for 'strong Fascist tendencies'. Finland, Latvia, Lithuania and Trinidad rejected it merely 'because the picture is of the gangster type'.

The film was made because DeMille thought he had something left to say, after *The Godless Girl*, about the state of modern youth. Opening in a high school, where kids are shown preparing for adult responsibilities by taking on the roles of 'District Attorney' and 'Chief of Police', the scene shifts to a Jewish tailor, who is attacked and shot by a local racketeer because he has refused to pay for 'protection'. A student witness is clubbed down. His outraged friends are told the law is helpless: a judge shows them the huge book of 'Rules of Evidence', telling them how difficult a conviction could be. When the racketeer, played by Charles Bickford, is put on trial, eighty-six witnesses give him an alibi, and he is acquitted. The students decide to investigate and find clues that lead them to the gangsters' night club, a rather staid joint in which the girls sing such ruffians' favourites as 'Three Blind Mice' and 'Rockabye Baby'. When the kids are discovered, one of them is shot, and a gun planted on the other. In their search for justice the kids take the law into their own hands, kidnapping the racketeer and putting him on trial before a 'night court' of hundreds of howling students. Dangling him over a pit of rats, they force a confession, as cops who have been tipped off race the gangsters rushing to rescue their boss. The student mob, carrying their prey on a rail, march en masse to the judge's chambers, lustily singing 'John Brown's Body', the District Attorney having ratified their kangaroo court with the words: 'These kids are deputy sheriffs – they acted on my authority.' The judge offers his congratulations to 'these heroic young men'.

No wonder the Dutch censors were nonplussed. The US censors, however, took a more sanguine view, Hays man James Wingate writing to Paramount executive A. M. Botsford on 24 July 1933:

The word 'punks' is sometimes censorable . . . [but] it seems that the spirit of the picture will prove acceptable. We do not believe it will be interpreted in any way as an attack on constituted authority, or a portrayal of lynch law, inasmuch as we noticed that you took care at all times to portray the boys as under control and working in harmony with the police department, having been appointed special deputies by the sheriff, and at the end the judge, mayor and district attorney were portrayed as being in sympathy with the boys' actions. We believe that on this basis this element in the story can be defended. We trust that the good reception it had at the preview will augur equally well for the general public acceptance of the picture throughout the country.

The Hays Office, it appeared, had a peculiar view of its own strictures against the depiction of lawlessness in motion pictures. One senses their relief that they were not being goaded, this time, with women's breasts, licentious dances or inappropriate vernacular phrases. One might have thought they would have paused at the scene of mob fury, as Bickford is dangled by a rope over the rats, the crowd yelling: 'Yah, you big ape! There isn't going to be any habeas corpus . . . we haven't got time for any rules of evidence . . . we want a conviction . . .'

Taking no chances, Paramount's publicists pumped this risible minor film as a ground-breaking epic: 'THE FIRST GREAT SPECTACLE OF MODERN TIMES! CECIL B. DeMILLE SHOWS US WHERE WE'RE HEADING IN "THIS DAY AND AGE." Startling in Sweep! Dramatic in Intensity! 5,000 New Faces! Pitting young courage against evil corruption . . . hurling their bombshell of defiance at the "vultures" who live on the fat of the land!' Released in August, the studio pitched the film as DeMille's twentieth-anniversary production as a film-maker, proposing that theatres should mount publicity 'milestones' depicting DeMille's classics – *The Squaw Man, Male and Female, The Ten Commandments, The King of Kings, The Sign of the Cross* – as all leading up to the masterpiece, *This Day and Age*.

Such a blast of publicity could not easily fail, and audiences turned up, though what people thought of the film is a moot point. *Variety* noted 'a highly improbable and fantastic story, but as done by DeMille, carries more than average audience appeal . . . DeMille has kept his story as free of bath-tubs as his previous extravaganzas have been free from racketeers . . . As a grosser it should be all right.' As indeed it was, keeping Adolph Zukor reasonably happy.

DeMille was, nevertheless, floundering about, uncertain what to do next. Robert Birchard reports that his next picture was planned to be a complete departure from his previous work – a futuristic disaster movie, 'The End of the World', based on a novel by Philip Wylie and Edwin Balmer, *When Worlds Collide*. (The book would eventually be filmed two decades later, in 1951.) But instead, DeMille and his crew hied off to Hawaii in September to shoot the second film of his Paramount contract, the satirical comedy *Four Frightened People*.

Cecil's weaving about between disconnected themes reflected at least in part the loss of Jeanie Macpherson, exiled from writing for him by studio fiat, though she still remained his number-one lady-in-waiting. He had managed to finagle back Anne Bauchens as editor midway through *The Sign of the Cross*, despite the studio's demand that he should use their cutter, Alexander Hall. Bartlett Cormack had written *This Day and Age*, but *Four Frightened People* was assigned to the more familiar Lenore Coffee, working in tandem with Bartlett. Miracle art director Mitchell Leisen had also departed, to begin his own directing career. And so Cecil sailed off to Honolulu to shoot his latest fancy on the islands of 'Maono Loa' and 'Maono Kea' in the 'South Pacific'.

The film opens abruptly on a ship whose crew has mutinied because bubonic plague has broken out on board. The passengers are ignorant of this, apart from our four frightened principals – played by Claudette Colbert, Herbert Marshall, Mary Boland and William Gargan – who cast off in a small boat towards the coastline of what

They shed civilization as they *shed their clothes!*

● Generations made them ladies and gentlemen ...a few hours in the jungle made them male and female! Primitive! Savage! Battling nature for life . . . each other for love!

A prim, timid school teacher

A quiet, serious research chemist

A scatter-brained social worker

A reporter gathering tomorrow's headlines

CECIL B. De MILLE'S
"FOUR FRIGHTENED PEOPLE"

with
Claudette Colbert   Mary Boland
Herbert Marshall   William Gargan
A Paramount Picture

is supposed to be Malaya. What follows is by way of a parody of civilization unmasked by savagery: Claudette Colbert's mousy schoolteacher becomes a mistress of the jungle, the world-famous reporter (Gargan) vies with the self-effacing chemist (Marshall), while society woman Mrs Mardick (Boland) ends up lambasting the hapless natives about their lack of birth control. Into the melange is tipped Leo Carrillo as Montague, a Malay who is more English than the English and who is eventually killed by a tribe of pygmies.

'They Shed Civilization As They Shed Their Clothes!' squawked the publicity. 'Generations made them ladies and gentlemen . . . a few hours in the jungle made them male and female!' 'The jungle is the great leveller,' contributed DeMille to the press book, 'it reveals the real person, for better or worse, under the veneer of civilization . . . In the jungle there was no use for civilized inhibitions, conventions, repressions . . . Life and love meant fierce struggle; and fierce struggle always means a ruthless revealing of what the individual actually is like.'

Yet the attempt to compare the picture to the old classic *Male and Female* rebounded, since even by 1934 few recalled the silent era as an ideal. The censors, as was their wont, complained about Claudette Colbert bathing apparently naked in a stream, though DeMille flim-flammed them with claims of body stockings and they meekly waved him through. Colbert in a leopard skin or clothed in leaves remain, nevertheless, the only memorable images in the swamp. At the end, after the four are rescued, the reporter writes his self-aggrandizing book, Mrs Mardick goes back into society, Marshall divorces his prim wife back home and finds Colbert in her old berth as a schoolteacher, teaching Malay geography.

The film flopped, despite Colbert and the publicists' desperation to jazz up the somewhat confused shoot, jabbering about the location in the

forest of Hau, an impenetrable tangle of twisted trunks and branches. Since primitive times, the Hawaiians have used the Hau branches as the outrigger part of their canoes, but it was forbidden to cut these sacred trees without a dispensation from the king or chief. In order to make room for cameras and equipment . . . DeMille ordered his crew to cut away some of this wired growth. Native Hawaiians . . . refused to do it, and the Hollywood grips had to do the work themselves. For days, the Hawaiians watched DeMille goggle-eyed, waiting for the heavens to open up and hurl thunder bolts at him. But when nothing so spectacular happened to the director, they began to wonder if, after all his imperious manner and bearing, he could be considered as a new type of Hawaiian chief . . .

DeMille returned to more hearings about his income-tax arrears and demands for cuts in the picture by Paramount executives, who did not share DeMille's enthusiasm for exotic locations. Adolph Zukor and company could not understand why DeMille had taken his eye off the rolling ball of profits generated by his period epics. By the end of the year, the die was cast, and 1934 ushered in the preparations for DeMille's return to grandeur, with *Cleopatra*.

'Henceforth, I am going to make only pictures of big, so-called epic character,' DeMille told the *Los Angeles Times* on 28 January 1934.

There are two reasons for this. One is the question of the employment, and the other the fact that if I make a light comedy like 'Four Frightened People' someone immediately starts referring to it as an epic, and the public is disappointed if it doesn't maintain that character. I didn't want 'Four Frightened People' to be taken that seriously.

At best, I can only produce two pictures annually and it will be far more satisfactory to make those films real 'epics' as they call them rather than to consider any compromise. I expect to make a religious drama this year and naturally that will be on a scale of magnitude. Pictures dealing with religion and spiritual things, especially the Bible, are always compensating, and in more than a monetary way. I have had many letters attesting to the other benefits, and that is, after all, the biggest satisfaction.

The peculiar fact, however, is that the next film of DeMille's dealing with a Biblical subject was not made until 1948 – *Samson and Delilah*. Neither Cleopatra nor Richard the Lionheart, the subjects of his next two films, appear in the Bible; Cleopatra, Julius Caesar and Marc Antony, of course, featured in the works of William Shakespeare and George Bernard Shaw.

But 'Forget Shakespeare and Shaw', DeMille wrote to his niece Agnes, having asked her to come over from London – where she was arranging two ballet numbers for a revue – to arrange an exotic oriental dance for him set on Cleopatra's barge. (His letter was written, Agnes notes, 'for some unexplained reason, on cloth, like the *Book of the Dead*'.) The dance was to be part of the key scene in which Cleopatra seduces Marc Antony and prevents him from attacking Egypt and taking her off to Rome in chains. DeMille told Agnes: 'I am giving these lovers their first human chance.' It was all part of 'Uncle Ce'''s growing conviction that what he did and believed was unshakeably right. As Agnes wrote in her memoir *Speak to Me, Dance with Me*:

Cecil's pronouncements were given with total certainty: 'If' was the greatest poem in the English language; the best composers were Wagner and Tchaikovsky; Alma-Tadema was one of the finest painters, although he also liked Rubens. He stated the evaluation with less hesitancy than I have ever heard from professors, critics, or historians . . . Differing views were unthought of at his table.

Agnes also pointed out that 'Cecil was not outwardly pompous. He had wry humor and could tell jokes on himself. And he had wonderful charm. But he always got his way.' Life at 2000 DeMille Drive was as extravagant as ever, with Cecil holding forth as usual over dinner, and Constance ('Aunt Con') presiding over the small talk and gossip: 'The piano teacher's dog has been barking all night . . . Dinner lasted a long time and then they all drifted off to various pursuits and Aunt Con picked up her gaudy skirts and went to the wine cellar to find Uncle Ce a special bottle of Liebfraumilch. Aunt Con is idolized by the whole group. She doesn't give herself a minute's attention . . .' Uncle Ce would join the family at eleven after his day at the studio, and they discussed his and Agnes's ideas for the dance scene. 'I should love to do something mysterious, beautiful, new,' said Agnes. 'Not belly grinds and bumps.'

Uncle Ce's dance director, LeRoy Prinz, however, had other ideas. As Cleopatra and Marc Antony drink themselves silly, scantily clad girls would be winched up from the Nile in a giant fishnet. Girls in leopard skins would snarl and fight each other and be chivvied about by a whip-wielding hunk, before backflipping through fiery hoops. Agnes was not happy with this, as she had already begun developing her own style of dance which would eventually change that art in America. Prinz threatened to resign. Agnes learned Cecil's method, copied from Belasco: 'He asks everyone's opinions about everybody else's business, and afterwards does what he's made a custom of doing during the last twenty years.' He had a killing schedule:

Up at 6:30 a.m., he has breakfast at 7 with Aunt Con in her beautiful east bedroom, the sun pouring through the climbing roses. Off in his own car at 8:00, he drives through the Paramount gates at 8:10 and is on the set between 8:30–9:00 – lunches at 12:30 in the commissary. He is the only producer-director that doesn't demand a private dining room. Of course, his table is in the center and on a raised platform and all his staff sits with him.

Five hours' shooting from 1.30: 'He does everything (sets every camera angle . . . carrying a light gauge round his neck and a portable lens . . .) Breaks at 7:00. Rushes . . . for an hour or so and decisions as to selections for the cutter [Anne Bauchens] who keeps right up to the daily shooting with her rough cuts . . . Office conferences and business decisions until 10:30.' Then back to dinner with Constance, lasting till 1 a.m. 'He personally locks up the whole house, speaks to the night watchman, and goes to bed. I think he reads a little before sleep. Sometimes new scripts, more often the Bible – there's one by his bedside. He never gets more than five hours' sleep.'

Uncle Ce wanted Agnes to start her number on the back of a bull, naked and writhing. Agnes choreographed a dance with ten girls, but

DeMille's assistant and designer, Roy Burns and Ralph Jester, told her it was not something the director could photograph. As it turned out, 'belly grinds and bumps' were perfectly fine for DeMille, and in any case, it was merely one element of an enormously complex design in one of his most elaborate and exotic sets. Apart from many other distractions, Cleopatra's pet leopard, which was fortunately drugged, took a nip at DeMille's putteed calf. Claudette Colbert herself was unwell through much of the shoot, to Cecil's chagrin – 'she always was a bitch . . .' Both Agnes and the bull proved reluctant team players. The audition of her number proved vastly humiliating: dressers and make-up girls greased her hair and plucked her eyebrows; jewels were applied and then wrenched off her living flesh. And then the moment: 'Cecil sat in Cleopatra's great marble throne at the top of a flight of steps, the Sun of Horus behind his head. On his right sat Claudette Colbert, rebukingly lovely.' Agnes did her number, but DeMille only shook his head: 'Oh, no! Oh, no! . . . This has nothing . . . It has no excitement, no thrill, no suspense, no sex . . . What I would like is something like the lesbian dance in *The Sign of the Cross*.'

Story conference for *Cleopatra* (1934)

At which point, Agnes writes, she walked out. DeMille had humiliated his own niece in public, and it is clear that she never got over that moment: her disillusionment with Uncle Ce and her acerbic judgements on him date from this sour disaster. Agnes wrote, cryptically, at the end of her chapter on this debacle: 'Before I left Hollywood I treated myself to a superb fling with a wonderful young man. I had earned it in blood.'

DeMille shot *Cleopatra* in an amazing eight weeks between March and May 1934. Colbert was the obvious choice for the title role, but DeMille could not get Fredric March, his first choice for Marc Antony, as he was contracted elsewhere. By chance, so the tale goes, he came across an English actor with stage and screen experience, Henry Wilcoxon, who seemed ideal: big, brawny, brash and with the right kind of swagger. The addition of two great black Dobermanns that seem to pull him everywhere gave him just the right air of arrogance and vulnerability. Warren William, another English actor of more wooden good looks, became Julius Caesar. Ian Keith was a suitably thuggish Octavian, Joseph Schildkraut a suitably oily Herod, and C. Aubrey Smith excelled as Antony's chief general, Enobarbus, a hulking loyalist who tears off all his medals at the end in grief at his great commander's moral collapse due to his submission to the wiles of 'A Woman!'

For all Agnes's agony, *Cleopatra* is certainly DeMille's best sound epic, until the remade *Ten Commandments*, and ironically his most human talkie. There is a tinge of Gloria Swanson switching husbands in the quirky relationship between the queen, man-of-duty Julius Caesar and raunchy Marc Antony. The whole film, brought in at a crisp 104 minutes, is played tongue-in-cheek, with the script pitched at soap-opera level and containing frisky jests on the classical texts it derived from: 'You and your Friends, Romans, Countrymen!' Octavian rebukes Antony for his playing up to the crowd after Caesar's murder.

Freed of pious pomposity by the very absence of biblical connotations – no Christians and no Jews but a very campy Herod – Cecil could indulge in his orientalist fantasies to the hilt, despite later protestations that he took great pains to have researchers study the authentic costumes and art of ancient Egypt. From the front titles, carved majestically upon Egyptian stone and statue, *Cleopatra* evokes a classical European image of the orient, all pagan exhibitionism and as near nudity as the censor – whom Agnes claims was sitting at DeMille's side on the set – would allow. Without the spectre of religion – at least of the Judaeo-Christian kind – the attitude was more lax, even though the tightened Hays Code was about to be unleashed in July.

To the Miracle of the Short Shoot, we might add the Miracle of the Budget, which Adolph Zukor was willing to increase somewhat, but not by much, to under $900,000. This accounts for the incredibly economic battle scene between Octavian's Roman legions and the Egyptians led by Marc Antony and Cleopatra, which appears to incorporate unused scenes of the Egyptian charge in the desert from *The Ten Commandments*. Much of the sequence was put together in the effects department, with both Henry Wilcoxon and Ian Keith's close-ups matched optically with their troops. Crisp, short shots, cut with zip pans, prefigure the more frenetic cutting style we have become accustomed to in our own day. And the deployment of a relatively small number of extras – no more than a few hundred – clearly inspired Orson Welles's famous how-to-make-a-medieval-battle-out-of-almost-nothing in his 1966 Falstaff film, *Chimes at Midnight*. Horns toot, spears flash, feet trudge, horses' hooves and chariot wheels thunder and balls of fire are catapulted into the models of Cleopatra's shattered fleet. At the end, Marc Antony is left forlorn on a battlement, clipped of everything but his life, to thrust his sword into his own belly when he sees Cleopatra surrendering, unaware that she has given up Egypt to plead vainly for his life.

In a bow to his own silent Swanson oeuvre, DeMille provided what he obviously considered to be his own version of a feminist tract, in which the bragging men barking about women being good for nothing except as playthings are brought down by Cleopatra's wiles, although she reveals her own weakness in the end by falling for hunky Marc Antony. Patriotism comes a poor second, and in any case the rampaging Romans, scheming against and assassinating each other, are hardly civic models for a republic. Cecil is more sympathetic to his exotic Egypt, a place of mystery destroyed, as the jazz age was, by its hedonistic licence and the vulgar jackboots of secular conquest.

The movie's crowning scene, however, remains the great shot in the massive interior of Cleopatra's barge, when Marc Antony finally succumbs to a kiss and Cleopatra's raised close-up eyebrow gives the nod to her minions to set sail. Cinematographer Victor Milner, who received a well-deserved Oscar for the film, deployed a great crane shot, from the veils that descend upon the lovers, back along the length of the barge, its immense fluted oars swaying in unison, pulling back to reveal the oarmaster in the foreground, a muscular hulk in an Egyptian headdress beating the drum to the oarsmen, as drumbeat and oars suggest the pulsing of the lovers' sexual embrace. It is without doubt one of the great shots of the cinema: a brilliant blend of hokum, grandeur, grace, power and that intangible joy that only the movies, of all the arts, can produce, a shot that I have not forgotten since I first viewed the film many years ago.

Paramount really went to town with the movie, launching a mer-chandising campaign on the widest scale, recruiting Macy's, Wool-worth, A. S. Beck Shoes, Lux Soap and a host of other companies that would participate in tie-ins. There were 'Cleopatra sandals', 'Cleopatra perfume – Alluring and Lasting' and Cleopatra fashion styles – ladies' belts, compacts, cigarette cases and costume jewellery. 'Through two leading merchandising concerns,' the publicists told the theatre owners, 'hundreds of stores all over the country have already been contacted and are ready to display these items, co-operating with you when you play the picture.' Also featured: Feathered Modern Modified Cleopatra Head-Dress. 'Cleopatra had bangs – so modern women follow suit.' 'Hit Hard With Exploitation,' came the instruc-tion, using local slogans like 'If Cleopatra had lived in Blanksville she would have shopped for value at Marshall's.' And: 'Stage a Gala Cleopatra Ball . . . at a leading hotel under the sponsorship of a men's fraternal organization or a group of society women. This affair, which offers local citizens the chance to array themselves in the dazzling cos-tumes of Cleopatra's Egypt and Caesar's Rome, could easily wind up as the social event of the season.'

DeMille's merchandising had come a long way since displaying the latest gowns and bathing suits worn by Gloria Swanson and Bebe Daniels would cause ladies in the audience to raid their husbands' piggy banks to obtain them. This was now a fully fledged part of the industry, consumerism indeed come of age – and with the Depression still raging! Cleopatra balls, Cleopatra contests, Cleopatra's throne for 'street ballyhoo', school projects and history essays for pupils, a 'Talking Sphinx Lobby Stunt – Ask Questions of the Sphinx, silent for ages. It will answer with the voice of Cleopatra! Paint the shoulders and front of the body on a box made of compo-board, model in plaster the bas-relief of a face . . . opening should be made in the ears, connecting with a microphone inside the box . . . Get a girl who is quick-witted and ready with a come-back to do the answering . . .' There were cartoon serials for newspapers on the 'Events in the Life of the Glamorous Empress, Suggested by Cecil B. DeMille's "Cleopatra."' The publicists boasted 'Nine months of consistent, patron-creating publicity for this tremendous undertaking! The nation's best-read magazines, circulations totalling 20,000,000 monthly, spread the story month after month! Newspapers, with 30,000,000 daily readers, devoted thousands of columns to detailing its wonders! And, topping the whole campaign, the national lecture tour of Cecil B. DeMille! A tremendous, breath-taking build-up . . . greater than any before carried through for any picture.'

Oddly enough, the critics were not as bowled over by *Cleopatra* as they were by *The Sign of the Cross*. *Variety* defaulted to its sour mode, noting that the 'handpicked' audience at opening night was 'polite but not over enthusiastic. Consensus of opinion seemed to be that the film fails successfully to demonstrate the combination of extreme splendor with a story . . . Splendor and intimacy do not blend any more than the traditional oil and water. Each treads on the other's toes . . . It is on the pictorial angle, and almost wholly on that, that the success of the production depends. This is sufficient to make it a money picture.' Mordaunt Hall's *New York Times* review was more informative than either enthusiastic or hostile, commenting that the movie revealed DeMille 'in an emphatically lavish, but nevertheless a restrained mode'.

The audiences, however, flocked in large enough numbers to make the box office tinkle for Paramount and Adolph Zukor's cheeks to glow with a renewed commitment to future DeMille movies. In the budget for his next movie, Cecil would have almost half a million dollars more to cope with his needs.

When one watches *Cleopatra* seven decades later, with the ballyhoo long died down, the film endures, due in part to the blend of the personal and the spectacular achieved by DeMille but also very much due to Colbert herself. Against the odds, she succeeded in bringing the light touch of the comedienne to a role that could easily have been merely stylized and ridiculous but which instead resonates with grace and humanity. Beneath the hokum and the schlock, she supplies the movie with a heart, an element sorely missing, despite the lashings of sentiment, in DeMille features to come.

Exultant Pomp, and Silver Fanfares

From the *New York Times*, 12 May 1935:

GATEWAY INTO THE PAST:
The Year is 1190 When You Call on Cecil B. DeMille in Hollywood.
By Idwal Jones.

The massive iron door clicked behind me. Today was shut out by the sunlight, and I found myself in the twilight of the Middle Ages. Three or four barons in chain-mail were sauntering in a vast baronial hall hung with tapestry. Mastiffs were asleep on the hearth. In the shadows were lunging halberdiers, huntsmen, falconers, cupbearers and ladies-in-waiting. After a minute, all seemed logical. Alice's Wonderland and Hollywood are alike in that impossible things happen in them, and you are not surprised . . .

There could be no respite in Cecil DeMille's manifestations of the impossible. There were only shifts and changes in the Wonderlands that were painstakingly planned, designed, built, populated abruptly by a melee of actors, camera crew, lights, yelling assistants, carpenters, costumiers, chair carriers *et al.* and then torn down to make way for the next dream. After *Cleopatra*, Cecil had wanted to realize a project he had long wished to film, a pirate story, which morphed into a plan to adapt a biography published in 1930 by Lyle Saxon entitled *Lafitte the Pirate*. This was the tale of Jean Lafitte, a privateer who became a patriot in the war against the British in 1812. But various conflicts of title over the book and another play DeMille had purchased, *The Buccaneer*, led to the project being shelved. Another project, according to legend, emerged during one of the DeMille family's regular get-togethers, when Cecil took on all-comers in an 'open forum', an argument in which everyone else tried to challenge the master on some fact. Cecil's adopted son John, then twenty-two, suggested a film about the Crusades. Immediately, according to the *San Francisco Chronicle*: 'The young man must have been convincing, for the next morning a metamorphosis took place on the Paramount lot that could mean only one thing – the beginning of a DeMille picture.'

Howsoever the first seed was planted, it soon sprouted in the usual spectacular style, as the *Chronicle* essay written by Jeanette Meehan reported:

The dictionary doesn't list adequate adjectives with which to describe the screen's greatest box office director when he starts to work. Physically he becomes a machine. Emotionally he becomes a slave driver for a vast army of workers. He doesn't request, he demands absolute and unfailing efficiency from every member of his staff . . . No stone within a mile of him gathers any moss.

That morning began a seven-month intense research into history . . . In his inner office DeMille sat like a master puppeteer, working strings which connected him with 68 different studio departments employing between 2000 and 3000 workers. Through his door poured a deluge of players, props, costumes, artisans, craftsmen . . . Three secretaries, four telephones and dictating machine were swamped with routine. On his desk were 12 memorandum pads on which he made notes . . . From the Metropolitan Museum in New York came photographs of armor. New York armorers made exact copies of the originals and shipped them to Hollywood.

Then the real work began. The foundry, metal shop and blacksmith shop at the studio screamed with the sound of iron on iron. Helmets and spurs were produced by the carload. Huge shields were hauled to the wardrobe on trucks . . .

Of course, it was not all purely authentic – wood sprayed with silver lacquer was substituted for metal mesh, lest the extras collapse under the load. The property department turned out bows, arrows, siege ladders and an immense catapult for Richard the Lionheart to bombard the walls of Acre in Palestine – 'the largest single prop ever built for a motion picture'. (The massive ships of the silent 1925 movie *Ben-Hur*, directed by Fred Niblo, had long been forgotten.) A giant ram's head for the battering ram, a 35-ton siege tower – all was and is as movies decree:

[For] the siege of Acre, for example . . . 600 extras are used. Over each group of 100 extras is placed an assistant director. Each assistant then divides his group into subsequent groups of 10 extras each, from which he picks a competent extra as the boss of his particular ten . . . In order of their importance they relay the commands of the Grand Marshal who issues orders over the public address system – microphone and loud speaker. Over this public system DeMille rants, shouts, insults, hires and fires. He doesn't mince words. There's a reason.

'Each extra must be an actor,' maintains DeMille. 'In order to achieve uniformity of effect each must play an individual scene. You can't take a man from the lunch counter and lead him forth in a mood for battle. You've got to break him, mentally beat him; you've got to tear at his very entrails to make him give – to make him give things he doesn't know he's got.' . . .

The fight is on. The enemy is pelted with fireballs . . . One soldier gets his leg crushed under the great wooden wheel of the siege tower. Several catch on fire and either jump or are pushed into the artificial moat.

In his enthusiasm DeMille leans out from behind his barrier and gets a blunt arrow full in the face. Two horses get broken legs. The director gets red around the neck and rattles the inevitable gold coins in his pocket, Look out! It's coming!

'Who,' roars DeMille, 'is that cowardly cur over there? Who is that man who has no spunk or manhood or guts? Throw him out. THROW HIM OUT! This is WAR, not a pink tea for pansies!' And that's all he said that's printable.

DeMille and Loretta Young in characteristic relationship – *The Crusades*

As the Hollywood tradition requires, print the legend. *The Crusades* was DeMille's most out-and-out spectacle film since *Joan the Woman*, and certainly since *The Ten Commandments'* 'prologue'. Unlike his Joan of Arc tale, he could not rely on the charisma of Geraldine Farrar to galvanize the extras into falling into the moat. As the down to earth, slap-'em-on-the-back or punch-'em-in-the-face Richard the Lionheart, he cast Henry Wilcoxon, the obvious choice after his ebullient Marc Antony. Ian Keith, supporting actor both in *The Sign of the Cross* and *Cleopatra*, was cast as an unusually sympathetic Saladin. Since there had to be a love interest, DeMille's writers, Harold Lamb, Waldemar Young and Dudley Nichols (with a little creative input from, among others, Jeanie Macpherson, being eased into a hopeful comeback), exhumed Richard the Lionheart's queen, Berengaria, who apparently married him in Cyprus but then faded out of his tale, with no issue recorded of the marriage. Historical research points to Richard's homosexuality, but not in a film by Cecil B. DeMille! Thus Berengaria is brought to the fore in *The Crusades*, so that the publicists may trumpet 'The Flaming Chapters of One Woman's Love – Trapped by Two Worlds Locked in Titanic Conflict!', acclaiming Richard as 'Conqueror of Half the World – Fiercest Lover of the Ages!'

DeMille cast Loretta Young – birth name Gretchen and a former child star of the movies from 1917 – as the queen, whom Saladin returns chivalrously to her king after she is captured in a Saracen raid as the price of peace between Christians and Muslims. Her marriage to Richard is presented as the exchange demanded by the avaricious old King of Navarre for the cattle beef and grain the English Crusaders require for their voyage to Palestine. In a nice flight of fancy, DeMille has Richard too embroiled in his preparations for battle to marry Berengaria in person, so she is married, under the aegis of his minstrel, Blondel, to his sword.

This was also the first film in which Cecil cast his adopted daughter Katherine in a major role: as the pouting French princess Alice, whom Richard spurns, to the chagrin of the French king. One of Cecil's earliest silent actors, Pedro de Cordoba, appears in a cameo as 'Karakush', one of Saladin's minions, and C. Aubrey Smith turns up bearing a cross as the rabble-rousing Peter the Hermit.

The film is a curious addition to Hollywood's 'orientalist' cinema, progressing from a sterotypical brutalization of Christian captives by

Saracens in conquered Jerusalem towards the denouement, in which Queen Berengaria pleads a very modern cause – 'Whether we call Him Allah or God, shall men fight because they travel different roads to him?' – convincing Richard and Saladin to make peace and open up Jerusalem to Christians and Muslims alike.

DeMille was quite proud in later years of his even-sided view of the Third Crusade of AD 1190 and claimed it was 'one of my most popular pictures in the Middle East', though Robert Birchard quotes figures that cast some doubt on this. The opening scene alone would have caused groans in Arab cinemas, since history, Christian or Muslim, records Saladin's treatment of the Christians in his conquest of Jerusalem in 1187 as merciful compared with the atrocious massacre by the Crusaders who first took the city ninety years before – unmentioned by DeMille. Presenting Saladin as a gallant knight, and even as a soft-spoken lover, was less predictable, as he presents a positive contrast to the quarrelling Christian kings, and in particular, the treacherous Conrad of Montferrat, played with oily menace by Joseph Schildkraut.

The ambiguities of the film are, however, par for the course in Hollywood's view of the Arab east, before the establishment of the state of Israel in 1948 skewed the American cinema towards a more hostile posture. If Saladin is the perfect knight, he is also a compatriot of the bustling citizens of the silent *Thief of Baghdad*, which for all its exoticism portrayed a society functioning dynamically on its own terms. And though his amorous procedures are considerably less forceful than Rudolf Valentino's as *The Sheik*, they are still almost as gratefully acknowledged. The problem with DeMille's good intentions, and with his theme of the redemption of King Richard, who realizes that the sword alone cannot deliver Jerusalem, is that they are still cast in the spirit of hokum that had become Cecil's declared stock-in-trade.

And what hokum! Henry Wilcoxon's Richard hams it up, winning a fist fight with the blacksmith who is making his sword, striding forth and riding up and down in kingly armour and presiding over some of the 1930s' best-filmed cavalry charges, a crunching of horses and men on the battlefields of California's Palestine. Victor Milner, improving on *Cleopatra*, deployed a fluid camera with some splendid crane shots in the crucial Acre night siege. Massive fireballs fly across the battlements, men plunge into the moat, and all is as the Great

CONQUERER OF HALF THE WORLD
...FIERCEST LOVER OF THE AGES!

Richard the Lion-Heart! A sword of lightning! A heart of steel!...But he surrendered both to a beautiful Princess he had never seen!...He matched his strength against the savage armies of the East, and the fierce fury of eleven kings to get her—and won!

CECIL B. De MILLE'S
"THE CRUSADES"
with LORETTA YOUNG · HENRY WILCOXON
and a cast of many thousands...A Paramount Picture

Fieldmarshal of Hollywood decrees from his perch above, and often in the midst of, the fray. Loretta Young, displaying the full gamut from loathing the loutish king who uses her veil to wrap his horse's wounded leg to love when he chooses her over his expedient French alliance, presents a triumph of hairdressing over circumstance.

The magic of *Cleopatra*, however, eludes the film, and the marriage of the personal with the portentous that worked with Claudette Colbert does not stand the test of time. In its moment, however, DeMille was satisfied. The *New York Times*' Idwal Jones, now Hollywood's most tenacious stalker, reported, as the film faced its opening at the beginning of August 1935, on another of DeMille's innovations: the genuinely 'sneak' preview. As the tale was told, DeMille embarked on his yacht, the *Seaward*, from Catalina, to sail down the coast with his film cans. Eluding fleets of press men, his limousine left the docks and veered off to a small theatre in San Diego, whose patrons were not expecting anything more prominent than a minor western.

DeMille got out and whispered to the manager, who was stupefied at first then elated. The cans were whisked in . . . DeMille thought the laboratory conditions perfect. The subjects made a cross-section of America. They were neighborhood folk, with visitors to the fair, transients from an auto-trailer camp, legionnaires, shopkeepers, orange growers, a party of St. Louis shoe-factory workers, children, a sprinkling of Portuguese and Japanese fishermen . . .

As the pageant of the Middle Ages began to trundle across the screen, DeMille watched the faces of the audience in the reflected light. Since he was familiar with every inch of the film and every note of its recorded sound, he knew at any instant what was showing. He clocked the emotions of the watchers. It is a commentary on DeMille's mind that he cannot so much recall now an individual face but a composite face of that crowd.

His skill is in mob psychology. The avantguard cinematists, like Freund, René Clair and our Messrs. Hecht and MacArthur, go in for individual psychology, what the Germans call 'positivism,' or what we call behaviorism. All this DeMille is quite content to leave to the clinical avantguard. Give him the crowd, to flatten out with composed, glittering scenes and a prodigal and exultant pomp, the largess of a Durbar, and silver fanfares . . .

DeMille, Jones wrote, was particularly engaged with the audience's response to the film's music: as 'the vox humana stop was pulled out, the theatre was flooded with a music that was liturgical, a composite of the Gregorian chant, all the anthems ever heard, all the hymns ever sung in basilica, little tin Bethel and camp meeting, simple-pathetic airs keyed to exaltation and yet in the minor, four-octave chords – a language common to all time'.

Was it the lowest common denominator DeMille was seeking, like so many of the practitioners in today's Hollywood, or was it the widest common denominator, the holy grail of box-office appeal? How DeMille would have loved today's technical marvels, the crispness of the widest screen, the sonorous thunder of THX-Dolby and all the trimmings, the patter of rain coming from overhead speakers, the cries of the extras from the back of the hall. The 'sneak' preview gave DeMille the sense of an audience that was encountering the work free of expectation, of any premonition of what lay in store. Already, he realized, he was surrounded by those who knew, or thought they knew, what he was about or what he wanted, and would provide acclaim or abuse accordingly. Above all, he sought that mythical beast, the raw audience, America renewed in the pause of breath before the light beams struck.

The Crusades seemed to be a successful film, but by only grossing $1.5 million, just a hundred thousand over its costs, it showed a loss after taking into account all the promotional outlays. The lesson was, as Adolph Zukor was always pointing out, that period epics were simply too expensive and risky, the jackpot never guaranteed. Zukor himself would soon mark a quarter of a century in motion pictures, even more if one counted his penny arcade and nickelodeon days. And yet he too was fading away. DeMille had to make his deals with the new executives who were in charge of the 'bottom line'.

From 1936, DeMille embarked on a series of films set mainly in frontier America. If not quite classic westerns, they were historical sagas set at home rather than painted upon the broader canvas of religious wars at the frontiers of the 'known' world. As a new collaborator soon to join his team, Jesse Lasky Junior, would describe his mood in this period:

Epic Americana had always been, would always be box-office gold . . . DeMille had shrewdly lifted his own sights from the bathtub to Yankee mythology with *The Plainsman* and *The Buccaneer*. He now felt audiences were ripe for sweeping vistas of continent-taming tribulations. The thirties had regained prosperity without grandeur, sanity without sense of destiny. We needed to draw spiritual nourishment for the present from the past. We needed to regain a sense of purpose in the hangover from Prohibition and the materialistic disestablishment of the Depression. We had boozed away the American dream with Scott Fitzgerald and tasted the lusty cynicism of Hemingway and Dos Passos. Ripe time to produce chauvinistic fairy tales – thundering with rescuing cavalry, Old Glory cracking above the horse soldiers bugling into the wind, racing to save the settlers from the savages . . .

Jesse Jr was referring to his first full assignment as a writer for DeMille, on 1939's *Union Pacific*. But the passage reflects just as well the opening film in the series, *The Plainsman*, Cecil's first work with Gary Cooper, who would appear in three more of his films. By 1936, Cooper was a major star, with parts in twenty-odd silent and another twenty talkie pictures behind him, including *Morocco*, *A Farewell to Arms* and *Mr. Deeds Goes to Town*. DeMille cast him as Wild Bill Hickok in a rollicking tale of the taming of the frontier immediately after the Civil War. Buffalo Bill (James Ellison), General Custer (John Miljan), Calamity Jane (Jean Arthur) and Abe Lincoln all featured in the story.

As was to be the norm from now on, a bevy of writers cobbled the story together under the eagle eye of the boss. In this case, Waldemar Young, Harold Lamb and Lynn Griggs were credited, with Jeanie Macpherson adding material based on stories by Courtney Riley Cooper and Frank J. Wilstach. At least another three uncredited writers were on the team, a far cry from the days when DeMille and Macpherson would cook up a tale out of their imaginations or out of some pulp novel from which their fancy could take flight. As is often the case with such committee scripts, the result is less a coherent drama than a series of episodes wrapped around a basic plot about white men selling arms to the Indians and Cooper's fight to stop the villainous trader, Lattimer, played by a suitably unshaven Charles Bickford. A gruff love affair with Calamity Jane and friendship-rivalry with Buffalo Bill rounds off the tale.

It was the first original western DeMille had made (setting aside his two remakes of *The Squaw Man*) since 1917's *A Romance of the Redwoods* with Mary Pickford. His ideas of the west had changed intriguingly. The old silent west, that dangerous, anarchic place where even good intentions were blighted by a rough, amoral world, was now literally an empty plain upon which rugged, flawed heroes could find redemption in the patriotic project of America's manifest destiny. As the closing titles of *The Plainsman* declare: 'It shall be as it was in the past . . . Not with dreams, but with strength and with courage, shall a nation be molded to last.'

Critics pointed out that, with Wild Bill Hickok, Buffalo Bill and Calamity Jane as historical characters, there was nary a real plainsman in the lot. But authenticity in a DeMille film had long been reserved for the technicalities, not the content. In this department, DeMille was suitably loaded, as Idwal Jones pointed out in the *New York Times*: 'Practically all the pistols in "The Plainsman" came from DeMille's own collection. He owns eighty-six. Cooper owns forty-three. But the largest collection in Hollywood is 1,000, owned by J. S. Stembridge, owner of the gun room at Paramount Studio.'

There was gunplay galore in the film, and Indian torture, captive white women, ambushed cavalry mule trains and stereotyped Indians willing to trade Calamity Jane for Gary Cooper's musical watch. As Frank Nugent of the *Times* summed it up at the time: 'No saga of the plains . . . [but] an excellently contrived large-scale horse opera.'

Among the serio-comic Indians, however, there was a newcomer who barnstormed his way through a short cameo. As the tale is told by historian Anne Edwards, when the call went out for 'authentic Indians' to play in the movie, a young Mexican-American actor, Anthony Quinn, turned up, claiming to be a Cheyenne. 'Say something in Cheyenne,' said the casting director. '*Ksai Ksakim eledeki Chumbolum*,' said Quinn. He was taken swiftly into DeMille's office, together with an adviser 'who was supposed to know the Indian language'.

'*Xtmas ala huahua?*' the adviser said to him, in what Quinn was certain was phony Cheyenne, so he replied, '*Xtmas nava ellahuahua, cheriota hodsvi.*'

'Oh yes, he speak good Cheyenne,' the man told Cecil.

This was a fateful moment for the DeMille family, as, one year later, on 5 October 1937, Quinn married the boss's daughter, Katherine. By then, Cecil had discovered he was not an Indian. But the young man got by on his charm. In DeMille's next movie, *The Buccaneer*, Quinn played another role: as a pirate, Beluche. The marriage took place before the film shoot was over.

For the audiences that watched DeMille's films and gaped at the magazine features portraying his house and its ornaments – his weapons paraphernalia, illuminated manuscripts of Gregorian liturgy, medieval helmets, Hindu hatchets and graceful daughter Katherine among the artefacts – it was excusable if they imagined that, for him, life and movies were as one, a perfectly merged real-life fable. For Cecil B. DeMille at least, the Depression was a faded memory, and he could set his sights resolutely on conserving the values that went with his means.

Walking the Plank, or The Misadventures of Jesse Junior

When DeMille was marshalling his writers in preparation for *The Buccaneer*, twenty-six-year-old Jesse Lasky Jr tried his luck for the first time with his father's long-term colleague. Young Jesse had grown up in the Hollywood bubble and attended the inaccurately named Hollywood School for Girls, together with sons of stars like Douglas Fairbanks Jr and Noah Beery Jr, as well as DeMille's daughter Cecilia and another misplaced waif, Joel McCrea. He had travelled to Europe with his parents, Jesse L. and Bessie Lasky, and in 1936 had just returned from a trip to England, where he had helped to polish up a script by the already famous Alfred Hitchcock, *Secret Agent*. He had dabbled in poetry and some scriptwriting in Hollywood for films like *Coming Out Party*, *The Redhead* and *The White Parade*, all made in 1934. So he was not, in fact, appearing without credentials at DeMille's office, as he braved the daunting walk to the desk, past the 'photos of presidents he had helped elect, gifts from grateful stars, tokens of esteem from oil tycoons whom he had financed' and the burning spotlight turned on the supplicant's face, to ask for a job on his new movie. The tale is taken up in Jesse's own 1973 book, *Whatever Happened to Hollywood?*:

DeMille fingered the volumes of thin verse I'd sent him from England. 'Do you believe in God, Jesse?'

'Yes, sir. I think so.'

'Think so? But you don't know?' There was a dangerous – yes, ominous threat behind the question. A man might be burned at the stake for less than certainty.

'I believe in you, sir.'

'Not a bad beginning,' he allowed, thumbing one of my books. 'You write fair poetry. I wonder if you could write drama. Could you?'

Jesse pulled out some samples of dialogue he had prepared based on the story outline of *The Buccaneer*.

He took it benevolently: Zeus accepting an offering. He scanned it, then read it aloud slowly. Deliberately . . . He was making my dialogue sound like drivel – which no doubt it was. His eyes flicked up and I saw the blue-white rage that would be there on so many occasions. One hand slipped into the desk drawer and came out holding a revolver. He offered it, butt forward.

'If you want to destroy me, Jesse,' he hissed, 'use this. It's quicker!'

On this occasion, as Jesse tells the tale, DeMille rejected his script pages, except for one line, written for a scene in which the heroine, the Dutch girl, Gretchen, played by Franciska Gaal, has been made to walk the plank by the pirates. She is floundering in the waves with her pet dog when a boat carrying the film's hero, Jean Lafitte, played by Fredric March, and his lieutenant, Dominique, played by Akim Tamiroff, comes by. Jesse suggested Tamiroff should say: 'Do you hear that, boss? A barking fish!'

So DeMille took the line without adding the writer to his already busy team, although the record shows that Lasky was on board, though not for an on-screen credit. The crowded writers' barge included Edwin Justus Mayer, Harold Lamb, C. Gardner Sullivan and Jeanie Macpherson, whose adaptation of Lyle Saxon's book on Lafitte had sparked off the whole enterprise. Other uncredited writers included no less than Preston Sturges, Grover Jones – Paramount's regular fixer – and Emily Barrye.

As usual, too many cooks spoil the broth, and *The Buccaneer* certainly does not boast, to put it mildly, one of the screen's greatest texts. The plot bounces along, from a fine opening depicting President James Madison's wife giving a dinner to various senators and friends at the 'President's Palace' in August 1814, when the British march in and burn Washington. In good imperial form, the British generals finish the presidential dinner before using the candles to set fire to the mansion, the president's wife braving the fire to rescue the Declaration of Independence.

In *The Plainsman*, DeMille was dealing with a protagonist, Wild Bill Hickok, whose violence was portrayed as justified in the rough and ready law of the 'untamed' west. The American 'hero' in *The Buccaneer* is more problematic. Jean Lafitte, a Creole privateer, is introduced in the film by a Byronic verse: 'He left a Corsair's name to other times/ Linked with one virtue/ and a thousand crimes.'

Tempted both by British bribes and the promise of an American pardon, the pirate chooses to fight with Andrew Jackson's troops in the Battle of New Orleans of January 1815. History recounts that by that time the Treaty of Ghent, of 24 December 1814, had brought the war of 1812 between Britain and the United States formally to an end, but myth needs no formal sanction. The fact is left out of the film but noted in the souvenir brochure, which provides details of the research, spearheaded by DeMille in person: 'In March, 1937, De Mille led a research expedition – the only one he had personally conducted – into Louisiana.' Proceeding much as Henry Morton Stanley did in locating the missing David Livingstone in darkest Africa, DeMille, his associate producer, writer Mayer, publicist and secretaries 'spent three weeks endeavouring to uncover every vestige of Lafitte data the Mississippi delta country has to offer'. Apart from scouring the French Quarter and the Louisiana State Museum, libraries and private collections, the party also

. . . cruised 280 miles through the swamps of Lousiana, where the descendants of Lafitte's pirates still live.

Down through the winding bayous where Lafitte and his men, in pirogues, could quickly outdistance the swiftest pursuit, they chugged amid green hyacinth and towering cypresses hung with Spanish moss. In the distance, ducks rose and wheeled as 'black' as mosquitos – in a country where mosquitos at dusk are a velvet curtain that stings like a nest of adders.

Out to Grand Isle, Barataria, and the Gulf went the party. They talked to the shrimp fishermen, who live in green huts on stilts and proudly declare their ancestral links to Lafitte. They attended the fisherfolk dances, talked to the wives and sweethearts of the Cajuns and Baratarians. They photographed the old fort at the entrance to Barataria Bay, where Lafitte would hide his ships . . .

As usual, the research yielded a store of information for the construction of props, furniture, costumes and sets. Old flintlock rifles and pistols were purchased and used. Everything looks authentic but the film itself, which had to obey the immovable rule of being molded to the higher hokum that DeMille was sure his audience craved.

Although DeMille often wrote that he could not abide 'Yes men' and wished to have colleagues around him as strong-minded as himself, in practice his decisions were seldom successfully challenged. If

he made a mistake, it was more often than not left unrectified and could ruin an entire project. This was clearly the case with his choice for the female star of *The Buccaneer*, Franciska Gaal, a Hungarian actress and cabaret artiste who had appeared in a number of light-hearted Hungarian and German films, notably in 1933's *Scandal in Budapest*. She had been spotted by producer Joe Pasternak and then by Ernst Lubitsch, who recommended her as a Paramount star.

Bad acting by a professional in films is almost always the fault of the director, and so we must assume that Cecil B. DeMille simply did not understand Miss Gaal's comedic talents and miscast her badly in his film. At the time, however, he displayed his accustomed loyalty to his choice, preparing a special promotional short film for her with the working title 'Star Bright'. In this sketch, Cecil B. DeMille drives up to his residence to view in his own home cinema 'a European picture starring a young Hungarian girl', because, 'to DeMille, art is international'.

CS: *DeMille seated in projection room – low key lighting . . .*
DeMILLE: That's the girl, Bill! . . . That's her, that's Gretchen! Can't you see her opposite Fredric March in 'The Buccaneer?' She's petite, vivacious, spirited – can she speak English? (*He reaches for the phone without waiting for answer. To phone*:) Get me Budapest!

When Gaal comes on, she protests to DeMille: 'But I am afraid to go to America. I am not one of those beautiful Hollywood blondes.' DeMille: 'I don't want a typical Hollywood beauty. The woods are full of them. I want a fine emotional actress for the part I have in mind.' Miss Gaal, flouncing in bed, is still uncertain: 'But the United States is so big. And I am so little . . . Well, maybe I can leave in two weeks . . . One week? Oh you Americans! Well, I try. Goodbye Mr DeMille . . .' She hangs up the phone, springs out of bed and calls her little helpers: 'Hans . . . Julie . . . Bertha . . . Pack our things . . . we are going to America!'

Miss Gaal's English was not very good, and her appearance in the film is mawkish and embarrassing. She would make two more films in the US and then disappear from the American screen, though she graced the Broadway stage for a while.

DeMille's other choices were more appropriate, though star Fredric March's French Creole accent is a little more grave than necessary and Akim Tamiroff's clowning is overblown. At the time, however, he was a wow with audiences, who loved his scene-stealing antics, facial tics and his character's continual reminders to all and sundry that he had been 'Napoleeone's favorite gunner'. The 'barking fish' line also got a laugh. Anthony Quinn chalked up a second appearance for DeMille, as Beluche, another Lafitte stooge. Hugh Sothern provided a fine, earthy General Andrew Jackson, and Walter Brennan began a long line of chin-wagging western eccentrics as the general's coonskin-cap orderly, Ezra Peavey.

Despite being marketed as another DeMille spectacle, with 6,000 extras of all castes and nationalities portraying Lafitte's army of outcasts and deserters, chosen on the principle enshrined in the casting sheets of 'Men without stomachs and women without red fingernails', there is not a great deal of spectacle in the film. DeMille and cinematographer Victor Milner once again, as in *Cleopatra*, built montages of battle out of dramatic moments, flourishes, explosions, shouting faces and falling bodies. The best scene is probably the muster of Lafitte's scattered men from the bayous, the Creole calls bringing forth an armada of small boats gliding towards the camera in twilight.

The film is another DeMille rarity, and one can only speculate on why it dropped out of distribution for so long. Presenting the British as the colonial oppressors was historically accurate but fell out of favour less than two years after the movie's release, when the Second World War pitted the British against Nazi Germany. The gala opening in New Orleans attracted a massive crowd and tumultuous applause. *Variety* deserted its usual gloomy critique of DeMille to proclaim the film 'a cinch for big boxoffice returns around the world . . . Production is ultra all the way . . .'

Spectacle apart, the film demonstrates the lengths to which DeMille, following traditional American iconography, will go to present the redemption of an American cut-throat as a patriot, as long as he has literally waved the flag. Just as Jesus Christ redeems the sins of mankind, so are hands red with blood washed clean by the embrace of the American cause. In the end Jean Lafitte is a flawed DeMille hero and sails with Gretchen into exile, not because he has taken so many innocent lives as a pirate or because of his past as a slave trader (which the film ignores), but because one of his lieutenants, against his orders, had burned an American ship and murdered all but one of her passengers, including Lafitte's upper-class lover's sister. Lafitte hanged his erring lieutenant but accepted responsibility for the massacre. For DeMille, Byron's 'one virtue', however, clearly outweighs the 'thousand crimes'. That virtue, of course, is the choice of liberty, the one card that trumps all the rest.

Within less than a month of *The Buccaneer*'s opening in February 1938, DeMille was already engaged in preparations for his next film, *Union Pacific*, a saga of the construction of the cross-America railway. This time, DeMille hauled Jesse Lasky Jr into the writers' engine room from the start. Called into the director's office, Jesse found a railroad spike waved in his face. 'Know what this is, Jesse?' 'A railroad spike.' As Jesse wrote: 'He looked displeased . . . I would have done better with something like "A pin to secure the future of a nation." "A railroad spike," he mocked. "What would you call the quill that signed the Declaration of Independence? A feather?"'

Besides DeMille, Jeanie Macpherson was in the room. Now ageing and plump, Jesse noted that she 'always wore one color at a time, and today it was purple. Purple shoes, purple silk stockings, purple silk dress, purple straw hat with a purple-jeweled hatpin . . . An ancient boa drooped a pair of molting vixens down her heavy purple bosom.' DeMille was already exploring the individual shots of the film in his mind:

Wind-combed prairie – like a vast, almost uncrossable sea between east and west. A moat of separation bridged only sporadically by the occasional Pony Express rider – or the rocking Concord stages of the Wells Fargo – racing the arrows of death . . . Sweat, blood, and steel. That's what built the Union Pacific! Yes, and whisky and sin – in portable hells of corruption following the railroad builders, siphoning their wages away in the saloons, brothels and gambling dens under the tents that followed the ever westward-pushing end of track!

Lasky portrays Jeanie Macpherson in this meeting as 'no longer toothsome, long since fallen from favor, haunting his corridors like a ghost of paradise lost, hoping for occasional invitations to be present at meetings like this'. In fact, DeMille, awash with writers, no longer needed her, and she was present only due to his stubborn loyalty. Lasky pictures her as a nervous wreck, dropping pencils and notebook on the floor. 'Goddamn it, Jeanie, if you can't hold a pencil in your hand, write with it in your teeth!' Cecil shouts. But his anger, as ever, just as quickly cools, as he cajoles his minions: 'I'm just trying to get you fellahs to see how it was. Get the dust of history out of your brains and start smelling drama!' And he is off again:

'Get this – and get it into your guts and your souls! The theme of this picture. Lads from the Old World come to the New – to fight its war and bind its wounds – with bandages of steel! Steel track – red with the blood of the lads who lay it – forging a nation and a destiny – lads who could scarcely pronounce its name, America!' It had come out like a nasal battle cry . . . 'I want train wrecks. I want to see the explosions of steam and bursting boilers! Iron guts! I want to boil on those prairies, and freeze in the Sierras. I want to smash through the barricades of mountain ranges of snow and ice. I want a love story that nobody has ever got on the screen, and I want human drama! Suspense. Not just "Will they make it or won't they make it?" which any damn fool can write. I want a snake under every bed! . . . I want to see Abe Lincoln's dream – come to life!'

Beyond the hyperbole and the shouting, what DeMille was planning was in essence a remake of John Ford's famous silent western,

The Iron Horse, filmed on location in northern California and Nevada in 1924. As was his custom, DeMille nominally based the screenplay on a published book, this time Ernest Haycox's *Trouble Shooter*. This provided the main character, Jeff Butler (played by Joel McCrea), who is employed to oversee the security of the Union Pacific railroad. The published source gave DeMille a necessary protection against the swarms of litigants who, since *The Ten Commandments* and before, had plagued him with plagiarism suits.

As Lasky described the process, DeMille employed a hierarchy of writers, led by chief adapter Jack Cunningham, 'a wheezing, bone-dry veteran', with Walter DeLeon, 'small, worried, seasoned, good at dialogue and ferreting out nuggets from mountains of research', and C. Gardner Sullivan, 'the methodical giant who composed sequences of short shots and elborately prepared camera angles that were calculated to give DeMille pictures a tremendous sense of visual place'. Then there was uncredited input from at least five more writers, Jeanie Macpherson included. Lasky was tasked, among other plot issues, with the invention of the bits of business that characters were to do while delivering lines: one character plays with a knife, another spits, a girl is always smoothing her hair, 'a man is always checking to see that his fly is buttoned before entering a room. Little clues to personality . . . The classic film example is George Raft's repeated tossing of a coin.' Lasky was supposed to think up and describe 'a personal idiosyncrasy, for practically every character in the film'.

DeMille's scripts bulged with these instructions, many of them additions scrawled all over the margins by the director. DeMille did not like ad-libs and was once, Lasky recounts, undesirably upstaged by Akim Tamiroff wiggling his ears while allowing another character to precede him into a railroad car, thus stealing the scene. Editor Anne Bauchens removed the wiggle forthwith.

DeMille, wrote Lasky, 'used writers like a general who counted no costs and spared no feelings . . . Some writers were quite literally driven to drink, or into massive epic sulks or sudden resignations.' To one desperate tirade by a writer Cecil riposted once: 'Don't you dare get mad at me! . . . I'm the only one who gets mad on a DeMille picture!' On *Union Pacific*, Lasky was goaded at the production crew's lunch table for his failure to come up with an adequate piece of shtick for the villainous railroad saboteur, played by Brian Donlevy:

'Jesse refuses to tell me what Brian Donlevy does with his hands, gentlemen! Don't you find that rather selfish on his part? . . . I suppose you will say, "Oh, let the director think up everything . . . " Well, damn it, I happen to believe that good screenwriting means finding ways to make an actor REAL on the screen! Not with a lot of talk – but with actions large and small – or I might as well hire a few clothing-store dummies and dub in the lines!'

Eventually Lasky came up with the idea that the villain would clip his cigar, dunk the end in a glass of whisky and put that end in his mouth while lighting the tip. 'That way he can smoke and drink at the same time . . . It's erotic . . . a faintly phallic suggestion the censors would be sure to miss.' 'Good, Jesse! Put it in the script at once! We'll try it!'

Pretty soon Lasky was initiated into the inner circle of colleagues who were invited up to the 'Paradise' ranch to wear the Russian blouses, a site forbidden to wives. Alas, he could not report on any of the orgies witnessed by Charles Bickford, nor the collection of erotica reputed to be in Cecil's private bungalow, which Jesse never entered. All Jesse could say was, 'His fetishes, if any, were a passionate hatred of red nail polish on actresses and a penchant for small, well-shaped feet. All agents knew this and warned their actresses accordingly.' But once admitted, Jesse Jr was expected to work assiduously on the script, drunk or sober. DeMille himself always rose before 6 a.m., to swim in his pool, chop wood, shoot deer or whatever else took his fancy in the acreage of his private kingdom.

Despite the consistent stories of DeMille's incessant bullying and the human casualties that peeled off right and left, both crew and cast of his movies could see that the boss drove himself harder than any of his satraps and minions. A striking demonstration of this occurred towards the end of the shoot of *Union Pacific*, in January 1939, when DeMille collapsed and had to undergo a prostate operation. Production was shut down for three weeks. 'Then one morning an ambulance nosed through Paramount Studio's DeMille Gate,' Lasky wrote, 'and word spread around the lot: The Boss had returned. We hastened to the set to witness a display of sheer guts and stamina. His face a gaunt mask, DeMille, still aboard his litter, was strapped to the platform on the great camera boom . . . Now there was no escape from his watchful eye . . . I might be chatting with some pretty actress behind a wind machine when suddenly the angry invalid would be whipped through the air, descending in his ice-packed cradle to hiss in my ear, "Why are you wasting my time, Jesse? . . . You're supposed to be a writer. There are laws in this state against taking money under false pretences!"'

Union Pacific wrapped at the end of February 1939 and was released at the end of April, to great acclaim. Frank Nugent of the *New York Times* stated that as a 'big, old-fashioned De Mille show', it was 'easily the best he has made in years'. This judgement certainly stands the test of time, as even at an inflated length of two hours and twenty minutes, the movie is DeMille's best sound-era western, and one of his best sound pictures in all. Joel McCrea, not having to impersonate a real-life American hero – although DeMille did claim he was a composite of several researched figures – is able to portray the first of his classic figures of frontier integrity. He is pitted against his old army buddy, gambler Dick Allen (played by Robert Preston), who becomes an agent of the whisky-cigar chewing Donlevy against the entrepreneurs building the railway. As ever in DeMille's American epics, there are the visionary capitalists galvanized by Abe Lincoln's desire to see America united east to west and greedy money men out for their personal advantage against the ideal of 'manifest destiny'. In the middle, of course, there is the girl, Mollie Monahan – 'post-mistress at end of track' – simple, Irish, headstrong and caught between Preston and McCrea. DeMille wanted to cast Claudette Colbert, but she turned him down. For once, circumstance prevented Cecil from making a mistake, and he cast Barbara Stanwyck, who gives her full energy to the film.

Most probably only DeMille knew this, but Mollie derived in no small part from a character in his father Henry's first successful play, *The Main Line*, of 1886: she was Positive 'Possy' Burroughs, the Western Union operator who saves a runaway train and who was always 'improvin' herself generally till there ain't a man on the section can hold a pack of cards agin' her'.

The plot line, despite the plethora of authors, was straightforward: Mollie loves Dick but is attracted by Jeff's honesty and courage in seeing off all threats to the railway. When Dick robs the pay train for the saboteurs, she agrees to marry him in order to protect him when the stolen pay sack is hidden in her cabin. The two friends are set against each other, but when a train is attacked by Indians they are once again united against a common threat. Jeff lets Dick escape, but at his wedding to Mollie, Jeff turns up to take him in. This time

Cecil B. DeMille's **UNION PACIFIC** BARBARA STANWYCK and JOEL McCREA

Mollie helps Dick escape. At the great ceremony of the striking of the golden spike to symbolize the meeting of east and west, as the railway engines from either side meet, Dick appears to reclaim his wife, but then is shot trying to prevent the villain (Donlevy) from killing Jeff. Jeff has to break the news to Mollie, with the laconic coda: 'We'll meet him again, at end of track.'

Frank Nugent wrote: 'Say that for the picture: it is an encyclopedia of frontier adventure in which every anticipated peril is hazardously encountered, every predictable plot-turn affably realized . . . DeMille spares nothing, horses or actors . . . Even when nothing is happening he manages to keep his screen alive. He stages a romantic dialogue on a hand-car hemmed in by grunting bison, a tender farewell in a caboose surrounded by whooping redskins, his sentimental death scenes in a gambling hell and beneath the smoking fragments of a wrecked locomotive. When he has a chance for real action, of course, the sky's the limit – Indian raids, shooting scrapes, brawls, fist-fights, train robberies, fires, chases and trestle breaks.'

In a real sense, all western railway films derive from the first famous movie of the genre, Edwin S. Porter's *The Great Train Robbery* of 1903, those mere ten minutes that set many an early pioneer of the movies off on an inevitable path. For once, DeMille did not need to induce the higher hokum artificially: it was endemic in the source, the myth of the west itself, the frontier ethos, true or imagined, that was so eagerly adopted as a counter to America's real-life confusions, challenges and disappointments. Jesse Lasky Jr told the tale of a journey the writers made with DeMille during the preparation to meet a ninety-eight-year-old grandpappy who was said to have worked on the railway. Prodded by his family to tell the movie folk his stories, he grumbled: 'Stories? Weren't no stories . . . It was there, and there weren't no stories to it. The damn fools made up the stories after. Damn fools who never was nowhere.'

It was as if, Lasky suggested to DeMille, the people who were actually there 'lived in a language of action, or they probably couldn't have done it'. There was no need of the story if you had lived the reality. All the rest was embellishment. But embellishment, of course, was the very habitat of Cecil B. DeMille.

REEL FIVE

So Shall It Be Written, So Shall It Be Done!

'The Ink-throwing Behemoth – Leviathan!'

To Mr Mervyn LeRoy,
Metro-Goldwyn-Mayer Studios,
Culver City, California
From Ted Bonnet,
Paramount Pictures Inc. Publicity Department

February 25, 1942

Dear Mr. LeRoy:

Mr deMille tells us that you have been good enough to request suggestions as to how to introduce him at the Academy dinner.

To begin with, it occurs to me that you might provoke a chuckle by pointing out that to you has been delegated the most unnecessary job of the evening – introducing Cecil B. deMille to Hollywood.

As you may know, Mr. deMille and Paramount are celebrating their 30th joint motion picture anniversary with the world premiere of his 66th [*sic*] production, REAP THE WILD WIND, in Hollywood next month . . .

You know that his THE SQUAW MAN, which he filmed in the old barn that has since been rehabilitated into the present Paramount gymnasium building, was the first Paramount production . . .

The difference between the barn and Paramount's big new stage 16, which I believe is the largest sound stage in Hollywood, reflects the progress that motion pictures have made.

Mr. deMille has received many honors for his pictures throughout the world. He is not called 'the old master' for nothing . . . In his long career, he has become almost a 'one man institution' on the American scene. And Hollywood will unite next month to do him honor. John B. Kingsley, president of the Chamber of Commerce, has even proclaimed the week of March 15th–21st as 'deMille Week' to spotlight the double anniversary and the premiere . . .

To refresh your mind on his career, I am enclosing a copy of his biography, in which you may find some facts useful to you.

Sincerely, Ted Bonnet.

Neither Mervyn LeRoy nor anyone else in Hollywood needed much coaching in C.B.'s biography, since it was being trumpeted from countless journals in the land at this time. 'The Shadow of Cecil B. DeMille Looms Large Over the Screen Capitol,' was Idwal Jones's headline in the *New York Times*. 'DeMille, after thirty years of making pictures on the old lot, feels he is just warming up to do some real work.'

As ever, the DeMille machine showed no signs of slowing down. Films and banking aside, in 1942 DeMille was in the sixth year of another subsidiary career: as host of a one-hour radio show, the *Lux Radio Theater*. Sponsored by Lever Brothers in New York, the CBS show was broadcasting from Los Angeles weekly radio versions of Hollywood movies, with their original stars or new casts. As the host, DeMille introduced Marlene Dietrich, Clark Gable, William Powell, Al Jolson, Barbara Stanwyck, Claudette Colbert and almost everyone else in the movie constellation, every Monday evening from 1 June 1936 until 24 April 1944, well over four hundred programmes. The show boasted at its peak an audience of 40 million listeners. It was this, more than his films, that made DeMille's voice familiar in almost every household in America.

DeMille was to leave the show in 1944, in circumstances that were crucial to his inexorable journey towards the right of the political spectrum. In 1939, however, he was still in the mainstream of American patriotic zeal. In that year, which led up to cataclysmic events in Europe, Cecil, allowing minimal time to recover from his operation, roped Jesse Lasky Jr and Jeanie Macpherson into his latest project, a documentary film to be made as part of the celebrations of the New York World's Fair. The idea was to use stock footage 'from every picture dealing with American history ever produced by anyone on earth', which Anne Bauchens would cut together at breakneck speed. Cecil's assignment for his writers was: 'I want the history of the United States, stressing the theme of liberty, on my desk by five o'clock today.'

The picture would be called *The Land of Liberty*, and it was ready for release in June 1939. It was presented as containing a thousand sequences from one hundred and twenty-five different pictures – feature films, documentaries and newsreels – with the aim, as its historical adviser, Professor James Shotwell of Columbia University, explained, of being 'the drama of a free people after it had achieved freedom'.

The usual drama accompanied its construction, with DeMille throwing tantrums at his writers, accusing them at one point, Lasky recalled, of reducing America's history to 'a lunatic's valentine accompanied by a greeting-card drivel. You are either totally insane, or dedicated to the destruction of my reputation as a film maker.' By now Lasky had grown used to these tirades, and Jeanie Macpherson offered and rescinded her umpteenth resignation. Critics, however, were kind to the finished film, with Frank Nugent of the *New York Times* calling it 'a fascinating record and a tribute to Hollywood as well as our democracy . . . It serves to remind us of the cinema's skill in evoking the past, of its ability to make a permanent record of the present.' What sort of record was not under challenge in those days of recovery from the Depression and before the war that was to come.

The box-office success of *Union Pacific* netted DeMille a four-picture deal from Paramount. Once again the scribes were gathered, seven in all, with Jesse Lasky Jr squeezed in the front ranks. This time the source was home-grown: Cecil's own 1908 play, *The Royal Mounted*, though the finished film, *North West Mounted Police*, bore little resemblance to the original creaking horsedrawn vehicle, apart from its setting, the Canadian north-west, and the Mounties who were its inevitable heroes.

This would be DeMille's first film in Technicolor, and the cinematographers, Victor Milner and W. Howard Greene, had to contend with the immense camera that contained the three-strip film. Earlier Technicolor features, such as *The Adventures of Robin Hood* and *Dodge City*, showed that action movies could be as dynamic in this system as any other, but *North West Mounted Police* appears to us today a pretty slow and lumbering piece. The paralysis was clearly not in the camera but in the writing department. As Jesse Jr so aptly witnessed, DeMille had made the writing process into a cluttered nightmare of divide and rule, resulting in a script that satisfied the boss but could be dead on the screen. DeMille's credo – he wanted his films to be led by action rather than fancy words or clever dialogue that showed off the writer's prowess but left the audience cold – left a legacy that, unlike much of his previous oeuvre, would not stand the test of time.

From 1940 to 1944, amid the battles of the Second World War, DeMille made three films, all in colour – he never returned to black and white – adding to his Mountie saga the sea story *Reap the Wild Wind* in 1942 and the 'true-to-life' *The Story of Dr Wassell*, released in 1944. Of the three, *Reap the Wild Wind*, starring John Wayne, still swashes and buckles handsomely, if to no great intellectual effect, while the other two count among DeMille's weakest vehicles.

If one looks at the films produced in Hollywood in this period, one can list Orson Welles's *Citizen Kane* and *The Magnificent Ambersons*, Hitchcock's *Rebecca*, *Suspicion* and *Shadow of a Doubt*, John Ford's *The Grapes of Wrath*, William Wellman's *The Ox-Bow Incident*, Frank Capra's *Meet John Doe* and Michael Curtiz's *The Sea Hawk*, *The Sea Wolf* and *Casablanca*, to name but a few – among the best the studio system could offer, even in wartime. The prosecution might afford to rest, were it not for the unavoidable fact that all three of DeMille's films of this period were commercially successful, *Reap the Wild Wind* spectacularly so, and even the two that I have classified as duds were well received by critics at the time. In terms of the 'bottom line', film-making as a business, DeMille remained supremely confident.

He certainly flung himself with his usual verve into his Mountie picture, contributing, in his own now well-known and sonorous voice, an introduction over the mountainous landscape: 'The Canadian North West . . . Here the first traders from the Old World intermarried with the Indians of the plains and the forests to found a new race, the Mestis of Canada . . . Here for two centuries the half-breed hunters and trappers multiplied and prospered, a law unto themselves . . .' As newcomers, 'surveyors and homebuilders' pushed west, 'bringing laws of land and property' and threatening the old ways, a revolt, led by Louis Riel, broke out in 1885, and only 'a handful of hard riding men in red coats stood between Canada's destiny and the rebellion'.

Destiny, of course, trumped everything, including justified grievances, and in the grand tradition of colonialist narratives the rebels are seen falling under the influence of a brute, Jacques Corbeau, who is being hunted from across the border by Dusty Rivers, Texas ranger. DeMille first considered Joel McCrea for the role, but signed on Gary Cooper, who rides through the movie in his surliest and most laconic mode. Lasky reports that the star invoked his own authority over the script, reducing two long, wordy passages to their essence: 'Nope' and 'Yup.' Preston Foster and Robert Preston

played two Mounties who represent duty and impulse respectively, with the latter seduced from his post by the lusty 'half-breed' Louvette, Corbeau's daughter, played in a lascivious if somewhat demented mode by Paulette Goddard. She came fresh from her role as Hannah in Chaplin's *The Great Dictator*, and got the role, legend recounts, by dressing up as the character, stomping into Cecil's office in full costume and putting her foot on his desk. For the good woman, April Logan, betrothed of stiff-backed Preston Foster, DeMille cast the English actress Madeleine Carroll. Akim Tamiroff provided the inevitable comic relief as a Mestis sidekick, Duroc. Somewhere in the movie, among the Indian also-rans, Cecil's old flame Julia Faye was browned up as 'Wapiskau' and Lon Chaney Jr played 'Shorty'.

By now DeMille was Hollywood's favourite living legend, celebrated in multiple essays, articles, press puffs and recyclable myths. 'The pappy of them all . . . a clear-eyed, physically superb gent of 59 who . . . goes serenely along making one movie after another for the usual $1,500,000, and keeps on getting rich,' wrote John Chapman in the *Chicago Sunday Tribune* on 15 September 1940.

On the set the DeMille temper is notable, and ineffective, because everybody knows it's an act. (His father's partner, Belasco, used to smash his watch in fits of anguish, then weep that it was his dear mother's watch . . . He never ran out of watches.) During shooting of 'Northwest Mounted' he addressed a company of 500 over loud-speakers for five minutes, saying he wanted absolute quiet. A couple of minutes after he'd finished he saw an extra girl whisper to a companion, commanded her to come up to the platform.

'I just spent five expensive minutes telling this company I wanted absolute quiet,' he bellowed over the p.a. system. 'Now I want you to tell the whole company what you said.'

The quivering extra, after more urging, said:

'I said I wonder what time the old baboon is going to let us go to lunch.'

The howl that went up told DeMille he wouldn't get any more work done for a while.

'Right now!' he said.

That 'Right now!' or 'Lunch!' resounded through a plethora of identical tales told about different DeMille movies, as well as the noted habit the director had of jingling 'lucky' ceremonial gold coins in his pocket. Another witness, assistant Cullen ('Hezi') Tate, who claimed to have been with DeMille since 1916, told about another scene in *North West Mounted Police*, featuring three hundred Indians, Gary Cooper and the rest of the cast, which was not going well, prompting DeMille to pick on the hapless assistant and bawl him out, till the crowd felt so sorry for him that they pitched in and did the scene properly. 'And did I feel hurt?' related 'Hezi'. 'I did not. I know what he was yelling at me for. It was the "DeMille system." When he really means to bawl you out, he gets you alone in his office and talks to you without even raising his voice. And, boy, it hurts. You know, he's been a kind of foster father to me. I love the old goat.' This story was related, appropriately, in Paramount's press release for the film.

This was the point at which DeMille attempted to revive his old idea of 'The Queen of Queens', the Virgin Mary story, which was effectively kiboshed by Father Daniel Lord. DeMille abandoned, for the moment, any thoughts of returning to the Bible as his fount – at any rate, not the New Testament. Instead, he turned to a tried and tested movie material source, the *Saturday Evening Post*, which had published a sea story by Thelma Strabel set on the Florida coast in 1840. The tale would be adapted by a triumvirate consisting of Jesse Lasky Jr, Charles Bennett and Alan Le May, with the usual additions by all and sundry, including Jeanie Macpherson. The three main writers were taken aboard DeMille's yacht, the *Seaward*, for a good dose of the briny and told to get on with it. Miss Strabel, DeMille told Lasky, had 'given us pretty pictures of sails and sunsets shining through a lady's auburn hair. What I want in this subject are storms and sinkings and salvage . . . the creak of rigging . . . the bite of hurricanes . . .'

The usual shuffling about for the main roles ensued. Errol Flynn was unavailable, so John Wayne would be the errant Captain Jack Stuart, with Paulette Goddard in another assertive female role as Loxi Claiborne, inheritor of her father's salvage business. The inevitable rival, Stephen Tolliver, would be played by Ray Milland, and the thoroughly bad egg in the omelette would be Raymond Massey as King Cutler, a salvage boss who gets his business by scuttling vessels.

Wayne was not very happy with the characterization of Jack, who lacks the proper heroic fibre, until he redeems himself at the end by saving his rival's life. It is Tolliver, the upper-class toff, who turns out to be the moral centre of the story, rather than he-man Jack. The plot line was complicated, with twists and turns of fortune and love, and sufficient storms, sinkings, fist fights and snarling protagonists to keep DeMille and his audience happy. There was also a *coup de cinéma*, an underwater battle between John Wayne and a giant octopus which attacks him and Ray Milland while they are diving to examine a wreck. This idea came up, Lasky claimed, in one of the writers' brainstorming sessions with the director, who was demanding a denouement that would match his *Union Pacific* train wreck or the opening of the Red Sea in *The Ten Commandments*. 'What', he would say, 'would fascinate Eskimos in their igloos, harness harassed housewives, rivet restless children?' Charles Bennett came up with the solution, the human enemies who have 'become allies against the common danger . . . this ink-throwing behemoth, this leviathan!'

Man against nature, at the bottom of the sea, in Technicolor! Well, it had worked in print for Jules Verne . . . The special-effects team constructed the leviathan out of sponge rubber, with thirty-foot tentacles that were jerked about by electrical motors and limbs and eyes operated from a switchboard. The whole thing was as realistic as rubber octopuses generally are, but one can note that, for their work on *Reap the Wild Wind*, the effects team – Farciot Edouard, Gordon

CECIL B.
DeMILLE'S
MIGHTY
SPECTACLE

REAP THE WILD WIND

COLOR BY
TECHNICOLOR

STARRING

**JOHN WAYNE
SUSAN HAYWARD
RAY MILLAND
PAULETTE GODDARD**

with Raymond Massey · Robert Preston · Charles Bickford · Walter Hampden · Janet Beecher Produced and Directed by Cecil B. DeMille
Screenplay by Alan LeMay, Charles Bennett and Jesse Lasky, Jr. Based on a Saturday Evening Post Story by Thelma Strabel · A Paramount Re-Release

Jennings and William L. Pereira – won 1942's Academy Award for special effects, while Louis Mesenkop won the award for sound.

The press announced that for his sixtieth birthday, on 12 August 1941, DeMille would don a diving helmet himself and supervise the underwater battle in person, though the *New York Times*'s Frank Nugent cast some doubt on that in a long magazine essay celebrating the anniversary, published on 10 August. 'CB's road to glory', the critic pointed out, 'is paved with the broken hearts of his critics. He is always proving the boys wrong. At 60 he is well-endowed with material things: a mansion, no less, on a street officially named DeMille Drive . . . a 1,200 acre rattlesnake-infested ranch in the Sierras [*sic*] which, not inappropriately, he calls "Paradise"; a 106-foot Diesel-powered schooner . . . and a private fortune which, even in these post-depression days, is safely up in seven figures. And has he any thought of retirement?'

DeMille replied to Nugent: 'Mrs DeMille was asking the same question the other night . . . She was saying directing was very exhausting, that at least I might consider just producing. Then she turned the light out and said, "Of course, you understand I've only been talking to myself."'

More and more, Mrs Constance DeMille was becoming a kind of ghost in the machine. During the filming of *Reap the Wild Wind*, however, tragedy struck the family, when the three-year-old son of Katherine and Anthony Quinn, Christopher, wandered off into the adjacent property of W. C. Fields and drowned in his ornamental lily pond. Fields was as devastated as his neighbours, his famous hostility to children being one of his contrary inventions. Katherine was marked for life by this accident, which sent her 'into a lifelong study of religions that dealt with the afterlife'. Cecil, in turn, became overprotective of his other grandchildren, particularly Cecilia's five-year-old daughter, also Cecilia, or 'Citsy'. The child would often stay in a small ante-room off his bedroom, close at hand, with Constance in another connecting bedroom.

As if to mirror this personal misfortune, dark days descended on America when, on 7 December, Japan launched her air attack on Pearl Harbor.

A stage was being prepared upon which DeMille could play a role he had cast for others many times on the screen . . .

Two-gun Cecil: The Misunderstood Hero

On 10 March 1942, in the wake of the ceremonial Academy dinner, the grand and the grandiloquent of Hollywood gathered again at the site of the old Vine Street barn for a luncheon, after the unveiling of a bronze plaque. Jesse Lasky Sr and Samuel Goldfish-Goldwyn were there, as were Louis B. Mayer, A. P. Giannini and surviving cast members of DeMille's earlier films, including Bill Farnum, Hobart Bosworth, Julia Faye, Jack Holt, Raymond Hatton, Monte Blue, Conrad Nagel, Noah Beery, Leatrice Joy, Richard Dix and William Boyd. Cecil introduced them and read out a letter from his brother William, now professor of drama at the University of California, who did not attend, quoting: 'You seem to have won your 30-year war, and don't let success go to your head. You must have been clean all your life because you are always mentioned in connection with bathtubs.'

DeMille's speech acknowledged those who had helped him and also those who had passed away: Dustin Farnum, Theodore Roberts, Wallace Reid, Agnes Ayres, James Neil, Oscar Apfel and colleagues Rudolph Valentino and Douglas Fairbanks Sr, who had all 'taken their last curtain call and gone on to the next production'. He acknowledged his long-term collaborators, like Jeanie Macpherson and his first secretary Ethel Wales, and reminisced about the barn, the site of his first films and also the place from which 'I used to dress for flying every afternoon and from here we started the first commercial aviation company in the United States that maintained scheduled flights between three cities'. He spoke about the motion-picture industry as the 'fifth estate', after the three 'estates' of the clergy, nobility and common people and Edmund Burke's 'fourth estate' of the press – with radio as the 'sixth estate' – and then continued:

Today the motion pictures hold the same place in the war effort that a standard bearer does in an army. Theirs is the task of holding high and ever visible the values that everyone is fighting for.

But we can do even more. Motion pictures are the greatest unifier the world has ever known. Through them one people may become acquainted with another; one people may grow to understand one another; one people may grow to admire and even love one another . . .

We stand today at the tag end of one age and on the brink of another. To our generation has been given the opportunity of pioneering a whole new world! Destiny has marked us for great adventures and high achievement. But there are tough times ahead – tougher than we old pioneers went through.

Two weeks later, Cecil had the satisfaction of a successful opening of *Reap the Wild Wind*, the audience responding to its rambunctious hogwash at a time of deep anxiety and horror, as hundreds of thousands of young men and women departed to fight America's most hazardous war. At this moment, the Japanese were overrunning the islands of the Philippines and Indonesia, and US forces were besieged on Bataan. Bosley Crowther wrote in the *New York Times*: '"Reap the Wild Wind" is a picture which represents the quintessence of make-believe. But who, in this time of trouble, is going to take exception to that?'

On 26 March, DeMille was honoured with another lunch, this time sponsored by the Associated Motion Picture Advertisers and held in the grand ballroom of the Waldorf-Astoria in New York. Here he was praised by Will Hays and Gloria Swanson, but it was clear his mind was not on the festivities, as the *Times* reported:

The only sombre note was sounded by Mr. DeMille, who dwelt upon world conditions. Likening liberty to a woman – 'a beautiful, desirable and very jealous woman' – he warned that 'no woman likes to be taken for granted' and urged the nation to 'get mad, forget hours and profits, roll up its sleeves, spit on its hands and go to work.

'The stupidity of partisanship is treason in these times, whether it be partisanship of capital, labor or government,' he declared. 'The job of motion pictures is to help bring home a full realisation of this crisis and of the deadly peril that lurks in internal squabbles . . .

'In the midst of battles and convoy departures to foreign lands, of bombing raids and disturbing headlines, we have in our power to show a lonesome soldier what home looks like, to mirror to him and to all men the joys of freedom. We can give harassed America relaxation and rest and, occasionally, even an hour of peace and laughter.'

The associated advertisers gave him an illuminated parchment scroll 'in honor of his contributions to the film industry'. But DeMille was searching for a vehicle that could clothe his fine words and sentiments with meaning. A film about the Mexican 'Rurales' was touted, but shelved. The usual Hollywood fund-raising benefits for the troops were clearly not sufficient. At the end of April, a package of Hollywood celebrities, including Groucho Marx, Cary Grant, Jimmy Cagney, Bing Crosby, Claudette Colbert, Merle Oberon, Pat O'Brien, Stan Laurel and Oliver Hardy, was due to depart from Washington on a 'Hollywood Victory Caravan', a morale- and fund-raising trip across the country by train. But on 28 April, one of President Roosevelt's regular 'fireside chats', broadcast on radio throughout the nation, provided Cecil with a subject.

Marking 'nearly five months since we were attacked at Pearl Harbor', the president spoke of the army and navy forces that were now in combat all over the world. He marked the Russian counter-offensive against the Nazi invasion, the battles in the Mediterranean and opposition in France to the declaration of a pro-Nazi government in Vichy. He called for unprecedented sacrifices and gave accounts of three specific acts of heroism by Americans overseas. One of them was the example of a doctor, Corydon M. Wassell, 'a missionary, well known for his good works in China. He is a simple, modest, retiring man, nearly 60 years old, but he entered the service of his country and was commissioned a lieutenant commander in the army.'

Dr Wassell's claim to President Roosevelt's attention, and that of his nation, was his stubborn heroism in remaining with his patients, naval officers and crew who had seen action off Java and who were too injured to be evacuated by ship to Australia when the Japanese drew near. Refusing evacuation, Dr Wassell improvised stretchers and transport to take the men to the coast till they could be put aboard a small Dutch ship, which was bombed and machine-gunned from the air. 'Dr. Wassell took virtual command of the ship, and by great skill avoided destruction, hiding in little bays and little inlets,' till they could reach safety in Australia. The official report, Roosevelt read out, said that Dr Wassell was 'almost like a Christ-like shepherd devoted to his flock'.

DeMille used the president's broadcast in the trailer for the film he was to produce, showing himself listening and calling his studio boss, Frank Freeman: 'Are you listening to the President? . . . I think it'll make a great picture – what do you say I make it my next?' He certainly moved into rapid action, whisking the good doctor from Australia to Los Angeles in order to get his story in detail. Author James Hilton was added to a stripped-down team of Alan Le May and Charles Bennett (with the usual uncredited input from Jeanie Macpherson). Jesse Jr was otherwise committed, assigned by the army to the Astoria studio to 'script films on the mysteries of rigging and maintaining barrage balloons'. DeMille had to wait to get his choice for the lead, Gary Cooper, who was shooting *Saratoga Trunk* at the time. DeMille used the time in intensive research – interviewing participants in the actual events and drawing up detailed designs and drawings for his Java hospital and naval war scenes. The budget would top $2,700,000, his highest to date.

Since Dr Wassell's 'back story' was complicated, DeMille simplified it to suit the drama. An Arkansas country doctor, Wassell had gone with his wife to work with the Episcopal missions in China, where she died in an accident. He remained in China till its internal wars forced him to leave in 1927. He then remarried and returned to regular doctoring, until the war with Japan brought him to Java. DeMille eliminated the first wife and made the second a missionary nurse whose picture prompts him to go to China, where they fall in love but part over a professional mishap involving a cure for river sickness. In the film, they meet again by chance at a Java train station. In reality, the second wife, Madeleine, was already married to Dr Wassell when he began his army service.

Dr Wassell himself was not particularly impressed by DeMille, Hollywood or even the president's broadcast, which, according to the *New York Times*, he hadn't heard. He refused to believe he had been mentioned in it for quite a while, calling the whole idea 'Heifer dust!' and telling his friends, 'That's nothing. George Washington used to talk about me in his speeches, too. Happens to me all the time.' Gary Cooper was obviously a good choice for the role, although the *Times* described Wassell as looking 'a little like Walter Huston'. About the prospective movie, the modest doctor told the newspaper: 'Personally I don't like it. But it's for Navy release, so I'll do anything I can.'

Naval co-operation, at a time when the forces were engaged elsewhere, was obtained by Paramount by the promise of a percentage of the gross receipts of the movie for the Navy Relief Society. In July, when Cooper was at last free, shooting began, ending in October

1943. The film opened on 26 April 1944 with a premiere in Little Rock, Arkansas.

While DeMille was filming, the tide of the war had turned, and the Japanese were losing ground in New Guinea, the Gilbert and Marshall Islands and on other battlefields. Allied casualties were heavy and the public's receptiveness to Hollywood heroics was tempered by the real cost and pain of the war. On the other hand, the New York premiere was held on 6 June, D-Day itself. Bosley Crowther of the *New York Times* commented on 7 June:

Considering his well-earned reputation for staging virtually everything he does, Cecil B. DeMille might be suspected of acting on a stupendous hunch . . . Imagine a De Mille war picture in New York on D-day! Mr. DeMille's press agents will have to be forcefully restrained. And, oddly enough, the picture is plainly and precisely the sort which gives every indication of having been made to catch the tide. For it is blood, sweat and tears built up to spectacle in the familiar 'DeMille' epic style . . . Mr. DeMille has screened a fiction which is as garish as the spires of Hollywood. He has telescoped fact with wildest fancy in the most flamboyantly melodramatic way. And he has messed up a simple human story with the cheapest kind of comedy and romance . . .

As Crowther noted, DeMille had used every cliché, cutting in 'some chummy little flashbacks of the doctor's modest sparking of a nurse', and 'has leered oafishly in the direction of a nicely shaped Javanese girl who attaches herself rather literally to one of the wounded men'. DeMille's discomfort in dealing with non-white characters, fuelled by the history of his exotic orientalism as it had flowered in *Cleopatra* or *Fool's Paradise*, was at odds with his fervent belief that films should make nations speak unto nations. It is salutary to realize that, in his entire oeuvre, all seventy films, there is not one modern black African-American character, let alone one with narrative value. The Javanese nurse, Tremartini, is played by white Carol Thurston, for whom this was the start of a bumpy career often playing native or American Indian girls. Authentic foreignness is represented by Scandinavian nurse Bettina, played by Signe Hasso. (Laraine Day played the main love interest.) At least there are some authentic Chinese actors in the flashback scene, but there is not a single Indonesian national in the entire featured cast. Race was one element of the grand human story that DeMille clearly felt he should leave well alone.

James Agee, in *The Nation*, was even more scathing in his critique of the picture:

I do not feel that I need to have been there to know that his [Wassell's] story is one of the great ones of this war; also, that it could be much better told through moving pictures than by any other means; also, that on both counts Cecil DeMille's screen version of it is to be regretted beyond qualification. It whips the story, in every foot, into a nacreous foam of lies whose speciousness is only the more painful because Mr. DeMille is so obviously free from any desire to alter the truth except for what he considers to be his own advantage.

Of course, DeMille could see no truth, at this point in his career and life, other than his own and deployed, as ever, the higher hokum: the sentimental nurse–soldier romances, the stalwart sacrifice, the crazy jeep chases amidst 'bombings, cannonadings, machine-gunnings and blasting to raise the roof'. All in all, Bosley Crowther wrote of the film's 'vivid Technicolor hues', 'they make for a very pretty and seductive DeMillitary display'.

At two hours and seventeen minutes, *The Story of Dr Wassell* remains a heavy diet of corn to consume. Cooper, professional as he is, plays it throughout with a kind of disapproving scowl. One might, after all, have preferred Walter Huston, who was at least closer in age to the fifty-eight-year-old Wassell. But the cod heroics sink the film, particularly, as James Agee pointed out, when it was supposed to celebrate genuine heroism – although, Agee himself had to admit, Dr Wassell, ever the modest Arkansas gent, professed to rather like the finished movie.

Cecil's disappointment with the critics, and his belief in his own star, had now meshed with his patriotic zeal in straining every sinew, as he saw it, for the war effort. But, as in the First World War – and well before then, if we recall his oft-mentioned desire to serve as early as 1898 – he chafed at the bit of civilian life. Just before Pearl Harbor, the record shows that he was once again eager to beef up his own military credentials, applying and receiving from the 'United Daughters of the Confederacy' a 'Cross of Military Service'. The application was based on the service of his grandfather, William Edward deMill, in the Confederate forces during the Civil War. Cecil's own rank was entered as 'Major Signal Army of United States', having been first commissioned 'Captain, Fifty-first Company, California Home

Guard', on 5 November 1917. The certificate was verified two days after the Japanese attack, on 9 December 1941, by Mrs Lulu Yonge Poland, president of the Nathan B. Forrest Chapter, and Mrs Glenn Voorhies, Chapter Recorder of Crosses, and finalized on 10 January 1942.

Apart from his movie contributions and tours to rally the troops, Cecil's direct Second World War service, at the age of sixty-plus, consisted of his local duties as the Laughlin Park air-raid warden. A picturesque account of this has been recorded by Carlotta Monti, the mistress of his neighbour W. C. Fields, in her highly embroidered memoir, *W. C. Fields and Me*. According to Ms Monti, DeMille was accosted on Fields's lawn, while plying his flashlight and wearing his regulation tin helmet, by the Great Comedian, wielding a pistol and accusing him of being a Nazi spy.

'I'm Cecil B. DeMille . . . I'm your neighborhood air raid warden,' says the interloper. 'We haven't had any air raids,' states the inveterate boozer, accurately. 'It's a preventive measure,' explains DeMille. 'You speak English well for a Nazi,' snarls Fields, 'where did you learn our language?' 'I was born here.' 'Oh, a traitor to your country,' rants Fields, 'another Benedict Arnold. There's a noose waiting for the necks of the likes of you.' Or so Ms Monti's fable unfolds.

Hollywood continued to wallow in its dreams, with W. C. Fields watching through his telescope for Japanese submarines. In the real world, however, DeMille was worried and fretting, not only over the progress of the war but also over the rising cost of his films and the stranglehold, as he saw it, of the unions representing his cast and crews.

This conflict had a long and complex pedigree. Union activity among film workers, in particular actors, stretched back to vaudeville days. On the stage, Actors' Equity had won an important strike in 1919 over wages and conditions. During the 1920s, the 'golden years' of Hollywood, the high salaries of stars and major directors were in great contrast to the meagre fees paid to ordinary actors, studio workers and technicians. The major craft union, IATSE, made some inroads but its management was heavily infiltrated, during the 1930s, by mob figures from the criminal empire that had been empowered by Prohibition. Screenwriters were poorly paid for years, prompting writers like Donald Ogden Stewart and John Howard Lawson, who had participated in two DeMille scripts – *Dynamite* and *Madam Satan* – to form the Screen Writers' Guild in 1933. (Lawson's militancy would lead him to join the Communist Party, whose membership would be a matter of searing controversy in the coming era of investigations by HUAC, the House Un-American Activities Committee.) Union unrest was rife in the months leading up to Roosevelt's New Deal reforms of the movie industry, which included the revised Hays Code of 1934.

As we have seen from DeMille's own Russian adventure and *The Volga Boatman*, sympathy for the Soviet Union was rife in Hollywood, not just among party members or even radicals but among liberals too. This sympathy was badly dented by the Moscow show trials of the mid-1930s, though the party members were unshaken in their faith. Nevertheless, there were liberals enough in Hollywood to organize in solidarity with Republican Spain in 1937, among them the usual suspects like Donald Ogden Stewart, Lester Cole and John Garfield, but also the unexpected, like Fredric March and John Ford.

Since the Russian Revolution, however, American union organizers had been painted by their opponents, employers and the political right as Bolsheviks and enemies of Freedom. As an employer, Cecil DeMille may have still had a soft spot for Russia, but he had none for the domestic left which campaigned for better working conditions in his own industry. His speeches in the aftermath of Pearl Harbor clearly reflected his disaffection with 'the stupidity of partisanship . . . of capital, labor or government', though it was particularly that of labour he was to judge as the greater 'treason'. The 'deadly peril that lurks in internal squabbles' was, in time of war, his greatest bugbear.

Despite this, DeMille was not among the vanguard of Hollywood right-wingers who began organizing against what they saw as undue communist influence in the film colony. Their bugbear was not only union activity but films like Michael Curtiz's *Mission to Moscow* of 1943, which harnessed Walter Huston and Ann Harding to the cause of the gallant ally, Stalin's Russia. In February 1944, directors Sam Wood, Clarence Brown, King Vidor, Victor Fleming and Norman Taurog, alongside other luminaries such as Walt Disney and Gary Cooper, unveiled a 'Motion Picture Alliance', declaring that 'we resent the growing impression that this industry is made up of, and dominated by, Communists, radicals and crack-pots. We pledge to fight . . . any effort of any group or individual, to divert the loyalty of the screen from the free America that gave it birth.' Future officers of this alliance would be John Wayne, Robert Taylor and Hedda Hopper, but not Cecil B. DeMille. His cause, at that time, was 'All Out for Victory', and his personal sacrifices were outlined in the press on 2 June:

Prime example of how the war has taken the high life out of Hollywood is the once mighty Cecil B. DeMille. The old tycoon of celluloid, bathtub and glamor, who for 30 years could obtain all the comforts of life by simply pressing a button, is now reduced to waiting on table at his house, tending the garden . . . and – believe it or not – washing his own socks . . . DeMille has a 20-year-old son in the rear ranks of the infantry, and his son-in-law holds a captaincy in the air corps. He has lost a valet and a writer to the draft; a butler, a maid and two gardeners to Lockheed, and the laundryman to a Japanese relocation center.

The Navy has taken his luxurious 106-foot yacht. The highest taxes in American history, plus the $25,000 salary ceiling, have put a serious crimp in his bankroll. And despite his close friendship with Rubber Director William Jeffers, he has to struggle along on a mere 'A' gas card.

Despite these hardships, he was serving as chairman of the Red Cross Blood Donor drive for the motion picture and radio industry, national co-chairman of United Nations Relief, representing the occupied Netherlands, and still producing and hosting his weekly radio show.

It was this show, the *Lux Radio Theater*, that was to ignite, in August 1944, the spark for his own massive 'internal squabble'. The flashpoint came over a decision by the American Federation of Radio Artists (AFRA), the radio workers' union, to levy one dollar on each of its members in order to fund a fight against a new Californian 'right to work' proposal – 'Proposition 12' – which sought to abolish the closed shop in the state. Members had to pay up by September or face suspension from the union. DeMille refused to pay his dollar, and the battle royal commenced.

News hit the stands on 15 November:

UNION MAY OUST DEMILLE

The refusal of Cecil B. DeMille, movie and radio director, to pay a $1 special assessment to the American Federation of Radio Artists may cost him his $5,000 weekly salary as a radio director, Claude L. McCue, union secretary, said today. If Mr DeMille does not reinstate himself as a member in good standing in the union within thirty days he will face possible expulsion or suspension for declining to pay . . . Mr McCue asserted. He said the agency producing Mr. DeMille's radio show prohibited the appearance of any artist not in good union standing.

This one would run and run and become Cecil's cause célèbre, his Rubicon, Valley Forge and Joan of Arc moment all rolled into one grand gesture of refusing Tribute to Tyranny. News on 2 December: 'The American Federation of Radio Artists today gave Cecil B. DeMille and other delinquent members until 5 P.M., Dec. 11, to pay up union assessments or be suspended from union membership and barred from the radio.' DeMille declared that he 'would give up his weekly radio program "rather than pay one single dollar in political tribute which acknowledges that I am no longer a free man."' He argued that the closed shop usurped his rights as a voter to make up his mind openly on any given proposition and bound him to a cause he opposed.

Proposition 12, in fact, had been defeated, and therefore the union was within its legal rights in California. On 6 December, DeMille's attorney, Neil McCarthy, filed an injunction against the union and obtained a 'temporary restraint', preventing the union from suspending him. On 24 January 1945, however, Judge Emmett Wilson dissolved his own restraint, ruling for the union. DeMille was by now on the warpath, vowing to take the case to the Supreme Court and declaring his hope that state legislatures would 'enact laws to wipe out the evils of which he complains'. He was duly barred from the radio show, and his last broadcast was, ironically, *Tender Comrade*, with Olivia de Havilland and Dennis O'Keefe, a version of one of Hollywood's most left-wing movies, directed in 1943 by Edward Dmytryk and written by Dalton Trumbo. The show went out on 22 January and terminated Cecil's almost nine-year stint. Lionel Barrymore replaced him as the *Lux Radio Theater* host.

At a St Patrick's Day dinner at Omaha on 17 March given by his friend, the railroad tycoon William Jeffers, Cecil turned up the rhetoric of his new cause:

'Too many business men and laboring men alike have been Neros who fiddle while the liberty of their country burns,' Mr. DeMille said. 'There has been built up in this country an unelected government, which is superseding in power and authority the elected government. And a dissenting voice raised against this unelected, but all-encompassing power, is condemned to obliteration whereas, in reality, he is only pleading for constitutional government for all.'

The producer said the country can only stop 'this abuse of power' if it 'organises for the right of the worker to be politically free.'

Mr DeMille said he was not speaking 'for or against a closed shop,' but declared 'a closed shop constitutes a monopoly of labor, and where any monopoly exists it should be controlled and regulated for the welfare of the community.'

This was not quite the all-out rant of the right, which saw no evil in the monopoly of capital and continued inveighing against communist infiltration, but the lack of proportion in Cecil's comments was by any standard sheer demagoguery. The underlying fact was that DeMille's acceptance of a closed shop for AFRA members would have undermined his own position as an employer of the workers in his own films. Throughout the war, the record shows that strikes and stoppages by film workers accelerated, on a variety of bread-and-butter issues with little or no political content. These were to culminate in major strikes at MGM, Warner Brothers and Disney studios in 1946. DeMille's stand for the principle of workers choosing to be members of a union or not was a stand for his own clear commercial interests.

On 11 April, *Variety* reported that the DeMille Political Freedom Foundation had been formed in Los Angeles, which would ensure 'the rights of everyone, union or non-union alike, to be politically free'. The announcement, by 'civic leader' Frank P. Docherty, also stated that 'the foundation favors unions and the right of men to bargain collectively', distancing DeMille from the far right. DeMille still had movies to make, and a head-to-head battle with union power would not be a very clever idea. His rhetoric, however, continued to build: 'Un-American Elements in Unions Hit by DeMille' headlined the *Los Angeles Times* on 4 July 1945. 'Un-American elements in the unions are condemning men and women to oblivion all over the country by denying them the right to work,' DeMille told an Advertising Club luncheon at the Biltmore. Declaring himself still 'a union member', DeMille insisted:

I am not talking about honest union members or honest union leaders of whom there are many with honest American purpose, but about union racketeers . . . Right now it is within the power of a few men to bottle up every seaport in the United States, close thousands of its factories, disrupt transport and communications and create a chaos which could only have violent revolution as its end . . .

DeMille continued to repeat his clarion call at every venue he could find, as in the July issue of the *Reader's Digest*:

A dissenter is branded as a 'labor hater' or 'fascist.' In reality, the dissenter is only pleading for constitutional government for all . . . speaking out against the injustice of one group imposing its will upon the others . . . You can stop this abuse of power, if you support the right of the worker to be politically free, and if you hang onto constitutional government as you would to a life raft in a boiling sea.

Having stormed the political heights – or plumbed the depths, depending on one's point of view – Cecil returned to base, and the movies. He had found a perfect subject to continue his series of patriotic Americana. After a spate in the contemporary world, he was returning to history with a new major project, decisively and aptly titled *Unconquered*.

With the Jawbone of an Ass: From Fort Pitt to the Philistines

And once again, to the familiar rattle of drums, the convocation of the writers – Jesse Lasky Jr and Charles Bennett, joined by devout Republican and hardboiled DeMille ally Fredric M. Frank, with the usual dabs from Jeanie Macpherson and one Norman Reilly Raine. More drum rolls for the planning and designs of colonial America, the battles upon the stockades, the casting of Gary Cooper in three-cornered hat and buckskins, Ward Bond as a stalwart blacksmith, veteran Henry Wilcoxon as a British Redcoat and bloodthirsty Indians, led – in one of cinema's wierdest casting decisions – by Boris Karloff as Guyasuta, Seneca chief. Reviving a publicity tool deployed for both *The Ten Commandments* and *The King of Kings*, DeMille commissioned a novelization of the movie, to be published concurrently with the picture, this time by author Neil Swanson. (The two Bible novels had been co-written by Henry MacMahon and Jeanie Macpherson.)

For the female lead DeMille returned to Paulette Goddard, with whom he had been rumoured to have had a fling during the making of *North West Mounted Police*. No amount of her feisty overacting could deter him. This time she would be Abigail Hale, an English convict who has chosen slavery in the New World over death by hanging in the old. The two men in her new life would be Gary Cooper and Howard da Silva as Martin Garth, a blackguard who, like the villain in *The Plainsman*, is selling guns to the Indians so they can make war on the whites.

In DeMille's America of 1763, indentured slavery is a wholly white affair, with scarcely a black face even among the crowds, let alone among the featured players. On board the docking slave ship, Paulette is the subject of a bidding war between evil da Silva and saintly Cooper, as Captain Christopher Holden, who keeps adding sixpence to Garth's bid so as to save her from his clutches. Garth, however, buys her back through a subterfuge, laying the ground for future rivalry. In a trans-racial twist, the tale gives Garth an Indian wife, played inscrutably by Katherine DeMille, who continually refers to herself in the third person as 'this one'.

All DeMille's attempts to paint a historically accurate background to the story – with scenes depicting a young Colonel George Washington and the two British surveyors, Mason and Dixon, drawing boundaries between future states – come to nought, as the director neglects to provide convincing characters, plot points or dialogue. Technicolor cinematographer Ray Rennahan, who had filmed the colour sections of *The Ten Commandments*, as well as classics such as *Becky Sharp*, with co-credits on John Ford's *Drums Along the Mohawk* and King Vidor's 1946 *Duel in the Sun*, provided lush forest and mountain scenes for the movie. But too much credibility had already been lost in the scripting process. As Jesse Lasky recalled, Wilfred Buckland, DeMille's old art director, came to the office during a script discussion over the action-packed scene of Cooper's escape with Paulette from the Indians. They were canoeing towards a

Unconquered – Gary Cooper hiding from the script?

waterfall. How could they save themselves? Buckland, possibly remembering a similar scene in Buster Keaton's *Our Hospitality*, suggested that Cooper could grab a tree branch protruding through the waterfall, and with the combined weight of man and woman, swing into a cavern and safety. Lasky queried: 'Could an audience believe it?' DeMille answered: 'An audience will believe what it sees.'

However it was engendered – and Lasky undermines this account somewhat by placing the story, and the scene, in the wrong film, *North West Mounted Police* – the heroic rescue is in the movie. But any residual credibility it might have had has already been diminished by the sequence of Paulette's captivity among the Indians and Cooper's appearance to save her, walking as if by magic through the smoke of a gunpowder flash and tricking the chief with a compass, making its magnetic arrow point inexorably towards him as he is laden down with knife and tomahawk. No amount of hoka-heying by the tribe's hapless medicine man can turn the arrow away, and Cooper walks off with Paulette.

DeMille's casting of Karloff is incomprehensible until one realizes his obvious intention is to paint the Indians as horror-picture savages, bloodthirsty, ignorant and treacherous. Even Bosley Crowther of the *New York Times* had to comment that the film was 'as viciously anti-redskin as *The Birth of a Nation* was anti-Negro long years back'. (One might note that even the prejudiced Griffith often portrayed Indians in a much more positive way, as in his early short, *The Indian and the Child*, of 1908.) Other scenes of frontier life, such as a vintage bathtub scrub for Paulette Goddard in a log-cabin barrel, fail to ignite any real sparks.

Phil Koury, one of DeMille's office assistants on the movie, tells another tale of the film's faltering plot lines. At a first showing of the rough cut of the picture at the studio, an unnamed newcomer dared to respond to DeMille's oft rhetorical query to the assembled viewers: 'I'd like to have you tell me what you think of the picture.' The newcomer, misunderstanding the requirement, said: 'It's a very great picture,' and then, 'but there is one thing, Mr. DeMille. I don't like the ending. It makes a fool out of the villain.'

The newcomer pointed out what should have been obvious, that in the final shoot-out between Gary Cooper and da Silva at Fort Pitt, the villain, who has been painted throughout the movie as a shrewd but ruthless schemer, 'tries to grab his gun out of the holster on the horse saddle, swing round and try to shoot down a man who's already got the draw on him. It doesn't make sense.'

'If what this man says is true,' said DeMille, 'we might just as well throw this picture into the ashcan.'

As well they might. But DeMille had spent a staggering $4.3 million on the film, his highest budget to date. Watching the film, it is difficult to figure out what the money was spent on, even factoring in rising post-war costs. What wonders DeMille had wrought with *Cleopatra* for a fraction of that sum, twelve years before!

Ominously, just before the picture's shoot began, long-time collaborator Wilfred Buckland shot himself and his son William, who had been in a state mental hospital after a nervous breakdown. Wilfred's last art-direction job for DeMille had been the stunning Zeppelin set for *Madam Satan*, his first assignment after a long hiatus following 1923's *Adam's Rib*. Apart from DeMille's films, he could find few jobs in the business and eked out a living as a production illustrator. He was eighty at the time of his death, in July 1946.

Then, on 26 August, Jeanie Macpherson died, having been diagnosed a few months before with an inoperable cancer. DeMille sat with her for many days at the hospital, watching another part of his life, his closest collaborator, and in a real sense, his alternative wife, depart. They had not been lovers for many years, but she took with her much of the fire and bravado that had marked his golden silents.

Unconquered failed at the box office, signalling to DeMille that his run of luck with patriotic epics was over.

Beyond the film set, however, his own real-life saga as a true-born patriot was escalating by the month. In September 1945, with the war in the Pacific over and in the wake of his tub-thumping in the *Reader's Digest* and elsewhere, he was awarded a gold Americanism Medal by the Wall Street Post 1217 of the American Legion. Despite warnings from William Green, the president of the American Federation of Labor, that giving DeMille a medal would 'seriously affect the present amicable relationship' between the AFL and the Legion, the award was made, citing DeMille's 'courage, sacrifice and non-temporizing struggle for the liberties of all'.

In his acceptance speech, at a ceremony on the steps of the Subtreasury Building in New York which marked the 156th anniversary of the adoption of the Bill of Rights, DeMille spoke to a crowd of 3,500 Wall Streeters and coast-to-coast over ABC radio, decrying the new 'tyranny' of unions. 'When one man or group has the power to decide who shall work and who shall not, that is a national cancer – a cancer that must be cut out before it renders our country too weak to resist the poisons of totalitarianism.'

His barrage continued through the following year. In February 1946, the headline in the *Los Angeles Times* following his speech at the 433rd inaugural banquet of the Los Angeles Realty Board, held in the Ambassador Hotel's Embassy Room, read: 'DeMILLE CALLS ON HONEST LABOR TO PURGE SELF OF UNCLEAN BOSSES'. 'DeMILLE URGES UNITY OF CAPITAL AND LABOR', said the *Examiner*.

Continuing into 1947: 'CECIL B. DeMILLE ASKS LAW BAN CLOSED SHOP. DeMILLE APPEAL TO CONGRESS: DON'T LET UNIONS SWAY YOU.' It is salutary that DeMille's appeals were mainly made to legislators, financiers or extremely rich people at honorary dinners rather than to ordinary union members, who were not eager to heed his call. As the months went by, Cecil's rhetoric made less and less mention of 'honest' unions and bound his arguments closer and closer to those who thundered against communist infiltration into almost every corner of American life.

In February 1947, DeMille formally testified before the Senate Labor Committee, urging the banning of 'jurisdictional strikes'. He argued that closed-shop provisions intimidated workers, and that 'in some cases, he has found the same "fear" among union members as among workingmen in Russia'. In April, he was back in court, to appeal for his right to be reinstated in the radio union despite refusing to pay his one-dollar charge. In June, it was 'DeMILLE LAUDS SCOUTS AS FRONT LINE DEFENSE AGAINST COMMUNISM' in the Los Angeles *Citizen-News*:

Honoring Eagle Scouts of the San Fernando Valley Council, held last night in Eaton's Rancho, DeMille stated: 'The communists are our enemies, the enemies of the boys here tonight . . . Let us not wait for atomic bombs to fall on our cities, or barricades to be set up in the streets before we act. If we value liberty for ourselves and our children, we must fight our enemies in the schools, the churches, industries and labor unions. We will make no truce with them. Now is the time to act in order to keep America free from totalitarian and communistic powers.'

His old friend, railroad mogul William Jeffers, was present, as well as Los Angeles police chief C. B. Horrall and the Rev. Harley W.

Smith, president of the Studio City Rotary Club. DeMille was now fully engaged politically, inveighing against opposition to the new Taft-Hartley bill to curb unions as '90 per cent manufactured by union leaders'. Later in June, speaking to the National Association of Retail Grocers in San Francisco, he returned to the claim that American workers lived in fear of speaking freely despite the Bill of Rights, 'because we have in America a weapon as powerful as the Gestapo or the Soviet secret police. That weapon is the closed and union shop controlling the right to work.' And in October – the month in which full-blown hearings of the House Un-American Activities Committee began in Washington into Hollywood's infiltration by communists, with subpoenas against forty-three film-industry people, including nineteen 'unfriendly' witnesses – DeMille spoke to four hundred women of the Better Film Council of Chicagoland and other women's clubs, churches and parents' groups, urging, 'You mothers hang on to American freedom . . . for freedom is like a clock and can run down before you know it. This whole nation is the result of individual liberty, the opportunity to go ahead. Opportunity is greater than security. Opportunity leads on. Security makes you fat, wrinkled and old.'

These were certainly attributes DeMille was determined to avoid. By this time, Cecil was well advanced in planning his next picture, a return, for the first time in over fifteen years, to ancient times and his first Old Testament epic since *The Ten Commandments* of 1923. The title would be *Samson and Delilah*.

DeMille had nursed this project for a long time. The first treatment, he claimed, had been written by Harold Lamb as far back as 1932, in the wake of *The Sign of the Cross*, but it got waylaid by *This Day and Age*. As usual, the project had its multiple sources. In case the Bible itself were not enough, Cecil had obtained the rights to a novel called *Judge and Fool*, written by Vladimir (Ze'ev) Jabotinsky, founder and leader of the Zionist Revisionist movement until his death in 1940. The book on Samson was Jabotinsky's only full-length novel, and alongside the inevitable apologia for Jewish settlement in Palestine, it contained other plot points that could be of use, as well as functioning as the required copyright bulwark against the plagiarism suits that had plagued Cecil's previous biblical films.

Plot points and 'back story' were needed, as the story of Samson in the Bible takes up a mere four chapters of the Book of Judges. We are given the bare bones of his astounding strength and prowess and his battles against the Philistines unto his spectacular demise, as well as the tale of his birth to his previously barren mother, translated in the King James version as 'Lo, thou shalt conceive, and bear a son, and no rasor shall come on his head, for the child shall be a Nazarite unto God from the womb'. Though the Hebrew *nezir elohim* merely means monk or abstinent for the Lord, the word 'Nazarite' presented Samson to Christianity as a prototype Christ, if a more attractively militant one to DeMille in his embattled present state.

Embarking on the usual period of research and development, DeMille set his new researcher, Swiss-born Henry Noerdlinger, on a quest for biblical-era background and chivvied Jesse Lasky Jr and Fredric Frank into boiling the results down into a Hollywoodable script. The first story conferences were held in July 1946. According to Phil Koury, DeMille claimed that 'I really got part of the idea for Samson and Delilah from an old Hindu story about a courtesan who loved a priest. She was the mistress of an emperor and when the emperor found out about the priest he had the courtesan's feet, hands and breasts cut off and he threw her on a dung heap outside the city, and then the priest came and sat with her.'

Eventually, the talk got round to the Bible and the ways in which the ancient story could be told for a modern movie audience: '*If ye had not ploughed with my heifer ye had not found out my riddle . . .* That's what Samson says when the guests tell him the answer to the riddle, and he is mad as hell. Every time the Spirit of the Lord comes upon him he goes out and rips about ninety people apart . . . and when he got mad he was strong as hell.'

Perhaps DeMille missed his vocation as an evangelical preacher, or as he often claimed, he found a deep satisfaction in returning to those Bible tales his father used to tell at home. There was better balm to be had here than in ranting about unions to realtors in Los Angeles. Though claiming to find his inspiration in the great art of Michelangelo, Rubens and Gustave Doré, it clearly was a great sex and tough-guy story at its root, however the Spirit of the Lord might have shaped it.

For Delilah ('one lady barber who made good', in Mae West's immortal words), DeMille considered the latest screen siren, Rita Hayworth, but the job eventually went to Hedy Lamarr, née Hedwig

Eva Maria Kiesler. The Viennese-born actress had caused a scandal when she appeared nude and simulating an orgasm in a Czech film, *Extase*, in 1932. DeMille selected her late in the day after screening her 1938 debut US film, *Algiers*.

Samson and Delilah was the film that inspired Groucho Marx's comment that he would never go to a film where 'the man's tits are bigger than the woman's'. The casting of Victor Mature was also a delayed decision – DeMille had considered Cary Grant, Mr Universe Steve Reeves and even Douglas Fairbanks, Jr. Mature certainly had the physique, and the added advantage of being, in fact, a fine, and on occasion, subtle actor, though he annoyed DeMille with his distinct lack of enthusiasm when it came to wrestling a lion in person.

The eventual basic treatment, as summarized in the censor's file on the movie – Joe Breen of the Motion Picture Producers and Distributors Association of America was still firmly in the saddle – shows how the Book of Judges had been rendered for consumption:

SYNOPSIS:
Story about Delilah who, seeking revenge, discovers the secret of Samson's strength and betrays him to the Philistines.

Samson, the young Danite whose amazing feats of strength bring him renown, loves Angela Lansbury, daughter of a Timnath merchant, and wishes to marry her despite the fact that she is a Philistine and the cruel Philistines have held his people in subjugation for forty years.

His rival for Angela Lansbury's hand is Henry Wilcoxon, Military Governor of Dan. Angela Lansbury's younger sister, Delilah, loves Samson passionately and, hoping to win his love, helps him gain the attention of George Sanders, the Saran of Gaza, ruler of the land, in a lion hunt during which Samson kills a lion with his bare hands.

Samson gets to marry Angela Lansbury, but Delilah plans revenge, getting it at the wedding feast when Samson's riddle is given away by his wife at Delilah's prompting. 'Disillusioned, Samson fights the Philistines – the battles resulting in the deaths of Angela Lansbury and her father. Delilah's love for Samson turns to hate and she vows to bring him low.'

Thus is the whole biblical tale – of physical strength being only an attribute of divine favour in the cause of freeing the Israelites, which is withdrawn due to earthly lust – made into a standard lovers' tiff. Bible stories were ever interpreted according to taste and audience, from sombre sages to wide-eyed schoolchildren. The censor board, by the by, was interested less in plot than in the ticking of boxes on its 'Film Content Analysis Chart', noting 'If Professional Character is Unsympathetic', 'If Foreign Race or National is Shown', 'If Drinking Is Shown – wine – beer – hard liquor – unidentified'. Are there any courtroom scenes, weddings, burials, prayers, and how are they treated: 'Victor Mature prays to his God, and the pagan Hedy Lamarr also says a prayer.' 'Is social acceptability of drinking indicated?' Yes. Types of crime shown: 'Theft – There are also killings and caravan robberies which are not being considered as "crime" but rather as resistance to invaders.' Indeed. 'Fate of Criminal – Heroic Suicide.' This kind of thing would continue until the 1960s, with the Code finally yielding to a new system of advisory ratings as late as 1968.

DeMille's conviction that he could square the circle of the higher hokum, biblical fabulism and cinematic realism would lead to many droll moments, fodder for the DeMille legend: how he strutted around the set testing out the jawbone of an ass with which Samson slays the Philistines, forcing Henry Wilcoxon to defend himself with his javelin as his director demonstrated the ferocity required for the scene; how Jesse Lasky almost wrestled the lion, after Victor Mature held back, the trainer holding Hollywood's oldest, most toothless and most amiable lion, Jackie, ready for the fray. Some tales claimed that Victor Mature was afraid of everything – lions, wind, swords, falling temples – and had to be ever coaxed into action. In fact, his amiable nature invests Samson throughout with a kind of reluctance to commit mayhem which is perfectly in keeping with the tale.

Life magazine sent writer John Bainbridge to witness DeMille on the set, and he carried back the usual tales of the chair boy, the mike boy and another 'perpetual attendant . . . a sturdy, youngish woman who wears sunglasses indoors and is known as the Field Secretary. Her main task is to take down in shorthand practically everything DeMille says during his working hours. From morning till night she hovers near him, never out of his earshot, recording dozens of momentous notes such as "Remind me to inspect the idol in the temple – also the fire in his belly," or "Get haircut," or "Will need more feathers for the banquet scene" . . . Since DeMille may get some of his best ideas while eating, his Field Secretary always sits next to him at lunch, notebook at hand.' (This would have been Berenice Mosk, right-hand lady extraordinaire.)

As ever, DeMille lunched with his staff at a permanently reserved table at the Paramount commissary. Nobody would eat until he took his place. If he had a guest, the secretary would place a note beside him with the guest's name and why he was there, but 'DeMille doesn't necessarily follow this cue'. Phil Koury noted that DeMille would suffer from lapses of memory and had to have these procedures rigorously in place to keep up with all the endless minutiae of production. *Life*'s Bainbridge recorded that DeMille was fond of holding forth about his family tree: 'He is exceedingly proud of all of its branches and twigs and often points out that if his forebears, who came from Holland to what is now Manhattan 300 years ago in a ship called the *Gilded Beaver*, had held on to the real estate they acquired, the family would now own more of downtown New York than the Astors.' It does not seem he ever referred to the other branch of the tree, but Cecil had long since snipped the Jewish genes from his stem.

Nevertheless, here were the biblical Danites and their Philistine oppressors, an ancient Gestapo with full pagan credentials. The final temple scene was the most troublesome of the shoot, with the arena set in which Samson strained at the columns combined with a model 'itself the size of a very comfortable house, being eighty feet square and sixty feet tall at its highest point'. It was designed to collapse when small charges of dynamite, controlled from a central switch-board, were detonated. As the *New York Times*'s Thomas Brady described the first attempt, late in November 1948:

The climax was to occur when a forty-foot image of the god Dagon fell on puppet models of the Philistine court and crushed the enemies of Samson. With five cameras photographing the scene, an engineer set off the charges, but the idol toppled only part way over and remained suspended, leaving the Philistines apparently unhurt . . . Reconstruction of the model temple will cost about $15,000 . . . with three crews of men at work to get it restored in a hurry. In the meantime regular photography of full size, close-up scenes of the temple disaster is proceeding on another sound stage at the studio.

The film of *Samson and Delilah* did not set new benchmarks in vulgarity, sexuality, lewdness, piety, spectacle, violent action, sadistic whipping, the presentation of wild animals and divine miracles, costuming, props or special effects – though all these elements are present in the picture. Critic Simon Harcourt-Smith, writing in the British magazine *Sight and Sound* in 1951 and dubbing DeMille 'The Siegfried of Sex', wrote of his 'inane stories, inaner dialogue, decrepit clichés' uniting with a showman's taste so that 'one is goaded, irritated, sometimes even shocked by his pictures. Yet, grudgingly, when one sees *Samson and Delilah*, as when one saw *The Sign of the Cross* nearly a generation ago, one recognises a mastery – repellent, monstrous, blatant perhaps, but a mastery, not to be denied . . . We may not like what Cecil B. de Mille sets out to achieve; but we must grant that he achieves it with absolute precision. The arc through which the bare midriff wriggles, the parabola of the sadistic lash, are evidently calculated to a nicety, as a great chef might weigh the condiments for one of his sauces. We are hardly surprised to hear that *Samson and Delilah* is packing the cinemas of Lisbon, Antwerp, Calcutta and Hong Kong.'

When we goggle at the film's multiple absurdities – its intercut shots of a stuntman wrestling a weary lion and Victor Mature strangling a prop, George Sanders dressed up for a Beverly Hills fancy-dress party in mock-Minoan style, Delilah munching an apple on a garden wall, Angela Lansbury throwing a javelin at a fake lion skin, the jawbone of an ass laying out a straggling line of extras in a 'narrow defile', and so on – are we not watching the pilot movie of the entire Cinecittà sword-and-sandal cycle, from Maciste unto Ulysses and Hercules against Samson, albeit those open-air cinema concoctions had an honourable home pedigree of their own? But lines such as Samson's rebuff to Delilah as she hurls herself at his bloody pectorals after he has seen off the lion – 'One cat at a time!' – surely have their own peculiar immortality. And is DeMille not parodying the proselytizing, consumerist, give-the-public-what-it-wants ethos of Hollywood itself? As a pack of dwarves goad blinded Samson in the Philistine arena, below the plaster-and-sawdust model of the great god Dagon, is it not DeMille himself, crippled and enchained by the twin pillars of studio Mammon and the tyrannical unions, straining to bring down this fake tinsel temple of deceit? Is he, as Harcourt-Smith suggested, 'the resurgent god of bad taste', repenting his vanguard days as the constructor par excellence of consumerism with the desirable gowns of Swanson and the ground-breaking contours of arts moderne and deco by jumbling everything up in a new Babel of images, a Technicolor junkyard of styles, furnishings and Sunday-school Nativity attire? Are we laughing at him or is he laughing at us? Or is he, despite it all, to be taken, in his own burnished self-image, as the very epitome of the wide-eyed, wise, ageless child, sincere and unashamed?

John Bainbridge of *Life* continued his description of his sojourn at the DeMille set with the aftermath of Samson's humiliation as a beast of burden turning a great stone mill, after he has been captured following Delilah's night-time barbering session that removed the hairy source of his strength:

I walked over to Victor Mature's dressing room to ask him about his interpretation of Samson, from the spiritual standpoint. 'Hiya, kid,' he said. 'Come in and park it. I'll be right with you.' Samson was busy at the moment studying a racing form. 'Jeez,' he said, 'this is a wonderful pastime.' After Samson had made a phone call to put a bet on the fifth race at Bowie, I asked him what he thought of his current role. 'Jeez, it's great,' he said. 'These whiskers, they're driving me nuts. They put 'em on with glue, spread glue all over my face. It's a great part, really great.'

Before Samson had time to discuss his role at greater length, he was interrupted by a visit from a woman wearing horn-rimmed spectacles, who said she was preparing an article for a screen magazine on what various actors

Victor Mature and Hedy Lamarr – 'Jeez, this is a great part!'

and actresses would do if they could live their lives over again.

'What would you do, Mr. Mature?' she asked.

'I would write to mother more often,' Samson said.

There was not much doubt what Cecil B. DeMille would do – the same as he had done the first time round. As Bainbridge walked back with Mature to the set, DeMille was slipping off his coat to the chair boy without even looking and seating himself on the great camera crane, ready to be raised thirty feet up in the air. '"Jeez, look at him," Samson said. "He's a genius, that kid."' And as the *Life* reporter watched DeMille preparing the dungeon mill-stone scene, an extra on the set whispered to him:

'This is the first DeMille picture that will give the customers corn that's been ground.'

'I'm Ready for My Close-up'

In May 1949, Cecil B. DeMille took on his most unexpected role: as an actor in another director's movie. Billy Wilder's *Sunset Boulevard* was conceived as a grand satire on the virtual highs and real-life lows of Hollywood life, the tenuous and frustrating life of the grubbing screenwriter and the delusions of the has-been silent star, Norma Desmond, bravely taken on by Gloria Swanson. Swanson had been out of the movies since 1934, with one minor foray (1941's *Father Takes a Wife*) since then. She had made only five talkie pictures since her silent days and had gone through another two husbands. Stage work had alternated with business forays into clothes design and cosmetics, and she had begun a television show in 1948, only to quit after abdominal surgery. A call from Wilder, who had co-written her 1934 film, *Music in the Air*, brought her back to Paramount, despite her recent operation.

The film Wilder and writer Charles Brackett had prepared was a bizarre reunion of the once great, like Erich von Stroheim, who had directed her in *Queen Kelly* – his last, and severely curtailed, silent movie – and in cameos, Buster Keaton, Anna Q. Nilsson and H. B. Warner as her regular bridge partners at the Desmond mansion. These were the 'waxworks' described in the voice-over of screenwriter Joe Gillis, a role intended for Montgomery Clift that went instead to William Holden.

With Swanson on board, DeMille was a *sine qua non*, and Cecil submitted to a key scene in which he receives his former star on the Paramount sound stage, where Wilder reconstructed a sequence from *Samson and Delilah*. As DeMille's assistant Phil Koury described the event:

There were four scenes, each requiring two hours and an average of seven 'takes.' Throughout this wordless combat between two techniques of film

DeMille and Gloria Swanson in Billy Wilder's *Sunset Boulevard*

direction, DeMille radiated kindness and fatherly concern, with Wilder demonstrating a monumental sense of management to the crowd of curious that jammed Stage 5 for the occasion . . .

DeMille appeared on the set wearing his trademark – field boots and riding breeches and coat of French, narrow-wale-corduroy – remarking, 'The front of the camera is a new and strange world to me.'

The scene called for DeMille to be told by an aide that Norma Desmond has arrived at the studio to see him. An assistant says: 'She must be a million years old,' to which DeMille ripostes: 'I hate to think where that puts me. I could be her father.' The usual call for retakes is given. As Koury describes: 'DeMille begins to look round, grinning. "This is the fifth take. Am I that bad?"' Wilder calls for another take. DeMille: 'I don't suppose Paramount will pick up my option after this.'

DeMille is totally at ease in the scene, as befits someone who created his own image and fulfilled it for the public for the last thirty-six years, despite his admission that, from stage days, 'I'm afraid I was always a very poor actor.' But only of other parts, not playing himself. In fact, the DeMille scene is the only one in Wilder's movie in which the director accepted a bowdlerized, tame vision of Hollywood rather than the coruscating cartoon he drew of its deranged, delusionary core. There is no DeMillean yelling through his megaphone, no bullying of extras and assistants nor demands for the impossible realism of a nonsensical script. All is fatherly compassion for the star who shared the best moments of his growing fame. Nevertheless, he does not hire Desmond, and the studio's phone calls to her house are merely to rent the magnificent old car in which von Stroheim drives his 'madam' about town. A Hollywood director is a Hollywood director after all.

Throughout this period, DeMille continued holding forth about his beef with the unions and the perils of communism. Speaking in June 1948 at the Kiwanis International Convention in Los Angeles, attended by 11,000 delegates representing 2,200 clubs, DeMille predicted that 'at least 5,000,000 decent, idealistic good Americans will vote the way the Communist party wants them to vote for their new third party next November', resulting in the next US Congress containing 'for the first time in our history a disciplined group of legislators, who unwittingly or wittingly, will be following the leadership of a foreign power rather than the interests of the American people'. The Kiwanis, an all-male organization dedicated to helping children in poor communities, accordingly adopted a resolution to work 'to eradicate communism', the ideological requisite of the hour. A year before, Cecil had lost his appeal against the radio union, which the courts ruled had been acting in its rights as DeMille, a union member, was bound by its rules.

Cecil continued to claim that he was concerned above all with individual rights, having told the *Los Angeles Times* in May 1948 that 'the individual has been battered from both sides. Business management has treated him like a commodity or tool. Union management has lorded it over him as if he were a serf or a slave.' He was pleased that the Taft-Hartley 'right to work' bill had been passed – over President Truman's veto – but agitated for an amendment making it clearer that federal law would 'protect the right to work absolutely and at all events'. In May 1949, in Denver, he addressed a crowd at an 'I Am an American Day' rally at the city auditorium, speaking of 'the light of freedom' which flamed in the dark days of eighteenth-century kingly despotism:

Now, in the 20th century, it still burns in a world menaced by the darker despotism of commissars. How long it will burn depends on how you and I answer the question 'Are you an American?' not with our lips but with our lives . . . Mark this well. This cancer of brutal collectivism is not confined to Europe or Asia. Its cells are working here spreading their poison through the vital organs of our national body.

He then ranted on, declaring that America's enemies wanted peace but it was 'the kind of peace that lulls us into false security and lets them do their work of rotting from within as silently as moths, as deadly as cancer . . . Consolidating their conquests of Poland, Hungary, Romania and Czechoslovakia; gaining time to settle with Marshal Tito; swallowing China with its teeming millions; reaching over Asia, from the Sea of Japan to the Indian Ocean, tightening inch by inch, the iron ring with which they hope to embrace both the Atlantic and the Pacific, with us in the middle.'

Defenders of DeMille's political conduct in this period point out that, despite all this, he did not appear as a witness in the Hollywood witch-hunt that the House Un-American Activities Committee launched in October 1947. Friendly witnesses like Walt Disney, Jack Warner, Louis B. Mayer and actors Adolphe Menjou, Robert Taylor, Ronald Reagan and Gary Cooper rushed to denounce communists in the movie ranks, while 'unfriendly' witnesses, mainly writers like Ring Lardner Jr, Dalton Trumbo, Alvah Bessie and Bertolt Brecht, were called and badgered to name names. In this process, eight writers and two directors (Herbert Biberman and Edward Dmytryk) were sentenced to jail for defying the committee – among them ex-DeMille scriptwriter John Howard Lawson. Various appeals delayed their incarceration until June 1950. The blacklisting of any writer, actor or other movie employee questioned in hearings without providing names was already in full swing. DeMille had a fright during the casting of *Samson and Delilah* when his candidate for Miriam, the village girl who pines for Samson, Olive Deering, appeared on one of the committee's ubiquitous 'lists'. But somehow, conveniently, she was classified as 'clean'.

DeMille, however, did not need to appear as a witness, as despite his chequered past in the Moscow-friendly annals, he was quite clearly a part of the prosecution. He had just spread his net much further than his own industry. His credentials as a commie hunter in Hollywood would pretty soon be established in any case. No one was in any doubt about his position, and in February 1949, the powerful and politically acceptable American Federation of Labor's Hollywood Film Council, representing the Screen Actors Guild and the crews' union, IATSE, withdrew from the Motion Picture Industry Council when DeMille was named its chairman. DeMille denied he was 'anti-labor' and eventually this tiff was patched up.

Meanwhile, and for the sixty-ninth time, there was a new DeMille film in the offing. Confounding expectations, as was ever his wont, it was neither a biblical film nor an epic of patriotic Americanism. Instead it was a circus picture. As the *New York Times* announced on 22 June 1949: 'PARAMOUNT IS SET FOR FILM ON CIRCUS: De Mille To Make "The Greatest Show on Earth" Under Deal With Ringling Brothers'.

Many people might have assumed this was merely a hoax, but the project was under way. Cecil's assistant Phil Koury wrote about the film's genesis: 'The circus idea germinated from an old desire to do a "stream of civilization" story centering in a railroad station, "where great drama passes in review every day."' DeMille had pondered this for years, 'but could not make it into the kind of "Grand Hotel" format he had in mind. However, he feels he has the same dramatic ingredients in the circus story.' Family historian Anne Edwards wrote that, in effect, DeMille had pinched this idea from David O. Selznick, producer of *Gone with the Wind*, the one movie DeMille would have loved to emulate. Selznick had told the press in April 1948 that he was going to film a circus story with the Ringling Brothers and Barnum and Bailey, on a blockbuster budget of $6 million. The circus people held out for a large piece of the cake, and Selznick withdrew. Cecil succeeded in getting Paramount executives to pledge $250,000 to Ringling Brothers for the right to use their facilities and their famous title slogan. The circus owners needed the money, as they were still living down the consequences of a major fire in the big top at Hartford, Connecticut, in June 1944, when one hundred and sixty-seven of their customers perished. Their contract with the studio stipulated that, whatever the movie contained, it would not show the 'tragic fire at Hartford, Connecticut or any other circus fire in which patrons were injured'.

In an unusually personal approach to research, and perhaps in relief at getting away from the political arena, DeMille joined the circus in person for its summer tour of 1949. As Koury described it:

Since joining up in Chicago Aug. 5 for a three-week jaunt, DeMille has virtually become the circus' fourth ring – a relentless, tireless figure, constantly on the move in the steaming heat of the big top. For hours each day he has peered through his camera viewer, with the savage determination of an errant Watson on the search for melodramatic clues. In getting these ideas on composition, he has become an object of considerable wonderment to spectators. The stalking figure in breeches, boots and sport shirt is observed darting in and out amid leggy chorines, squinting at the Bengal tigers or climbing to a platform ninety feet above the center ring (a feat for a person half of DeMille's sixty-eight years) as slim, spangled bodies fly through the air.

Cecil took with him his fourteen-year-old granddaughter, Cecilia ('Citsy'), who was having the time of her life with the troupe, once being allowed by granddad to ride one of the elephants in the 'pre-show' parade. Koury reports that two elephants had been named 'Samson' and 'Delilah', presumably to make sure product placement worked well both ways.

DeMille later stated that *The Greatest Show on Earth* was the toughest production he had ever worked on. Apart from his practical research, he screened every circus picture he could lay his hands on and devoured volumes on circus history. However, he was disappointed with many of their 'nostalgic reflections upon a life once known'. The circus, he wrote in the *New York Times* in December 1950, was not just 'a place of spangles and tinsel, of sleek "resinbacks," of funny clowns . . . This is only the veneer. There is more to the circus – its spirit as a fighting machine, a thing struggling constantly against accident, flood and storm, forcing its way forward because its people know only one credo – "the show must go on."'

One senses DeMille's instinctive identification with this central ethos of all the performing arts, given added force by his own steely voice that would introduce the opening scenes of the film:

We bring you the circus, a pied piper whose magic tunes call children of all ages . . . into a tinsel and spun-candy world of reckless beauty and mounting laughter . . . of stepping horses and high flying stars. But behind all this the circus is a massive machine whose very life depends on discipline, motion and speed. A mechanized army on wheels that rolls over every obstacle in its path. It meets calamity again and again, but always comes up smiling . . . A fierce, primitive fighting force, that smashes relentlessly forward against impossible odds . . .

A metaphor, perhaps, not just for DeMille's own progress through

TECHNICOLOR

Paramount presents CECIL B. DeMILLE'S "THE GREATEST SHOW ON EARTH"

life but for America herself, at this hour that the forces of righteous-ness identified as the time of greatest challenge? The hero of this chal-lenge, as the tale developed, would be Brad, the circus manager, played by Charlton Heston in his second Hollywood role (it was his fourth film; the first two, in which he was featured as *Peer Gynt* and *Julius Caesar*, were directed by David Bradley). Heston's moody perfor-mance as a gambler in William Dieterle's noirish *Dark City* (released in 1950) got him the part, once DeMille was convinced the actor was not just 'dour' and 'sinister' but had a sense of humour. He would be the flawed Nietzschean superman who would drive the circus along, even at the price of harming the ambitions of his trapeze-artist lover, Holly (played by Betty Hutton), by replacing her in the top spot with a box-office star, The Great Sebastian – to be played by Cornel Wilde.

In December 1951, DeMille gave Hollywood gossip queen Hedda Hopper more details about his summer stint:

I took Cecilia, my granddaughter, and Gladys Rosson, and Fred Frank, one of the authors, and we played one-night stands all through the Northwest and lived with the circus. We bunked in the circus tents, ate with them. You get to know them. You see 2,800 eggs fried at the same time. I wanted to get a shot of that so much. I haven't room for half of what I have . . . There are 28 languages spoken under that big top. Like a League of Nations in operation . . . These people – I saw them in blow downs – I saw them when these terrible storms that ripped the thing to pieces, when the flyers were up – the audience panicked and the wonderful flyers didn't come down . . . There were a thousand wonderful shots there in fifteen minutes . . .

For the assigned writers, this was the first time they were tasked with producing a script based on contemporary American life. In fact, it was the only DeMille production since 1933's *This Day and Age* that was set in present-day America. The writers were Fredric Frank, Barré Lyndon and Theodore St John. Jesse Lasky Jr missed out on the film as he was in Italy in 1949 trying to make European movies with an independent producer, Nat Wachsberger. He and the other writers of *Samson and Delilah* had been summarily dismissed by DeMille at the end of its shoot. Cutting costs ruthlessly, DeMille addressed them at the final commissary lunch and said: 'Well, that's it, fellahs. Good job. You're finished. Collect your final check and go home after lunch.'

Jesse relates his astonishment, as the writers were used to being held over for the next project, and in any case they were legally allowed at least two weeks' severance pay. When apprised of this, DeMille went into one of his funks about the crass treachery of minions who should have been glad to be part of the great 'brotherhood of effort that doesn't watch clocks or count pennies, but gives all to the endeavor'.

From his own point of view, DeMille, recalling the multiple resignations of Jeanie Macpherson, did not regard this as a permanent rift and cabled Lasky in Rome to 'COME HOME STOP ALL IS FORGIVEN.' But Lasky ignored this and missed out on the Academy Award that the writers of *The Greatest Show on Earth* won for the film in 1953.

While preparing for the picture, *Samson and Delilah* finally opened just before Christmas 1949. In New York, the film premiered in two theatres, the Paramount and the Rivoli, both besieged by crowds of 3,500 people, as *Times* critic Bosley Crowther duly reported: 'The lines stretched on both sidewalks for almost the entire block.' Crowther noted the sumptuousness of 'a spectacle that out-Babels anything he's done. There are more flowing garments in this picture, more chariots, more temples, more peacock plumes, more animals, more pillows, more spear-carriers, more beards and more sex than ever before' – though that last is debatable. 'Does it all make for entertainment?' Crowther asked. 'That quite frankly depends. If you are looking for historical drama, for poetic tragedy – no. But if you'll settle for gold-plated pageants, for muscular episodes and for graphic inducements to wolf-whistling, then "Samson and Delilah" is for you.'

Samson and Delilah played to packed houses in America and abroad through 1950, making a very healthy profit. DeMille was assured of his almost $4-million budget for *The Greatest Show on Earth*. Research and preparation continued, and Cecil scaled down his political tub-thumping, for a while. In June, he presided over the seventy-sixth annual convention of the Shriners (the Ancient Arabic Order of the Mystic Shrine), acting as Grand Marshal. Membership of a Masonic order was an old tradition among performers, vaudeville, stage and film artists – Harold Lloyd and Oliver Hardy being prominent examples. One hundred thousand members partici-pated on this occasion, and mercifully the threats of communism and union militancy were not mentioned. But in October, a major row broke out in Cecil's own union, the Screen Directors Guild.

The Taft-Hartley Act passed in June 1947 had banned the union closed shop and also mandated that union officials should sign a loy-alty oath that declared their repudiation of the Communist Party. After unsuccessful legal challenges, the law was upheld by the Supreme Court in May 1950. At the Screen Directors Guild, board members, including the president, Joseph L. Mankiewicz, signed the oath. But when Mankiewicz left in June on a long European trip, DeMille and fourteen other board members (including Clarence Brown, Frank Capra, Tay Garnett, Henry King, George Marshall, Leo McCarey, William Seiter and Andrew Stone) met on 18 August and decided, as they explained in a lengthy telegram of 14 October, that: 'In conformity with the anticommunistic belief of the members of SDGA all those seeking membership in the Guild should be obliged to sign a non communistic oath.' The bylaws of the guild were accordingly revised and referred to the membership. According to the cable, 618 ballots were mailed: 547 members voted yes, 14 voted no and 57 did not send back their ballots. Mankiewicz returned to New York on 24 August, and all hell broke lose in the guild. Mankiewicz accused the board members of forming a blacklist and opposed the move. The instigators accused him of opposing the democratic will of the membership and demanded his recall from the presidency.

These were the times in which they lived: the Cold War was at its height; from July 1948 to May 1949, there was the Berlin Blockade, in which the Soviet forces in Germany shut off land communication with the old capital, prompting a western airlift; in February 1949, the takeover of China by the Red Army of Mao Tse-tung was complete and the argument over 'Who lost China?' began raging in the US; in September 1949, the Russians tested their first atomic bomb; and then, on 25 June 1950, the communist army of North Korea invaded the South. The US, under a UN mandate, scrambled to launch a 'police action' in Korea. By the end of 1950, China would commit her own forces to the war.

On the home front, in January 1950 Alger Hiss, a State Department official, was convicted for perjury over his denial that he had passed state secrets to Whittaker Chambers, an ex-communist who had shifted to the right. In March, Klaus Fuchs, a German-born physicist and former member of the German Communist Party, was convicted in England of passing hydrogen-bomb secrets to the Soviet Union. On 17 July, Julius Rosenberg, a small-time engineer and trade-union activist in New York, was arrested and accused of being part of Fuchs's spy ring. His wife, Ethel, was arrested in August. Their case would become a cause célèbre.

This was not the moment, clearly, for the stalwarts of Americanism to go soft on the communist menace. Of the 'Hollywood Ten' who had defied the HUAC inquisition, nine were in jail by June 1950. It was not surprising that, faced with what they would have thought was a bona fide board decision, the vast majority of Screen Directors Guild members voted to accept the oath of loyalty.

The split between the DeMille fifteen and Mankiewicz became front-page news. Twenty-five 'liberal' directors came to Mankiewicz's aid, among them Billy Wilder, Elia Kazan, John Huston, John Farrow, Fred Zinnemann and Mark Robson. All of them, however, signed the 'loyalty oath' to ensure, according to the new bylaws, that they were guild members of 'good standing'. They petitioned for a general meeting of the guild, and a meeting of the board of directors was held 'to consider the proxy form to be used at the big gathering'. As reported by Thomas Brady in the *New York Times* on 22 October: 'John Ford, who, although a conservative, had not joined in the fight, spoke forcibly to the effect that the guild should concern itself with professional matters exclusively.'

The special meeting was held on Sunday night, 22 October, at the Beverly Hills Hotel. Almost all of Hollywood's 'helmsmen' were present, and the proceedings have duly entered legend. Joe Mankiewicz described the tense meeting years later, as DeMille spoke, and according to Mankiewicz emphasized the foreign-sounding names of his opponents – Jo-sef Mankievitz, Billy Vilder, Fred Zeenemaan, etc. – suggesting their subversive and communist links. As Mankiewicz told writer Peter Bogdanovich:

All during this, I was wondering, and I knew quite a few others were wondering, what John Ford thought. He was kind of the Grand Old Man of the Guild and people could be influenced by him. But he just sat there on the aisle wearing his baseball cap and sneakers, didn't say a word. Then after DeMille had made his big speech, there was silence for a moment and Ford raised his hand . . . 'My name's John Ford,' he said. 'I make Westerns.' He praised DeMille's pictures and DeMille as a director. 'I don't think there's anyone in this room,' he said, 'who knows more about what the American public wants than Cecil B. DeMille – and he certainly knows how to give it to them.' Then he looked right at DeMille, who was across the hall from him. 'But I don't like you, C.B.,' he said. 'And I don't like what you've been saying here tonight. Now I vote we give Joe a vote of confidence – and let's go home and get some sleep.' And that's what they all did.

The *New York Times* revealed that the grand membership meeting began at 7.30 p.m. and continued till 3.00 a.m. on Monday morning. DeMille, 'leader of the board majority, made a tactical blunder by challenging the political bona-fides of the Mankiewicz supporters – a blunder which rallied even conservative members to their side. The blow which finally defeated the DeMille faction, however, came from George Stevens, a board member who had not previously engaged in the fight. He took the floor, offered his resignation, and charged the DeMille group with conspiring to push through a mail recall of Mankiewicz without convening the membership.' Ford's intervention put the seal on Stevens's counter-thrust, after many ordinary members like Delmer Daves and Don Hartman expressed their outrage at DeMille's accusations, Hartman speaking of 'paper hat patriots who stand up and holler "I am an American" and that no one else is'. Ford's suggestion that the entire board of directors should resign and a new board be elected was adopted by the meeting.

Bruised, but not beaten, Cecil returned to his true vocation: making movies. Shooting began on *The Greatest Show on Earth* in January 1951 and continued till the end of May, with additional shots taken up till August. It was the longest shoot of all DeMille's films, due to the complications of the shifting locations. DeMille expanded later to Hedda Hopper: 'It was the toughest production problem to solve that I have had presented to me in the 39 years I have been making pictures. You cannot light a big top so you have to invent a new light . . . If I could not get the light I could not make the picture . . .' Technicolor had to come up with new film-stock solutions to allow the massive interior of the circus tent to be filmed with the lighting available at the time. Camera movements had to be tailored to the task: 'You can't carry cameras up on booms over 10,500 people in the audience. You are giving directions to four cameras placed in four different places so that you would have to work out shots to such an extent beforehand in your head . . .' A normal situation in a controlled studio but not in the context of a three-ring circus, where so many things are going on at once, as the film featured not only its stars, stand-ins and extras but many of the Ringling Brothers–Barnum and Bailey acts as well.

Once edited, with veteran Anne Bauchens still at the splicing table, the film ran for two and a half hours. After a few months of suitable razzmatazz and promotion, it opened at Radio City Music Hall in New York in January 1952. Once again, DeMille proved that in his own department, at least, he could do no wrong, and it proved the most profitable of his movies, bringing a net profit of over $6 million, half of which went to the producer-director's own coffers.

The film still resonates with its celebration of the old-style circuses, killed off by new attitudes to the treatment of the animals that made the three-ring shows so distinctive: the parade of elephants, the caged lions and tigers, the horses and trained chimpanzees. But over and above this, DeMille celebrated the camaraderie and community of the circus folk, united in a common cause. It is achievement for achievement's sake, life as both spectacle and freak show: the old-style parade through small towns, drawing the crowd with its brass band and baby elephants and clowns towards the big top, where escape from reality reigns supreme; the audience's thrill at the risks taken by the acrobats ever tinged with a sadistic expectation of a gut-wrenching disaster.

DeMille's story revolved round the rivalry of the high-wire artists Holly and The Great Sebastian, vying with each other in dangerous manoeuvres till the latter falls without his safety net and is crippled. Two sub-plots relate the machinations of commercial rivals to cripple the circus – aided by the jealous elephant trainer whose girl Sebastian is flirting with and who helps wreck the circus train – and the tale of Buttons, a clown played by James Stewart, who hides behind his great painted red smile the secret of a crime committed in his previous life as a surgeon: the mercy killing of his wife. This part of the story brought DeMille into conflict with the Catholic Legion of Decency, who issued a condemnation of the film for this theme, which they claimed was treated sympathetically. DeMille protested that a crime had been committed and atoned for, as Buttons saves the wounded Brad and others in the train-wreck scene. But the Legion of Decency's Christianity was too robust to accept atonement. Ironically, DeMille was also condemned by some extreme Protestant Masons, who disliked an early scene in which a Catholic priest blesses the circus train as it leaves town. No matter that the scene was based on fact.

The train crash provided DeMille with an apotheosis of train crashes past – from the time-bending inferno of *The Road to Yesterday* to the snowy derailment of *Union Pacific*: a tangle of twisted metal, careening carriages and wild beasts thrown free of their cages, the terror mitigated by human heroism, the ultimate disaster survived. And when the circus parade, bandaged like a troupe of wounded warriors, draws the crowd towards the skeleton masts of the big top to the tune of 'Yankee Doodle Dandy', DeMille's metaphor is fully engaged.

One wonders why Cecil B. DeMille waited so long to make a movie based on real-life people in their working lives, pursuing their own and their audiences' dreams with great panache and proper melodrama. Some critics still accused him of 'schmaltzing' it all up, but for once the higher hokum and its subject combined to present a carnival worthy of the label 'Glorious Technicolor'. DeMille's peers thought so, and perhaps in relief, perhaps to encourage him to continue along this path, voted him a long-delayed Oscar, to go with the writers' award, for best picture of the year. He was also honoured with the Irving G. Thalberg Award for 'creative producers whose bodies of work reflect a consistently high quality of motion picture production'.

Into the Home Stretch: Towards Mount Sinai Resurgent

The autumn of 1950 saw the beginning of the publication of a series of articles written by DeMille with Phil Koury relating, in eighteen weekly instalments, the various tales of his career. This mini-book was syndicated to over thirty newspapers. In this dry run for an auto-biography, Cecil represented his life as he wished, carving out his own narrative, beginning with the boyhood influence of his Episcopal father.

DeMille was keen, as he passed his sixty-eighth birthday, to emphasize his religious credentials. An earlier essay, written by one William Gammon in the *American Weekly* in November 1949, had outlined a curious early epiphany which, DeMille was quoted as say-ing, established his 'real baptism in the faith of my fathers'. This somewhat cloying tale of early religiosity begins with the more secu-lar interests of little seven-year-old Cecil and his older brother Will, who precociously 'pored over Dickens and Thackeray, Macaulay and Carlyle. Cecil also discovered Plutarch; the lives of the ancients fasci-nated him.'

No mention of the Champion Driver here. Apparently, in March 1889, father Henry De Mille 'brought home an important announce-ment: Christ Church had hired a full-fledged Episcopal clergyman who would conduct daily services during Passion Week'. Mother De Mille laid out the boy's Sunday best: 'black shoes and long black stockings, black worsted knee-breeches, a black broadcloth vest that buttoned to the neck . . . a short black coat with silk lapels and a huge white lace collar'.

Not at all enthused, the boy went off, only to find that he was the only one in the congregation. The red-bearded clergyman, however, was not deterred from conducting his full service:

Scarcely glancing at the empty pews, he turned toward the altar and knelt.

The passion of consecration was in the clergyman's voice as it rose to the rafters, and Cecil was embarrassed. He felt like an eavesdropper.

His prayers concluded, the clergyman rose and turned to the empty church. His glance fell on the boy and he smiled. It was a warm smile, a smile full of dignity and sincerity . . . Cecil's feeling of guilty intrusion vanished in the warmth of that smile. It was as though the clouds had parted, drenching the world with sunshine and brightness.

As the service proceeded through the reading of the Epistle and Gospel texts, the boy participated, giving the responses in a ringing, childish voice.

The boy left the church to carry with him forever the boon of the clergyman's benediction, 'the Peace of God, which passeth all understanding.'

'Without my own personal conviction,' DeMille told Mr Gammon, 'I could not have carried the story of Jesus of Nazareth to the 650 million people who have witnessed it.'

DeMille told Hedda Hopper that he considered his greatest achievement, 'besides marrying Constance', to be *The King of Kings*. 'It has never missed a week's playing in 25 years,' he told her, 'seen by more people than any picture ever made – and it has been shown free to the poor of half the world. I sent a print out to Madam Chiang Kai-Shek at her request, for hospitals and troops of Formosa.' And he sent another print for screening to captured North Korean prisoners of war – '18,000 prisoners spellbound sitting and looking at it'. As well they might be.

In the first episode of his syndicated story, Cecil related a more homely early epiphany:

My father had one spectacular weakness. He loved to have his head rubbed. We children knew of this weakness and used it to our advantage.

Each evening it was father's custom to read a chapter from the Old Testament and one from the New . . . We hated to have him stop, so we used to sit on an arm of his chair and take turns gently rubbing his head. Soothed and relaxed, he kept on reading into extra chapters.

Our consciousness of the Bible as a dramatic book was deepened by the family's weekly visits to art galleries in New York. Father stood behind us in kindly but restraining fashion, explaining the magnificent coloring of Rubens, the marvellous lighting of Rembrandt and the symmetric compositions of Doré . . . In each Bible picture I have brought to life one or more of Doré's great illustrations . . .

The next dozen and a half episodes enlarged on Cecil's long path towards his abiding goal of bringing his father's stories to life in the movies. 'The motion picture was a struggling young art, and the world of finance had grave doubts about its future. There was a great fear of costume pictures in the industry . . .' So all of Cecil's career – all the bathtub scenes, the many beautiful actresses, from Bebe Daniels and Gloria Swanson through Leatrice Joy and Claudette Colbert – became a journey to its predetermined sacred goal. The series included the tale of how Colbert wouldn't consider holding a snake for her death scene till DeMille came in wrapped in a huge Mexican boa constrictor and then offered Claudette her harmless little adder. '"Oh, that little thing!" she said, relieved, and reached for it.' DeMille also covered the mystery of the fifty-foot prop idol in *Four Frightened People*, whose appearance and disappearance non-plussed the inmates of the local lunatic asylum in Hawaii; the financial struggles; tales of his Soviet trip; discovering that *The Godless Girl*, shorn of its last reel, was being used as an atheist tract; his pearls of wisdom and comments on doctors – 'As a boy I remember the old general store philosopher in our town saying that a man was a coward if he needed a doctor more than twice a lifetime. "At birth and at death," he would say . . .' – the struggles of the censors with scripture; old family problems with William, who lacked faith in the film business . . .

There was an entire episode on 'How He Values Women': 'Unless beauty is fanned by that inner spark known as personality, it is of no use on the screen . . . In interviewing a girl for a picture, I look for personality in two things – eyes – those "windows of the soul" – and voice, with perhaps a hasty glance at her feet.' Other episodes focused on producers' troubles, on his travails with lawsuits, and on a man called Kratzman who kept hounding him to make a film about Jeremiah. There were recycled stories about the awakening drugged leopard in *Male and Female*, and close to the end of the series, a warning to screen stars that 'Freedom Is Our Heritage'. The loyalty oath, DeMille declared, was a 'Gauge of Spirit'. Mixing his history somewhat, DeMille wrote: 'The spirit that founded this nation was, at the same moment, both a loyalty oath and a rejection of the principles of Communism . . . A man has the right to remain silent, assuming he is willing to accept the consequences of his silence. As an American he has the right. But he does not have the right to be silent when his silence is decisively un-American.' The communists, he wrote, call America's private enterprise 'American Imperialism', but

if imperialism meant 'feeding millions of men, women and children
. . . spreading to other countries the idea of free speech, a free press,
freedom of religion, free elections . . . then it's bred in the bones of
every real American. And he should be proud and stand up for it.'

The tub thumping resumed as the exhausting period of the circus
shoot ended, with various patriotic groups praising DeMille for his
outspoken stand on behalf of America: he received honours from
national social-science society Sigma Tau Sigma, at Los Angeles City
College; a gold medal from the Sons of the American Revolution; and
on his seventieth birthday, on 11 August 1951, a huge birthday card
with eight hundred signatures by 'government officials and theater
owners from every part of the world addressed to "The Greatest
Showman on Earth,"' presented to him at Paramount Studios.
DeMille told his adorers that he hadn't begun to make 'all the films
he would like to make'. 'I would like to start on Page One of the Bible
and begin making pictures . . . Then I would like to start on Page One
of American history and go right down to the latest dispatch from
Korea.'

DeMille was at the height of his power and fame as he turned seventy. No film director was more famous or had been in the headlines
for so long. None had made so much money for himself or the industry. In 1942, Hollywood Chamber of Commerce president John
Freeman had estimated that up to that date DeMille's films had
'returned $55,000,000 in film rentals from a gross intake of
$200,000,000, and had been seen by approximately 800,000,000
ticket buyers'.

But strange to tell, DeMille was still not certain, despite all the
Bible thumping, what his next picture might be. Hindsight leads to an
obvious conclusion, but real life is more confusing. To some newsmen DeMille still mentioned the 'Queen of Queens' project, or
'Helen of Troy', or even his unfulfilled idea of 'scienti-fiction', though
George Pal had just produced *When Worlds Collide*, which DeMille
had once touted. In April 1952, he won the Golden Peanut Award
from the National Peanut Council for his circus film and then hied off
to Europe to receive a French gong, the La Victoire Award, for
Samson and Delilah. The Belgian Film Festival invited him to nomi-
nate his list of '10 best films of the half century', and he modestly
included four of his own – all his Bible pictures.

Then suddenly, at the end of April, DeMille announced the dissolution of his own production company, citing the burden of 'corporate income taxes, excess profits tax, franchise taxes' and other burdens that 'left no opportunity for the retention of sufficient capital to bring about the accomplishment for which the company was originally organized'. Calling himself a 'small businessman', he went on the warpath against a new enemy, the 'Exorbitant Tax Structure'. He turned his stock over to his daughter Cecilia and her husband Joseph Harper, his lawyer Neil McCarthy, personal secretary Gladys Rosson and 'others'. In other words, the money remained safely in his control. DeMille went on a lecture tour, had a Chair of Drama endowed in his name at the University of Southern California, and then told newsmen in May he was working on preparations both for 'Helen of Troy' and a new film with a 'Boy Scout' background, later mentioned as a biopic of scout founder Robert Baden-Powell.

Commie bashing continued, with DeMille and Alliance College president Arthur P. Coleman protesting to Congress about the use of the mail service to spread 'communistic propaganda'. In June, he told the LA Chamber of Commerce that President Truman was afraid of the 'invisible government' that was still running the country, stating that 'there can be no compromise of a system of freedom under God and a Godless system'. The great conflict of the day was still 'the light of freedom and the darkness of slavery'.

In August, Cecil and Constance celebrated their golden wedding anniversary. The entire family gathered for the occasion. DeMille was aged seventy-one and four days. The secret of happiness, he said, was 'Just find a patient, gracious lady – and let her run things.'

In December, DeMille had another grandchild, the fifth child of Katherine and Anthony Quinn. The press reported the child, Valentina, as their fourth, missing out the boy who had drowned in W. C. Fields's lily pond. Pressures within this marriage were breaking it up, and soon Quinn would depart on a European voyage which would see him make five films in Italy, including Federico Fellini's La Strada. The clock was winding down on Cecil B. DeMille's phantasm marriage of total fidelity that could contain in its idyllic boundaries both multiple mistresses and the most pious Christianity. Constance was already frail, aged almost eighty and beginning to exhibit symptoms similar to those of the condition we know today as Alzheimer's disease.

Still, no one really expected DeMille to retire, and indeed, in February 1953, the first mention was made of the film that would crown his career. In the same week that both DeMille and actor Montgomery Clift were among the eight hundred recipients of a 'Freedom Award', Cecil told a press meeting in New York, on 25 February, that he was 'going slowly' on his new picture, *The Ten Commandments*. The reason, he said, was that he wanted to be alert for new technical developments in the movies. He had been caught out, with *The Godless Girl*, by the arrival of sound, and Hollywood was now experimenting with three new formats: Cinemascope, Cinerama and 3-D.

'You can just say', he declared, 'that "The Ten Commandments" will be made in the most advanced form of film production available at the time I start shooting.' Some people, he said, were putting their faith in a gadget, not a drama. But any medium would only be 'as good as the idea it distributes – and not better'.

The research that went into DeMille's remake of his 1923 classic was the most extensive he had ever undertaken, and perhaps the most extensive of any Hollywood film. Cecil tasked the very thorough Henry Noerdlinger with this project, which involved consulting 950 books, 984 periodicals, 1,286 clippings and 2,964 photographs, according to the efficient Swiss himself. The results were boiled down to a two-hundred-page book published by Noerdlinger with the University of Southern California Press in 1956. The notes run the gamut through the biblical narrative and its various interpretations, ancient sources like the historian Flavius Josephus and Philo of Alexandria's *On the Life of Moses*, Jewish Midrash, the Koran, the vast literary corpus of Egyptology, sources on language, usage and the various characters of the tale, and archaeological evidence regarding all aspects of life under the pharaohs, particularly the era of Rameses II. They covered the architecture of the buildings, the ritual and the countless illustrations that have survived of almost every aspect of ordinary life, such as the tilling of the soil, fishing in the Nile, the methods of quarrying and working stone, Egyptian crafts, the dwellings of the labourers, fabrics and colours, costumes and adornments of both men and women, hair styles among the Egyptians and the Hebrews, perfume, incense and cosmetics, jewellery, eating habits and entertainments of the time, dancing and musical instruments. The entire preparations, art designs, research materials and production papers of the second version of *The Ten Commandments* take up about 450 boxes of the 1,800-odd that comprise the Cecil B. DeMille collection at Brigham Young University in Utah. Apart from Griffith's *Intolerance*, it is doubtful that more people were employed to design, build, sew, tend, feed and service any other movie production, before or since.

It was to be his own testament. As Cecil noted in a long speech given to mark the movie's gala opening in 1956, in which he reiterated the themes of 1923: 'The Ten Commandments are not outmoded relics of a barbaric age. They are as true and valid and real as the day they were burned into tablets of stone by the Finger of God ... What I hope for our production of "The Ten Commandments" is that those who see it shall come from the theatre not only entertained and filled with the sight of big spectacle, but filled with the spirit of truth – that it will bring to its audience a better understanding of the real meaning of this pattern of life that God has set down for us to follow ... Moses is Everyman – in his pride, his bitterness at God allowing evil to befall his people, and in his reluctance to do God's work. The life of Moses was a life of struggle and defiance, of daring and sorrow, a life of love and battle, of sacrifice and murder, a life of achievement and disaster, humiliation and glory.'

A life, give or take the murder, not unlike that of a more modern hero, Cecil Blount DeMille himself?

A 'Spiritual Acetylene Torch'

Everything was going to be bigger and better than before. This time there would be no limited prologue and the extended agony of a modern story to ram the moral home. This would be, in the words of Jesse Lasky Jr, a grand 'Victorian pageant play' to suit a grand Victorian man. This time, with colour and the new VistaVision process, there would be no white sands of Guadalupe standing in for the yellow dunes of Egypt – this time it would be the real thing.

DeMille's description of the circus well fitted his own production in full swing: 'a massive machine whose very life depends on discipline, motion and speed'. In September 1954, the company set out for Egypt from New York, DeMille recalling to the press that the first time he had filmed this story, 'Paramount fired me' for spending a mere $1 million. This time, he was planning to hire in Egypt 30,000 people and 15,000 animals. One scene alone, the Exodus, would employ 20,000 extras. Entire local villages would be hired to take part.

First of all, however, DeMille had to negotiate the shifting sand dunes of Egyptian politics. When he had first tentatively considered the remake, Egypt was still a British satrapy, nominally independent and ruled by the obese and profligate King Farouk, whose legitimacy was of doubtful provenance. In 1948, his incompetent armed forces had failed to dislodge the Jewish armies from southern Palestine, leading to the vast Palestinian Arab exodus which was a matter of national shame. In July 1952, a revolt by Egyptian army officers overthrew the monarchy and forced the king into exile. DeMille had to negotiate, not with an easily procured potentate, but with a revolutionary regime. At this point, however, the regime was anti-British but not anti-American, as America's secret services scrambled to ensure that the post-colonial Middle East stayed on the right side in the Cold War. Good, if fragile relationships existed between the US

and the head of the Egyptian officers, General Naguib, and with the real power behind him, the young and charismatic Colonel Gamal Abdel Nasser. In April 1954, Egypt was declared a republic, with Naguib as president and Nasser as prime minister. By November, when DeMille was already filming in Egypt, Naguib had been deposed and succeeded by Nasser. Major problems with the west, the nationalization of the Suez Canal, Egypt's alignment with the Soviet Union and the Suez crisis pitting the country against Israel, France and Britain still lay in the future.

Henry Wilcoxon, né Richard the Lionheart and now DeMille's associate producer, described his and DeMille's meeting with the new power in somewhat colourful terms to author Katherine Orrison for her book on the making of *The Ten Commandments, Written in Stone*:

Our state car whisked us away from Naguib's headquarters and across Cairo. The car pulled up at a military encampment. We were instructed to step out onto a red carpet. We were led into a tent with four chairs set on top of an exquisite Oriental rug . . . In a matter of minutes, Colonel Gamal Abdel Nasser himself strode in, filling the tent with blinding charisma that was all dark burning eyes, flashing white teeth and impeccable English.

'Hen-ry Wil-cox-on!' he exclaimed, 'I would know you anywhere! So exciting of you to visit my country!' He hastened over to shake my hand . . .

DeMille, apparently, was ignored for the moment, as Nasser remembered the Lionheart of *The Crusades*, a most popular film due to its sympathetic treatment of Saladin, although the record shows it actually did poor business, as we have seen, in the Arab world. Nasser would have been much too young to have seen the first *Ten Commandments*. The Egyptian flattery overlay a genuine welcome, as a major Hollywood production and the dollars it would bring were an obvious boon to a regime seeking legitimacy with the US and aware that the old British colonial power would try, sooner or later, to shake it out of its seat. DeMille's pre-existing relationship with the American University in Cairo would have ensured good contacts, and the best of them was in any case the US ambassador to Egypt, Jefferson Caffery. So it was a little cheeky of Wilcoxon to claim that 'all of Egypt was put at our disposal by my number-one fan'.

Indeed, sizeable portions of the Egyptian army, dressed up to the nines as Pharaoh's charioteers, were deployed in the desert locations outside Cairo and on the Red Sea coast, with a host of civilian Cairenes and villagers as the Twelve Tribes of Israel. The first scenes shot for the film, however, were on the Sinai peninsula, in the vicinity of Mount Sinai itself.

The mountain is located in the centre of the southern tip of the Sinai, in a landscape of rugged desolation which can be seen in the background of the movie as Moses toils up the slopes towards his divine destiny. Even chief cinematographer Loyal Griggs's Technicolor-VistaVision cannot do justice to this rocky panorama, in which Mount Sinai itself is merely one of a range of mountains, not in themselves of prodigious height, but which tower over the ochre desert. (The adjacent Mount Catherine is 400 metres higher than Mount Sinai.) The blasting heat, even in October, the burning sky and the quiver of history in the air could drive the most acute atheist to peculiar visions. The only human habitation is the ancient and venerable Greek

Orthodox monastery of Saint Catherine, to which DeMille and his crew repaired in their convoy of vehicles from the seaside oil terminal of Abu Rudeis. There would have been no asphalted road in 1954, and white markers had to be set out for the larger crew that was to follow. At the monastery, the legendary method of access used to be a basket winched up the wall, but it appears that DeMille and co. had a more mundane way in through a gate. Once there, as described by stills photographer Ken Whitmore to Katherine Orrison: 'The company bedded down for the night in the individual monks' cells – very plain, rude affairs with a shelf for a bed and a simple straw mattress on top . . . DeMille was given the archbishop's quarters – "deluxe" accommodation consisting of a suite of three rooms with a sixteenth-century bed and a bathtub with no water pipes . . .'

Whitmore seems to have missed out on the monastery's most noted peculiarity – the skulls and bones of the monks who had lived and died there over the centuries. But there the movie pilgrims were, looking over their first spectacular Sinai sunrise.

The identification of the site as the biblical Mount Sinai is apocryphal, and in subsequent scenes of God's fiery cloud cover the mountain is set apart in the studio. But it was a clever move on DeMille's part to begin the shoot in this austere setting. Unlike almost any other epic film of that period or before, set in the contrived atmosphere of a studio backlot or even a 'lookalike' environment like Guadalupe, the genuine aura of the primal location set the tone for the two months that followed, even if there was, off screen, a pukka Cairo catering company that saw to the Hollywoodians' profane needs.

The next scenes shot, west of the Red Sea, brought in Pharaoh banishing Moses and his cohorts pursuing the freed Children of Israel. DeMille had cast Yul Brynner as Pharaoh after seeing him on stage in *The King and I*. His trademark stocky confidence and pure shaven head occupied the role of Rameses II to perfection, and the great catchphrase he was given – 'So let it be written, so let it be done!' – remains the perfect DeMillean motto. The contrasting physical presence of Charlton Heston as Moses underlies the testosterone battle between them that fuels the movie, as muscles are flexed, chests jutted out and nostrils flared. Heston was not, oddly enough, Cecil's first choice for the part, as he had his heart set on William Boyd, the Volga Boatman, Mr Hopalong Cassidy, for the role. Luckily for the

'So let it be written, so let it be done!'

film, Boyd was not keen on the adventure, though he did turn up as a guest at the shoot. The role was clinched for Heston when DeMille compared his features with Michelangelo's great sculpture of Moses. What was good enough for Michelangelo was good enough for DeMille.

Cecil deliberated long over his female principals, settling in the end on Anne Baxter as the Moses-loving but Pharaoh-marrying Nefretiri, Yvonne de Carlo as Jethro's daughter Sephora and Nina Foch as the princess who draws baby Moses from the bullrushes. Cedric Hardwicke made a splendidly regal Sethi, father of Rameses II and adoptive father of Moses. John Derek manifested actual personality as Joshua, and John Carradine hid behind his own bushy face-growth as Moses' brother Aaron. Among the minor delights, Vincent Price camped it up nicely with his whip as the master builder, and Edward G. Robinson provided the Schildkraut touch as the nasty Hebrew overseer and skeptic, Dathan.

The writers, ingathered again, were Aeneas Mackenzie, Jesse Lasky Jr, Jack Gariss and Fredric Frank. Mackenzie had been writing screenplays of period and adventure movies since 1939 – *The Private*

Lives of Elizabeth and Essex, with Errol Flynn, was one of his first co-credits. Lasky praised him as 'a fine film dramatist and a walking encyclopedia of obscure information'. Lasky himself was back in the fold, forgiven for previous *lèse-majesté*. With his usual nose for the risk of plagiarism, DeMille contracted three spurious sources – *Prince of Egypt* by Dorothy Clark Wilson, *Pillar of Fire* by the Rev. J. H. Ingraham and *On Eagles' Wings* by Rev. A. E. Southon – giving ringing endorsements of the 'ancient texts', Philo, Josephus, Eusebius, Jewish Midrash and – pause for a separate credit – the Holy Scriptures, all emphatically out of copyright.

Lasky's position in this maelstrom of verbiage was, he later noted, a decision by DeMille that 'I was the company Hebrew. The fact that I'd never been bar-mitzvah, or even inside a synagogue, and had in boarding-school been a leader of the Christian Endeavor Society, was completely ignored.' A Jew was a Jew. So DeMille would stride up to him, the ritual coins jingling in his pockets, and say: 'I want you to write me the first feast of Passover. Write it from the heart of a Hebrew . . . You've got to dig. Into yourself. Your ancestors. Just as I go back to that baron at Hastings, fighting beside William the Conqueror, when I need courage.'

The usual yelling fits would ensue on occasion, when DeMille accused Lasky of reducing 'a great moment in the saga of mankind to Hollywood theatrics'. According to Lasky, DeMille then spat on his script. Lasky resigned, but of course was immediately back at work.

DeMille was at his best, as many witnesses verify, in his general-ship of this mightiest of his cinema battles. Often imperious to the crew, he was diligent with his actors, high or low. Eugene Mazzola, who played Rameses' first-born as a small boy, recalled the quality of the direction: 'He never demanded. He asked me to "try" things. "Can you try to be more surprised?" Or, "What I'm trying for is . . ." It was always very personal. No yelling. No bullying . . . And never – never did he ever "act out" or read a line for me.' As he had ever stated, DeMille hired the actors to act, and his expectation that they would do their best often brought out the best in their performances, no easy task with the portentous biblical dialogue.

The script, in line with many of DeMille's screenplays, contains a great deal of 'novelistic' detail that prescribes mood as well as dia-logue and technical descriptions, like the first sight of Pharaoh Rameses I: 'seated in a chair of state upon a low dais, is aged, his immobile hawk face chiseled into granite lines by time. Behind him stand the Fanbearer-at-the-King's-Right and a Captain of the Palace Guard. Below the chair, a scribe sits cross legged on the steps, with writing materials upon his knees. To one side, below the dais, a Sardinian swordsman in horned helmet above narrow, savage eyes is on duty as a personal bodyguard . . .'

Seldom was a film so thoroughly prepared, storyboarded and analysed in advance, with sumptuous colour drawings of costumes and sets which could form on their own a great volume of distinctive popular art. As with all scripts, scenes were omitted in the final film, including a lengthy opening sequence of the divine Creation itself, Genesis encapsulated from The Beginning: 'In the vast darkness of infinity, little tongues of fire come to life, swirling in pre-destined patterns of divine movement,' as the narrator – DeMille himself, of course – intones: 'Day and night – sun and stars – heaven and earth created He them . . .' The script instructs the camera to record the 'blazing finger of God', and in the seas, 'the camera starts to move up the sloping bank to shore – as though it were the first living creature to crawl out of the deep . . . Dissolve to: THE YOUNG, NEW WORLD IN THE DAWN OF TIME, a prehistoric vista of mountains and valleys clothed with primeval vegetation.' In the event, most of this, and the visualization of the 'first figure of Man' and Woman – 'a vague, shadowy figure, suffused in unearthly light – the fulfillment of man's first dream of beauty' – was left out. But there was so much to leave in . . .

Among the many spectacular scenes in this most inherently spectacular of films, the Exodus itself stands out as the most crowded crowd scene in movie history. Whether there are twenty or thirty thousand people in the great overhead crane shot in which the freed slaves move out below the stone gods of Egypt into the desert is moot. The point is that you are aware these are people, each with his or her own quirk of movement, and not a sea of computer-generated things dictated by machine 'intelligence'. Somehow there is a great satisfaction in reality, even if it's the reality of ersatz grandeur, that instead of fooling perception pleases the eye. DeMille uses his signature method of controlling a crowd, setting myriad individual tasks for the extras to do, whether it is to rein in a goat, collect a child's doll, pull a donkey, witness a new birth in a cart, haul bundles, or in the most poignant self-reference in the scene, carry an emaciated H. B. Warner, Christ in *The*

King of Kings, as a dying grandfather bearing a few twigs which may be planted after he is gone in the Promised Land. Another familiar figure, Henry Wilcoxon, pressed into service in addition to his production duties, manfully shadows the Queen of Egypt as a sombre Egyptian captain. He is the one who says, 'I have known battle for thirty years, Pharaoh, but I have not known fear until tonight,' when the 'Angel of Death' fog of God's plague of the first-born drifts across Yul Brynner's balcony.

The great Exodus scene masked another drama, which occurred during one of the master shots. As the Children of Israel marched off into the wilderness, their director was stricken with a heart attack as he was clambering up a ladder to his vantage point. Luckily he managed to climb down on his own, and his granddaughter Cecilia and staff were soon on hand. Satisfying himself that 'I got the shot', he was ushered off. But against doctor's orders, he was back on the set on a stretcher the next morning. Three days later, he had to return to the US, and the remaining location photography was handled by Loyal Griggs, with Cecilia standing in for her grandfather. He was well enough to resume the shoot, back in the studio, from the end of March 1955.

The legends of *The Ten Commandments* have already filled one book and could fill several others: the actors itching under the 'full body make-up' that turned them into properly brown Egyptians; the special-effects challenges, such as using a water hose with a red dye to simulate Moses' staff turning the Nile red from its tip, the animated pillar of fire, the popcorn used for the Plague of Hailstones and the unused Plague of Frogs scene, in which hundreds of rubber frogs were prepared whose legs could be moved from a central keyboard like the giant octopus of *Reap the Wild Wind*. A screen test was apparently shot with Anne Baxter 'screaming as they hopped up and down in her room and on her bed'. According to Lasky, this test footage was 'the hot ticket on the Paramount lot that summer', adding wistfully: 'I wonder where that footage is today . . .'

The *coup de cinéma* was, of course, the parting of the Red Sea, achieved using a tank at the Paramount lot with ramps down which the water would cascade, and then combining matte paintings, miniatures and the water flowing in and reversed back out with the Egyptian location shots. On the big screen – and compared to seamless CGI effects – disbelief is not completely suspended, but the garishness of the scene, its air of high drama, Technicolor, VistaVision and the Gustave Doré compositions make it work precisely as it was intended: a 'state of the art' cinematic miracle, with Henry Wilcoxon and his colleagues bubbling in the water briefly, instead of the soldier-dummies used in the 1923 version. 'And the waters returned, and covered the chariots, and the horsemen, and all the host of Pharaoh . . . But the Children of Israel walked upon dry land in the midst of the sea . . .'

Unlike the tableau sequences of the silent 'prologue', the VistaVision version filled in the gaps of the biblical story itself – between the time when the babe Moses is drawn from the Nile by Pharaoh's daughter and brought up as her son and the day when the grown man strikes down the Egyptian who is mistreating his people. Noerdlinger's research into several sources turned up the idea that Pharaoh Rameses II, son of Sethi, whose sister rescued Moses, had a mysterious elder brother who might have inherited the throne. Was this the original Moses? DeMille and his writers constructed the narrative of a fatal rivalry between half-brothers. This was, if one looks back, a familiar DeMille story device, used as early as 1915's *The Unafraid* and then again in *Triumph*, in 1924. The entire plot line can be seen as a return to Cecil's most enduring theme, the reversal of fortune, played out literally on a biblical and cosmic scale. The low are raised high, the most high humbled in the dust. The DeMillean 'dilemma' being, for Moses, should he take the throne as Pharaoh to gain power to free his people or should he take the divinely ordained, and much thornier, path, to walk through fire to be their deliverer?

One can see, at last, where that original theme came from: those elegiac evenings at home, rubbing father's scalp by the fireside as the ancient stories flowed. The strength of the plot is, of course, in its primal aspect: if, as legend has it, there are only thirty-six or twelve or six basic stories from which all human narratives flow, this is certainly one of them, if not the most enduring since Cain and Abel. To the brew can be added the genesis of the Patriarch and Deliverer, and Woman's Fall, ensnared by jealousy and lust.

The culminating scene, upon Mount Sinai, is a whirl of fiery finger-of-God effects chiselling the Ten Commandments upon their tablets of stone, as special-effects man William Sapp explained to Katherine Orrison: 'I'm back of the rock during the scene, lighting the gunpowder that makes the words and the shape of the tablets. Heston's tablets were those and granite tablets. Mr. Heston's stand-in worked with a lightweight plaster pair I made for camera rehearsals and lighting setups.' As Heston cowers before the might of the words, the Children of Israel down below are disporting themselves with the Golden Calf constructed by order of the heretic Dathan. As this was 1955, a puritanical time in America, with the censor still wielding the sword as the angel of morality, DeMille's instructions for the scene were for it to be more of a 'Sunday school orgy'. The extras gyrate and scamper about below the golden idol, as Joan Woodbury, who played Korah's wife, recalled to Katherine Orrison: 'I got sick, but I went on with the orgy. The oil the prop master put on the golden calf to make it look bright and shiny gold aggravated my emphysema. The oil got all over my wig and clothes when I had to rub up against the golden calf, and I'd wind up nauseous and gasping for breath . . . night after night I'd stagger home and lie in a hot tub, trying to soak – then scrub – Max Factor's "Dark Egyptian" body makeup off my skin . . .' And all the while DeMille's own stentorian voice intones, as

if bemoaning his own recalcitrant flock: 'They were as children who had lost their faith . . . and they cast off their clothes . . . and there was manifest all manner of ungodliness and works of the flesh, even adultery, and lasciviousness, uncleanness, idolatry and rioting and wrath, and they were filled with iniquity and vile affections . . .'

One might note that these lip-smacking words (and the unashamed reproof of adultery) do not derive from the relevant chapters of the Book of Exodus, which makes do with the making of the Calf, burnt offerings and naked dancing, but from other sources chosen for added detail, just as the Ten Commandments themselves, in Exodus, are merely the beginning of a long list of commandments of complex ritual lasting eleven chapters which are equally sacred to observant Jews. DeMille's tale, adult as it appears in the telling, remains the devout child's summary.

And lo, the tablets are smashed, the heretical punished and the sinning tribes made to wander in the wilderness for forty years until the entire generation of the Golden Calf blasphemers is consumed; and Moses himself, with an astonishing head of white curls and Michelangelesque white beard, wanders alone up Mount Nebo, within sight of the Promised Land but forbidden to enter.

DeMille's vision of the Hebrew creation myth, in its Mosaic chapter, is devoutly fundamentalist, or more precisely 'literalist', right from the opening shafts of light through the clouds and the primal message – 'And God said let there be light, and there was light . . . and man was given dominion over all things upon the earth, and the power to choose between Good and Evil – but each sought to do his own will, because he knew not the light of God's law. Man took dominion over man, the conquered were made to serve the conqueror . . .' – but with a nod to present-day schisms: 'And freedom was gone from the world.' And to the end, as Moses walks off, the last image, the glowing tablets of the Law and the legend: 'So it was written, so it shall be done.'

The entire saga ran for three hours and thirty-nine minutes, the longest and, at over $13 million, the most expensive Hollywood movie made to date. I recall seeing it at what must have been the age of ten at its opening in Israel, at the Zion Cinema in Jerusalem, in all its glory, complete with intermission for ice cream. I knew not, at the time, the Hollywood whence it came, which was summed up by Laurel and Hardy, Disney's *Treasure Island* and *The Wizard of Oz*.

This was, undoubtedly, a worthy successor, though Lasky's Feast of Passover scene occasioned some drollery among the ruder element. After all, its semi-Hassidic intonements were several thousand years out of kilter. But we all loved the Finger of God, the terrible pestilent claw reaching down from the sky to strike down the first-born of Egypt. Memorable too, though we had no idea of its source, the stirring Wagnerian majesty of the score by Elmer Bernstein, thundering and rolling over the hills.

'So let it be written, so let it be done.' Ironically, the film opened in November 1956, just a few days after the cessation of hostilities prompted by Israel's invasion of the Sinai peninsula and the ensuing war with Egypt, part of the British and French scheme to overthrow the Suez Canal-snatching Colonel Nasser. The Egyptian army was smashed, and archaeologists, rabbis and scholars trekked down the peninsula, launching a politically charged argument about the real location of Mount Sinai. Israel was dislodged from the Sinai, after the failure of the British–French 'Suez War', by American pressure.

Even among the inevitable plaudits for the film, there were caveats from some church elements, namely a Reverend Edward O. Miller of New York's Episcopal church – of DeMille's own patrimony – who 'contrasted the "fundamentalism" of the motion picture with what he termed the view of Christianity and Bible scholarship . . . Instead of the Ten Commandments being shown as the product of the "thrilling, centuries-old struggle and yearning of mankind for moral uprightness," he said, they are depicted as cut verbatim into stone tablets by "a sort of spiritual acetylene torch."' In Egypt, the film had already been condemned as early as November 1954 by at least one newspaper, *Al Hillal*, as 'Zionist propaganda'. Taking its lead, curiously, from an anti-Zionist Jewish activist, Alfred Lilienthal, whom DeMille had met at an early press conference, the journal claimed the film 'tries to convince the world that the Sinai Peninsula does not belong to Egypt . . . but that it is a part of Israel . . . This picture will make millions – and these millions will be used to further the Zionist cause . . .' The editor called for the Arab League to convene a conference 'for the purpose of banning this picture in all Islamic and Arabic countries'.

Since the hoo-ha over *The King of Kings*, DeMille was not *persona* most *grata* with American Jewish institutions, but this time some did rush to give him awards: a statuette of Michelangelo's *Moses* from the Cinema Lodge of B'nai B'rith and a citation scroll from the Massachusetts Committee of Catholics, Protestants and Jews. Cecil also got a Grand Lodge Achievement Award from the Masons and a place among the nine Great Living Americans from the United States Chamber of Commerce. The other recipients of this honour in 1957 included an Olympic gold-medal winner, an air-force flyer who had flown at 1,900 miles per hour, the artist Norman Rockwell and one J. J. Warren, of North Brookfield, Massachusetts, breeder of 1956's hen of the year.

For DeMille, the long period of chiselling his film upon those tablets of celluloid was a time of gain and of loss. Early in the process, in 1953, he had lost Gladys Rosson, his right-hand woman and lover for almost his entire lifetime, who died of cancer in June of that year. Then, on 5 March 1955, his brother William died at Playa del Rey, just before the start of the studio shoot of the picture and while Cecil was still recuperating from his heart attack. The newspapers noted the passing of the 'playwright, screen director, producer and author of books and numerous articles for periodicals'. Two hundred people gathered with the family, including Jesse Lasky and colleagues from the University of Southern California's drama department, which William had founded in 1941. His ashes were placed in the Cecil B. DeMille Memorial in Hollywood Memorial Park Cemetery, in the shadow, even after death, of the little brother who had surpassed him.

Later the same month, Cecil's granddaughter Cecilia was formally engaged to Major Abbas El Boughdadly, who had swept her away during the location shoot in Egypt, when he played Pharaoh Yul Brynner's charioteer. They would be married in July in San Francisco in twin ceremonies: a Muslim marriage at the Egyptian consulate and a civil marriage at City Hall. Cecil presumably bit his lip and accepted the edicts of love and fate. In August, there was another wedding, as adopted son Richard de Mille married Margaret Belgrano van Fossen in Pasadena, a second marriage for both. Cecil's bombshell to Richard of his true genesis as William's son remained a family secret until revealed by Richard himself years later.

At the end of the year, the Screen Producers' Guild honoured DeMille with a Milestone Award for his 'historic contributions to the art of the motion picture'. Though *The Ten Commandments* received a host of nominations for the 1956 Academy Awards, it won only one, for visual effects. DeMille was not even nominated for best director. That was won by George Stevens for *Giant*, while best picture was won by *Around the World in 80 Days* – Todd-AO trumping VistaVision. In the higher hokum stakes, DeMille was already a dinosaur.

By 1956, the great furore of the House Un-American Activities Committee's Hollywood hearings had died down, the Hollywood Ten had been released from jail and Senator Joseph McCarthy's blitz on communists everywhere had come and gone. The aftermath was evident in the continued blacklisting of writers who laboured on in a shadowy world of proxy credits. Mainstream Hollywood was well and truly scared off any radical projects and was happy with conformity and family values, with musicals set to plug the gap where social conscience once had a place. Nevertheless, change was not quite banished: there was teenage rebellion, which reared its head with James Dean and gyrated with Elvis Presley. Liberal Hollywood had not died away; it had merely retired to lick its wounds – a fairly long lick, as it turned out. But DeMille's grandiose religio-political drum roll was perhaps an unwelcome reminder of the schism that had scarred the Garden of Eden of the grand celluloid dream.

The Ten Commandments, with all its kitsch Sunday-school *folie de grandeur*, cosmic hokum and deliberately portentous dialogue, retains its place, in the end, as a supreme example of Hollywood craft and professionalism, executed by a director who had developed that craft from the earliest days of his experiments with form and content at the Lasky 'barn' in 1914. DeMille wanted to inspire his audience, and certainly people responded in many ways to the grand spectacle he had provided, but his desires as a lay preacher of moviedom and his visceral instincts as a film-maker may not have been as synchronous as he might claim.

When all is said and done and one sits down to experience the apotheosis of Cecil B. DeMille as it unfolds on the screen, one might be struck, not by the vision of the achievement of freedom, but by the sheer savagery of the piece. Against the brutality of the tyrant, Rameses-Stalin, with his whip-wielding thugs, chains and forced-labour battalions, the God of the burning bush and the fiery mountain deploys his panoply of violent retribution: his ten plagues, his random despoliation of the kingdom, his ethnic slaughter of the Egyptian first-born, the blood smeared on the lintels of the Hebrews' houses a potent ancient symbol of separation and exclusion. Pharaoh's arrogance in clinging to his false gods is, as in the source, the root of all evil. Fear of the Lord is the governing force. When the errant Children of Israel, as Moses' brother Aaron says in the Book of Exodus, 'are set on mischief', DeMille's Moses cries at them: 'Those who will not live by the Law, shall die by the Law!' And so an entire generation is condemned. These can hardly be said to be a people who, in any modern sense of the term, have a 'free' will. They require the divine whip to lash them towards their destiny.

One might ponder future events, as an America fifty years on from DeMille's epoch unleashed its own neo-divine thunderbolts against other tyrants in the same crucible of the ancient near east.

EPILOGUE

'A Man Is No Better Than What He Leaves Behind Him'

In *The Ten Commandments*, the 'Voice of God' – an electronic amalgam of the voices of Charlton Heston and DeMille – intoned, when asked to identify itself: 'I AM THAT I AM . . .' And when asked what message there was for the Children of Israel, the voice answered: 'Thou shalt say . . . I AM hath sent me unto you.'

DeMille was *sui generis*, an original voice that decided at the end to settle on being a megaphone for what he saw as scriptural truth. In his speech accepting his Milestone Award in 1956, DeMille argued for a historical understanding of his profession and his craft, for the preservation of its classics and for an understanding of its impact around the world:

When leaders of nations tell us, as the highest officials of Egypt and Burma have told me – that as boys they derived their conception of the world, their ideas of right and wrong, from American motion pictures, they bring home to us our awe-inspiring responsibility. It is a sobering thought that the decisions we make at our desks in Hollywood may intimately affect the lives of human beings, men, women and children throughout the world . . .

As an innocent American abroad, DeMille may have taken the polite comments of his hosts far too seriously, or perhaps he realized that they masked a deeper psychological truth. Today, we take Hollywood America's hegemony of ideas for granted, beside a host of influences from other elements of American popular culture that are flung out by the long arms of huge corporations. But DeMille was ever anxious, in his rhetoric, to square the circle of art and Mammon:

We are responsible as artists and as molders of men's thoughts.

We have a duty to our art and a duty to the audiences for whom we make our pictures . . .

We must keep these two responsibilities clearly in view all the time. If we do that we may be able to keep our industry free of the forces which threaten to corrupt it from within and the forces which threaten to cramp and stifle it from without.

Our greatest danger from within the industry is the worship of the golden calf – the temptation to care nothing about what we put on the screen as long as it makes money.

Of course, DeMille agreed, any business must make a profit, but even if vice makes a higher profit than virtue, it would be 'treason to the human spirit – and treason to the art we serve' to succumb. Life, he declared, 'is a warfare between good and evil', and the dramatic film-maker must portray both and oppose the censorship which would reduce all narrative to a 'sentimentalized . . . untrue picture of human existence'. This depiction of the grand drama of good and evil, in motion pictures, was his life's work, 'and every foot of it in film, and every minute of it in time, has been an adventure which I would not exchange for anything else in the world'.

DeMille saw himself and his art as a Light Unto Nations, with a declared goal of 'promoting the concepts of brother-hood regardless of race and religion'. In this, he was more of a politician than a film-maker, prone to demagogic statements that could hardly stand the test of a close view of his work. His life, as his niece, Agnes de Mille, pointed out in an extended review of his life in *Esquire* magazine in 1964, was riddled with contradictions:

He was the most famous person in Hollywood; yet he seldom mixed in any public shenanigans, the gala openings, restaurants, parties, and such. He kept absolutely to his own circle. He went home nights.

He made illicit sex and tangled marital arrangements a national export; yet he himself, although wreathed with rumors like Jupiter's brow, remained fixed beside his wife . . . He introduced exoticism into the national domestic décor, but the bathtubs in his own house were plain, straight, white, and for cleanliness only . . .

He prided himself on being a profound biblical scholar, and a great part of his career was devoted to dramatizing and propagandizing the Old Testament, but he never once cast a recognisable Jew in any role except to portray villainy.

He skirted plain obscenity in his work, but he remained, in his speech before women, always prudish, and considered Ernest Hemingway and D. H. Lawrence salacious . . .

He could be the hardest and the most terrifying man I have ever met, yet he sat beside many a deathbed because in the last moments it was his voice that was needed for comfort, his strength and his faith. People called for him when they were dying . . .

He himself expired on 21 January 1959, having suffered a second, more serious heart attack on 18 June 1958, just two days after testifying yet again to Congress in Washington against union restrictions and the 'right to work'. On 12 August, his seventy-seventh birthday, he had attended another honorary lunch at Paramount studios. He had continued to plan and talk up future productions since the wrap of *The Ten Commandments*. There was the continuing project of a film on Baden-Powell and the founding of the Boy Scout movement, to be produced and possibly directed by Henry Wilcoxon, though scripting had not even begun. There was 'Project X', an epic on space exploration that DeMille himself would direct. This had no script either. There was a Jesse Lasky Sr project called 'The Big Brass Band', but Lasky himself died in 1958. One last project was completed under Cecil's nominal supervision: a remake of *The Buccaneer*, with Yul Brynner in the Jean Lafitte role, and directed, for lack of anyone else, by Anthony Quinn. The result was a lacklustre mess that only worsened his heart condition. Charles Higham describes him screaming with rage as he surveyed the film's rushes.

But there were to be yet more honours: the Exalted Order of the White Elephant from the King of Thailand, a junior high school in Long Beach named after him, civic honours in Berlin, the French Legion of Honour and a Paris Medal of Honour in October 1957, Man of the Year from the Salvation Army, the 1958 'Fame' Award of Achievement, etc., etc., etc.

A laudatory article in the *Los Angeles Times* in May 1958 was headlined: 'C.B. DeMILLE – CAESAR IN TOUCH WITH PEOPLE'. The quality he had that people most overlooked, said fellow movie pioneer Sam Goldwyn, was 'repose'. Even after his heart attack, he would rise at his home at 9 a.m., breathe deeply for a few moments and then do 'his regular 12 morning pushups. Feeling refreshed, as he says, he then started hoisting dumbbells, 26 times with a pair weighing 12 pounds and 26 times with a lighter pair.' After that, the usual lunch at the Paramount commissary, 'where he greeted his guests – two ranking German industrialists, two Camaldolese hermit monks, two Boy Scout leaders, two nuns, a schoolteacher from Cape Town,

South Africa, and a 40-year-old woman fan from Ohio, who immediately handed him two poems about herself to read – "So you will know me better."' There were still periods of retreat to the 'Paradise' ranch, but whatever energetic goings-on had enlivened it in the past, it was now just a place for rest. DeMille 'went for a walk through his private wilderness with some 30 deer following . . . thinking ahead to his next picture . . .'

In August, he was photographed together with Anne Bauchens, his loyal editor since *We Can't Have Everything* in 1918. Most of his long-term harem had passed away in his loyal service. Apart from Bauchens, only Julia Faye, who had been given small parts to the end, e'en unto the *Commandments* (as Elisheba), would outlive him, dying in 1966. Anne Bauchens lasted till 1967. Her contribution to keeping the DeMille narratives flowing, through thick and thin, was incalculable. In 1947, she had told the *New York Times* that *The Ten Commandments* (silent version) was 'the most difficult picture she has had to edit. DeMille used sixteen cameras and shot enough film for ten pictures', a task for the editor which could 'lead you to one of three things, fame, drink or the nearest psychiatrist.' She added: 'That is why there are only eight women cutters in Hollywood . . . they die young . . .'

Neither she nor her boss, however, suffered that fate. After attending the New York premiere of the remade *Buccaneer* on 22 December 1958, DeMille returned home, but his condition worsened rapidly. Anne Edwards describes one of his last days, when son-in-law Anthony Quinn came to see him; as Quinn later told Edwards: 'He was dressed in a flannel robe. We sat in the courtyard near the long hall library . . . I knew it was the last time I would see him . . . As I got up to leave . . . I said: "You know in Europe I learned a very nice thing! . . . Men hug each other on saying good-bye." I took the frail man in my arms. He made a feeble attempt to hug me. In that minute out of twenty-odd years we became father and son . . .' And then he was gone. He died with Cecilia and her husband, Joseph Harper, by his bedside.

And there were eulogies galore: 'Movies Lose a Monarch'; 'Entire City Pays Tribute' in Los Angeles. Hedda Hopper: 'We'll never see his like again.' The ceremony at St Stephen's Episcopal Church in Hollywood was simple, but the entombment was in the $250,000 mausoleum he had endowed for himself and his family in the lake section of Hollywood Memorial Park Cemetery. His wife, Constance, was eighty-five and 'unable to attend the funeral services', as she was said to be confined to her bed at the time – in fact, unable to comprehend the news. A thousand people gathered inside and out-side the church, a 'Who's Who' of Hollywood, from Alfred Hitch-cock down. Pallbearers included Sam Goldwyn, Henry Wilcoxon, Henry Noerdlinger, lawyer Neil McCarthy and Adolph Zukor, him-self eighty-six years old. The Reverend Owings recited 'selected read-ings from an old bible given to Mr. DeMille when he was eleven years old'. The readings included verses from the Epistle to the Romans and the Gospel according to St John and the 91st and 121st Psalms: 'He that dwelleth in the secret place of the most High shall abide under the shadow of the Almighty.'

In his will, DeMille left the bulk of his multimillion-dollar estate to his daughter Cecilia and the rest to his three adopted children and their children. 'The producer's will left nothing to his widow Constance, but it stated his love, respect and admiration for her and said she was already provided for.' Cecilia filed for guardianship of her mother, whom she said was 'incompetent to handle her own affairs' because of 'old age and mental deterioration'. Constance died on 17 July 1960, succumbing finally to pneumonia.

Among the many condolences for DeMille, from friends, peers and public figures – including one from 'all his friends in the F.B.I.' deliv-ered by J. Edgar Hoover – was a short one-liner by Jerry Lewis: 'Heaven's gain is our loss.'

What then might be the verdict of the recording officer standing at the other end of the lost bridge of *Feet of Clay*? Would there be the usual balance of good and bad deeds, or a massive clippings file of reviews, from *Variety*, the *Hollywood Reporter*, the *New York Times*, all the way down to the *San Jose Courier*?

In his life, he could have been, apart from a movie director, many things: piratical entrepreneur, airline pioneer, banker, engineer, politi-cian – state governor, even presidential candidate? In truth, he lacked an attribute absolutely vital for a working politician: the willingness to sell out when expediency requires, to compromise for power alone, to play the long game. He was always impatient for results, and although he could bide his time when necessary and navigate the thorny deal-making back rooms of the movie business, he would always demand to be back as soon as possible in the thick of the action on the set.

He was a doer, not a talker, and this was evident from his stage days, when he discovered, more by error than trial, that he was not in fact destined for fame as a writer. Writing was brother William's forte and passion, and the younger brother, as younger brothers do, sought to emulate him. William was an intellectual and social moralist, and so Cecil thought he should be too. The Henry Georgian and Charles Kingsleyan ideas did seep into his work, but they were soon sidelined in the Champion Driver's overwhelming urge for drama and action. And yet he became the more acute observer, in the language of images, of the absurdities and sub-terfuges and mendacities of the social scene. He portrayed America's rush to a new consumerist paradise after the First World War, but his own relatively easy access to fame set him apart from that desperate scramble, and the sermons of his nineteenth-century father began beating a louder and louder drum roll of disapproval of the devil-may-careness of the age in his mind. In the end, there was no alter-native for all those drunken, hedonistic, bemasked jazz babies but to parachute out of a lightning-struck Zeppelin over their Gomorrah, New York.

When Cecil, as a sideline to his doing, did begin to talk, as union scourge and anti-communist ranter, he spoke, in the main, demagogic nonsense, though the current generation of American political evan-gelists might do well to canonize him as a precursor of their latest chapter in patriotic 'manifest destiny'. For those who recall the days of the Hollywood blacklist, DeMille is counted as one of those who stood aside, already installed in the enemy's tent, opening a flap now and then to his own quarters for some forbidden cast member that he nevertheless required. Though he never testified formally to the HUAC, at other ceremonial banquets he was turning the spit on which America's enemies, real or imagined, were roasted.

But there comes the question always posed in the sound-bite world of instant analysis: What was he really like? Was he really the tyrant of legend, bullying his staff, vulgarizing both sex and religion, the 'Sol Hogwasch' of a British columnist's satire, 'who is always yearn-ing to slip a chariot race into his current "mammoth" production of "Wuthering Heights"'? The 'Siegfried of Sex'? Or was he at heart a simple family man, never happier than when at home with his devoted wife and grandchildren, a benign patriarch who in Richard de Mille's memoir was someone who always showed his love for his children, adopted or not: 'He sort of looked at you, and you felt included'?

Like every man of charisma, he inspired great loyalty, even among those, like his writers, whom he repeatedly browbeat and scolded like recalcitrant children. As many of his long-term crew members and staff recalled, he became like a father to them, perhaps more aptly like an old-time shepherd of his flock.

What did all these tantrums and sudden demonstrations of power reflect? Was he, paradoxically, a man with deep feelings of inadequacy? Shall we deploy Freud to fathom his extremes of Old Testament wrath and New Testament forbearance? With so massive an ego, how great the id?

Setting long-distance psychoanalysis aside, this might not be a difficult question to answer. Cecil Blount DeMille was brought up in an age and an environment in which religion was a natural part of nurture: to any devout monotheist, man is a puny, inadequate being faced with the perfection and awesome power of the Almighty. His path in life involves gaining an understanding of his inadequacy and the struggle to find an answer to the age-old question: How should I live my life? The challenge posed by the religious to the secular in an age of 'enlightenment' then became: If religion ceases to be your moral compass, what, then, is? DeMille decided, like Dostoyevsky, that if God is dead, all is permitted, and he inveighed against this from the 1920s onwards. In the end, like a sulphur and brimstone pastor, he could only stand firm upon his mountain peak and thunder out: 'The Law is the Law!'

And yet he broke at least one of the Ten Commandments repeatedly: Thou Shalt Not Commit Adultery. As is the case with transgressors, there were many excuses and implied licences from his legally wedded wife for his personally sanctioned harem. In this, no doubt, DeMille was a hypocrite, as he was a hypocrite when he held forth at rich people's dinner parties about the evil of unions that sought by means he decided were, in his own commercial interests, illegitimate, to improve workers' earnings and conditions.

One might point out that a man who needs to browbeat his wife by leaping on top of the furniture, or to allow the bully in his heart to trump the compassionate husband could be said, in some sense, to lack confidence. As one may recall from the anguished letter Cecil sent his wife before setting out on his film career, in which he held forth about his rampaging sexual demons, there was a peculiar honesty in this marriage typical of the private contracts married people make for reasons that abide in their hearts. As DeMille's children recalled, their mother was a virtual saint, continually ministering to others, fulfilling the most infuriating archetype of modern feminist antipathy. Whatever her own hidden doubts about all this, she carried them with her to the grave.

As for his own sexual kinks, however they were played out in the bedroom with his lovers and whatever the speculation about his famous 'foot fetish', the more revealing aspects are, as I have argued, there for all to see in his films. From the threat of eye gouging in 1915's *The Unafraid*, the torture and burning at the stake of *Joan the Woman*, the rape by the soldiers in *The Little American*, the desert-island disrobings of *Male and Female* – with the fantasy martyrdom of Gloria Swanson – the great hairy-chested slavemaster of the first *Ten Commandments*, the despoliation of *The Volga Boatman*, the sadistic warders of *The Godless Girl* and through to the whippings, tethered girls and dwarves spitted by Amazons in *The Sign of the Cross* and beyond, the DeMille world is full of undressed and tormented women and bare-chested men heaving in some agonized lust, whether it be of power or religious fervour. Indeed, if one wishes to indulge in current obsessions with gender mystification, one might enquire into the significance of DeMille's casting sessions in 1956, in which male aspirants to various roles in *The Ten Commandments* were required to remove their shirts, or the import of the heaving torsos of Moses, Pharaoh, Joshua *et al.*, the latter nicely subject to the lash of Vincent Price. But one must leave this to the scalpels of professional film theorists, ever ready to apply wild speculation, whether the shoe fits or not.

Suffice to say that, between sex and God, Cecil B. DeMille found a niche that was uniquely his own. And in this regard the accusations of vulgarity, coarseness, exploitation and disingenuity which have always dogged him are, I think, somewhat beside the point. It is the essence of religion, whether monotheistic or otherwise, to regard the control and governance of sexual desire as one of its foremost principles and aims. And clearly, the only way to prevent Nefretiri leaping upon Charlton Heston's bare nipples or Vincent Price lashing his

Joshuas without restraint is to deploy divine intervention, the same Ten Commandments that are, without equivocation, THE LAW. And if DeMille himself has special dispensation from any part of this, it is, no doubt, by dint of his devotion to the rest. In this too, alas, he was a true pastor, if not obviously a perfect one.

In the end, as one always seeks to arrive at some summation, we can note that DeMille wrote his own epitaph, in the heading of his Milestone Award lecture: 'A Man Is No Better Than What He Leaves Behind Him.' It appears to me self-evident that what is important in the life of any artist is the art. For someone like DeMille, with his seventy films directed over a period of forty-two years, his voracious appetite for work and non-stop application, what is left after the gossip about his private life abates can only be the films themselves: a celluloid cathedral of the Hollywood that he in large part created and shaped.

But what was left behind was also an idea, and I have tried to trace the path by which DeMille, who at one time was the epitome of American exploitation and the movie guru of its developing consumer society, turned into a maverick who worked from the hub of that commercialization to cast his thunderbolt warnings of divine retribution. These bolts were cast out of a historical tradition that preceded urban America, the 'graven images' of photography and the cinema, the Golden Calves of great corporate concerns, 'all manner of ungodliness' and material heresies. This idea, of America as not only a frontier society but a reprise of the biblical narrative of rebirth and revelation, was endemic in much of the nation's religious discourse from earliest pioneer times, most strikingly in the Mormon replication of the Exodus in the brethren's march through the wilderness towards a new Promised Land. But in the cinema it was DeMille who defined it, with the formidable power and mass distribution of all the resources of corporate communication, the 'media' that envelops global culture in our own day.

In 1955, when DeMille wrote to the Fraternal Order of Eagles about the primal significance of the Ten Commandments and their eternal answer to the question of how we should live, he was plugged into an existing project of the Order. This was the distribution of thousands of framed versions of the Ten Commandments to the Order's various 'aeries' and to juvenile, district and municipal courts, as well as to politicians, business leaders, ex-President Truman and

Pope Pius XII. DeMille, never one to pass up a promotional opportunity, agreed with the Eagles to expand the project into a series of stone monuments to be placed in courthouses throughout the land. Paramount chipped in by offering the presence of leading actors to unveil the monuments, and in return the Fraternal Order of Eagles 'urged its members to support the Ten Commandments movie'.

The monoliths were made of Carnelian granite, the closest that could be found to genuine Mount Sinai stone, and featured the Commandments, the American flag and eagle, the all-seeing eye of God superimposed on a triangle (the basic masonic sign), two stars of David and the Greek monogram Chi-Rho, the Christ. They were four, five and six feet tall, the largest weighing 2,500 lbs. In keeping with the agreement, Charlton Heston presided over the unveiling of one monolith in North Dakota, and Yul Brynner over another in Milwaukee. Eventually, up to 4,000 stones were placed in various civic centres and courthouses all over the US.

Half a century later, nationwide controversy broke out over these very stones. Civil Liberties Unions in several states began legal proceedings to declare them unconstitutional, violations of the separation between church and state. In Duluth, Nebraska, Kentucky and Austin, Texas, the secular and the religious warred over the monuments. In 2004, the United States Supreme Court took up the Austin case, and religious conservatives rose to the challenge: 'The Ten Commandments could be the [biggest] blockbuster religious liberty case that the Supreme Court has seen in a really long time . . . it's finally here,' declared Mathew Staver, of the Kentucky Liberty Council.

On the other side of the argument, a liberal cleric, the Reverend Barry W. Lynn of Americans United for Separation of Church and State, affirmed that 'the Ten Commandments is a religious document. Its display is appropriate in the houses of worship but not at the seat of government.'

And so disunity, bitter contention, discord, pious wrath and anger over a clash of principles washed in a sea of rage over the arena in which Cecil B. DeMille had wished to implant the ideas of a consensual law, respect for mutually agreed values, national harmony and freedom from strife.

His film legacy, intriguingly, is also divisive. Once the King of Hollywood, he has been often excoriated as excessively old-fashioned, a tyrant, an overblown windbag and faker whose movies lacked humanity and whose idea of freedom was the freedom to do as he liked for his own aggrandizement and profit alone. British critic Gilbert Adair wrote in 1999 that 'he "filled in" the Bible as an infant fills in a colouring book, selecting only the gaudiest and most lurid of hues . . . There does exist one cinematic genre that would seem to be absolutely moribund: the biblical spectacle. Not only is it inconceivable that another will ever be made, but it's almost equally inconceivable that anyone will now care to take another look at those, DeMille's included, that have already been made.'

Of course, the critic wrote those words before our world was shaken by a renewed battle of religious fervours, between the old east and the 'new-old' zealots of a Christian America, and before the resurgence of 'faith-based' cinema in Mel Gibson's *The Passion of the Christ*, a film that out-lurids anything DeMille might have conceived, but with none of his prodigious pictorial skill. As I have tried to show, DeMille's biblical films form just one peak in a mountain range of movies, most of them still wreathed in the fog of lost memory that has yet to be fully recovered. Once the fog clears, one can see the full extent of the achievement, from the dynamic play of experimentation in the new full-length 'feature' motion picture through to the dazzling marriage of social satire and commerce, the largely unsung masterpieces of the early 1920s and the beautifully wrought epic *The King of Kings*. DeMille embraced this journey with enormous vigour, displaying a level of energy uncommon even in that time of discovery, when the art was malleable, the craft was being developed and each new day dawned like an explorer's morning.

One does not have to agree with the political views of any artist to evaulate and appreciate the art. Much depends on how narrow your choice is of who you are willing to learn from. For myself, I am certainly an opponent of the ideas DeMille propagated in his 'Crusade for Freedom' in the 1940s and 1950s. I find much of his behaviour in this period loathsome and offensive. His was one of many prominent but reckless voices that laid the ground for the assault by Senator Joseph McCarthy on the rights of employment and free speech of so many American citizens and so many of DeMille's fellow workers in film, television and radio. And yet the films of his own great Golden Age have been an unexpected joy to discover, an undervalued treasure trove of totally achieved, totally controlled movies that defined his own peculiar America in his own peculiar way – before he 'found the truth'. And once he had found his 'truth,' he began the long decline, which nevertheless was punctuated with majestic flourishes that will, with their own distinctive skill and manner, stand a more rigorous and long-sighted test of time.

The granite stones may well be removed from the courthouses, but the intangible echoes of those many strange, uplifting, infuriating, perplexing narratives, with their raw emotions and often bemused characters dancing in the puppet show of their outrageous master of ceremonies, will endure as long as the movies themselves – in whatever form or medium our own technological Golden Calves might mutate them into – will endure.

SELAH.

And the rest is beams of light, in the dark . . .

APPENDICES

Acknowledgements

This is an unauthorized biography, my first attempt at this particular creature. The estate of Cecil B. DeMille informed me that it could not assist me in my endeavour. Thus informed, my publishers and I decided to construct our tale from the voluminous amount of primary information available in the public domain. The family archive, domiciled in Provo, Utah, has been in any case well grazed by previous scholars, and retains no significant secrets. DeMille's mighty pyramid of production files, irrascible notes to fellow film people and primary texts have either been published or are duplicated in other archives. I am thus indebted to the usual suspects in the following archives: to Barbara Hall and all who man the ship at the Margaret Herrick Library at the Academy of Arts and Sciences in Los Angeles; to Rod Bladel and crew at New York Public Library's Performing Arts archive; and to staff at the BFI in London. As our decision has been to relate DeMille's saga largely through his films, I am indebted to staff at the BFI's film archive; to Mark Quigley and staff at the University of California at Los Angeles; to Rosemary Hanes and staff at the Library of Congress Motion Picture Division; to Ned Comstock at the Film and Television Library at the University of Southern California; and in particular to Jared Case at Eastman House in Rochester, New York, for opening my eyes to the marvels and curiosities of Cecil B. DeMille's largely unseen silent oeuvre. A special debt of gratitude is acknowledged to Pat Silver-Lasky, author of *Screenwriting for the 21st Century*, for opening up the files on Jesse Lasky Jr and much raconteurship and good advice on that pivotal period in Hollywood and in DeMille's career. Thanks as ever to the indefatigable Joel Finler in London, to Clyde Jeavons and, as ever, to Mairi, who doesn't like Cecil B. DeMille. 'Unauthorization' has in any case freed me to make my own judgements of DeMille both as man and film-maker and to explore his manifold contradictions and complexities without fear or favour, to the best of my abilities.

Photographs and illustrations courtesy of the Joel Finler Collection;

the British Film Institute; Library of Congress Motion Pictures Division; Getty Images. Movie 'lobby cards' courtesy of Pat Silver-Lasky, from the Jesse L. Lasky Jr Collection.

Notes on Sources

Abbreviations

AMPAS: Margaret Herrick Library, Academy of Motion Picture Arts and
Sciences, Los Angeles.
BFI: British Film Institute Library, London.
LOC: Library of Congress, Motion Picture Division.
MPN: *Motion Picture News*.
MPW: *Moving Picture World*.
NYDM: *New York Dramatic Mirror*.
NYPL: New York Public Library of the Performing Arts, New York.
NYT: *New York Times*.
USC: University of Southern California Doheny Library.

Prologue

xi 'Yesterday was the Exodus . . .' Charlton Heston papers, AMPAS.
xii 'There were thirty-eight . . .' Hortense Myers and Ruth Burnett, *Cecil
B. DeMille, Young Dramatist*, Bobs-Merrill Co. Inc., 1963, p. 193.
xii 'an old pre-revolutionary house . . .' Anne Edwards, *The DeMilles. An
American Family*, Collins, 1988, p. 21.
xiii 'We were moving slowly . . .' etc., *Photoplay*, December 1919.
xiii 'I am a great believer . . .' ibid.

Chapter 1

3 'The first DeMil house . . .' Cecil B. DeMille, *Autobiography*, W. H.
Allen, London, 1960, p. 5.
4 'in which she played . . .' etc., Anne Edwards, op. cit., p. 14.
5 'You all remember the story . . .' NYPL, Henry De Mille folder.
6 'August 12th my little boy . . .' etc., DeMille, op. cit., p. 2, 3.
6 'I do not for a moment . . .' NYDM, 17 October 1891, NYPL.
7 'The first thing to be accomplished . . .' NYT, 24 June 1888.
7 'a scene representing . . .' NYPL, clippings.
7 'PRAIRIE F. . . .' *The Main Line*, from *The Plays of Henry DeMille*
(*America's Lost Plays series*), Indiana University Press, 1940, p. 3.
8 'Gas lamps were ingeniously concealed . . .' quoted in Craig
Timberlake, *The Bishop of Broadway, The Life & Work of David
Belasco*, Library Publisher, New York, 1954, p. 60.

9 'Mr. DeMille discovered . . .' etc., *The Illustrated American*, 4 March 1893, NYPL.

10 'From the calf love . . .' ibid.

10 'parted from her lover . . .' etc., *Brooklyn Daily Eagle*, 6 November 1890, NYPL.

11 'the war of classes . . .' etc., NYT, 18 August 1891, NYPL.

11 'to the place of great distinction . . .' David Belasco, *The Theatre Through Its Stage Door*, Harper & Bros, 1919, p. 94.

11 'died in his prime . . .' *Brooklyn Daily Eagle*, 12 February 1893, NYPL.

Chapter 2

13 'Mother made each of us . . .' DeMille, op. cit., p. 37.

13 'the combined advantages . . .' etc., clipping, NYPL.

14 'When Mr De Mille died . . .' etc., *New York Sun*, 5 March 1905, NYPL.

15 'He worked with untiring patience . . .' ibid.

15 'Have thy tools read . . .' Charles Kingsley, quotes (various websites).

16 'He lived and worked . . .' essay by Agnes George de Mille on www.progress.org/books/george.html.

16 'Theoretically the man is utterly backward . . .' letter to Friedrich Sorge, 30 June 1881, quoted on *www.cooperativeindividualism.org/marx_henrygeorge.html*.

17 'was a state occasion . . .' Anne Edwards, op. cit., p. 32.

17 'ingeniously arranged . . .' etc., DeMille, *Autobiography*, ibid., p. 40,41.

18 'Cecil found the house . . .' Hortense Myers and Ruth Burnett, op. cit., pp. 108–9.

19 'If something isn't done soon . . .' ibid., pp. 117–8.

19 'When I was nine . . .' quoted in Richard de Mille, *My Secret Mother, Lorna Moon*, Farrar Straus & Giroux, New York, 1998, p. 25.

20 'written a play that is . . .' *New York Sun*, 5 March 1905, NYPL.

20 'Kind-hearted publicists who . . .' DeMille, op. cit., p. 44.

20 'Miss Rebecca Adams . . .' NYT, 17 August 1902, NYPL.

20 'kept down to family members . . .' Anne Edwards, op. cit., p. 35.

21 'Although the weather . . .' NYT, 31 March 1903, NYPL.

Chapter 3

22 'intelligent effort . . .' NYT, 5 February 1905, NYPL.

22 'a pleasant antidote . . .' Glen Hughes, *A History of the American Theatre 1700–1950*, Samuel French, New York, 1951, p. 339.

23 'a charming, modest man . . .' Brooks Atkinson, *Broadway*, Limelight Editions, 1985, p. 54.

23 'The ideal play . . .' NYT, 15 September 1907, NYPL.

24 'Billy: What's up . . .' William de Mille, *Strongheart*, playbook, NYPL.

24 'somewhat rather tiresome "race question" . . .' NYT, 31 January 1905, NYPL.

24 'Cecil B. DeMille was capital . . .' clipping, September 1905, NYPL.

25 'Marie: Are you the bearer . . .' *The Pretender*, playbook, NYPL.

26 'DeMille worked for two . . .' *The Bookman*, February 1907, NYPL.

26 'Scene: The Desert . . .' etc., *Son of the Winds*, playbook, NYPL.

27 'wooden railroad coaches . . .' etc., DeMille, *Autobiography*, ibid., p. 48.

27 'against an interesting background . . .' etc., *New York Sun*, 5 March 1905, ibid., NYPL.

29 '[It is] the story of . . .' clipping, *New York Mirror*, 1906, NYPL.

29 'All along there are laughs . . .' NYT, 2 October 1906, NYPL.

30 'JACK: Of all the concentrated . . .' *The Genius*, playbook, NYPL.

30 'Cecil was barely twenty-one . . .' etc., Richard de Mille, op. cit., p. 18.

Chapter 4

32 'wild shrieking melodrama . . .' etc., *America's Lost Plays*, Vol. XVIII (David Belasco), Indiana University Press, 1965 (1940), p. 172.

33 'Mary Pickford . . .' etc., NYT, 4 December 1907, NYPL.

33 'It was my fortune . . .' David Belasco, op. cit., p. 163.

33 'Romantic impulse . . .' ibid., p. 166.

33 'clever man . . .' etc., George Jean Nathan, *Legend's End, David Belasco*, 1917. Quoted in *The American Theatre as Seen by Its Critics*, Montrose J. Moses and John Mason Brown (Eds), W. W. Norton & Co., New York, 1934.

34 'The great American play? . . .' *The Bookman*, February 1907, NYPL.

34 'There are four stages to a murder . . .' NYT, 7 April 1908, NYPL.

34 'I felt the same . . .' etc., *The Royal Mounted*, playbook, NYPL.

35 'O'Brian: Oh, Major . . .' ibid.

35 'A Story-Book Play . . .' NYT, 7 April 1908, NYPL.

36 'You and I are worthy . . .' etc., *The Stampede*, playbook, NYPL.

36 'The roar of the stampeding cattle . . .' ibid.

37 'a beautiful dragonfly . . .' DeMille, op. cit., p. 54.

37 'lovable old Dutchman . . .' NYT, 29 January 1911, NYPL.

37 'a novel by Mrs Oliphant . . .' NYT, 11 February 1911, NYPL.

38 'it is no new thing . . .' quoted in Anne Edwards, op. cit., p. 43.

38 'twenty-five hundred cards . . .' *The Columbia Monthly*, Vol. VIII, April 1911, NYPL.

38 'The Truth of the Unreal . . .' etc., American Academy of Dramatic Arts, 1906, NYPL.

40 'There are many people who think . . .' NYT, 21 April 1907, NYPL.

40 'I think we are on the eve . . .' *The Bookman*, ibid., NYPL.

40 'Money talks . . .' *The Land of the Free*, playbook, NYPL.

41 'Every age has its own code . . .' NYT, 1 October 1911, NYPL.

41 'will make railway . . .' etc., NYT, 20 September 1911, NYPL.

Chapter 5

43 'My daydreams for years . . .' etc., Jesse L. Lasky with Dan Weldon, *I Blow My Own Horn*, Victor Gollancz Ltd, London, 1957, p. 16.

45 'I went to see Mrs. H. C. DeMille . . .' etc., ibid., p. 88.

45 'Cecil and I eyed each other . . .' ibid.

46 'all-satisfying . . .' *The Billboard*, 20 January 1912, NYPL.

46 'In producing "California" . . .' *Pittsburgh Gazette*, 1 December 1911, NYPL.

46 'threatened with demolition . . .' etc., *The Billboard*, 29 November 1913, NYPL.

47 'the story of a swindling antiquarian . . .' NYT, 30 January 1912, NYPL.

47 'One pretty and charming song . . .' *New York Mirror*, 9 October 1912, NYPL.

49 'woman will have gained . . .' NYT, 6 February 1912, NYPL.

49 'Jesse, I'm pulling out . . .' etc., Lasky, *I Blow My Own Horn*, Victor Gollancz, London, 1957, p. 91.

Chapter 6

53 'I told the clerk . . .' etc., Lasky, op. cit., pp. 94–5.

53 'well-known theatrical . . .' MPN, 20 December 1913, BFI.

54 'made a careful study . . .' MPW, 11 July 1914.

55 'multiple reel motion picture . . .' *The Billboard*, 29 November 1913, NYPL.

56 'the moving picture man must try . . .' MPW, 11 July 1914, p. 186.

56 'When contemplating entry . . .' MPW, 11 July 1914, p. 214.

57 'I had seen a few motion pictures . . .' DeMille, op. cit., p. 63.

58 'Ever since the first ingenious . . .' MPW, 3 January 1914, BFI.

60 '1. Mess room . . .' *The Squaw Man*, script, USC.

63 'FIRST LASKY PRODUCTION . . .' MPN, 28 February 1914, BFI.

63 'the touches of great beauty . . .' etc., MPW, 28 February 1914, BFI.

64 'The actors appeared . . .' DeMille, op. cit., p. 82.

Chapter 7

66 'I did not suspect . . .' in Anne Edwards, op. cit., p. 49.

66 'When I first went out . . .' 14 January 1914, NYDM, NYPL.

67 'it was necessary . . .' *New Jersey Times*, 16 January 1914, NYPL.

68 'The piece . . . displayed more novelty . . .' *Vogue*, 15 December 1913, NYPL.

71 'to supply the exhibitor with . . .' MPW, 30 May 1914.

72 'In the heart of the West . . .' etc., on-screen titles, *The Virginian*, 1914.

73 'a deserving success . . .' MPN, 19 September 1914, BFI.

73 'in the main . . .' *Variety*, 11 September 1914, BFI.

74 'William C. DeMille . . .' MPW, 26 September 1914, BFI.

Chapter 8

75 'Suddenly I was in California . . .' etc., William C. de Mille, *Hollywood Saga*, E. P. Dutton & Co., New York, 1939, p. 65.

75 'Flannel shirt, khaki trousers . . .' *New Jersey Star*, 10 July 1915, NYPL.

76 '60,000,000 persons . . .' *New York Record*, 5 February 1915, NYPL.

77 'For the past six months . . .' MPW, 6 June 1914, BFI.

77 'were indeed generous . . .' etc., MPW, 13 June 1914, BFI.

77 'No – absolutely no! . . .' *Movie Pictorial*, 4 July 1914, NYPL.

80 'translation of domestic melodrama . . .' Sumiko Higashi, *Cecil B. DeMille and American Culture: The Silent Era*, University of California Press, 1994, p. 55.

82 'a shining star in the Paramount sky . . .' MPW, 21 November 1914, BFI.

83 '"Hello Bill," he said . . .' etc., William de Mille, *Hollywood Saga*, ibid., p. 67.

83 'If it can go on the screen . . .' DeMille, op. cit., p. 101.

84 'if we showed only half the actor's face . . .' DeMille interview in Kevin Brownlow's *Cecil B. DeMille, An American Epic*, TV documentary, released by Independent Artists, July 2004.

Chapter 9

87 'such a series of . . .' MPW, 27 March 1915, BFI.

87 'of mixed French . . .' etc., Charles Higham, *Cecil B. DeMille*, Dell, 1976, p. 39.

88 'She behaved rather . . .' etc., ibid., p. 40.

90 'My wife's my mistress . . .' Richard de Mille, op. cit., p. 21.

90 'often brought home children . . .' Anne Edwards, op. cit., p. 74.

92 'must express the thoughts . . .' William de Mille, op. cit., p. 22.

92 'Therefore it must deal . . .' ibid., p. 25.

92 'the comedy by-play . . .' *Variety*, 11 June 1915, BFI.

92 'surpasses many of the previous . . .' *Variety*, 18 June 1915, BFI.

93 'some of the finest scenery . . .' MPW, 12 December 1914, BFI.

93 'make a movie version . . .' NYT, 14 February 1915, NYPL.

94 'brought back from her conquests . . .' MPW, 8 May 1915, BFI.

Chapter 10

95 'Tears of Audience . . .' The Billboard, 24 February 1912, NYPL.

95 'Subtitle: "HONEST" HEINE . . .', etc., *Kindling*, script, USC.

98 'The story . . . is extremely morbid . . .' *Variety*, 16 July 1915, BFI.

98 'A Genuine Film Masterpiece . . .' MPW, 3 July 1915, BFI.

99 'Worse than ignorance . . .' ibid.

100 'met at the train . . .' *Photoplay*, August 1915, NYPL.

101 'Cecil de Mille . . . declares Miss Farrar . . .' *Photoplay*, September 1915, NYPL.

102 'As work progressed . . .' etc., Geraldine Farrar, *Such Sweet Compulsion*, The Greystone Press, New York, 1938.

103 'Just twenty years later . . .' William de Mille, *Hollywood Saga*, ibid., p. 154.

105 'minimizing diffuse light . . .' Lea Jacobs, 'Belasco, DeMille and the development of Lasky Lighting', *Film History*, Vol. 5, 1993, BFI.

105 'The producer for the legitimate stage . . .' NYT, 12 September 1915, NYPL.

Chapter 11

107 'in spite of . . .' *Variety*, 31 December 1915, BFI.

107 'The natives won't forget her . . .' MPN, 28 August 1915, NYPL.

108 'Ten million persons . . .' MPN, 9 October 1915, BFI.

110 'I was always taught that . . .' *Motion Picture Magazine*, November 1924.

111 'features like this one . . .' MPW, 25 December 1915, BFI.

111 'here certainly is . . .' *Variety*, 31 December 1915, BFI.

113 'the moral dilemma . . .' Higashi, op. cit., p. 93.

113 'get underneath the veneer of society . . .' NYT, 15 September 1907, NYPL.

114 'fifth in importance . . .' NYT, 2 January 1916, NYPL.

Chapter 12

115 'Aunt Constance gave him his dinner . . .' Agnes de Mille, *Dance to the Piper, Memoirs of the Ballet*, Columbus Books, London, 1987, p. 38.

115 'a residential paradise . . .' *Architectural Digest*, April 1990.

116 'silk Russian blouses . . .' etc., DeMille, op. cit., pp. 152–3.

116 'beautifully bound . . .' Charles Bickford, *Bulls, Balls, Bicycles &*

Actors, Paul S. Eriksson Inc., New York, 1965, p. 172.

116 'before his mother, Bebe . . .' Agnes de Mille, op. cit.

117 'like a Pasha . . .' ibid., p. 40.

117 'represent an outlay . . .' MPN, 11 March 1916, BFI.

120 'DeMille's growing sense of staging . . .' Robert S. Birchard, *Cecil B. DeMille's Hollywood*, The University Press of Kentucky, p. 80.

120 'Mae Murray . . .' MPN, 29 July 1916, BFI.

121 'The title for the picture . . .' MPN, 30 September 1916, BFI.

121 'an absorbing personal story . . .' DeMille, op. cit., p. 155.

124 'a woman of flesh and blood . . .' ibid., p. 155.

124 'Farrar was given . . .' Agnes de Mille, op. cit., p. 20.

125 'To prevent any fakiness . . .' etc., *Photoplay*, January 1917, BFI.

127 'During the burning . . .' Agnes de Mille, op. cit., p. 21.

127 'For my climax at the stake . . .' Geraldine Farrar, op. cit.

128 'above all a director's picture . . .' MPW, 13 January 1917, BFI.

128 'hardened motion picture . . .' *Variety*, 29 December 1916, BFI.

Chapter 13

130 'a Timely, Up-to-the-minute . . .' MPN, 21 April 1917, BFI.

130 'our director-general . . .' Jesse L. Lasky, op. cit., p. 111.

130 'we'll commission you if . . .' etc., DeMille, op. cit., p. 176.

131 'There were two places . . .' Jesse L. Lasky, op. cit., p. 111.

133 'pout for effect . . .' *Variety*, 18 May 1917, BFI.

136 'Prominent foreign film men . . .' MPN, 16 June 1917, BFI.

136 'Ages ago . . .' *The Woman God Forgot*, script, USC.

137 'When I first saw Kosloff . . .' Agnes de Mille, op. cit., p. 52.

138 'the feathered attire of the men and women . . .' etc., Geraldine Farrar, op. cit.

Chapter 14

140 'she went to the victim's home . . .' Agnes de Mille, op. cit., p. 38.

141 'Our decision to spend . . .' MPN, 29 September 1917, BFI.

141 'Sixteen hours is frequently . . .' MPN, 3 November 1917, BFI.

142 'suggestive settings . . .' MPW, 21 July 1917, BFI.

142 'The present obvious method . . .' MPW, 21 July, BFI.

143 'Fade in. Int . . .' *The Whispering Chorus*, script, USC.

147 'Tremble, holding the single rose . . .' ibid.

148 'as a feature production . . .' *Variety*, 5 April 1918, BFI.

148 'We have found out it isn't necessary . . .' MPW, 21 July 1917, BFI.

149 'Simplicity, directness . . .' 'Topics in Stageland', 17 March 1918, unsourced clipping, NYPL.

149 'What the public demands today . . .' quoted in DeMille, op. cit., p. 193.

Chapter 15
153 'Seymour bathing suits will be . . .' *Theatre* magazine, February 1919, NYPL.
154 'Police Take Notice . . .' MPN, 20 April 1918, BFI.
155 'Peace for the Exhibitor . . .' MPN, 7 December 1918, BFI.
156 'Cecil B. DeMille nearly starved . . .' *New Jersey Telegraph*, 29 September 1918, NYPL.
160 'All the characters are drawn . . .' MPN, 8 June 1918, BFI.
160 'An admirable product . . .' *Variety*, 31 May 1918, BFI.
161 'the society which revolves around . . .' MPN, 20 July 1918, BFI.
162 'Think it very serious . . .' Jesse L. Lasky Collection, AMPAS, Los Angeles.

Chapter 16
163 'I had come to see Gloria Swanson's clothes . . .' *Picture Play* magazine, March 1919, NYPL.
164 'Mr Goodstadt started to tell me . . .' etc., Gloria Swanson, *Swanson on Swanson, An Autobiography*, Michael Joseph, London, 1980, p. 93.
166 'Gorgeous Gowns . . .' etc., MPN, 1 February 1919, BFI.
168 'The most moving scene . . .' Goria Swanson, op. cit., p. 102.
169 'as the middle class became more immersed . . .' Sumiko Higashi, op. cit., p. 155.
170 'worked in some good sex stuff . . .' *Variety*, 30 April 1920, BFI.
170 'He [DeMille] stimulates a keen . . .' *Photoplay*, December 1920, BFI.
171 'Women get into a habit of picking . . .' ibid.
172 'It's amazing . . .' etc., *Photoplay*, May 1921, BFI.

Chapter 17
174 'The vast majority of our younger set . . .' *Photoplay*, August 1919, BFI.
176 'it looks as if the Cecil B. DeMille . . .' *Variety*, 2 May 1919, BFI.
177 'Millions Invested . . .' MPN, 9 August 1919, BFI.
178 'Santa Cruz Island . . .' *Picture Play* magazine, October 1919, NYPL.
178 'It would not be good taste . . .' J. M. Barrie, *The Admirable Crichton* (1902), from *The Plays of J. M. Barrie*, Hodder & Stoughton, London, 1928.
178 'LORD LOAM: Can't you see . . .' ibid.
179 'Crichton (to Lady Mary): A king! . . .' ibid.
180 'Mr DeMille had saved the most dangerous . . .' Gloria Swanson, op. cit., p. 119.
181 'I could hear the lion breathing . . .' ibid., p. 122.
182 'a velvet tray covered with . . .' ibid., p. 123.

Chapter 18

184 'THE HEART AND SOUL . . .' NYDM, 12 June 1920, NYPL.

188 'has taken upon himself . . .' MPN, 30 October 1920, BFI.

188 'the "faith cure" episode . . .' *Variety*, 22 October 1920, BFI.

188 'all this may be impressive . . .' NYT 18 October 1920, NYPL.

191 'Anatol, an idle young bachelor . . .' Arthur Schnitzler, *Anatol, a Play*, translated 1901(?), from 'Gaslight' website http://gaslight.mtroyal.ab.ca/anatol.htm.

Chapter 19

196 'not a good picture . . .' *Variety*, 26 August 1921, BFI.

196 'power of public opinion . . .' etc., MPN, 23 April 1921, BFI.

197 'people who go out deliberately . . .' introduction to Leonard Merrick's *A Chair on the Boulevard*, from Project Gutenberg website, www.gutenberg.org/dirs/etext06/7chbd10.txt.

203 'alligator den . . .' MPN, 29 April 1922, BFI.

Chapter 20

206 '"Before you were born . . . "' Richard de Mille, op. cit., p. 55.

207 'a very beautiful young lady . . .' DeMille, *Autobiography*, ibid., p. 214.

212 'DeMille at his bizarre best . . .' MPN, 17 February 1923, BFI.

212 "a silly, piffling screen play . . .' *Variety*, 1 March 1923, BFI.

213 'He has been criticized . . .' MPN, 30 December 1922, BFI.

Chapter 21

214 'It's just like we're living in dem times . . .' quoted in 'A Sanctuary out of the Exodus,' by Marshall Weiss, www.jewish-theatre.com/visitor/article_display.aspx?articleID=424.

214 'A quantity of high priced liquor . . .' NYT, 23 February 1923, NYPL.

216 'hydraulic engineers . . .' MPN, 14 July 1923, BFI.

216 'Take dat off'n you . . .' quoted in Marshall Weiss, op. cit.

216 'Old men, infirm of step . . .' ibid.

217 'represented the biggest single . . .' MPN, 14 July 1923, BFI.

220 'stood on a rock . . .' quoted in Marshall Weiss, op. cit.

221 'The scene should look like a group . . .' *The Ten Commandments*, script, USC.

221 'Departed is the picturesque splendor . . .' brochure, Famous Players-Lasky Corporation, 1923, author's collection.

221 'is the garden variety . . .' *Ten Commandments*, 1923 folder, AMPAS, Los Angeles.

222 'a girl who doesn't bother . . .' etc., ibid.

223 'For hours preceding the start . . .' MPN, 5 January 1924, BFI.

224 'the bill for Pharaoh's . . .' DeMille, *Autobiography*, ibid., p. 236.

225 'A great picture . . .' MPN, 5 January 1924, ibid., BFI.

225 'uninspired . . .' NYT, 22 December 1923, NYPL.

225 'mob the box offices . . .' *Variety*, 27 December 1923, BFI.

226 'It took almost a whole day . . .' Anne Edwards, op. cit., p. 10.

226 'Ground-penetrating radar . . .' Associated Press report, 10 November 1999, quoted at www.welcometosilentmovies.com/news/newsarchive/tencommand.htm.

226 'a bottle of Quality and Purity . . .' ibid.

Chapter 22

227 'Putting It Over Right . . .' *Triumph*, press book, Library of Congress (LOC).

228 'the most morbid . . .' MPN, 20 December 1924, BFI.

228 'Nationwide Idea Contest . . .' etc., *Triumph*, press book, op. cit.

229 'Originality and subtlety . . .' NYT, 21 April 1924, NYPL.

229 'to us this is the worst picture . . .' NYT, 27 April 1924, NYPL.

230 'While the wife is away . . .' MPN, 27 September 1924, BFI.

231 'one man told us . . .' NYT, 28 September 1924, NYPL.

231 'Then one sees a shot . . .' etc., ibid.

231 '(*Amy, thinking Kerry dead* . . .)' etc., *Feet of Clay*, script, AMPAS.

233 'real picture! . . .' etc., *Feet of Clay*, press book, LOC.

233 'on purple notepaper . . .' Charles Higham, op. cit., p. 106.

233 'DeMille had turned Catalina . . .' ibid., p. 107.

234 'intended to eliminate waste . . .' MPN, 3 May 1924, BFI.

234 'political censorship is un-American . . .' MPN, 23 August 1924, BFI.

234 'We can do this work together . . .' etc., ibid.

Chapter 23

236 'a dramatic exposé . . .' *The Golden Bed*, press book, LOC.

236 'selling like hot cakes . . .' ibid.

238 'Lillian Rich, Jeanie, and Claire West . . .' Charles Higham, op. cit., p. 111.

239 'Reel 6, Roll 5 . . .' *The Golden Bed*, script, AMPAS.

241 'It is not your (cash) advance . . .' Robert Birchard, op. cit., p. 198.

241 'Mr. DeMille, his wife . . .' NYT, 11 January 1925, NYPL.

241 'I will produce pictures of the same calibre . . .' MPN, 24 January 1925, BFI.

242 'technically, Cecil B. DeMille's fantastic . . .' NYT, 25 January 1925, NYPL.

242 'We are willing to let you have . . .' Robert Birchard, op. cit., p. 202.

243 'make a film on the life of Christ . . .' DeMille, op. cit., p. 245.

243 'a graphic picturization . . .' etc., MPN, 25 July 1925, BFI.

243 'Big in theme . . .' ibid.

244 'one of the most vividly sensational . . .' etc., *The Road to Yesterday*, press book, LOC.

246 'I came away filled with admiration . . .' etc., NYT, 19 July 1925, BFI.

247 'DeMille adheres tenaciously . . .' NYT, 1 December 1925, NYPL.

Chapter 24

248 'Columbia's sword unsheathed . . .' MPN, 19 April 1919, BFI.

248 'First Pictures out of Russia . . .' MPN, 7 July 1923, BFI.

249 'Theodore Kosloff has approached me . . .' letter, 26 September 1921, Adolph Zukor collection, AMPAS.

250 'As to Kosloff . . .' letter, 14 October 1921, ibid.

250 'It reminded me of mankind's . . .' DeMille, op. cit., p. 248.

254 'Feodor demands the privilege . . .' *The Volga Boatman*, press book, LOC.

254 'weird Hollywood dream . . .' NYT, 14 April 1926.

255 'every State in the Union . . .' MPN, 3 April 1926, BFI.

256 'sharp decline . . .' MPN, 13 March 1926.

256 'The Deluge will come as a suggestion . . .' MPN, 17 April 1926, BFI.

256 'The Master-Craftsman . . .' MPN, 29 May 1926, BFI.

Chapter 25

258 'AT NO TIME . . .' brochure, *King of Kings*, author's collection.

259 'Ziegfeld at his most sumptuous . . .' *Played by Ear, the Autobiography of Father Daniel A. Lord, S.J.*, Image Books (Doubleday), 1959, p. 254.

259 'H. B. Warner, playing the part . . .' ibid., pp. 254–5.

259 'He was a strange and fascinating blend . . .' ibid., p. 255.

259 'to treat all classes fairly . . .' quoted in Robert Birchard, op. cit., p. 221.

260 'the most despised character . . .' NYT, 13 June 1926, NYPL.

260 'a love story that would satisfy . . .' *Played by Ear*, op. cit., p. 257.

261 'DeMille at his most DeMill-ish . . .' ibid.

262 'the effeminate, sanctimonious . . .' DeMille, op. cit., p. 253.

262 'walk through make-believe . . .' etc., *Played by Ear*, op. cit., p. 258.

262 'Some of the largest sets . . .' etc., MPN, 6 November 1926, BFI.

263 'tremendous in its lesson . . .' *Variety*, 20 April 1927, BFI.

263 'so reverential is the spirit . . .' NYT, 20 April 1927, NYPL.

263 'the greatest sermon of all time . . .' MPN, 29 April 1927, BFI.

263 'looks predestined . . .' *Variety*, 20 April, ibid.

263 'Filmdom's Most Notable . . .' Hays Office memo, MPPDA *King of Kings* file, AMPAS, Los Angeles.

264 'a competent and attractive young woman . . .' *Dearborn Independent*, 9 April 1927, AMPAS.

264 'you will appreciate the value . . .' MPPDA memo, 12 April 1927, AMPAS.

264 'dean of American rabbis . . .' etc., Felicia Herman. 'The Most Dangerous Anti-Semitic Photoplay in Filmdom', in *The Velvet Light Trap*, No. 46, autumn 2000, BFI.

265 'more of a five and ten cent Shylock . . .' etc., ibid.

266 'The entire sisterhood . . .' note in MPPDA *King of Kings* file, AMPAS.

266 'The King of Kings has awakened in my soul . . .' etc., DeMille scripts, USC.

269 'All of a sudden, his voice boomed . . .' Anne Edwards, op. cit., p. 103.

271 'It was completely dreadful . . .' *Played by Ear*, op. cit., p. 261.

Chapter 26

272 'INSIDE A CINEMA CZAR'S . . .' *Brooklyn Eagle*, 9 September 1928, NYPL.

274 'a production task unparalleled . . .' etc., MPN, 7 October 1927, BFI.

275 '[I] understand the inmates . . .' Robert Birchard, op. cit., p. 229.

276 'that our behavior depends . . .' Frederick Lewis Allen, *Only Yesterday, the Fabulous Twenties*, Bantam Books, 1946 (1931), New York, p. 224.

276 'DeMILLE INDICTS . . .' *Motion Picture* magazine, May 1928, BFI.

277 'commending the idea . . .' etc., NYT, 19 February 1928, NYPL.

278 'After working for several hours . . .' NYT, 11 March 1928, NYPL.

281 'Vivid! Colorful! Realistic! . . .' MPN, 26 January 1929, BFI.

282 'King Vidor Decries Dialogue Films . . .' MPN, 14 July 1928, BFI.

282 'Talking pictures will never . . .' ibid.

282 'So-called sound pictures . . .' MPN, 1 December 1928, BFI.

282 'predicted that in five years . . .' MPN, 25 August 1928, BFI.

282 'CECIL B. DEMILLE QUITS . . .' NYT, 3 August 1928, NYPL.

Chapter 27

287 'swaggering and burly . . .' quoted in Charles Bickford, op. cit., p. 143.

288 'The party at the DeMille . . .' ibid., p. 161.

288 'A sturdily built bronzed man . . .' etc., ibid., p. 162.

288 'preference in women . . .' etc., ibid., pp. 167–8.

289 'most impressive in those prohibition days . . .' etc., ibid., p. 171.

289 'A girl, beautiful, blonde . . .' ibid., p. 177.

290 'a mess of corn . . .' etc., ibid., pp. 193, 196.

290 'a master of technical detail . . .' NYT, 28 December, 1929, NYPL.

292 'There is quite a lot of lisping . . .' NYT, 15 November 1928, quoted in Donald Crafton, *The Talkies: American Cinema's Transition to Sound*, 1926–1931, University of California Press, 1997, p. 277.

292 'Scene 1: Courthouse . . .' *Dynamite*, script, AMPAS.

Chapter 28

296 'an illegal rate of interest . . .' NYT, 9 July 1928, NYPL.

297 'as producers we regard ourselves . . .' NYT, 21 August 1929, NYPL.

298 'I think in some ways it broke William . . .' etc., Agnes de Mille, 'Goodnight, C.B.', *Esquire*, January 1964, NYPL.

299 'I used to be insulted . . .' *Los Angeles Times*, 24 November 1929, AMPAS.

301 'Page 3: 10: (Bob) "I'm not sorry . . ."' *Madam Satan* folder, MPPDA files, AMPAS.

Chapter 29

305 'I was struck . . .' DeMille, op. cit., p. 284.

306 'Nothing you have heard about it . . .' quoted in Kevin Brownlow, op. cit.

306 'It was a land of . . .' DeMille, op. cit., p. 283.

306 'Funerals, one old horse . . .' quoted in Charles Higham, op. cit., p. 158.

306 'thrilling muster . . .' DeMille, op. cit., p. 282.

306 'two experiments started . . .' Higham, op. cit., p. 159.

307 'Russia is the most interesting . . .' etc., clipping, 7 December 1931, AMPAS.

307 'The DeMilles journeyed . . .' ibid.

309 'HOLLYWOOD'S SOCIAL UPHEAVAL . . .' *Variety*, 19 January 1932, BFI.

311 'indefinite vacation . . .' etc., *Variety*, 3 May 1932, BFI.

311 'contract with Paramount . . .' *Variety*, 23 August 1932, BFI.

312 'THE LOVES, THE BLOOD-LUST . . .' *Sign of the Cross*, press book, LOC.

313 'THE FAITH OF CHRISTIANS . . .' etc., ibid.

314 'the red-headed woman . . .' ibid.

314 'something else caught the lion's . . .' etc., Phil A. Koury, *Yes, Mr. DeMille*, G. P. Putnam's Sons, New York, 1959, p. 25.

315 'I will write a play . . .' NYT, 20 November 1932, NYPL.

316 'ordinarily we would have been . . .' MPPDA files, AMPAS.

316 'The picture "The Sign of the Cross" . . .' ibid.

317 'Spectacle of a type . . .' *Variety*, 6 December 1932, BFI.

317 'there is an abundance of imagination . . .' NYT, 1 December 1932, NYPL.

317 'Multitudes in Rome were then oppressed . . .' *Sign of the Cross*, press book, op. cit.

Chapter 30

319 'strong Fascist tendencies . . .' etc., MPPDA files, AMPAS.

320 'The word "punks" . . .' *This Day and Age* folder, MPPDA files, AMPAS.

320 'THE FIRST GREAT SPECTACLE . . .' *This Day and Age*, press book, LOC.

321 'a highly improbable . . .' *Variety*, 29 August 1932, BFI.

322 'They Shed Civilization . . .' *Four Frightened People*, press book, LOC.

323 'forest of Hau . . .' ibid.

323 'Henceforth, I am going to make . . .' *Los Angeles Times*, 28 January 1934, AMPAS.

324 'Forget Shakespeare and Shaw . . .' etc., Agnes DeMille, *Speak to Me, Dance with Me*, Atlantic Monthly Press, 1973, p. 212.

325 'He asks everyone's opinion . . .' ibid., p. 222.

325 'Up at 6:30 a.m . . .' etc., ibid., p. 223.

326 'Cecil sat in Cleopatra's great marble throne . . .' ibid, p. 230.

329 'Cleopatra sandals . . .' etc., *Cleopatra*, press book, LOC.

331 'polite but not over enthusiastic . . .' *Variety*, 21 August 1934, BFI.

331 'in an emphatically lavish . . .' NYT, 17 August 1934, NYPL.

Chapter 31

332 'GATEWAY INTO THE PAST . . .' NYT, 12 May 1935, NYPL.

332 'The young man must have been . . .' *San Francisco Chronicle*, 30 June 1935, AMPAS.

333 'The dictionary doesn't list adequate adjectives . . .' ibid.

333 '[For] the siege of Acre . . .' ibid.

336 'one of my most popular pictures . . .' DeMille, op. cit., p. 314.

338 'DeMille got out and whispered . . .' etc., NYT, 4 August 1935, NYPL.

339 'Epic Americana had always been . . .' Jesse L. Lasky, Jr., *Whatever Happened to Hollywood?* Funk & Wagnalls, New York, 1973, p. 150.

340 'Practically all the pistols . . .' NYT, 10 January 1937, NYPL.

340 'No saga of the plains . . .' NYT, 14 January 1937, NYPL.

341 'Say something in Cheyenne . . .' etc., Anne Edwards, op. cit., p. 143.

Chapter 32

342 'DeMille fingered the volumes . . .' etc., Jesse L. Lasky, Jr., op. cit., pp. 132–3.

344 'In March, 1937, DeMille led . . .' etc., Paramount souvenir brochure, AMPAS.

346 'CS: DeMille seated . . .' etc., 'Star Bright' script, *The Buccaneer* folder, AMPAS.

346 'Men without stomachs . . .' souvenir brochure, op. cit.

347 'a cinch for big boxoffice . . .' *Variety*, 12 January 1938, BFI.

347 "Know what this is, Jesse?' . . .' Jesse L. Lasky, Jr, op. cit., pp. 150–1.

347 'always wore one color . . .' ibid., p. 151.

348 'Wind-combed prairie . . .' etc., ibid., pp. 151–2.

348 'Get this . . .' ibid., pp. 153–4.

349 'a wheezing, bone-dry veteran . . .' etc., ibid., p. 156.

349 'a man is always checking to see . . .' ibid., p. 170.

349 'used writers like a general . . .' etc., ibid., p. 156.

350 'Jesse refuses to tell me what Brian Donlevy does . . .' etc., ibid., pp. 171–2.

350 'His fetishes, if any . . .' ibid., p. 166.

350 'Then one morning an ambulance . . .' ibid., p. 185.

351 'big, old-fashioned DeMille show . . .' NYT, 11 May 1939, NYPL.

352 'Say that for the picture . . .' ibid.

353 '"Stories? Weren't no stories . . . "' Jesse L. Lasky, Jr, op. cit., p. 159.

Chapter 33

357 'Dear Mr. LeRoy . . .' Paramount press release, 25 February 1942, AMPAS.

358 'The Shadow of Cecil . . .' etc., NYT, 15 February 1942, AMPAS.

358 'from every picture . . .' etc., Jesse L. Lasky, Jr, op. cit., p. 189.

358 'the drama of a free people . . .' NYT, 16 June 1939, NYPL.

359 'a fascinating record . . .' ibid.

361 'The pappy of them all . . .' etc.., *Chicago Sun Tribune*, 15 September 1940, AMPAS.

362 'And did I feel hurt? . . .' Paramount press release, AMPAS.

363 'given us pretty pictures . . .' Jesse L. Lasky, Jr, op. cit., p. 216.

363 'What would fascinate Eskimos . . .' ibid., p. 219.

364 'CB's road to glory . . .' etc., NYT, 10 August 1941, NYPL.

365 'a lifelong study of religions . . .' Anne Edwards, op. cit., p. 157.

Chapter 34

366 'You seem to have won . . .' *Daily Variety*, 11 March 1942, AMPAS.

366 'I used to dress for flying . . .' ibid.

367 '"Reap the Wild Wind" is a picture . . .' NYT, 27 March 1942, NYPL.

367 'The only sombre note . . .' ibid.

368 'nearly five months . . .' etc., NYT, 29 April 1942 – 'The President's Broadcast', NYPL.

369 'script films on the mysteries of rigging . . .' Jesse L. Lasky, Jr, op. cit., p. 234.

369 'That's nothing. George Washington used to talk about me . . .' NYT, 28 June 1942, NYPL.

370 'Considering his well-earned reputation . . .' NYT, 7 June 1944, NYPL.

371 'I do not feel that I need . . .' *The Nation*, 10 June 1944, quoted in Gene Ringgold & DeWitt Bodeen, *The Films of Cecil B. DeMille*, The Citadel Press, 1969, p. 334.

371 'United Daughters of the Confederacy . . .' document in AMPAS file.

372 'I'm Cecil B. DeMille . . .' Carlotta Monti, *W. C. Fields and Me*, Prentice-Hall Inc, 1971, pp. 190–1.

373 'the stupidity of partisanship . . .' NYT, 27 March 1942, NYPL.

373 'we resent the growing impression . . .' Larry Ceplair and Steven Englund, *The Inquisition in Hollywood, Politics in the Film Community, 1930–1960*, 2003 (1979), University of Illinois Press, p. 211.

374 'Prime example of how the war . . .' clipping, 2 June 1944, AMPAS.

374 'UNION MAY OUST DEMILLE . . .' NYT, 15 November 1944, NYPL.

375 'The American Federation . . .' NYT, 2 December 1944, NYPL.

375 'would give up his weekly . . .' NYT, 5 December 1944, NYPL.

375 'enact laws . . .' NYT, 26 January 1945, NYPL.

375 'Too many business men . . .' NYT, 18 March 1945, NYPL.

376 'the rights of everyone . . .' *Variety*, 11 April 1945, AMPAS.

376 'Un-American Elements in Unions . . .' etc., *Los Angeles Times*, 4 July 1945, AMPAS.

377 'A dissenter is branded . . .' *Reader's Digest*, July 1945, AMPAS.

Chapter 35

380 '"Could an audience believe it?" . . .' Jesse L. Lasky, Jr, op. cit., p. 198.

380 'as viciously anti-redskin . . .' NYT, 19 October 1947, quoted in Ringgold and Bodeen, op. cit., p. 339.

380 'I'd like to have you tell me . . .' etc., Phil A. Koury, op. cit., pp. 150–1.

381 'seriously affect the present . . .' *Los Angeles Times*, 23 September 1945, AMPAS.

381 'courage, sacrifice . . .' NYT, 7 September 1945, NYPL.

382 'When one man or group . . .' NYT, 26 September 1945, NYPL.

382 'DeMILLE CALLS ON HONEST LABOR . . .' *Los Angeles Times*, 9 February 1946, AMPAS.

382 'DeMILLE URGES UNITY . . .' *Los Angeles Examiner*, 9 February 1946, AMPAS.

382 'CECIL B. DeMILLE ASKS LAW . . .' *Herald Express*, 14 February 1947, AMPAS.

382 'DeMILLE APPEAL TO CONGRESS . . .' *Los Angeles Citizen-News*, 21 February 1947, AMPAS.

382 'in some cases, he found the same "fear" . . .' *Los Angeles Times*, 15 February 1947, AMPAS.

382 'DeMILLE LAUDS SCOUTS . . .' *Los Angeles Citizen-News*, 6 June 1947, AMPAS.

383 '90 per cent manufactured . . .' *Los Angeles Examiner*, 12 June 1947, AMPAS.

383 'because we have in America . . .' *Los Angeles Times*, 27 June 1947, AMPAS.

383 'You mothers hang on to . . .' *Chicago Tribune*, 16 October 1947, AMPAS.

384 'I really got part of the idea . . .' Phil A. Koury, op. cit., p. 213.

384 '*If ye had not ploughed with my heifer* . . .' ibid., p. 215.

385 'SYNOPSIS: Story about Delilah . . .' MPPDA files, AMPAS.

386 'Disillusioned, Samson fights . . .' ibid.

386 'Film Content Analysis Chart . . .' ibid.

387 'perpetual attendant . . .' *Life*, 5 December 1949, NYPL.

387 'He is exceedingly proud . . .' ibid.

388 'The climax was to occur . . .' NYT, 23 November 1948, NYPL.

388 'The Siegfried of Sex . . .' Simon Harcourt-Smith, *Sight and Sound*, February 1951.

389 'I walked over to Victor Mature's . . .' *Life*, 5 December 1949, NYPL.

390 'Jeez, look at him . . .' etc., ibid.

Chapter 36

391 'There were four scenes . . .' NYT, 29 May 1949, NYPL.

393 'at least 5,000,000 decent . . .' NYT, 11 June 1948, NYPL.

393 'the individual has been battered . . .' *Los Angeles Times*, 12 May 1948, AMPAS.

394 'Now, in the 20th century . . .' etc., clipping, 16 May 1949, AMPAS.

395 'The circus idea germinated . . .' NYT, 'With DeMille Under the Big Top', 21 August 1949, NYPL.

396 'Since joining up in Chicago . . .' ibid.

396 'a place of spangles and tinsel . . .' NYT, 3 December 1950, NYPL.

397 'I took Cecilia . . .' interview, 10 December 1951, Hedda Hopper Collection, AMPAS.

398 'Well, that's it, fellahs . . .' etc., Jesse L. Lasky, Jr, op. cit., p. 265.

398 'The lines stretched on both sidewalks . . .' NYT, 22 December 1949, NYPL.

399 'In conformity with the anticommunist . . .' telegram, 14 October 1950, Albert Lewin Collection, USC Cinema and Television Library.

400 'John Ford, who, although a conservative . . .' NYT, 22 October 1950, NYPL.

401 'All during this, I was wondering . . .' Peter Bogdanovich, *John Ford*, Studio Vista, London, 1967, p. 19.

401 'leader of the board majority . . .' NYT, 29 October 1950, NYPL.

401 'paper hat patriots . . .' quoted in Scott Eyman, *Print the Legend, the Life and Times of John Ford*, Simon & Schuster, 1999, p. 382.

402 'It was the toughest production problem . . .' Hedda Hopper Collection, op. cit.

Chapter 37

404 'real baptism in the faith . . .' etc., 'The Faith of Cecil B. DeMille', *American Weekly*, 20 November 1949, AMPAS.

404 'Scarcely glancing at the empty pews . . .' ibid.

405 'besides marrying Constance . . .' Hedda Hopper Collection, op. cit.

405 'My father had one spectacular weakness . . .' *Los Angeles Examiner*, 29 October 1950, AMPAS.

406 'The motion picture was a struggling . . .' ibid.

406 '"Oh, that little thing . . ."' *Los Angeles Examiner*, 12 November 1950, AMPAS.

406 'As a boy I remember . . .' *Los Angeles Examiner*, 10 December 1950, AMPAS.

406 'Unless beauty is fanned . . .' *Los Angeles Examiner*, 14 January 1951, AMPAS.

406 'The spirit that founded this nation . . .' *Los Angeles Examiner*, 25 February 1951, AMPAS.

407 'government officials and theater owners . . .' *Los Angeles Times*, 11 August 1951, AMPAS.

407 'I would like to start . . .' *Los Angeles Examiner*, 12 August 1951, AMPAS.

407 'returned $55,000,000 . . .' *The Hollywood Reporter*, 11 March 1942, AMPAS.

408 'corporate income taxes . . .' *Los Angeles Times*, 29 April 1952, AMPAS.

408 'invisible government . . .' etc., *Los Angeles Times*, 26 June 1952, AMPAS.

408 'Just find a patient . . .' *Los Angeles Times*, 17 August 1952, AMPAS.

409 'You can just say . . .' *Los Angeles Daily News*, 2 March 1953, AMPAS.

410 'The Ten Commandments are not outmoded . . .' Paramount press release, AMPAS.

Chapter 38

413 'Our state car whisked us away . . .' Katherine Orrison, *Written in Stone, Making Cecil B. DeMille's Epic, The Ten Commandments*, Vestal Press, p. 19.

414 'The company bedded down for the night . . .' ibid., p. 88.

416 'a fine film dramatist . . .' Jesse L. Lasky, Jr, op. cit., p. 298.

416 'I was the company Hebrew . . .' etc., ibid., pp. 300–1.

416 'He never demanded . . .' Katherine Orrison, op. cit., p. 121.

416 'seated in a chair of state . . .' *The Ten Commandments*, script, Jesse L. Lasky Jr Collection, courtesy of Pat Silver-Lasky.

417 'In the vast darkness of infinity . . .' etc., ibid.

418 'the hot ticket on the Paramount lot . . .' Katherine Orrison, op. cit., p. 39.

419 'I'm back of the rock during the scene . . .' ibid., p. 75.

420 'I got sick, but I went on with the orgy . . .' ibid., p. 130.

422 'contrasted the "fundamentalism" . . .' NYT, 3 December 1956, NYPL.

422 'tries to convince the world . . .' *Al Hillal*, November 1954, AMPAS.

423 'playwright, screen director . . .' *Los Angeles Times*, 9 March 1955, AMPAS.

Epilogue

429 'When leaders of nations tell us . . .' February 1956 in the Journal Library of the Screen Producers' Guild, AMPAS.

429 'We are responsible . . .' etc., ibid.

430 'He was the most famous . . .' Agnes de Mille, *Esquire*, January 1964, ibid., NYPL.

431 'C.B. DeMILLE – CAESAR . . .' etc., *Los Angeles Times*, 11 May 1958, AMPAS.

432 'the most difficult picture . . .' NYT, 6 April 1947, NYPL.

432 'He was dressed in a flannel robe . . .' Anne Edwards, op. cit., p. 217.

433 'selected readings from an old bible . . .' *New York Herald Tribune*, 24 January 1959, NYPL.

433 'The producer's will left nothing . . .' *Mirror*, 28 January 1959, AMPAS

434 'who is always yearning . . .' Simon Harcourt-Smith, op. cit.

435 'He sort of looked at you . . .' Richard de Mille, op. cit., p. 13.

438 'urged its members to support . . .' Sue A. Hoffman, 'The Real History of the Ten Commandments Project of the Fraternal Order of Eagles', www.religioustolerance.org/hoffman01.htm

438 'The Ten Commandments could be . . .' Georgia headlines, 16 January 2006, www.accessnorthga.com/news/ap_newfullstory.asp?ID=47625.

438 'the Ten Commandments is a religious document . . .' ibid. (Note also article 'The God Racket, from DeMille to DeLay' by Frank Rich, *New York Times*, 27 March 2005.)

439 'he "filled in" the Bible . . .' *Independent on Sunday*, 4 July 1999, AMPAS.

Chronology, Plays and Films

30 January 1853: birth of Matilda Beatrice Samuel.

4 September 1853: birth of Henry Churchill De Mille.

1 July 1876: marriage of Henry and Beatrice.

25 July 1878: birth of William Churchill de Mille.

12 August 1881: birth of Cecil Blount de Mille (later DeMille).

23 May 1891: birth of Agnes Beatrice de Mille, died 12 February 1895.

1898: Cecil attends Pennsylvania Military College.

1899: Cecil attends American Academy of Dramatic Arts.

February 1900: Cecil debuts as actor in *Hearts Are Trumps* (bit part).

16 August 1902: marriage of Cecil B. DeMille and Constance Adams.

1901–1903: Cecil has parts in plays: *To Have and To Hold, Are You a Mason?, Alice of Old Vincennes, Hamlet.*

September–December 1905: Cecil appears in *The Prince Chap.*

November 1913: incorporation of Jesse L. Lasky Feature Play Company.

22 December 1913: lease of Burns and Reiver studio in Hollywood.

29 December 1913: commence shoot of *The Squaw Man.*

Plays by Henry C. De Mille
John Delmer's Daughters, a comedy in 3 acts, 1883
The Main Line, 1886
The Wife, a play in 4 acts, 1887
Lord Chumley, a play in 3 acts, 1888
The Charity Ball, a comedy drama in 4 acts, 1889
Men and Women, a drama of our times, in 4 acts, 1890
The Lost Paradise, a drama in 3 acts, adapted from the German play by Ludwig Fulda, 1897

A Play by Beatrice de Mille and Harriet Ford
The Greatest Thing in the World, a play in 4 acts, 1900

Plays by Cecil B. and William C. de Mille
The Pretender, a play in a prologue and 4 acts, 1901 (?)
The Genius, a comedy in 3 acts, 1904
The Royal Mounted, a play in 4 acts, 1908
Son of the Winds, 1910
The Stampede, a play in 3 acts, 1910
After Five, a farce-comedy in 3 acts, 1913

Plays by William C. de Mille

Strongheart, a play in 4 acts, 1904
(*The Genius*, a comedy in 3 acts, 1906)
The Warrens of Virginia, 1907; *Classmates*, 1907
(*The Royal Mounted*, 1908)
The Land of the Free, a play in 3 acts, 1910
The Woman, a play in 3 acts, 1911
Rollo, a sketch, 1912; *At the Florists*, a sketch, 1912
50 Years from Now, a tragedy of the future, in one act, 1912
Food, a tragedy of the future, 1912; *The Man Higher Up*, a dramatic
    sketch, 1912
Votes for Fairies, a playlet in one act, 1912
(*After Five*, a farce comedy in 3 acts, 1913)
The Squealer, a sketch, 1914; *In 1999*, a problem play of the future, 1914
Deceivers, a play in one act, 1914; *Poor Old Jim*, a sketch in one act, 1914
The Forest Ring, a play in 3 acts (with Charles Barnard), 1921

Comedy sketches by Cecil B. DeMille for Jesse L. Lasky

California, January 1912
The Antique Girl, January 1912
In the Barracks, 1912

Plays Produced by Cecil B. DeMille

The Wishing Ring, 1910; *Speed*, 1911; *The Marriage-not*, 1912; *Cheer Up*,
    1912

Cecil B. DeMille Filmography

DeMille's filmography fills several published books, and the credits will
only be summarized here. For further details, see Robert Birchard's *Cecil B.
DeMille's Hollywood*, and Gene Ringgold and DeWitt Bodeen's *The Films
of Cecil B. DeMille*. Fullest available credits can also be found at
www.imdb.com (the Internet Movie Database).

Note on film duration: a reel of silent film would run from 12 to 15 minutes depending on the hand-cranked speed.

Silent Films

The Squaw Man

Produced and directed by Cecil B. DeMille and Oscar C. Apfel. From the
play by Edwin Milton Royle. Cameraman: Alfred Gandolfi.
With Dustin Farnum, Red Wing, Monroe Salisbury, Winifred Kingston,
Billy Elmer, Foster Knox, Joe E. Singleton, Haidee Fuller. 6 reels. Released
February 1914.

The Virginian
Produced and directed by Cecil B. DeMille. Script by DeMille from the novel by Owen Wister. Cameraman: Alvin Wyckoff. With Dustin Farnum, Winifred Kingston, J. W. Johnston, Sydney Deane, Monroe Salisbury, Anita King, Billy Elmer, Tex Driscoll. 4 reels. Released September 1914.

The Call of the North
Produced and directed by Cecil B. DeMille. Script by DeMille from the novel by Stewart Edward White and play by George Broadhurst. Cameraman: Alvin Wyckoff. Art Director: Wilfred Buckland. With Robert Edeson, Theodore Roberts, Winifred Kingston, Florence Dagmar, Horace B. Carpenter, Milton Brown, Vera McGarry, Jode Mullaly, Sydney Deane, Fred Montague. 5 reels. Released August 1914.

What's His Name
Produced and directed by Cecil B. DeMille. Script by DeMille from the novel by George Barr McCutcheon. Cameraman: Alvin Wyckoff. Art Director: Wilfred Buckland. With Max Figman, Lolita Robertson, Sydney Deane, Dick LaStrange, Fred Montague, Theodore Roberts and Cecilia de Mille as Phoebe. 5 reels. Released October 1914.

The Man from Home
Produced and directed by Cecil B. DeMille. Script by DeMille from the play by Booth Tarkington and Harry Leon Wilson. Cameraman: Alvin Wyckoff. Art Director: Wilfred Buckland. With Charles Richman, Theodore Roberts, Mabel van Buren, Fred Montague, Monroe Salisbury, Jode Mullaly, Horace B. Carpenter, Anita King. 5 reels. Released November 1914.

Rose of the Rancho
Produced and directed by Cecil B. DeMille. Script by DeMille from the play by David Belasco and Richard Walton Tully. Cameraman: Alvin Wyckoff. Art Director: Wilfred Buckland. With Bessie Barriscale, J. W. Johnston, Jane Darwell, Dick La Reno, Monroe Salisbury, Jeanie Macpherson as Isabelita's daughter. 5 reels. Released November 1914.

The Girl of the Golden West
Produced and directed by Cecil B. DeMille. Script by DeMille from the play by David Belasco. Cameraman: Alvin Wyckoff. Art Director: Wilfred Buckland. With Mabel van Buren, House Peters as Ramerrez, Theodore Roberts as Rance, Anita King, Sydney Deane, Raymond Hatton as Castro, Jeanie Macpherson as Nina. 5 reels. Released January 1915.

The Warrens of Virginia
Produced and directed by Cecil B. DeMille. Script by William de Mille from his own play. Cameraman: Alvin Wyckoff. Art Director: Wilfred

Buckland. With Blanche Sweet as Agatha Warren, House Peters as Ned Burton, Page Peters, James Neill, Mabel van Buren, Marguerite House, Dick La Reno. 5 reels. Released February 1915.

The Unafraid
Produced and directed by Cecil B. DeMille. Script by DeMille from the novel by Eleanor M. Ingram. Cameraman: Alvin Wyckoff. Art Director: Wilfred Buckland. With Rita Jolivet as Delight Warren; House Peters as Stefan; Page Peters as Michael; Theodore Roberts, Billy Elmer, Lawrence Peyton. 4 reels. Released April 1915.

The Captive
Produced and directed by Cecil B. DeMille. Script by DeMille and Jeanie Macpherson. Cameraman: Alvin Wyckoff. Art Director: Wilfred Buckland. With Blanche Sweet as Sonya; House Peters as Mahmud; Page Peters as Marko; Theodore Roberts as Turkish officer. 5 reels. Released April 1915.

The Wild Goose Chase
Produced and directed by Cecil B. DeMille. Script by William de Mille. Cameraman: Alvin Wyckoff. With Ina Claire, Helen Marlborough, Raymond Hatton, Theodore Roberts. 5 reels. Released May 1915. *Missing film.*

The Arab
Produced and directed by Cecil B. DeMille. Script by DeMille and Edgar Selwyn, from the play by Edgar Selwyn. Cameraman: Alvin Wyckoff. Art Director: Wilfred Buckland. With Edgar Selwyn, Gertrude Robinson, Horace B. Carpenter, Billy Elmer, Raymond Hatton, Theodore Roberts, Irving S. Cobb. 5 reels. Released June 1915. *Missing film.*

Chimmie Fadden
Produced and directed by Cecil B. DeMille. Script by DeMille from the play and book by E. W. Townsend. Cameraman: Alvin Wyckoff. Art Director: Wilfred Buckland. With Victor Moore as Chimmie Fadden; Raymond Hatton as Larry; Mrs. Lewis McCord as Mrs. Fadden; Anita King as Fanny; Ernest Joy, Camille Astor, Tom Forman. 5 reels. Released June 1915. *Missing film.*

Kindling
Produced and directed by Cecil B. DeMille. Script by DeMille, from the play by Charles A. Kenyon. Cameraman: Alvin Wyckoff. Art Director: Wilfred Buckland. With Thomas Meighan as Heine Schultz; Charlotte Walker as Maggie Schultz; Raymond Hatton as Steve; Billy Elmer as Rafferty, Lillian Langdon as Mrs Burke-Smith; Florence Dagmar as Alice; Tom Forman as Dr Taylor. 5 reels. Released July 1915.

Maria Rosa

Produced and directed by Cecil B. DeMille. Script by William de Mille from the play by Angel Guimera. Cameraman: Alvin Wyckoff. Art Director: Wilfred Buckland. With Geraldine Farrar as Maria Rosa; Wallace Reid as Andreas; Pedro de Cordoba as Ramon; Anita King as Ana; Ernest Joy, Horace B. Carpenter, James Neill. 5 reels. Shot in June 1915; released May 1916.

Carmen

Produced and directed by Cecil B. DeMille. Script by William de Mille from the novel by Prosper Mérimée. Cameraman: Alvin Wyckoff. Art Director: Wilfred Buckland. With Geraldine Farrar as Carmen; Wallace Reid as Don José; Pedro de Cordoba as Escamillo; Horace B. Carpenter as Pastia; Jeanie Macpherson as Gypsy girl. 5 reels. Released October 1915.

Chimmie Fadden Out West

Produced and directed by Cecil B. DeMille. Script by DeMille and Jeanie Macpherson from stories by E. W. Townsend. Cameraman: Alvin Wyckoff. Art Director: Wilfred Buckland. With Victor Moore as Chimmie Fadden; Raymond Hatton as Larry; Mrs Lewis McCord as Mother; Florence Dagmar as Betty. 6 reels. Released November 1915.

The Cheat

Produced and directed by Cecil B. DeMille. Script by Hector Turnbull. Cameraman: Alvin Wyckoff. Art Director: Wilfred Buckland. With Fannie Ward as Edith Hardy; Sessue Hayakawa as Tori; Jack Dean as Dick Hardy; James Neill, Utake Abe, Hazel Childers, Dana Ong. 5 reels. Released December 1915.

The Golden Chance

Produced and directed by Cecil B. DeMille. Script by DeMille and Jeanie Macpherson. Cameraman: Alvin Wyckoff. Art Director: Wilfred Buckland. With Cleo Ridgley as Mary Denby; Wallace Reid as Roger Manning; Ernest Joy as Mr Hillary; Raymond Hatton as Jimmy the Rat. 6 reels. Released December 1915.

Temptation

Produced and directed by Cecil B. DeMille. Script by Hector Turnbull. Cameraman: Alvin Wyckoff. Art Director: Wilfred Buckland. With Geraldine Farrar as Renee Dupree; Theodore Roberts as Otto Mueller; Pedro de Cordoba, Raymond Hatton, Elsie Jane Wilson, Sessue Hayakawa. 6 reels. Released January 1916. *Missing film.*

The Trail of the Lonesome Pine

Produced and directed by Cecil B. DeMille. Script by DeMille from a play

469

by Eugene Walter and novel by John William Fox Jr. Cameraman: Alvin Wyckoff. Art Director: Wilfred Buckland. With Charlotte Walker as Jane Tolliver; Thomas Meighan as Jack Hale; Theodore Roberts as Judd Tolliver; Earle Fox as Dave Tolliver. 5 reels. Released February 1916.

The Heart of Nora Flynn

Produced and directed by Cecil B. DeMille. Script by Jeanie Macpherson from a story by Hector Turnbull. Cameraman: Alvin Wyckoff. Art Director: Wilfred Buckland. With Marie Doro as Nora Flynn; Elliott Dexter as Nolan; Ernest Joy, Lola May, Billy Jacobs, Peggy George, Charles West. 5 reels. Released April 1916.

The Dream Girl

Produced and directed by Cecil B. DeMille. Script by Jeanie Macpherson. Cameraman: Alvin Wyckoff. Art Director: Wilfred Buckland. With Mae Murray, Theodore Roberts, James Neill, Earle Foxe, Charles West, Mary Mersch. 5 reels. Released July 1916. *Missing film.*

Joan the Woman

Produced and directed by Cecil B. DeMille. Script by Jeanie Macpherson. Cameraman: Alvin Wyckoff. Art Director: Wilfred Buckland. With Geraldine Farrar as Joan of Arc; Wallace Reid as Eric Trent; Raymond Hatton as King Charles VIII; Tully Marshall as L'Oiseleur; Theodore Roberts as Cauchon; Hobart Bosworth, James Neill, Charles Clary, Lawrence Peyton, Horace B. Carpenter, Cleo Ridgley, Lillian Leighton, Marjorie Daw, Walter Long. 10 reels (?), 137 minutes. Released January 1917.

A Romance of the Redwoods

Produced and directed by Cecil B. DeMille. Script by DeMille and Jeanie Macpherson. Cameraman: Alvin Wyckoff. Art Director: Wilfred Buckland. With Mary Pickford as Jenny Lawrence; Elliott Dexter as 'Black' Brown; Raymond Hatton, Tully Marshall, Charles Ogle, Walter Long, Winter Hall. 7 reels. Released May 1917.

The Little American

Produced and directed by Cecil B. DeMille. Script by DeMille and Jeanie Macpherson. Cameraman: Alvin Wyckoff. Art Director: Wilfred Buckland. With Mary Pickford as Angela Moore; Jack Holt as Karl von Austreim; Raymond Hatton as Count Jules de Destin; Hobart Bosworth, Walter Long, James Neill, Norman Kerry, Wallace Beery, Sam Wood, Colleen Moore. 6 reels. Released July 1917.

The Woman God Forgot

Produced and directed by Cecil B. DeMille. Script by Jeanie Macpherson.

Cameraman: Alvin Wyckoff. Art Director: Wilfred Buckland. With Geraldine Farrar as Tecza; Wallace Reid as Alvarado; Raymond Hatton as Montezuma; Hobart Bosworth as Cortés; Theodore Kosloff as Guatemoco; Walter Long as High Priest; Julia Faye as Handmaiden. 6 reels. Released November 1917.

The Devil Stone

Produced and directed by Cecil B. DeMille. Script by Jeanie Macpherson from a story by Beatrice De Mille and Leighton Osmun. Cameraman: Alvin Wyckoff. Art Director: Wilfred Buckland. With Geraldine Farrar, Wallace Reid, Tully Marshall, Hobart Bosworth, Mabel van Buren, James Neill. Released December 1917. 6 reels. *Only two last reels survive.*

The Whispering Chorus

Produced and directed by Cecil B. DeMille. Script by Jeanie Macpherson from a novel by Perley Poore Sheehan. Cameraman: Alvin Wyckoff. Art Director: Wilfred Buckland. With Raymond Hatton as John Tremble; Kathlyn Williams as Jane Tremble; Elliott Dexter as George Coggeswell; Noah Beery, John Burton, Guy Oliver, J. Parke Jones, Tully Marshall, James Neill; Walter Lynch, Gustav von Seyffertitz and Edna Mae Murray as the Faces, and Julia Faye as Girl in Dive. 7 reels. Released March 1918.

Old Wives for New

Produced and directed by Cecil B. DeMille. Script by Jeanie Macpherson from the novel by David Graham Phillips. Cameraman: Alvin Wyckoff. Art Director: Wilfred Buckland. With Elliott Dexter as Charles Murdock; Florence Vidor as Juliet Raeburn; Sylvia Ashton as Sophy Murdock; Theodore Roberts as Berkeley; Wanda Hawley as young Sophy; Helen Jerome Eddy as Norma Murdock; J. Parke Jones as Charley Murdock; Marcia Manon as Viola; Julia Faye as Jessie; Gustav von Seyffertitz as Blagden; Edna Mae Cooper, Tully Marshall, Lillian Leighton. 7 reels. Released May 1918.

We Can't Have Everything

Produced and directed by Cecil B. DeMille. Script by William de Mille from the novel by Rupert Hughes. Cameraman: Alvin Wyckoff. Art Director: Wilfred Buckland. Editor: Anne Bauchens. With Kathlyn Williams, Elliott Dexter, Wanda Hawley, Sylvia Breamer, Raymond Hatton, Theodore Roberts, Tully Marshall, Thurston Hall, Sylvia Ashton. 6 reels. Released July 1918. *Missing Film.*

Till I Come Back to You

Produced and directed by Cecil B. DeMille. Script by Jeanie Macpherson. Cameraman: Alvin Wyckoff. Art Director: Wilfred Buckland. Editor: Anne

Bauchens. With Bryant Washburn as Captain Strong; Florence Vidor as Yvonne; G. Butler Clonbough as Karl von Krutz; Winter Hall as King Albert of the Belgians; George E. Stone as Jacques; Julia Faye as Susette. 7 reels. Released September 1918.

The Squaw Man (first remake)

A Cecil B. DeMille production, directed by Cecil B. DeMille. Script by Beulah Marie Dix from the play by Edwin Milton Royle. Cameraman: Alvin Wyckoff. Art Director: Wilfred Buckland. Editor: Anne Bauchens. With Elliott Dexter as Jim Wynnegate; Ann Little as Naturich; Theodore Roberts as Big Bill; Katherine MacDonald as Diana; Tully Marshall, Herbert Standing, Monte Blue, Charles Ogle, Helen Dunbar. Released December 1918. 6 reels. *Only final reel survives.*

Don't Change Your Husband

A Cecil B. DeMille production, directed by Cecil B. DeMille. Script by Jeanie Macpherson. Cameraman: Alvin Wyckoff. Art Director: Wilfred Buckland. Editor: Anne Bauchens. With Gloria Swanson as Leila Porter; Elliott Dexter as James Denby Porter; Sylvia Ashton as Mrs Huckney; Lew Cody as Schuyler van Sutphen; Theodore Roberts as The Bishop; Julia Faye as Nanette; James Neill, Ted Shawn. 7 reels. Released January 1919.

For Better, For Worse

A Cecil B. DeMille production, directed by Cecil B. DeMille. Script by Jeanie Macpherson from an adaptation by William de Mille of a play by Edgar Selwyn. Cameraman: Alvin Wyckoff. Art Director: Wilfred Buckland. Editor: Anne Bauchens. With Gloria Swanson as Sylvia Norcross; Elliott Dexter as Dr Edward Meade; Tom Forman as Richard Burton; Wanda Hawley as Betty; Raymond Hatton as Bud; Theodore Roberts, Sylvia Ashton, Winter Hall, Jack Holt. 7 reels. Released May 1919.

Male and Female

A Cecil B. DeMille production, directed by Cecil B. DeMille. Script by Jeanie Macpherson from the play *The Admirable Crichton* by James M. Barrie. Cameraman: Alvin Wyckoff. Art Director: Wilfred Buckland. Editor: Anne Bauchens. With Gloria Swanson as Lady Mary Lasenby; Thomas Meighan as Crichton; Lila Lee as Tweeny; Theodore Roberts as Lord Loam; Raymond Hatton as Ernest Wolley; Julia Faye as Susan; Mildred Reardon, Maym Kelso, Rhy Darby, Lillian Leighton, and Bebe Daniels as King's Favorite. 9 reels. Released November 1919.

Why Change Your Wife?

A Cecil B. DeMille production, directed by Cecil B. DeMille. Script by

Olga Printzlau and Sada Cowan from a story by William de Mille. Cameraman: Alvin Wyckoff. Art Director: Wilfred Buckland. Editor: Anne Bauchens. With Gloria Swanson as Beth Gordon; Thomas Meighan as Robert Gordon; Bebe Daniels as Sally Clark; Theodore Kosloff as Radinoff; Sylvia Ashton as Aunt Kate; Maym Kelso, Clarence Geldart. 8 reels. Released May 1920.

Something to Think About

A Cecil B. DeMille production, directed by Cecil B. DeMille. Script by Jeanie Macpherson. Photography by Alvin Wyckoff and Karl Struss. Art Director: Wilfred Buckland. Editor: Anne Bauchens. With Gloria Swanson as Ruth Anderson; Elliott Dexter as David Markley; Monte Blue as Jim Dirk; Theodore Roberts as Luke Anderson; Claire McDowell as Housekeeper; Julia Faye, Mickey Moore, Theodore Kosloff as Clown. 7 reels. Released October 1920.

Forbidden Fruit (remake of The Golden Chance)

A Cecil B. DeMille production, directed by Cecil B. DeMille. Script by Jeanie Macpherson. Photography by Alvin Wyckoff and Karl Struss. Art Director: Wilfred Buckland. Editor: Anne Bauchens. With Agnes Ayres as Mary Maddock; Forrest Stanley as Nelson Rogers; Clarence Burton as Steve Maddock; Theodore Roberts as James Mallory; Kathlyn Williams as Mrs. Mallory; Julia Faye as Maid. 8 reels. Released February 1921.

The Affairs of Anatol

A Cecil B. DeMille production, directed by Cecil B. DeMille. Script by Jeanie Macpherson, Beulah Marie Dix, Lorna Moon and Elmer Harris from Arthur Schnitzler's play *Anatol*. Photography by Alvin Wyckoff and Karl Struss. Art Director: Paul Iribe. Editor: Anne Bauchens. With Wallace Reid as Anatol; Gloria Swanson as Vivian; Elliott Dexter as Max; Wanda Hawley as Emilie; Theodore Roberts as Gordon Bronson; Bebe Daniels as Satan Synne; Monte Blue, Agnes Ayres, Julia Faye, and Theodore Kosloff as Nazzer Singh. 9 reels. Released September 1921.

Fool's Paradise

A Cecil B. DeMille production, directed by Cecil B. DeMille. Script by Beulah Marie Dix and Sada Cowan from *The Laurels and the Lady* by Leonard Merrick. Photography by Alvin Wyckoff and Karl Struss. Editor: Anne Bauchens. With Conrad Nagel as Arthur Phelps; Dorothy Dalton as Poll Patchouli; Mildred Harris as Rosa Duchene; Theodore Kosloff as Rodriguez; John Davidson as Prince Talaat-Ni; Julia Faye as Samaran; Clarence Burton, Jacqueline Logan, Guy Oliver, Kamuela Searle. 9 reels. Released December 1921.

Saturday Night

A Cecil B. DeMille production, directed by Cecil B. DeMille. Script by Jeanie Macpherson. Photography by Alvin Wyckoff. Art Director: Paul Iribe. Editor: Anne Bauchens. With Edith Roberts as Shamrock O'Day; Conrad Nagel as Richard Prentiss; Leatrice Joy as Iris van Suydam; Jack Mower as Tom McGuire; Julia Faye as Elsie Prentiss; Theodore Roberts as Uncle Van; Edythe Chapman, Sylvia Ashton, John Davidson, James Neill. 9 reels. Released January 1922.

Manslaughter

A Cecil B. DeMille production, directed by Cecil B. DeMille. Script by Jeanie Macpherson from the novel by Alice Duer Miller. Photography by Alvin Wyckoff and L. Guy Wilky. Art Director: Paul Iribe. Editor: Anne Bauchens. With Leatrice Joy as Lydia Thorne; Thomas Meighan as Daniel O'Bannon; Lois Wilson as Evans; John Miltern as Governor Albee; Julia Faye as Mrs Drummond; George Fawcett, Edythe Chapman, Jack Mower, Dorothy Cumming, Sylvia Ashton, James Neill, Mickey Moore; Raymond Hatton as Brown; Mabel van Buren, Dale Fuller and Ethel Wales as Prisoners. 10 reels. Released September 1922.

Adam's Rib

A Cecil B. DeMille production, directed by Cecil B. DeMille. Script by Jeanie Macpherson. Photography by Alvin Wyckoff and L. Guy Wilky. Art Director: Paul Iribe. Editor: Anne Bauchens. With Elliott Dexter as Prof. Nathan Reade; Anna Q. Nilsson as Mrs. Ramsay; Milton Sills as Michael Ramsay; Pauline Garon as Mathilda Ramsay; Theodore Kosloff as King Jaromir; Julia Faye as 'the Mischievous One'; George Field, Clarence Geldart, Robert Brower, Clarence Burton. 10 reels. Released March 1923.

The Ten Commandments

A Cecil B. DeMille production, directed by Cecil B. DeMille. Script by Jeanie Macpherson. Photography by Bert Glennon, Edward S. Curtis, J. Peverell Marley and Fred Westerberg. Technocolor Photography by Ray Rennahan. Art Directors: Paul Iribe and Francis McComas. Editor: Anne Bauchens. Technical director: Roy Pomeroy.
Cast in prologue: Theodore Roberts as Moses the Lawgiver; Charles de Roche as Rameses; Julia Faye as Wife of Rameses; Estelle Taylor as Moses' Sister; James Neill as Aaron; Lawson Butt as Dathan the Discontented; Clarence Burton as Taskmaster; Terrence Moore as Pharaoh's Son; Noble Johnson as Bronze Man.
Cast in modern story: Richard Dix as John McTavish; Rod La Rocque as Dan McTavish; Edythe Chapman as Mrs McTavish; Leatrice Joy as Mary

Leigh; Nita Naldi as Sally Lung; Robert Edeson, Agnes Ayres, Charles Ogle. 14 reels. Released November 1923.

Triumph

A Cecil B. DeMille production, directed by Cecil B. DeMille. Script by Jeanie Macpherson from the novel by May Edington. Photography by J. Peverell Marley. Editor: Anne Bauchens. With Rod La Rocque as King Garnet; Leatrice Joy as Ann Land; Victor Varconi as William Silver; Theodore Kosloff as Varinoff; Robert Edeson, Charles Ogle, Julia Faye, George Fawcett, Zasu Pitts. 9 reels. Released April 1924.

Feet of Clay

A Cecil B. DeMille production, directed by Cecil B. DeMille. Script by Beulah Marie Dix and Bertram Milhauser from the novel by Margaretta Tuttle. Photography by J. Peverell Marley and Archibald J. Stout. Art Director: Paul Iribe. Editor: Anne Bauchens. With Rod La Rocque as Kerry Harlan; Vera Reynolds as Amy Loring; Julia Faye, Robert Edeson, Theodore Kosloff, Ricardo Cortez, Victor Varconi, William Boyd. 10 reels. Released September 1924. *Missing Film.*

The Golden Bed

A Cecil B. DeMille production, directed by Cecil B. DeMille. Script by Jeanie Macpherson from the novel *Tomorrow's Bread* by Wallace Irwin. Photography by J. Peverell Marley. Art Director: Paul Iribe. Editor: Anne Bauchens. With Lillian Rich as Flora Lee Peake; Rod La Rocque as Admah Holtz; Vera Reynolds as Margaret Peake; Henry B. Walthall as Colonel Peake; Theodore Kosloff as Marquis de San Pilar; Warner Baxter as Bunny O'Neill; Julia Faye, Robert Edeson. 9 reels. Released January 1925.

The Road to Yesterday

Cecil B. DeMille Pictures. Directed by Cecil B. DeMille. Script by Jeanie Macpherson and Beulah Marie Dix from the play by Beulah Marie Dix and Evelyn Greenleaf Sutherland. Photography by J. Peverell Marley. Art Directors: Paul Iribe, Mitchell Leisen and Anton Grot. Editor: Anne Bauchens. With Joseph Schildkraut as Kenneth Paulton; Jetta Goudal as Malena Paulton; William Boyd as Jack Moreland; Trixie Friganza as Harriet Tyrell; Julia Faye as Dolly Foules. 10 reels. Released November 1925.

The Volga Boatman

Cecil B. DeMille Pictures. Directed by Cecil B. DeMille. Script by Lenore Coffee from the novel by Konrad Bercovici. Photography by Arthur Miller, Peverell J. Marley and Fred Westerberg. Art Directors: Mitchell Leisen, Max Parker and Anton Grot. Editor: Anne Bauchens. With William Boyd

as Feodor; Elinor Fair as Vera; Robert Edeson as Prince Nikita; Julia Faye
as Mariusha; Victor Varconi as Prince Dimitri Orlaff; Theodore Kosloff as
Stefan. 11 reels. Released April 1926.

The King of Kings

Cecil B. DeMille Pictures. Directed by Cecil B. DeMille. Script by Jeanie
Macpherson. Photography by J. Peverell Marley, Fred Westerberg and J. A.
Badaracco. Art Directors: Mitchell Leisen, Anton Grot and Dan Sayre
Groesbeck. Editors: Anne Bauchen and Harold McLernon. With H. B.
Warner as Jesus; Dorothy Cumming as Mary; Jacqueline Logan as Mary
Magdalene; Rudolph Schildkraut as Caiaphas; Joseph Schildkraut as Judas;
Victor Varconi as Pontius Pilate; Ernest Torrence as Peter; James Neill,
Joseph Striker, Robert Edeson, Sydney D'Albrook, David Imboden, Robert
Ellsworth, John T. Prince, Charles Belcher, Clayton Packard and Charles
Requa as Apostles; William Boyd, Sam DeGrasse, Majel Colman, M.
Moore, Julia Faye, Theodore Kosloff. 18 reels, 155 minutes. Released April
1927, re-released as sound/music version, 1928.

The Godless Girl

Cecil B. DeMille Pictures. Directed by Cecil B. DeMille. Script by Jeanie
Macpherson with title and dialogue sequences by Beulah Marie Dix.
Photography by J. Peverell Marley. Art Director: Mitchell Leisen. Editor:
Anne Bauchens. With Lina Basquette as The Godless Girl; George Duryea
as Bob; Eddi Quillan as Bozo; Marie Prevost as Mame; Noah Beery as
Head Guard; Mary Jane Irving, Clarence Burton, Gertrude Quality, Kate
Price, Hedwig Reicher, Julia Faye, Emily Barrye. Final reel with spoken dia-
logue. 12 reels. Released March 1929.

Sound Films

Dynamite

A Cecil B. DeMille production for MGM. Directed by Cecil B. DeMille.
Script by Jeanie Macpherson. Additional dialogue by John Howard
Lawson and Gladys Unger. Photography by J. Peverell Marley. Art
Directors: Cedric Gibbons and Mitchell Leisen. Editor: Anne Bauchens.
With Charles Bickford as Hagen Derk; Kay Johnson as Cynthia Crothers;
Muriel McCormack as Katie Derk; Julia Faye as Marcia Towne; Conrad
Nagel, Joel McCrea, Robert Edeson, William Holden, Tyler Brooke. 126
minutes. Released by MGM December 1929. Silent version also released.

Madam Satan

MGM. Produced and directed by Cecil B. DeMille. Script by Jeanie
Macpherson. Additional dialogue by Gladys Unger, Elsie Janis and
(uncredited) John Howard Lawson. Photography by Harold Rosson. Art

Director: Wilfred Buckland. Costumes by Adrian. Music and lyrics by Clifford Grey, Herbert Stothart, Elsie Janis and Jack King. Dance Director: LeRoy Prinz. Sound by J. K. Brock. Editor: Anne Bauchens. With Kay Johnson as Angela Brooks; Reginald Denny as Bob Brooks; Roland Young as Jimmy Wade; Lillian Roth as Trixie; Elsa Peterson, Boyd Irwin, Tyler Brooke; Theodore Kosloff as 'Electricity'; Abe Lyman and his Band. 115 minutes. Released October 1930.

The Squaw Man (second remake)
MGM. Produced and directed by Cecil B. DeMille. Script by Lucien Hubbard and Lenore Coffee from the play by Edwin Milton Royle. Additional dialogue by Elsie Janis. Photography by Harold Rosson. Editor: Anne Bauchens. Music: Herbert Stothart. With Warner Baxter as Jim Wynn; Lupe Velez as Naturich; Eleanor Boardman as Diana; Paul Cavanagh as Lord Henry Kerhill; Charles Bickford as Cash Hawkins; Roland Young, Lawrence Grant, Mitchell Lewis, Raymond Hatton, Victor Potel, Julia Faye. 107 minutes. Released September 1931.

The Sign of the Cross
Produced and directed by Cecil B. DeMille. Script by Waldemar Young and Sidney Buchman from the play by Wilson Barrett. Photography by Karl Struss. Art Director: Mitchell Leisen. Editor: Anne Bauchens. With Fredric March as Marcus; Elissa Landi as Mercia; Claudette Colbert as Poppaea; Charles Laughton as Nero; Ian Keith, Vivian Tobin, Arthur Hohl, Harry Beresford, Nat Pendleton. 125 minutes. Released November 1932.

This Day and Age
Produced and directed by Cecil B. DeMille. Script by Bartlett Cormack. Photography by J. Peverell Marley. Art Director: Roland Anderson. Editor: Anne Bauchens. Music: Howard Jackson, L. Wolfe Gilbert and Abel Baer. With Charles Bickford as Garrett; Judith Allen as Gay Merrick; Richard Cromwell as Steve Smith; Harry Green as Herman; Oscar Rudolph as Gus; Eddie Nugent, Billy Gilbert, Ben Alexander, Guy Usher, George Barbier, Charles Middleton. 86 minutes. Released August 1933.

Four Frightened People
Produced and directed by Cecil B. DeMille. Script by Bartlett Cormack and Lenore J. Coffee from the novel by E. Arnot Robertson. Photography by Karl Struss. Art Director: Roland Anderson. Editor: Anne Bauchens. Music: Karl Hajos. With Claudette Colbert as Judy Cavendish; Herbert Marshall as Andrew Ainger; Mary Boland as Mrs Mardick; William Gargan as Stewart Corder; Leo Carrillo as Montague; Tetsu Komai, Chris Pin Martin, Joe De La Cruz, Ethel Griffies. 95 minutes. Released January 1934.

Cleopatra

Produced and directed by Cecil B. DeMille. Script by Waldemar Young and Vincent Lawrence. Photography by Victor Milner. Art Directors: Hans Dreier and Roland Anderson. Costumes: Travis Banton. Editor: Anne Bauchens. Montage sequences: William Cameron Menzies. With Claudette Colbert as Cleopatra; Henry Wilcoxon as Marc Antony; Warren William as Julius Caesar; Gertrude Michael as Calpurnia; Joseph Schildkraut as Herod; C. Aubrey Smith as Enobarbus; Ian Keith as Octavian; Ian McLaren, Arthur Hohl, Leonard Mudie, Irving Pichel, Claudia Dell, Eleanor Phelps; Harry Beresford as Soothsayer. 100 minutes. Released August 1934.

The Crusades

Produced and directed by Cecil B. DeMille. Script by Harold Lamb, Waldemar Young and Dudley Nichols. Photography by Victor Milner. Technical Effects: Gordon Jennings. Art Directors: Hans Dreier and Roland Anderson. Costumes: Travis Banton. Editor: Anne Bauchens. Music: Rudolph Kopp. With Loretta Young as Berengaria; Henry Wilcoxon as King Richard; Ian Keith as Saladin; Katherine DeMille as Alice; Joseph Schildkraut as Conrad; Alan Hale as Blondel; George Barbier, William Farnum, Hobart Bosworth, Lumsden Hare; C. Aubrey Smith as The Hermit. 125 minutes. Released August 1935.

The Plainsman

Produced and directed by Cecil B. DeMille. Script by Waldemar Young, Harold Lamb, Lynn Riggs, additional material by Jeanie Macpherson, based on stories by Courtney Riley Cooper and Frank J. Wilstach. Photography by Victor Milner. Art Directors: Hans Dreier and Roland Anderson. Editor: Anne Bauchens. Musical Direction: Boris Morros. With Gary Cooper as Wild Bill Hickok; Jean Arthur as Calamity Jane; James Ellison as Buffalo Bill Cody; Charles Bickford as John Lattimer; Helen Burgess as Louisa Cody; Porter Hall, Paul Harvey, Victor Varconi; John Miljan as General George Custer; Frank McGlynn as Abraham Lincoln. 113 minutes. Released January 1937.

The Buccaneer

Produced and directed by Cecil B. DeMille. Script by Edwin Justus Mayer, Harold Lamb and C. Gardner Sullivan. Based on an adaptation by Jeanie Macpherson of *Lafitte the Pirate* by Lyle Saxon. (Uncredited writers: Preston Sturges and Jesse Lasky Jr.) Photography by Victor Milner. Art Direction: Hans Dreier and Roland Anderson, Editor: Anne Bauchens. Musical Score: George Antheil. With Fredric March as Jean Lafitte; Franciska Gaal as Gretchen; Margot Grahame as Annett de Remy; Akim Tamiroff as

Dominique; Walter Brennan as Ezra Peavey; Ian Keith as Crawford; Douglas Dumbrille as Governor Claiborne; Hugh Sothern as Andrew Jackson; Anthony Quinn as Beluche. 125 minutes. Released February 1938.

Union Pacific
Produced and directed by Cecil B. DeMille. Script by Walter DeLeon, C. Gardner Sullivan and Jesse Lasky Jr from the novel *Trouble Shooter* by Ernest Haycox. (Uncredited writers: Frederick Hazlitt Brennan, Stanley Raub, Jeanie Macpherson, Harold Lamb and Stuart Anthony.) Photography by Victor Milner. Art Directors: Hans Dreier and Roland Anderson. Editor: Anne Bauchens. Music: Sigmund Krumgold and John Leipold. With Barbara Stanwyck as Mollie Monahan; Joel McCrea as Jeff Butler; Robert Preston as Dick Allen; Brian Donlevy as Sid Campeau; Akim Tamiroff as Fiesta; Lynne Overman as Leach; Lon Chaney Jr as Dollarhide; Anthony Quinn as Jack Cordray. 135 minutes. Released April 1939.

North West Mounted Police
Produced and directed by Cecil B. DeMille. Script by Alan Le May, Jesse Lasky Jr and C. Gardner Sullivan. (Uncredited writers: Jeanie Macpherson, Frank Wead, Clements Ripley and Bartlett McCormack.) Photography by Victor Milner and W. Howard Greene. Art Directors: Hans Dreier and Roland Anderson. Editor: Anne Bauchens. Music: Victor Young. With Gary Cooper as Dusty Rivers; Madeleine Carroll as April Logan; Preston Foster as Sergeant Jim Brett; Robert Preston as Ronnie Logan; Paulette Goddard as Louvette Corbeau; George Bancroft as Jacques Corbeau; Akim Tamiroff as Dan Duroc; Lynn Overman, Walter Hampden; Lon Chaney Jr as Shorty; Wallace Reid Jr, Robert Ryan, Julia Faye. Released October 1940. Technicolor, 126 minutes.

Reap the Wild Wind
Produced and directed by Cecil B. DeMille. Script by Alan Le May, Charles Bennett and Jesse Lasky Jr from the novel by Thelma Strabel. (Additional writing by Jeanie Macpherson.) Photography by Victor Milner and William V. Skall. Underwater photography by Dewey Wrigley. Process photography (Oscar, 1942): Farciot Edouard, Gordon Jennings and William L. Pereira. Art Directors: Hans Dreier and Roland Anderson. Sound (Oscar 1942): Louis Mesenkop. Editor: Anne Bauchens. With Ray Milland as Stephen Tolliver; John Wayne as Captain Jack Stuart; Paulette Goddard as Loxi Claiborne; Raymond Massey as King Cutler; Robert Preston, Lynne Overman, Susan Hayward, Charles Bickford, Walter Hampden, Louise Beavers, Victor Varconi, Raymond Hatton, Julia Faye, Monte Blue, J. Farrell Macdonald; Hedda Hopper as Aunt Henrietta. Released March 1942. Technicolor, 123 minutes.

The Story of Dr Wassell

Produced and directed by Cecil B. DeMille. Script by Alan Le May and Charles Bennett based on the story of Commander Corydon M. Wassell and the story by James Hilton. Photography by Victor Milner and William Snyder. Art Directors: Hans Dreier and Roland Anderson. Editor: Anne Bauchens. Music: Victor Young. With Gary Cooper as Dr Wassell; Laraine Day as Madeleine; Signe Hasso as Bettina; Carol Thurston as Tremartini; Dennis O'Keefe, Carl Esmond, Paul Kelly, Stanley Ridges, Elliott Reid, Philip Ahn, Barbara Britton. Released April 1944. Technicolor, 140 minutes.

Unconquered

Produced and directed by Cecil B. DeMille. Script by Charles Bennett, Fredric M. Frank and Jesse Lasky Jr from the novel by Neil H. Swanson. (Uncredited writers: Jeanie Macpherson and Norman Reilly Raine.) Photography by Ray Rennahan. Art Direction: Hans Dreier and Walter Tyler. Editor: Anne Bauchens. Music: Victor Young. With Gary Cooper as Captain Christopher Holden; Paulette Goddard as Abby Hale; Howard da Silva as Martin Garth; Boris Karloff as Chief Guyasuta; Ward Bond as John Fraser; Cecil Kellaway, Virginia Campbell, Henry Wilcoxon, C. Aubrey Smith, Victor Varconi; Raymond Hatton as Venango Scout; Katherine DeMille as Hannah. Released October 1947. Technicolor, 146 minutes.

Samson and Delilah

Produced and directed by Cecil B. DeMille. Script by Jesse L. Lasky Jr and Fredric M. Frank, based on a treatment by Harold Lamb and the novel *Judge and Fool* by Vladimir (Ze'ev) Jabotinsky. (Uncredited writer: Jeanie Macpherson.) Photography by George Barnes. Effects and process photography by Gordon Jennings, Farciot Edouart and Wallace Kelley. Holy Land photography by Dewey Wrigley. Art Directors: Hans Dreier and Walter Tyler. Editor: Anne Bauchens. Music: Victor Young. Choreography: Theodore Kosloff. With Victor Mature as Samson; Hedy Lamarr as Delilah; George Sander as The Saran; Angela Lansbury as Semadar; Olive Deering as Miriam; Henry Wilcoxon as Ahtur; Russ Tamblyn as Saul; Julia Faye, Fay Holden, William Farnum, Victor Varconi, John Miljan, Fritz Leiber, Mike Mazurski. Released October 1949. Technicolor, 131 minutes.

The Greatest Show on Earth

Produced and directed by Cecil B. DeMille. Associate Producer: Henry Wilcoxon. Script by Fredric M. Frank, Theodore St. John and Frank Cavett (Oscar, 1952). (Uncredited writers: Stephen Longstreet, Luther Davis and Sidney Biddell.) Photography by George Barnes and J. Peverell Marley. Art

Direction: Hal Pereira and Walter Tyler. Editor: Anne Bauchens. With
Charlton Heston as Brad; Betty Hutton as Holly; Cornel Wilde as
Sebastian; Dorothy Lamour as Phyllis; Gloria Grahame as Angel; James
Stewart as Buttons; Emmett Kelly, Henry Wilcoxon, Lyle Bettger, Lawrence
Tierney, Julia Faye, John Ringling North. Released January 1952.
Technicolor, 152 minutes.

The Ten Commandments (remake)
Produced and directed by Cecil B. DeMille. Associate Producer: Henry
Wilcoxon. Script by Aeneas Mackenzie, Jesse L. Lasky Jr, Jack Gariss and
Fredric M. Frank from *Prince of Egypt* by Dorothy Clark Wilson, *Pillar of
Fire* by Rev. J. H. Ingraham, *On Eagles Wings* by Rev. A. E. Southon, the
ancient texts of Philo, Josephus, Eusebius, the Midrash and the Holy
Scriptures. (Uncredited writer: Edmund Penney.) Photography by Loyal
Griggs, J. Peverell Marley, John Warren and Wallace Kelley. Art Directors:
Hal Pereira, Walter Tyler and Albert Nozaki. Music: Elmer Bernstein.
Editor: Anne Bauchens. With Charlton Heston as Moses; Yul Brynner as
Rameses; Anne Baxter as Nefretiri; Edward G. Robinson as Dathan;
Yvonne de Carlo as Sephora; John Derek as Joshua; Sir Cedric Hardwicke
as Sethi; John Carradine as Aaron; Debra Paget, Nina Foch, Olive Deering,
Ian Keith, Julia Faye, Woody Strode, Abbas El Boughdadly. Released
November 1956. Technicolor, VistaVision, 220 minutes.

Synopses of selected DeMille archive films covered partially or in passing in text

Call of the North, 1914
Title: 'A Factor of the Hudson Bay Company was Lord of all temporal
existence. Under his displeasure men were thrust unarmed into the wilderness. If starvation failed, his Indians did not. This was called the Journey of
Death.'
While the all-powerful factor goes on a journey up north to a remote cabin,
a trapper, Rand, tries to woo Jack Wilson's daughter, but she does not
respond. The factor, injured in a fall, comes across Wilson's log cabin, is
taken in and flirts with the daughter. He decides to marry her, outraging
Rand, who convinces the factor that she is flirting with his friend, Graeme
Stewart. The factor orders Graeme out on the Journey of Death, leaving his
young son in the care of Indians. Five days later, floundering in the snow,
Graeme dies, and an Indian reports the death to the factor.
  Twenty years later: the factor is in supreme control of the north, living
with his daughter, Virginia. Graeme's son, Ned Stewart, now trades in defiance of the company. An old Indian tells him how his father died. The
treacherous Rand is now the factor's enforcer, and Ned is caught and ban-

ished from the territory. He reaches 'civilization' alive, and recovers to set off back north. On the way, he rescues one of the factor's men, Pickard, from a trap. Ned is recaptured, but the man he rescued brings him a rifle. Virginia learns Ned is to take the Journey of Death, and having learned his identity as Graeme's son, claims it was she who gave him the gun. The factor sends young Ned, as he had his father, on the Journey of Death. Meanwhile, Rand is shot by Pickard's wife and confesses he had caused the factor's jealousy against Graeme twenty years before. The factor realizes his injustice . . . Ned is rescued and brought back to the factor for the final atonement, and he canoes off down the river.

The Warrens of Virginia, 1915

Among the aristocratic Warrens of Virginia, there is a quarrel over slave ownership, as a black mammy brings their drinks. The door opens to bowing black servants, as the whites dance. News of the shots fired at Fort Sumter is brought. Ned Burton is immediately estranged from his sweetheart, Agatha Warren, as he is from the North. Four years later, Lee's ragged army hopes for help and supplies.

While the women at home pick silver to be melted, a supply train leaves from Lynchburg. Ned Burton, now a Northern officer, is ordered to infiltrate and deceive the Southern enemy by having himself captured with fake papers. His moral dilemma: deceiving his old friends and sweetheart. As a captured prisoner, he meets Agatha Warren again, and she accepts his proposal of four years before, despite his being a Yankee. She finds his dispatches on him and is torn between her love and duty. She gives the dispatches to her people. The Southern army marches towards the supply train, thinking they are saved, while the Union army prepares its ambush. Agatha begs forgiveness from Ned, but he says: 'I don't believe I'm the man to whom you should give your first kiss.' The supply train is ambushed and destroyed. General Warren realizes the trick, and Ned is ordered to be shot as a spy. The General gives Agatha a pass to give to Ned so that he can escape and 'run like a coward', but he tears it up. Ned is sentenced at the Appomattox Court House, but news comes that the war is over and the South has lost. Two years later: 'Peace, unweaponed – Conquers every wrong.' Ex-General Warren and Agatha are in their garden, shelling peas, as a black boy plays a lute. A Yankee general visits Warren, bringing Ned Burton. Despite his continuing anger, Warren reconciles as, seen from a window looking out into daylight, Ned walks off.

Chimmie Fadden Out West, 1915

In contrast to scenes of New York Bowery life, a rich railroad magnate, Van Cortland, plots to send the local wide boy Chimmie out west so he can pretend to make the greatest gold strike in the world. The suckers will then hire a record-breaking train from the magnate. Meanwhile, Chimmie tells his girl, 'the Duchess': 'I wonder if we kin ever git enough coin so's that we can git spliced.' Chimmie agrees to go out west for $10,000, crosses Death Valley with a mule, arrives at a frontier town, spends money and boasts of his strike, causing a fake gold rush. His girl travels out only to find him with a saloon girl. His brother rides the roads to get to him. Chimmie plans his wedding and the magnate celebrates by selling 'a Million Shares of Stock'. But Chimmie's brother tells all to the duchess, and she tells her groom: 'I won't marry a thief!'

Chimmie confronts Van Cortland and orders him to buy back the fake stock. He leaves them his fancy coat but keeps the pants. He gets the girl and turns to the audience at the end, as he kisses her, to say: 'Wot dye mean, I lost my gold mine?' FADE OUT.

Trail of the Lonesome Pine, 1916

After the Civil War, there is warfare between the government and the Tollivers, 'moon-shiners' who want to 'maintain their ancient right to operate without a licence – and defend their belief to the death'. Hales arrives as a new revenue man to clean things up, but June Tolliver volunteers to keep the new revenuer off the family trail. She faints by the pine as he strolls up, and when he carries her to her cabin, he is captured by the Tollivers. He is bound and spoonfed by June, who tells him: 'They do say I make the eatin'est hoe-cake – if yo' all care for it!'

Hales gets her to light his pipe and starts a fire in the hut to loosen his bonds and escape back to town. He joins a posse at a shoot-out at the moonshiners' shack, confronting June and her shotgun. He tells her: 'You can't shoot me, because you love me!' They kiss, and she says: 'I reckon I do love yo' – but I'll shoot your head off – if yo' cross that door!' The moonshiners escape through a tunnel. A spy sends a message to the Tollivers, saying Hales is coming by the south trail, but only June can read, and she sends her family in the other direction to ambush the posse. But the message is false, and the Tollivers ambush Hales, wounding him and taking him back to the cabin. June convinces her love-struck cousin Dave to ride for a doctor. Dave brings the posse and doc under a flag of truce. Hales recovers and offers the Tollivers freedom if they promise to stop a-moonshinin'. Old Judd shoots Dave for his betrayal. Healed, Hales bids June farewell by the lonesome pine, promising to return to wed her, and walks off into the woods.

Till I Come Back to You, 1918

In Belgium, Yvonne, a farm girl, is married to the Prussian von Kurtz, a martinet who beats her son, Jacques. King Albert stops by in his car, on his way to exile, notices Jacques playing Napoleon and tells him: 'Take care of my country – till I come back to you.' Von Kurtz returns, vowing to send Jacques to an orphanage. Later, as the war continues, Jefferson Strong of the 'Big American Brothers' witnesses the capture of von Kurtz. American officers decide to fake a letter from von Kurtz to his wife introducing Strong as a friend, so that he can get through the lines. Strong gets to Yvonne's house. Meanwhile, in the orphanage, a German inspector asks the kids who is the greatest man in the world. Jacques answers: 'Albert, King of the Belgians.' Jacques is taken home to be punished by his father. Strong has to impersonate von Kurtz, but reveals his true identity to Jacques and Yvonne.

Meanwhile, von Kurtz escapes, heading home. In the town, the Yanks are tunnelling beneath a German 'liquid fire' chamber. The Belgian orphans discover they are to be sent to German munition factories to slave and starve. Jacques remembers his king's admonition and returns to help the kids escape. He leads the orphans to Yvonne's farmhouse. They see 'von Kurtz' in German uniform, but Strong tells them: 'Don't be afraid, kiddies, I'm an American!' They try to escape through a tunnel, but Yvonne leads them by mistake to the powder chamber. Strong prevents an explosion and holds the tunnel alone against the advancing Germans. The Yanks confront von Kurtz, who is shot down. Strong explains his actions but must face an American court martial. Jacques goes to find King Albert, who comes down to save Strong. King Albert vows that, once the Yanks have driven out every vestige of 'the terrible hun', 'then I will come back to you'.

Select Bibliography

History of the American Cinema Series, University of California Press

Balio, Tino, *Grand Design, Hollywood as a Modern Business Enterprise, 1930–1939* (Vol. 5), 1993.
Bowser, Eileen, *The Transformation of Cinema, 1907–1915* (Vol. 2), 1990.
Crafton, Donald, *The Talkies, American Cinema's Transition to Sound, 1926–1931* (Vol. 4), 1997.
Koszarski, Richard, *An Evening's Entertainment, The Age of the Silent Feature Picture, 1915-1928* (Vol. 3), 1990.
Musser, Charles, *The Emergence of Cinema, the American Screen to 1907* (Vol. 1), 1990.

Books on Cecil B. DeMille and Related Hollywood and Stage Topics

Belasco, David, *The Theatre Through Its Stage Door*, Harper & Brothers Publishers, New York, 1919.
Bickford, Charles, *Bulls, Balls, Bicycles and Actors*, Paul S. Eriksson, Inc., New York, 1965.
Birchard, Robert S., *Cecil B. DeMille's Hollywood*, University Press of Kentucky, 2004.
Brownlow, Kevin, *Behind the Mask of Innocence*, Jonathan Cape, London, 1990.
Brownlow, Kevin, *The Parade's Gone By*, Secker and Warburg, London, 1968.
Ceplar, Larry and Englund, Steven, *The Inquisition in Hollywood, Politics in the Film Community, 1930–1960*, University of Illinois Press, 2003.
de Mille, Agnes, *Dance to the Piper*, Columbus Books, London, 1987.
de Mille, Agnes, *Speak to Me, Dance with Me,* An Atlantic Monthly Press Book, Little, Brown & Co., 1973.
DeMille, Cecil B., *Autobiography*, Ed. Donald Hayne, W. H. Allen, London, 1960.
de Mille, Richard, *My Secret Mother Lorna Moon*, Farrar, Straus & Giroux, New York, 1998.
de Mille, William C., *Hollywood Saga*, E. P. Dutton & Co., Inc., 1939.

Doherty, Thomas, *Pre-Code Hollywood, Sex, Immorality and Insurrection in American Cinema 1930–1934*, Columbia University Press, New York, 1999.

Edwards, Anne, *The DeMilles: An American Family*, William Collins Sons & Co., London, 1988.

Essoe, Gabe and Lee, Raymond, *DeMille: The Man and His Pictures*, Castle Books, New York, 1970.

Finler, Joel L., *The Hollywood Story*, Wallflower Press, London, 2003.

Higashi, Sumiko, *Cecil B. DeMille and American Culture: The Silent Era*, University of California Press, 1994.

Higham, Charles, *Cecil B. DeMille*, Dell, 1976.

Irwin, Will, *The House that Shadows Built* (life of Adolph Zukor), Doubleday, Doran & Co., New York, 1928.

Jobes, Gertrude, *Motion Picture Empire*, Archon Books, Hamden, Connecticut, 1966 (unique detailed look at the business history of pioneer Hollywood).

Koury, Phil A., *Yes, Mr. DeMille*, G. P. Putnam's Sons, New York, 1959.

Lasky, Jesse L., *I Blow My Own Horn*, Victor Gollancz Ltd, London, 1957.

Lasky, Jesse L., Jr., *Whatever Happened to Hollywood?* Funk & Wagnalls, New York, 1975.

Lord, Daniel A., *Played by Ear, the Autobiography of Father Daniel A. Lord, S. J.*, Image Books, Doubleday, 1959.

MacMahon, Henry and Macpherson, Jeanie, *The Ten Commandments, A Novel*, Grosset & Dunlap, New York, 1924 (novelization of the film).

Macpherson, Jeanie and MacMahon, Henry, *The King of Kings, A Novel*, Grosset & Dunlap, 1927 (novelization of the film).

May, Larry, *Screening Out the Past: The Birth of Mass Culture and the Motion Picture Industry*, Oxford University Press, New York and Oxford, 1980.

Myers, Hortense and Burnett, Ruth, *Cecil B. DeMille, Young Dramatist*, the Bobbs-Merrill Company, Indianapolis and New York, 1963.

Noerdlinger, Henry S., *The Documentation to the Motion Picture The Ten Commandments*, University of Southern California Press, 1956.

Orrison, Katherine, *Written in Stone, Making Cecil B. DeMille's Epic, The Ten Commandments*, Vestal Press, Maryland, 1999.

Ringgold, Gene and Bodeen, DeWitt, *The Films of Cecil B. DeMille*, The Citadel Press, New York, 1969.

Sklar, Robert, *Movie-Made America: A Cultural History of American Movies*, Vintage Books, New York, 1994.

Sloan, Kay, *The Loud Silents, Origins of the Social Problem Film*, University of Illinois Press, Urbana and Chicago, 1988.

Swanson, Gloria, *Swanson on Swanson: An Autobiography*, Michael Joseph, London, 1981.

Timberlake, Craig, *The Bishop of Broadway: The Life & Work of David Belasco*, Library Publishers, New York, 1954.

Walsh, Frank, *Sin and Censorship: The Catholic Church and the Motion Picture Industry*, Yale University Press, 1996.

Wright, Melanie J., *Moses in America, The Cultural Uses of Biblical Narrative*, Oxford University Press, 2003.

Index

All DeMille's films are indexed under 'DeMille, Cecil B.: films', with a substantial main entry marked in **bold**. Illustrations are in *italics*.